Comerica, Conduent, and the U.S. Treasury Betrayed Veterans and Other Victims

Ignoring Identity Theft is Profitable for the Abusers

J.B. Simms
with Dianne Helm

ERIK PUBLISHING

Publisher's Cataloging-in-Publication Data

Names: Simms, J.B., 1953- . | Helm, Dianne, 1959- .
Title: Comerica, Conduent, and the U.S. Treasury betrayed veterans and other victims : ignoring identity theft is profitable for the abusers / J.B. Simms with Dianne Helm.
Description: St. Augustine, FL : Erik Publishing, 2023.
Identifiers: ISBN 9798218194369 (pbk.)
Subjects: LCSH: Conduent. | Comerica Bank. | United States. Department of the Treasury. | Banks and banking -- United States. | Financial services industry -- Corrupt practices -- United States. | Political corruption -- United States. | BISAC: BUSINESS & ECONOMICS / Banks & Banking. | POLITICAL SCIENCE / American Government / General. | POLITICAL SCIENCE / Corruption & Misconduct.
Classification: LCC HV6769.S56 2023 | DDC 364.16 S--dc23

Table of Contents

Jackie Densmore and J.B. Simms

Jackie Densmore

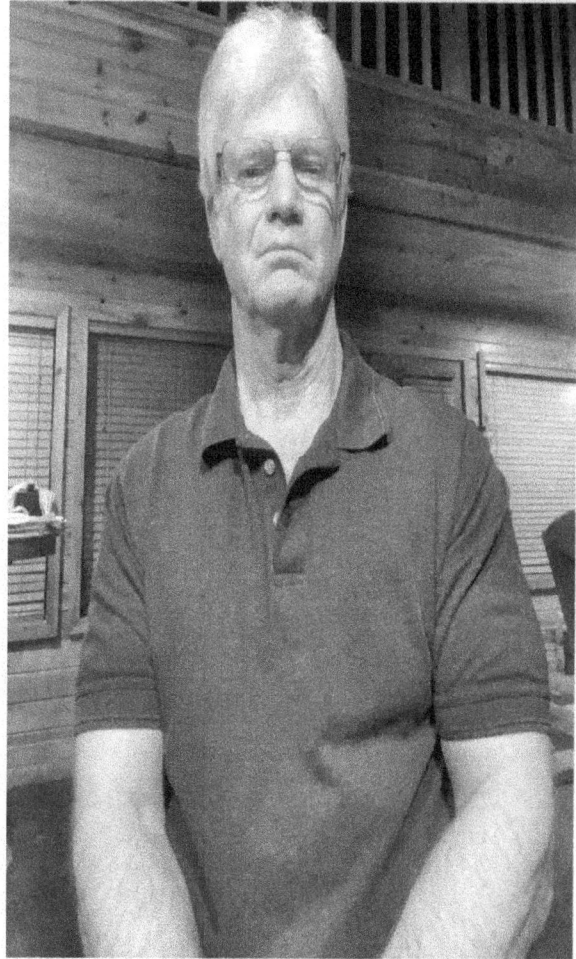

J.B. Simms

Acknowledgments

Jackie Densmore, my fellow plaintiff in the federal lawsuit against Comerica Bank and Conduent, has been by my side, in my ear, and the two of us became joined at the hip during this case for almost 5 years. We talked at all hours of the night, and to the victims. Jackie would call anytime, knowing at the time that I was in California, and she was in Boston, with no apology. Jackie joined me nine months after I began this attack against Comerica Bank, Conduent, US Treasury OIG, Social Security, Bureau of Fiscal Service, and the Veterans Administration. These five years together were tough for both of us. Jackie and I drove the bus on this case and our results would not have happened without Jackie. Thank you, Jackie; you have my heart.

Dianne Helm listened to this story beginning in December 2019 when I visited her for 3 months when she lived in St. Petersburg, Florida. I met Dianne in the spring of 2009 in Los Angeles at a book fair at UCLA. Dianne was a book publisher and editor. I began compiling the emails while I was in her apartment during my visit as I thought about writing this book. Dianne edited the manuscript chapters I presented to her and we went back and forth with our edits. Her experience in editing was a great help to me. Thank you, Dianne, for your time and patience.

My son, Major Joe Simms, USAF, had to listen to his father talk about this case from the beginning. His support, encouragement, and input were very important to me, and Joe will tell you that his dad is a bit crazy but driven.

I thank the 103 victims for trusting me enough to reach out to me personally. Well over $350,000 was recovered for these victims whose fraud claims were denied. You lit a fire in me to help others, and I thank you.

Preface
"The Direct Express Evil Triumvirate: Comerica, Conduent, and US Treasury "

You could be at the drugstore ready to pay for prescriptions related to your military service-related disability, buying an internet cable for your cousin's television, standing at an ATM attempting to make your monthly cash withdrawal, presenting your Direct Express debit card to a clerk fifty miles from your home to purchase fuel for your automobile, using your Direct Express card to pay for your rent, or buying groceries for your children who receive Social Security disability entitlements. You receive this message from the clerk or the screen of an ATM: "Your card has been declined."

You tell the clerk, "I know there is money in my account" as you become embarrassed. You are overwhelmed. You become scared as you inspect the Direct Express telephone app to inspect your Direct Express account and see hardly any money in your account. The transactions you see tell you that someone other than you charged one or more transactions to your account. The charge is "Pending." You do not know what "Pending" means; all you know is you have no money, and the pending charge has reduced your balance and access to your money.

If you could not access your Direct Express account from your telephone, you had to go home to access your Direct Express account on your computer. The drive to your house was full of anxiety; "I have no money." You see the fraudulent transactions on your computer and know you have no way to communicate with a "Direct Express person" by using email. You have no answers.

You see a balance of $15 in your account. You checked your balance before leaving home and saw your Social Security deposit of $600 in your account. Now you have no money.

If this terror of having no money is not enough, you now must call the telephone number located on the back of your Direct Express debit card to get answers. The real torture begins. If you think you were victimized by a fraudster, just wait until you call the telephone number you found on the back of your debit card. The telephone number is to a call center, and you believe this is the call center for your Direct Express debit card. You call the number. There is no answer. The call center telephone continues to ring. You call again. Still no answer, and there is no answer for more than an hour, maybe two.

After an hour or two, a person answers your call to the call center. You are told that the pending fraudulent transactions cannot be stopped even though you did not make the transaction. You live in Denver, CO and someone used your card in San Francisco, or you live in Hawaii and your card was used in Long Island, NY. Maybe your card was used to purchase perfume to be shipped to India. The attendant at the call center is someone you think works for Direct Express, but NO ONE WORKS FOR DIRECT EXPRESS. You think Direct Express is a "company." The attendant tells you the transaction which you claim is fraud must be paid and you can dispute it later. You ask where the charges were made to your card. You are told your money was withdrawn from an ATM in Atlanta; you live in Ohio. The fraudster had to have a "card" to do this, but the attendant is not listening to your story and does not care.

The attendant tells you a new card will be sent to you. The attendant sends an automatic message to the mailroom and a fraud questionnaire is sent to you.

You are then told you must fill out the questionnaire and mail it to an address in Texas for the Fraud Department to "investigate" your claim. The questionnaire is to be mailed to you, and if the fraud department does not receive the returned questionnaire packet within ten (10) days of it being mailed to you (you are now responsible for the US Postal Service delivery), your fraud claim will be denied. The Fraud Unit has no way to determine exactly "when" your questionnaire was received by you, so your claim will be arbitrarily declined. No investigation begins until the fraud packet is returned to the bank.

Notice of your fraud claim, no matter how obvious the fraud, will never be acknowledged by alerting someone at the call center. You do not know that the call you made to the call center was technically and legally "notification," but you will be held hostage (and your money) until you return the completed fraud packet. You were not told that you could write your narrative of your fraud experience and email it to a fraud department. You tell the attendant that you want to talk to someone in the Fraud Department, but the attendant tells you there is no telephone number for the fraud department, then your call is transferred to "another level" and you wait on hold for an hour, and the call is dropped. Nothing will be done until you get the Fraud Packet in the mail.

You are screaming, angry, and scared. You have no money. Rent must be paid. The kids must eat. Medicine must be purchased. You need your money now.

You look at the front of your Direct Express debit card. You see the name of a bank: Comerica Bank. You have never heard of that bank, so to the internet, you go.

First stop, Better Business Bureau. You file a report.

Second stop, you find something called the Consumer Financial Protection Bureau. You file a report.

Third, you might make a report with the Federal Trade Commission.

One of these agencies responds and tells you they sent the complaint to what you thought was Direct Express, but you see that your report was sent to Susan Schmidt of Comerica Bank. After contacting Ms. Schmidt, Vice President of Comerica Bank, she tells you she will be forwarding your complaint to a Customer Advocacy office of Direct Express.

Wait a minute. Why was Ms. Schmidt forwarding your problem to someone else? What is a Customer Advocate? Where is Direct Express? Comerica Bank's name is on the debit card. Why was Susan Schmidt sending you to another company? Susan Schmidt worked for Comerica Bank. The Better Business Bureau and Consumer Financial Protection Bureau forwarded your complaint to Susan Schmidt. "Comerica Bank" is printed on your Direct Express debit card.

You receive a telephone call from a person who identifies themselves with a first name who said Susan Schmidt referred your call to them. They tell you they work for the Customer Advocacy division of Direct Express. You were still thinking "Direct Express is a company" but there is no company named Direct Express. You were told your case was assigned to a fraud unit, and it might take up to 90 days for "them" to decide if your fraud complaint was valid. If the fraud packet was not completed and returned in time (considering mailing time), your fraud claim would be denied.

Back to the internet.

You see that a person named J.B. Simms has posted information about fraud issues and violations of federal banking laws by Comerica Bank regarding Direct Express cardholders. The first thing you learned is there was no "Direct Express" company; Direct Express is a program, created by the Bureau of Fiscal Service which is a division of the US Treasury. The Bureau of Fiscal Service (BFS) granted the contract to Comerica Bank to run the Direct Express program.

You see the hundreds of posts by persons being victimized as you are being victimized.

Another revelation you read from Mr. Simms's comments was that Comerica Bank did not operate the call center for Comerica Bank; the call center was operated by a company named Conduent. You were thinking "Why did I not know this?"

You read the information provided by Mr. Simms that tells how the Direct Express program was operated, who approved it, and the fact that the Bureau of Fiscal Service (BFS) was found to have failed to oversee the program they created and oversee the bank (Comerica Bank) to whom they gave the contract. Comerica Bank is the Fiscal Agent of the Direct Express program, and two audits from OIG Treasury revealed inept behavior by BFS.

Mr. Simms refers you to Sonja Scott, a US Treasury agent, who seems to be attentive to the complaints against Comerica Bank. After you tell Ms. Scott your story you think something might happen to make Comerica Bank listen to you.

Ms. Scott informs you that your complaint will be forwarded to a person at the Bureau of Fiscal Service (BFS). That is no comfort.

Wait a minute; BFS is the division of the US Treasury that gave the contract to Comerica Bank, and it was OIG Treasury (where Sonja Scott works) that published two reports which were critical of BFS for failing to oversee Comerica Bank. Why would you send a problem to the agency which caused the problem in the first place? No one at BFS will make Comerica Bank comply with any banking regulation or law. BFS was "in the bag."

BFS had no intention of advocating for any Direct Express cardholder, but Ms. Scott did what she was told to do and referred the complaints to Santaniello and BFS.

This was the nightmare of the Direct Express cardholder. The call center was operated by Conduent. Attendants at Conduent admitted they had no knowledge of banking laws (Regulation E), and the Conduent fraud unit could not differentiate fraud from valid transactions. Comerica Bank (Susan Schmidt) would not admit authority over Conduent. Nora Arpin (Senior VP at Comerica) denied any responsibility on the part of Comerica (Arpin was the direct contact person, the "bag lady" for Comerica's federal payments). Thomas Santaniello, the Congressional Liaison of BFS, refused to allow Direct Express cardholders access to the decision-making group referred to as the "Evaluation Team" that decided which bank (referred to as a Fiscal Agent) was to be awarded the Direct Express contract.

No one was accountable.

BFS created this problem by awarding the Direct Express contract to Comerica Bank three times, knowing Comerica Bank had to hire Conduent as a sub-contractor to administer the program. Comerica Bank falsified information on each application regarding their capabilities to obtain the contract and to handle the program (having no

adequate infrastructure in place). Comerica Bank got the contract, then returned to BFS to request additional millions of dollars to assist in "infrastructure." The cake had been baked and no one was supposed to figure out who was responsible, but we knew.

Office of Inspector General (OIG), Department of Treasury, assisted in the coverup by publishing bogus reports and refusing to acknowledge subpoenas and Freedom of Information requests, as did OIG Social Security. Simms directly advocated for well over a hundred victims and recovered over $350,000 for the victims by confronting Conduent and Comerica Bank. Over 65% of the victims who contacted Simms received full refunds. The cabal of BFS, Comerica Bank, Conduent, OIG Treasury, and Social Security was exposed. Direct Express cardholders continue to be victimized, including military veterans using the Direct Express program to receive their Social Security benefits.

To give the readers an example of the frustration with the contradictions and malfeasance of federal agencies, below is a flyer found in envelopes containing Social Security checks:

Above is the insert that Social Security used to threaten persons receiving Social Security checks (rather than a direct deposit). There are people preferring to receive their Social Security payments by check (mostly older recipients and those not computer savvy) and the Social Security Administration did not publicize that a recipient could request a waiver, which allowed recipients to legally opt for a paper check.

At the time of this writing the attorney for the plaintiffs (including Jackie Densmore and me) opted for mediation without the consensus of the plaintiffs. Comerica's lawyers do not want publicity for the abuse their clients suffered as a result of Comerica Bank and Conduent's banking law violations. Employees of Social Security OIG, Bureau of Fiscal Service, and lawyers employed at OIG Treasury do not want their corruption publicized. They get what they deserve, and the hundreds, if not thousands, of victims will be heard.

Below are passages taken from the website of the Social Security Administration website:

Controls over the Enrollment Process with the Direct Express® Debit Card
Program (Limited Distribution)

(A-15-12-21273)
To determine the effectiveness of controls over the beneficiary enrollment process for the Direct Express®
Debit Card Program.
BACKGROUND
In April 1996, Congress passed the Debt Collection Improvement Act of 1996 (DCIA), which requires that, as
of January 1999, Federal payments, subject to certain exceptions, be made electronically. In September 1998,
the Department of the Treasury (Treasury) issued a regulation to implement the provisions of the DCIA. The
regulation requires that individuals who file claims for Federal benefits on or after May 1, 2011 be paid by
electronic funds transfer (EFT). All Individuals are required to receive Federal payments by EFT after March
*1, 2013, **unless they have a waiver.***
RESULTS OF REVIEW
We determined the controls over the enrollment and post-entitlement processes for beneficiaries in the Direct
Express® Debit Card Program could be improved.
CONCLUSION
SSA, Treasury, and Comerica play critical roles in administering the Direct Express®
Program to SSA beneficiaries. All parties depend on their respective authentication and
matching processes to enroll authorized beneficiaries and representative payees in the
payees in the Direct Express® Program.

Notice the mention of the waiver, and "*We determined the controls over the enrollment and post-entitlement*
processes for beneficiaries in the Direct Express® Debit Card Program could be improved."
SSA rammed the Direct Express program down the throats of the most vulnerable recipients. Nothing
improved. There were no effective investigations and complaints ignored.

The "zero-liability" advertised by Mastercard was a joke. They blocked our calls.
What is it worth to experience the loss of your identity? How would you feel knowing your Social Security
number was being used by many criminals and your bank accused you of making transactions thousands of
miles from your home? Comerica Bank had no security features for Direct Express cardholders, but they did for
their regular customers.

This the story of how J.B. Simms, with fellow victim Jackie Densmore, defended Direct Express cardholder
victims against the corruption and malfeasance of Comerica Bank, Conduent, Bureau of Fiscal Service, the
Social Security Administration, and the Office of Inspector General of US Treasury.

Introduction

This description of the Direct Express program was taken from the following quote from an audit published by the Office of Inspector General, Department of Treasury:

In 2008, the Bureau of the Fiscal Service (Fiscal Service)1 established the Direct Express® Debit MasterCard® program (Direct Express), a program that allowed federal beneficiaries to receive benefit payments electronically using a prepaid debit card. Effective March 2013, individuals, with limited exceptions, could no longer receive federal payments by paper check and would have to either receive the payments by direct deposit to a bank account or through the Direct Express prepaid debit card. 1 (OIG 14-031) 1

To accomplish our objectives, we reviewed: (1) Fiscal Service's considerations in initiating the program, (2) Fiscal Service's financial agent selection process and the selection of Comerica as the Direct Express financial agent, (3) the terms of the financial agency agreement (FAA), (4) how an amendment to the FAA to compensate Comerica was vetted and approved, and (5) Fiscal Service's monitoring of the FAA. We interviewed officials and staff with Fiscal Service, Comerica, the Federal Reserve Bank of Dallas, and the Social Security Administration (SSA). We also reviewed Fiscal Service's policies and procedures, and examined documents related to the origination and administration of the FAA. Additionally, we visited two call centers that handled Direct Express calls to gain an understanding of call center operations.2(OIG 14-031.) 2

The first few chapters of this book will include conversations I had with Comerica Bank, Conduent, officials from the US Treasury, Bureau of Fiscal Service, Social Security, and victims of the Direct Express debit card program. The chronology will include emails with federal officials, commentary, and exhibits including communication with my closest ally and fellow victim, Jackie Densmore. Some emails were edited for clarity and passages of emails were deleted for space. Important passages of emails were included in the book.

In the minds of Direct Express debit cardholders, there was an illusion of a company named Direct Express that was perpetrated by Comerica Bank, Conduent, and Bureau of Fiscal Service (also referred to as BFS and will be referred to as BFS) which is a division of US Treasury. Comerica Bank contracted with BFS to operate the Direct Express debit card program. The Direct Express cardholders were subject to the dictates of who they thought were" Direct Express employees" but the Direct Express cardholders were not talking to employees of a company named Direct Express.

Direct Express is not a company. Direct Express is a debit card program created by the Bureau of Fiscal Service (BFS), Department of Treasury, to disburse federal payments (Social Security, VA benefits, Civil Service, and more) to persons either not having a bank account or choosing a debit card to receive payments.

Comerica Bank perpetrated this charade to protect themselves and Conduent from individuals [persons] researching the companies, determining how Comerica Bank got the original contract and renewed contracts with our federal government, and concealing violations of federal banking law. A little research was all that was necessary to find the truth; maybe a little more than a little.

Conduent is not a bank. Although some employees have worked at a bank (few) these employees are not familiar with debit card banking laws. If a person thinks they are talking to a Direct Express employee, they are talking to a Conduent employee.

Persons using the same Direct Express debit card as I was using were experiencing the same neglect and violation of banking law Regulation E as myself. When I found out that banking laws were being violated, persons were not being reimbursed for fraudulent transactions, and that federal investigative audits were not complete or comprehensive, I flew into a rage and went into action.

More than one hundred persons contacted me personally from January 2018 through April 2019 to help them get their money that was taken by fraudulent means and through no fault of their own. The Bureau of Fiscal Service victimized veterans who receive VA benefit checks, Social Security recipients (Retirement, Disability, and Supplemental Security Income (known as SSI), civil service employees, and others.

This story is not only about what I experienced and accomplished, along with the assistance of Jackie Densmore; this story is about the betrayal of veterans and other citizens, some disabled, some caring for disabled children, by our government, Comerica Bank, and Conduent.

During this journey, a victim named Jackie Densmore (from Massachusetts) joined me to defend the victims, exposing the corrupt federal program and corrupt federal employees. We also caused the Veterans Administration to create a new division of the VA (Veterans Benefit Banking Program) as the VA ceased its association with Treasury and stopped endorsing the Direct Express program.

You will read the accounts of victims in the program who lost their monthly entitlements from the Veterans Administration (VA) and the Social Security Administration (SSA), the lies and cover-up by federal and banking officials, what we did to help the victims, and how we went after the abusers.

The Direct Express cardholders thought Comerica Bank (and Conduent) were supposed to follow "a law." The law is Regulation E (15USC1693) and the subsequent regulations from the Federal Reserve and the FDIC. The following is a summation below:

Comerica Bank is a member of the Federal Reserve and must abide by regulations based upon law, 15USC1693. A summation of regulations in the Code of Federal Regulations, Title 12 Code of Federal Regulations Paragraphs 205.6 and 205.11, is listed below.

The duties of the financial institution (Direct Express/Comerica Bank, (the financial institution).

(A) Must acknowledge the first call to the call center giving notice of the fraud.

(B) Is allowed to decide to conduct no investigation, noticing fraud immediately and reimbursing the cardholder

(C) Must begin the investigation immediately upon receiving verbal notice.

(D) Cannot wait for written reports from the cardholder to begin the investigation.

(E) Must give full provisional credit within 10 days of reporting fraud if the investigation can take up to 45 days.

(F) Cannot hold cardholder liable for knowing about fraudulent activity if circumstances such as hospitalization or travel are a factor.

(G) Must give a record of the complete investigation if requested.

(H) Cannot hold cardholder liable for any negligence or trusting behavior, i.e., give access information to a family member, or caregiver, to access funds on behalf of the cardholder.

The motivation of banking officials to violate federal law, and federal workers who allowed the criminal acts only to become codependent in the process by enabling crimes and ignoring victims, is up to you to determine.

This is the story of my fight, along with Jackie Densmore, against agencies of our government that knowingly victimized Social Security recipients.

The revelations were shocking.

Chapter One
Treasury, BFS, Comerica, Conduent, and Direct Express

Our government approves contractors who want to sell their products and/or services. Obtaining a contract to furnish a service or a product to our government is something that businesses and entrepreneurs covet. The Direct Express program was created by the US Treasury and is administered by the division of US Treasury known as Bureau of Fiscal Service (BFS). Treasury needed a bank to run the Direct Express program and Treasury advertised to banks that it was entertaining bids to run the program. Here is an explanation of how the program began. Below are outtakes from three different audit reports:

Office of Inspector General (OIG) Treasury Report 14-031
Published March 26, 2014
Fiscal Service Needs to Improve Program Management of Direct Express

In April 1996, Congress passed the Debt Collection Improvement Act of 1996 (DCIA) requiring that all non-tax federal payments made after January 1, 1999, be paid by electronic funds transfer (EFT). In its effort to implement DCIA, in September 1998 Treasury issued regulations2 which provided that individuals receiving a federal benefit, wage, salary, or retirement payment shall be eligible to open an electronic transfer account (ETA)3 at a federally insured financial institution that offers ETAs.[3]

Pursuant to its authorities, in January 2007 Fiscal Service directed a financial agent, JPMorgan Chase Bank, NA (JPMorgan Chase), to conduct a 1-year pilot program to provide unbanked federal beneficiaries the option to receive federal benefit payments electronically. (12 USC § 90, Depositaries of public moneys and financial agents of Government, provides that the Secretary of the Treasury may select financial agents in accordance with any process the Secretary deems appropriate. The Federal Deposit Insurance Corporation defines unbanked as lacking any kind of deposit account at an insured depository institution.) [4]

Fiscal Service set eight performance metrics for evaluating the pilot program. Eight (8) months into the 1-year pilot, in September 2007, Fiscal Service declared that the success of the pilot supported a national rollout of the program, as the pilot met 3 of the 8 performance metrics – Cost to government of disbursing a payment, Cost of card to beneficiary, and Overall customer satisfaction; Fiscal Service also determined that another metric, Losses due to fraud and unauthorized use, was not material.[5]

Fiscal Service announced in September 2007 that it was seeking applications from financial institutions to serve as the financial agent that provides beneficiaries the option of using a prepaid debit card for receiving federal benefit payments electronically. Fifteen (15) institutions responded to the announcement, and Fiscal Service established a financial agent selection process for Direct Express.[6]

After reviewing average costs within the debit card industry, Fiscal Service decided not to use a cost model or otherwise create a cost estimate to price the program due to the short time to select a financial agent and belief that pricing would be determined by competition. In addition, Fiscal Service did not develop a quality assurance surveillance plan for monitoring the selected financial agent's compliance with the FAA.[3] Direct Express was established by the Department of the Treasury's (Treasury) Financial Management Service. Effective October 7, 2012, Treasury consolidated the Financial Management Service with the Bureau of the Public Debt, and re-designated it as the Bureau of the Fiscal Service. Although most matters discussed in this report occurred while the program was administered by the Financial Management Service, we refer to Fiscal Service throughout this report [7]

In 2008, the Bureau of the Fiscal Service (Fiscal Service)1 established the Direct Express® Debit MasterCard® program (Direct Express), a program that allowed federal beneficiaries to receive benefit payments electronically using a prepaid debit card. Effective March 2013, individuals, with limited exceptions, could no longer receive federal payments by paper check and would have to either receive the payments by direct deposit to a bank account or through the Direct Express prepaid debit card. [8]

Although we do not take issue with the selection of Comerica as the financial agent for Direct Express, Fiscal Service could not support its determination that Comerica would provide the lowest cost/highest quality service to the cardholders at the time of its selection. Also, Fiscal Service did not document its evaluation of Comerica's full technical capabilities, including Comerica's stated capacity to process and accommodate a nationwide prepaid debit card program for federal beneficiaries. [9]

Fiscal Service entered into an FAA with Comerica, effective January 3, 2008, which stated that Comerica would not charge any fees to the government or any government agency and may charge cardholders only the card usage fees prescribed in the FAA. Although the cost of Direct Express was originally free to the government, Fiscal Service amended the FAA, effective March 31, 2011, to provide compensation to Comerica of $5 per new enrollment processed on or after December 1, 2010, and up to $20 million for infrastructure development support (of which $12.7 million was paid as of June 2013). We found that Fiscal Service did not identify, consider, or document all the available options before deciding whether and how much to compensate Comerica for operating the program. [10]

According to Fiscal Service officials, the rationale to compensate Comerica was based on increased demand for the Direct Express card as a result of the "all-electronic mandate." (The "all-electronic mandate" refers to Treasury's December 22, 2010, amendment to its regulation to require recipients of federal non-tax payments to receive payment by EFT, effective May 1, 2011.) Fiscal Service anticipated that the mandate would result in enrollments increasing to between 3 million to 4 million cardholders by 2013. Another consideration was that Comerica's revenue did not meet the bank's expectations because of how Direct Express cardholders used the card (e.g., cardholders were by and large withdrawing cash when benefit payments were loaded on the cards instead of using the cards for purchases, resulting in less interchange income to Comerica). [11]

We believe that amending the FAA to compensate Comerica, in effect, served to guarantee a minimum volume of business and level of compensation. Furthermore, Fiscal Service did not validate the revenue and expense information from Comerica before amending the FAA to compensate Comerica and did not adequately validate infrastructure improvements before paying Comerica. Fiscal Service's decision to pay Comerica for infrastructure development support could also provide Comerica with a future competitive advantage in the rebid of the FAA. [12]

The last paragraph above, noting that the Fiscal Agent Agreement (aka FAA) was "amended" to allow Comerica Bank to be compensated (the original 2008 contract did not allow for Comerica Bank to be paid a fee), is evidence Comerica Bank did not have the infrastructure which Comerica Bank presented (falsely) on the application to become the Fiscal Agent of the Direct Express program.

Office of Inspector General (OIG) Treasury Report 17-034
Published January 24, 2017
Direct Express Bid Evaluation
Documentation Requires Improvement

In 2008, the legacy Financial Management Service₁ entered into a financial agency agreement (FAA) with Comerica Bank (Comerica) to operate the Direct Express® Debit MasterCard® Program (Direct Express). The program allows beneficiaries to receive Federal benefit payments electronically, using a prepaid debit card. In 2014, the Bureau of the Fiscal Service (Fiscal Service) rebid the Direct Express FAA and selected Comerica as the financial agent₂ for an additional 5 years, effective January 3, 2015. [13]

General Accounting Office (GAO) Report 17-176
Published January 25, 2017
A Report to Congressional Requesters.

The Department of the Treasury's (Treasury) use of financial agents has evolved as it has moved from paper to electronic transactions in response to changes in technology and new laws. Treasury has a long history of using financial agents to support its core functions of disbursing payments and collecting revenue. Since the 1980s, Treasury has used agents to move from paper to electronic transactions as it has modernized its systems. For example, Treasury began using financial agents to collect tax revenue electronically in response to a 1984 law and to make payments electronically in response to a 1996 law. Such changes have continued since Congress enacted a permanent, indefinite appropriation in 2004 for Treasury to reimburse financial agents, after which Treasury began including in its annual budget the total amount paid to financial agents. Compensation to financial agents has grown from $378 million in fiscal year 2005 to $636 million in fiscal year 2015, partly due to increases in the number of debit and credit card payments made to federal agencies that are processed by financial agents. While Treasury discloses in its annual budget the total amount paid to financial agents, it has not fully disclosed in a central location information about individual agents, including their compensation and services provided. Treasury officials said they are not required and have not determined a need to publicly disclose compensation under each financial agency agreement. According to an Office of Management and Budget directive on open government, transparency promotes accountability by providing the public with information about government activities. Greater disclosure and transparency could enhance the accountability of Treasury's use of financial agents by informing the public and Congress about how much and for what purposes it is spending federal funds to obtain services from financial agents.

The Bureau of the Fiscal Service (Fiscal Service)—the largest user of financial agents within Treasury— developed its financial agent selection process (FASP) guidance to document the steps and internal controls that its program offices generally are expected to follow in selecting and designating financial agents. The guidance provides assurances that a FASP is effective and efficient, documents key information, and complies with applicable laws and regulations. The guidance directs program offices to maintain an administrative record of key documents generated during a FASP. GAO selected five financial agents designated between 2010 and 2015 to review their administrative records but could review only four because the record for one was not created. None contained all the documents listed in the guidance, but three contained the majority. For example, the record for myRA®, a new retirement savings program using a financial agent to provide custodial services, contained 6 of 11 key documents— missing, for example, certain planning and approval documents. As a result, the records varied in the extent to which they complied with Fiscal Service's guidance, including controls. In November 2015, Fiscal Service revised its guidance to require not only program offices to deliver an electronic copy of their administrative records to the Bank Policy and Oversight (BPO) Division but also BPO to use a checklist to ensure that the records are complete. The 2015 guidance was not in effect for the records GAO reviewed. However, BPO's implementation of the new procedure should provide assurances that future designations are in compliance with the FASP guidance, including controls.

Within Treasury, the Bureau of the Fiscal Service (Fiscal Service) is responsible for the department's basic functions of collecting and holding federal taxes and other revenues and making federal payments. Fiscal Service (and its predecessors) has a long history of using financial agents to help support these functions, and Fiscal Service currently has financial agency agreements with nine financial institutions.

According to Fiscal Service officials, by using financial agents, the department is able to leverage the existing banking infrastructure and avoid the expense of creating a separate government banking system to provide these basic services. Treasury compensates Fiscal Service's financial agents using the permanent, indefinite appropriation, and in fiscal year 2015 Treasury paid Fiscal Service's financial agents $636 million.[14]

3

Below is the chart from GAO 17-176 (January 25, 2017) detailing the Fiscal agents for Bureau of Fiscal Service
[15]

Table 3: Payments Management Programs Using Financial Agents

Program	Program description	Financial agent	Effective date of financial agency agreement
Trust Fund Accounting and Commissary System	The Trust Fund Accounting and Commissary System allows the Bureau of Prisons Central Office and federal prison sites to electronically manage inmate trust fund monies from the time inmates enter the federal prison system until their release. The Trust Fund Accounting and Commissary System also manages all operations of the trust fund for the benefit of the inmates.	Bank of America, National Association	May 3, 2000
Stored Value Card - Navy Cash	The Navy Cash card is a reloadable prepaid debit card that contains both a closed-loop function used on Navy ships and a MasterCard branded open loop function that can be used ashore.	JPMorgan Chase Bank, National Association	August 14, 2003
U.S. Debit Card	The U.S. Debit Card provides a prepaid option for federal agencies to disburse federal payments through electronic funds transfer. The U.S. Debit Card provides various options for executing payments; producing agency reporting requirements; providing branded or nonbranded cards; creating spending limitations and allowances as required; and supporting end users with customer service.	JPMorgan Chase Bank, National Association	October 1, 2008
Stored Value Card - EagleCash & EZPay (Funds	The Stored Value Card Funds Pools Program establishes and maintains funds pools that back Stored Value EagleCash and EZPay Cards.	Bank of America, National Association	January 1, 2010
Non Traditional Alternative Payments	The Non Traditional Alternative Payments Settlement Account is an account in which transactions to alternative payment providers, such as mobile banking technologies and web-based payment systems are processed.	Wells Fargo Bank, National Association	October 16, 2014
Direct Express	The Direct Express card is a prepaid debit card available for federal benefit recipients who lack an account at a financial institution and who are required to receive their benefits electronically.	Comerica Bank	January 3, 2015
Stored Value Card - Navy Cash Open Loop	The Navy Cash Open Loop function is being transitioned from JPMorgan Chase to PNC Bank.	PNC Bank, National Association	July 20, 2015
Military Meal Checks	Military Meal Checks allows the Department of Defense to issue third-party drafts to new military enlistees and trainees for the purpose of purchasing meals while in travel status away from a military installation.	PNC Bank, National Association	July 27, 2015

Chapter Two
There is no Direct Express "Company"

When I enrolled to receive my Social Security monthly payments in 2015, the online Social Security enrollment site recommended that I set up the monthly payments on a Direct Express debit card if the payments were not to go into a conventional bank account. I had no idea the money WAS being sent to a bank, Comerica Bank, and that I would be given an account number at that bank. I signed up and began receiving my monthly Social Security payment.

After approximately 16 months money was twice stolen from my Direct Express debit card account; the first time in January 2017 and then again in December 2017. When I figured out that people at the call center were not going to go to contact the merchants and determine the nature of the fraud, I had to contact the merchants both times to recover the money I lost.

You would think the bank would investigate the fraud I reported and make an inquiry of the merchant to see if the transaction appeared fraudulent. Neither the bank, Comerica Bank, nor their call center, contacted any of the merchants.

Fraudsters were buying video game memberships, online dating apps, vacation trips, perfume, leather jackets, and other online memberships.

After the second fraud episode which was discovered on Saturday, December 9, 2017, I began trying to find out how persons were twice able to steal money from my debit card account. I had to contact the merchants both times and "convince" them that the charges were fraudulent because I knew Comerica bank and the call center were not going to be helpful. The merchants agreed to return my money both in January 2017 and December 2017, however, they had not been contacted by Comerica Bank to be notified that the transactions were fraudulent. The common denominator regarding both instances of fraud was Comerica Bank, which did nothing to help recover my money, nor was the bank willing to acknowledge the fraud and subsequently credit my account. Research revealed Comerica had violated federal banking laws regarding acknowledging notice of fraud, provisional credit upon notification, and conducting investigations.

After becoming aware of fraudulent charges, I called the call center both times and was told the pending charges (which were blatantly fraudulent) could not be taken off my account. The attendant said she would send the matter to the fraud unit, but she could not forward my call. The fraud unit cannot receive an incoming call from a person at the call center. Customers cannot directly contact the fraud unit.

Having been a private investigator first licensed in 1981 and licensed for over 25 years, fraud and other criminal activity were nothing new to me. I operated my agency for 19 years. Before that, I was in banking for a few years. I had sources and instincts.

After figuring out how my debit card account was hacked, and by whom, I was interested to know why the people at Comerica Bank allowed this to happen and failed to follow up on the fraud claim.

I did what most victims do; I contacted the Better Business Bureau. Then I contacted the Consumer Financial Protection Bureau. Neither responded directly to me; they both directed my complaint to Susan Schmidt of Comerica Bank. I just filled out online forms and submitted the forms to the "black hole" of the internet hotline links.

After hearing nothing from the Comerica Bank fraud unit, I decided to start digging.

Wednesday, December 13, 2017, was to be a busy day. The internet revealed Comerica Bank had a division called Corporation Quality Assurance and the telephone number was in Detroit, Michigan. I called the number at 2:10 pm, received a recorded voice message, and left a message of my own. The voice message I left would be particularly important at a later date.

Afterward, I found a fax number on the Direct Express website, and at 4:14 pm I faxed a copy of my debit card statement sheet which revealed 6 fraudulent transactions on my debit card account.

Two days later, on December 15, 2017, I received an email from a person named James stating he was a Customer Advocate for Direct Express. On the same afternoon, as I was walking my friend's dog, I received a call from a person named James who sent me the email. I told James I had faxed a copy of my statement noting the fraud to the telephone number found on the website. James was an empty-headed arrogant putz, telling me he had my fax in his hand. After telling him this was my second fraud report and demanding to know what he was going to do, he refused to connect me to a fraud investigator. I ended the call.

On December 13, 2017, a report was filed with the Better Business Bureau regarding Comerica Bank. I thought this was the thing to do, but I soon realized that all complaints to the BBB went straight to the Comerica Bank office in Detroit.

Wednesday, December 20, 2017

Ann Atkinson aatkinson@austin.bbb.org
Wed, Dec 20, 2017, 9:02 AM
to me:
In that case, your best source for the next steps would be a regulatory agency that could assist you in taking action against the business. You may want to reach out to the Texas Department of Banking. Or the Attorney General's Office:
Regards,
Ann Atkinson, Alternative Dispute Resolution Specialist
Better Business Bureau, 1805 Rutherford Ln, Ste. 100, Austin, Texas 78754
p: 512.206.2824

Beginning an hour after I discovered the fraud on Saturday, December 9, I spent the next few days dealing with Zulily, the company where two of the fraudsters charged my account. After the Zulily Customer Service personnel cooperated in a limited manner, I found the attorneys for Zulily and left messages at the telephone numbers I discovered. That opened the doors to more information, and the Zulily Customer Service employees began cooperating. Eventually, I determined that the fraudsters were buying perfume and a brown leather jacket to be sent to India.

After gentle persuasion, the Zulily attendant gave me the address from which the merchandise was ordered, and I determined the location was a restaurant named House of India in Columbia, Virginia. Law enforcement jurisdiction of this area is handled by the Howard County Sheriff's Department, so I contacted them and sent them a narrative of the incident alerting them that fraudsters were operating in their area.

Zulily refunded my charges. Comerica and their call center (later I determined this was not their call center, but a subcontractor third party) tried to take credit for the refund. There were a few menial hacks for a few dollars, and when Comerica saw that Zulily refunded large amounts of two purchases, Comerica credited the small fraudulent charges.

After alerting the Howard County Sheriff's Department to the fraudsters from India being in their county, I became curious as to how and why Comerica Bank was allowing this fraud and why there were no investigations by a Comerica Bank Fraud Unit.

I was having an issue with Susan Schmidt referring me to a "Customer Advocate" and not addressing the matter herself. What was the purpose of a Customer Advocate? Why could no one see the fraud, which was perpetrated thousands of miles from me, the cardholder?

Susan Schmidt's response to the Consumer Financial Protection Bureau and the Better Business Bureau was such that she was to pass the problem to someone at "Direct Express." Wait, there is no company named Direct Express, so who was the person to whom Schmidt was sending my fraud complaint? The man named James said he represented Direct Express, and he was useless. I needed to talk to Schmidt.

On Wednesday, January 24, 2018, I again tried to reach Schmidt of Comerica Bank by telephone. I called and left a message for her on December 13, 2017, and no one returned the call. I thought the recorded message would be received and the call returned. I was wrong to assume the call would be returned.

On this later date, I dialed the number I saw listed in Schmidt's reply to the Consumer Financial Protection Bureau. A person named Susan Rutledge took the call. Ms. Rutledge stated her telephone number was (313) 222- 9302, that Schmidt was not at work that day, and she was in the same office as Schmidt. I explained the fraud matter and that the complaint from the Consumer Financial Protection Bureau was routed through Susan Schmidt and subsequently to a "Customer Advocate" who stated he worked for Direct Express. Was Susan Schmidt supposed to push the button and reimburse fraud victims? I asked Ms. Rutledge to leave a message for Schmidt to call me.

After having received no call from Schmidt over the next few hours, I called Rutledge again, was transferred to a voice mail for Ms. Rutledge, and left a message. Afterward, I called Schmidt at (313) 222-7934 and got her voicemail as well.

Thursday, January 25, 2018

The call from Susan Schmidt, Comerica Bank

12:00 pm

The return call from Susan Schmidt of Comerica Bank was received and Ms. Schmidt admitted she had received the complaints from the BBB and the Consumer Financial Protection Bureau. (I made complaints to several other agencies as well). Schmidt stated Comerica Bank manages the Direct Express program. I questioned how my account was handled. Ms. Schmidt stated she would forward my concern that day to a person with Direct Express named Steven who was in Austin, TX.

I asked Ms. Schmidt about my call and the voice message I left approximately six weeks prior for her office on December 13, 2017. She admitted that the telephone number I called was a number answered in her office area. I then asked if Comerica Bank kept the recording of the messages. She stated they did. I then asked her to research the records to find the call. She immediately stated there was no record of my call, which was a lie.

I found it interesting that this was the same office, Corporate Quality Division at Comerica Bank, which I had contacted over 6 weeks prior, and they never returned my call. Schmidt, of Comerica Bank, evidently did not return telephone calls, she also ignored my message of December 13, which was never returned. It appeared the Corporate Quality Division of Comerica was equally culpable as any fraud or customer service personnel associated with the Direct Express program.

In the meantime, I was attempting to do end-of-year tax work. I discovered that the Direct Express program did not allow customers to view their transactions before 90 days. This caused me hardship.

The "Direct Express" call: case closed?

Immediately after the call ended with Ms. Schmidt of Comerica, I received a call at 12:16 pm from James of Direct Express. James stated he considered the matter of my fraud complaint closed. I told him I wanted to see the investigation that took place on my account. James refused to provide a copy of the investigation. I quoted Regulation E to him, advising him I was entitled to a copy of the investigative report. I then asked James if he had banking experience and if he had taken AIB Courses. James stated," I do not have to tell you that."

(AIB, American Institute of Banking, is a banking educational institution that offers classes addressing different banking subjects. Banking employees must take AIB courses to progress in the ranks in the banking industry. All the reporting and regulatory agencies I contacted which were supposed to protect consumers kept referring me to other places. No one took responsibility or enforced compliance with federal banking laws upon Comerica Bank. The watchdog agencies sent me to Susan Schmidt of Comerica Bank.

On January 26, 2018, I received an email from the Customer Response Center of the Federal Deposit Insurance Corporation, which regulates Comerica Bank as a state-chartered bank. The email stated my complaint was being forwarded to the Consumer Financial Protection Bureau (CFPB).

My impression of the email I received from the FDIC was that their email to me was a "scripted, canned reply." I stated I had contacted the CFPB which simply sent the complaint to Comerica Bank (Schmidt in particular) without an investigation. I also noted that Comerica Bank was given constructive notice of fraud, as defined by Regulation E (the federal banking law, 15USC1693) when I left the voice message as a recording at Susan Schmidt's office on December 13, 2017.

I filed a second complaint with the CFPB.

Monday, February 5, 2018

The ineffective Consumer Financial Protection Bureau (CFPB)

I had been calling many people at regulatory and reporting agencies only to continue getting the run-a-round. I was getting weary. The only thing that kept me going was the fact that I knew I was not the only victim out there and that no one was going after Comerica harder than me.

I decided to call the Consumer Financial Protection Bureau again.

At 12:08 pm I called the headquarters at (202) 435-7000. I talked to a lady identified as Keosha who was in the Consumer Complaint Division. Keosha was polite and when I asked her direct questions concerning the purpose of her agency and the fact that the CFPB has enforcement authority but is never used, her answers were shocking. She stated the following:

1. My case(s) against Comerica Bank was being closed.
2. CFPB cannot investigate each complaint.
3. Keosha did not know the threshold number of complaints that start an investigation.
4. I needed to hire a private attorney.

I began searching the internet and found complaints by people having a Direct Express debit card. There was a website named "Pissed Consumer" and I saw several complaints, so I submitted my experience with the Direct Express program and my contact information. This was to be the beginning of a long ride. This would lead to over a hundred people contacting me directly.

I began receiving telephone calls and emails from victims. I had no idea how much work I was creating for myself, but I knew others would not be as forceful as me to get my money and to make someone accountable. From this point on I will paste the narratives of the people who contacted me. The narratives are in chronological order but there are a few instances when the dates do not appear to be in order. There might have been a few conversations before the emails were sent, but the names of the people are in the correct order in which I was contacted. There will be typos, sentence fragments, and grammatical errors within the email, copied as written by the original sender or recipient.

These communications were sent from victims of financial fraud, and they were contacting me because Comerica Bank and their call center had failed to abide by Regulation E.

Sunday, February 25, 2018

Victim Number 1-Brian (Gainesville, Florida)
9:19 pm
"Some kid hacked my son's Play Station account and got my Direct express (or should I say Direct access) card info and in 6 hours he banged me for $284.00.
He bought several games and game packs that he downloaded. When I saw this I almost snatched my son up but he swore it wasn't him and showed me his downloaded games. He was telling me the truth. So I called Sony and they said that you could see that the IP address was different and the little *** was downloading a game now. They stopped it and froze his account. They gave me a claim number and told me to contact my bank to file a complaint. They told me to give them the claim number they had just given me and when they contact them they would refund my money because you could see that they were fraudulent charges. They just needed my bank to contact them basically and it would be a done deal because it was an obvious theft.
I contacted Direct Express then printed the form they told me they needed and they would take care of it within 10 to 14 working days of receiving it. Filled the form out with the claim number from Sony on there and a comment about what Sony said then mailed it that day. Three weeks later I called to see what was going on and was told a decision was made and they were not at fault so my claim was denied.
Thanks, Brian
Banks and insurance companies have so much power they think they are above the law and are too powerful to be messed with and I am sick to death with it. They are the true axis of evil in this world."

Monday, February 19, 2018

Victim Number 2-Paul (Las Vegas, Nevada)
8:26 PM email to me
Hello J.B.,
"My name is Paul from Pissed Consumer website. Found this email address on the internet and not the Erik Publishing site. Noticed that approx. 180 other individuals have contacted you about their Direct Express problems. I would like to introduce my problem with Direct Express as well. My only difference is that they stole sothing from me and I stopped them in their tracks. I am at a very distrusting stage and I'm certain that you understand. Have we found a way to communicate with each other and know who we are speaking with as of yet? This is what really frightens me the worst. If you have anything you can add in order for us to feel comfortable with this, I'm listening. Thank you and look forward to speaking with you,"
Paul ordered a new Direct Express debit card. The customer service personnel employed by Conduent sent the request to the company named Fiserv which printed cards. Someone intercepted the shipping of the card through FedEx and had the card delivered to an area north of Miami, FL. When Paul did not receive his card, he found the bogus FedEx account and the destination of his new card. Paul ordered another card, and luckily Paul's card arrived before the Direct Express debit card arrived in Florida.
Paul's encounter will appear again.

Tuesday, February 20, 2018

Victim Number 3- (Mt Vernon, WA)
Email received: The cardholder lost $915. His funds were electronically withdrawn from his Direct Express account.

Victim Number 4- Dean (Philadelphia, PA)

Dean emailed me. We talked. The notes are below.

Dean is 47 years of age. From January 29, 2018-February 7, 2018, he lived on North Broad Street, Philadelphia. Dean was transported by ambulance to a hospital. All identification was left in his apartment. While in the hospital, SSA money was deposited into his account. Someone broke into his apartment and stole his bank card (all personal documents were left at the apartment). His Direct Express debit card was used at an ATM (the thief found his PIN in his room). $725 taken. Dean could not pay rent- had to move into a homeless shelter.

Thursday, February 22, 2018

The Day of Revelation

At 2:01 pm I called the FDIC at (877) 275-3342. A lady answered the call and told me the FDIC did not oversee the Direct Express program or Comerica Bank (oddly the Comerica Bank website stated Comerica Bank was insured by the FDIC). I was referred to the Federal Reserve OIG (Office of Inspector General) at (855) 411-2372.

At 2:26 pm a call was placed to (855) 411-2372. This was the number given by the Federal Reserve OIG which oversees Consumer Financial Protection Bureau. I talked to an operator named Asha.

Asha was given the following case numbers given to me by the CFPB:171229-27440881 and 18103-2747258. (After filing a report in December 2017, the CFPB was contacted again, and a subsequent number was given).

The following is what was learned from Asha on this date, February 22, 2018:

Comerica Bank/Direct Express program has 414 complaints, spanning 17 pages on her computer screen.

The CFPB does have enforcement authority but hardly ever uses that authority.

The CFPB cannot investigate each complaint.

Asha did not know the threshold number of complaints against a bank that would generate an investigation.

Asha referred me to the CFPB Ombudsman at (855) 830-7880.

I then called OIG SSA (Social Security Administration) at (800) 269-0271 and submitted a complaint to their office.

I realized the money I was receiving on my Direct Express card was my Social Security money. I figured I would report this to the Social Security Administration.

Below is the email I received from the Social Security Administration:

OIG Hotline OIG.Hotline@ssa.gov
Thu, Feb 22, 2018, 5:31 PM to me
Social Security Administration
Office of the Inspector General
Allegation Management and Fugitive Enforcement Division
We have received your recent internet communication of potential fraud, waste, and/or abuse in Social Security Administration programs. Thank you for taking the time to send us your report. Your allegation will be carefully reviewed. Federal law prohibits the disclosure of any information relating to allegations of potential wrongdoing; even to the person who filed the initial report. Therefore, we will be unable to provide you with any information relating to actions we may take. However, if you have additional information that you wish to add to your report, please contact us using one of the following:
Internet:http://oig.ssa.gov Mail: Social Security Administration
Office of the Inspector General
Allegation Management and Fugitive Enforcement Division

Sending a complaint to a "hotline" for any federal agency might generate a response but rarely results in any corrective action.

Friday, February 23, 2018

Victim Number 5- Nancy, Los Angeles

Fraudulent charges were found on the SSA payment for her two disabled children. The charges were from Johannesburg, South Africa on February 1, 2018

Page One- $1,035.94 Page Two- $312.48 Total-$1,348.42

Nancy stated in an email:

On more than one ocassion money has just. Been fradulently taken out of my account and don't get it back this last time feb 1 I get my two sons ssi money in there 1,300 or something all of it stolen from my account same day by fradulent charges from company's in Africa when I. Called them to tell them it wasn't me they said wel do u know who I said no then they tell me it takes 90 days I gotta fill out papers and send them back I did now everytime I.call to check status they either hang up on me or can't help me I had to pay rent and bills and I couldn't because someone decided to steal my ssi benefits and these people don't give a fuck there horrible last time my money dissapared I had to file complaint with BBB to finally get something back but this is not right it can't be how there running this neway thanx for replying I'm in California Too Los Angeles actually/

The money was recovered a month or so later, then Comerica took the money back again. The Conduent people could not see the fraud.

Saturday, February 24, 2018

I began receiving telephone calls from more victims. A lady named Nancy from Los Angeles called me after I emailed her my telephone number. Nancy lived in Los Angeles and had two handicapped children. Her children's Social Security money was fraudulently taken by a person in Africa. Nancy told me she had never been to Africa. I told her the person she needed to call. She would get back to me later.

During the previous year, I wrote and published a book entitled *Friendly Fire at the Veterans Hospital*. I learned that cabinet-level offices and other agencies have divisions within their agencies referred to as the Office of Inspector General (OIG). I knew that the state banks regulated by the FDIC were accountable to the Consumer Financial Protection Bureau, and the watchdog of this agency was the Federal Reserve OIG. I contacted the Federal Reserve OIG on Feb 22, but I needed to see if an OIG report existed within Treasury concerning the Direct Express program and Comerica Bank. Maybe there would be a report somewhere that I could read.

This was the turning point of the case.

I went to the internet and found OIG Treasury Audit 14-031. The findings of the report were that the Bureau of Fiscal Service, which operates the Direct Express program and awarded the original contract to Comerica Bank in 2008, needed to improve the management of the Direct Express program. There were many suggestions made for improvement. There were no references in later reports that improvements had been made.

I realized that Comerica Bank bid to become a Fiscal Agent of the Bureau of Fiscal Service. As a Fiscal Agent, Comerica was to dispense money to recipients of Social Security, Veteran Affairs Benefits, and a few other government agencies. If the recipient person did not have a bank account or chose to receive their benefits on a credit card, the funds were placed onto a Direct Express debit card. The card was associated with Comerica Bank.

When OIG Treasury Audit 14-031 was published on March 26, 2014, the Commissioner of the Bureau of Fiscal Service was David A. Lebryk (who later took a different position at BFS and is employed at BFS as of this writing).

The following passages were found in OIG Treasury 14-031:

To accomplish our objectives, we reviewed: (1) Fiscal Service's considerations in initiating the program, (2) Fiscal Service's financial agent selection process and the selection of Comerica as the Direct Express financial agent, (3) the terms of the financial agency agreement (FAA), (4) how an amendment to the FAA to compensate Comerica was vetted and approved, and (5) Fiscal Service's monitoring of the FAA. We interviewed officials and staff with Fiscal Service, Comerica, the Federal Reserve Bank of Dallas, and the Social Security Administration (SSA). We also reviewed Fiscal Service's policies and procedures and examined documents related to the origination and administration of the FAA. Additionally, we visited two call centers that handled Direct Express calls to gain an understanding of call center operation. [16]

Although we do not take issue with the selection of Comerica as the financial agent for Direct Express, Fiscal Service could not support its determination that Comerica would provide the lowest cost/highest quality service to the cardholders at the time of its selection. Also, Fiscal Service did not document its evaluation of Comerica's full technical capabilities, including Comerica's stated capacity to process and accommodate a nationwide prepaid debit card program for federal beneficiaries. [17]

Fiscal Service entered into an FAA with Comerica, effective January 3, 2008, which stated that Comerica would not charge any fees to the government or any government agency and may charge cardholders only the card usage fees prescribed in the FAA. Although the cost of Direct Express was originally free to the government, Fiscal Service amended the FAA, effective March 31, 2011, to provide compensation to Comerica *of $5 per new enrollment processed on or after December 1, 2010, and up to $20 million for infrastructure development support (of which $12.7 million was paid as of June 2013). We found that Fiscal Service did not identify, consider, or document all the available options before deciding whether and how much to compensate Comerica for operating the program.[18]*

According to Fiscal Service officials, the rationale to compensate Comerica was based on increased demand for the Direct Express card as a result of the "all-electronic mandate."6 Fiscal Service anticipated that the mandate would result in enrollments increasing to between 3 million to 4 million cardholders by 2013. Another consideration was that Comerica's revenue did not meet the bank's expectations because of how Direct Express cardholders used the card (e.g., cardholders were by and large withdrawing cash when benefit payments were loaded on the cards instead of using the cards for purchases, resulting in less interchange income[7] to Comerica).[19]

The primary source of income to Comerica from Direct Express is interchange income.[20]

BFS did not document the lack of infrastructure presented by Comerica Bank in its application for the contract. Also, Comerica Bank got the bid by initially agreeing to take no money (no pay) for operating the program. Comerica Bank returned to BFS at a later date to be paid tens of millions of dollars for "infrastructure" which included paying the call centers, a task ultimately performed by a company named Conduent. This was the plan all along: Comerica Bank would do what was necessary to get the contract, knowing their lack of infrastructure was concealed, noting the call center would be operated by a third party, and Comerica would return to BFS to be paid. (One of the prerequisites for being the Fiscal Agent was that the infrastructure was to have been in place at the time of the submission of the application. Comerica Bank falsified the application.)

Now it was clear: There was never a company named Direct Express. Direct Express was the name of a program, not a company. Comerica Bank contracted with a call center company named Conduent to handle the accounts (call center, customer service, fraud department) while Comerica Bank stated in their application to BFS that Comerica Bank did have the infrastructure to handle 5 million accounts. This was the first lie.

Years later it was learned Comerica Bank did not reveal that Conduent would be the custodian of all records of the Direct Express program. Comerica Bank housed no cardholder records. This explained why Schmidt referred me to Conduent employees; Comerica Bank had no cardholder records.

The footnote on Page 7 of Treasury Audit 14-031 report noted that cardholders were not using the debit cards to interact with merchants, which was the reason Comerica Bank gave to justify returning to take more money from Treasury.[17] Comerica Bank should have known the cardholders were older persons who were not used to using debit cards for small purchases. They made big cash withdrawals from an ATM and paid for purchases using cash.

We believe that amending the FAA to compensate Comerica, in effect, served to guarantee a minimum volume of business and level of compensation. Furthermore, Fiscal Service did not validate the revenue and expense information from Comerica before amending the FAA to compensate Comerica and did not adequately validate infrastructure improvements before paying Comerica. Fiscal Service's decision to pay Comerica for infrastructure development support could also provide Comerica with a future competitive advantage in the rebid of the FAA.[21]

All of the six finalists offered pricing at no cost to the government.[22]

Comerica Bank knew it was going back to be paid. It is hard to believe Lebryk and others at BFS were not privy to the devious Comerica plan. The revelation that paying Comerica would give Comerica an advantage as the incumbent during the rebid fell on deaf ears. Lebryk and BFS had their reasons for awarding the contract to Comerica Bank; reasons they kept secret.

We acknowledge the importance of Direct Express to achieve the goal of DCIA and Treasury's "all electronic mandate." However, as discussed in our report, we are concerned with Fiscal Service's administration of the Direct Express program, its enforcement of the terms of the FAA, and its overreliance on the financial agent for decision-making information. Also, we found that Fiscal Service's documentation supporting key decisions and the ongoing monitoring of a program involving tens of millions of taxpayer dollars and the delivery of payments to millions of Federal beneficiaries was often lacking.[23]

It was apparent OIG Treasury had no faith in BFS or Comerica Bank to handle the Direct Express program, but no one was made accountable to the cardholders.

It looked like the tail (Comerica Bank) was wagging the dog (Bureau of Fiscal Service and OIG Treasury) but it was later discovered that the tail might have been the subcontractor used by Comerica Bank to operate the call centers; Conduent.

Fifteen (15) institutions responded to Fiscal Service's announcement for a financial agent for Direct Express. After an initial review, Fiscal Service determined that all but two of the applicants met the requirements of the financial agent selection process.[11] Fiscal Service conducted a preliminary evaluation of the remaining 13 applicants to determine whether each applicant:

• Was qualified to act as a financial agent
• Had partners or affiliated organizations with which Treasury had no concerns
• Was qualified to issue MasterCard- or Visa-branded debit cards nationwide
• Was able to establish reloadable debit card accounts insured by the Federal Deposit Insurance Corporation and subject to Regulation E[12] protection
• Was able to establish and staff an enrollment and customer service call center with U.S. citizens or lawful resident aliens no later than January 2008
• Had sufficient experience issuing debit cards

[12]Regulation E, set forth by the Board of Governors of the Federal Reserve System, outlines the rules and procedures for electronic funds transfers and the guidelines for those who sell and issue electronic debit cards. Rules for consumer liability for unauthorized card usage fall under this regulation as well.[24]

Not only had Comerica Bank falsified their bid submission by stating Comerica, *"[W] as able to establish reloadable debit card accounts insured by the Federal Deposit Insurance Corporation and subject to Regulation E protection"* [25] but flagrant violations of Regulation E on my account (and others to be seen later) proved that Comerica Bank had no intention of abiding by Regulation E. Sadly, BFS was not going to hold Comerica Bank accountable and OIG Treasury was not going to enforce the law.

A critical concept in federal procurement regulations is that quality assurance surveillance plans be put in place to determine if the government is actually receiving the goods and services it purchased in accordance with the contract. Fiscal Service did not develop a quality surveillance plan to determine if the government and cardholders were receiving services in accordance with the FAA.[26]

OIG Treasury stated that BFS had no follow-up plan to see how Comerica Bank was servicing the cardholder. *Comerica has not consistently met some service level requirements in the FAA and Fiscal Service has not enforced these requirements.[27]*

Hidden within a paragraph on Page 23 was the following passage:

We found that the customer satisfaction surveys were conducted annually, not monthly. Fiscal Service was satisfied with the frequency of the surveys and we do not consider this non- compliance with the FAA to be a significant issue. As an observation, however, we do note that the surveys were not independent (i.e., conducted by a party reporting directly to Fiscal Service), but rather conducted by a company commissioned by Comerica and MasterCard.[28]

Comerica Bank was cooking the books. The "satisfaction surveys" were conducted by a subcontractor of Comerica Bank and MasterCard, not independently commissioned by BFS. Comerica Bank was in effect "grading their own test papers."

The first sentence in the Concluding remarks of OIG Treasury 14-031 is below:

Although Fiscal Service's decisions to create Direct Express and select Comerica as the program's financial agent were reasonable, we are concerned with Fiscal Service's administration of the Direct Express program, its enforcement of the terms of the FAA, and its overreliance on Comerica for decision-making information. Fiscal Service did not construct an independent government cost estimate during the financial agent selection process or before amending the FAA to determine whether the costs Comerica incurred or may incur in performing services for Direct Express were reasonable and fair. Particularly surprising to us was that Comerica never formally asked Fiscal Service for a change in the FAA to provide compensation.[29]

BFS had given Comerica Bank and Conduent free reign. Not only was there no enforcement of the terms of the FAA (Fiscal Agent Agreement) by BFS, but Comerica Bank also never formally submitted the request for funding after receiving the bid; the funding (which was not part of the original FAA) was received by a mere undocumented hint to an unidentified person or persons at the Bureau of Fiscal Service. Culpability, malfeasance, or failure to perform, as documented in the inadequate audit by OIG Treasury, failed to produce tangible evidence of Comerica's subsequent funding upon obtaining the bid for an unfunded contract.

OIG Treasury 14-031 was a joke. This was not a credible investigation and dictates from OIG Treasury were not enforceable. Little did I know that the second audit, OIG Treasury 17-034 was no better.

Below are outtakes from Treasury OIG 17-034 published January 24, 2107. This was the second audit of the Direct Express program which was created by BFS.

Fiscal Service followed applicable laws, regulations, policies, and procedures when selecting Comerica as the Direct Express financial agent. However, we noted concerns with the documentation of the bid evaluation.

12

These included simple errors and other issues with form and substance that could make it difficult for Fiscal Service to justify its award decisions, especially given that Fiscal Service selected a proposal with higher out-of-pocket costs to the government and less savings to the cardholders.[30]

So, what was the justification for awarding Comerica the bid the second time?

Transition costs are of particular interest since an overemphasis of these costs could result in an insurmountable advantage in favor of the incumbent. Such an advantage could restrict future competition by discouraging potential bidders from submitting a proposal if they perceive that it would be overly difficult for another bidder to unseat the incumbent. This situation could also provide an incumbent with undue leverage over the Federal Government in negotiating future terms, conditions, and compensation.[31]

In May 2014, Comerica and Bank A separately gave oral presentations further detailing their proposals and answering questions from Fiscal Service.[32]

In April 2019 Thomas Santaniello of BFS refused to allow Jackie Densmore and me, both victims of Direct Express fraud, from testifying before this group. BFS was operating in the shadows, protecting the "decision-makers."

According to Fiscal Service's Evaluation of Applicants, both Comerica and Bank A were capable of delivering a service that would meet or exceed all of the technical requirements in the solicitation. This evaluation document also stated that Bank A's proposal would be less costly to the cardholders, but transitioning the FAA to a new financial agent would involve significant and unavoidable disruptions to both the cardholders and the benefit agencies and would be more expensive to the Federal Government. Accordingly, Fiscal Service selected Comerica to continue operating Direct Express.[33]

The fix was in. The cake was baked. Comerica Bank submitted inaccurate information to get the federal contract.

We have concerns with the bid evaluation documentation that could make it difficult for Fiscal Service to justify or defend its award decision. In addition, several documents in the FAA file contained inaccurate and/or incomplete information.[34]

BFS ignored inaccurate and incomplete information submitted by Comerica Bank. OIG Treasury failed to specify the documents or information, which made them as guilty as BFS. There was a connection between OIG Treasury and BFS employees; they both drank from the same trough.

Transition costs are of particular interest, especially if an overemphasis is placed on the weight of these costs in the bid evaluation. If the emphasis placed on transition costs is not properly tailored to the lifecycle of the program underbid, it could result in an insurmountable advantage for the incumbent. Such an advantage could restrict future competition by discouraging potential bidders from submitting a proposal if they perceive that it would be overly difficult for another bidder to unseat the incumbent. This situation could also provide an incumbent with undue leverage over the Federal Government in negotiating future terms, conditions, and compensation.[35]

BFS made certain that Comerica obtained the "leverage" necessary to be awarded the new bid. It appeared that the "deep pockets" of Conduent were the genesis of the scam.

File Documents Contained Incorrect and Incomplete Information

The Fiscal Service FAA file contained documents such as the Evaluation of Applicants, the Direct Express FASP12 Scoring Methodology, and the FASP Execution Plan to record the rationale, assumptions, plans, and support for selecting the financial agent for Direct Express. The file included documents that contained incorrect and incomplete information. Specifically, the following documents contain examples of incorrect and incomplete information.

The Evaluation of Applicants document approved in August 2014 contains these statements and inaccuracies:
"The cumulative cost to the government of selecting Comerica would range from $38 million to $42 million." Separate supporting documentation showed a range of $35 million to $42 million.
"Direct Express had 5.2 million active accounts in May 2015." May 2015 was 9 months after Fiscal Service approved the document, and separate supporting documentation showed that Direct Express had about 3 million active accounts as of May 2014, the time of the evaluation.

"Comerica's surcharge-free network has 100,000 locations." Comerica's oral presentation to Fiscal Service in May 2014 included a reference to 85,000 surcharge-free locations.

The Direct Express FASP Scoring Methodology document contains a statement that "the pessimistic scenario's estimated transition costs are $63.92 million." A different page of the document (and the separate Evaluation of Finalists document) showed the "pessimistic" total as $59.08 million.[36]

Comerica Bank overstated the number of active accounts by 2.2 million. Comerica Bank overstated the number of surcharge-free network locations by 15,000. This was more evidence of submitting false documents to obtain the cherished government contract.

A note in the appendix of the report was noted:

Note E – To address this recommendation, Fiscal Service intended to establish the Financial Agent Oversight Group, a working group tasked to establish oversight policies, including a standard checklist for document retention. Fiscal Service established the working group and as of March 2016, adopted the oversight policies related to FAA documentation. Fiscal Service also told us that appropriate documentation was maintained for Direct Express and that they had closed the recommendation internally. Although Fiscal Service improved file documentation since our last audit, further improvement is needed. Our current audit disclosed that important FAA file documents contained incorrect and incomplete information. Accordingly, this report addresses this finding and related recommendations.

We recommend that the Fiscal Service Commissioner improve the documentation of FAA bid evaluations by ensuring that (1) factors under consideration are presented in comparable terms and the rationale for selecting factors and weights used is adequately described and (2) accurate and complete documentation is maintained for FAA files.[37]

At the end of the second audit, the following was discovered:

We appreciate the courtesies and cooperation provided to our staff during the audit. Major contributors to this report are listed in appendix 4. A distribution list for this report is provided as appendix 5. If you wish to discuss the report, you may contact me at (202) 927-5904 or Greg Sullivan, Audit Manager, at (202) 927-5369.

/s/

Kieu T. Rubb
Audit Director[38]

I saw someone I could call.

I studied the audits. There was no record of interviews with Conduent employees. Conduent was not mentioned. Conduent was operating the call centers and had access to all five million Direct Express cardholders. If OIG Treasury "investigated" Comerica and Conduent, there was no evidence of this in either OIG Treasury report. I knew something was fishy. No one was doing their job.

The call center Comerica Bank was using was not part of Comerica Bank; the call center for the Direct Express program was not operated by Comerica Bank, nor was the call center operated by a company named Direct Express. Again, there is no company named Direct Express. The call center was operated by a company named Conduent.

Conduent was determined to have been a subsidiary of Xerox. The workers at Conduent who were masquerading as Direct Express call center and "Customer Advocacy" employees were violating Regulation E which governed Comerica Bank, and thus Conduent. Conduent was not a bank but was performing banking functions. How does that happen?

Sunday, February 25, 2018

An email came in first thing this morning. A man named Brian from Philadelphia wrote that his Direct Express account had been hacked through his son's Play Station account. The IP address was not that of Brian's. He lost $284.00. Brian contacted who he thought was Direct Express. Brian was told it would take 10-14 days to get his money back; that was three weeks ago. I gave him the phone number for Susan Schmidt at Comerica Bank. Here is what Brian emailed to me:

Some kid hacked my son's Play Station account and got my Direct express (or should I say Direct access) card info. and in 6 hours he banged me for $284.00.

He bought several games and game packs that he downloaded. When I saw this I almost snatched my son up but he swore it wasn't him and showed me his downloaded games. He was telling me the truth. So I called Sony and they said that you could see that the IP address was different and the little *** was downloading a game now. They stopped it and froze his account. They gave me a claim number and told me to contact my bank to file a complaint. They told me to give them the claim number they had just given me and when they contact them they

14

would refund my money because you could see that they were fraudulent charges. They just needed my bank to contact them basically and it would be a done deal because it was an obvious theft.
I contacted Direct Express then printed the form they told me they needed and they would take care of it within 10 to 14 working days of receiving it. Filled the form out with the claim number from Sony on there and a comment about what Sony said then mailed it that day. Three weeks later I called to see what was going on and was told a decision was made and they were not at fault so my claim was denied.   Thanks, Brian   Banks and insurance companies have so much power they think they are above the law and are too powerful to be messed with and I am sick to death with it. They are the true axis of evil in this world.

Monday, March 26, 2018

Today was the day I would confront OIG Treasury. I studied both reports. I knew the name of the audit director would be found at the end of the report, and I found the name of Kieu T. Rubb as an auditor on the latest OIG report. The telephone number (202) 927-5904 was listed as the telephone number for Ms. Rubb.
The following is an account of the beginning of my experience with OIG Treasury.
9:15 am
T (202) 927-5904 OIG Treasury Audit Director Kieu T. Rubb (signed OIG audit)- Voice Mail referred to Paulette Battle, (202) 927-5400 as the new auditor.
Other names on the final page of the OIG report were:
Michael J. Maloney (202) 927-6512
Christen Stevenson (202) 927-8117
9:16am
T (202) 927-5400 OIG for Paulette Battle- transferred to Paulette Battle. I gave info to Ms. Battle that the two previous OIG audit reports were inadequate, the call center employees were ill-suited to handle banking customers, and Susan Schmidt lied to me regarding having no record of a voicemail message I left in December. Ms. Battle was polite, and receptive, and offered to take the matter to her boss.
958am
After a bit of confusion with her email address, a follow-up email was sent to Ms. Battle. A second telephone call was made to reach Ms. Battle. She stated she had received the email and again would refer it to her boss. The conversation with Paulette Battle would be the event that set everything into action.

Thursday, March 1, 2018

A website was discovered related to the Bureau of Fiscal Service, Department of Treasury. I emailed a complaint to this address. I figured this would be a "black hole" of a hotline email, but I sent it anyway.

Monday, March 5, 2018

I was wondering if the Board of Directors of Comerica Bank had any idea of the violations of Regulation E by Comerica Bank and Conduent as well as the two OIG Treasury reports.
I looked at the website for Comerica Bank, found the names of some of the members of the Board of Directors, and made the following contact:

11:58 am
T (727) 423-3481 Michael E. Collins, Comerica Board Member- Left message with Tony Collins- voicemail
1216pm
I emailed Blake Collins info@blakecollinsgroup.com

Tuesday, March 6, 2018

Researching Comerica Board Members was my first activity.
913am T (480) 214-7400 for Roger A Cregg- ext. 7402: left message, voicemail.
Reginald Turner- emailed him at rturner@clarkhill.com
Jacqueline P. Kane- Clorox, T (925) 368-7979: left message, voicemail
Roger A Cregg- AV Homes Inc. (480) 214-7400-ext 7402: left message, voicemail.

Wednesday, March 7, 2018

2:28 pm
I talked to Dean who was in Philadelphia. He was homeless because of the fraud charges on his account. He could not pay his rent. Dean had to be hospitalized. The thief must have found his ATM card and PIN written in his checkbook while ransacking his apartment. There were only three credit cards in his "purse": Fingerhut, Mastercard, and Victoria's Secret. I gave him the number for Susan Schmidt and the Conduent people.

Pissed Consumer

During my research into Comerica Bank and entities involved with the Direct Express program, I came upon a website named Pissed Consumer. I wished the name of the site were more pleasing, but I had to look at the site. The way I came upon the site was simply doing a "Google search" for Comerica Bank and Direct Express and up popped Pissed Consumer. There were hundreds of complaints but no real posts with solutions.
I posted my first entry at Pissed Consumer. I gave readers names, telephone numbers to call, and a quick blurb on Regulation E. I wanted the victims to be a bit more conversant in the banking law (Reg E) so they would be able to be more specific in their arguments to Conduent and Comerica Bank. The invitation was made for victims to contact me, and a class action suit would be explored.
Over the next few months, my phone started ringing and emails started appearing.

Thursday, March 8, 2018

Dean from Philadelphia texted me. He contacted Susan Schmidt and Susan Rutledge at Comerica Bank. Dean received no help from them. Dean was now stuck in the homeless shelter after having been discharged from a hospital in Philadelphia. His money was gone, and he had no debit card. It was no surprise Schmidt would not help him.

Tuesday, March 13, 2018

10:55 am
T Consumer Financial Protection Bureau- talked to Daniel- All complaints are considered. Sent to Ms. Ross- referred to (855) 830-7880 CFPB Ombudsman. Transferred- left voice message.

Wednesday, March 14, 2018

It was time to research Nora Arpin, a Sr. VP at Comerica Bank. Arpin was found to be an officer in a prepaid bank card organization known as the Network Branded Prepaid Card Association. Arpin was representing Comerica Bank. I wondered what her associates would think of her knowing she was violating federal banking laws and violating the Fiscal Agent Agreement made between Comerica Bank and BFS of the US Treasury.

Thursday, March 22, 2018

There would be times I would receive follow-up emails or calls from victims.
Below is a note I made regarding Nancy Hernandez:
Nancy Hernandez- Finally got money.
Was supposed to get $1,495, got $1,348 (-147)
Nancy needs to send me a copy of her charge sheet.

I used LinkedIn as a business connection program, which sometimes doubled as a social media platform. On this date I notice two persons had viewed my profile:
Nora Arpin (Govt Electronic Solutions, Comerica Bank)
Mitch Raymond (Payments Executive, Conduent)
It was interesting that these people associated with the Fiscal Agent contract, and the subject to two OIG Treasury Audit reports would be looking at my profile. Oddly neither shielded their identity. Were they being brazen or stupid?
I was addressing many inquiries on Pissed Consumer. I was not prepared for the deluge of calls I was about to receive.

Friday, June 1, 2018

Victim Number 6-Hassan, Philadelphia, PA

On June 1, 2018, Hassan, a man from Philadelphia, PA, was receiving his Social Security benefits on a Direct Express debit card. Money that had been deposited on his debit card had been withdrawn from two ATM locations operated by Citi Bank, in Manhattan, NYC. I advised Hassan to fax the information to the person named as the Customer Advocate of Conduent and call Susan Schmidt (Comerica). He talked to Christine (Customer Advocate) and got his money returned within a week. Christine was found to be the only Conduent employee who was helpful to the fraud victims.

The number of victims calling me was about to explode. I did not to get much sleep. I would soon be gaining an associate, and we would be exposing lies from the bank officials and government employees.

Make a New
Year's resolution
you can keep.

Reduce stress in the new year.
Convert your paper check
to an electronic payment
with direct deposit or a
Direct Express® card.

Chapter Three
Enter Densmore: All Hell Breaks Loose

From June 2018 through the first part of August 2018, there was not much activity from victims contacting me, but that was about to change. I was hearing nothing from Treasury, but I continued to write emails and make calls for the victims who had called me.

There was one incident which should be told. My identity was stolen for the third time. This time the theft seemed to have originated with the Social Security Administration (SSA). Someone contacted SSA using my identity and changed my address. I had no idea it had happened and found out only because I went to the Social Security office to ask a question about insurance.

I was curious about insurance (Medicare) and I needed an explanation of Medicare Part B and C. I had never been sick enough to stay overnight in a hospital. I decided to go to the Social Security Office in Fresno to get some answers. It was learned from the clerk at the Social Security office that someone used my identity to change my address.

After returning to my apartment, I filed the following police report online, stating that I learned that my identity had been stolen. I hoped would be able to find out who did this.

Tuesday, July 3, 2018

FRESNO POLICE DEPARTMENT SUMMARY INCIDENT REPORT
General Information
Incident Type   Identity Theft
Report Date   07/03/2018 07:11 PM
Narrative
Incident Description
On the morning of Tuesday, July 3, 2018, I arrived at the Social Security office located at 640 W. Locust Ave, Fresno, CA. The time of arrival was approximately 9:00 am.
Upon giving identification to the clerk at the Social Security office, she advised me that the address on the account was different from the address on my California driver's license. The clerk verbally gave me the address she had, which I heard was on a street named Hollywood in Coarsegold, CA. Upon arriving in Fresno in late November to temporarily care for a lady, we traveled to Coarsegold in late November. I paid cash for a meal at a restaurant and did not use a debit card. This has been confirmed by viewing and copying my bank statements; no charges have been made on the card in Coarsegold, CA.
The clerk politely advised me she could not give me a copy of the screen she was viewing, nor could she orally give me the specific information, other than a person at the suspicious address made the change of address from my address in Placentia to the address in Coarsegold on June 19, 2018.
Upon returning to the residence of my friend, I created an online account with the Social Security Administration and accessed my account. The false address observed by the clerk at the Social Security office was immediately observed by me. The person responsible for changing the address misspelled the name of Coarsegold in two places, but upon examining the address, it does refer to an accurate address.
The identity thief gave the following address: (redacted) Holiday Dr," Cosrsegod", CA 93614. You will note that the first "s" in the city name was accidentally inserted as an "s" and should have been an "a" since the letters are adjacent on the keyboard. The letter "l" is missing in the last part of the city name, and should have preceded the last letter, "d".
I called the local sheriff's department having Coarsegold within its jurisdiction and was directed to make a report with your agency.
I have made copies of the pages from my Social Security page, which can be submitted to an investigator from the Financial Crimes unit. I look forward to presenting this information to an investigator. As stated, I can be reached at (803) 309-6850.
I am willing to prosecute.

Someone got into my Social Security account and changed my address. I was fortunate to have been able to return to my apartment and find the address used by the fraudster. You would think this would be a slam dunk for law enforcement, however, that would be wrong. Over the next year, I pushed to have the occupants of the residence interrogated. I learned they were interviewed, but the sheriff's department which had jurisdiction refused to allow me to see the incident report. Sounds like a bit of home cooking.

Thursday, August 2, 2018

I started getting results (or just got the attention of Comerica Bank and Conduent) by giving victims a direct telephone number to Susan Schmidt at Comerica as well as Nora Arpin.

Below is a typical email I began receiving. Every case was a nightmare.

Date: Thu, Aug 02, 2018, 12:43 pm
To: jbsimms
"...I'm a Disabled Veteran and I was robbed of $900 and a service fee of $1.50 through a bank transfer they claimed on 08/01/2018 and woke up to it today 08/02/2018. I filed a fraud report and will file a police report tomorrow."
August 9, 2018
I contacted everyone you told me, but no one responded. Then on Wednesday, the money was credited in my account. As soon as my new card comes, the sooner, I can transfer my money to my new bank. That's all I know, thanks.

This was amazing. Why couldn't all the cases be this easy? The truth is they all were this easy to solve but there was no rational reason for the delays and the violation of federal banking law.

I told the victims how to get their money back by telling them who to call and to send emails but I had no idea what was about to happen, and the calls were about to explode.

Sunday, August 12, 2018

Jackie becomes my partner

My life changed this day. I got a call from a lady in Massachusetts named Jackie who told me that she was the caretaker for her brother-in-law, who was a military veteran receiving VA disability checks as well as receiving a Social Security check. Over $800 was missing from the Social Security payment account; the money had been deposited onto a Direct Express debit card.

Jackie and I talked. I told Jackie who to call and what to say. Jackie learned that her brother's Social Security payment of over $800.00 which was to have been paid at the first of August had been compromised and the money was stolen in Florida. Jackie was animated. She was angry, very angry.

The money from the account for her brother-in-law was taken by a black woman in Hollywood, Florida. The black woman went into a Walmart, showed identification to a person at the Customer Service desk, and was paid the money that was supposed to have been paid to Jackie. The black woman used an identification that allowed her to represent herself as Jackie. When Jackie learned this, she was livid.

We discussed the many aspects of her case and other victims. I told Jackie about a victim named Paul in Nevada whose reissued debit card was shipped to an address in Miramar, Florida. I put Jackie in touch with Paul. The person who hijacked Paul's debit card could have been the same person responsible for stealing Jackie's identity.

Jackie went into proactive mode. We discussed store security, store video, police, etc. Conduent was not helping. I gave Jackie the phone numbers and email addresses for Nora Arpin and Susan Schmidt at Comerica Bank.

Jackie contacted the store security at Walmart. She hired a private investigator. The in-store security camera enabled us to see the fraudster, and the private investigator found the address of the person who tried to redirect Paul's card. It appeared to be the same woman.

A police report filed by Jackie with local police did not generate any help. A subsequent investigation by U.S. Treasury revealed that the federal investigator botched the case. This federal investigator was a Treasury "Special Agent" who never contacted the alleged fraudster. The agent stated the video did not reveal a legible license tag on the car, but the agent never looked at the video of the arrival of the fraudster in the parking lot. What an idiot.

Jackie reached out to a writer employed by America Banker magazine named Kate Berry. Ms. Berry (furthermore to be known as Kate). The arrival of Kate into the mix was important by partnering with Jackie and me.

Jackie was trying to coordinate between the police, the private investigator, and Walmart security to investigate the fraud on the Direct Express card used by her brother-in-law to receive his Social Security benefits. More victims would be contacting me.

Monday, August 13, 2018

Jackie did not play around. I explained how I had been ignored by Comerica and Conduent and Jackie had experienced the same thing. This was a new game and a new day with Jackie joining me. After explaining to Jackie about my chat with Paulette Battle, Jackie fired off an email to Ms. Battle.

From: Jackie
Date: August 13, 2018, a.m. 1:13:48 PM EDT
To: [Paulette Battle] battlep@oig.treas.gov
Subject: Jacqueline (redacted) claim number 1-49014789 reference number 79965312
Hello Paulette
Thank you for taking the time to speak to me about this serious matter. As discussed, I am the payee on my brother-in-law (redacted) social security disability. He gets his funds deposited on the 3rd of each month onto a Direct Express card. On Aug 2, 2018, a person claiming to be me called into direct express stating their card had been damaged and that they wanted a MOENY GRAM sent to the rep from Direct deposit then transferred to a Walmart in Hollywood FL!!!!!! Transaction number 13373783747 in the amount of $814.32 at 5:29 pm . I am beyond upset that Direct Express would authorize this since it has been explained to me by social security that a money gram is never to be sent in fact against policy's. The money should have gone back to social security. I am being told this will take up to 45 days until investigation is completed by Direct Express which again is against the law! I don't know what is going on with Comerica bank and direct express, but I have found overwhelming complaints about similar situations where money is being stolen from these accts. I would like a follow up on this immediately. Direct Express has been no help!! I cannot believe the us treasury would have a contract with such a corrupt company. I have emailed governors and state officials regarding this and am prepared to take this issue to the top. No one should have to go through this again. With all the complaints online as well as being in contact with JB Simms I know that I am not alone and many many others who my attorney will be contacting. I appreciate your time and look forward to speaking with you soon
Jacqueline

One of my clients during my active PI years was a USAF fighter pilot. I reached out to him because Jackie's brother-in-law is a disabled veteran. I was desperate for a connection to someone who could help.
Jackie was a combination of enthusiasm and rage. How could Comerica ignore her claim of fraud when an obese black woman presented herself as Jackie (who is quite white) and Comerica and Conduent ignored this?

I told Jackie about Paul in Nevada, and that the fraudster might be the same for both Jackie and Paul. Jackie and Paul communicated and exchanged information.
Jackie was crazy busy on the internet. She found an article printed in the Dallas Morning News about victims of Comerica and Conduent.

I told Jackie about Nora Arpin of Comerica and Mitch Raymond on March 22, 2018, from Conduent looking at my profile on LinkedIn. Jackie found the following info on the American Banker website:

Nora Arpin is responsible for the strategy, development, compliance and client relationships of the Government Electronic Solutions team within Comerica Bank's well established Public Sector & Specialized Services practice. Among her group's responsibilities is the management of the U.S. Treasury's Direct Express program which provides millions of Federal Benefit Recipients with electronic deposit of their benefits on a prepaid card. She has more than 40 years of dedicated banking experience, including 25 years of treasury management experience and 10 years of retail banking experience.[39]
https://www.americanbanker.com/author/nora-arpin

Arpin was the link between BFS and Comerica Bank. Jackie was now onto Arpin.
After finding the article about Arpin in American Banker, Jackie went to the source and found a writer from American Banker. The writer stated he would talk to his boss.
This was good. Having Jackie onboard with me was going to be the best thing that could have happened.

Jackie also received the following email from Treasury Agent Sonja J. Scott, Office of Investigation.

From: "Scott, Sonja L." ScottS@oig.treas.gov
Date: August 14, 2018, at 2:08:00 PM EDT
To: Jackie (redacted)
Subject: Complaint re Direct Express
We have received your complaint and referring the matter to the Bureau of Fiscal Service who manages the
Direct Express Program. Sonja
ASAC Sonja L. Scott
US Department of Treasury
Office of the Inspector General
Office of Investigations

Sonja Scott responded to Jackie and Sonja had no idea she would be associated with us for almost two years and over a hundred emails.

Jackie was talking with Paul in Nevada. I felt we were ready to expose something big. The fraud experienced by Jackie, Paul, and others could not be isolated. We needed more voices.

Wednesday, August 15, 2018

Jackie sent me this email.
From: Kate Berry (American Banker)
Date: August 15, 2018, at 3:23:10 PM EDT
Subject: American Banker…
Hi Jackie –
My colleague John forwarded your information to me.
I just got off the phone with Jim Simms talking about Direct Express and Comerica.
I'm working on this and wanted to chat before I reach out.
Do you have time to chat?
Best,
kate

This was a great development. Kate was to become one of our greatest allies. Dozens, maybe hundreds, of emails were to be exchanged between Jackie, me, and Kate Berry. I had not heard of American Banker magazine, so I thought maybe Jackie could sell this thing and get some attention to the fraudsters victimizing the cardholders. The victimization was not perpetrated only by unknown people; it was being done by Comerica Bank, Conduent, and the Bureau of Fiscal Service.

Jackie and I were trying to put the story of the fraud in her brother-in-law's account in Florida together with Paul's fraud to see if there was a connection. Paul found out that the delivery of his debit card had been diverted so he called who he thought was Direct Express when it actually was Conduent. He knew the name of the fraudster and the address.

Here is what Paul told us:
The card was delivered to Alexis. When I saw that the card arrived there, I phoned Direct Express to let them know to cancel the card. Took 45 min on hold to get a hold of them and when they finally got the card shut off; 10 min. later is when Alexis tried to activate it. I received part of my money that evening and the remainder of it the next day through money orders from Direct Express. Meanwhile, Direct Express ordered me a new card and had it sent to me.

Alexis was the thief. She had received Paul's card. He was fortunate that he was smart enough to determine what was happening and alerted Conduent before the card arrived at Alexis' home address.

I knew that this was not the first fraud performed by Alexis. She had to be part of a crew of fraudsters, but who was going to catch them?
My thought was to help the victims get their money from Comerica and Conduent. Law enforcement officers, mainly investigators, were lazy and wanted you to solve the crime before coming to them. Jackie and Paul had proof of the fraud, but no law enforcement agency cared. It would get worse.

Date: Wed, Aug 15, 2018, 8:33 am
To: jbsimms
I have been on disability since 2011 and was receiving my disability in a regular checking account. About 2 -3 years ago I switched over to the Direct Express card to try to avoid some of the fraud I had been experiencing For the past 8 years I have been a caretaker for my mom due to Alzheimer's/Dementia. 2 years ago, Social Security office made me my mom's representative to receive her Social Security checks. I was waiting for a direct express card for her but they put both of our payments on my card. In August of 2017 I requested a print out of my past transactions and found a $1046. charge to my card from Walmart. I know i didn't spend that amount at Walmart so as soon as I could I called Direct Express about this charge. They had to put in a dispute form. I finally received an answer from them stating that it had been too long for them to look into this charge further unless I had a good reason why I took so long to question the charge.
I have been spending way too much time on the phone and computer trying to get these issues resolved and it seems that No one seems to care that i as a disabled human being is having so much trouble just trying to get the full amount owed to me from my disability check and I cannot afford it. I have to be on a strict budget and with them moving money out and in on my account without my knowledge is extremely stressful to me. I suffer from PTSD and the fact that I can't depend on them to do what they are supposed to with my money my anxieties are at a high level. I cannot even change my direct deposit now to a real bank unless I go in person to the office and with no car and no money. I cant get into town to do this. I feel stuck and taken advantage of. Please help me. Thank you.

I found an email address for Nora Arpin, so decided to send her an email.

From: jbsimms
Date: Thu, Aug 16, 2018, 12:19 pm
To: Ntarpin@comerica.com
Cc: Jackie
Dear Ms. Arpin,
It came to my attention that you and Mitchell Raymond (of Conduent) have viewed my profile on LinkedIn. That revelation was quite telling in the context of my experience with Direct Express, the call centers, the Customer Advocacy office, Susan Schmidt, and Susan Rutledge.
Susan Schmidt's office received a telephone voice message from me that was never returned. Schmidt admitted the calls were recorded, and refused to research the call after I proved the call was ignored. Susan Schmidt has since denied knowing my identity, probably after hearing the 3 calls from the crow.
The Customer Advocacy attendant, James, was a waste of a hire. I hear he is gone. A lady named Christine, who supposedly was laid off, was the only intelligent person with whom I came into contact. I recommend she be rehired.
I have been contacted by more than a dozen disaffected customers of Direct Express and have helped them navigate the murky waters of accountability with respect to Comerica in order for them to receive their money. One of these persons is Jackie Densmore, who is the caretaker of a disabled Marine, who has been trying to recover the money which was fraudulently stolen from Derek's account. Direct Express allowed a fraudster to allow the money in the account to be redeemed in Hollywood, Florida while Derek lives in Massachusetts. The delay of reimbursement is unconscionable. This man served his country. This man, as other Veterans, does not deserve the disrespect you have heaped upon them. I hope you can contact any of your relatives who are Veterans and tell them what you allow to happen to other Veterans. Look them in the eye and tell them that you allow an incompetent call center, advocacy center, fraud department, and the office of Susan Schmidt, to scoff at the Veterans, mothers of dependent children, and other disabled persons.
If you or Raymond, or your counsel, have the integrity to contact me, I will be glad to read your reply. I am certain you and your cohorts will be contacted by persons other than me who will attach accountability and consequences for your actions, and lack thereof.
Sincerely,
J.B. Simms

Below is the "automatic reply" I received from Nora Arpin.

"I am out of the office with minimal access to email. I will respond to your message when I return."

Nora Arpin continued to be the person who was the direct link between BFS and Comerica Bank. She had fooled the Network Branded Prepaid Card Association into believing she was ethical. A telephone call was made to the headquarters of this association (202) 548-7200) on August 29, 2018 and a voicemail message was left.

I began sending Jackie copies of the OIG Treasury Reports and contact information for Nora Arpin and others. While I was going after Nora Arpin, Jackie was contacting the office of Elizabeth Warren, her senator.

From: casework@warren.senate.gov
Date: August 16, 2018, at 6:30:52 PM EDT
Subject: Thank You for Contacting Me
Dear Jacqueline,
Thank you for contacting my office regarding your case. I know this matter is of great concern to you and I sincerely hope I can be of assistance.
Attached is a Privacy Act Waiver Form authorizing my staff to advocate on your behalf. Please take a moment to fill it out and return it. In addition to the waiver form please take the time to briefly summarize your issue; the agency in question, any actions you have taken so far, and your desired result. Please include the summary with your Privacy Act Waiver form.
Once my office receives this form and summary we will be able to look into this matter. If you have any questions regarding this issue, please contact Jessica Wong from my staff at (617) 565-3170.
I look forward to being of service to you.
Sincerely,
Elizabeth Warren
United States Senator

Friday, August 13, 2018

Victim Number 13-Kenneth: Aurora, Colorado

Kenneth went to a pharmacy to fill a prescription for medication to address his PTSD. No money was in his Direct Express account. It was later learned that a person in San Francisco spent Kenneth's money at a Walgreens store. The amount missing was $750.00. Below is more of the story.

I received a call from Kenneth who lives in Colorado. The following is a synopsis of the call.

On August 1, 2018, Kenneth was at a doctor's office. He left the doctor's office to get medication. Kenneth receives monthly deposits onto his Direct Express card for SSDI, and PTSD, in the amount of $750 per month. Upon arriving at the pharmacy, Kenneth attempted to pay for his prescription with his Direct Express card. He was told there were no sufficient funds for the purchase. He checked his app on his phone, and the money showed $0.00 in his account. Kenneth called the telephone number on the back of his Direct Express debit card. No response was received. Kenneth tried to call customer service. He spent 2 hours on the telephone with them and got nowhere,

Afterward, Kenneth went to see his psychiatrist named Rita. While Kenneth was sitting in the room with Rita, Rita called the telephone number on the back of the Direct Express card and she got a customer representative to answer. The customer representative said to Rita "we know he did not do this. We have to send a fraud packet and the fraud unit will have to determine fraud. It takes a week to get to the fraud unit." The call was made on a Friday, and the operator told the psychiatrist to call back on Monday.

It was learned that a person had used a Walgreen store in San Francisco to withdraw the money (no further details are available). The operator was told this was a fraudulent transaction and that he is in Aurora, Colorado. Kenneth was mailed a package from the "Fraud Unit" of Direct Express. He filled out the forms and mailed them back to Direct Express.

Kenneth was in Colorado. The fraud occurred in San Francisco. How hard was it to prove that this was fraud, and that Kenneth was due to receive provisional credit until Conduent did their investigation? I knew there was to be no investigation because no one "investigated" the fraud om my account or the fraud on the accounts of other victims who had contacted me.

I directed Kenneth to print his statement, circle the fraud, and fax the info to Direct Express. I also directed him to call Susan Schmidt in Detroit and advise her that he had talked to Jim Simms, and that he (Kenneth) knew Schmidt had spoken to Jackie earlier today.

I told Jackie about Kenneth. Jackie contacted Kate Berry and told her that another person (Kenneth) had become a victim.

Friday, August 17, 2018

Kenneth called me to tell me a couple things. Kenneth received a telephone call from a person named Ralph Babb from Comerica Bank. Babb apologized for the problem Kenneth was having with his account. Kenneth did not know that Ralph Babb was the CEO of Comerica Bank.

Ralph Babb? The CEO of Comerica Bank? Apologize? Boss of Arpin and Schmidt and Rutledge? How the hell did Babb find out about Kenneth's calls to Schmidt? This was amazing news that we got to the top, the CEO. We thought things would change, but nothing changed. Babb would resign, taking millions of dollars as severance, and the same game would continue from Arpin and Schmidt.

Soon after Kenneth got the call from Babb, Kenneth called me to tell me his money had been returned to his account. Yeah, he was thanking Jackie and me, but it took all of us, including the psychiatrist, to get this done. Kenneth then talked to Kate Berry, the reporter from American Banker. He told Kate that the money came back after Ralph Babb called and apologized.

Enter Kate Berry in to the mix

Berry, Kate
Sun, Aug 19, 2018, 7:48 PM
to Jackie, me
Just responding to a couple of emails here on Sunday night. Thanks for sending -- and Reg E is a huge deal, this is a regulatory violation for sure! I write about Reg E. I have to check if any companies have been held accountable for Reg E, though. As you know, there are lots of regulations on the books that when a bank doesn't abide by them, it doesn't mean a regulator is going to fine them or penalize them in any way.
This seems to be the important point on Reg E:
But in these cases, banks must generally provide consumers with a provisional credit to their account within 10 days of the bank receiving the error notice.
Jim, to your other point, why don't they stop the charge when you're alerting them of the charge? Perhaps they can't -- which seems hard to believe. Kb
Berry, Kate
Tue, Aug 21, 2018, 2:11 PM
to me, Jackie
Just wanted to let you both know that Comerica told me they shut down the Cardless Benefit Access Service, which is the program that sends Money grams when the card goes missing, and they were sending benefits to fraudsters in other states.
FYI
more later.

Kate had talked to Arpin. Jackie had gotten Arpin's attention, and after being confronted by Kate Berry, Arpin "threw us a bone" and shut down an entire program, the Cardless Benefit Access Service. Arpin thought this gesture would make us go away. Arpin was wrong; we had much more to do.

Berry, Kate
Tue, Aug 21, 2018, 8:47 AM
to me, Jackie
Hi guys -
Comerica delayed the interview -- in a very bizarre way.
So, now I'm talking to Nora tomorrow, same time, 11 a.m. EST.
What a boondoggle!
Let me know if you hear anything else. I'm writing the story today and will fill you in on any developments. Do you know if Kenneth Tillman got his disability money reimbursed?

J B Simms
Tue, Aug 21, 2018, 4:16 PM
to Kate, Jackie
Talked to Kenneth. The CEO of Comerica called him. Yes.Ken was a bit out of it, and did not get the name, but man identified himself as the CEO.Apologizing. Told Ken to get confirmation of the man's name.

Jackie
Tue, Aug 21, 2018, 4:32 PM
to me
I bet it was Ralph Babbs. Susan Schmidt is in his office.

Berry, Kate
Fri, Aug 24, 2018, 7:43 PM
to Jackie, me
Hi Jackie, J.B. --
Wanted to let you know that my editor held the story for a day to give Treasury time to respond.
I will send you both a link when it posts.
They might just hold off until Monday, not sure yet.

Friday August 24, 2018

Jackie's shot across the bow

Arpin called Jackie at 6 pm on this day. Arpin had gotten the message that the money designated for Jackie's brother in-law had been stolen by a black woman near Ft. Lauderdale at a Walmart store. Arpin told Jackie that the program implemented by Comerica Bank, allowing customers to obtain money from their accounts at Walmart stores, was being stopped. Jackie questioned Arpin about how a black woman could identify herself as a white lady from Massachusetts and have Jackie's identifying information. Jackie asked Arpin why she had not replied to emails from J.B. Simms, which, of course, is me. Arpin never responded to me. Arpin told Jackie she did not know J.B. Simms. Arpin was lying to Jackie and Jackie confronted Arpin. Arpin had looked at my profile on LinkedIn on Mach 22 (five months prior to calling Jackie) and had received my emails. After Jackie pounded Arpin with the evidence, Arpin admitted knowing about J.B. Simms. The money was then returned to Jackie's account.

Arpin told Jackie that the Cardless Benefit Program used by the fraudster was being shut down and things were not handled correctly.

Let me put this into perspective; Arpin was calling Jackie "after hours." The conversation lasted well after 6 pm, and we had to wonder what was really motivating Arpin. Plus, Arpin lied to Jackie about not knowing about J.B. Simms. Jackie was to become my closest ally.
Jackie called Kate Berry and me and told us about the conversation with Arpin.
Arpin did not ask about Jackie's brother-in-law, the disabled veteran whose Social Security money had been stolen.

Berry, Kate
Aug 27, 2018, 7:21 AM
to Jackie, me
Did you get a copy of the story? I sent a link......

Below is the article written by Kate Berry and published August 26, 2018. This was the beginning of our validation.

Comerica scrambles to address fraud in the prepaid benefits program

By Kate Berry

August 26, 2018, 1:51 p.m. EDT

Comerica Bank has shut down a component of its prepaid card program for federal benefits recipients after a recent spate of fraud cases.

Fraudsters have exploited security flaws in Comerica's Cardless Benefit Access Service to drain accounts belonging to federal beneficiaries, including retirees who receive Social Security benefits and veterans who rely on disability payments to make ends meet.

The service, which Comerica says is now discontinued, was part of the Direct Express program, a partnership between the Texas bank and the U.S. government that allows users without bank accounts to access their funds through prepaid cards.

The Cardless Benefit Access Service allows consumers to withdraw funds if they have lost their card, even when they are away from their home state. But in hundreds of cases the program allegedly dispensed funds to fraudsters, who had previously gained access to cardholder data and posed as the benefits recipients.

"Direct Express didn't put up a red flag, even though they had all the information about the money being wired to Florida, when we live in Massachusetts, but they just sent the money," said Jackie Densmore, the caregiver for her brother-in-law, Derek Densmore, a disabled Marine who receives benefits. "We were thinking it was safe because it's the U.S. Treasury."

Cardholders allege that criminals — potentially working with insiders, such as call-center employees or third-party card manufacturers — stole Direct Express card numbers, addresses and three-digit card identifiers, enabling them to make fraudulent online purchases. In some cases, criminals also called Direct Express to report cards as lost or stolen, or to have PIN numbers changed, and had payments routed to MoneyGram locations where they could pick up a check and cash it.

Several victims of fraud claim Comerica has been slow in reimbursing them their money and in some cases has even suspended their accounts pending an investigation, restricting them from accessing new benefits payments. In some instances, they say Direct Express also charged cardholders fees to reissue and activate new cards after a fraud had been committed.

"Direct Express is holding customers hostage as a result of their own incompetence," said J.B. Simms, an author and retired private investigator, who complained to the program after discovering fraudulent charges on his Direct Express account in December 2017.

Comerica shut down the cardless service on Aug. 18 and, victims said, took more concerted steps to return cardholders' funds only after American Banker raised questions about the allegations of fraud. Some accountholders, including Simms, have been complaining to Comerica for months.

Comerica said that it believes the Direct Express fraud is limited to the cardless service, and that one employee at a Direct Express call center has been fired over the security breach. Comerica has oversight of the Direct Express program but outsources the main call center function to Conduent, a publicly traded conglomerate in Florsham Park, N.J.

"Criminals have found a way around the controls that we put in place to safeguard cardholders," said Nora Arpin, a Comerica senior vice president and director of government electronic solutions. "We've taken action to shut down the Cardless Benefit Access Service and have begun an investigation."

Arpin said "only a few hundred cardholders" were affected, or just 0.13% of Direct Express' 4.5 million prepaid debit cardholders.

Conduent declined to comment and referred all calls to Comerica.

The federal government oversees benefits payments through the Bureau of the Fiscal Service, an arm of the Treasury Department.

"The Bureau of the Fiscal Service is working with the Treasury Office of Inspector General, Comerica and its partners to effectively address bank card fraud and other consumer concerns, and protect the more than 4.5 million Direct Express benefit recipients who rely on this program for their monthly federal benefits," said Thomas Santaniello, a spokesman for Treasury's Bureau of the Fiscal Service.

Call centers targeted by organized fraud rings
Arpin laid the blame squarely on organized fraud rings that are known to target call centers. In the case of Direct Express, she said, the fraudsters used data acquired from prior breaches to impersonate cardholders and steal government-issued benefit payments.

"There isn't a single aspect of the payments system — credit cards, checks, cash — that doesn't experience fraud," Arpin said. "We very much empathize with the fact that there are circumstances in which being without the money is a very difficult situation for the cardholder."

For the defrauded cardholders, however, the loss of monthly federal benefit payments has caused untold financial havoc. Cardholders describe having panic attacks, being unable to pay their rent and spending hours trying — unsuccessfully — to get reimbursed by Direct Express.

Cardholders allege that Direct Express typically refused to reimburse them their money when they lodged an initial complaint, and that program operators claimed the bank would first have to conduct an investigation.

Under Regulation E, the bank has 45 to 90 days to investigate fraud a claim. However, consumers can get their funds restored more quickly if they submit a written statement alerting Direct Express that they were a victim of fraud. The bank then has 10 days from receiving the statement to send a provisional credit to the consumer.

'So I can pay my bills and purchase my medicines'

One of the more harrowing stories came from Kenneth Tillman, a Marine Corps combat veteran in Aurora, Colo., who suffers from post-traumatic stress disorder.

On Aug. 1, Tillman went to a pharmacy to buy medicine but his Direct Express card was denied. When he checked the Direct Express app on his phone, it showed a zero balance.

"I went into a panic mode," he said.

He said he initially spent two hours trying to get through to Direct Express and finally drove to his therapist's office. They contacted the call center together.

After finding three fraudulent charges at a Walgreens store in San Francisco, Direct Express suspended Tillman's account. But a call center employee refused to issue Tillman a credit for his roughly $750 in monthly benefits, he said.

"They told me it would take 90 days to get my money if they determined it was fraud, even though the lady told us it was fraud," Tillman said.

Later that day, Tillman was admitted to a hospital, where he was treated for a week for pneumonia, said Rita Roberts, his therapist and a founder at New Start Recovery, an Aurora, Colo., counseling center.

"He's been sick since the moment this happened because he couldn't handle the stress," Roberts said.

Tillman said when he was released from the hospital, on Aug. 17, he sent a letter to Direct Express, which required a written statement in order to start an investigation and give him a credit for his funds.

He wrote in the statement: "I need my [Social Security Disability Insurance] payment to be immediately reimbursed to me so I can pay my bills and purchase my medicines."

Paul Katynski, 59, a disabled maintenance supervisor, called Direct Express on Feb. 6 to get the balance on his account, but instead got a recorded message that his PIN did not match. He reset his PIN. A day later, $1,971 in disability benefits were drained from his account.

"I knew something was wrong when I went to get my money and there was no money," Katynski said.

He immediately called Direct Express, which told him that he had reported the card as lost.

"I said, 'I don't think the card is lost, since it's right here in my hand,' and I had to convince Direct Express that I was me," he said. "It was scary."

With his rent already due — and fearing an eviction notice — Katynski asked Direct Express to send him a MoneyGram, but they would only send $1,000, or half his benefit payment, he said.

In the meantime, Direct Express shipped out a new prepaid card and gave Katynski the tracking number, he said.

A day later, he called to get a delivery update and found the card had been re-routed to an address in Miramar, Fla. Another call to Direct Express, and a 40-minute hold, and he was able to cancel the second card, averting another fraud.

Direct Express charged him $59 in fees, which relates to him receiving and activating two new cards, as well as receiving two MoneyGrams that he needed to pay his rent.

"This is a lot of money that people are stealing and it happens every day, and it's sad, and no one is doing anything about it," Katynski said.

'Purely for the cardholder'

However, Tillman, Katynski and others say Comerica ultimately reimbursed them all of their missing funds and fees, but only after American Banker had contacted them.

Arpin defended the bank's policy to suspend beneficiaries' prepaid accounts immediately after a fraud complaint, saying it is meant to protect accounts from any further fraud.

"Card suspension is purely for the cardholder," she said. "If we identify the fraud through our scanning systems, then we reimburse the cardholder within 10 days. When fraud is identified before the cardholder calls us, we'll make an outbound call. If we can't reach the cardholder, we'll temporarily suspend their card."

But some cardholders disputed the processes and procedures used by Direct Express, saying they got no help from the call center or Comerica, even after providing information about fraud that could have allowed law enforcement to track down the criminals.

Derek Densmore, of Bourne, Mass., the disabled Marine, was distraught after $814 in disability payments got routed to a MoneyGram at a Walmart superstore in Hollywood, Fla., said his sister-in-law, Jackie Densmore. (As his caregiver, she is the payee on his Direct Express account.)

When she called Direct Express on Aug. 3 to check the account balance, there was a recording saying the debit card had been canceled and a new one would be sent in the mail. Densmore waited until Aug. 10, but by then, her brother-in-law's benefits had been stolen. She was shocked that Direct Express did not call her to check before sending his benefits via MoneyGram to another state.

Frustrated at not being reimbursed, she searched social media for information about Direct Express and Comerica's operation of the program. She came across Simms, the retired investigator, who had posted his contact information on Facebook. They began talking and sharing notes.

Simms had reported improper charges on his Direct Express account in December 2017. But he had no luck getting the money reimbursed by Direct Express.

He ultimately got reimbursed $234 back from Zulily, the merchant where fraudulent charges for clothing and perfume had been made, he said.

He claims criminals who stole Social Security and disability benefits "could have been stopped if Direct Express or Comerica had a fraud unit that could communicate with customers and law enforcement."

"The red tape you have to go through to get to these people is insane," Densmore said. "Disabled veterans and the elderly don't stand a chance when their money is taken and they give no answers."

Cardless service met a need, but carried risks

Arpin said the Cardless Benefit Access Service, launched in August 2017, addressed a need to provide cardholders with access to their funds in an emergency if they were not in possession of their cards.

There were "unfortunate situations where somebody didn't have their [Direct Express] card and was in a state other than where they live," she said, "One of the challenges we've had with the program is that cardholders are often without their cards and they were looking to get access to their money faster."

She declined to describe the bank's security measures to prevent fraud, citing confidentiality.

She said Comerica's oversight of the Direct Express program includes visiting the call centers several times a year and listening monthly to recordings of calls to assess how the Conduent-run call centers are performing.

Conduent is a global provider of diversified business services that operates in 11 different industries, with offices from India to Jamaica. In July, two U.S. senators called for an investigation into allegations that Conduent billed customers for inaccurate electronic tolling charges in Florida and Michigan.

Julie Conroy, the research director in Aite Group's retail banking practice, said organized crime rings are attacking call centers more than ever before.

"Organized crime rings will go to great lengths to infiltrate contact centers," Conroy said. "There should be more controls over authentication, what is a genuine request and confirming that it is the actual consumer."

Treasury's IG performing follow-up audit of Direct Express

Comerica won the government contract to oversee Direct Express in 2008 and the contract was renewed in 2014, despite some criticism by the Treasury OIG in prior audits over how the program was being run.

In June, the Treasury's OIG issued an "engagement memo" to Treasury related to the Direct Express program. The memo informed the Bureau of the Fiscal Service of a follow-up audit to determine if program administrators had responded to 14 recommendations included in IG audits in 2014 and 2017.

"Two months ago, we notified Fiscal Service that we were going to undertake a corrective action verification study to see if the recommendations we made were followed up," said Rich Delmar, counsel to Treasury Inspector General Eric Thorson.

The recommendations included that the program assess the costs and burden of the program to the cardholders; establish a quality assurance surveillance plan to monitor and document Comerica's performance, including service-level requirements; track Comerica's revenues and expenses; and periodically assess whether the bank's compensation is "reasonable and fair."

The OIG expects to complete its audit by the spring of 2019, Delmar said.[40]

Arpin was playing this fraud off as a rare occurrence, but she shut down the Cardless benefit program as a result of Jackie Densmore.

Delmar commissioned an investigation in late June and never told me. I assumed Delmar thought we would not find out about the investigation. It was learned the "Engagement" which created this investigation was made June 18, 2018. Kate found this out, but Delmar did not tell Jackie or me that my call to Paulette Battle on February 26, 2018 was quite effective.

Santaniello was involved in the coverup. The statement by Santaniello in Kate's article proved that.

Should we have felt vindicated? No, we did not. Delmar and Arpin hid information from us. Schmidt lied to me about returning calls and the function of Conduent. Conduent employees, who handled over five million retirement and benefit accounts for US citizens, were incompetent and Comerica knew it.

Monday August 27, 2018

Jackie and I were glad that Kate Berry sent us a copy of the article she wrote. Jackie and I were so happy. What we did not understand at the time that the employees working at Comerica, BFS, and Treasury had no shame; Kate Berry could write and expose malfeasance but those responsible were not to become apologetic or accountable. Comerica, Conduent, and Treasury (the Direct Express Evil Triumvirate) simply "hunkered down" and prepared to protect themselves and each other; if one falls, they all fall.

Ben Dupré <bendupre@gmail.com>
Mon, Aug 27, 2018, 11:43 AM
Dear Mr. Simms,
My name is Ben Dupre. I'm a consumer protection attorney in the San Jose, California area.
I am helping a disabled individual that had a traumatic experience with Comerica Bank.
I'm looking to speak with others who may have had similar bad experiences with Comerica Bank.
And I came across a recent article where your story was part of others' story that have had similar very bad experiences with Comerica Bank.
Do you have any time to have a short chat?
Sincerely,
Ben

I talked to Dupree. He wanted affidavits from Jackie, McPhail, and me to help with their case. He wanted witnesses, not clients. We agreed to help Dupree.

Monday, Aug 27, 2018

7:36 AM
J B Simms
Mon, Aug 27, 2018, 7:36 AM
to Kate, Jackie
Just did.
Glad to see that OIG did agree to do audit.
They never informed me.
Evidently, they "got the message."

Berry, Kate
Mon, Aug 27, 2018, 7:46 AM
to me
What did you think of the story?
Sometimes when people are involved in a story, they don't always like it.
But I think it at least caught the attention of Comerica, Treasury and Conduent.
Will anything change? I doubt it.

Kate Berry (American Banker)
Mon, Aug 27, 2018, 9:19 AM
to me, Jackie
A lot of details ended up on the proverbial cutting room floor just because of space and focus.
My editor wanted to focus on the stories that the consumers -- you guys -- told, because the allegations were so compelling.
Because Treasury has the main oversight of Comerica for the program, the CFPB info got cut. Under Mick Mulvaney, and the Trump administration, the CFPB likely would not take action anyway, they would punt to the Treasury.
We'll see what happens.
I agree that if an attorney takes this case and files a purported class action, that will get a lot of notice!
I will keep on any developments and please send me any follow-up info. you have.

From: jbsimms
Date: Tue, Aug 28, 2018, 2:33 pm
To: Ntarpin@comerica.com
Cc: Jackie
Dear Ms. Arpin,
During your conversation with Ms. Densmore, you stated you would be contacting me on the following Monday. No contact was received. You then were notified that you were to be interviewed by Ms. Berry of American Banker. I still have not received any contact from you.
After reading the article published by Ms. Berry, it was noted that you directed that the cash advance program with respect to Walmart be discontinued. While you chose to focus on that program and blamed the criminals for compromising your "security measures," it was your security measures (or lack thereof) that have allowed the criminals to thrive. The lack of supervision, knowledge, and understanding of security and the criminal element, along with your lack of concern, have injured many people. Your use of statistics (as I refer to Mark Twain) does not justify what has happened.
I want to know when Comerica is going to publish the closing of this program, and the dismantling of what is supposedly the Fraud Unit of Direct Express.
You did read that the OIG will be investigating this matter, and I am the source of this investigation. I was the person talking to the OIG auditor in February, over six months ago. The auditor's name is Paulette Battle. This matter should be handled in a transparent manner. I will be monitoring this matter as I field calls and emails from disaffected Direct Express customers.
I suggest you speak with your board members (four of whom have been contacted by me) to establish a committee of customers to make sure Comerica does not continue to violate federal banking laws and subject customers, including Veterans and other retirees, to the same abuse and neglect as has been the practice of Comerica.
Sincerely,
J.B. Simms

Later in the day, I got a call from another victim. Mark Miller's wife received a letter from Conduent. Conduent was denying fraud claims before any investigation was conducted.

Mark Miller (victim)
Attachments
Aug 27, 2018, 2:46 PM
to JB.Simms
Jim here is info you requested; this is my email account I am her husband thank you.

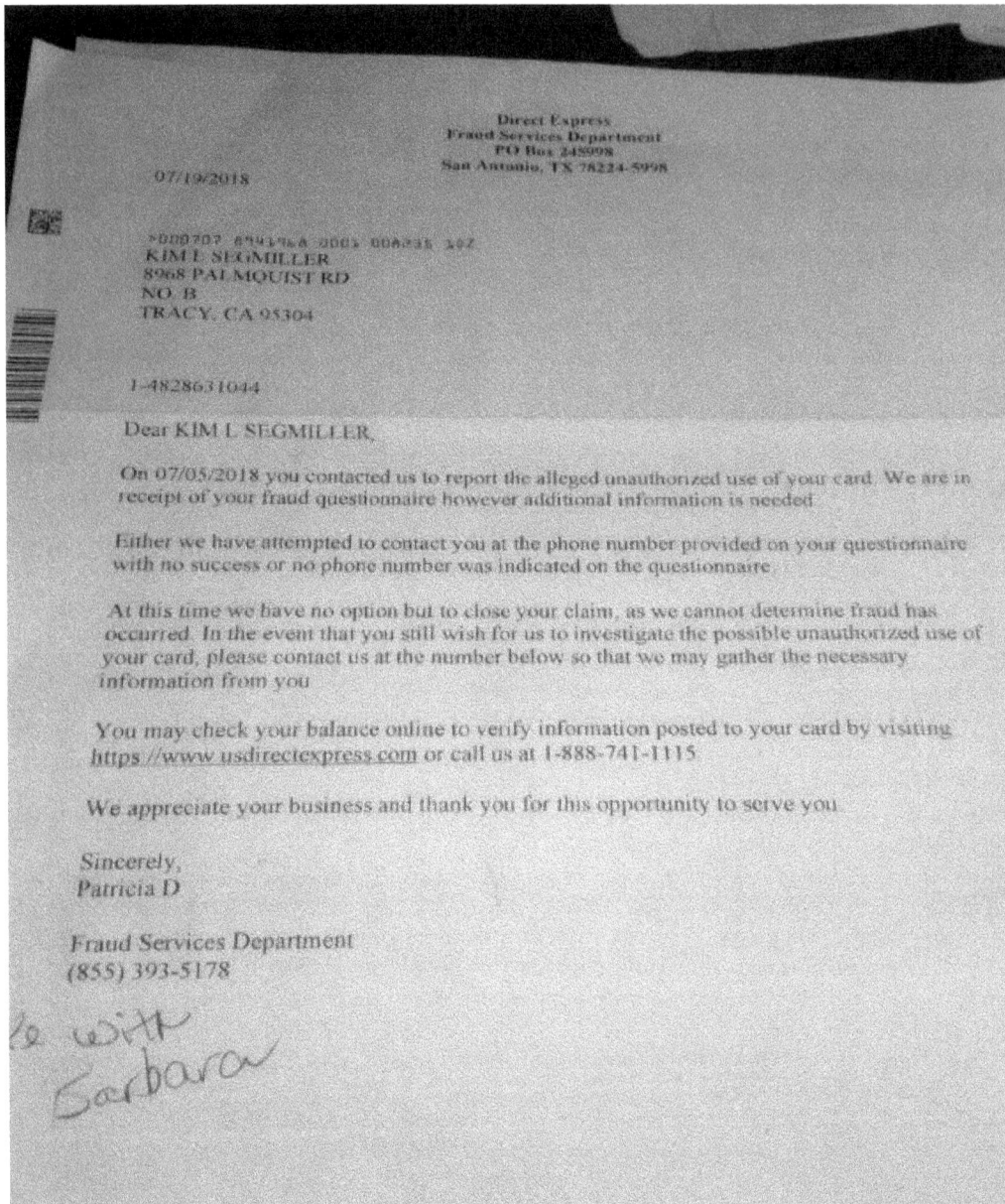

Direct Express
Fraud Services Department
PO Box 245998
San Antonio, TX 78224-5998

07/19/2018

KIM L SEGMILLER
8968 PALMQUIST RD
NO. B
TRACY, CA 95304

1-4828631044

Dear KIM L SEGMILLER,

On 07/05/2018 you contacted us to report the alleged unauthorized use of your card. We are in receipt of your fraud questionnaire however additional information is needed.

Either we have attempted to contact you at the phone number provided on your questionnaire with no success or no phone number was indicated on the questionnaire.

At this time we have no option but to close your claim, as we cannot determine fraud has occurred. In the event that you still wish for us to investigate the possible unauthorized use of your card, please contact us at the number below so that we may gather the necessary information from you.

You may check your balance online to verify information posted to your card by visiting https://www.usdirectexpress.com or call us at 1-888-741-1115

We appreciate your business and thank you for this opportunity to serve you.

Sincerely,
Patricia D

Fraud Services Department
(855) 393-5178

le with Barbara

The above photo is a prime example of what Conduent was doing. They were sending out preprinted denials without looking at the fraud reports. The letter is not specific. No one looked at the claim. They just ignored it.

J B Simms
Tue, Aug 28, 2018, 10:29 AM
to Kate, Jackie
Dear Kate,
Thank you for getting the article out. Hopefully, this will be the jumping-off point for accountability.
Jackie has some people jumping.
Thanks again. Maybe there will be a follow up.

Wednesday August 29, 2018

Berry, Kate
Wed, Aug 29, 2018, 11:54 AM
to me
Thanks, Jim - I see you're still doing more to get the word out, which is great!!
It's a full-time job stopping crooks, especially high-level corporate crime.

Emails were flying between Kate, Jackie, and me.
I shared the info about Nora Arpin and her membership with the National Branded Prepaid Card group.
Below is an inquiry I sent to this group:

I, and scores of others, have experienced identity theft as holders of Direct Express debit cards, administered by Comerica. The persons at Comerica who are the link between Fiscal Services of the US Treasury is one of your own, Nora Arpin. The lack of diligence on the part of Comerica to adhere to federal banking regulations and protect cardholders was documented in an article written by Kate Berry at American Banker, which was published Monday, August 27, 2018. I hope others within your organization take note. A reply would be welcomed.

Nora Arpin was a board member of the National Branded Prepaid Card organization.

J B Simms
Wed, Aug 29, 2018, 1:52 PM
to Jackie, Kate
I just left a nice vm [voicemail] for cfpb ombudsman.
Their recorded message stated they would be the agency to call to keep consumers from having to contact other agencies.
You should listen to it (855) 830-7880
Absolutely the most incredulous thing I ever heard (other than my son's stories about where he had been).
If you get a chance, call the number and listen. If you have a way to record and transcribe it, do it.
They will like me as much as Nora likes me.

Friday, August 31, 2018

From: jbsimms
Date: Fri, Aug 31, 2018, 11:44 am
To: Richard Delmar (OIG Treasury)
Cc: Jackie
Dear Mr. Delmar,
Since my communication with Paulette Battle approximately six (6) months ago, and after reading the article in American Banker magazine earlier this month, it appears as though my efforts to point out the inadequacy of the previous OIG reports were fruitful. My personal experience with Direct Express/Comerica, my banking experience, my banking resources, and my former official vocation have all contributed to my shock at the fact that Comerica is allowed to violate federal banking laws as well as have an inbred atmosphere of secrecy and lack of accountability. The OIG of Treasury never investigated the Fraud Unit, or if it ever existed. Direct Express was directed to shield its victims of identity fraud from their rights to repayment by Comerica Bank officers.
I will not go into detail in this writing, but I am certain you are privy to the communication I have had with Paulette Battle in February 2018. It was quite odd that your office had come to the conclusion that an audit/inspection/investigation was necessary, and this decision was made two months ago. Since that time, Ms. Densmore had to contact Ms. Battle, and Ms. Battle (through no fault of her own) did not convey the plan for the audit to Ms. Densmore, which, according to the magazine article, was scheduled two months prior. I will assume Ms. Battle would have been aware that this decision had been made.

It is not certain whether I will be asked to be the contact person for the cardholders who have been victimized by Comerica, after they were victimized by online fraudsters. We will be communicating directly with you to make you aware of the issues and to ensure transparency between your office, the investigations, and the public. I look forward to discussing this matter with you next week if possible.
Sincerely,
J.B. Simms

Wednesday, September 5, 2018

Richard Delmar, who was head legal counsel for OIG Treasury, would become a main player in this story.

From: jbsimms
Date: Wed, Sep 05, 2018, 8:43 am
To: Richard Delmar (OIG Treasury)
Cc: Jackie
Dear Mr. Delmar,
I copied, and am pasting, a copy of an email that was forwarded to me from Jackie Densmore. The reason I am sending this to you is that the boilerplate template response did not address the fact that elementary security procedures and well as follow-up with the "fraud unit" could have stopped this abuse of Derek Densmore but would prevent the abuse of future cardholders. It was also noted that the person who sent the email to Ms. Densmore did not sign the email nor give a telephone number to call and debate the legitimacy of the "concern" for Derek Densmore, a disabled war Veteran, or Ms. Densmore. Derek deserves to face anyone in yours or any office in Fiscal Services who has caused him emotional harm. Derek faced an enemy of your freedoms on the battlefield; Fiscal Services owes him the respect to face his enemies at Fiscal Services instead of hiding behind unsigned emails.
This matter will be pursued by Ms. Densmore and I feel she will pursue the matter to make this a public relation nightmare, naming names and making persons accountable for the pyramid of wrongdoings of Fiscal Services, and the US Treasury for allowing Fiscal Services to run free as three-year-old with no parent at Chuckie Cheese.
Nora Arpin (Comerica) and Mitchel Raymond (of Conduent) have conducted their due diligence of me. I hope they have given you the results of their research.
Read the email below. Since you have not replied to my email of 4 days ago, maybe you will respect Derek Densmore enough to contact his caretaker, Jackie.

From: Direct Express <Direct.Express@fiscal.treasury.gov>
Date: September 4, 2018, 6:58:21 PM EDT
To: Jackie
Subject: Your Inquiry to the Treasury Office of Inspector General
Dear Ms. Densmore:
Your inquiry to the Treasury Office of Inspector General regarding your Direct Express® card was referred to the Bureau of the Fiscal Service (Fiscal Service). We understand that you are a representative payee for your brother-in-law, Derek Densmore, a disabled veteran who receives Social Security benefit payments, and that you receive Mr. Densmore's payments electronically on a Direct Express® card. The Direct Express® card program was established by the Fiscal Service in support of a Congressional mandate to deliver federal benefits and other non-tax payments electronically. Comerica Bank is Fiscal Service's financial agent that operates the program.
We understand that, unfortunately, you were a victim of fraud as the result of a fraudster who stole your personal information and used that information to access the funds from your Direct Express® card account. Direct Express® card account holders are protected by Regulation E and other safeguards available to consumers; and, we understand that your stolen funds were fully refunded to you on August 16, 2018, following your report to Comerica Bank on August 10, 2018.
Fiscal Service will continue to work to protect federal benefit recipients from payment fraud and to maintain the overall integrity of the Direct Express® program.
Office of Legislative and Public Affairs
Bureau of the Fiscal Service
U.S. Department of the Treasury

See the reference to Reg E above? OIG Treasury had been conducting "investigative audits" that were basically a coverup of Comerica Bank violations and lack of supervision by the Bureau of Fiscal Service.

Tuesday, September 7, 2018

The telephone call from Jackie that Delmar would never forget

I called Jackie. She told me she had wanted to hear from someone in Treasury about the investigation that was taking place which Delmar revealed to Kate Berry. Delmar was the spokesman for Treasury who told Kate Berry that an audit/investigation had begun as a result of my complaint to Paulette Battle on February 26, 2018. Jackie got Delmar's telephone number for Delmar from a source.

Jackie called Richard Delmar this day, Tuesday, September 7, 2018. Delmar identified himself, Jackie identified herself, and Jackie lit into him with a loud unpunctuated run-on sentence as if being projected from a firehose.

Delmar disconnected the call.

Jackie called Delmar back. "Listen, you motherfucker, don't you ever fuckin' hang up on me, do you hear me?" A conversation then began.

Jackie pointed out to Delmar she read the article published by Kate Berry, and she wanted to know about the investigation he mentioned to Kate, plus the facts surrounding the failure of Comerica Bank and Conduent to investigate fraud and their violations of Regulation E. Delmar stated that OIG Treasury would be investigating all these issues.

Treasury was going to publish another "audit" and cover up for Comerica and Conduent as they did in the previous two published audits. This was proven when OIG Treasury published audit 19-041 on July 29, 2019, a year later, which was full of inaccurate information and justifications to excuse malfeasance on the part of the Bureau of Fiscal Service, which was the division of Treasury that awarded the Direct Express contract to Comerica Bank.
Jackie then asked Delmar why Delmar "never responded to J.B. Simms but responded to Kate Berry?" Delmar denied being familiar with J.B. Simms, but after being pressed for the truth, Delmar admitted he had an unanswered email from J.B. Simms on his computer. Delmar told Jackie he would respond to Simms.

Jackie was on a roll. She called Michael Jackman (the aide for US Rep. Keating from Massachusetts). Jackman told Jackie he would send questions to Delmar.
Delmar emailed Jackie and stated he would answer questions from Jackman.
Jackie called me and we talked about Kate's article. We decided we had to find Gale Stalworth of OIG of Social Security; they need to be involved.

At 1:01pm Jackie texted: "Sara (Soc Sec OIG) (410) 966-8385." *We want OIG of Treas and Soc Sec to work together"* was the text.

Having Jackie onboard will turn out to be the best thing that could happen.

From: "Delmar, Richard K." <Richard Delmar (OIG Treasury)>
Date: September 7, 2018 at 1:28:48 PM EDT
To: jackie
Subject: Direct Express/Comerica
Ms. Densmore – I'm writing to assure you that Treasury OIG takes your concerns seriously, as it does its oversight responsibility for the Direct Express program.
If you have information relating to misconduct, inefficiency, or mistakes in how the program is executed, specifically or generally, I would appreciate you relaying it here,
so our Audit and Investigations programs can review it. Thank you.
Rich Delmar
Counsel to the Inspector General, Department of the Treasury

I sent Jackie the address for the FOI (Freedom of Information (Act) to be sent to the Treasury. This address was found on the Treasury website. This is the text of the email I sent to Jackie.

By U.S. Mail to:
U.S. Department of the Treasury
Bureau of the Fiscal Service (Fiscal Service)
Attn: FOIA Disclosure Office/Room 508B
3201 Pennsy Drive, Building E
Landover, MD 20785
By Fax: 202-874-5484
Online at: https://www.treasury.gov/foia/pages/gofoia.aspx
Phone Number: 202-874-5602

Note this address. The FOI was sent to this email address, and faxed, but (spoiler alert) Treasury will deny receiving the FOI and it would be a year before we got the information we requested.

Use this info to make contact after the FOI is mailed and faxed:
Address:
FOIA Request
Department of the Treasury
Washington, DC 20220

Spoiler Alert": OIG Treasury did not respond for 11months until Jackie kept making demands. Treasury contacted Jackie in August of 2019 stating they found the FOI request.

Tuesday September 11, 2018

Jackie told me this morning she called Sara Lizama of the Social Security at (410) 966-8385. Jackie told her about all the complaints about Comerica Bank and wondered why Social Security never investigated the Direct Express program. Jackie pointed out the complaints all over the internet.

Date: *Tue, Sep 11, 2018 2:33 pm*
To: *Richard Delmar (OIG Treasury)*
Cc: *Jackie, ntarpin@comerica.com, designnmind@yahoo.com*
Dear Mr. Delmar,
It is apparent to me that both you and Ms. Arpin (Comerica Bank) are reluctant to engage me in verbal or written communication, even after both of you acknowledged to Ms. Densmore that you "intended" to reply to an email from me which was, as you hesitatingly acknowledged, in front of you. While I do applaud Paulette Battle (OIG Auditor) for engaging me in conversation and email in February 2018, it was not until the article in American Banker magazine was published that it was announced that Ms. Battle did, indeed, talk to "her boss" and let the boss know that the OIG reports of the FAA of Comerica Bank was severely lacking.
Ms. Arpin and her assigns (Susan Schmidt, Susan Rutledge, and others) did all they could to shield the cardholders from the mysterious fraud unit by using a Customer Advocate office to deny the violation of Regulation E Section 226.12(b)(2)(iii)(3) to victims of identity theft after Direct Express, at the direction of Comerica, directed funds to be withheld from victim cardholders before giving cardholders a chance to deny the debit transaction. I do believe the employees of Direct Express or Comerica with whom I communicated were a bit surprised that I knew the definition of an "AIB Course" and that I had completed some courses before opening an investigative agency.
Nowhere in either audit was there evidence of any direct contact with any Direct Express employee, Fraud Unit Manager, or anyone at Comerica who be accountable for violation of the above-named statute or any within Regulation E. The relationship between Fiscal Services and Comerica is cloaked with secrecy, and the motivation by Fiscal Services employees to be complicit with Comerica's abhorrent behavior begs the question as to the motivation of said Fiscal Services employees, to include David Lebryk, Cherly Morrow, and Kim McCoy.

I would assume that Mr. Thorsen, based upon his military career, would find the victimization of fellow Veterans a bit distasteful, and I can only assume that this practice has been hidden from Mr. Thorsen. Hopefully, I will see a statement from Mr. Thorsen to the media concerning this behavior by Fiscal Services. This email will serve as a formal request that Treasury OIG not only include the stories of victimization by me, Derek Densmore and his caregiver Jackie Lynn Densmore, Paul Katynski, and Kenneth Tillman, but that the four of us will be able to give a written response to the findings and the procedure used by Treasury OIG to flesh out the genesis of banking regulations being violated, the failure of Treasury OIG to be knowledgeable of banking organization, and the true motivation of Fiscal Services to fall prey to the "end game" of Comerica to be paid by the taxpayers and victimize Veterans and other taxpayers.
Sincerely
J.B. Simms

Wednesday, September 12, 2018

I decided to see what Nora Arpin's "peers" at the National Branded Prepaid Card Association thought of Kate Berry's article. Below is the notation from my notepad.

150pm t (202) 617 3086 NBPCA pub relations- Kate Allen
She knows about the article written by Kate Berry (American Banker) but did not publish this on the site of NBPCA. She was to contact board members of this organization (Nora Arpin is the Vice Chair of the National Branded Prepaid Card Association). She "is running out to catch a train and cannot talk."

Since Kate Allen did not want to talk about Nora Arpin and Comerica Bank, I decided to send her an email.

Subject: Comerica, Nora Arpin, et al
From: jbsimms
Date: Wed, Sep 12, 2018 2:26 pm
To: kallen@theheraldgroup.com, Cc: Jackie Densmore
Dear Ms. Allen,
Thank you for agreeing to speak with me as you were hurrying to "catch a train." Although our conversation was abbreviated, and you acknowledged reading the article published in American Banker, there are matters which you might not be aware.
As you read in the American Banker article, Rich Delmar, Chief Counsel to the Inspector General of Treasury, was quoted as having knowledge that the OIG of Treasury made a decision 3 months or so ago to conduct an inspection/investigation of Comerica Bank. This investigation was requested by me in February, 2018 through the Chief Auditor, Paulette Battle, to whom I gave information which prompted this impromptu inspection. I do have banking experience, and you can google my name or Erik Publishing to see my additional professional experience.
As the representative of the media company which is contracted with the National Branded Prepaid Card Association, I would have thought one of the board members would have published a response to the piece in American Banker but considering that the person at Comerica Bank who will be one of the subjects of this investigation is a board member (having accolades galore), it is no surprise that no one at the NBPCA has opined.
You suggested that I call the office of the NBPCA. I mentioned that I had called and left messages. These calls were made on August 29, 2018 at 9:58am (Pacific Time) and on September 5, 2018 at 10:42am (Pacific Time). No reply was received.
I look forward to your reply when you contact the board members concerning my ignored calls, as well as the fact that the NBPCA has not commented on the piece in American Banker, since the matter under investigation affects each member of this organization. It would also be interesting to know how you came about this article. The person being copied is Jackie Lynn Densmore, who is also named in the article. Jackie, along with Ken Tillman of Colorado, contacted me for my input upon being victimized. Paul Katynski did how own investigation after his identity was stolen, and we have compared notes for months concerning the matter with Comerica and its contract with Treasury, among other issues.
Thank you again for taking the time to speak with me, and I am certain we will talk again. Ms. Densmore might be the person you will speak with.
Sincerely, J.B. Simms

Thursday, September 13, 2018

Victim 7 Debra-Texas

Debra emailed and then she called me. Her Direct Express debit card was stolen, used while she was in the hospital. The amount she lost was $1,103.00. On September 1, 2018, Debra checked her balance and noticed a charge for $1,103 .00 to Amazon and ATM withdrawals which she did not make. The date of the fraud was August 31, 2018.On September 1, Debra had to call many times to get an operator and she reported the fraud immediately to the Conduent call center. I told Debra to make a police report and call Schmidt and Arpin at Comerica. Debra learned that her money had been withdrawn from the credit paid on account November 13, 2018, seventy- four days later. Debra was pleased to get her money.

From: jbsimms
Date: Thu, Sep 13, 2018, 12:03 pm
To: Richard Delmar (OIG Treasury)
Cc: Jackie
Dear Mr. Delmar,
I was encouraged to hear that Ms. Densmore was able to gain your ear with respect to this unfortunate matter of the oversight of the operation of the Direct Express program by Comerica Bank. Ms. Densmore advised me that you would be "reaching out to me" and for that I am grateful.
Your call will be very important to me, and I do not want to miss your call. If you would contact me via email to set up a time to chat, I will be glad to accommodate your schedule.
I look forward to our conversation.
Sincerely,
J.B. Simms

September 14, 2020

Delmar, Richard K. <Richard Delmar (OIG Treasury)>
Sep 14, 2018, 11:11 AM
to me, Michael, Jackie, Kate
Treasury OIG has been reviewing how BFS and Comerica have executed the Direct Express program for several years and has identified problems and recommended corrections in that execution.
We continue to conduct those reviews, as well as actively investigating allegations of misconduct involving the program. To clarify, our previous Direct Express work was focused on BFS' efforts to award the FAAs and not on the details of fraud monitoring and customer service. Our new audit and investigative work focus on issues raised by Mr. Simms and Ms. Densmore. Mr. Simms's criticism to the contrary, our prior work, as all our work, complied with all GAO and CIGIE standards and is objective and independent, as the Inspector General Act requires.
Rich Delmar
Counsel to the Inspector General
Department of the Treasury

Delmar admitted that investigations were taking place. This is important to remember because Delmar would later deny the existence of any investigation to avoid revealing documents involving the connection between Comerica Bank (Arpin) and Bureau of Fiscal Service (Santaniello).

Jackie got Delmar's attention.

Now it was time to research the GAO, the General Accounting Office.

Monday, September 24, 2018

Below is an email Delmar sent to Michael Jackman, an aide to US Representative Keating (MA).
It was good that Jackie contacted Keating, and that Jackman became involved. Delmar's interaction (emails) with Jackman became one promise after another, and the promises were never kept. Delmar danced around Jackman because he could.

From: Delmar, Richard K. <Richard Delmar (OIG Treasury)>
Sent: Monday, September 24, 2018, 10:51 AM
To: Jackman, Michael <Michael.Jackman@mail.house.gov>
Subject: Treasury Direct Express - Inspector General action
Mr. Jackman – following up on our previous communications about Treasury OIG's oversight of the Direct Express program.
In addition to our current audit work, our Office of Investigations is meeting with responsible officials at BFS and Comerica to discuss the Direct Express program and the fraudulent activities affecting it.
We will evaluate the steps already taken by Comerica and their sub-contractor to make the system and its processes more robust and resistant to identity theft and other frauds.
In addition, we will review what they are doing to analyze frauds and their own possible vulnerabilities, as well as how they report problems.
With our financial crime and forensic expertise, we will add value by identifying security gaps and proactive steps they can take, including the provision of more real-time information to us.
Thank you for your interest. I'll keep you advised of developments.
Rich Delmar
Counsel to the Inspector General
Department of the Treasury
Richard Delmar (OIG Treasury)

From: Michael Jackman (Aide to Rep. Keating)
Sent: Monday, September 24, 2018, 1:14 PM
To: Delmar, Richard K. <Richard Delmar (OIG Treasury)>
Subject: RE: Treasury Direct Express - Inspector General action
Thank you, Rich. I appreciate your response and would ask that as best you can, please keep me abreast of any developments from these meetings.
Michael Jackman, District Director
Office of Congressman Keating (MA-09)

At this point I became aware of the importance of Jackie. This was the beginning of thousands of hours of emails and conversations. Some of the conversations were about Jackie's manicure and cats in her house.

Switch today.

Make the change on our site
or over the phone, now!

¡Haga el cambio en nuestra pagina de
internet ó por telefono, ahora!

GoDirect.gov
1-800-333-1795

**Phone operators are available
Monday–Friday | 9 a.m–7 p.m. EST**

You can also visit your bank or credit union.

Para español, visite

DirectoasuCuenta.gov

Converting your paper check to
an electronic payment is easy.

All you will need is your:

* Social Security number

* Information from your most
recent federal benefit check
or claim number

* Date of birth *FOR DIRECT EXPRESS®*

* Financial institution's routing
transit number *FOR DIRECT DEPOSIT*

* Account number and account
type (checking or savings)
FOR DIRECT DEPOSIT

DIRECTEXPRESS

DIRECT DEPOSIT
Simple. Safe. Secure.

1120

40

Chapter Four
Bureau of Fiscal Service and OIG Treasury on the Run

We went after the Bureau of Fiscal Service and OIG Treasury as the victims poured in.

Jackie and I had a false sense of accomplishment. Persons at Comerica, Conduent, OIG Treasury, and Social Security (including Delmar, Arpin, Schmidt, and Lizama) were communicating with us not because they were admitting errors; they were reacting to inquiries because they got "caught" being greedy, lazy, and unaccountable.

Thursday, September 19, 2018

Victim Number 8-Don: Scottsdale, Arizona

Don contacted me after finding my contact information on the Pissed Consumer website. On August 31, 2018, fraud was detected on Don's Direct Express debit card. Don immediately reported the fraud amount to the Conduent (Direct Express) call center; $431.00 was wired to Rapid Cash, Kansas City, KS from a Cash Advance location in Washington State. Afterward, he called the office of Rapid Cash and learned that the fraud originated in Washington State.

Don called Conduent (Direct Express) on August 31, canceled his card, and filed a claim for fraud. Paperwork was sent to Don (from Conduent/Direct Express Fraud Department) which was filled out and returned to the address for Direct Express.

This fraud occurred before Mr. Otto was aware the deposit had been made to his account.

Don called Susan Schmidt of Comerica Bank, using the telephone number I posted on the internet. On Wednesday, September 19, 2018, Mr. Otto called Susan Schmidt, of Comerica Bank. Schmidt hung up on Mr. Otto when he mentioned the Treasury Department.

At 6:51 pm I received an email from Don; he got his money back, all in one day.

Saturday, September 22, 2018

Victim Number 9-Harold: Darlington, SC

Henry's daughter called me. Her father, a retired Veteran, was a victim of fraud in his Direct Express account. Amounts ranging from $4,000 to $7, 000 were diverted to a Green Dot debit card account, The crime was reported to Direct Express and the Darlington (SC) County Sheriff's Department on July 23, 2018. Direct Express had not reimbursed the funds. The total loss was $30,000.00.

This matter was noted in an email submitted to Kate Berry (American Banker) (American Banker), Nora Arpin, Richard Delmar (OIG Counsel), and Jackie Densmore on this date, Saturday, September 22, 2018

Sunday, September 23, 2018

Research was conducted to connect the dots. Santaniello was quoted in Kate's article. The Treasury website identified Thomas Santaniello as being assigned to the Legislative Affairs Office of the Bureau of Fiscal Service. He was the watchdog. Claire Santaniello- Security and Exchange Compliance for Pershing, a BYN Mellon company

The website Anonymous Watchman posted on May 14, 2018, a telephone number of (888) 851-1920, and that the Federal Reserve Board regulates Comerica. Interestingly I had contacted the FRB OIG about Comerica Bank violating Regulation E, and no one was interested.

The time had come to dig a little deeper and find the best source to identify a nemesis, a former employee of BFS Treasury.

Christen Stevenson

3/2016 to present- Director of Audits and Investigations, US House of Representatives

2/10-10/15- (5 yr,9 mo) Audit Manager – US Treasury

05-07- Internal Auditor-Fed Res Bank, Chicago

I had to dig deep to find Stevenson. She had attempted to avoid detection by ceasing the activity in some internet areas, but it is hard to hide from a hungry animal.

Research on Green Dot, the debit card used by the fraudster who took $30,000 from Victim Number 9, revealed the following:

Rajeev V. Date, UC Berkley, Harvard, Fenway Summer- Owner

7315 Wisconsin Ave, Suite 960 West, Bethesda, MD 20814, (202)864-6231

Rajeev Date would be a target. He was withholding information from the McPhail family.

Monday, September 24, 2018

A Green Dot Board Member was contacted. It was Rajeev V. Date. He refused to assist the victim or discuss the matter. The coverup continued.

Now it was time to target the Consumer Financial Protection Bureau.

From: CFPB Ombudsman <CFPB_Ombudsman@cfpb.gov>

Date: Mon, Sep 24, 2018 9:38 am

To: "jbsimms@erikpublishing.com"

Mr. Simms – Thank you for contacting the CFPB Ombudsman's Office.

The CFPB Ombudsman's Office provides an independent, impartial, and confidential resource to informally assist individuals, companies, consumer and trade groups, and others in resolving issues with the CFPB. For more information about the CFPB Ombudsman's Office, please see www.consumerfinance.gov/ombudsman. Your voicemail indicated that you were seeking to put our office on notice regarding an article that was being published. You had also shared that you were seeking to speak with someone regarding things that are happening in regard to consumers. Could you please share further information so that we may determine how we may assist?

We look forward to your response,

CFPB Ombudsman's Office

Tel: 202 435 7880

Delmar, Richard K. Richard Delmar (OIG Treasury)

Mon, Sep 24, 2018, 1:39 PM

to Jackie, me

Ms. Densmore – thanks for your call earlier today. For your information, and yours, Mr. Simms, here is the email I sent to Rep. Keating's staffer earlier today.

A special agent from our Office of Investigations will contact you as our investigation progresses following up on our previous communications about Treasury OIG's oversight of the Direct Express program. In addition to our current audit work, our Office of Investigations is meeting with responsible officials at BFS and Comerica to discuss the Direct Express program and the fraudulent activities affecting it.

We will evaluate the steps already taken by Comerica and their subcontractor to make the system and its processes more robust and resistant to identity theft and other frauds.

In addition, we will review what they are doing to analyze frauds and their own possible vulnerabilities, as well as how they report problems.

With our financial crime and forensic expertise, we will add value by identifying security gaps and proactive steps they can take, including the provision of more real-time information to us.

Thank you for your interest. I'll keep you advised of developments.

Rich Delmar

Counsel to the Inspector General

Department of the Treasury

What would Delmar tell Keating?

I emailed Delmar copies of the timeline of the Victim Number 9 fraud.

Scott, Sonja L. ScottS@oig.treas.gov

Mon, Sep 24, 2018, 10:54 AM

to me

I and a Treasury OIG auditor would like to interview you telephonically next week. Please let us know your availability. Thank you. Sonja

ASAC Sonja L. Scott

US Department of Treasury

Office of the Inspector General

Office of Investigations

Rajeev Date
Green Dot Debit Card
(202) 864-6231
0842am (pst)
A telephone call was received from Mr. Date. He acknowledged his association with Green Dot and was told of the fraud involving Victim Number 9. Mr. Date was very receptive, stating he would research the matter.

Rajeev Date lied; he never returned the call or addressed the matter. It would take over 2 years to get the information from Comerica about the identity of the fraudster. The McPhail family would suffer accusations of complicity by Jon Chally, one of the attorneys for Comerica Bank. Chally's clients were liars.

Below is the email I sent to the daughter of Victim Number 9. I copied Jackie, Nora Arpin, and Richard Delmar.

Green Dot debit card president lied about the McPhail investigation

J B Simms
Mon, Sep 24, 2018, 9:30 AM
to Marteshia, Jackie, Kate, Nora, Richard Delmar
I just received a call from Rajeev V. Date, a member of the Board of Directors of Green Dot, with Green Dot being the debit card to which your father's (Harold McPhail) deposit account at Direct Express was victimized. Mr. Date took your telephone number and he told me he would have someone at Green Dot contact you concerning this fraudulent transaction.
As I told Mr. Date, this matter was dismissed by the "fraud unit" of Direct Express/Comerica Bank. The rationale used to justify the dismissal of your claim (totaling over $30,000) is not clear, nor is the justification valid. I see from the police report (attached), and your bank statements that you sent me, that the fraud occurred on February 13, March 6, April 4 and April 17, totaling $23,000. This does not include the monies taken in July.
If Comerica Bank/Direct Express is denying your claim based upon the fact that a time factor had expired upon reporting the claim, I suggest to you that Comerica Bank/Direct Express has liability with respect to the fact that transactions of this denomination should have gotten the attention of the least intellectually gifted person at Direct Express and caused no concern to them. Someone at Direct Express might have known about this and ignored this.
Also, the people at Direct Express and Comerica Bank are aware that retirees and other recipients do not regularly look at their statements and have no concern until either a family member looks at the statement or a withdrawal is denied. Comerica Bank/Direct Express use the timeline parameters to avoid liability for fraud, and to cover up the fact that they failed to put safety features/notification systems in place as do other financial institutions. Comerica has been paid tens of millions of dollars to operate Direct Express, but they are not spending the money to protect their cardholders; the money is going "somewhere else."
Green Dot Debit Card is a member of the National Branded Prepaid Card Association, of which Nora Arpin (Comerica Bank) is a Board Member. Let's hope Mr. Date has someone at Green Dot to communicate with you, validate your claim, and if necessary, shame Comerica Bank into acknowledging their failure to protect your father, and reimburse him for their failure.
Mr. Delmar, Counsel for the Treasury OIG, should take this failure into account, and communicate this to the investigators who are said to be conducting an interim investigation of Comerica Bank, and Nora Arpin. Sincerely,
J.B. Simms

From: jbsimms
Sent: Monday, September 24, 2018, 11:10 PM
To: CFPB Ombudsman
Cc: Kate Berry (American Banker) (American Banker); Jackie
Subject: RE: Your Voicemail to the CFPB Ombudsman's Office
Thank you for your email. I contacted your office months ago, and since the consensus is that the CFPB is impotent and does not enforce its own policies (as witnessed by the failure to investigate the 400+ claims against Direct Express/Comerica), your email was refreshing and encouraging.

Tuesday, September 25, 2018

Victim Number 10-Charity: Lexington, North Carolina
Fraud dates:
$102.50 7/4/2018 ATM Withdrawal- 1020 S. Main St, Lexington, NC
$102.50 $203.95 7/4/2018 ATM Withdrawal- 4929 E Hwy, 704 E Madison (Stokes County)
$200.00 7/3/2018 ATM Withdrawal- 107088 NC Hwy 704, Madison, NC (Stokes County)
$25.00 7/3/2018 Dollar General Madison, NC $25 cash back
$531.45 Total
The Fraud Claim was made on July 10, 2018.
Victim Number 10 was in a hospital in Winston Salem, NC on these dates the fraud took place. Conduent refused to give provisional credit within 10 days Conduent refuses to contact banks owning ATMs used in fraud Conduent refuses to acknowledge police reports. Conduent refuses to contact police. The card was not loaned or given to anyone.

Wednesday, September 26, 2018

Tamara Christian
KOVR Television- CBS affiliate
(916) 374-1361 KOVR Television- CBS affiliate
tchristian@kovr.com KOVR Television- CBS affiliate
A telephone call was received from Ms. Tamara Christian, KOVR Television- CBS affiliate. She was a consumer reporter at KOVR and produced a piece about Direct Express. She has had little cooperation from OIG Treasury, specifically a dismissive email from Thomas Santaniello, Office of Legislative Affairs at the US Treasury.
Email communication would be established, and Ms. Christian requested an interview.

From: "Christian, Tamara A"
Date: Wed, Sep 26, 2018, 4:32 pm
To: Jbsimms
Dear Mr. Simms,
My name is Tamara Christian; I'm a Consumer Producer for the CBS station in Sacramento, Ca.
I just read the article in, American Banker, regarding the Direct Express Program through Comerica, I jumped out of my cubical when I read your comment.
You see, I've been investigating this debacle for several months. I've tossed FOIA's at the Office of Comptroller/Department of Treasury/ Government Accountability Office ...etc., with no real results. And of course, reaching out to Comerica, but I've been met with the usual talking points and no real answers.
Our Consumer Unit has put a few stories to air, but I'm looking for the smoking gun.
I would be beyond thrilled to talk with you and hear what insights you have.
Please give me a call at your earliest convenience at (916) 374-1361.
Thank you for your time.
Sincerely,
Tamara

I called Tamara. She replied.

Hi Jim,
* It was a pleasure to chat with you. Here is a link to one of the stories we've put on air...*
https://sacramento.cbslocal.com/2018/05/22/stolen-social-security-benefits/
This is what we've been trying to figure out for months.
Do you have the answers to any of the following questions.
We want to know:
How much the Direct Express program costs to run?
How much Comerica gets paid to run it?
Who is monitoring the direct express program?
What sort of government accountability does direct express held to?

Has the program ever been audited for consumer satisfaction and financial accountability?
How many Direct Express customers reported fraud on their accounts in 2016 and 2017?
Out of those reported fraud cases, how many lead to an immediate provisional credit during the investigation?
Thank you,
Tamara

Below is the email which was sent to me from Tamara Christian and is the response Tamara received from Susan Schmidt of Comerica Bank. Schmidt got her answers from Nora Arpin of Comerica Bank.

From: "Christian, Tamara A"
Date: Wed, Sep 26, 2018, 5:20 pm
To: jbsimms
Everything below is from Comerica…………
Answers to your questions are below from Nora Arpin. Please let me know if you need anything else.
Thanks,
Susan
• *How many fraudulent charges were reported to Comerica by Direct Express cardholders for calendar years 2016, and 2017?*
Comerica regularly validates that it's fraud rate for the Direct Express program is among the lowest in the industry. We use third party sources for this validation, however specific fraud data is not released to the public by any company in the card space due to the verified likelihood of increased criminal activity if this type of information were to be shared. The card networks do not release this type of information publicly and strongly discourage their Issuers from releasing this type of information publicly as a security measure.
• *What is Comerica's policy regarding provisional credits, during a fraud investigation?*
The Direct Express program follows Regulation E with the exception that we give cardholders a longer period of time to report an unauthorized transaction (90 days vs. the 60 days in the Regulation). Regulation E states the conditions in which provisional credit is given. The Direct Express program adheres to the terms of Regulation E. The specific language from the Regulation may be found below:
Time limits and extent of investigation— (1) Ten-day period. A financial institution shall investigate promptly and, except as otherwise provided in this paragraph (c), shall determine whether an error occurred within 10 business days of receiving a notice of error. The institution shall report the results to the consumer within three business days after completing its investigation. The institution shall correct the error within one business day after determining that an error occurred.
(2) Forty-five-day period. If the financial institution is unable to complete its investigation within 10 business days, the institution may take up to 45 days from receipt of a notice of error to investigate and determine whether an error occurred, provided the institution does the following:(i) Provisionally credits the consumer's account in the amount of the alleged error (including interest where applicable) within 10 business days of receiving the error notice. If the financial institution has a reasonable basis for believing that an unauthorized electronic fund transfer has occurred and the institution has satisfied the requirements of § 1005.6(a), the institution may withhold a maximum of $50 from the amount credited. An institution need not provisionally credit the consumer's account if:(A) The institution requires but does not receive written confirmation within 10 business days of an oral notice of error.
• *Once fraud is reported, how often are people receiving an immediate provisional credit? (please see the below combined answer to this question and the next one)*
• *How long does an average fraud investigation take to complete?*
While it may seem like we should be able to obtain enough information from the cardholder over the phone to complete the investigation right away, that usually isn't the case. The Direct Express program, like most (if not all), Financial Institutions request paperwork to assist with the investigation. That paperwork plays a critical role in assisting the investigation which is why it is requested. If the paperwork is received by the 10th business day, provisional credit is given which is in compliance with Regulation E. The exception to the request for paperwork is when it is very clear that there have been 3rd party fraud (i.e. the fraud team identifies a transaction as potentially fraudulent before the cardholder calls in to dispute the transaction, etc.). In those cases, we fast track the resolution, and the cardholder receives credit to his/her card in 10 days or sooner. Each and every investigation is unique—there is no average time to complete an investigation as the facts in each case dictate the time to completion.
Tamara Christian, KOVR-TV SACRAMENTO, CA

Wednesday, September 26, 2018

A telephone call was received from Ms. Christian. She had received little cooperation from OIG of Treasury, specifically a dismissive email from Thomas Santaniello, Office of Legislative Affairs at the US Treasury. Email communication would be established, and Ms. Christian requested an interview.

Friday, September 28, 2018

Sonja Scott (OIG Treasury)
Fri, Sep 28, 2018, 2:07 PM
to me
No transparency issues. We will be asking general questions as to what occurred, when, to whom etc. We will then have specific questions based on information that you have already provided. I do not have a list. I just wanted you to know that we are trying to keep questioning focused and limit our discussion to an hour, if possible. We can always speak again. We do not normally audio record these interviews but will make you aware if that becomes desired.
Sonja

Monday, October 1, 2018

Victim Number 11-Teresa: Kentucky
From: Teresa Hodson
Date: Mon, Oct 01, 2018 4:39 pm
To: jbsimms
I was receiving my ssi benefits thru Direct Express then the end of 2016 my money was fraudulenty taken from a company overseas after that I closed down my account with them and in March 2018 started my benefits coming to a private checking account no problem for months then today when my benefits are to be put in that account I had nothing contacted ssa was told it was sent to Direct Express for some reason and no one knew why...called direct express on hold for hours finally was told August 23 someone posing as me opened the account got a card and today took out every dime. I have filed all necessary reports etc. But I don't have a dime to pay my rent, eat nothing. Comerica bank direct express this seems to be something they have had trouble with before. I'm told if I get my federal money back it could be 60-90 days. I just don't know what to do at this point Direct Express did not protect my money or my information. Thank you.

After sending Teresa the names, email addresses, and telephone numbers of persons she needed to contact, Teresa sent me the following email:

On October 16, Teresa sent me this email. This is the emotion I was hearing from the victims:
Jim I'm in tears. I just called direct express to try to track down my money. The guy now says it's been flagged, and social security needs to verify who I am so they can release the money and put it on another care. It's literally driving crazy I'm pretty strong but this is the most wearing thing ever. I just called Alisha who is with direct express who gave me her direct line it's the 4th message I've left this week but tonite I totally unloaded and I mean bad I was just done. So I just left a message for Ms. Lozama? Just asking her to please help me with this. I'm just spent.

This was a typical email, mostly from people receiving Social Security and very limited income. This was breaking my heart.
I continued researching the Comerica/Conduent/BFS connections and stumbled across the General Accounting Office, GAO.
There was a report GOA 17-176 published by the GAO which was very critical of the lack of transparency of the Bureau of Fiscal Service in reporting the amount of money distributed to each Fiscal Agent, including Comerica Bank.

Tuesday, October 2, 2018

J B Simms
Oct 2, 2018, 8:10 AM
to Jackie, Sonja
I am on a train, traveling. Unexpected day trip. Hopefully, tomorrow's call can be scheduled.
Thank you, and I look forward to addressing the issues. Jim Simms

I spent the day of October 2, 2018, being interviewed by Tamara Christian in Sacramento, CA

Christian, Tamara A
Tue, Oct 2, 2018, 6:08 PM
to me
Jim,
It was truly a pleasure meeting you! I can't thank you enough for making the trip up here.
I hope this story is just the tip of what is to come and I'm happy that you're a part of that.
I have no doubt that we'll be chatting soon.
Sincerely,
Tamara

Meeting with Tamara was the beginning of more media exposure. Tamara and her producer were shocked by Comerica Bank and Conduent ignoring the victim.

Wednesday, October 3, 2018

Paul Katynski
Wed, Oct 3, 2018, 11:53 AM
to me
Just finished meeting with Sonja. Went very well and I guess that I'm not the only victim of Alexis Grimsley. I guess the information I compiled will aid them in arresting her. Thanks for the help, Paul

Date: Wed, Oct 03, 2018, 6:37 pm
To: CackleyA@gao.gov
Dear Ms. Clackley,
I am involved in a matter with Treasury and Social Security OIG offices, and the matter at hand also involves the CFPB. I have been in touch with the CFPB and see that this agency is not operating as its mandate demands.
I want to discuss this matter with you or the person in OIG of Fed Reserve who would handle this matter. The Federal Reserve has a copy of my complaint.
Please contact me and advise me of my options. This matter will involve a number of agencies, and all are culpable.
Sincerely,
J.B. Simms

Thursday, October 4, 2018

Victim Number 12- Bob
Bob emailed me and stated the following:

October 4, 2018
$755 was sent to a Wells Fargo Account. Comerica not responding.

Bob's money was sent to a Wells Fargo account the same as McPhail's money was sent to the Green Dot account.
I gave him the names and contact information of Richard Delmar and Sonja Scott at OIG Treasury. This victim found me on Facebook after Rob Ferry named me as an administrator of the Facebook page. Some of his messages were from Facebook, some were emails.

Thanks, Jim, I called Sonja and just got a recording but, left a message telling her that I just talked to you and also left a message on what happened and how this is my only source of income and if I don't get my money back soon I will be evicted and all my utilities shut off and I cant buy any food. Plus all the late fees I will incur. And that waiting on their form and then possibly another 45 days for investigation is unacceptable. I need my money now.

Here are emails from Bob which followed:

Hi Jim, I just got an email back from Richard Delmar saying he got my email, the same email I sent to you with a snapshot of my Direct Express account showing the IVR transfer. Richard was very receptive and he said he will get right on it. I want to thank you Jim for all you do.

Hi Jim, you really got the ball rolling for me. I can't tell you how appreciative I am. I already had Comercia bank call me and just a little while ago Calvin from Advocacy from Direct Express. I wanted to forward this to you because he sent me the claim form PDF so I don't have to wait the 5 to 7 business days for the mail. And also he gave me the FAX number to send the claim information to, or you can email him at this address. I already faxed and emailed my claim to him. So, I will let you know when it's resolved. Again, I can't express to you how thankful I am for all that you do. Something needs to be done to those fraudsters.

You are doing a fantastic job Jim. I am so glad I found you. I had a full refund on the illegal money transfer in just 2 days. They even refunded me the express shipping charge to get a new card. I got the new card on the 3rd day. So, all in all I had all my funds back and ready to use in 3 days thanks to you.

He got Delmar on the phone but received no answer from Nora or Schmidt. We knew that Treasury, and the Bureau of Fiscal Service, was involved with this operation. BFS approved the contract with Comerica Bank, and we were after BFS for not only approving the contract, but for ignoring the problems.
Below is the email from Jackie.

Thu, Oct 04, 2018, 10:30 pm
To: jbsimms
JB do we know how long bob was without his money? This info super important when taking with Sonya if you could put a list together and by the way Brady kicks ass. 😆

Friday, October 5, 2018

Victim Number 12-Bob
Subject: RE: Direct Express
From: Bob
Date: Fri, October 05, 2018 8:23 am
To: "jbsimms
The Advocacy of direct Express called me this morning letting me know all my funds are available. I said good because I should be getting my card today because I paid 13 dollars for express shipping. Which, I told her I shouldn't even be charged for that since none of this was my fault. She said she will credit my account for the 13 dollars. So, it all worked out well thanks to you Jim. I couldn't imagine not having any money for 45 days or more. Not even 15 days. I really think they should have paid me something for all the stress I went through because of their lack of security. I hope after all this is over they lose their contract and some people even arrested. It needs to go to a bank that has the infrastructure to handle a big contract like this. And not some shady company as Direct Express where its almost impossible to get a hold of someone when retirees and disabled vets are relying on their checks to live. I woke up last night because I just remembered I had an autopay bill coming out of my check on the 5th of every month. Luckily I have another credit card and was able to make a one time payment. People lose their homes and much more if they don't get a check. And late fees and everything else starts acquiring. I thank God I found you and for all the help you gave me to get my money back the next day it happened. I thank God for people like you who fight for us little people.
Sincerely,
Bob

From time to time, Delmar and Scott appeared to be concerned with the victims. I was cautiously optimistic that since Delmar commissioned an investigation that they realized OIG Treasury had done a terrible job during the first two OIG audits.
This optimism did not last long.

The beginning of being the Facebook page Moderator

The email below was received from Rob Ferry. The work I had been doing got the attention of the moderator of a Facebook page that was dedicated to assisting Direct Express victims.

Subject: Rob Ferry made you a moderator of the group Against Direct express scamming people.
From: "Facebook" <notification@facebookmail.com>
Date: Fri, Oct 05, 2018, 6:06 am
To: Jim Simms
Re: Facebook
Rob Ferry made you a moderator of the group Against Direct express scamming people.

I became the moderator of the Facebook page that victims of the Direct Express program had joined. Bob allowed me to change the name of the Facebook page to Direct Express Cardholder Victims. I began posting educational links and documents for the victims to read. The number of victims increased rapidly.
I had been trying to get the CFPB to be accountable. This email below was encouraging but no one helped.

Date: Fri, Oct 05, 2018, 8:49 am
To: JBSimms
Cc: "Cackley, Alicia P" <CackleyA@gao.gov>
Mr. Simms:
I am contacting you on behalf of Ms. Cackley. To discuss matters involving CFPB with its IG, you should contact the IG staff at the Federal Reserve, which serve as its inspector general.
The following staff should be able to assist you:
Mark Bialek
Inspector General of the Board of Governors of the Federal Reserve System and the Bureau of Consumer Financial Protection, Mark.Bialek@frb.gov
Peter Sheridan, Associate Inspector General for Audits and Attestations, Federal Reserve Board and Bureau of Consumer Financial Protection 202-973-5009 Peter.j.sheridan@frb.gov
Melissa M. Heist, Associate Inspector General for Audits and Evaluations, 202-973-5024
melissa.m.heist@frb.gov

None of these people ever assisted me or any Direct Cardholder victims, nor would they address the fact that their agency failed to adhere to their legal obligation.

From: Cackley, Alicia P
Sent: Friday, October 05, 2018, 11:37 AM
To: Goebel, Cody J
Subject: FW: CFPB investigation
Hi Cody,
Could you please contact the gentleman whose email is below and provide him with the information he is seeking about CFPB's IG? I am traveling back from San Francisco right now and can't really deal with it. He also left me a voicemail, so you can reach him by phone at (803) 309-6850 if that is easier.
Thanks,
Alicia

Saturday, October 6, 2018

Victim Number 14-David: Colorado Springs, Colorado
Colorado Springs, CO Veteran Benefits
10/1/2018, 999.83 Noticed money missing- a debit for 999.83 to a ZIONS BANK - posted 10/01/2018 at 17:31:55; called an IVR MONEY TRANSFER. There was also a 1.50 charge for a IVR TRANSFER FEE. I spoke to a guy who was all business and no" I'm Sorry this happened" and was advised of what they would be

doing when included questions that seemed accusatory in presentation - did you lend someone your card? did you family use it without your permission? are you sure you did not authorize this?

The customer service at Conduent accused the victim of authorizing the transfer.

Tuesday, October 9, 2018

Victim Number 15-Felicity: North Carolina
Email from Felicity:
September 6, 2018- $283.00 was taken from DE account Facebook message: Jim. Ive filled report to bbb. Im enroute to making calls to susan on monday. What else do i need to besides staying alive with nothing to support me. Please help me.
September 12, 2018- Discharged from Trust Point Hospital. Purse was returned in a zipped, transparent plastic bag. All contents were emptied from the purse into the plastic bag. I inquired about the condition of my belongings. I was given a yellow sticky-note upon which was written the name of "Stephanie" to call if anything was missing. When speaking to william i tried to explain whatt was going on and that i had decomped. Basically all of the people i spoke with told me was not their problem. So now im told to resubmit a different version of what i think happened.

Below is more of an email I received from Felicity:

So i found you on the internet. Ive been in tears i can not prosecute based on info because they will not provide me with an address to the terminal. I cant eat. I cant even enjoy my life after the fact. The exboyfriend gets off again for his crack addiction while i suffer. The exboyfriend is now long gone.
And im left here with nothing. All of this has caused me a great deal of humilation and emotional distress. Thank you

Getting emails like the one below was becoming a regular thing. Many times, I had to give the victims the names and telephone numbers of the persons at Comerica and Conduent, and tell them what to say, and they would get results.
Below is the email from Felicity that made this worthwhile.

Date: Thu, Oct 25, 2018, 8:53 am
To: "jbsimms
Hi Jim
I got the money in my account.

Below is the timeline of my contact with Felicity:

September 16, 2018- Notice fraud on DE account. Called DE
September 19, 2018- Received fraud packet.
September 24, 2018- faxed packet info to DE
Tuesday, October 9, 2018- Contacted Simms
Thursday, October 25, 2018- received funds.
Some of what I was doing was working, but we were going after Comerica and Conduent. You should notice that Conduent had not contacted Felicity from September 24 through October 9 when Felicity called me. I did with her as I did with others; I told her to tell them they had violated Regulation E and that Simms had been called.

Tuesday, October 9, 2018

From: OIGHotline <oighotline@frb.gov>
Date: Tue, Oct 09, 2018, 12:23 pm
To: jbsimms
Mr. Simms:
The Office of Inspector General (OIG) of the Board of Governors of the Federal Reserve System (Board) and

the Bureau of Consumer Financial Protection (the Bureau) has received your October 8, 2018, complaint regarding the Bureau complaint process. Thank you for bringing your concerns to the attention of our office. This OIG is the independent oversight authority for the Board and the Bureau, focused on auditing and investigating matters of fraud, waste, or abuse relating to the agencies' programs or operations. Our office is not authorized to oversee the activities of financial institutions, to engage in the program responsibilities of the agencies we oversee, or to conduct matters deemed not to be within our jurisdiction. The OIG reviews all complaints to determine whether they are appropriate for audit, investigation, or evaluation. Please note that our office is unable to investigate or intervene in an individual consumer complaint against a financial institution.

Please note, we are unable to provide status updates regarding a complaint once it is submitted to the OIG Hotline, referred to the Board or the Bureau, or referred to the appropriate internal component of the OIG (i.e., Investigations or Audits and Evaluations). However, if additional information is needed from you regarding your complaint, someone from our office will contact you directly.
Thank you,
OIG Hotline

This was their job. This was how they allowed Conduent and   Comerica to continue their fraud.

Wednesday, October 10, 2018

Sonja Scott, OIG Treasury. Office of Investigations

For some strange reason, I trusted Sonja Scott, but I knew her hands were tied by Delmar and the attorneys at OIG Treasury.
From: "Scott, Sonja L." <ScottS@oig.treas.gov>
Date: Wed, Oct 10, 2018, 10:40 am
To: jbsimms
Cc: Jackie
Thank you. I just spoke with Ms. McPhail. I also contacted the SA OIG today.
Sonja

We were trying to merge the human element with the fact that Comerica and Conduent were ignoring the victims and violating banking laws.
Why wasn't OIG Treasury going after the Bureau of Fiscal Service? The answer became clear; all Treasury employees were covering for each other.

From: jbsimms
Sent: Wednesday, October 10, 2018, 1:34 PM
To: Sonja Scott (OIG Treasury)
Cc: Jackie
Subject: RE: tears of victims
Thank you for being receptive.
I gave your number to Felicity Palma. Her card was stolen, used while she was in the hospital, and Direct Express and Comerica are so inept they cannot understand that there is a security camera at the atm where her card was used. Law enforcement claims the loss did not meet the threshold to make them concerned. I told her to make the criminal complaint regardless of what she is told.
Outsourcing the call center, outsourcing the "fraud unit", and a Customer Advocacy Department which shields the fraud unit, all need to be discontinued. Comerica has to hire a call center and fraud unit personnel to work specifically for Direct Express. I have not read the FAA, but if the FAA states that a call center be created, not outsourced, this should be addressed. I cannot address that specific issue, but there is so much malfeasance on the part of Comerica, and lack of performance by Fiscal Services, Social Security, and CFPB, it might seem difficult to know where to start. I know your jurisdiction is limited, but your office has enough to keep you busy. I suggest taking over the office of Nora Arpin and Susan Schmidt by government officials as a coup.
Jim Simms

Subject: RE: tears of victims
From: "Scott, Sonja L." <ScottS@oig.treas.gov>
Date: Wed, October 10, 2018, 9:39 am
To: "'jbsimms, Jackie, Tamara Christian
Kate Berry (American Banker)), Richard Delmar (OIG Treasury) oig.media@frb.gov, Nora Arpin (Comerica Bank)
I will speak to anyone who wants to speak with me. We are conducting an audit on the program and have opened investigations on individual cases. Sonja

From: jbsimms
Sent: Wednesday, October 10, 2018, 12:33 PM
To: Jackie; Tamara Christian; Kate Berry (American Banker); Delmar, Richard K. <Richard Delmar (OIG Treasury)>; Sonja Scott (OIG Treasury); oig.media@frb.gov; Nora Arpin (Comerica Bank)
Subject: tears of victims
Jackie, Kate Berry, and Tamara Christian understand what I am going to tell you. The others, government and bank employees, have no idea the damage caused by Comerica Bank to the lives of the persons they victimize. I am receiving texts from a victim who is crying. I have talked to her over the past few days. I will be calling her momentarily. She is at a police station to file a report. Direct Express knows about the crime but has not reported the crime and is not communicating with law enforcement.
I have defended victims for decades in many different scenarios. My telephone rings and I get email messages because people are helpless.If you want to listen to a woman cry because the bank and the agencies charged with regulating the bank are not helping her, I will gladly give her your telephone number.
This should not be happening.

I then sent the documents on the McPhail case to Sonja (Victim 9).

Thursday, October 11, 2018

8:08 am
I received a call from Tiffany J.- OIG hotline coordinator
She stated she cannot regulate the work of CFPB. She stated I need to contact my representative congressman. I can ask that policy be changed. She denied that the mandate of the CFPB was to investigate. She refused to give a threshold of cases that would spark an investigation. The telephone was disconnected by Tiffany after about 20 minutes. She could not take the heat.

The CFPB was useless. They made broad statements trying to make the public believe that they were advocates for the consumers. The administrators of the agencies were lazy and lied to the consumers. Nothing was being investigated.
Subject: Harold McPhail and the $30,000 electronic fraud
From: jbsimms
Date: Thu, Oct 11, 2018, 12:16 pm
To: "OIGHotline" <oighotline@frb.gov>
Cc: Sonja Scott (OIG Treasury), Sarah Lizama (SSA OIG), raj.date@fenwaysummer.com, "Marteshia McPhail", Nora Arpin (Comerica Bank), "Jackie"
Dear Tiffany J.,
I am sending this email on behalf of Marteshia McPhail's father, Harold McPhail. If you think a $30,000 fraudulent activity report would meet the threshold of having an investigation conducted, I encourage you to review these documents and share this matter with the CFPB.
As our conversation started this morning, I contend that the CFPB is not performing its duties as noted on the website for the CFPB and that the Fed Res OIG does have the mandate of investigating the failure of performance by the CFPB. The responsible party at Comerica Bank, Nora Arpin, is well aware of this matter and she is not responding.
Hopefully, these attached documents need no explanation. Mr. Date, a board member of Green Dot, has been aware of this matter for weeks, as have other copied governmental OIG offices.
The information attached is more comprehensive than the majority of the complaints filed with the CFPB.

Until your office decides that your mandate is to respond to and investigate the CFPB, as is your charge, these reports will continue to come across my desk, as more victims look for help.
Sincerely, J.B. Simms

A copy was sent to Rajeev Date, the CEO of Green Dot.

Date refused to assist the McPhail family, knowing they lost $30,000 to fraud.

Friday, October 12, 2018

I sent this email to Sonja Scott after studying Reg E. I sent this to Sonja Scott in reference to the fraud on the account of Harold McPhail.

J B Simms
Fri, Oct 12, 2018, 12:34 PM
to Sonja, Sara, Jackie, Marteshia
Pardon me for trying so informally. I am in a gym.
During my search for the part of the statute directing banks to submit all information regarding violations of federal law, I found an opinion, I believe from the FDIC, that states the 60-day time restriction for reporting can be bypassed due to extenuating circumstances, namely "being in hospital."
Ms. McPhail stated that her father was in the hospital during April, for approximately a month. Comerica Bank/Direct Express operate a rogue operation, determining which laws they wish you to obey. I will send all of you the link a bit later.
Jim

Thursday, October 18, 2018

Victim Number 16-Clara: Lindsay, CA
Jackie got a call from a woman in Kingman, AZ, 71 yoa, Clara Braunreiter and gave the woman my telephone number. Clara was missing a lot of money.

I called Clara. She did not know how much she lost. Calvin (from Conduent) called her but she did not want to talk to Calvin until she talked to me. She had been in the hospital many times during the past year, sometimes in Los Angeles. Money is missing from her account. She did not know the amount.

In 10/2018 over $997.00 monies were paid to PayPal (Taco Bell, Amtrak (Washington, DC, and more. She called Calvin at (512) 250-7630 and left a message on voice mail. Calvin called and told Clara she had to fill out a fraud packet, and an investigation might take 3 months.

I advised Clara to call Nora Arpin and Sonja Scott.

Clara was disabled. Her health was bad. There was no way Clara would be able to fill out a fraud packet. Conduent was using this fraud packet to keep from paying people.

Friday, November 9, 2018

There was a restaurant nearby my apartment where I edited my books and worked on this Direct Express/Comerica mess. On this day I was at the restaurant when it closed at 9 pm. I had many emails to return, and the staff would let me stay after closing time as they mopped the floors.

The journey back to my apartment was a walk of about 15 minutes. I happened to be walking past a bank building when my phone rang.

It was Clara. She told me she checked her account and a deposit of $ 1,843.00 had just been placed into her account. Clara had to get to an ATM and get the money out before Comerica took back the money.

Clara had never used an ATM. I told her to go to an ATM and call me and that I would walk her through the procedure. She called back the next day and told me she got the money out. A person was at the ATM and helped her. Clara had to go to the ATM a couple of times to get her money.

I was so happy for her. How could Comerica and Conduent jointly be so evil to ignore the victims? It took pressure, and we were applying the pressure.

Sunday, December 2, 2018

At 10 pm Clara called: $700 had been taken from her account by Conduent. No explanation was given.

The following day I sent an email to Sara Lizama of Social Security OIG and told her about the issue with Clara.

Tuesday, December 4, 2018

Over the past two months, I was on the telephone many times with Clara. Now that Conduent took money from her account, I told Clara to demand a copy of the "investigation" that Conduent performed which authorized them to take her money. Clara called Calving at the Conduent Customer Advocacy for Direct Express; Calvin refused to send Clara a copy of the investigation.
Clara was entitled to a copy of the investigation. Conduent was violating federal banking regulations.
This is what was going on; we pushed for the money. Conduent wants to take 3 months. They then debit the account on the first of the month.
Dirty people.

Thursday, October 11, 2018

Jackie had been pushing the office of Senator Elizabeth Warrant to become involved. Senator Warren, along with Senator Hatch, were the senators who requested the Office of Inspector General to investigate the lack of transparency with regard to the dispensing of funds by the Bureau of Fiscal Service. The Bureau of Fiscal Service dispensed funds through "Fiscal Agents" which would distribute funds to recipients. The Bureau of Fiscal Service was not revealing federal funds disbursed to each Fiscal Agent, only reporting the whole of the disbursement by the agency.
Jackie wanted Senator Warren's office to address how Comerica Bank got the contract and the fact that Comerica Bank was violating Reg E on a regular basis.

From: Woolheater, Ashley (Warren) [Ashley_Woolheater@warren.senate.gov]
Sent: Thursday, October 11, 2018, 1:05 PM
To: Berry, Kate
Subject: Exclusive follow up: Comerica
Hi Kate,
 We haven't been introduced yet; I'm the new press secretary in Senator Warren's DC Senate office. She's preparing to send letters to Comerica, SSA, and the VA pressing for answers about the security breaches and fraud schemes (Comerica) and about why the agencies chose to partner Comerica. I'd be happy to share these with you, if useful or connect, if you have further questions. We'll probably issue a public release in a day or so.
Ashley

We were hoping Kate's involvement would prompt some accountability.

Friday, October 12, 2018

Date: Fri, Oct 12, 2018, 10:21 am
To: jbsimms
Cc: felicity, Jackie
As always, all victims can contact me and provide me with any police reports or information. Thank you. Sonja
ASAC Sonja L. Scott
US Department of Treasury
Office of the Inspector General
Office of Investigations

Jackie had been talking to Kate Berry (American Banker) (American Banker) for a while. Today Kate sent us an email which gave us a bit of encouragement.

On Oct 12, 2018, at 11:58 AM, Berry, Kate wrote:
Hi Jim, Jackie --
I wanted to let you know that Sen. Elizabeth Warren's office is putting out a release soon on Comerica --- see the email exchange below.
Also wondered if you've contacted the CFPB ombudsman.
https://www.consumerfinance.gov/about-us/blog/cfpb-ombudsmans-office-celebrates-first-ever-ombuds-day/
I see all your emails and have been mired in other stories (I'll send you my latest!)

Where are you in chatting with the OIG and others? Are you getting satisfying comments back from them that they are conducting an investigation? It's very difficult to know.
Just letting you know as well that I will be out of the office for a few days, I'm moving, but you can always text or call my cell.
best, Kate
We thought someone would help. Maybe Warren will help.

Jackie
Oct 12, 2018, 9:43 AM
to Kate, me
Kate !
This is fantastic news !!! I have been swamping her office will all emails and phone calls so glad they are finally moving on this . As far as progress , Sonja has been a big help trying to get funds back for victims and also track down fraudsters in Florida . It seems that they have had several cases regarding fraud in Florida Paul spoke to Sonya and told him my story as well I believe there was other cases to and when I spoke to Sonya they apparently were questioning somebody in Florida haven't heard back yet on status.
Michael Jackman from Congressman Keating's office has now forwarded all of the emails and Victim's information to Congress is financial bureau they are looking it over and requested more info from Mr. Jackman which is a good sign.
Mr. Delmar has had numerous phone calls with victims and clearly realizes there is a huge problem even admitting it to one of the victims.
Sarah from the Social Security office still drags her feet and setting up an investigation so hopefully once on your contacts her it'll make her move her feet even faster
JB and I will continue to fight , although very tiring at times we push forward .
Please keep us posted with any new developments , thank you so much Kate
 Good luck with the move
Jackie

Tuesday, October 16, 2018

Jackie did her job. She got the attention of Senator Elizabeth Warren who was deliberating running (again) as a candidate for the presidential nomination from the Democrat Party. I sent a number of documents and a synopsis to issues to be addressed.

Senator Warren sent letters to VA, SSA, and Comerica Bank. She requested answers to questions regarding fraud victims. The deadline for response was October 31, 2018.

Subject: Request for official OIG investigation of CFPB, and inquiry from Brian E.J. Martin, CFPB
From: jbsimms
Date: Tue, Oct 16, 2018 11:37 am
To: Mark.Bialek@frb.gov, Peter.j.sheridan@frb.gov
Cc: "Cody Goebel" <GoebelC@gao.gov>, "Jackie", "Kate Berry (American Banker) (American Banker)", ClackleyA@gao.gov, Sonja Scott (OIG Treasury), michael.jackman@mail.house.gov
Dear Mr. Bialek and Mr. Sheridan,
I received an email from Mr. Goebel which included your email addresses. The email from Mr. Goebel was sent to me as a response to an email I sent to Ms. Clackley on October 3, 2018.
The OIG of both US Treasury and the Social Security Administration are in direct contact with me concerning the matter of Comerica Bank/Direct Express. I have been attempting to see a bit of accountability from the CFPB after my complaint was sent to that agency (171229-2740881 and 180127-2811418, same complaint was duplicated by CFPB).
Jackie (copied above) has enlisted the assistance of Senator Elizabeth Warren and Rep. Bill Keating (staff member copied above) to validate ours and expose the more than 400 complaints filed with the CFPB against Comerica Bank/Direct Express.
I received a telephone call last week from a female who identified herself as "Tiffany J." being a worker at the FRB Hotline. While we discussed the lack of compliance of the CFPB for 30 minutes (the call was interrupted before we ended the call), Tiffany attempted to defend the work of the CFPB by noting an investigation of another matter which had taken place. When pressed for a "threshold" of complaints necessary for the victims, SSA recipients and Veterans, to have their collective complaints investigated, Tiffany could not answer the question.

This email is, as were communications to OIG of Treasury and OIG of SSA, a formal request for an OIG audit and investigation of the CFPB with regard to Comerica Bank/Direct Express, and the lack of adherence to the mandate of this agency which has enabled and encouraged Comerica Bank/Direct Express to violate tenants of Regulation E and subject citizens, including Veterans and disabled Veterans, to emotional, psychological, and financial horrors.

Today I noticed that an enforcement attorney of the CFPB, namely Brian E.J. Martin, viewed my LinkedIn page. If any of you have contact information for Mr. Martin, please invite him to email me with a direct telephone number so we might talk.

Sincerely,

J.B. Simms

The Federal Reserve was ignoring us. Months later Comerica Bank became a member of the Federal Reserve, and Bialek and Sheridan must have known of their application. If they would claim they did not know, you would think the information of violation of Regulation E would have gotten their attention, but they did not care.

The daughter of Victim Number 9 (McPhail) called me. She said her dad received a letter stating the $30,000 loss was in a "Fair Hearing Status." The Fair Hearing Status was a bogus label for stopping all investigations and refusing to give a copy of any investigation to the McPhail family. The following email was sent to Customer Advocacy of Conduent for clarification.

I sent hundreds or close to a thousand or more emails on behalf of victims. The fraud Mr. McPhail experienced was not investigated by Green Dot, Mastercard, nor Conduent.

From: jbsimms

Date: Wed, Oct 17, 2018 9:23 am

To: advocacy@usdirectexpress.com

Cc: "Marteshia McPhail" , "Jackie" , Sarah Lizama (SSA OIG), "Sonja Scott"

Dear Advocacy Office:

My name is J.B. Simms. My Direct Express account was hacked twice; January 2017 and December 2107. I am very familiar with your Customer Advocacy office, and the fact persons use pseudonyms as names so as not to be accountable to customers or the authorities. I have been asked to make an inquiry concerning a number of victims of Direct Express, and one is Harold McPhail.

Harold McPhail was a victim of theft from his Direct Express account in the amount of $30,000.00. His daughter, Marteshia McPhail, has been in touch with your office, with a lady named Caitlyn. The telephone number for Ms. McPhail is (843) 260-5604. Your office has been aware of this matter for weeks and Mr. McPhail has not received his money. This request specifically is to determine the definition of a "Fair Hearing Status" and the names of the persons who are involved in this designation. I believe this designation does not exist.

If you need additional documentation on the matter involving Mr. McPhail, contact his daughter and tell her. We have all the documents which prove Direct Express fell short in their duty to protect this customer.

This matter has been brought before the OIG of Treasury and the OIG of Social Security, as you see the copied emails in the header. I will not go into the inadequacy of the Direct Express program, the skill level of the employees, or the lack of protection of cardholders. Those issues are being investigated by persons and agencies which hopefully will eliminate persons who are deemed incompetent.

Have one of your people contact me via email or call me at (803) 309-6850 and tell me what a "Fair Hearing Status" actually is. In the meantime, I will be in contact with Ms. McPhail and her father. Sincerely,

J.B. Simms

Wednesday, October 17, 2018

12:50pm

I telephoned (888) 555-5577 Conduent Fraud- an idiot answered the phone. I asked a supervisor, he hung up. I called back, and got a supervisor named Mely. who gave me fax number (210) 334-6597. Stated she was in Texas.

Neither spoke plain English.

I thought I was not supposed to have this fax number, but it became useful.

Subject: Pending investigation
From: jbsimms
Date: Wed, Oct 17, 2018 1:52 pm
To: advocacy@usdirectexpress.com
Cc: "Jackie", "Bob Czzowitz", "Teresa Hodson", "Marteshia McPhail", "felicity palma", Sonja Scott (OIG Treasury), Richard Delmar (OIG Treasury), Sarah Lizama (SSA OIG)
FYI:
I am receiving calls from people who cannot get any satisfaction from not only your Customer Advocate office but also your Fraud Unit.
Today, I sent you an email to which you have not responded. This is not unusual for Direct Express.
Within the email, I brought to your attention that your office has been delaying reimbursement for two persons, and I am adding another within this email. The other persons being copied are Chief Counsel for Treasury OIG, and the OIG office of Social Security.
Teresa Hodson, named above, was told that her monies are available to be accessed. She activated her card, and now she is getting messages that she has to validate herself in person. You people put that restriction on her account, not her. Her monies should have sent to her weeks ago, and now Direct Express persons are making up rules as they go along.
Marteshia McPhail's father, Harold McPhail, was a victim of a $30,000 fraud. Transactions were sent from within Direct Express personnel to a Green Dot debit card. Ms. McPhail told me she had been talking to a person named Caitlin, who said the matter was in Fair Hearing Status. Fair Hearing Status? What the hell is that? Direct Express was sent all necessary information, the cardholder was in the hospital, and Direct Express did not notice transfers of $7,000, $6,000 and $4,000 to a different debit card? This man, Harold McPhail, served his country in Vietnam, and continued his service until 1986. This is how you treat our Veterans?
When I called the telephone number for the Fraud Unit, (888) 545-5577, one person whose English was not understandable, hung up the telephone when I asked for a supervisor. I called back, got a person who spelled her name as "Mely' and whose English was marginal. These people have no respect for our Veterans because they are not from our country. This is how Direct Express/Comerica saves money; they get minimum wage people to handle bank fraud cases.
Another lady, Felicia Palma, had her card stolen and a withdrawal in an amount approximately $250.00 was taken. She was in the hospital, as was Mr. McPhail. Ms. Palma cannot get any satisfaction from this organization called Direct Express. Her $250.00 is just as important as anyone's money.
In December 2017, my account was hacked, I made a complaint to the BBB, was shuffled off to Susan Schmidt (who no longer answers her telephone, having designated that task to secretary) then to a person who went by the name of "James" within the Advocacy office. He knew less about banking law than my dog. I had to get my money from the merchants. My account is easy to find.
I want to talk directly to the person in charge of the Fraud Unit and the person in charge of the Advocacy office. My telephone number is (803) 309-6850. When the OIG of Treasury, Social Security, Federal Reserve, and Veteran Affairs comes to your office, they will want answers as well.
I am a retired private investigator and now an author. This is going to be a great book.
Sincerely.
J.B. Simms

Victim 11: Teresa

From: Teresa
Date: Wed, October 17, 2018, 7:11 pm
To: jbsimms
Do you have any idea what it feels like for someone to stand up for you with wanting nothing in return, giving us a voice where we are not being heard? Jim from the bottom of my heart thank you, I'll ride this with you til the end. God bless.

Thursday, October 18, 2018

Victim Number 17- Vera: New Jersey

Vera, a retired elderly lady never looked at the balance on her account until her daughter check her balance. They saw charges for Lyft trips in California from January through August. Vera's claim of fraud was denied. Vera lived in New Jersey, knew no one in California, and her card "never left my side."

I created a spread sheet. The total taken by the thief using the Lyft card from January through August was $1,156.82.

Conduent denied the fraud claim. Lyft refused to cooperate.

Friday, October 19, 2018

I emailed Calvin at Conduent Customer Advocacy for Clara Braunreiter and Felicity.
9:21am
I called (888) 545-5577 Fraud Unit- The person answering the call stated:
"…[t]his is a call center run by Conduent. No email, just fax."
This was the first admission that the people answering the phones under the name of Direct Express do not work for Direct Express: They work for Conduent.
I do not know why this was not exposed before this date. Now we had more to investigate.

Victim Number 18- Malaine -Michigan

From: *Malaine*
Date: *Fri, Oct 19, 2018, 9:24 am*
To: *jbsimms*
Hello,
I found your email address on the Direct Express Facebook page. On October 4, 2018 I found that $637.00 plus a $1.50 fee had been transferred from my Direct Express Account the previous evening. I did not authorize said transfers. I contacted Direct Express immediately and they shut my card down and supposedly sent me the paperwork to fill out. When I didn't receive the paperwork I called again and was told I could fax a statement into them. I did this on the 10th of October but they never got it. I faxed it again on the 15th and they still hadn't received it. Luckily I received the paperwork on the 15th, I filled it out and mailed it back that day. They did not receive it until the 18th. The delays conveniently put it past the 10 days required. When I finally got through to them today they said that I should receive a decision within 45 -90 days. I do not have time for this. This is my disability money and it is all I get. I have already rescheduled both my Oncologist and Pulmonologist. I just don't know what to do so any help you could give me I would greatly appreciated.
Thank You,
Malaine

Oct 19, 2018, 12:46 PM,
JBSimms wrote:
Dear All,
I called the Fraud Center for Direct Express. The telephone number called was (888) 545-5577. A person who was obviously struggling with the English language answered the call. I asked for the email address for the Fraud Unit. She stated that the Fraud Unit for Direct Express does not have an email account, and that the only way to send documents to the "Fraud Unit" was by fax.
I asked for the fax number. The lady said, in a very halting manner, "The number 1, dash, 210, dash, 334, dash, 6597." This confirmed the person who answered the call was reading from a script.
She said the fax would be received in Texas. She would not reveal her location, but said she works for a call center. I asked for the name of the call center. She put me on hold, and came back and stated, "The company name is Conduent. That is all I can tell you."
Now it is confirmed. The Customer Service and the Fraud Unit have been outsourced to persons who have no banking training. These are call center operators. Comerica Bank pays Conduent to take the calls from Customer Service and Fraud, exposing personal data to all call center personnel, and none of the persons at the call center have the knowledge or expertise to handle banking matters, much less abide by Regulation E.
Mr. Bialek and Mr. Sheridan, I have requested the OIG from your office to investigate why the CFPB has ignored all complaints lodged against Direct Express/Comerica. I repeat that request here.
The customer service and fraud units of Direct Express are shams. The advertising by Comerica touting the safety of the debit card accounts is false. The party is over.
Sincerely,
J.B. Simms

1012am I telephoned Clara Braunreiter- no answer
1043am I telephoned Direct Express customer advocacy (512) 249-3597 transferred to x2668, voicemail.
1053am I telephoned Direct Express Cust Advocacy, Calvin (512) 250-7630 left a message on voice mail.
144pm I telephoned Calvin (512) 250-7630- left a message on voice mail.
145pm I telephoned Clara Braunreiter- (928) 530-8581- she said there had been no word from Calvin. She was to call the call center.

Saturday October 20, 2018

Jackie and Paul Katynski were trying to convince Sonja that their cases were linked. The fraud upon Paul's account was probably the same person in Florida who took the money from the account of Jackie's brother-in-law.

Jackie
11:47 AM
to Sonja Scott, me, Paul
Sonja
I'm sorry to be flooding you with all this info but I do feel that Paul and my case are related, in fact, if they are we might be able to find the mole in these cases, I have circled in red important key info :
⬤First picture shows you that my hired PI had found where subject lives even pulled her deed and found that she owns the condo
⬤Second picture shows that Paul's card was routed to this address
⬤Third picture shows the same address for UPS
When I contacted Hollywood PD
Det. Campbell told me he has far too many cases which lead to no arrests with these fraud cases , I had told him about Paul's case even gave him her name . Begged him to pull Wal-Mart tape which he did do but says the woman on the tape is not the same woman however my PI learned that her family lives across the street and may have been the ones in Walmart. I'm not sure but I think you said you were questioning someone in FL hopefully this info will help.
Jackie

Tuesday, October 23, 2018

At 943am I talked to Victim 17 Vera who lives in NJ. Vera was 61 years of age and received $1,250 per month in Social Security. Her daughter found that at least $985 was missing. She started receiving Social Security disability in August 2017. Her Direct Express card never left her side.
She called Nora Arpin; she was to get a call from Nora on Thursday, Oct 25.
 Nora Arpin never called Vera.
Vera faxed me her statements, and I created a spreadsheet. All charges were in California by a fraudster using Vera's card for Lyft travel.
Sometime later, Vera got a letter from "Direct Express"- they offered to pay only 3 months ($137) and Vera would lose 7 months of charges.

From: jbsimms
Sent: Tuesday, October 23, 2018, 11:37 AM
To: Jackie; Kate Berry (American Banker) (American Banker); Christian, Tamara A
Cc: Sonja Scott <ScottS@oig.treas.gov>; Sarah Lizama (SSA OIG)
Subject: Look who viewed my LinkedIn page
I have had two people, lawyers, from the CFPB view my profile. Here is the latest.
The first one was Brian E.J. Martin, Enforcement Atty of OIG Fed Reserve
Heather Brown is in the Financial Education and Impact section. I think the word impact will be appropriate when we are done.
There is a Consumer Advisory Board at the CFPB. What a waste of time these people are. We will identify and contact them to listen to their denials.
Hats off to Ms. Lizama and Ms. Scott. I see your involvement.
Jim Simms

Federal employees were checking out my internet presence.

From: "Christian, Tamara A"
Date: Tue, Oct 23, 2018, 11:38 am
To: jbsimms
As long as they don't put a price on your head

Subject: Direct Express Dispute: Malaine
From: Malaine
Date: Tue, Oct 23, 2018, 2:50 pm
To:
Hi,
I don't know how to thank you. The money was put back into my account and I have opened a checking account at my local credit union. Unfortunately, I have to wait until December for the Social Security to transfer it over but at least I will be free of Direct Express. It was so nice to set up om Doctors appointments and buy groceries. Again Thank You very much.
Malaine
There is the evidence the Conduent Fraud unit is inept.

Wednesday October 24, 2018

Comerica was Treating Direct Express cardholders as second-class citizens

I found the Comerica Bank website and found the security measures offered to Comerica Customers and compare credit/debit card safety features:

ID Monitor: Equifax programs
Standard Monthly Security fee: $9.99
Better: $12.99
Best: $16.99
Offered to Comerica Bank customers, not Direct Express cardholders.

Thursday, October 25, 2018

Conduent Fraud Division admits no knowledge of Regulation E

909am
Jackie called me.
She called the Conduent fraud unit managing the Direct Express debit cards. A person named Lillie talked to Jackie and said she "works for Conduent." Electronic fraud was sent to the Dispute Team. It usually took cardholders 45-90 days to get their money returned. DE card is not a bank card; Regulation E does not apply. She sees a lot of fraud, mostly electronic fraud. DE accepts child support and alimony.
Jackie told me to call and get info from Conduent. She gave me the phone number and it was my turn. Below are my notes of the call. Some of this was exciting and some was disturbing.
The following are notes from the conversation I had with two persons after I called the Fraud Unit of Conduent who were supposed to be investigating fraud report submitted by Direct Express cardholder.

11:04am PST T (888) 545-5577 DE Fraud (Conduent)
Talked to Emanuel. I had to give all my identifying info before he would talk to me.
He was not familiar with Regulation E.
He is employed by Conduent. After some persuasion, learned his company ID # 8382002
"This is a call center. My number was on his screen."
My account was referred to Soc Sec for "Consent Based Process" which he could not explain.
(my Soc Sec ID was hacked in June, 2018, which is prob what he is seeing on screen)
He cannot fax or email me any information.
"This is a legitimate department of Direct Express. We handle banking disputes."
(Remember, this is a call center employee, not a banking specialist)
I asked him "Does my debit card fall under Regulation E with regard to electronic disputes?"

His answer was:
"I cannot disclose that."
Do you send all disputes to the Dispute Department?
"We do disputes here in this office."
When asked who pays his wages, he stated, "I cannot give you my personal information; that would be absurd."
It was then that he revealed his identification number.

I was then transferred to a "supervisor." I was sent to Gustov. I gave my information. Gustov asked if I was a private investigator. Evidently my account had been flagged.

There was an alert on my account. Gustov kept trying to move the conversation back to my account, stating that my dispute of December 2017 was closed.

He stated I needed to go to the Social Security office. I told him I am not making any changes, and this conversation is not about my personal account.

When asked if my fraud against my debit card was covered under Regulation E, Gustov stated:

"I suppose (the Direct Express was protected by Regulation E); I cannot discuss policy with you. You must check the Direct Express website for more information."

After many requests, Gustov gave his employee ID # 8382057.

Oddly, the employee number for Gustov is higher than Emanuel. What makes Gustov a supervisor?

Regarding Regulation E, I got two answers:

Emanuel- "I cannot disclose that."

Gustov- "I suppose so."

The conclusion drawn from this phone call was the following:

Conduent employees handle banking disputes.

Neither attendant was familiar with Regulation E.

The fraud unit (Conduent) cannot/will not fax or email Direct Express cardholders.

This just hit me: In December 2017 (prob the 13th) when I faxed info to the Fraud Unit, I called the Customer Advocate within a few minutes. The Customer Advocate (James) stated he had the fax "in my hands."

The Fraud Unit call center must be next to the Customer Advocate area, or operators co-mingle their job descriptions based upon the number being called. A person can be an Advocate on one call and a Fraud Unit person on the next call.

We still did not know where the disputes go for this 60–90-day deliberation.

More evidence of malfeasance: The hidden General Accounting Office report

I found GAO Report 17-176 that would further expose OIG Treasury and BFS.

First-page synopsis was killer; the lack of transparency at the Bureau of Fiscal Service was rampant. The following pages cited problems at BFS:

P 24 Compensation, P 25 Conflict of Interest, P 27 Records not complete, P 31 Req for Exec Action

Subject: General Accounting Office audit requests Fiscal Service Transparency
From: Jackie
Date: Sat, Oct 27, 2018, 3:51 pm
To: jbsimms@erikpublishing.com
Wow how did you find this?!?!
On Oct 27, 2018, at 6:44 PM, jbsimms wrote:
https://www.gao.gov/assets/690/682274.pdf
Above I have sent you the link to the entire report from which the two attachments were taken. The attachments are the first and second pages of the GAO report of Fiscal Services, and the need for individual fiscal agent payments to be available to the public, the citizens. If Fiscal Services only gives a yearly total of payments to companies having a Fiscal Agent Agreement with Fiscal Services, the public and Congress has no way of monitoring the operation of individual agreements.
This lack of transparency on the part of Fiscal Services emboldens, encourages, and enables FAA recipients (Comerica Bank in particular) to use "creative bookkeeping" and allows Fiscal Services employees to fail to make FAA recipients accountable.
This also encourages gratuities to be paid to Fiscal Services employees who administer the agreements.
I present to the office of Senator Warren, Ranking Members of the Armed Services Committee and Banking Committee, as well as Treasury OIG, this document to prove that this matter which began with my telephone

call to a Treasury OIG auditor in February 2018, was addressed in published form by the GAO in January 2017, and ignored.

Maybe if someone had read this report, even the two attached pages, Comerica Bank would not be terrorizing and victimizing veterans and other recipients from Social Security and Veteran Affairs.

Sincerely,

J.B. Simms

The above email was sent to all known persons at Treasury and copied to Jackie.

Tuesday, October 30, 2018

Santaniello plays the cover up game with a TV reporter

From: "Christian, Tamara A"

Date: Tue, Oct 30, 2018, 10:01 am

To: jbsimms

Hi Jim,

For the last week, I've been emailing and calling Tom Santaniello at Fiscal Service to get the number of Direct Express Cardholders for the state of California.

In the past he provided us with the national numbers and Sacramento numbers, however, it has come to the point where I feel that he is blowing me off intentionally.

He's not returned a single phone call or email. I was hoping you can give me some insight as to why this might be. I know Fiscal Service is feeling the heat but these are just numbers of cardholders, what is your take?

Sincerely,

Tamara

No one wanted to talk to Tamara.

From: CFPB Ombudsman <CFPB_Ombudsman@cfpb.gov>

Date: Tue, Oct 30, 2018, 10:46 am

To: jbsimms

Mr. Simms – Thank you for your email. As you may know, the CFPB's consumer complaint process is designed to obtain a response from the company. More information about the Bureau's process can be found on the agency's website at this link.. We understand that the CFPB does not investigate individual complaints or serve as an individual's advocate. At the same time, the consumer complaints do inform the Bureau's examination of the companies and enforcement of the consumer financial protection laws as further described on www.consumerfinance.gov.

 If you would like to provide further feedback for the CFPB's consideration, you may do so at the agency's Tell Your Story resource at this link: https://www.consumerfinance.gov/your-story/

Thank you again,

CFPB Ombudsman's Office

Tuesday, October 30, 2018

Victim 19 Marilyn - Nevada

Las Vegas, NV Lost card. The customer service lady who took info made error in address.

It was later learned Marilyn's new card never arrived. The lost card had $260 on card. Customer service. Customer service put Nebraska vs Nevada (NE vs NV) and now Marilyn had her money and it was going into her bank account. Direct Express took out a fee of $13.50 for UPS and Marilyn just wrote it off.

This was typical of Conduent employees.

Wednesday, October 31, 2018

Jackie told me someone at Comerica Bank had talked to Sen Warren office. We were having trouble getting information from Senator Warren's office to include the responses from the letters she sent.

Chapter Five
Politics and Games

Thursday, November 1, 2018

Jackie sent me an email; Comerica sent pages of answers to Warren. Abby Webber is to look at answers. That was encouraging but Senator Warren had not shared the answers with us. That made us a bit suspicious but dealing with Senator Warren was Jackie's job.

It was a daily occurrence that I received telephone calls and emails from victims. My days began early while I was living on the West Coast. It was not unusual to be awakened at 6 am or earlier by victims.

Vera, the disabled victim from NJ, was not able to send an email to Conduent. I sent the following email to Conduent on her behalf. Conduent used the name "Advocacy, Direct Express as their way not to expose themselves. Parts of the email are edited. Subject

From: jbsimms
Date: Thu, November 01, 2018, 11:10 am
To: "Advocacy US" <advocacy@usdirectexpress.com>
I am sending this to you on behalf of the cardholder listed below:
Unknown to Ms. Best, her debit card information was being used by a fraudster, who opened a Lyft account and took dozens of rides each month, beginning in January 2018. Even if the low balance alert had been implemented by Ms. Best, this fraud would not have been detected. The fraud occurred in California.
The Lyft persons stated that the account was opened by a person using a name similar to that of Ms. Best. Ms. Best lives in NJ; the charges are in California.
I explained to Ms. Best that Direct Express "personnel" are employees of Conduent, and do not interact with merchants or law enforcement; they simply answer the telephone. Ms. Best is being copied in this correspondence. You have her telephone number on file, but I will give it to you to confirm this: Nora Arpin, of Comerica Bank, spoke with Ms. Best last week, but failed to call her on Thursday as promised. I ask that you contact her immediately to refund all Lyft charges from her account, dating back to January 2018. Attached is a copy of the first page of the January statement of Ms. Best.
Best.
Sincerely,
J.B. Simms

Saturday, November 3, 2018

Victim Number 20: Katherine- Colorado
Dispute at lodges in Big Bear, Big Bear Village $200, and Honey Bear Lodge $222. Got provisional credit of $354, then credit was reversed next day.
Waited 1:45 min to talk to Cust Serv- Cust serv wanted Katherine to mail a copy of her driver license and her Social Security card.

Victim Number 21: Andrea -Pennsylvania
The following was mailed to me on 11/3/2018.

Mr. Simms, Hello, my name is Andrea. I'm writing on behalf of my significant other, Jeremy, who is a disabled SSI recipient, and a Direct Express cardholder. I apologize in advance if this is longwinded.... On 10-9-18 we ran some errands. We're in a small town about an hour south of Pittsburgh - using his Direct Express card for two purchases. A local McDonalds (at 13:13), followed by a purchase at Walgreens (at 13:33).
That night, we logged on to Direct Express website to check the balance (as we typically do, just to "balance the checkbook" so to speak), and noticed the balance was incorrect. Clicked on the list of transactions and saw one at a Champs sporting goods store, in Valley Stream New York (store #14596) for $206.39, at 18:36. Quickly looked in his wallet, and there was the card. NOT lost or stolen. His card has never been lost or stolen in the past - never an issue with Direct Express until now (has been a cardholder since 2009 or 2010.) He doesn't use it often for shopping online - it had been over a month since an online transaction took place. So how did this happen? No clue. He immediately called Direct Express in a panic. The lady told him the debit to Champs

Sports was still pending, it needed to be posted before anything could be done on their end. He said "Aren't you able to put a stop on that transaction? A hold until we sort this out? Something? Because it's clearly fraudulent - I couldn't have made a purchase at Walgreens in my town at 13:33, then at Champs in Valley Stream NY by 18:36..." She said No, no. just keep an eye on your account until it's posted, then call us back. And if you do believe someone is fraudulently using your card, you should report it to your local police.

Victim Number 22: Jackie -Massachusetts
Jackie became my partner fighting Comerica Bank and Conduent in August 2018. Jackie was the administrator of VA and Social Security benefits being paid to her brother-in-law. Jackie's identity was used to fraudulently take money from a Walmart store located in Miramar, Florida.

Victim Number 23: J.B. Simms- California
I was hacked twice; January 2017 and December 2017. It was after the December hack that I began investigating and fighting on behalf of other victims.

Victim Number 24: Lisa- Tucson, Arizona
$264.78 missing Caregiver took card information after buying provisions for the victim who is disabled. Lisa got evicted. Eviction hearing Wed Nov 21.
Fraud noticed Fraud reported Requested copy of investigation November 21, 2018

Lisa was evicted from her home on November 26, 2018. No provisional credit was given, and no investigation was conducted.
I sent an email to Arpin on behalf of Lisa Mena, requesting a copy of the investigation.

This case broke my heart. I received dozens of emails. I made dozens of calls to Lisa's landlord, Comerica Bank, and Conduent on behalf of Lisa. As noted, I sent an email to Nora Arpin on behalf of Lisa requesting a copy of the investigation. No one at Conduent responded.

Monday, November 5, 2018

Victim 24 Lisa sent me an email. She was on the verge of being evicted. I was helpless.
Here is what I sent to people who could have helped her.

From: jbsimms
Date: Mon, Nov 05, 2018, 1:42 pm
To: Sonja Scott (OIG Treasury) Sarah Lizama (SSA OIG), Kate Berry (American Banker)
Cc: Nora Arpin (Comerica Bank) "Advocacy US" <advocacy@usdirectexpress.com>,
mark.bialek@frb.gov, Peter.j.sheridan@frb.gov, "Lisa Mena"
Lisa,
I am copying the above persons on your email and thank you. Comerica Bank is responsible for creating a false "customer Advocacy" department staffed with Conduent call center persons. There is no fraud unit. No persons are familiar with banking laws, or have taken an AIB course (and yes, I have taken AIB courses as a banker, and made A's in all my courses). The Federal Reserve is supposed to be monitoring the CFPB, and they have been copies on this email as well.
Jackie and I will not stop until all victims are compensated, and Comerica is no longer a fiscal agent of the US Treasury. A criminal probe is being requested.
Jim

Below is an email from the daughter of Victim 9, a Vietnam War veteran. Her father would eventually be included as a plaintiff in the federal lawsuit with 8 fellow plaintiffs suing Comerica Bank and Conduent.

From: Marteshia
Date: November 5, 2018, at 12:00:32 PM EST
To: Kate Berry
Cc: Jackie
Subject: Direct Express Assisted needed
Hi Kate,
My name is Marteshia McPhail, daughter of Harold McPhail Sr., a retired disabled veteran of the United States. My father has a Direct Express account, and that large sum of money was transferred from his account onto a Green Dot card. Each of the transactions was done using a computer, but each time the associate at Direct Express, said someone would change his account information then, performed the fraudulent transactions. My father does not have a computer, internet services or a green dot card. This happen between the periods of Feb 2018 until, April 2018. My father contacted them to file a fraud investigation and has yet to receive any of his money back.
He was advised to do a police report, if he would like to pursue his case. He completed a police report, responded to their request/questionnaire, called several times, but yet to get any of his money. The last we hear after speaking to Caitlin on 12Oct2018, that his claim was in a fair hearing status. When trying to reach that department or get answer or resolution, we are constantly routed from one associate to the next, before being hung-up on.
I was looking for Direct Express physical address on 23Sep2018 and found Jackie contact information, then contacted her. She said you was able to resolve her case and I am hoping you can do the same for my father. Please contact me to discuss this matter further or provide options or suggestions on what I can do next. My contact information is below. Thanks for your time.
Kind Regards,
Marteshia

Clara, Victim Number 16, began calling more often because Conduent was ignoring her.

At 9:05 am Clara, Victim Number 16, called me. Conduent had not replaced her money. She first called me on October 18, 2018. Clara received a call from Conduent that advised her that her complaint file was closed. I told Clara we were not done with Conduent and Comerica Bank. I would fight further for her. She had lost well over $997.00 and could not get Conduent to investigate her fraud claim; they simply denied the claim.

Clara needed her money. Calvin was doing what Conduent and Comerica usually did; postpone and hope the victim cardholder became weary and stopped challenging the dismissal of fraud claims. I advised Clara to call Nora Arpin of Comerica and Sonja Scott (Treasury OIG).

After talking to Clara, I called Calvin (512) 250-7630. Calvin was familiar with my telephone number and never answered my calls, so I left a message on his voicemail. I advised Calvin to "give Clara her provisional credit and investigate what you want because there is no one at Conduent qualified to investigate anything."

At 11:13 am I again called Clara. Clara told me she would send me her statements. I advised her to fax the packet to Calvin at (877) 507-0012. The time I took with Clara was not out of the ordinary. I was working all day fielding calls and emails. These victims had no one to help them.

Along with sending victim information, we began sending documents to people at OIG Treasury. On this date, I sent a copy of the General Accounting Office (GAO) 17-176 report which exposed the Bureau of Fiscal Service's lack of transparency regarding dispensing funds.

This battle against Comerica Bank and Conduent became a battle with the Department of Treasury, including the Bureau of Fiscal Service and OIG Treasury. There were times I thought Sonja Scott cared that citizens were being victimized by a failed program created by the Bureau of Fiscal Service, a division of Treasury. I emailed Sonja Scott a copy of the GAO Report 17-176. Sonja Scott was all we had, so we continued to send victim information to Scott.

From: jbsimms
Date: Mon, Nov 05, 2018, 11:54 pm
To: Sonja Scott (OIG Treasury)
Cc: "Jackie"
Dear Ms. Scott,

Forgive me for shoveling documents to you of which you might be aware, but the revelations I found in this document proved a couple of things: Fiscal Services lacks transparency, it has not been corrected, and the Chief Counsel of Treasury was deeply involved in the approval of all Fiscal Agency Agreements.

These are issues that I would like to discuss with you before others opine in the media. Of course, Ms. Densmore is copied and consulted in all my correspondence.

This GAO report seems to be a thinly veiled slight in the direction of the OIG of Treasury, which is consistent with my motive for contacting Ms. Battle in February, pointing out the deficiencies in the report, and requesting an investigation into a specific area that was ignored.

Your receptiveness to victims (Best, Braunreiter, McPhail presently) is refreshing and hopefully, this will continue. Comerica has lost its vigor in the past month to solve problems.

I am asking for transparency within the Treasury OIG report even before it is published. I have no problem talking with specific persons assigned to investigate this matter. You know I am familiar with the workings of an investigation of this type, and banking operations and regulations are not foreign to me. My sources within the industry are valuable assets to me to enlighten me with respect to how things "should be." One of the persons who were under my charge while working at a bank before I became a PI was the son of a man who owned a bank and was consolidated with a larger bank, of which I worked.
Jim

Tuesday, November 6, 2018

After reading GAO Report 17-176 it became clear that I needed to contact Michael Clements who was the gentleman whose name and contact information was printed at the end of the report, (202) 512-8676, Michael Clements (Gen Acct Office)

From: jbsimms
Date: Tue, Nov 06, 2018, 9:19 am
To: Michael Clements (Gen Acct Office)
Cc: "Jackie "
Dear Mr. Clements,

I am involved in a major investigation of the Direct Express program which is being administered by Comerica Bank. Comerica Bank, as the above referenced report reveals, is one of the eight (8) entities which are fiscal agents of the US Treasury that receive funds to disburse.

The GAO report 17-176 was very enlightening. I would like to discuss the interest the GAO might have with respect to the investigation being conducted by Treasury OIG and supposedly Social Security OIG into the matter of mismanagement of the Direct Express program by Comerica Bank.

This matter has gained the attention of Senator Elizabeth Warren, and she sent a letter to the CEO of Comerica Bank and the acting commissioner of Social Security to get answers. These answers were received last week, and we have been unable to review them due to political activity.

You may reach me at (803) 309-6850 and the above email address. Ms. Densmore is being copied on this correspondence, having had her identity stolen which compromised benefits for her brother-in-law, Derek Densmore, a disabled US Marine.
I look forward to communicating with you.
Sincerely,
J.B. Simms

Now it was time to send an email to Ms. Lizama at Social Security.

From: jbsimms
Date: Tue, Nov 06, 2018, 9:38 am
To: Sarah Lizama (SSA OIG) Cc: Jackie
Dear Ms. Lizama,
After speaking with Ms. Densmore this morning, I related that I have not heard from victims Harold McPhail, Clara Braunreiter, or Veralyn Best that they had reached you. It is heartbreaking for them to call and continue to tell me they left messages and no one is doing anything.
I have not had any answer to a simple question about my identity having been stolen.
Jackie and I discussed that the OIG of Social Security has not announced a formal investigation into the matter of identities of Direct Express recipients being stolen by fraudsters. We believe your office will find that Social Security recipient complaints to Direct Express are not being handled by banking professionals, but by call center workers.
Simply put: Is the OIG of Social Security (or has OIG of Social Security) committed to formally investigate this matter of Direct Express and Comerica Bank on behalf of recipients of benefits from your agency? Based upon information supplied to you, and the discussions you have had with victims, I would assume your office would commit to putting out the big fire rather than dousing small fires when they pop up.
J.B. Simms

I was constantly sending emails to Kate Berry. Kate believed us. Kate had more to do than listen to Jackie I and me every day, but sometimes Kate pushed for answers. We were grateful for her help. Now Kate was going after the main player of Comerica Bank, Nora Arpin.

Subject: American Banker......FW: Direct Express Assisted needed
From: "Berry, Kate"
Date: Tue, November 06, 2018, 10:17 am
To: Nora Arpin (Comerica Bank) Cc: Sonja Scott (OIG Treasury)
Hi Nora -
I just got off the phone with the daughter of Harold McPhail Sr., a retired disabled veteran whose Direct Express account was targeted by fraud to the tune of $30,000! I repeat -- $30,000!
When we spoke for the story I wrote in August, you said that Comerica had discontinued the Cardless Benefit Service that was responsible for fraudsters draining the accounts of federal beneficiaries.
Fraud at Direct Express is rampant, and out of control, and Comerica is failing beneficiaries.
I am writing again about this specific fraud because of the vast sums involved, and the fact that Direct Express has failed to launch a real investigation follow-up directly with Mr. McPhail or his daughter Marteshia, who is trying to get her father's money back. According to Marteshia, Direct Express sent them two of the same form letters, asked to file a police report and has done nothing since.
Frankly, I have to ask: What is going on with this very broken system Comerica has set up? Who is looking into this widespread fraud?
I need a response by my deadline, which is Thursday.
best, kate

From: jbsimms
Date: Tue, November 06, 2018, 10:30 am
To: "Berry, Kate", "Nora Arpin (Comerica Bank)"
<Nora Arpin (Comerica Bank)>
Cc: "ScottS@oig.treas.gov" Sonja Scott (OIG Treasury), "Marteshia McPhail"
Sarah Lizama (SSA OIG), Richard Delmar (OIG Treasury),
Michael Clements (Gen Acct Office), "Advocacy US" <advocacy@usdirectexpress.com>, Jackie
Thank you, Kate, for addressing this issue. I have the bank statements showing the monies taken from Mr. McPhail's account. I also spoke directly with Mr. Date of Green Dot debit cards. This was done in September. All the agencies, Comerica (Arpin) Direct Express Advocacy (Conduent call center employees), Social Security (Lizama), and Treasury (Scott and Delmar) had been contacted. The Direct Express people (call center persons, not banking personnel) had no clue why they were not repaying this money. If Comerica has the same safety features for Direct Express as they offer their customers, this would never have happened.
I applaud you, Ms. Berry. You will make a difference when others of us are ignored.

It was time to confront Green Dot and the fraud experienced by veteran Mr. McPhail.

From: jbsimms
Date: Tue, Nov 06, 2018, 12:22 pm
To: pr@greendot.com
Cc: raj.date@fenwaysummer.com
I am assisting a person whose bank account was defrauded of $30,000.In late September, I tt Raj Date, one of your board members about this. Mr. Date has not contacted anyone in your company to report this crime. We have all the relevant numbers to identify the criminal. Mr. Date was given the identifying information.A writer from American Banker is going public with the story. She called me this morning.
Sincerely,
J.B. Simms

Thursday, November 8, 2018

The number of victims who had contacted me was growing. I sent the current list of 24 victims to Jackie.

From: Jackie
Thu, Nov 8, 2018, 5:03 AM
to ScottS, me, kate berry
Ms. Scott
I would like answers to what's going on in Florida. You are the Senator and have you contacted their office? I also want to know about my case and if anyone has yet to contact the Hollywood police dept Det Campbell considering the woman is on tape that stole Derek's money. I am growing very impatient with my questions not being answered.
Thank you.
Jackie

Jackie sent another email moments later.

Words cannot describe the anger I have seen all these complaints listed in here from California no wonder Ms. Christian was all over this reporting I would like to know who the senator for California and how to contact them.. Rich Delmar did you ever get Ms. Christian the number of cardholders in CA?!?
Also I would like to know the number for Massachusetts as well.
Sonja have you looked into CA as well?

Sonja Scott replied:
Scott, Sonja L. Sonja Scott (OIG Treasury)
Thu, Nov 8, 2018, 11:22 AM
to Jackie, lisamena73@yahoo.com, me
We have spoken and she sent me information that I have forwarded to our Bureau of Fiscal Service rep. Sonja

I had enough of Conduent employees ignoring fraud victims. I had to send an email to Calvin at Conduent (Customer Advocacy) on behalf of Clara.

It was interesting that Conduent had a division referred to as "Customer Advocacy." These people advocated for no one.

From: jbsimms
Date: Thu, Nov 08, 2018, 5:12 pm
To: "Advocacy US" <advocacy@usdirectexpress.com>
Dear Calvin,
Here is how this is going to work.
Clara Braunreiter is faxing me a copy of her bank statements, which show the fraud. I will be faxing this information to you because it is not fair for Ms. Braunreiter to have to spend an additional one dollar per page to fax you and me. I have an investigative background and banking knowledge which will allow me to examine

the transactions. I, along with others, am monitoring the activity of the "Customer Advocacy" office and have assisted approximately 25 persons to date.

After the fax is sent to (877) 507-0012, I will be scanning the documents and sending you the documents in an attachment. It might be appropriate for you to contact Ms. Braunreiter to confirm receipt of the fax and/or the email which I will be sending you.

These transmissions, fax and email, will satisfy the arbitrary parameters you placed upon Ms. Braunreiter by telling her that if you did not receive the information concerning the fraud within 10 days, you were going to close the case. You will be receiving copies of the same information which you readily have available to you on your computer. Making Ms. Braunreiter send documents to you, with her not owning a computer or being tech savvy, was an undue burden that she did not deserve from you or your Conduent colleagues.

You will have this information in front of you tomorrow. I will make sure you have the information.
Sincerely,
J.B. Simms

I was able to reach Mr. Clements at the General Accounting office by telephone at 1:30 pm. He was receptive as I described how victims of the Direct Express and the lack of transparency as cited in GAO 17-176 needed to be given attention. He was great. I was excited that he validated my position.

I asked that he commission a new investigation subsequent to GAO 17-176. He agreed to do so but he needed Senator Warren or another person from Congress needed to send a written request for him to commission a new investigation or audit.

Jackie called me and she told me she tt Kate. Kate told Jackie that she received an email from Wendy Bridges, who was at SVP Comerica Bank. Bridges were directed by Nora Arpin to begin responding to email inquiries. Wendy Bridges stated the $30,000.00 reported as fraud by Mr. McPhail was being called theft, not fraud. SVP Wendy Bridges also stated to Kate Berry that she" [w]as getting inaccurate information from J.B. Simms." Bridges were getting her marching orders and her narrative from Nora Arpin.

From: jbsimms
Date: November 8, 2018, at 5:50:00 PM EST
To: "Ashley Woolheater" <Ashley_Woolheater@warren.senate.gov>, Abby_Webber@warren.senate.gov
Cc: "Jackie ", Kate Berry (American Banker), "Michael Clements" <Michael Clements (Gen Acct Office)>, "Tamara Christian" <tchristian@kovr.com>
Subject: Request for GAO investigation of Fiscal Services FAA with Comerica Bank
Dear Ms. Woolheater and Ms. Webber,
Pursuant to a telephone conversation I had with Michael Clements (email address above, telephone (202) 512-7763), I am contacting you and your constituent, Jackie to request that you contact Mr. Clements of the General Accounting Office on behalf of Senator Warren and request a formal investigation of the Department of Treasury. Bureau of Fiscal Services, with regard to the Fiscal Agency Agreement between Fiscal Services and Comerica Bank. If this request needs to come directly from your constituent, Ms. Densmore will forward this email, or an edited version, to your office to comply with your protocol.

You are aware of the victims in this matter, the questionable procedures which Comerica Bank created and allowed with regard to the administration of Direct Express, and that the OIG of Fiscal Services is now conducting an investigation of this matter after having the facts brought to their attention. OIG of Social Security has been active to an extent in this matter, and the OIG of the Federal Reserve (which oversees the Consumer Financial Protection Bureau) is aware of the investigations but has not responded as of this date.

I thank you for your proactive approach in this attempt at accountability for our veterans and others who have been subjected to the rogue and selfish actions of Comerica Bank.
If there are any questions, please do not hesitate to contact your constituent, Ms. Densmore.
For your approval, I will attach the GAO report 17-176 which was signed off by Mr. Clement. I ask that you read the synopsis on Page 2 for an overview of the report.
Sincerely,
J.B. Simms

Jackie was being ignored. She was getting the list of victims I was sending. We both were frustrated. We were the only people listening to the victims. The stories were heartbreaking.

Jackie Densmore
Thu, Nov 8, 2018, 5:08 AM
to ScottS, Sarah Lizama (OIG Social Security), me, Kate Berry (American Banker), tchristian, michael.jackman, Richard Delmar (OIG Treasury), Abby
Words cannot describe the anger I have seen all these complaints listed in here from California no wonder Ms. Christian was all over this reporting I would like to know who the senator for California and how to contact them.
Rich Delmar did you ever get Ms. Christian the number of cardholders in CA?!?
Also, I would like to know the number for Massachusetts as well.
Sonja, have you looked into CA as well?

Friday, November 9, 2019

Conduent sent a multi-page questionnaire and investigated the cardholder and not the criminal. The questionnaire asked intrusive questions and when the victim had filled out the form, some were made to feel that they caused the fraud, as if they were a lady "asking for it" being perceived as being dressed provocatively.

Regulation E did not forbid a cardholder from allowing a trusted person (caregiver, relative) to use the card, with permission, to buy provisions for a disabled cardholder. Unauthorized transactions could always be contested.

I emailed many people at Comerica Bank, Conduent, and federal employees copies of Regulation E and the regulations created from the law by the FDIC and Federal Reserve.

On this day I took my laptop computer to a local eatery to work on victim cases. The eatery closed at 9:00 pm. I went there many times for a change of environment to think about and coordinate this venture.

As I was walking home, my telephone rang at 912pm. It was Clara. She got her money back $1843.00. We were both laughing with joy. She stated she would have to try to get the money from an ATM, but she had never used an ATM. I gave her a bit of instruction.

Remember that Calvin said would take 3 months for Clara to get her money if they decided to do so. The pressure and exposure worked. I was overjoyed.

Saturday, November 10, 2018

Victim Number 25: Cherylene – Riverside, California
I am hearing impaired.
May 6, 2018 Called Direct Express after finding fraud, $947.98.
Credit reporting agencies
May 8, 2018 Mailed fraud packet
June 22, 2018 Called DE Customer Service- advised did not receive fraud packet. Case closed. June 23, 2018 Faxed documents- Case opened
June 30, 2018 Called DE Cust svc. Found dispute, not started working on case August 2018 Called many times. Received diff info each call
October 20, 2018 Customer Service adv fraud case pending
October 22, 2018 Demanded to talk to supervisor, Heather, said to stop harassing
November 9, 2018 Talked to friendly supervisor, no record of dispute.
Nov 10- contacted Simms
Nov 15- $900 was put on account. they wouldn't give me a direct answer to my question on why the first representative I spoke with said all accounts are not active then spoke with supervisor who offered to close the account and I mentioned I thought it was closed but its been active so then there are actual ones. Charges that are theirs they keep being off point and said they closed my account and hung up on me

Called again: and did a three-way call with them. And direct express discussed who was responsible to pay me back my refund as soon as direct express customer service answered the credit supervisor hung up on me. Just thought you should know thank you.

No monies were put back in the account until after she talked to me. I directed Cherylene who to contact and what to say. It worked.

Conduent screwed with this account for 6 months. I got her money returned in 5 days. See the email I sent to Wendy Bridges on November 12.

Monday, November 12, 2018

After having been contacted by Victim Number 25 (Cherylene) on November 10, and knowing she would not be able to make her point to Comerica or Conduent, I sent the following email to Wendy Bridges, who Nora Arpin designated to begin receiving emails. Nora Arpin did this because victims were contacting Nora and she did not want to deal with the victims.

Subject: Fraudulent charges on the account of Cherylene Bruins
From: jbsimms
Date: Mon, Nov 12, 2018, 9:47 am
To: wwbridges@comerica.com
Cc: Kate Berry (American Banker), Jackie "Cherrylene Bruins" <cherrylene.bruins@gmail.com>, Sonja Scott (OIG Treasury) Sarah Lizama (SSA OIG), Nora Arpin (Comerica Bank)
Dear Ms. Bridges,
With today being the observance of Veterans Day, you will be off today, and I will not be expecting a reply until tomorrow. It appears Ms. Arpin has "handed the baton" to you, so I assume you are the "point-person" for questionable happenings affecting cardholders of Direct Express.
The emails I have received from Ms. Bruins are distressing but not unusual, as I have read and heard countless stories of dismissive and harmful interaction received by cardholders from the Conduent outsourced call center personnel hired and contracted by Comerica. Ms. Bruins is hearing impaired and has experienced inhumane service from Conduent persons posing as Direct Express representatives.
The persons posing as fraud unit and customer advocacy personnel read from a script and are not helpful to Ms. Bruins, which is why I am reaching out to you on her behalf.
Attached you will find a record of the transactions which Ms. Bruins claims are fraudulent. I bring your attention to transactions dated December 1, 2017, and April 3, 2018. Both transactions reflect a $303.00 ATM withdrawal, having the notation "FRBKSDI   IN, HOUSTON" which is a code for the transaction which has not been deciphered. If Ms. Bruins claims she was not in Houston on that date, three things need to be revealed: (1) the location of the ATM (2) the time of the transaction (3) the video of the transaction.
If you have a source within the Fraud Department of Comerica Bank that can identify the code written on that transaction, that would be helpful. Since the "fraud unit" of Direct Express consists of Conduent call center workers, there is no expectation that anyone identifying themselves as Direct Express employees will, or have ever, interacted with merchants, other banks, or law enforcement. I have no problem directing Ms. Bruins to the Houston Police Department (if Houston was the location of the transaction) and helping her. This was the job of a person designated as a Fraud Unit of Direct Express employee.
These Direct Express cardholders have suffered enough. If you would like to read the email account sent to me by Ms. Bruins, I will be glad to do so.
Ms. Bruins is copied on this email. If you would like to communicate directly with her, any attention to this matter from anyone at Comerica Bank would be welcomed.
The attachment and the notes are from Ms. Bruins. There are no subjective comments from me or others on the attachment.
Your assistance in this matter will be a welcomed step toward the appearance of goodwill on the part of Comerica Bank.
Sincerely,
J.B. Simms

Research was conducted regarding Conduent's refusal to credit Mr. McPhail the $30,000 of which he was defrauded. Mr. McPhail was in the hospital when some of his money was stolen.
I found a reference to Staff Opinions in FDIC Regulation 6500[37] which addressed delays in reporting fraud.

Subject: found the cite about hospitalization
From: jbsimms
Date: Mon, Nov 12, 2018, 10:19 pm
To: "Marteshia McPhail"
Cc: "Jackie ", Kate Berry (American Banker)
I found it.
This came from the Supplement, which is Staff opinions, at the FDIC regulations.
Remember, the FDIC regs were taken from the CFR (Code of Federal Regulations) and changed around a bit in the language.
The Federal Reserve version, listed as FDIC 6500 Regulation E Supplement (as in 12 CFR 205) stated:
Extension of time limits
Supplement
FDIC Reg 6500-1005
6(b)(4) Extension of Time Limits
1. Extenuating circumstances. Examples of circumstances that require extension of the notification periods under this section include the consumer's extended travel or hospitalization.

HOSPITALIZATION! Conduent did not know the law, and neither did Comerica.

There it is.
Also, just because the bank sent statements (or post them on his account) there is no conclusive evidence he saw them.

Tuesday, November 13, 2018

I emailed Wendy Bridges and Abby Webber (Senator Warren's office). Abby wanted to know who had not been paid, and Wendy Bridges needed to know she was not going to be able to ignore us.

Subject: Cooperation in assisting victimized Direct Express customers
From: jbsimms
Date: Tue, Nov 13, 2018, 10:46 am
To: wwbridges@comerica.com
Cc: "Jackie ", Kate Berry (American Banker)
Dear Ms. Bridges,
Since Ms. Arpin has designated you as the new "go-to" person with respect to inquiries and legal issues presented by recipients of government funds dispensed by Direct Express, you will now be made aware of the heart-wrenching stories of persons having lost money due to fraud, and the fact that all Direct Express employees (Conduent call center employees, in reality) are impotent when it comes to solving the problems. While a number of federal agencies are investigating the role Comerica Bank has played while administering the Direct Express program, and the adherence to the Fiscal Agency Agreement (which is not part of your role as designee by Nora Arpin), I will be forwarding issues and emails to you for your inspection and personal experience. This will be a time for "face-saving" for Comerica Bank, and we hope your cooperation will reflect a conscientious and honest mindset.
While I do not expect you to communicate directly with me (as was the decision of Nora Arpin), the email address and telephone numbers of the victims which were sent to me via email will be forwarded to you. I will be glad to communicate with any verified compliance officer of Comerica Bank or any verified person employed by Comerica Bank assigned to a fraud unit. Direct Express has no fraud unit composed of persons having a banking background, and one refused to tell me the number of AIB courses he had completed.
Some of these problems can be solved easily. Some need law enforcement involvement which was a task the Conduent employees were not capable of performing.
I have a list of 25 persons who have contacted me. Many of these people had their monies returned after contacting me and/or Ms. Densmore. These people trust us more than they do Direct Express or Comerica Bank.
I look forward to your offer of cooperation. My background and experience are easy to find.
Sincerely,
J.B. Simms

Jackie was busy working on getting Elizabeth Warren to follow up on her ultimatum to Comerica, Treasury, and Social Security to return the answers to the questions she submitted.

Jackie
Nov 13, 2018, 5:28 PM
to ScottS, me, Abby, Ashley_Woolheater, Sarah Lizama (OIG Social Security), Richard Delmar (OIG Treasury), kate. berry, michael.jackman
Ms. Scott,
I am emailing you tonight to inform you that someone tried to gain access to my chase credit card luckily this bank actually has brains and contacted me before they could charge anything. something as simple as this to protect me and my credit that Direct Express could not do, which is disgusting considering the amount of money Comerica got when they got the contract.
Funny thing is I never had anyone try to use my identity or try to gain access to my credit cards until the breach with Comerica's call centers.
Maybe this all could have been stopped if they spent the money to protect the cardholders instead, they spent the money on God knows what?!?!
If Comerica investigated my case maybe my information would not have been compromised like it is now.
I will repeat this again and maybe someone investigating this will do the job they were hired to do:
A woman in Hollywood FL went into Walmart pretending to be me and cashed in on Derek's money. This woman knew my name address, phone number and social security number. Hollywood police Dept has this woman on tape!!!!! I mean how hard is this job for investigators?!?
This woman could be behind recent attempt of chase card, considering you claim there are investigators in FL , I want to know who and a phone number in charge of my case.
Enough is Enough, if I have to hire an attorney to represent me I will at this point.
I am tired of not getting answers.
I work extremely hard to withhold my credit score and my personal information. As you may recall my money was not stolen my brother in laws was as he is a retired Marine who served our country after 9/11. I was never made whole, instead I will now need to protect my identity for the rest of my life for this.
Ms. Scott, I would like a follow-up call tomorrow with some answers.
Jackie

Victim Number 26: Ronald -California
Ronald called me. He used a card in the casino in April 2018. Somehow, he lost his card but had not used his card after leaving the casino. The next time he went to use his card was May 3. Ronald 1,500 taken. The card was also used for prison inmate calls.
Looks like the money was deposited, then drained on May 3 and 4.

Wednesday, November 14, 2018

From: Jackie
Date: November 14, 2018, at 9:20:03 AM EST
To: Wendy <wwbridges@comerica.com>
Subject: Education on the company you work for
Dear Ms. Bridges,
Allow me to introduce myself, my name is Jacqueline Densmore. You may have heard about me in reference to the American Banker report on shutting down the cardless benefit program with Direct Express / Comerica after my identity was stolen along with my Brother in laws money thru a money gram.
I first want to point out to you since you apparently are Nora Arpin's gatekeeper some important facts, below are links that people have written about the fraud and corruption as well as all the complaints cardholders have had regarding Direct Express / Comerica.
I think you should take the time and educate yourself first before saying that victims' stories are exaggerated, your lack of compassion and intelligence tells me you will not hold your position very long.
Your scare tactics with reporters will not work, I have reached out to all major media outlets, reporters, and senators as I'm sure you are aware. You see it's not just one victim it's thousands so when you say your card has a 94 percent satisfaction rating, I found that hysterical. The proof is among these links of the dissatisfied customers and the ones that are still coming forward. So, the real numbers will come out in the various audits that are now being conducted thanks to all the victims that have come forward to TELL their stories and thanks

to J.B. Simms whom I consider a huge advocate for these victims. Make certain your bank and the programs that it runs are seriously in question so I would get your facts correct before you attack reporters and victims. I will remind you again, Nora Arpin has already come forward admitting security breaches and fraud associated with the Direct Express program as well as all the links below, too many to list actually. Comerica / Direct Express damaged its reputation when it allowed unqualified employees to run their call centers to save a few bucks.
Thank you for your time.
Sincerely,
Jacqueline Densmore

Wednesday, November 14, 2018, 2:17 PM
Lizama, Sarah Office of the Inspector General <Sarah Lizama (SSA OIG)> wrote:
Hi, Jackie,
The Congressional Liaison for SSA OIG is Walter Bayer. You will have to contact your congressperson or representative's office to complete a Privacy Release form (which you should be able to do online). They then send your request to Mr. Bayer who directs it for response by the OIG. I understand from our discussion that Senator Warren's office has probably already contacted SSA's Office of Legislative and Congressional Affairs, this is just another avenue.
Sarah Lizama Office of the Inspector General, Staff Assistant 410-966-8685

J B Simms
Wed, Nov 14, 2018, 6:44 PM
to Kate, Jackie
Marteshia said in text: "Hi All, Just checking In.
I did get a call from an Inspector General who said he should be coming to town to interview my dad and investigate the case. Hopefully, this will bring a final resolution."
This will be huge news if this family gets their money back.

I telephoned Victim 24 Lisa Ann to check on her. His phone had been disconnected. I then began to review her emails. I found her address and determined the address was at Somerset Apartments and found a telephone number for the supervisor of the apartments (who was evicting Lisa Ann). I eventually tt a lady named Christine who worked for Community Bridges. The lady told me she did not know if Lisa Ann was evicted so I pleaded the case for Lisa Ann. I told her Lisa Ann's telephone was disconnected and asked that she pass along a message that I called.

Eventually, Lisa was evicted, and I was devastated.

No one at Conduent was listening and no one was investigating anything. No one at Comerica Bank was making Conduent accountable. The Bureau of Fiscal Service was no help. Sonja Scott was telling us her hands were tied.

I sent an email to Wendy Bridges of Comerica Bank and told her of the issue with Lisa Ann.

From: jbsimms
Date: Wed, Nov 14, 2018, 11:45 am
To: wwbridges@comerica.com
Cc: "Jackie ", "Lisa, Nora Arpin (Comerica Bank) Kate Berry (American Banker)
Dear Ms. Bridges,
Below are emails from Lena Mena, and my email to her. I believe this information has been forwarded to Ms. Arpin. I could check my outgoing mail to confirm that Ms. Arpin was made aware of this.
This matter is one of the symptoms of the problem. You appear not to be culpable with respect to the deal made with Fiscal Services, but the imminent PR fallout probably will come across your desk. Now that Ms. Arpin put you into the mix, you will be hearing more stories like what happened to Lisa Mena, and what Jackie Densmore and I have had to do to help these victims of Direct Express and Comerica Bank.

I sent an email to Lisa a day or so ago. No answer was received. You see from the email that Ms. Mena was to call Ms. Arpin. It has not been confirmed that the call was made, but eventually, the truth will be learned about the call.

This fraud is evident; a third-grader would understand this. You will no longer be insulated from the emotional damage suffered by the victims.

I am afraid Lisa has been evicted, and worse.

Her housing director, Christine Evans, can be reached at (520) 419-2634. HIPPA laws prohibited her from identifying Lisa as a recipient of care, but she took my number. She understands.

If Lisa has no phone, and no computer access, how is she to know if her monies have been put back into her account? If you think I embellish and exaggerate, read Lisa's words, not mine.

J.B. Simms

Thursday, November 15, 2018

From: jbsimms
Date: Thu, Nov 15, 2018, 10:22 am
To: "Jackie ", Kate Berry (American Banker)
Cc: Nora Arpin (Comerica Bank) wwbridges@comerica.com, "Advocacy US"
<advocacy@usdirectexpress.com>, "Cherrylene Bruins"
This is what greets me every morning.
There is no use expecting results from Direct Express, which is manned by Conduent call center workers.
I want Cherrylene to know she is not forgotten.
If Direct Express/Comerica/Conduent cannot find the ATM where Cherrylene lost $606, and know she has no need for monthly credit reports, the decision-makers need to be held accountable for victimizing recipients.

Subject: Re: the issues
From: Cherrylene
Date: Wed, November 14, 2018, 4:55 pm
To: jbsimms
Im on it, i called Liza today it kept disconnecting the call im not sure why, however the interpreter said it could be either the phone line connection issue or her answering machine is full, i will try again first thing first tomorrow however i have to attend social security office tomorrow with some paper works i have another severe issues with social security for four years myself and my daughter s case struggling with ss about my daughter s deafness and my overpayment. Attempted to hire lawyers for it but they immediately declined me an attorney due to that it's overpayment smh
Anything i should grab to do while im at the office??
Also please please bear with me if i dont answer in while or sometimes a day or two i will try my best to go to the library to check emails i do not own a phone i usually borrow my mother's.
Reason of delays of responding is due to i had lost my place with eviction we are soon to be homeless by the 26th of this month ive struggled to make ends meet but couldnt when direct express and ssi/ssa stopped our payment in such short notice and struggling 4 years with ss i ve fell further deep till i couldnt catch up anymore
.
Please i am not neglecting and want this done and out of my hands asap i will try to buy a phone however bear with me. thank u so much Jim im glad u reached out to me truly appreciate you. good evening

This will be a day Franklin Lemond will always remember

Jackie Densmore
Thu, Nov 15, 2018, 2:04 PM
to Kate Berry (American Banker), me
Attorney contact info 📣 📣 📣
I think this is it guys !!!!
So excited right now

Jackie contacted a lawyer who might be interested in representing the victims. The lawyer was Franklin Lemond.

From: Franklin Lemond <flemond@webbllc.com>
Date: November 15, 2018, at 5:00:43 PM EST
To: Jackie
Subject: Comerica - EPPICard - Direct Express
Jackie,
I enjoyed speaking with you today about your experiences with the Direct Express program and Comerica Bank. I look forward to speaking with you again soon. In the meantime, I wanted to make sure you have my contact info.
Thanks,
Franklin

Franklin's life would change.
I was very worried about Lisa. She got my message and sent me the following email.

Lisa
Thu, Nov 15, 2018, 4:03 PM
to me
I was told by the VP of Commercia Bank Nora Arpin that she was not able to return my dispute money being that a pin was used as well as the "Spokeo" charges for $40-60 dollars because i had something similar to that website on my history, so it wasn't likely unauthorized. She "sympathized" as she put it with my situation about being evicted stating she once had a niece who was in a situation similar to mine where she could not pay her rent and was possibly being evicted and that it was unfortunate but there was nothing she could do that point. She made the phone call to me approximately at 8:00 pm AZ time so it came as rather a surprise to see her number pop up. I spoke to her assuring her it was not my authorized charges and I can't believe there was nothing more that could be done and she said you were quoting the law wrong to people and that this was the thing she had to explain to people because they are not responsible for anything like a credit card would be responsible for because it is a prepaid card the money is handled differently and covered by the bank differently. I told her i didn't agree but that i was thankful for her help. That was the last time i spoke to anyone. She said specifically in my case it wouldn't be reimbursed because my card wasn't stolen it was considered a theft and is have to pursue that with my local police department here only. I only assumed you were aware of my outcome and i apologize for not messaging you. I was very discouraged and i have eviction court now on the 21st. Right before Thanksgiving. I am so depressed.
Thank you for checking in, Lisa

Friday, November 16, 2018

The first email I read this day was from Cherrylene; she got her money, $900. I was so happy for her.

Research was part of my work. I was looking for the "silver bullet" to stop this victimization of these innocent people. I reviewed Pissed Consumer, Consumer Affairs.com (where I found 184 reviews critical of the Direct Express program) and also reviewed the Direct Express website.

I wanted answers and accountability. I was regularly sending emails to Jackie, and we both were sending emails to Richard Delmar, Chief Counsel, and Sonja Scott, both of OIG Treasury.

Jackie
Fri, Nov 16, 2018, 12:36 PM
to Richard Delmar (OIG Treasury), me
Ok, Mr. Delmar, you neglect to answer any of my emails claiming you are looking into the questions, well at this point I would like to speak with your supervisor please forward your name and number to me.
Thank you, Jackie

Mr. Delmar responded immediately.
Delmar, Richard K. (OIG Treasury)
Fri, Nov 16, 2018, 12:37 PM
to Jackie, me
please call me - 202-927-3973

Jackie called Delmar. Delmar told her: *"Don't you ever ask for my supervisor. I told you I am working with Jackman. What else do you want?"*

We were not making friends. Delmar was about to get a dose of Jackie.

Saturday, November 17, 2018

Victim Number 27: Cynthia- Conyers, Georgia
Cynthia called me. Her account was drained of $1570.
Monies were used at the Best Buy store in Minnesota. I did research while we were on the phone and found the store was located at Best Buy store: 1000 West 78th St., Richfield, MN 55432.

Date: Sat, Nov 17, 2018, 9:23 am
To: jbsimms
Good morning,
My account was drained of $1570.
For many years my son's SSI and now his SSA benefit would go to the United States government-recommended US Direct Express site. On November 1st the bank sends me an email that stated they were happy to provide me with my online username.
On November 2nd US Direct Express sent another email that alerted me that my son's funds were below $100. I was out of town, but I immediately called to see if they could stop payment on the $500+ purchase to Best Buy among other outrageous purchases that were pending. When I go to the account's history the $500 purchase is no longer a part of the history. Plus there is no record of the money returning to the account. The customer service representative stated that she could not close the account and that once the purchases were no longer pending then the account would be closed, and another card would be issued to me.
She advised me to call daily. On November 4th I called again and there were still 2 outstanding pending payments, but the customer service rep. closed the account. He stated that a new card would be issued via mail.

Monday, November 19, 2018

Victim Number 28: Lori -Louisiana
Money taken by Chase bank atm on Nov 6. Got info. Gave numbers of persons to call
11/20 tt Lori- she to go to the bank and call police
11/21 tt Lori- she called Cherry @ Comerica (sub for Wendy). Cherry sent Lori to Money taken by Chase bank atm on Nov 6. Got info. Gave numbers of persons to call
11/20 tt Lori- she to go to the bank and call the police.
11/21 tt Lori- she called Cherry @ Comerica (sub for Wendy). Cherry sent Lori to Schmidt, who stated she would look into this.

Below is the text I received from Lori:

Yes Jim I immediately got a credit back on my account after I spoke to Ms Cherry. Then I received a letter about a month later stating that it was the ATM that kept my money. I thank you for your assistance on this matter. You helped me out extremely. Lori

Victim Number 29: Larry-Idaho
Larry called.
Money and debit cards were sent to Georgia. Sonja Scott got the email and was looking into it. Sent Larry email directing him.
Got an email Monday November 26, 2018- got his $1006. Money was sent to bank in GA. Larry is in Idaho.
12/4- Larry email. Got money, cannot access card.

Email from Larry:
The payment I am supposed to have for December shows that it is on the new card that they sent me to return the funds stolen from me in November. Direct Express has locked me out of it, so I can't use it. They told me I had to return to Social Security, which I did twice yesterday. Social Security said that there is no reason I can't use the card as it was authorized for last month. I opened a checking account at a reputable bank I've used in

the past and will start receiving my money direct deposit to that account starting in January. Social Security was very helpful with the new account, and practically cheered for me for leaving Direct Express. There is absolutely no doubt that Direct Express is intentionally withholding my December money from me. Do not trust Direct Express. The investigation has been completed, so there is no reason other than thievery by them for me not having my money this month.

Tuesday, November 20, 2018

Here is an email I sent to Larry, and I copied persons at Treasury, Social Security, Senator Warren's office, and Kate Berry.

From: jbsimms
Date: Tue, Nov 20, 2018, 10:34 am
To: "Larry "
Cc: Sonja Scott (OIG Treasury) Sarah Lizama (SSA OIG), "Abby Webber"
<Abby_Webber@warren.senate.gov>, "Jackie ", Kate Berry (American Banker)
Larry,
I know this is a tedious matter, having to contact all these people. Jackie and I have over 25 people who have reached out to either or both of us, and the numbers keep climbing.
If you would, keep Jackie and me informed with your progress, or lack thereof. You might know by now that Direct Express is a shell for Conduent call centers. I have spoken to a number of persons in the Customer Advocacy section and the Fraud Section of Direct Express and have determined, without question, that all these people are call center persons, outsourced by Comerica Bank, and:
1. Do not contact merchants on behalf of Direct Express cardholders to protect and investigate charges.
2. Do not contact or refer information to law enforcement on behalf of Direct Express cardholders.
3. Have not taken any AIB courses which qualify them to discuss any banking subject with customers
4. Shield the fact that all workers under the heading of Direct Express are, in fact, call center persons.
5. Susan Schimdt, SVP of Comerica, takes all complaints from BBB and CFPB and forwards the complaints directly to the Customer Advocate of Direct Express (which is a call center person).
6. Conduent employees do not have the intellect to determine fraud on an account.
7. Conduent employees are not familiar with Regulation E, 12CFR205. I asked two of them; they did not know what it was. I have their identification numbers.
8. Comerica hired call center persons to handle Direct Express customers.
9. Social Security has been compromised, and their statements of "investigations" being performed have never been confirmed. Jackie and I are victims of Soc Sec breaches, and we speak from experience.
Keep good notes. Copy Jackie and me on your progress. We have recovered money for over 12 persons and will work to have yours recovered and the thieves arrested.
Make certain you file a local police report.
Jim Simms

I knew that I needed to get the GAO to conduct a new investigation. Jackie and I began trying to get Elizabeth Warren's office to request another GAO investigation, so we copied Abbey Woolheater (Senator Warren's aide) in emails to Michael Clements (the author of GAO 17-176). That would be simple, we thought. The GAO would conduct a more thorough investigation than would OIG Treasury and would be objective.

I decided to write this book and knew I had to review emails, which were the timeline and narrative of the Direct Express nightmare. I had over 4000 sent emails and over 2300 incoming emails on one email address account I used.
I had the same mantra for all victims, but the number of victims was multiplying so fast I could barely keep up.

Tuesday, November 20, 2018

J B Simms
Tue, Nov 20, 2018, 2:42 PM
to Jackie, Abby
This is the issue in which the GAO was involved. We also have the Jan 2017 GAO report which I forwarded to you both.
As was stated to me by the author of the above-mentioned GAO report, and based upon our conversation, the author stated that a new investigation of Comerica/Fiscal Services/Social Security, et al, will be initiated by the GOA simply upon the receipt of a request from someone in the office of a member of Congress.
The trail has been blazed, let's go down the trail.
Jim

Wednesday, November 21, 2018

940am Talked to Lori Matherne- she talked to Schmidt today. Got a person named Cherry, who was nice. She directed Lori to Advocacy.

1230pm- I received a call from Franklin Lemond, the attorney who emailed Jackie. Oddly, Franklin was from the same city in South Carolina where I lived for over 40 years. We hit it off well and realized there would be a lot of work to do.

After talking to Franklin, I sent an email to Arpin on behalf of Lisa Mena, requesting a copy of the investigation. A provision within Regulation E mandates that anyone having proprietary information about fraud can report the fraud, so now I was demanding the investigation.

From: Cynthia Clark
Date: Wed, November 21, 2018, 4:28 pm
To: jbsimms
Hey James,
I tried to contact EZ Konnections, LLC to ask about the expenditures made at the company. What I found to be amazing is the company NEVER asked what day, time and how much was spent. Their reply was going to your bank for answers. I believe that they are a part of the motley crew of thieves as well as Wirecash.com. I placed a complaint with the BBB in NJ for EZ Konnections. I had to pay the State of NJ $6+ to get the business license and address since the company refused to give me a name and address of the owner. The owner's name is Arun Kumar Upadhyay and he used to work at Merrill Lynch.
Wirecash refuses to return my call but I will work on them next.
Wish me luck and happy hunting!
Cynthia D. Clark

Thursday, November 22, 2018

Thanksgiving was not a day off. Emails had to be answered.

The first email would be to Cynthia Clark, of Georgia, whose son's Social Security funds were spent in Minnesota.

Work on documents was also performed.

Jackie sent an email address to Eric Thorsen, Commissioner of OIG Treasury. Thorsen did not respond.

I mailed a letter to the Sheriff of Madera County concerning the hacking of my Social Security address.

I called Lisa Mena. Lisa told me she had been living in a motel since she was evicted. It is sad when you are evicted because you were the victim of a $300 fraud transaction. I reminded her she needed a copy of the investigation, even though we were getting no cooperation from Conduent.

Pissed Consumer complaints continued to be filed, and I answered questions online and allowed some victims to contact me personally.

Saturday, November 24, 2018

From: jbsimms
Date: Sat, Nov 24, 2018, 9:22 am
To: "Cyn C"
if you have the email address of the Customer Advocate (basically a sham office, but you have to use it, and that is where Calvin is) send this to them:
advocacy@usdirectexpress.com
Is this the company which needs investigating, "Wirecash.com"?
You evidently lost money to Wirecash and Best Buy. What is going on with Best Buy?
Any response from Comerica? I am almost done dissecting the sections of Reg E which apply to Direct Express customers.
First thing is giving them notice, which you have done.
Next, send Calvin an email at the above email address and advise them that you are entitled to a full credit if the investigation takes more than 10 days. The investigation begins the moment you give notice, not when they send a packet or when they receive it. I will attach a copy of what I have done, minor corrections or formatting might be necessary, but I want you to see the law.
No one at Direct Express/Conduent think you would know that there are laws that they must follow. Don't be shy; I know you are not shy.
Jim

Sunday, November 25, 2018

Victim Number 30: Dawn-Oklahoma
Below is an email from Dawn.

My name is Heavenly Dawn Jewell. my husband passed away on 10-31-18 in Tulsa from no brain activity. Rob and the guy Darrell MILLUS Was the one who was there and he stole my husband wallet that had his direct express card. so I called and had the card replaced. Well the money is there but now it has been in a fraud account and now my rent is due and so r my bills and I can no one to help me so I would appreciate it if you can help me.

Cynthia Clark sent a list of the fraudulent transactions:

From: Cynthia Clark <msmcdoogle@yahoo.com>
Date: Sun, Nov 25, 2018, 4:18 pm
To: "jbsimms@erikpublishing.com" jbsimms
1. Nov. 1-Google transaction for Target-$39.36 occurred at 12:06:25 IN CA-online
2. Nov. 2-Global Mobile (EZ KONNECTIONS)-$116.67 occurred at 00:13:18 in NJ-online
3. Nov. 2-WireCash.com (Forex Express)-$367.71 occurred at 00:41:00 in CA-online
4. Nov. 2-Best Buy-$21.49 occurred @ 00:01:33 in Richfield, MN online- store-0994
5. Nov. 2-BestBuy-$39.76 occurred @ 7:41:00 in Richfield, MN online store-0994
6. Nov. 3-Best Buy-$21.49 occurred@ 07:41:00 in MN transaction #-805575076326-instore
7. Nov. 3-Best Buy-39.76 occurred @ 08:53:57 in MN transaction #-805576745849-instore
The above transactions were from my on-line bank history.
Below is the transaction timeline that Calvin provided:
1. WireCash.com charge of $367.71 posted on 11/3/18
2. Global Mobile Konnections -$116.67 posted on 11/3/18
3. Best Buy Com charge of $21.49 & $429.99 share the same transaction # of 805575076326 posted 11/3/18
4. Best Buy Com charge of $39.76 & $494.99 share the same transaction # of 805576745849 posted 11/3/18
5. Google pay for Target-$39.36 posted 11/8/18

It was noted that I contacted Best Buy on 11/3/18 to dispute charges but nothing was done to stop delivery. Why? The biggest discrepancy that I see is Calvin's history all say Best Buy Com. Whereas my online accounting have stores 0994(online) and 8550. My Best Buy case#-219691202.
I am totally confused.

Since the 4th I have called several times but whenever I put in my card information a recording comes on and states that my card is in the mail and then hangs up. I received the bank card on the 11th day after closing the compromised account. I have been referred to the company's advocate.

Monday, November 26, 2018

J B Simms
To: Eric Thorsen <Thorsene@oig.treas.gov>
cc: Jackie Densmore
date: Nov 26, 2018, 1:49 PM
subject: Direct Express and veteran abuse
Dear Mr. Thorsen,
I am having to send this from my phone, and not my business email.It is our hope that Mr. Delmar has kept you in the loop on the matter of the failure of Fiscal Services, Comerica Bank, and how this affects veterans.
This is personal for Ms. Densmore and me; her brother-in-law is a disabled vet, and my son is active. Their info is easy for you to find.We would like interaction with you, directly.
Sincerely,
J B Simms

Thorsen would never contact me. He was Delmar's boss and had been at OIG Treasury during both OIG audits. Jackie sent the following email to Sonja Scott, OIG Treasury, Division of Investigations.

Jackie Densmore
Mon, Nov 26, 2018, 5:08 PM
to ScottS, me
Good evening. Ms. Scott wanted to follow up with you after our call today, no one has yet to contact me in regard to my case (Florida OIG) so I was wondering if you would be so kind as to send another email or direct me to the investigator's supervisor.
I'm also requesting Mr. Thorsen's email and direct telephone line, I must have written it incorrectly when we spoke today. I needed more coffee probably lol.
JB and I sent you an email on another 2 victims today with phone numbers listed in emails can you please reach out to them (Cynthia Clark and Kenneth Roussin)
Still waiting to see a list if you have one on who you spoke to and the progress that way, we can keep track.
I'm also interested in the conversation we had about multiple investigations going on in multiple states regarding direct express fraud, do you know how many separate investigations are going on and which states are involved? It would help since victims are all spread out.
When we spoke, I voiced my concerns about the call centers (Conduent) leaking information as already admitted by VP Nora Arpin in the American Banker Article. My question is why would the call centers not be incorporated with these investigations? Can you address this with your office and see if they can include it in the present investigations?
Please let me know what your thoughts are on this as well as my requests in the email.
Thanks again,
Jackie

Scott, Sonja L. Sonja Scott (OIG Treasury)
Tue, Nov 27, 2018, 5:08 AM
to Jackie, me
I spoke to the case agent as well as his supervisor. You should be receiving a call from him. Sonja

Monday, November 26, 2018

A Michigan resident's Direct Express care used in NY

Victim Number 31: Ken- Lake City, Michigan
An email from Ken is below:

From: Kenneth Roussin
Date: Mon, Nov 26, 2018, 2:39 pm
To: jbsimms
Good afternoon,
I'm Ken Roussin. I am currently going through a nightmare with Direct Express.
On Nov. 09, 2018, My Direct Express Debit Card was compromised with 2 unauthorized charges. I called Direct Express to report this. They said one moment please. They told me where these 2 charges were made from...A different state and they were made online.
They told me they could not do anything for 5 days and I should call them back, meanwhile, they would open an investigation that day and I should call Direct Express back on Nov.14th,2018.
I called them on Nov.14th,2018. They said they would mail me paperwork to fill out and I must have them returned in 10 business days.
The forms did not arrive in my mailbox until Nov.24th,2018.
I filled out the forms and then called Direct Express and told them I didn't receive the forms until Nov.24th,2018.
They told me they were sorry for the delay, but I could Fax the forms today Nov 26, 2018.
I have Faxed the forms. It's been 16 days and the money still isn't on my card. These Unauthorized charges were made online from a different state as I still have possession of my card. Can you assist me in this matter?
Ken Roussin
There were 2 charges made on Nov.09/2018 One charge was $173.80. The 2nd charge was for $104.61 I was told by Direct Express, these were made online to a Champs Sports store in New York. I live in Lake City Mi.
There were 2 charges made on Nov.09/2018 One charge was $173.80. The 2nd charge was for $104.61 I was told by Direct Express, these were made online to a Champs Sports store in New York. I live in Lake City Mi.

Subject: DE Issues
From: "Scott, Sonja L." Sonja Scott (OIG Treasury)
Date: Tue, November 27, 2018, 6:11 am
To: "'roussinkenneth@aTt.net'" Cc: 'Jackie ', jbsimms
We have received your complaint and have forwarded to the Bureau of Fiscal Service which oversees the DE Program. We have had very good success when working with the BFS in getting these matters resolved. Sonja ASAC Sonja L. Scott
US Department of Treasury, Office of the Inspector General. Office of Investigations

Tuesday, November 27, 2018

Subject: DE Issues
From: "Scott, Sonja L." Sonja Scott (OIG Treasury)
Date: Tue, November 27, 2018, 6:11 am
To: Roussin Kenneth
Cc: Jackie, jbsimms
We have received your complaint and have forwarded it to the Bureau of Fiscal Service which oversees the DE Program. We have had very good success when working with the BFS in getting these matters resolved. Sonja ASAC Sonja L. Scott
US Department of Treasury, Office of the Inspector General

Why can OIG Treasury not understand that BFS is the culprit?
They cannot because the last two OIG reports let BFS off the hook, and OIG is covering for itself.
Somehow, I liked Sonja. I felt she was trapped in the web of OIG Treasury and could not help as she wanted.
How she thought the Bureau of Fiscal Service would help anyone was beyond me.

I received an email from Larry Fenwald email; Larry got his money, $1066.00. I also got an email from Ken Roussin email; he was reimbursed today as well.

I continued to point out Reg E failures of Comerica Bank to Sonja Scott.

From: *jbsimms*
Date: *Tue, Nov 27, 2018, 9:06 am*
To: *"Scott, Sonja L." Sonja Scott (OIG Treasury)*
Cc: *"Abby Webber" <Abby_Webber@warren.senate.gov>, "Jackie "*
Dear Ms. Scott,
Thank you for your attention to these matters. Jackie and I receive cases at random times. I have a list of close to 30 victims.
Lisa Mena is a sad case; evicted, now in motel, because a caretaker took her info and used close to $250 at places Ms. Mena did not visit. I have statutory evidence that M.s Mena is not liable ("negligence" or trust does not make the cardholder liable).
If you would like to discuss 12CFR205.6 and 12CFR205.11, and the blatant violations committed by Comerica and enabled by Fiscal Services, I will enlighten you and those who would be privy on speaker.
The GAO report published in January 2017 is an indictment of Fiscal Services and Comerica. I received verbal confirmation from the author of that publication that when he receives the request from Senator Warren's office, the GAO will initiate a follow-up investigation.
I look forward to your reply.
JB Simms

Subject: Your Direct Express Fraud Claim
From: Kenneth Roussin
Ken got his money back. This was another victory, proving the fraud department of Conduent was a fraud.

Date: Tue, November 27, 2018, 4:00 pm
To: jbsimms
Jim...Good News. I got my money back case is closed. You have been a great help.
American Banker called me. I told them you were also assisting me.
They had nothing but great things to say about you...
So, I will pay this forward and help other people in the situation I was in.
Once again...Thank You.
Ken

Sometimes I had to send 20 emails a day to victims and the feds. The workday began early and some days up to ten hours were spent working to help the victims.

Victim Number 32: Carlos (Cynthia)-pa
November 27, 2018, Cynthia called.,
She previously worked for Vinnie Parco Husb SSA Disabled, ret law enforcement.
The money was funded on 10/24. 10/26 declined. Called DE on 10/26. Found out that a duplicate card was ordered and sent to 9201 Fairway Court, Jonesboro, GA 30236. Cynthia is in PA.
1259pm Cynthia Wells (570) 535-5685 prov111.lost@gmail.com
10/24 husb card funded
10/26 declined at a store. Called DE Cust svc- canceled the card. Got the address where the card was sent:
She worked for Vinnie Parco in NYC years ago.
Has a letter from Brandon 11/9 (Conduent customer service). Had to issue another card
10/26 first call 30 phone calls to reach cust svc
11/6 card sent
Someone in Georgia had soc sec card and Ga DL. Cards sent out on 10/26- were sent to GA
She filed a complaint with BBB (Sherry Brauer) and FTC
BBB must have referred to Comerica, then to Brandon at Advocacy
11/29 DE to expedite new card

Was there a Georgia connection? The Direct Express card was sent to Jonesboro, GA. How was the address changed on the account? Did someone walk into a Social Security office in GA with false identification and request an address change? It was more likely the address was changed through a person encoding the address at the call center, Conduent.

Bank fraud includes defrauding bank customers, not just the bank

What the fraudsters were doing was bank fraud. In Shaw v US, defrauding a citizen also is bank fraud.

I mentioned earlier that the fraudsters were committing bank fraud, even though the "target" appeared to be the customer and not the actual bank. I referred to the Supreme Court case of Shaw v. United States. Below is the text of the opinion hand down by the Court.

SHAW v. UNITED STATES CERTIORARI TO THE UNITED STATES COURT OF APPEALS FOR THE NINTH CIRCUIT No. 15–5991. Argued October 4, 2016—Decided December 12, 2016 Petitioner Shaw used identifying numbers of a bank account belonging to bank customer Hsu in a scheme to transfer funds from that account to accounts at other institutions from which Shaw was able to obtain Hsu's funds. Shaw was convicted of violating 18 U. S. C. §1344(1), which makes it a crime to "knowingly execut[e] a scheme . . . to defraud a financial institution." The Ninth Circuit affirmed. Held: 1. Subsection (1) of the bank fraud statute covers schemes to deprive a bank of money in a customer's deposit account. Shaw's arguments in favor of his claim that subsection (1) does not apply to him because he intended to cheat only a bank depositor, not a bank, are unpersuasive. First, the bank did have property rights in Hsu's bank deposits: When a customer deposits funds, the bank ordinarily becomes the owner of the funds, which the bank has a right to use as a source of loans that help the bank earn profits. Sometimes, the contract between the customer and the bank provides that the customer retains ownership of the funds and the bank only assumes possession; even then, the bank has a property interest in the funds because its role is akin to that of a bailee. Hence, for purposes of the bank fraud statute, a scheme fraudulently to obtain funds from a bank depositor's account normally is also a scheme fraudulently to obtain property from a "financial institution," at least where, as here, the defendant knew that the bank held the deposits, the funds obtained came from the deposit account, and the defendant misled the bank in order to obtain those funds. Second, Shaw may not have intended to cause the bank financial harm, but the statute, while insisting upon "a scheme to defraud,"[42]

These fraudsters were committed to bank fraud and Conduent was supposed to give all criminal activity to Comerica Bank, which in turn (according to Nora Arpin) was to report all criminal activity to OIG Treasury. Persons at Social Security claimed they were unaware of the fraud, which meant they were either ignoring complaints from recipients or not receiving any notification from OIG Treasury. All this depended upon all parties doing their jobs, which appeared to be a lot to ask.

Wednesday, November 28, 2018

Comerica Bank discriminates against Direct Express cardholders in security

From: jbsimms
Date: Wed, Nov 28, 2018, 6:43 pm
To: Nora Arpin (Comerica Bank) "Wendy Bridges" "Advocacy US" <advocacy@usdirectexpress.com>
Cc: Jackie, Kate Berry (American Banker)
Dear Ms. Arpin, Ms. Bridges, and other persons involved/interested in the protection of Direct Express customers,
While discussing the issue of "alerts" with victim Cynthia Clark (Conyers, GA) whose account was hacked for approximately $1,500.00, a number of issues came up. One subject was the poorly trained personnel at Conduent, lack of knowledge of banking laws, etc, then we focused on the "alerts" that Comerica/Direct Express claims keep their customers safe and protected. Let me explain a few things, and draw an analogy that you will never forget, and maybe not forgive. The analogy could be used as a closing argument (yes, I have represented my company in many civil matters, even having to sue a law firm for a fee and won a jury verdict) against Comerica Bank. When the litigation reaches the courts, you just might hear this again.
Many banks offer different levels of protection for their cardholders. BMO Harris Bank offers free alerts, giving the customer a "cafeteria style" option package for protection. BMO Harris offers alerts as to transaction type, merchant type, dollar amount, geographic location, international transactions, and more. Comerica does not

offer these levels of protection to Direct Express customers. Many of the over 30 persons who have contacted me would never have been victimized if Comerica offered these protections. We are just scratching the surface, and you know that.

Comerica Bank offers a three-tier level of protection for their customers, costing $9.99, $12.99, and $16.99, and is called "ID Monitor" run by Equifax. Direct Express customers are not afforded the option for security that Comerica Bank offers their customers.

If a person, as Ms. Clark, receives an alert that her balance has been reduced to $150.00, and she sees a fraudulent pending charge on the account which was made 1000 miles from her home, she cannot remove the pending charge, her money is frozen, and the care for her son, and herself, is compromised. If she was able to have protection as BMO Harris Bank has for its customers, this would never have happened.

Comerica offers a "low balance" alert. If your balance reaches the low threshold you choose (for example, you choose to be "alerted" if your balance reaches $150.00 or below) this only protects persons whose spontaneous spending habits need to be reined in, and/or they have no idea how much money they have. This alert does not protect against fraud as advertised. Once the low balance has been reached, and there are "fraudulent pending" charges on your account or even fraudulent charges which were paid, Direct Express will not stop the pending charges, nor do they automatically give provisional credit within 10 days as mandated in 12CFR205.11(c)(2)(i). So, the customer is held hostage by persons who do not know the law, and the customer is left with no options. There was no protection.

Let me use an analogy of the "protection" advertised by Comerica Bank. If you do not understand, call me and I will help you.

Using the "low balance alert" feature offered by Comerica Bank for Direct Express for safety and protection is the same "safety feature" used by a man performing coitus or experiencing specified friction; when his "balance" of seminal fluid reaches a low level, having expelled an unexpected flow from his reservoir, he is "alerted" by an involuntary spasmodic reaction. He cannot retrieve any of the flow (i.e., fraudulent charges) that left him. After this experience, a person from Comerica Bank offers the man a condom.

Two issues should be addressed here: (1) the condom would not allow the man to "collect his loss after the fact" and (2) putting on the condom "after the fact" would not only be an exercise in futility but would be an awkward if not impossible exercise in itself.

Let the jury decide if the safety measures touted by Comerica Bank for Direct Express would protect a blue dress or a recipient of government funds.

Jim Simms

Many legal statutes were being sent to Cynthia Clark in GA. I wanted Cynthia another victim, to be armed with the law when addressing Comerica Bank and Conduent.

Michael Clements at GAO was helpful, but we just could not get Warren to help.

J B Simms
Wed, Nov 28, 2018, 1:27 PM
to Michael, Jackie
Dear Mr. Clements,
We spoke a month or so ago with respect to having your office authorized to begin a new investigation of Fiscal Services/Comerica Bank based upon the revelations I gave you.
You stated you would be receptive to beginning another investigation if you were requested by a member of Congress. While we have reached out to Sen Warren's office to contact you to fulfill that prerequisite, we have other members of congress who are aware of this matter.
My question is this: would a request from any member of Congress fulfill the prerequisite for you to begin a new investigation? I will be glad to communicate with you concerning the 30+ persons who have contacted me, and the interaction I/they have experienced at the hands of Comerica Bank, being enabled by Fiscal Services.
Thank you very much.
Jim Simms

Clements, Michael E <Michael Clements (Gen Acct Office)>
Thu, Nov 29, 2018, 6:17 AM
to me
Mr. Simms.
Any Member can submit a request. However, to balance the demand for our work with our available resources, we have a prioritization process. I've pasted the language from our Congressional Protocols below. But, in general, requests from leadership receive priority. That's why Senator Warren, who is the Ranking Member of the relevant committee, was a good option.
Thanks.
Mike

Jackie got an email from Jackman (Rep. Keating office)- He agreed to talk to persons at Social Security.
11:23 am, I called Marilyn Haas, left a message, and got a voice mail.
She returned the call- got her money back. DE charged her for UPS $13.50; bad.
Her initial loss was $230.00. She had to give her sister's address because the attendant wrote down the zip code wrong. The call center person said the zip code was invalid; the call center person entered NE (for Nebraska) instead of NV (Nevada). She did not recognize the city, or it is assumed she thought NE sounded like NV.

2:50 pm, Cynthia Clark (Conyers) called- she got some money back on the card.
Got Best Buy money back. The original amount in total was $985.00. DE kept $500.
Money was fraudulently sent on Global Connect /Wire Cash.

Talked to Andrea Junelle-Jeremy and got the $206.39 credited on 11/23. This was to the Champs store in NY. This was another victory against Comerica and Conduent.

Thursday, November 29, 2018

Michael Clement- GAO- received email. Will start investigation if member of congress asks.
Sent copy to JD, KB, and Abby Webber of Warren office.
We needed Sen. Warren to authorize this, and we will be on our way.

Victim Number 33: Peter- Florida
November 29, 11/29/2018 called. $700 taken from ATM. Claim denied. Talking to Brandon in ADV. Peter was getting very involved helping. Original claim dated August 31, 2018.

From: Peter DeGrandis
Date: Thu, Nov 29, 2018, 8:27 am
To: jbsimms
Dear jbsimms, (I got your contact info via a google post)
I am having a hellish Kafkaesque nightmare of an experience dealing with Direct Express. i received a final letter determining they would not insure stolen funds from my account. I filed police reports and requested film footage from the bank where my funds were withdrawn and stolen. I made it clear I want to press charges against the thief and have done all require to provide Direct Express with the information they need to provide me with the insured funds they are responsible to provide me, but this did little to get results.
Please help, I don't know where I can turn to resolve the corrupt actions of this criminal bank. They did little to investigate my claim, instead, they opted to justify my loss as my fault and are making the claim that I am the criminal and thief in question. They are a sickening organization and should be stripped from their place as a financial service provider for the government.
Please help,
Peter DeGrandis

This is what happened to Peter DeGrandis: his wallet and phone were stolen.Peter was from Boston. Been dealing with this for 3 months.The thief accessed the atm at midnight August 31 took $700.
Two transactions, back-to-back
9/1-6:30am new card issued.
He talked to Susan Schmidt; she refers to the man in Cust Advocate- Brandon
Brandon (Conduent) called last night, 11/28/ 2018. No resolution

Comerica Bank to follow the regulation of the Federal Reserve

15USC 1693(the law) VS 12CFR205 (Federal Reserve regulation based on the law- Reg E)

We see that 15USC1693 is the law; 12CFR205 is the Federal Reserve regulation derived from the law. Comerica Bank became a member of the Federal Reserve Bank and was subject to the provisions of the regulation as of November 6, 2018, when Comerica Bank was admitted as a member of the Federal Reserve.

From: "Jackman, Michael" <Michael.Jackman@mail.house.gov>
Date: November 29, 2018, at 2:48:20 PM EST
To: Jackie
Subject: RE: Must read !!!! It's a hearing on direct express that involves your agencies.
Jackie – Social Security OIG has reached out to me; they will be sending me contact info for the appropriate agent to whom you can report your incident and other incidents you are aware of -they have been auditing this situation for years and are interested in "data points" that can be part of their review of the DE program. I will forward the email once I receive it with contact info etc.
--Mike Jackman

Friday, November 30, 2018

Wendy was now acting like Nora.

Subject: Claim # 1-5038786775]
From: "Bridges, Wendy" <wwbridges@comerica.com>
Date: Fri, Nov 30, 2018, 7:54 am
To: "jbsimms@erikpublishing.com" jbsimms
I will be out of the office on Friday, Nov. 30, and will return to the office on Monday, Dec. 3. If you need immediate assistance, please call Frances Cherry at 214-462-4441.
Thank you!

From: Cynthia Clark
Date: Fri, Nov 30, 2018, 9:46 am
To: jbsimms
Hey there,
I am happy to say that I got the remaining funds today. I thank you so much for your guidance.
However, I want to remain in the trenches to assist others who have had similar experiences such as ours. The work has just begun. Count me in.
Cynthia D. Clark

Laater Cynthia wrote to me:
Done! The next month's monies have already dropped into a new account. I have withdrawn 98% of the monies deposited today in the Direct Express account. I plan to close out my DE account within 2 weeks.
Lastly, I have requested a copy of the completed report from Calvin.I may start blogging. Who knows.
Give Jackie my thanks. When will we all meet for our "Kumbuya" moment?
With heartfelt thanks,
Cynthia

J B Simms
Fri, Nov 30, 2018, 5:37 PM
to Jackie, Abby, Ashley_Woolheater, ScottS, Michael. jackman, Sarah Lizama (OIG Social Security), Kate Berry (American Banker)
I nailed the fact that Direct Express "employees" do not exist. There is no Direct Express call center, Advocacy, or Fraud Unit: all are staffed by Conduent call center employees.
Fraud is rampant and there seemed to be no remedy until Jackie, Kate Berry and I pushed forward.
Kate nailed the fact that Treasury OIG secretly authorized a new investigation based on my contact with an OIG auditor in February.

Comerica fooled Fiscal Services into thinking infrastructure was being created. Comerica and Fiscal Services did not expect a retired PI to be able to read and understand Regulation E.

The worst thing that ever happened to Comerica Bank, Conduent, and Fiscal Services was my account being hacked twice, Jackie being hacked, and Jackie finding Kate.

Every entity that has a responsibility, public or private sector, will be exposed and held accountable.
Merry Christmas.

From: J B Simms
to: Jackie Densmore
cc: Ashley_Woolheater@warren.senate.gov,Abby Webber <Abby_Webber@warren.senate.gov>,
Kate Berry,"Scott, Sonja L." Sonja Scott (OIG Treasury), Sarah Lizama <Sarah Lizama (SSA OIG)>
Date: Nov 30, 2018, 5:56 PM
Subject: Look at the trash they try to sell you on the company against fraud, WHAT A JOKE !!!
I have proof that the Conduent employees, disguised as Direct Express personnel, know anything about Regulation E, and Comerica uses Conduent to abide by Regulation E parameters. I have time, date, and employee identification numbers of two persons in the Fraud Unit, for whom the English language was a challenge, and neither knew anything about the banking regulations. The responses to my question, does Conduent abide by Regulation E, the answers were:
1) I cannot divulge that information
2) I suppose so
Conduent was aware of the problems when Comerica was given the second bid by Fiscal Services. Let's see what Treas OIG does with this. You people know I have been down these paths.
Get your popcorn early and get plenty of it. This is going to be a big show.

Jackie found the check waiver form as Treasury was denying persons to get paper checks.

Saturday, December 1, 2018

Subject: Re: Claim # 1-5038786775
From: Cynthia Cl
Date: Sat, December 01, 2018, 6:21 am
To: jbsimms
$985.32 on November 28th. $525.70 on November 30th.
The $985 is from Best Buy. Calvin said the $525 is the provisional credit.
The account has zero balance and I plan to close it within 2 weeks. At my age people only have one chance to try to fool me. Direct Express has used up its one chance.

Jackie Densmore
Sat, Dec 1, 2018, 1:16 PM
to ScottS, me
Happy Saturday Sonja!
I hope you enjoyed your birthday; I know it's Saturday but wanted to send to you since my Monday is crazy busy.Mr. McPhail's daughter ($30,000 victim) contacted me this weekend and said nobody from the OIG treasury special agent team has contacted them back regarding their case so they are requesting a follow up email / or call to let them know what's going on and who is in charge of their case. Can you please send her case agent an email requesting them to contact her or him?
Thanks Sonja!
Jackie

Scott, Sonja L. Sonja Scott (OIG Treasury)
Sat, Dec 1, 2018, 1:54 PM
to jackiedenzz@yahoo.com, me
Just exchanged emails with the case agent. He has spoken to McPhail s daughter and a fed attorney in reference to the matter. Not sure if he has spoken to McPhail...

So, Sonja had talked to a federal attorney about this case?

Sunday, December 2, 2018

Victim Number 34: Carol-Texas

My account was compromised somehow even though I was in possession of my card. They made 3 withdraws from my daughters account within seconds of each other, one for 302.00, the second for 202.00, and the third for 82.00, on June 9, 2017, at an ATM at a Racetrack gas station (3310 S. Cooper St, Arlington, TX, 76015).

From: Carol Gilmer
Date: Sun, Dec 02, 2018, 7:36 pm
To: jbsimms
Hello Sir,
My name is Carol Gilmer and I had an issue with Direct Express not refunding my money that someone had compromised my account.
This has been over 1 year ago, and I am constantly calling them fighting to get my money.
Do you have any additional advice for me?
Any help would be much appreciated.
Thank You
Carol Gilmer

From Carol:
Well, I finally got the paperwork from Alisha and to my disappointment it was NOT an investigation report at all.
It was copies of what I originally sent to them along with the loss prevention sheet (nothing more then a check list) and copies of where it shows the transactions.
So the reason it was denied is because I had conflicting information. It shows I need to send a police report which I originally did and they also sent me a copy of it back so if it is conflicting to them because I did send the police report...hum..
So u disputed it and resent the paperwork again along with the police report and this time I added an additional note stating for them to contact the detective and provided his phone number.
It doesn't show anywhere if they called the detective or not but at this point, I would say they did not.
The bottom line is there was no effort on their part to truly investigate my issue because it didn't fall into what they consider fraud therefore I was denied and the case closed.
I have not recovered my monies that someone took from my account so at this point I do want to have my name put on the list.

I was continually calling and emailing Sarah Lizama and Sonja Scott for all these victims.

Carol had requested an investigation 6 months before and Comerica never gave her a copy of the investigation. (On 1/31/19 I emailed Carol- demanding an investigation again.)

Victim Number 35- Brian: Texas
The following is the email received from Brian.

Point of Sale transaction
I am a disabled cancer patient and I have to survive on Social Security Disability as my sole source of income. On Oct. 25/2018 my fiance and I visited a local Metro Pcs store here in our new town of Midland Texas to receive a phone upgrade, I've been using Direct Express and Metro Pcs phone carrier for several years and was never informed that I was eligible for a cell phone upgrade at Metro PCS.
I asked about the 2 lines, because I've always had 4 lines for $25.00 each line with unlimited data. The service rep. told me that it looked like my plans were changed, Metro Pcs store employees had not only deceived and lied about me about the sale, but they also removed 2 lines without my knowledge or consent to do any of their activity, creating a serious problem. We demanded to speak to a supervisor at the store.
I spoke to Direct Express today and the agent told me that my case was closed yesterday because it was missing 2 requested documents (which were provided) they also said that I never exchanged the cellphone for a return or exchange which is also not true. In fact I went back to the store the following day Oct.26th, to do just that and was denied a refund, as well as denied conversation, I brought my son in law as a witness and can verify

every word I'm saying. Direct Express also has a policy that if the request for a dispute is made that after 10 days a provisional credit would be issued until the investigation is complete, however, they don't honor any of their policies.

Comerica Bank and Green Dot collude to hide the theft of $30,000 from McPhail

from: *J B Simms*
to: *"Scott, Sonja L." Sonja Scott (OIG Treasury)*
cc: *"Jackie, Marteshia McPhail. Kate Berry*
date: *Dec 2, 2018, 3:04 AM*
subject: Re: Mr. McPhail case

The persons assigned to conduct investigations for a federal prosecutor will be an FBI agent. The person who contacted Ms. McPhail did not comport himself as an FBI agent. If you are authorized to make a referral to the US Attorney office which covers Florence, SC, based on the information you have, please advise us. I have no problem determining federal jurisdiction, nor discussing this with the US Atty myself.

This matter will always involve records of Green Dot, which I believe is headquartered in the area of Pasadena, CA. Since the fraudulent account is said by Comerica to be in the name of the victim, the victim has the right to retrieve the record of transactions.

Any person from Comerica Bank or any entity assigned by Comerica Bank to investigate this matter need also to be investigated to determine the origin of their pronouncement that the Green Dot card was obtained by the victim, thus their ridiculous denial of fraud and imposition of liability upon Mr. McPhail.

I am grateful for your assistance. J.B. Simms

We needed Sonja Scott to investigate this fraud.

Monday, December 3, 2018

Victim Number 36: Toney-Kentucky

Call from Son Trenton who is the payee. Trenton is on disability. Two checks come: one retro from back money for Toney.

Trenton - $306, Toney- $454

Toney pays rent with Trenton's card

Money gone

Toney called Soc Sec- Tt Ms. Brown- Trenton has "another card."

Toney called DE- could not get thru- excessive call volume

Advised who to call.

An email was received from Toney later that day:

Toney got her money. Son has schizophrenia, disabled. She has two cards. Call volume is too high to get thru. Two payments of $306 and $454 per month were deposited on one Direct Express card. Somehow a new card was issued but was not requested. The $454 payment cannot be accessed.

12/4- She emailed the next day. She opened a bank account for son. I advised her to demand a copy of the investigation and immediate provisional credit.

On Tue, Dec 4, 2018, at 4:16 AM Toney Ritter wrote:
Mr. Simms,
It was a pleasure talking to you yesterday! Direct Express suddenly fixed the problem concerning my account! I could not have done this without your help!! Today, I am getting my son his own checking account then off to Social Security. Have a Wonderful Tuesday!!
Thanks Again

12/5-I called her Toney. I asked for update.

Toney texted me: "got son's money back."

"Thank the Lord there is someone out there that may help."

Victim Number 37: Katrina-PA
I talked to Nick, husband of Katrina. The card is an EPPI-card (child support). The fraud totaled $13-$1500. Katrina filled out paperwork. The state refunded part of the money $400. Nick called customer service, nightmare at the Direct Express call center.

Victim Number 38: Patricia-PA
December 1, 2018, Screenshot of account:
MeMe Live $346.83 (Card purchase) MeMe Live (International Purchase fee) Shipping (pending) $0.73. from Missouri.
I advised Patricia to email a copy of the statement to Conduent and demand a copy of the investigation.
3/5/19- I received email from Wollin (who initially contacted me on behalf of Katrina and Patricia. Patricia did get her money recovered promptly, within the 10 days allowed under the law. Your assistance was greatly appreciated. She also is no longer using her card and has her payments set up through a bank now.

Victim Number 39: Lisa- Corpus Christi, Texas
From: Lisa Tower
Date: Mon, Dec 03, 2018, 10:09 pm
To: jbsimms
Hi I woke up this morning and called to check my balance to find all was gone .00:00 deposit 21:30 one ATM transaction took it all. I live in Corpus Christi Tx the ATM transaction was made in Atlanta Georgia I called direct Express cause I have the card in my hand and they are telling me I only have been issued the one that is in my hand. So, I don't understand how it was used at atm many states away from me. But as if having all the money I have to live on for the month, rent due, and everything they put my account in negative by charging me 13.50 for shipping and $4.00 to replace the card I am holding in my hand . My rent was due today and I now owe direct Express money I can't believe this is happening. I faxed to them what happened called back to ask when I would have the money back was told 45-90 days and given have a good day. I live month to month on very little I have no other income. I have been crying off and on all day, I don't know what to do i filled a police report and I can pickup tomorrow to fax to direct Express. I don't know if you are still helping others. I have never been through this, and I don't know where to go from here.
Any suggestions would be greatly appreciated. Thank you for your time.

I jumped on this. Lisa looked at her transactions and determined the transaction was made on her Direct Express Card at 21:30 at an ATM at 3235 Peachtree Rd NW, Atlanta GA in the amount of $783.00.
Lisa had read my posts and she did the right thing; she reported the fraud to Direct Express. On 12/3/18 she filed the police report and emailed the information to Conduent (Direct Express Customer Advocacy) on 12/4/2018.
She called Nora Arpin and Wendy Bridges. Arpin returned the call. Lisa learned there were many attempts made on her card from outside the country but since the balance was zero, they could not get any money. Nora Arpin did not return calls to everyone and never returned a call to me.

Subject: Fraud on my Direct Express Card
From: Lisa Tower
Date: Wed, December 05, 2018, 8:03 am
To: "Nora Arpin (Comerica Bank)" <Nora Arpin (Comerica Bank)>
Cc: jbsimms
A transaction was made on my Direct Express Card at 21:30 at a ATM at 3235 Peachtree Rd NW, Atlanta GA $783.00 my entire S.S. was taken. I live in Corpus Christi, Tx and haven't traveled out of Corpus Christi in over 12 years. I have the card with me that was said to be used at this ATM (i did not lose my card or give my number out). I did not make this withdraw and it has left me in a terrible situation. I need to pay rent and this is my only income. I have filed a police report here in Corpus Christi, Tx. The case # is 1812030118 with Sgt Collier badge # 11823. I am a single mother. I feel robbed twice ...I now owe direct Express (due to the first thief not leaving enough) to replace a card I didn't lose. I have faxed direct Express, filed a police report, made and a complaint to BBB. The direct Express website to sign up says, again and again, this card is "safe" ... For who thieves???? All I get from direct Express and fraud reps is 45-90 days and "have a good day". I live month to month on very little. Someone took it all from me in one transaction and no one seems to care. The last fraud rep I spoke with at direct Express told me from him looking at my account it was obvious fraud there were many

failed attempts from different countries and he began to name them. So why 45-90 days? Again I now owe direct Express, a late fee of $50 for my rent, and Monday I guess no medication for the month. I guess it's my fault I have no one to borrow from. How much is this "safe" card going to cost me as of today with card replacement and late fee on rent I am at $67.50.

I gave email and fax numbers to all victims so they could make direct contact with Comerica Bank and Conduent. Same instructions. Very tiring, but these people have nowhere to turn.

Tuesday, December 4, 2018
Subject: Automatic reply: Fraud on Direct Express Card
From: "Arpin, Nora T" <Nora Arpin (Comerica Bank)>
Date: Tue, Dec 04, 2018, 5:39 am
To: jbsimms
I am out of the office with minimal access to email. I will respond to your message when I return.

Victim Number 40: Yvette-Colorado
"Over a course of 1 year total amount is $975 and $575 was missing this month alone and yes I've left messages on the lady's voice mail you told me to call from there several in fact and nothing I even went to social security and no one cares to help me or can give me a valid explanation has to where's my money and why haven't it been returned I reported the fraudulent activity going on the first time it happened and no one can give me no answers or return my calls"

I gave Yvette telephone numbers to call.An email from Yvette is below:

J B Simms
Wed, Dec 5, 2018, 12:40 PM
to jbsimms
is it possible that I can go to social security to let them know what's happening. My card was suspended and I already have threats from my landlord or the person I'm staying with that if I need to pay my rent and if I don't have my money by this evening that I have to find somewhere else to go you think that's possible that they can help me or like give might give me my check that direct Express suspended like I don't want her I need this is putting me through so much frustration I'm going through there's so much that this has been putting me through emotional distress like I can't deal with this right now

Jackie needed to tell her story about the fraud that affected he brother-in-law's account.

From: Jackie Densmore
Sent: Tuesday, December 04, 2018, 11:36 PM
To: CFPB Ombudsman <CFPB_Ombudsman@cfpb.gov>
Subject: Direct express fraud / Comerica Bank Attn: Wendy Kamenshine
Hello and this is my story,
I am writing this email concerning fraud that is happening all over the country with these treasury-recommended debit cards for federal benefits. Millions of Americans collect their benefits through a prepaid debit card called Direct Express. The cards are issued by Comerica bank, because the treasury wanted to save a few bucks they decided to push these cards on anyone who collected benefits by sticking a paper in with their paper checks stating that their benefits would automatically be enrolled in this program by a certain date.
my brother-in-law Derek Densmore is a 100 percent service-connected disabled veteran who suffers from severe mental illness and collects SSDI. I was appointed his payee for his Social Security Disability. We enrolled in the Direct Express program thinking it was a safe choice for his funds as it was stated in all the letters we had received and that the US Treasury had RECOMMENDED!
On August 3, 2018, I called the number on the back of the Direct Express card to see if his monthly Benefits had been deposited into his account (they are deposited on the 3rd of every month) and the recording stated that a new card had been mailed out. I thought it was strange so I got the Direct Express card out and looked at the expiration date to see if it had expired, the date was fine and the expiration date was 2022. I waited a couple of days to see if the card would come in the mail, but no card arrived.
I had tried to call several times but was unable to get anyone on the phone.

On August 10, 2018, I tried again, and this time was successful in reaching a supervisor. Marquelin badge #8122609 had taken the call, she first varied the account by my name, address, and social security number. She put me on hold to review the account and when she got back on the line she stated someone had called on August 2, 2018 (a day before my brother-in-law Derek's benefits would be deposited into his account) claiming to be me (name address and social security) this person stated they had damaged the card and wanted Direct Express to send a money gram so they could access the funds. I told the supervisor that I had not requested such a thing! She quickly realized that this was a fraud case. She looked further into the account and stated that she had no clue as to where the money was sent because the rep who requested the money gram did not notate the account properly. I became extremely upset that

my brother in laws funds was stolen and that the company that gave his money away had no records of where it was sent. She informed me she was going to open a claim but that I would need to fill out paperwork that would need to be mailed out to me before the Direct Expresses fraud department could even investigate this.

I hung up the phone upset and very angry that my identity had been stolen and even worse my disabled brother in laws money. I called back immediately and sat on hold over 45 min. Once I finally got a human being I asked for a supervisor. Nikki badge number 8123084 took the call. I explained what had happened and gave her the claim and reference number. I begged her to try to find the location so I could contact local police. She reviewed the acct and stated that it had been sent to a Walmart.

She could not tell me the location though. She stated I should file a police report in my town which is Bourne Ma and also that if I wrote a letter to Direct Express explaining what had happened it would speed up the investigation process. I asked her why they had no passwords on the accounts like mother's maiden name or why Direct Express wouldn't try to call me after a request like a money gram was going to be sent before it was sent as a precaution against theft or identity fraud. she stated to me that because these cards are issued to the disabled and elderly that they couldn't remember the passcodes and were getting locked out of their accounts. I asked her how would someone know when the benefits were going to be released she stated oh that's easy everyone's benefits get either deposited on the first or third of the month !!! The person called on the second which makes me believe it was an inside job.

I quickly left work and drafted a letter to the fax number she had given me and headed to Staples to send it. She said once received they wait 24 hours and then submit it.

I went to the Bourne police dept and officer Harrington and officer Gelson took the report. I had given her all the info including a copy of my license and the Direct Express card. Report will be enclosed.

Derek was extremely upset and insisted on coming back to the station to make sure they were going to look into this for him and also very concerned someone had all my information and knew where we lived. I guess that goes back to him being a marine. Very protective. We spoke with Sargent Perry who we know from doing well-being checks on Derek in the past. So Derek felt somewhat at ease knowing Sargent Perry was going to be looking into this case too.

On August 11, 2018, I had called Direct Express again for another over 45 min wait time and asked for a supervisor. I spoke with Domingue who I did not get the badge number again she varied me by name address and social security number. I informed her of everything that had happened and asked if she received the fax, she paused first told me to know then pressured her again with the same questions and asked her if this line was being recorded she quickly told me to hold on. She came back about 3 min later and told me yes, they did receive it but would not likely even be addressed until Monday as the fraud dept only works Monday to Friday.

Sunday, I became extremely stressed, so I started searching on the internet about Direct Express and came across numerous articles about this corrupt company and other victims with stories similar to ours. I was shocked how could the US Treasury be recommending these cards knowing of all the fraud that was going on? I dug deeper and even found a Facebook page on Direct Express. All the people's stories, unable to pay their rent or get their medicine or feed their children from people stealing money off these cards. And every story ends with nobody will help me. I thought of my brother-in-law and how that could be him if my husband and I didn't take care of him and that with his mental illness would be unable to do. I was a victim too because I was the payee they stole my identity and all I was doing was caring for the family who served our country and I was honored to do it. While researching I came across an article about a botched bid run by the feds that puts Comerica Bank in the hot seat for problems with benefit cards (Dave Lieberthe watchdog columnist with Marina Traham) the article which I will be sending Sheds light on the corruption. I noticed the name watchdog and linked it to a JB Simms with a phone number he listed to help on these fraudulent cases with Direct Express so I gave him a call. He too was a victim, he had told me his story and I told him ours. He told me his frustrations and that he had a list of other victims of these scram Scenarios. Names, dates, and victims phone numbers, I couldn't believe how many other victims he had tried to help but going up against this bank is *protected by so much corruption and mismanagement and I was seeing all of it for the first time, scary to have to go through it felt like our lives were turned upside down I mean I had to call all my creditors and pay $5 on each credit bureau to have my own social frozen because Massachusetts allows them to charge that, which is crazy if you are a victim and your money was stolen how could you pay that it's a twisted requirement, especially for people on the federal benefits. When you open a claim with the direct express, they will not refund your money right away they tell you up to 45 days until investigators resolve a claim. Now remember these victims are disabled, elderly, and veterans and this could be the only money they have to live on and they are without the money for no cause of their own.*

I was extremely hopeful when I contacted Mr. Simms, he had been through it with Comerica Bank the whole thing money was stolen not once but twice. After numerous phone calls and emails, nobody would help. He sent me a list of numbers on direct express that I did not have and instructed me to call and leave messages he also told me to contact money gram and get them to tell me where it was sent so I could tell the police. I knew he was sending us on the right track I found the money grams number on Sunday it was not easy getting a representative to give me transaction number 13373783747 and the location to which it was sent. It was sent to a Walmart in Hollywood Fl and cashed in the amount of $814.39 at 5:29 pm. I quickly called the Hollywood police department and filed a report with officer Quartell report number 126354. She said a detective would be contacting me at the end of the week and I informed her of the urgency of the videotape for Walmart but said had to wait for them to contact me. Exhausted I hung up the phone.

Monday, August 13, I went to the Taunton social security office to talk to them about what I could do to protect myself and also if there was a way to stop future deposits to direct express. We arrived at 8:49 am and there was already a line out the door people had been in line since 8:00 am I knew it was going to be a long day for Derek and me. We waited for hours and finally sat in front of Ms. Grace. Who listened to our story and also had gotten her supervisor to find out the next steps. Ms. Grace had told us her supervisor was away from her desk but would put a request for paper checks up until 3 months then he would have to go direct deposit. She gave me her supervisor's name and number Ms. Walker. We left, and I contacted Ms. walker to see what she was going to do since they had recommended this card company and it was federal money that people were stealing. She informed me that once social security deposits the money it's up to direct express to make sure it gets to the Recipient. It's not their job we cannot blame them. Just completely baffled about the lack of responsibility they are willing to take and the sheer disrespect they have for the people who are in that program makes me sick!

I then contacted the Hollywood police and spoke with Det. Campbell 954 967 4411

I asked him to see if a report was submitted and he confirmed it had but was not finalized at that time. I told him the whole story and even gave home the reference number claim number and even transaction number at Walmart and the time that the crime had occurred. He said he would go to Walmart to see what he could find out but the likelihood of them catching the person is very unlikely; so unlikely not worth getting the tapes since he probably won't recognize the person. I still have not gotten an answer from Walmart.

Mr. Simms did tell me about a story involving a victim who lived in Nevada. His card was highjacked to a location in Miramar Fl 7 miles from Hollywood Florida. I did relay that to the detective maybe cases were linked. The man in Nevada has not gotten his funds.

I received a call from Becki she is from the cardholder Advocacy group 313 222 3907

She wanted to let me know she received the compliment and that it was being sent over to fraud unit I asked her if she had seen a lot of these cases come across her desk on direct express and she stated (tons)!!!

I look forward with speaking with you.

Thank you for your time.

Jacqueline Densmore and Derek Densmore

Wednesday, December 5, 2018

T Lisa Tower- (361) 442-9796- lost $783.00 in one transaction
Need address of Wells Fargo ATM in Atlanta (she is in Corpus Christi)
She had to repeat her SSN 4 times to Conduent call center person.
Attendant said there had been a bunch of attempts from diff countries on her account.
Lisa called Nora Arpin. Lisa got money back.

Thursday, December 6, 2018

From: "Jackman, Michael" <Michael.Jackman@mail.house.gov>
Date: December 6, 2018, at 10:37:55 AM EST
To: Jackie
Subject: RE: GAO
Jackie - let me look into the GAO request. My initial research indicates that the request would have more authority if it were coming from the chair of a committee, such as the Committee on Financial Services, which is the committee I had engaged with in October to see if they had done any review of the Comerica/Direct Express situation. I will check in again with them to see if they have made any progress.
As for Social Security, I had been in contact with the OIG, and it seems that Senator Warren's office had already contacted them. I believe the OIG will be reaching out to you directly.
--Mike Jackman

From: Lisa Tower <lisatower100@yahoo.com>
Date: Wed, Dec 05, 2018, 4:37 pm
To: jbsimms
Hi, I just checked my account and they have credited the transaction back to me. Not their fees but I am so thankful to you for all your help!!!! I can't say thank you enough for taking your time out to help me. This is the first time anything like this has happened to me it felt like I was getting nowhere with direct express. They said i would get the card today but there is no mail today cause of holiday. Hopefully the new card will come in tomorrow. But really can't say to you THANKYOU enough!!!

Was I happy? Yes, I was happy. List got her money the same day she contacted me. Arpin responded. We got Arpin's attention.

Thursday, December 6, 2018

Subject: RE: Question occurred to me
From: "Clements, Michael E" <Michael Clements (Gen Acct Office)>
Date: Thu, December 06, 2018, 11:46 am
Mr. Simms.
We conducted the prior work at the request of Senators Hatch and Warren. I'll also add that GAO conducts performance audits of programs v. investigations of individuals' problems with a program. IG offices typically handle those issues, and we have a fraud unit that addresses fraud-related problems.
Thanks.
Mike

Jackie Densmore
Dec 6, 2018, 11:41 AM
to Abby, AshleyWoolheater, me
It has come to my attention that Sen. Warren as well as Hatch both requested the original investigation by the GAO and had good reasons for doing so.
With all the evidence Mr. Simms and I have summited to your office with what's been going on with this program the very first thing that should have been done was to have the GAO investigate.
Your office already knew the procedure and has neglected to act on this.
I am beyond upset and am demanding an answer as to if you have contacted Mr. Clements and have supplied him with the necessary paperwork to get this investigation started!
I will remind your office that a lot of eyes are on this so the next step is to show Massachusetts residents as well as all the victims that you will do what's right and make the request for the GAO to get involved.
I have heard nothing but crickets from your office since we last spoke on the conference call dated 11-29-2018.
I will be waiting for your response, I'm also again requesting a meeting with the Sen. Warren
Jackie

The brush-off from Senator Elizabeth Warren

From: "Webber, Abby (Warren)" <Abby_Webber@warren.senate.gov>
Date: December 6, 2018, at 3:46:23 PM EST
To: Jackie
Cc: "Wong, Jessica (Warren)" <Jessica_Wong@warren.senate.gov>
Subject: RE: Requesting a status update
Hi Jackie,
Thank you for your continued interest. I appreciate the information you have shared with us, as protecting consumers is Senator Warren's top priority. Unfortunately, these matters can take a bit of time to sort out. As we discussed, Senator Warren and her oversight team are working hard on this issue, and I am happy to speak with you when we know more. Additionally, we encourage you to have victims contact their home state Senators to assist them with specific casework requests to ensure they are quickly addressed.
Best,
Abby

This is part of an email from Lisa Mena. This was breaking my heart. There was no pattern to helping:

'They have no idea what all this has done to me I can't describe how out of place I feel being a burden to my generous few friends who don't have means themselves but are helping me but find that I am grateful, and I thank God every day that goes by I eat and shower that's what I'm thankful for cause to me right now that's a hellva lot to ask for. Thanks Jim."

I emailed Nora Arpin- I thanked her for help with Lisa Tower and needed more responses from Conduent.

Sunday, December 9, 2018

A wake-up call to Comerica, Conduent, and US Treasury

From: jbsimms
Date: Sun, Dec 09, 2018, 11:20 am
To: Nora Arpin (Comerica Bank) "Wendy Bridges" <wwbridges@comerica.com>
Cc: "Jackie ", Kate Berry (American Banker), Richard Delmar (OIG Treasury), "Advocacy US" <advocacy@usdirectexpress.com>, Sonja Scott (OIG Treasury) Sarah Lizama (SSA OIG), "Abby Webber" <Abby_Webber@warren.senate.gov>, "Michael Clements" <Michael Clements (Gen Acct Office)>
Dear Ladies,
Maybe your life is pristine. Maybe you do not have to face anxiety, fear, then have to experience someone taking your money because of greed and accepting ineptitude because the victims are the "great unwashed." This is what you have done to Mr. Fennwald and his family. This is the fear, anxiety, and cortisol rush pulsing through his vein. You did the same thing to Kenneth Tillman, Derek Densmore, and countless other veterans. You have done this to persons who became homeless after you emboldened Conduent to continue to make decisions with persons' money and their lives.
I see no evidence that Conduent has given any of the more than 35 persons, with whom I and Ms. Densmore have come into contact, a copy of the investigation assigned to the fraud experienced by the cardholder. The dots have been connected. If Ms. Bridges alleges I or anyone else manufactures facts, read this for yourself. This man's PIN was changed five (5) times by a fraudster, and Comerica never placed the same security measures on the Direct Express card as they offer their regular customers.
You have not contacted me directly. I know how to solve these problems, and I have shared the fixes with others.
I gave away two pair of handcuffs in 2006, which were used to capture fugitives and put them back in jail. As I say, the dots have been connected. I suggest, when we are done, you ask for the Smith and Wesson cuffs; they have a double locking mechanism that keeps the cuffs from getting tighter as you move around.
You know where to find me.
J.B. Simms

Nora Arpin never communicated with me.

Monday, December 10, 2018

Sen. Elizabeth Warren's office refuses to allow an investigation of US Treasury

Subject: a very disturbing development
From: jbsimms
Date: Mon, Dec 10, 2018, 12:30 pm
To: "Michael Clements" <Michael Clements (Gen Acct Office)>
Cc: "Jackie "
Dear Mr. Clements:
A former constituent of Massachusetts, and a victim of Comerica Bank, was directed by me to contact the office of Elizabeth Warren, to assist in being reimbursed for the fraud on his account, which totaled approximately $700.00. The gentleman did make contact, the staffer did state she would assist the cardholder.
The cardholder then asked the staffer about having Senator Warren's office make the gesture to you and ask for a follow-up investigation of the malfeasance of Comerica Bank and the enabling by Fiscal Services. The cardholder sent me the following email:
"It was very clearly stated by Abby (in so many words) they will not pursue or support a GAO investigation... Warren's previous interplay with this issue has seemed to forge a relationship between Warren and Comerica and against any further pursuit of action against their conduct and our cause at this time."
I could only respond honestly to this to you on the telephone, not via email. This excerpt is distressing in many ways.
I have sent a request to the office of Senator Hatch. I know he is retiring. I left voice mail messages at both his Salt Lake City office and his Wash DC office. I also left an email on his website.
Your office is the only office that will be objective. If and when your office can commission another investigation, I have a yet unrevealed source to pass along.
Thanks.
Jim

From: jbsimms
Date: Mon, Dec 10, 2018, 3:47 pm
To: "Jackie ", Kate Berry (American Banker)
Conduent Political Action Committee contributed $5,000 to the Democratic National Committee in July 2018.

The political contributions kept them safe.

Tuesday, December 11, 2018

Toney Ritter
Tue, Dec 11, 2018, 4:55 AM
To: me
I did call and was told there is not a paper trail of any wrongdoing due to me receiving my son's SSI funds. That said I am telling everyone that will listen about the direct express doing's. I don't know if this helps but it sure can't hurt!
I went to the Social Security Office and submitted a request for my son's funds to be direct deposit into his new checking account.
I'm afraid of what might have happened if I did not contact you. It's a sad and scary world when people are willing to steal from
the disable and seniors, and we don't get enough money to live on in the first place, to have these people (criminals) stealing it!! Wow!!!
I Can't Thank You Enough, Mr. Simms
You Truly Are a Blessing!!

This touched my heart. These are victims. They were victimized by our government.
Emails to Nora Arpin were answered automatically, stating she is out of the office with limited email access. What the hell does that mean?

Victim Number 41 -Hope-New Mexico

Hope learned from Conduent that someone changed her address to an address in Florida and changed her email and phone. The change was made prob 11/27-28. Charges on her account were from out of state and out of the country.

From: hope Gearhart
Date: Tue, Dec 11, 2018, 12:41 am
To: jbsimms
Direct Express recently have been screwing me around after reporting unauthorized transactions on my account. the way they've treated me (except Claudia), you'd think I was barbecuing puppies for breakfast. Here's my bitchfest I've written for anyone who will listen attached.
Fraud noticed: November 16, 2018, lost $673.32.
Fraud reported: November 16, 2018
Reimbursement: Wednesday, December 19, 2018, Charges were from Ukraine

Hope sent an entertaining and volatile email. I did not publish the "bitch-fest", but Hope got her money back within a week of contacting me.

Victim Number 42-Joy: California

UNAUTHORIZED DEBITS ARE AS FOLLOWS:
Fraud dates:
September 9th: 2018 $4.95- (Pure Face & Skin) (authorized)
September 24th: $4.90 " (unauthorized)
September 24th: $88.98 (Organic Skin) (unauthorized)
September 22nd: $89.95 (Pure Face & Skin) (unauthorized)
October 22, 2018: $89.95 (Pure Face & Skin) (unauthorized)
October 25th, 2018: $88.98 (Organic Skin) (unauthorized)
November 22, 2018: $89.95 (Pure Face) (unauthorized)
November 23, 2018: $88.98 (Organic Skin) (unauthorized)
Total Amount of unauthorized Charges: $541.05

I sent emails to Joy on 12/11 and 12/20/18.
This is from Joy:
12/20/18
Hello and thank you for the email. Unfortunately, I have only received a portion ($356.00) to date of the total ($560) that I reported being taken from my account without my authorization. It has been over a month now since I reported the fraud to Direct Express. I have not received any correspondence from them regarding the remaining outstanding balance or the investigation into the matter. Although I have reported the Company that initially committed the fraud to the police. Hopefully they can put a stop to Companies who prey on unsuspecting consumers who use "trick" Marketing practices and techniques in order to gain access to consumers.

On 1/23/19 I emailed Joy- asked for a breakdown. her reply:

Hello Jim and thank you for the follow-up. After I emailed you and filed the complaint as per your recommendation, I did finally receive payment from Direct Express in the form of a credit for the items listed below in your email.

I did some research for Cynthia Clark, whose funds were used at Best Buy in Minnesota. I emailed and listed the violations of Regulation E for her, noting that she needed to demand a copy of the investigation. I forwarded this to Wendy Bridges and Jackie.

There were patterns of fraud from time to time. Jackie's and Paul's fraud were from the same place in Florida. Fraud was also experienced at Champs in NY by Roussin (2 hacks, 173.80 and 104.61) and Andrea Junelle ($206.00). Even after pointing out patterns of fraud, the people at Conduent never "connected the dots" and continued to victimize the cardholder.

Charity called me. She was still trying to get her money. She told me she tt the Conduent worker named Kevin on November 30. Kevin (Conduent) asked for Charity's diagnosis of her illness. Why? This was none of his business. The Conduent people were looking for any reason to harass the victim cardholders.

Victim Number 43-Harrell-Los Angeles, California
Fraud reported: 11/14/2018 $5,106.45.
Fraud Dates: 11/6, 11/7, 11/13
Fraud Continued: 11/14, 11/19, 11/20
Fraud paid: December 14 (posted Dec 16) $5106.45, $3,780.02, $4,600.00= $13,486.47

Harrell contacted me on Tuesday, December 11, 2018. Below is part of his email to me.

I am writing to you after reading all of your posts on this matter and im finding some hope. I was recently awarded disability and was to finally receive my backpay of which was approx 20k. As they sent me the new card on Nov 3rd, they also must have sent another card elsewhere and continued to send me new cards to me that were already voided as the fraudster managed to have one sent to them to an "updated" address. I have been hospitalized over the matter due to anxiety and released hoping it would be resolved but i see that they are denying my disputes. I've since asked social security to start sending my monthly payments to my Wachovia account of which i did not know that was even an option as it was suggested by social security that i use Direct Express. I will probably be following up with a phone call to you now. Im out of Los Angeles.
Any reply or suggestion ill take as ive been in shambles and live in my Car. Was hoping to move into an apt with that money.

Harrell's caregiver knew Harrell had received a lot of money from Social Security. Harrell sent me a copy of his transactions and I outlined the fraudulent transactions. There were dozens of ATM withdrawals, motel room costs, a television, and fast food. Harrell sent the spreadsheet I created for him to Conduent and told them I was involved.
Conduent had denied his fraud claim. Harrell received all his money within five days of contacting me.
I was pleased.

Harrell offered to pay me. Harrell was the only person of the more than one hundred person I assisted to offer to pay me. I was surprised but took nothing.

Wednesday, November 12, 2018

Subject: Re: card working?
From: Larry Fennewald
Date: Wed, December 12, 2018, 2:48 pm
To: jbsimms@erikpublishing.com
I've drained my card below $20. My wife came home last night, woke up to her dying this morning. She's in ICU now. I'm all out of answers right now.

I had researched debit cards offered by other banks and found that the debit card offered by the Bank of Montreal offered instant transaction notification. Comerica Bank did not offer any notifications for the Direct Express cardholders, but proprietary customers of Comerica Bank were offered a three-tier level of fraud protection.
I sent Jackie what I had found.

Thursday, December 13, 2018

1132am Hope called me: She called Alisha at Conduent. Someone called Conduent and changed physical address and email and phone number.

From: jbsimms
Date: Thu, Dec 13, 2018 1:39 pm
To: Sarah Lizama (SSA OIG)
Cc: "Jackie "
Dear Ms. Lizama,

With regard to my victimization via Social Security, I received a telephone call from the Madera County Sheriff's Department concerning the false address given to a Social Security worker on June 19, 2018. The investigator stated that an investigator interviewed the occupant of the false address, had no further leads, and closed the case.

I still need to know HOW my address was changed.

Secondly, you are aware that I receive calls almost daily from persons whose benefits have been compromised through Comerica Bank and Conduent call center employees. Many of the recipients are elderly and disabled, and it is quite an adventure for them to go to a Social Security office and present themselves and the dilemma. What can be done to assist these persons to escape from Direct Express and have their monies deposited in a bank or credit union via telephone? I understand confirmation is an issue, but if the bank account can be verified, and a banker can be contacted along with the recipient, it seems possible. I am simply planting a seed to assist persons from being victimized again by Direct Express, Conduent, and Comerica Bank.

If you could research the matter, and find a solution, you would save many people. I just got off the phone with a victim in NM who is 60 miles from a Social Security office.

Sincerely,
Jim Simms

The Social Security Administration was just as negligent as any office with regard to being duped by fraudsters. The issue I had with Social Security was they were ignoring my request for information concerning who and how this happened.

Saturday, December 15, 2018

This is the guy at Conduent who looked at my LinkedIn profile in March 2018:

Mitch Raymond- LinkedIn
03-08 Citigroup/customer service, Home Depot)

Sunday, December 16, 2018

Harrell emailed me; he got his money back. I called Jackie. I was relieved and excited.
Harrell got approximately $14,000.

Below is an email from Marteshia McPhail on behalf of her father:
dora jacobs
Sun, Dec 16, 2018, 2:17 PM
to advocacy, me
Hello,
I am checking the status of a investigation for my father, Harold McPhail. Since September his claim was in a fair hearing status, for 30,000 being fraudulent taken from his account. As of today, nothing has been return to his account.
Harold McPhail is the only authorized user on his account and has filed a police report and made a statement that he did not request or received any money from these transactions.
He would like his money returned immediately.
What is preventing this from happening? Why is this process taking so long?
Respond by email
Mardeemack

Comerica Bank, Green Dot, and OIG Treasury were all involved in this coverup. There would be more done for the McPhail family. I would be contacting law enforcement and OIG Treasury to find out why Mr. McPhail was being ignored.

Monday, December 17, 2018

From: jbsimms
Date: Mon, Dec 17, 2018, 12:55 pm
To: Nora Arpin (Comerica Bank) "Wendy Bridges" <wwbridges@comerica.com>, "Advocacy US"
<advocacy@usdirectexpress.com>
Cc: Jackie, Kate Berry (American Banker), Sonja Scott (OIG Treasury) Sarah Lizama (SSA OIG),
This copy of an email I just received is being forwarded directly to the persons responsible for victimizing a
person receiving cancer treatment. I know that Ms. Arpin has testified and submitted narratives (Barnett vs.
American Bank) and she knows how she will be perceived when the heirs of Mr. Shelly describe how Conduent
and Comerica ignored him, if Mr. Shelly fails to survive this bout.
Mr. Shelly simply asked for a copy of the investigation. My assertions that the Conduent call center workers
conduct no investigations have been validated.
The implications here are too much to ignore.
If Comerica and Conduent think they can navigate their way around liability in a courtroom, you will be
stepping into my arena. You have been given constructive notice and you have ignored Mr. Shelly and others.
Your liability has exceeded your professional position.
Do you see the email address for Mr. Shelley above? I respectfully suggest you have the Conduent persons
responsible for denying his claim to email him a copy of the investigation of his denial. If you have any
questions or would like an explanation, have one of your compliance officers call me at (803) 309-6850. Most
bank attorneys have never set foot in a courtroom and have never litigated. I will be glad to discuss banking
regulations, and civil, and criminal liability with any of them.
Jim Simms

Subject: Re: update
From: Brian Shelly <bScottshelly47@gmail.com>
Date: Mon, December 17, 2018, 11:31 am
To: jbsimms
Hello Jim,
I'm in agony due to cancer treatment. My request for a refund was denied, so I asked for a copy of the discovery
that Direct Express used to conclude that I was rightfully denied due to their investigation results. I received the
info; it was just copies of my complaint. No explanation, I called and was given the run-around don't have
anyone helping me. It's hard for me to do much of anything in my condition.
Thank You,
Brian Shelly

From: jbsimms
Date: Mon, Dec 17, 2018, 4:17 pm
To: "Sonja Scott" Sonja Scott (OIG Treasury)
Cc: Jackie, Kate Berry (American Banker)
I cannot believe what I am reading. I was doing some research on another military payment matter (DFAS)
which appears to be funded through the DOD.
While I was cruising through this GoDirect program, and Direct Express. Before we get done dismantling the
Comerica contract as a Fiscal Agent, you might tell your web designers to change the language on these two
links. It looks like Treasury has endorsed and recommends Direct Express.
I know our "interview" was postponed due to me being interviewed by a television station in Sacramento, but
the emails you received from me give you a pretty good idea of what I would tell you.
I hope your "investigators" don't try to "blow smoke" and patronize Fiscal Services. I might not be a Rhodes
Scholar, but I know the odor of rat.
While your investigators will be shielded by "we cannot disclose" umbrella, it would be nice to have a bit of
interaction. We just might be able to connect a dot or two that the investigators cannot or will not acknowledge.
The fact that Fiscal Services hid the fact that Comerica contracted out the management of the accounts should
be reason enough to prove they violated their contract or misrepresented their bid information.
After seeing the 7 other Fiscal Agents, it would be no leap to jerk the contract from Comerica and hand it off to
one of the other banks.

I am certain our views of Comerica and its oversight will be viewed before a Senate sub-committee before this is over.

Victim 44 Shirita-Ohio

An email was received from Shirita.

Victim was told by Conduent that her case was closed, and she cannot talk to a manager.

Victim did not know her card was missing; last saw card was Thanksgiving.

She Tt cop in Bardstown, OH. Card was used 3 times in a Walmart in Boardman, OH.

$580.00 taken out 11/30/18.

Money taken from Walmart, 1300 Doral Drive, Boardman, OH 44514

Williams called DE- was adv card was used for 3 transactions:

11/30/18 at 0056 $177.54

11/30/18 at 0058 $101.00 with cash back

11/30/18 at 0100 $101.00 with cash back Total $580.00.

12/17 Charisse W at Conduent called today; denied claim. advised Ms. Williams how to proceed.

12/18 rec'd copy of police report 3 pages. Sent email on behalf of Williams.

12/20 Claim was reopened.

1/15/19 Sent email. Asked for update.

Lisa Tower (from Corpus Christi, TX) emailed me. She got her money.

Tuesday, December 18, 2018

Putting Conduent on notice

From: jbsimms
Date: Tue, Dec 18, 2018, 11:22 am
To: "Advocacy US" <advocacy@usdirectexpress.com>, "Wendy Bridges" <wwbridges@comerica.com>
Cc: Jackie, "Lisa Mena"
Lisa,
I am forwarding this to Advocacy, and these are the people who are supposed to be sending you a copy of the investigation. There is a person in Advocacy who uses the name "Alisha" and is supposed to be a supervisor. Alisha works for Conduent and has no understanding of Regulation E. She has been told many times that you are entitled to a copy of the investigation which denied you your claim.
This will be a public relations nightmare for Comerica and is. Alisha has admitted to reopening cases only because Jackie Densmore and I became involved.
Aisha, I present to you the law, that you are to give Lisa Mena a copy of the investigation which led to the determination of the denial of her claim.
Sincerely,
J.B. Simms

The feeling of being ignored

Subject: Re: Being ignored
From: Lisa Mena
Date: Tue, December 18, 2018, 5:48 am
To: jbsimms
I know I have you and Jackie are the only keeping me sane and I know I have you and Jackie are the only ones keeping me sane and levelheaded and treated me as an actual victim like I am instead of a crook like direct express representatives. I feel thankful for the whole direction and support you have so easily given to me and continue to show me still to this day. Thank you and I will email them and contact them once again and request my investigative report of my dispute in detail to see how my decision was ultimately denied. Sad but these people treat the consumers of their product like they are not important or that anything we may ask is disregarded by them completely. They deserve to be given repercussions as to why they do not give me my report upon request. I am the consumer, not the crook.
Thanks, Jim & Jackie
Lisa A. Mena

Social Security Administration lies about "ongoing audits"

Subject: Direct Express Fraud
From: "Bayer, Walter Office of the Inspector General" <Walter.Bayer@ssa.gov>
Date: Tue, Dec 18, 2018, 2:27 pm
To: "jbsimms@erikpublishing.com" jbsimms

Mr. Simms,

As you can probably tell via our published audits and we take fraud against SSA's programs seriously and have frustrated many fraud schemes through our work. We also warn the public about potential scams. For instance, the latest scheme to appear (and grow) relates to impersonation scams, which have led to numerous alerts from our office.

We also share information about our ongoing and planned audits on our website).

Moreover, we work with Treasury OIG and other partners to audit and investigate potential abuse as it relates to SSA's programs. That said, we cannot discuss any ongoing or planned investigations in the same way we discuss our audits.

If you have particular allegations or information that you would like to share with us regarding potential fraud, waste, and/or abuse that can help us with this work, we welcome such information. And we will continue to share as much of our results as we can publicly via our audit reports and investigation summaries.

You can email me or reach me at (202) 358-6319 if you have any questions.

Thanks,

Walt Bayer

SSA-OIG Congressional Liaison

What a waste of time. The Social Security Administration, along with their Office of Inspector General (where Bayer worked) did nothing to help victims and continued to promote the corrupt Direct Express program.

Thursday, December 20, 2018

Another fraud case reopened at Conduent

540am

Shirita Williams called to tell me that Alisha (the person in charge of Conduent/Direct Express Customer Advocacy) called her; Conduent is going to reopen the case.

Shirita also called Wendy Bridges of Comerica and got her secretary; the secretary referred Shirita to Susan Schmidt.

This was great news and funny at the same time: we got the case "reopened "at Conduent Fraud Unit, then Wendy Bridges' secretary referred Alisha to Susan Schmidt. Nora Arpin referred everyone to Wendy Bridges and now Wendy is referring people back to Detroit and Susan Schmidt.

I called Franklin Lemond and advised him that Jackie and I are moving forward. We have victims who contact us every day.

Friday, December 21, 2018

Posted from VA website.

VA Urges Veterans to Sign Up for Direct Deposits

On March 1, 2013, VA will stop issuing paper checks. People who do not have electronic payments for their federal benefits by that time will receive their funds via a pre-paid debit card. Called the Direct Express card, it is issued by Comerica Bank as the financial agent of the U.S. Treasury.

This is what we had to tolerate. The VA was in the pocket of Conduent and Comerica. Our next target would be the VA. Seeing the VA endorse the Direct Express program was shocking, but the VA did not know about the victimization of the veterans. It would be my job to bring this to their attention.

Victim Number 45-Teresa-: FL
Fraud noticed: 12/9/2018

Fraud reported: 12/9/2018
Fraud credited: 12/26/2018
12/21/81 1207pm she called the office- she sent email to Calvin
She called call center with pending transaction on 12/9
Four transactions, total of $161.74 International transactions
Calvin was sent copy of December statement, showed fraud
MeMe Live, Taipei, Twn (Taiwan) China
Teresa tt a man, fraud investigator, evidently from Conduent. He had received many transactions from this
fraud between 12/1 and 12/10.

Children have no Christmas because of Comerica Bank and Conduent

From: Terasa Fogarty
Date: Fri, Dec 21, 2018, 11:37 am
To: jbsimms
Hi Mr. Jim, this is Terasa and I been talking to you on face book. I am really upset that it is Christmas, and my small grandkids don't understand adult stuff. But they do understand going to gramma and getting a Christmas gift...but this year my account had fraudulent charges that took all my money. Little lone not able to pay Bill's that will add more charges like late fees. I am on disability and have no means of other income. All this has me stressed out not knowing where to turn...The fraud department guy said MeMe Live charges is clearly fraud that he has had several calls between Dec 1 and dec 10th coast to coast about the MeMe live transaction on several people's Disability accounts. He said due to the several complaints they know its fraud, but they just don't know what it is connected to. He said wherever yours and everyone else card was used to make a purchase their system must have been hacked they just have to figure out what place. He said don't worry we know it's fraud. He said my paperwork has been scanned in and it's just a matter of time. He said to keep checking my account. He told me all this yesterday. I have called everyone you listed on Facebook and emailed them as well...I am really sad I am gonna have to tell my grandmother and kids I can't get them anything.

Subject: Re: Terasa about Direct Express fraud transaction
From: Terasa Fogarty
Date: Fri, December 21, 2018, 12:40 pm
To: jbsimms
I just called the fraud center and asked for a copy of the investigation, and she told me I had to wait for them to investigate and said thank you for calling and hung up on me.

From: jbsimms
Date: Fri, Dec 21, 2018, 1:40 pm
To: Richard Delmar (OIG Treasury)
Cc: "Jackie "
Mr. Delmar,
I just got off the phone with Terasa Fogarty. She mentioned that you tt her. Thank you for being receptive to her. I directed her to call you moments ago.
In layman's terms, here is an example of how stupid and untrained the Conduent employees are, and the indifference of Comerica Bank.
The charges, 4@$161.74, and other charges were to a MeMe.com account as an international transaction: TAIPEI, TWN. You and I both know this was from the capital city of Taiwan, Taipei.
Ms. Fogarty is in Alachua County, Florida. There is no pattern of her SSI payments using the MEME web account. This is evidently fraud. The Conduent person in "fraud" hung up on her.
Ms. Fogarty was to get immediate credit, no investigation was necessary for her to be without her money for 10 days. She has grandchildren. You can identify with a person losing a grandmother or abusing your mother or grandmother.
You do whatever you can do. She will be grateful, and I will be encouraged that someone will protect these mothers.
Jim Simms

We gave children the Christmas they deserved; funds were returned

Subject: Direct Express fraud charges
From: Terasa Fogarty
Date: Fri, Dec 21, 2018, 2:58 pm
To: jbsimms
Please email me back soon. I called Wendy Bridge who you told me to call and they said she was not over the direct Express that Sue Schmidt was. So I talked to her and told her everyone I have called and told them I was gonna get a lawyer and need a copy of my investigation and all extra charges I have related to this they will be held liable for...She told me she was gonna call Calvin and make a few other calls and call me back 25 minutes later Calvin called and said the money was put back into my account...Question do I need to go take it all out?

This was fast; we got the money back within a few hours. None of this would have happened if we did not push these people to do their jobs and adhere to the law.

Sunday, December 23, 2018

DeGrandis called- he got a call from Brandon (from Conduent) on Thursday. Brandon denied the fraud claim.

Tuesday, December 25, 2018

Christmas was saved again.

An email was received on Christmas morning. Below is the story.

Victim 46 Brittany-New Jersey
Fraud noticed: 12/10/2018 Fraud reported: 12/10/2018, $780.00.
Fraud amount credited: 12/25/2018.

Subject: Worst Christmas ever
From: Brittany Curry
Date: Tue, December 25, 2018, 7:38 am
To: jbsimms
Hello Mr. Simms,
Merry Christmas to you. I am not so happy. I filed a dispute with direct express the moment that I detected my card had been drained of my monthly benefits. I initiated the claim on 12/10 and began to do my research. I did everything by the book and thought for sure that according to their practice I'd receive my provisional credit on 12/24. I have Direct express over 1000 times along the way informing them that I need my credit in time for my son who believes in Santa and more importantly food. They assured me that since my paperwork was received on time that I should receive the credit but not guaranteed. I've been losing sleep night after night up until yesterday 12/24 when I called and received some great news that My credit was approved and deposited in my account. I informed the rep that I did not see this reflected in my account and he assured me that "they" have until the end of the business day to deposit the $780 and to rest assured that I will not have to ruin my son's Childhood because Santa is coming also for me to check my balance throughout the course of the day. Shortly before the end of the business day and maybe 100 times more in between I checked my balance and called the center and had only seen -11.00 still there in my account without increase. I immediately informed CSR of the issue, and no one can quite understand what happened to the provisional credit that is in fact documented in their system as a deposit. Please help I am running out of lies to tell my son about why we have not returned home so that he can see what Santa got.
Brittany

I sent Conduent one of my standard emails regarding violating Regulation E and the lives they were ruining.

Below is the follow-up email from Brittany:
12/28/18
Hello,
Yes, I received the deposit shortly after Christmas day. I am very thankful for your help.

Each time I received an email like this it made me happy for the victim and angry at Comerica Bank, Conduent, Bureau of Fiscal Service, OIG Treasury, Social Security, and all the criminals involved in this case.

Wednesday, December 26, 2018

Conduent is identified and lied about conducting an investigation

Subject: The big ass blink
From: jbsimms
Date: Wed, Dec 26, 2018, 5:54 pm
To: Jackie, Kate Berry (American Banker)
they blinked
they blinked
they blinked
Harrell Banoy kept asking for a copy of an "investigation" just like everyone else.
They ignored everyone else.
Harrell got a voice message from "Veronica" at (210) 334-6673 telling him that a copy of his investigation was being completed (yeah, right) and he should get it in 3 days or so.
Somewhere in the message, or the communication, Harold confirmed the person works for Conduent.
This is the opening of Pandora's other box. Now we can flood them with direct requests for reports to which the cardholders are entitled. We get one, and it might be crap, but this will be the beginning of another target to hit.
Harrell could not contact me except by text; he was en route to an AA meeting. Oh, Lord.
I found at least $15,000 of fraud in his case, and he got $13,800 back after I told him what to do.
I would never tell Jackie "What to do" because I like my nose right where it is.
Just had to share. They blinked.
Jim

An email was received from Cynthia Clark.
Conduent agreed to give her the credit for the fraud. This was good. Another satisfied customer.

Thursday, December 27, 2018

Today I worked on the case synopsis for Franklin Lemond. I had to sell the case to him, show him what had been happening, and brief him on the victims as well as the behavior of Comerica Bank, Conduent, and the federal officials who allowed this to happen.

Harrell Banoy was given this number by a Conduent employee named Veronica:
(210) 334-6673 on 12/26/18.
Research revealed this number is assigned to:
ACS State and Local Solutions
485 Quentin Roosevelt Road, Suite 595, Building 171, San Antonio, TX 78226
ACS was the original name of the company which was mentioned by Comerica Bank in the original FAA of 2018.

Subject: Re: card working?
From: Larry Fennewald
Date: Thu, December 27, 2018, 5:23 pm
To: jbsimms
I just wanted to tell you that I'm sorry I haven't got much done yet. My wife passed away Dec 24th. This is how she looked in 1971.

Larry attached a photo. His wife was lovely. My heart was broken.

Friday, December 28, 2018

I counted my victim list and had 45 victims on my list.
I even got calls and emails from victims on Christmas Day. These people were hurting.

106

Saturday, December 29, 2018

From: Terasa Fogarty
Date: Sat, Dec 29, 2018, 9:07 am
To: jbsimms@erikpublishing.com

Dec 9th, 2018, pending MeMe Live Charges.
Called direct Express on the card told to call back after the transactions cleared called back on Dec 10, 2018, and they canceled my card and started a fraud transaction dispute.
Dec 15th Nothing from Direct Express So I email a letter to the Card advocacy email Attn to Calvin. Told him I want my money back because they were fraudulent transactions, at the same time I did a complaint with consumer finance protection and called Calvin every 20 mins.
Dec 17th Spoke with Calvin 512 250 7630 at 1:55 pm after calling 8 times back-to-back. He then emails the fraud questionnaire and told me to fill it out and fax it back to 512 298 3461. I filled out the paperwork and fax it back the next day. I then emailed Calvin at advocacy@usdirectexpress.com. with a picture showing proof, it was faxed and had him email me to verify he got the fax...Meanwhile, I wrote another letter explaining the fraud and Regulation E and want my money back starting 10 days after the 1st call to the call center. On Dec 10th. I mailed it with my signature to the Direct Express payment processing center.
Customer Account service
P.O Box 245998
San Antonio, TX 78224-5998
I did that just so I could have proof I did contact them cause I was told you can't trust the advocacy center that you called them.
NOW Dec 17th getting papers faxed Dec 18,
Received an Email from Calvin on Dec 18th saying he received my fax.
Got a call back from Sarah at 410 965 1234
Dec 19 still No Money called fraud unit Number 888 545 5577 the lady told me when they process everything I would receive something in the mail that they have 45 days and she hung up on me
Dec 21 Called Sonja Scott at 202 927 5874 @ 3:49 PM no answer.
Called Wendy Bridges @ 214 462 4443 and was told that Wendy did not handle Direct Express but she would transfer me to the one that does. She gave me her name and number.
Sue Schmitt 313 222 7934 I spoke with her, and she got my information and told me she would check everything out and get back to me.4:00 pm
Dec 21, @4:44 pm Calvin called back and said the money was credited back to my account and I would receive a letter from them with all the information about the credit to my account.
Dec 21 @ 5:29 pm Sue Schmitt called me back and asked me if Calvin had called me back and also told me the account was credited...
SO It was a lot of calls and time and the process was stressful but finally it was lit back...This is the step I took for everything...some people may want to bypass writing the letter to the payment center but I advise you to do it for your protection to show you notified them and a receipt by doing signature on delivery.
Thanks for all you did to help me through this.

Teresa was just like all victims; frustrated and ignored. Comerica Bank and Conduent ignored victims, violated banking laws, and thought no one would make them accountable.

Comerica Bank and Conduent were ignoring victims: that was s their first mistake. I was not going anywhere, and with Jackie beside me, we would turn their world upside down.

Receive
your payment,
your way.

Convert your paper check
to an electronic payment
with direct deposit or a
Direct Express® card.

Chapter Six
Victims, A Lawyer, and the Government Coverup Exposed
2019: A new year and a new challenge

My days started early. I had to check my emails first thing. The battle with Delmar, Scott, Lizama, Bayer, Arpin, and Schmidt just drained the strength from me. The list of victims increased all the time. The stories change, but the pain is the same. No victim is getting any response regarding fraud on their Direct Express card accounts unless I contacted Comerica or Conduent, show the victims whom to call, or sometimes contact Sonja Scott and Delmar myself.

The next victim, Jennifer, a veteran, had a shocking story.

Wednesday, January 2, 2019

Jennifer Kreeger lost $1,300 of SSA benefits paid. Unauthorized ATMs withdrawals in Georgia.
12/31/18 Jennifer received a postcard mailed by Conduent on 12/27/18 stating an address change had been made to her account on 12/6/18.
Conduent waited 21 days to mail the notice of address change.
It was time for me to send out one of my emails.

From: *jbsimms*
Date: *Wed, Jan 02, 2019, 5:45 pm*
To: *Jackie Kate Berry (American Banker), Franklin Lemond (Plaintiff's Attorney), "Advocacy US" <advocacy@usdirectexpress.com>*
Cc: *Wendy Bridges (Comerica Bank), Nora Arpin (Comerica Bank), Richard Delmar (Treasury OIG), Sarah Lizama (SSA OIG), Sonja Scott (OIG Treasury), Michael Clements (US Gen Acct Office) Michael Jackman (Aide to Rep Keating), j4a958@cloud.com, Abby Webber (Aide to Sen Eliz Warren)*
I received communication from an Army veteran, Jennifer Kreeger, was victimized by a fraudster and now by Comerica Bank, Conduent, and Fiscal Services.
Let me begin by telling you that after talking to Ms. Kreeger, I was so enraged that if this had happened to a family member of mine, this would be a lead story on Fox, CNN, and Drudge.
Here is what I understand:
Ms. Kreeger receives approximately $1,113 per month from a service-related injury. This payment is from the VA is sent through Direct Express.
On December 30, 2018, Ms. Kreeger checked her balance, hoping her benefits would be deposited early because this was a holiday weekend. She saw a charge on her account, for an expedited item (it was a Debit Express card). Ms. Kreeger did not understand the charge. (See the $13.50 charge on the attachment).
On the following day, December 31, 2018, Ms. Kreeger checked her account again. She noticed an ATM withdrawal from an ATM located at 154 South Main Street ($1003.00) and Village Square Shopping Center ($123.00). These withdrawals were not made by Ms. Kreeger.
Ms. Kreeger called Direct Express (she did not know that "Direct Express" actually does not exist and that her call was being received by a Conduent call center persons). Ms. Kreeger cancelled the card and is having a new card sent to her current and correct address. She had not moved.
Ms. Kreeger went to get her mail after the call to Direct Express. There she found a post card (attached) upon which was printed that her address was changed 25 days earlier on December 6, 2018. By examining the face of the post card, it appears the post card was mailed on December 27, 2018, 21 days after the request for the change of address (referencing the date of the expedited fee for mailing a card).
Why did it take 21 days to mail the post card? It does not take 21 days to generate a post card.
Email and telephone information is on the account for Ms. Kreeger is known to Conduent. No one at Conduent contacted Ms. Kreeger.
If the notice of change of address was done efficiently, Ms. Kreeger would not have lost her money.
When Ms. Kreeger contacted me via telephone today, she was en route to filing a police report of the fraud. A copy of the report, being completed by a police officer, will be available soon.
Ms. Kreeger was directed by me to call Nora Arpin (Comerica), Susan Schmidt (Comerica) Wendy Bridges (Comerica) and Richard Delmar (Treas OIG). No answers were received from the Comerica Bank officers (this

was during office hours) and the call to Delmar resulted in hearing that Delmar is on furlough. We will determine who is sitting in his chair.

Ms. Kreeger then was directed to get someone on the phone at the Customer Advocacy office for Conduent/Direct Express. She talked to Brandon, who gave her erroneous information with respect that she was not getting her complete provisional credit until after she returned a completed form. He also stated the "investigation" would not begin until he received the completed packet of info, which he agreed to email to her. Brandon [at Customer Advocacy of Conduent] I hope your supervisor gives you a copy of this email. I suggest you have someone download a copy of 15USC1693 and read this to you very slowly. The investigation begins upon receiving notice of the fraud, which was on December 31, 2018. Complete provisional credit must be given if the "investigation" takes more than ten (10) days. The burden of proof is on Comerica Bank (Conduent is not a bank) to prove the transaction was fraudulent. The credit can be immediately give when fraud is obvious.

Ms. Kreeger researched the address of the fraud, and determined the crime was committed in Jonesboro, GA. This is not the first fraudulent transaction to be tied to Jonesboro, GA, but no one at Comerica or Conduent have any employees who can connect dots and see the pattern. Others of us see the pattern, and it is easy to see an in-house connection.

Pursuant to another paragraph of Reg E, any person having identifying information of a victim of fraud can report the fraud on an account. Since Ms. Kreeger called Conduent on 12/31/18, that was "notice." I suggest the Conduent Advocacy office attach this email to Ms. Kreeger's account.

Ms. Kreeger received no notice from Comerica Bank that her address had been changed. Most banks have notification alerts for such transactions and account modification. Comerica Bank has no security parameters. I have studied the security parameters for other debit cards and online banks.

Ms. Kreeger served her country. You people who have allowed this to happen to her will be held accountable, and I look forward to seeing each of you before a senate subcommittee. You will be in the hearing room when I address the committee before you speak.

J.B. Simms

The email would get the attention of someone.

Jackie found this article. It was published on May 11, 2018, and was applicable to Jennifer Kreegar as a veteran and the Veterans Administration endorsement of the Direct Express program. The VA was endorsing the Direct Express program and appeared to be unaware of the harm being experienced by veterans using this card. This was going be a huge battle with the VA.

How could the VA and SSA endorse a program that is full of corruption?

New Direct Express Debit Mastercard for VA payments

Easier, safer, faster

VAntage Point Contributor
Friday, May 11, 2018 10:00 am
Does anyone use paper checks anymore? Not many do, because they are costly, easy to misplace, and too much paper is bad for the environment.

VA is excited to introduce the Direct Express Debit Mastercard card for Beneficiary Travel and Compensated Work Therapy payments. This prepaid debit card is available to Veterans who don't have bank accounts or simply prefer to get their payments on a debit card.

Purchases can easily be made anywhere Debit Mastercard is accepted. You can get cash at retail locations, banks, credit unions, and ATMs throughout the world.

Providing Veterans easier, faster and safer access to their money is our top priority. Over 26,000 Veterans are receiving their Beneficiary Travel payments on debit cards. Electronic processing costs are considerably less than paper checks which also helps fund more services to Veterans.

You may be wondering if you can have direct deposit to your bank account and a debit card. You need to choose one or the other. But, either way you go, you will receive your money a lot faster and it's very safe and secure. We're trying hard to find new ways to serve you better. It's our way of honoring your service and empowering your health.

Visit the agent cashier at your local VA facility to sign up. Have questions about direct deposit or the Direct Express card? Customer service agents are available to help you. Call toll free 877-597-3055 Monday – Friday, 8 a.m. to 8 p.m. ET or visit www.usdirectexpress.com.

Thursday, January 3, 2019

I heard that the VA was having problems with the VA Secretary and some other persons in Washington. Changes were on the way, but that would not help us immediately. The exposure of the failure would sink one career and maybe save another.

Michael Clements at the General Accounting Office (GAO) was always receptive and helpful, but his hands were tied because members of Congress would not take the time to validate another GAO investigation of BFS.

Subject: RE: Jennifer Kreeger, a veteran, and violation of Reg E by
Comerica, Notice of Fraud
From: Michael Clements (Gen Acct Offc)
Date: Thu, January 03, 2019, 12:11 pm
To: "jbsimms
Depending on how Comerica is organized and its charter, it could be regulated by several different agencies. When I searched, I saw OCC and the Federal Reserve (which has authority over the holding company). FDIC has backup authority for banks with FDIC insurance, and also primary authority for banks not regulated by OCC or the Fed. Hope this helps.

Following this email, my reply is below.

On Jan 3, 2019, at 3:12 PM, jbsimms wrote:
I am having a hard time getting direct email or phone numbers for Margarita Devlin or Beth Murphy who is the Director of Compensation Service for Veterans Health Admin. Both persons need to know that the Go Direct card issued for veteran benefits, run by Comerica and Conduent, has no security parameters whatsoever. The frustrating thing is these people are so insulated.

This is where I started looking at LinkedIn for information regarding VA employees.

Stephanie Mardon- VA Assoc Chief Financial Officer

It looked like the VA was not going to cooperate. I would change that.

Victim Number 48: Dan- Alabama

Dan called me. His monies had been missing on regular basis.

After Dan had experienced the flu, he emailed me on Feb 2, 2019:

Just over one year ago, at&t was supposed to do an installation of Wi-Fi at a secure, high speed for a better price. The local rep could not get my direct express card to go through. he called the management office-a woman in the Philippines. She ran my card 5 times without telling me she was making multiple attempts. I asked and ordered her to stop. I did not get the installation and later called my card. $500. was gone! I called every at&t office, and no one but one employee, could explain nor care- no accountability, by them, or d. express! any real debit card.

Saturday, January 5, 2019

I worked on the Jennifer Kreegar case. I crafted more emails and talked to Jennifer. Our plan was to go after Conduent. They waited 21 days to contact her. This was outrageous. Jennifer was a disabled veteran. I was becoming more angry.

Sunday, January 6, 2019

Kreeger got her money from Conduent

Jennifer Kreegar called me - she got her money. It took only three days of us raising hell and sending emails to get her money. I was happy for her.

Little did I know that the calls I made to the VA on January 3 had gotten the attention of others at the VA. I looked at my LinkedIn account and found the following person has viewed my profile:

Paul Lawrence, Undersecretary for Benefits of Vet Affairs
Dr. Paul Lawrence was head of VBA- Veteran Benefits Association. The VA had endorsed this Direct Express program, and I was going to try to get changes made.

Over the next year I sent messages to Paul Lawrence and never once did Paul Lawrence ever contact me or engage me. He had failed at his job and did not want to hear that from me. Paul Lawrence never shied away from a photo opportunity, but he would never respond to me. I knew Lawrence had dropped the ball for the veterans he claimed to support.

Monday, January 7, 2019

Jackie found a great article and sent it to several us via email.

Jackie Lynn Densmore
Jan 7, 2019, 7:55 PM
to Abby, Michael, Sandra, Walter Bayer (SSA OIG), Sonja Scott (OIG Treasury), Franklin Lemond (Plaintiff's Attorney), me
Interesting considering this is dated 2014 and is still going on ????

Treasury Department Ignores Victims: Awards Comerica another 5 Years Contract

http://www.allgov.com/news/where-is-the-money-going/treasury-dept-ignores-fraud-charges-and-awards-comerica-5-more-years-of-providing-benefit-cards-to-elderly-and-disabled-140917?news=854278

Comerica Bank seemingly was on its way out of doing business with the U.S. Department of the Treasury after it was learned that the bank had exposed thousands of elderly and disabled Americans to fraud. But somehow it just got another deal with the agency...for another five years.
The Center for Public Integrity first revealed Comerica's foul-ups last year. An investigation showed thousands of individuals "had their Social Security and other benefits illegally rerouted to criminals' accounts because of weak fraud controls" at Comerica, Daniel Wagner reported.
The center also found that an "aggressive" marketing campaign by Comerica and the Treasury Department resulted in a million Americans being sent "Direct Express" benefit cards—used to distribute Social Security and disability payments—to people who didn't need or request them. This resulted in a financial gain for the bank, given that card fees are much higher than direct deposit into an account, which many of the card recipients already had.
On top of that, it was discovered that the Treasury Department had rewarded Comerica with $32.5 million for work it was supposed to do for free. The improper government payment turned the bank's potential 2013 loss of $24.2 million into an $8.4 million profit.
The findings were enough to prompt Treasury officials to announce that they would bring in another firm to handle the department's "Direct Express" services that Comerica allegedly botched.
And yet, the maligned contractor is still around.
The decision has caught the attention of Treasury's Office of the Inspector General, who now plans to review the steps that led to Comerica getting the five-year contract.
-Noel Brinkerhoff, Danny Biederman
To Learn More:
Treasury Extends Controversial Bankcard Deal with Comerica (by Daniel Wagner, Center for Public Integrity)
Federal Program to Pay Benefits without Checks Hurts Poor, Helps One Bank (by Noel Brinkerhoff, AllGov)

Victim Number 49: Jon Carnley- Alabama
A call was received from Jon Carnley.
I spoke to his caregiver- Leasa: John lost $468.88 at a Walmart in Andalusia, AL. Lost money at an ATM in Arizona (a fraudulent charge).
John was dealing with "Direct Express" Customer Advocacy (Conduent) and a person named Alisha (whose name I was familiar).
John called again; he was told by employee number 724831 at Conduent there was a security breach in the NJ Conduent branch office.
John and Leasa planned to go to Walmart and to the police to make a report.
1:20pm (January 7, 2019) Leasa called to tell me John had made a police report.

The police called Direct Express (Conduent) – The police told John that no investigation took place at Conduent Fraud Unit; all fraud decisions were based upon spending habits.

(This was no excuse for transactions thousands of miles away in Arizona).

Carnley told me, *"Direct Express let someone rob me of $500 in November and $40 in August. They denied my dispute. Money was taken from an atm at a casino. "*

It is believed that John was in a hospital when the money was taken. He had to borrow money from his mother to buy medicine.

On January 8, 2019, John called and said the security people at casino (where the ATM was located) contacted Conduent and Conduent refused to acknowledge the fraud.

I had given John the email address for the Conduent Fraud Unit and Customer Advocacy. Below is and edited version of what he emailed to the Conduent Customer Advocacy of the Direct Express program:

"On January 3 I purchased a money order at the Andalusia, Alabama Walmart for $464.88. On that same day within seconds of me purchasing the money order there was a ATM cash withdrawal of $182.50 off of my card from a Walmart in Arizona. The ATM withdrawal is fraudulent considering I can't be in two places at one time. On January 8th there was a money order purchased at the Andalusia, Alabama Walmart for $464.88. This is a fraudulent charge considering as of the 6th I have been in Pensacola Florida getting prepared to go to MD Anderson in Huston to begin treatment for my cancer. On January 15th I called the number on the back of my card and they transferred me to what they called the level 2 fraud department. I spoke with a gentleman by the name of Jim about the $464.88 fraudulent charge and was given the claim number 1-5114364376. On the 16th I spoke to David with the employee ID number 724831 about the fraudulent ATM withdrawal and was given the claim number 1-5121439872. David informed me that the New Jersey office had been compromised and there had been a breach."

Jon Carnley called Sarah Lizama of Social Security (I gave him the telephone number) at 5pm. She told him she would help.

John sent me an Instant Message at 8:33pm eastern time: "Got some money back. $554. still owed some. Claim denied."

John got some of his money returned to him. I was pleased with that, but it took my direction to make this happen.

Tuesday, January 8, 2019

Emails sent for Carnley as others

From: jbsimms
Date: Tue, Jan 08, 2019, 3:08 pm
To: "Advocacy US" <advocacy@usdirectexpress.com>
Cc: "Advocacy US" <advocacy@usdirectexpress.com>, Nora Arpin (Comerica Bank), Wendy Bridges (Comerica Bank), Jackie Lynn, Sarah Lizama (SSA OIG), Sonja Scott (OIG Treasury), Jon Carnley Walter Bayer (SSA OIG)
Dear Alisha, Brandon, Calvin, James, or whatever names are being used by persons at this Conduent call center,
Jon Carnley had $500 taken from his account at an ATM in a casino on Nov 2, 2018. The casino security camera spotted the thief as a female. Conduent was contacted and refused to cooperate with the casino personnel. This is consistent with Conduent employees, not having the intellect to conduct any investigation into any claim of fraud, thus exposing cardholders to resulting malfeasance on the part of Comerica Bank.
Mr. Carnley called the "fraud unit today (again a Conduent employee) using a Direct Express number. I heard the employee refuse to give Mr. Carnley his provisional credit. She told Mr. Carnley that his case was closed but Mr. Canley was never given a copy of any investigation. Upon researching the account, there was a fraudulent transaction in early August, which was discovered by Mr. Carnley months later. The fraud unit tried to tag these two transactions together. Today, Mr. Carnley was told that the August fraudulent transaction was not available. When he challenged it, this Conduent call center person in the fraud unit then said they will open an investigation into the August ($40) transaction but will not reopen the $500 fraud on November 2, 2018. When Mr. Carnley told the Conduent person that Reg E allowed her ten days to give him provisional credit, she said, "I am glad you are reading the law, but we are not giving you anything until we complete our investigation." That is as close to an exact quote as I can get, because I heard it myself.

A copy of this is being sent to Ms. Lizama of Social Security and Mr. Bayer of SSA OIG. Ms. Lizama is now involved.
I suggest you people at Conduent who have been assigned from washing machine parts to Direct Express bank cardholders begin bringing empty cardboard boxes to work.
J.B. Simms

Wednesday January 9, 2019

From: <advocacy@usdirectexpress.com>
Date: Wed, Jan 9, 2019, 10:33 AM
Subject: RE: Direct Express Inquiry - Jon Carnley
To: jon carnley
Hello Mr. Carnley,
 Your dispute 1-5047868331 was approved and issued a Final Credit of $504.00. A corresponding letter has been sent via regular mail as well.
 Brandon, Advocate, Cardholder Advocacy Group

Carnley called me to tell me he got his money. I had sent a "nasty-gram" to Conduent and the next morning he gets his money back. Pretty good, huh?

Email from Jackie Densmore to Senator Warren's office
Hello,
I am trying to get an update on the release of information that your office received from Comerica, VA and social security dated Oct. 30 2018.
Since I had contacted your office in AUG 2018 a total of 58 victims have come forward with the same story ..,, Their accounts have been drained by fraudsters and Comerica / direct express refuses to help them and return their stolen funds .
Given the extent of fraud that is going on with these prepaid debit cards our hope that your office would make this top priority but have failed to do so .
Instead my thought and all the victims thoughts is that Sen. Warren is using this in her back pocket to gain votes when needed.
I can assure you the more time that passes for these documents to be released will only lose her votes considering this is affecting Veteran affairs disability money , social security disability money and also Eppicard state benefits in multiple states.
We have heard nothing about what Sen. Warren plans to do.
Just recently Ms. Kreeger , a Disabled veteran who served our country had her account drained!
She was receiving Va money , not ssa money also a program run by direct express . I will tell you that the Veterans Affair Administration is outraged that is going on!
So if Sen. Warren claims to care about the veterans I strongly suggest she releases the information to the public, remember not one cardholder has been warned this is happening and ALL agencies have been put on notice!
I thank you and look forwarded to an update on progress and new developments.
Jackie Densmore

Jackie sent me an email:
Statement for the Record
Social Security Payments Go Paperless:
Protecting Seniors from Fraud and Confusion
The Honorable Patrick P. O'Carroll, Jr.
Inspector General, Social Security Administration
June 19, 2013
We have also reviewed the Treasury's Direct Express debit card program. Direct Express is a low-cost program, administered by Comerica Bank, which allows beneficiaries who do not have a bank account to access their Federal benefit payments with a debit card. About 3.2 million beneficiaries are currently enrolled in the Direct Express program.
We found SSA could improve its controls over the processing beneficiary transactions in the Direct Express program. When Comerica initiates and verifies identification for Direct Express enrollments with SSA, the

Agency matches a limited amount of beneficiary information against the Direct Express record to verify and approve the enrollment. SSA should work with the Treasury and Comerica to enhance identity verification for enrollment and incorporate SSA policies into the Direct Express program. For example, Direct Express should not allow multiple beneficiaries to enroll on the same card without SSA's explicit approval; and debit cards should not be sent to foreign addresses if residency is a factor in continuing eligibility for benefits, as in the Supplemental Security Income program.

In the last year, we have also issued audit reports that reviewed controls over direct deposit changes initiated by the Agency's national 800-phone number, in local Social Security offices, and through SSA's online applications. In several instances, we found that controls in place were not fully effective, and authentication methods could be improved.

The above passage was taken from: https://oig.ssa.gov/sites/default/files/testimony/6-19-13%20Direct%20Deposit%20Written%20Testimony%20FINAL.pdf

Fraudsters were contacting both the Direct Express program and SSA and assuming the identity of debit card holders or SSA recipients, or both. Fraudsters would give a new address and have the renewed debit card sent to the new address with minimal investigation conducted to verify the change of address.

My email to Franklin Lemond and copied Jackie:
I have been answering calls, emails, and texts all day. Headache. I have made it worse.
Victim from Alabama contacted me yesterday, and after a marathon of calls and emails, hearing that the fraud case was closed, I was able to convince the Cust Advocacy person (Brandon) to reopen the case, and money was immediately put into the victim's account. The victim had borrowed money from his mother to buy cancer medication. I hope you two understand that a poor person having cancer, living in southern Alabama, was victimized and the bank violated the law in so doing. This is a plaintiff lawyer dream.
I have dozens of cases like this.
The Cust Advocacy person, Brandon, told the victim that "JB Simms is a pain in our neck. Why did you call him?"
I am not the lawyer, but I know 15USC1693 and the FDIC Reg 6500. The law is simple. Once the law is quoted, and I a few personal points are made about the individual case, challenging the ethics and motives, money starts flowing.
Why do you think the McPhail case was escalated? I was on the phone with a board member of the company, Green Dot. Things get done.
My issue is this: just because the victims call me, or Jackie, and the bank is convinced to pay the victim, the victim suffered tortious damages of the illegal loss of the money for any period over ten days, loss of medicine, food, shelter, dignity, and suffered stress, anxiety, fear, depression, suicidal thoughts, shame, condescension, humiliation, and frustration that the bank not only did not follow the law, but flaunted the fact that the victim was unaware to cover the inadequacies of training.
The damages are like ordering off a menu at a hamburger joint: each case has meat and a bun, then add condiments and cheese and some cases are so egregious that they qualify as a "double chili cheeseburger."
I am collecting the money. I am directing the victims how to be repaid asap. If I forwarded these 50+ persons immediately to an attorney, it would not be effective.
My purpose is to get them reimbursed; the attorney will represent them to "make them whole."
As a former PI, my job was to make the attorney into a star. I did that very well.
I want to know the parameters and prerequisites which each victim must meet to be fully represented are considered and addressed.
Bottom line is just because I collected the money, the damages were not compensated. Jackie and I can coordinate all the victims who contact us. Once the cases begin to settle, the spigot will flow.
Jackie has done a spectacular job making her contacts. You know what I did, "convincing" Treasury OIG commission the investigation in February 2018.
Yes, all this can be done because I have done this before.
I simply want an assurance that after a person makes contact, and I put the wheel in motion to get the victim repaid, that Jackie and/or I can send the package to you and represent each victim.
Ultimately, my goal is to have Comerica lose the contract with Fiscal Services. Believe me, they do believe what I tell them, and the discovery from the lawsuits will be the nail in the coffin.
Those are the issues, in a nutshell. Jim

Thursday, January 10, 2019

Clements, Michael E ClementsM@gao.gov
Thu, Jan 10, 2019, 6:47 AM
to me
Mr. Simms.
Below is a link to a report that identifies the payment to Comerica. This is the total payment for the Direct Express Program. Our staff believes Fiscal Service told us that the specific terms of the financial agency agreements are non-public, which would include the fees for each individual account.
Mike
https://www.fiscal.treasury.gov/files/reports-statements/FinancialAgentReportFY2018.pdf

Jackie sent questions to Franklin Lemond about Comerica and the security breaches.

More media people were being contacted and responding. Sandra Chapman was contacted by Jennifer Kreegar. Below is Ms. Chapman's email to me.

Sandra.Chapman@wthr.com
Thu, Jan 10, 2019, 9:17 AM
Hi Jim,
My name is Sandra Chapman...I am a reporter at WTHR TV in Indianapolis.
We are working on a story regarding the fraud of government benefits from the government's contractor Direct Express / Comerica.
I would like to speak with you about complaints you have made. Is there a phone number where you can be reached?
Thank you,
Sandra Chapman, 13 Investigates Reporter

Jennifer Kreegar had gotten the attention of a news reporter. We were hoping more exposure would help us.

From: jbsimms
Date: Thu, Jan 10, 2019, 9:07 pm
To: Abby Webber (Aide to Sen Eliz Warren)
Cc: "Jackie Lynn", Kate Berry (American Banker)
Dear Ms. Webber,
You know that I am intimately aware of the violations, justifications, and rationalizations made by Ralph Babb to Senator Warren. The point is this: If the letter to Treasury and Fiscal Services was sent at originally written, your office allowed Babb to conduct an investigation of his bank. You used assertions made by Mr. Babb as an interpretative resource, and I saw no mention of Regulation E or the fact that Comerica Bank outsourced all customer related matters to untrained call center persons having no knowledge of banking laws.
If you need a part for your washing machine, a Conduent call center person would be the person you call, not for bank fraud matters.
Using assertions made by Ralph Babb of Comerica Bank as "evidence" of anything will detract from the credibility of your office and that of Senator Warren.
This is not political. This is not partisan. This is a blatant abuse by a fiscal agent of US Treasury to protect persons from whom they are being paid to protect.
Sincerely.
J.B. Simms

Senator Warren was putting out inaccurate and incomplete press releases. The edits that I wrote, requested by Warren's office, were being ignored.

Kate Berry published the following article in America Banker magazine:

Warren: Comerica fraud shows need for security fix in prepaid program

By Kate Berry

Published January 10, 2019, 9:43am EST

Sen. Elizabeth Warren, D-Mass., wants the Treasury Department to enhance fraud protection in the Direct Express prepaid program — now a partnership between the Texas-based Comerica Bank and the U.S. government — when the program's contract is rebid in 2020.

In a letter to be sent Thursday to Treasury Secretary Steven Mnuchin, Warren said hundreds of federal benefits recipients were victims of fraud in the program administered by Comerica. Direct Express allows users without bank accounts to access their funds through prepaid cards.

"The fraud detection and reimbursement process in the Direct Express program need to be examined with close scrutiny," Warren wrote in the letter, a draft copy of which was obtained by American Banker.

Sen. Elizabeth Warren, D-Mass.

"The fraud detection and reimbursement process in the Direct Express program need to be examined with close scrutiny," wrote Sen. Elizabeth Warren.

Bloomberg News

American Banker first reported in August that Comerica had shut down its Cardless Benefit Access feature after fraudsters drained accounts belonging to retirees who receive Social Security benefits and veterans who rely on disability payments. The cardless feature had allowed Direct Express users to withdraw their funds if they lost their card or were away from their home state.

Comerica's Direct Express program disperses roughly $3 billion in Social Security and disability payments to 4.5 million Americans who do not have bank accounts but who receive federal benefit payments electronically on prepaid debit cards.

Cardholders have alleged that Direct Express routinely refused to reimburse them after money was stolen from their prepaid debit card accounts. Federal regulations require that consumers be given provisional credit if they file a complaint and have the prepaid card in their possession.

In all, Comerica identified 480 cases of fraud and roughly $460,000 in money stolen from beneficiaries over a one-year period beginning in August 2017, when the Cardless Benefit feature was first introduced, Warren wrote.

Though Comerica has oversight of the Direct Express program through a contract with the Bureau of Fiscal Service, an arm of the Treasury Department, the bank outsources the main call center function to Conduent, a publicly-traded conglomerate in Florham Park, N.J.

Warren's six-page letter also was sent to Commissioner Kim McCoy of the Bureau of Fiscal Service.

The senator wrote that despite Comerica's claims that all the fraud victims have been made whole, the complaints by consumers about how the bank handled their account inquiries should get scrutinized.

"Comerica maintains that all 480 cardholders affected by the fraud schemes have received full reimbursement, but claims from my constituents and victims continue to raise questions," she wrote. "Victims maintain that Direct Express never contacted them about the fraud, there are hundreds of complaints on the Consumer Financial Protection Bureau's Complaint Database and the Better Business Bureau's website alleging unprofessional customer service and difficulties in the fraud reporting and reimbursement process."

In November, the Bureau of Fiscal Service said that it was rebidding the Direct Express contract. The contract was first awarded to Comerica in 2008, and was renewed in 2014 despite some criticism over how the program was being run.

Warren had previously pressed Comerica CEO Ralph W. Babb Jr. in October to respond to complaints from consumers over how the bank handled fraud complaints.

Comerica had claimed that accounts were not compromised through a cybersecurity breach of the bank, but rather that beneficiaries likely had their private identifiable information stolen from third parties, according to briefings Warren received from Comerica and Treasury's OIG.

"Comerica was not the victim of a cybersecurity breach," Warren wrote.

A spokesperson for Comerica was not immediately available for comment.

Comerica created the Cardless Benefit Access feature, originally called "Emergency Cash," to help cardholders who had left their cards behind in the aftermath of Hurricanes Harvey and Maria request and transfer money to a MoneyGram location.

"The systems set up to prevent fraud under the Cardless Benefit Access program were not robust enough to prevent fraud when criminals obtained [private identifiable information] from other sources," Warren wrote. "While no program is entirely fraud-proof, it is possible that a better designed program could, and would in the future, reduce the risks of this type of fraud."

Warren also wrote that officials with the Social Security Administration and Veterans Administration as well as the public were not adequately informed of the fraud. She asked Mnuchin to ensure that officials at the Social Security Administration and the Department of Veterans Affairs are notified promptly of any fraud affecting the program.

Warren also asked Treasury to guarantee that fraud issues "are resolved quickly with no cost of loss of benefits for program beneficiaries."

Warren, who has formed a presidential exploratory committee, has vowed to shine a spotlight on banking issues including data breaches while casting herself as an advocate of the working class.

"The Direct Express program was designed for individuals who don't have bank accounts, and for many of these Americans their federal benefits are their sole source of income that keep a roof over their head, pay for life-saving medications, and put food on the table," Warren wrote.

Kate Berry (Kate Berry covers the Consumer Financial Protection Bureau for American Banker.)

Elizabeth Warren was in the pocket of the bankers. Warren was not going to reveal anything. Transparency was a big issue, so I emailed Michael Clements to address the lack of transparency.

Friday, January 11, 2019

8:00am A conference with Franklin Lemond and Jackie Densmore lasted 45 minutes. Being awake and aware at 8am was normal while I was living on the West coast. We discussed the fact that Regulation E was limiting filing times for lawsuits depending upon the date of the fraud, and I told Mr. Lemond that I would be sending victim narratives to him.

An email was sent to Abby Webber of Senator Warren's office which included the critique of Warren draft. The draft I was sent was watered down and did not address the issues or make Comerica Bank accountable. I was under no illusion that Senator Warren would use my words, but we were hoping Senator Warren would be a bit more honest in her press release.

From: jbsimms
Date: Fri, Jan 11, 2019, 7:30 am
To: Abby Webber (Aide to Sen Eliz Warren)
Cc: "Jackie Lynn", Kate Berry (American Banker)
Dear Ms. Webber,
The thought of the proposed letter which was critiqued yesterday woke me this morning. The time here is 6:06 am.
Those of us who know are learning more "truths" every day know that the "evidence" cited in the "investigation" that Senator Warren is stating was performed was a reprinting, or regurgitation, of justifications and excuses presented by Ralph Babb to Senator Warren. Babb treated Senator Warren with the utmost disrespect by lying to her in his reply, and for Senator Warren to pen a letter to Treasury and Fiscal Services quoting Babb as a reference or source paints Senator Warren with a brush as though she were duped. Remember, I have been in touch with Treasury and Fiscal Services long before Senator Warren graciously agreed to represent her constituent, Ms. Densmore. I was the person who challenged Treasury OIG to commission a new investigation. I was the one who first examined the two Treasury OIG reports and reported the evidence of malfeasance among and between Fiscal Services and Comerica Bank. If my information was not credible, we would not be here discussing this today.
I beg of you to consider not quoting Babb as a credible source with respect to his editorial comments. Quote facts and figures, not the false praising of the accomplishment of Comerica Bank and its concern for Direct Express cardholders. They are the same as Whitey Bulger and FBI agent Connally; they are dirty.
Sincerely,
J.B. Simms

Victim Number 51: Daniel-Georgia
Daniel called – he lost $2,100 on 11/8/2018. He referred me to his wife; he was calling me on his phone in the car.
Daniel's wife (Lizzette) said money been coming out $200-$300 at a time.
I directed Lizzette to call Conduent- she talked to Alisha (manager at Conduent Customer Advocacy) who said she did not know J.B. Simms. (That was quite laughable).

1:42pm call from Lizzette- she talked to Alisha, then me. Alishia did not know about her case. Alisha was to mail statements to Lizzette.

From: jbsimms
Date: Fri, Jan 11, 2019, 3:37 pm
To: "Advocacy US" advocacy@usdirectexpress.com
Cc: Jackie Lynn, Sarah Lizama (SSA OIG), Walter Bayer (SSA OIG), Wendy Bridges (Comerica Bank), "Nora Arpin" ntarpin@comerica.com

Dear Alisha,

Today, you had a telephone conversation with the wife of Daniel McFadden. The lady with whom you spoke is named Lizzette. Her telephone number is (404) 840-3630.

Mr. McFadden called me while he was working and referred me to his wife, Lizzette. Ms. McFadden was telling me that increments of $200-$300 have been missing from their account. Basically, they know how much they are to receive, and the benefit amount is less than the amount shown by Social Security.

It is very interesting that you deny knowing who I am since the persons identifying themselves as Customer Advocates know who I am, have discussed me with other Direct Express card holders, and you have emailed me directly.

I advised the McFadden of the law. I read it to them. You and the rest of the Conduent employees know nothing about the law, notification, mandatory provisional credit, immediate notice, etc. I have had at least 50 people contact me concerning the Customer Advocacy area of Conduent.

I am not alone. There are others in the background who will are assisting me in ending this abuse. The less drama you create, the better. When this ends, Conduent will have no persons handling Direct Express matters, and you will be back to ordering parts for vacuum cleaners under warranty. You and the others should hope to be transferred by Conduent because the exposure of this abuse will not allow you to be employable any other place.

Treat these victims with the respect they deserve. If you are aware that Conduent employees are selling identification information, I suggest you speak directly to the FBI before they come to you. And yes, I have done this work before.

Sincerely,
J.B. Simms

Saturday, January 12, 2019

From: jbsimms
Date: Sat, Jan 12, 2019 10:13 am
To: "Advocacy US" advocacy@usdirectexpress.com
Cc: "Lisa Mena" , Sarah Lizama (SSA OIG), "Jackie Lynn", Sonja Scott (OIG Treasury), Walter Bayer (SSA OIG), "Franklin Lemond"

Dear Advocacy ("Alisha"),

I am forwarding this email to your office on behalf and with the permission of Direct Express cardholder Lisa Mena, as authorized by Regulation E, 15(USC)1693. I reported this fraud upon Ms. Mena's account months ago, and it is evident that you at Conduent, with the acknowledgment of Comerica Bank, have allowed violations of Regulation E to make Ms Mena homeless and humiliated. As stated by Ms. Mena, she has asked for validation of her fraud claim many times, and that validation, in the form of a copy of the investigation (to include all documents used to make the decision for dental), has surfaced or delivered.

Our investigation will reveal there are no persons assigned to Comerica Bank accounts (Direct Express and others) having the intelligence to interpret financial transactions to determine fraud. Your reluctance to produce the documents is further proof of this fact.

I suggest you contact Ms. Mena and send the copy of the investigation to her. Since your behavior has resulted in her transient living condition, I further suggest you send the result of the investigation immediately via email.

Sincerely,
J.B. Simms

Victim Number 52 Joe: Georgia

Below is the email message I received from Joe in Georgia:

Hours after receiving my November 2018 SS deposit into my Direct Express account, I received a low balance alert. I notified DE immediately of the pending fraudulent charges. I was told they could not stop the pending charges. My card was cancelled & I was mailed a new one in about 10 days. Only then was I able to contact them & dispute these charges, which I did; however, I had to wait another 10 days to receive the form by USPS to then submit in 10 business days. I met their ridiculous deadlines by returning the form by next day USPS, signature required. My claim was denied. The letter I received dated 12/15/2018 (received 12/24 2018) stated they had completed a through [thorough] investigation and could not confirm fraud had occurred. I called them 12/24/2018 and expressed my concern, then requested a copy of the documents on which they relied in making this determination.

I will continue with contacting BBB, treasury department, social media, local TV, radio, newspaper, etc. until I receive my $793.78.

I sent Joe the contact numbers for Conduent and briefed him on Reg E. He would use this information to try to get his money returned. It was not unusual for Conduent to deny a claim and ignore the cardholder, but I was having good results making Conduent reopen denied claims.

Monday, January 14, 2019

First thing this morning I received an email from Joe Almon, he sent me on Saturday. He got his money returned this morning. He talked to the fraud unit as I directed him to do, made notes. Merchant made the return $793.78.

I knew who was making the decisions, but the Conduent employees simply would not listen.

The merchant had to return the money while Conduent violated Regulation E.

It became necessary that I send Mr. Lemond the issues with Regulation E as I interpreted the law.

Subject: A layman's theory that will play into you hands, debunking the affinity for persons not repaid
From: jbsimms
Date: Mon, Jan 14, 2019, 6:15 pm
To: Franklin Lemond (Plaintiff's Attorney)
Cc: Jackie Lynn, Kate Berry (American Banker)
Dear Franklin,
I am a bit conversant with Reg E (15USC1693) and the regs created by diff agencies based upon 1693. I first will apologize for appearing to play lawyer, but I feel my theory was not created in a vacuum. While Comerica Bank has allowed violations of Reg E with no oversight until now, specifically in 1693g (Liability of Consumer) and 1693f (Error Resolution), I want to focus on one part which has been given little attention, and validate the work being done by Jackie Densmore, Kate Berry, and a few of the officials at various OIG offices.
After it is established that Comerica (I will use that label to include Conduent and Direct Express) is in violation any or all the following:
1693f(a)
1) not acknowledging the initial call as proof of notification
2) not beginning the investigation immediately upon notification
3) not reporting or mailing the results of the investigation within 10 days
1693f(c)
4) not receiving provisional credit in lieu of written confirmation
5) not concluding within 45 days
6) not providing report of investigation having no error within 3 days of the determination
1693f(d)
7) not providing full and complete investigation, to include all documents used in making the determination, upon request of cardholder,
plus, more that you might find, I feel that each victimized cardholder can be paid a flat fee for damages of each or all violation they endured.
I digressed a bit, but the initial reason for writing you was to give my thoughts on the passage below, having to do with treble damages.
The issue, which I have heard from other attorneys as well is this: "Send me people who have not received their money." I attempted to validate my work to immediately assist these victims during our conference on Friday, but now I have found a section in the code which not only validates the immediate action on behalf of the victim, it prompts Comerica/Direct Express/Conduent to indict themselves in an attempt to save face.
15USC1693f(e) Treble Damages
(e) Treble damages
If in any action under section 1693m 1 of this title, the court finds that-

(1) the financial institution did not provisionally recredit a consumer's account within the ten-day period specified in subsection (c), and the financial institution (A) did not make a good faith investigation of the alleged error, or (B) did not have a reasonable basis for believing that the consumer's account was not in error; or

(2) the financial institution knowingly and willfully concluded that the consumer's account was not in error when such conclusion could not reasonably have been drawn from the evidence available to the financial institution at the time of its investigation,

then the consumer shall be entitled to treble damages determined under section 1693m(a)(1) 1 of this title. The fact that I am able to motivate, cajole, annoy, irritate, or scare the people at Conduent to replace the money, which was fraudulently taken from the cardholders, plays right into an admission of violation of 15USC1693f(e) Treble Damages.

"The financial institution did not provisionally recredit a consumer's account within the ten-day period specified in subsection"

The reason the 50+ people have been assisted has been because they did not receive the provisional credit. If they had, they would not call.

"and the financial institution (A) did not make a good faith investigation of the alleged error"

There is no way Comerica can prove a good faith investigation was performed in any case. I have seen no communication with law enforcement and no contact with any merchant which was initiated by any Conduent worker. The have been asked to communicate with law enforcement, and I have seen no evidence of that. If they responded to law enforcement requests for locations of ATMs where fraud occurred, or communicated with banks/owners of ATMs, fraudsters could be readily identified. Conduent employees have never assisted in identifying a fraudster at an ATM.

"did not have a reasonable basis for believing that the consumer's account was not in error"

If you have collected no data, no reports, conducted no interviews, you cannot have any information from which to draw a conclusion. Actually, 90 percent of the time a Conduent person can see that the transaction in question was fraudulent, as in Wollin (Taiwan) Hernandez (South Africa), and mine which happened to be from Aruba (I called the place myself and convinced them to refund my money).

"the financial institution knowingly and willfully concluded that the consumer's account was not in error when such conclusion could not reasonably have been drawn from the evidence available to the financial institution at the time of its investigation."

The term "knowingly" implies the Conduent employees have the mental capacity and intelligence to interpret evidence, given that any evidence is to be examined. The Conduent people do "willfully" conclude a transaction was not in error but it is not known who actually makes the final call.

The term "could not reasonably have been drawn" is proven by the success I have had in enabling the cardholders to confront the Conduent "Fraud Unit" and many times have immediate reversal of a decision that the transaction(s) in question was not fraud.

The faster I can get a cardholder to make the telephone calls, send the faxes and email, and embolden them to confront Comerica Bank with their violations, the more likely it is that they get paid, and many do.

My point is this: If I can get a cardholder to do what is necessary to get their claim paid, they are happier. The fact that a reversal of the findings proves that the determination of fraud was not "reasonably drawn" and the rationale and evidence given by the cardholder reversed the "un-reasonably drawn" conclusion.

Thus, prima facie of violation of 15USC1693f(e) for Treble Damages. These victims, such as Jennifer Kreegar, Wollin, and Kenneth Tillman, are prime examples of this. I got Tillman and Kreegar their money.

If you look at the McPhail case, it was not until I contacted Green Dot that Conduent began an investigation, which means they violated Reg E as stated above, resulting in treble damages.

The did nothing, and after my involvement, they started trotting out investigative reports, claiming the Green Dot account was in Harold's name. They made the determination of no error based upon no evidence. This is as much work and prep as I have done in many years.
Jim

Franklin Lemond Franklin Lemond (Plaintiff's Attorney)
Mon, Jan 14, 2019, 3:41 PM
to Jackie, me
Thanks for these thoughts. I emailed Jennifer Kreegar agreement earlier today. Haven't heard back from her. Hoping to be on file no later than Friday, as next week I have travel obligations that will make my week hectic.
Franklin

Tuesday, January 15, 2019

Victim Number 50: Amica-Georgia

820am: I received a call from this victim. I sent email an email to confirm the information. Amica Mattox, RE Kevin Moore, McDonough, GA 30253

Monday January 28, 2019- sent text to Amica. I received an email, but no story was attached.

Wednesday January 30, 2019- I sent an email asking for full story on 2/13/2019 texted asking for update and info. I never received the full story.

Victim Number 53-Jody: Washington State

Fraud Detected: 12/2/2018
Fraud Reported: 12/2/201
Fraud credited to account: 1/28/2019.
ATM cash withdrawal 579 Garson Drive, NE, Atlanta, GA 22:57:45 12/0218
Lost $1003. Jody has small child. Referred by Cynthia Clark of Conyers, GA.

Jody called this morning. She lives in Brush Prairie, Washington. On 12/18/18 she saw money missing from her debit card account. She was to have a $750 deposit made, but her balance was $13. She called Social Security; the deposit was made.

Someone took $1003 on 12/2/2018, ATM, all at once as soon as the money hit her card account.

On 12/2/18 she talked to Conduent- they sent fraud packet for Jody to fill out and Jody returned the packet. She called Conduent customer service after returning the fraud packet and found out the address of fraud- 579 Garrison Drive, NE, Atlanta. (Research showed the address is a Wells Fargo Bank. Zip 30324)

1/15/19-I texted Jody at 745am. I advised her to email Conduent. Jody was going to the police since Conduent was not investigating her loss of $1003 and no provisional credit was given. The fraud was obvious; Conduent was simply ignoring her.

Jody received call at 11:36am on 1/28/19 from (512) 249-3599. Said money being put back. The claim was reviewed, and the refund was made. She did not know the name of person who called.

Kenneth Tillman (Denver, CO) called- He was going to have to talk to Mr. Lemond and we had to make his story simple but accurate:

> Went to Walgreens to pay for meds; money gone.
> Kept calling DE, long wait, no answer.
> Was told the referral takes a week to get to Fraud unit (Conduent).
> Went to psychiatrist Rita Roberts, New Start Recovery
> Rita Roberts called Direct Express (Conduent) from her office.
> Kenneth will be available to talk to Franklin Lemond for case.

Wednesday, January 16, 2019

Victim 54 Marisa-FL

Fraud detected: 1/3/2019
Fraud reported: 1/3/2019
Fraud location: H&M Stores and Victoria Secret, Modesto, CA
Credit returned to account: 1/16/2019.

From: Marisa Bloom
Date: Wed, Jan 16, 2019, 3:18 pm
To: jbsimms

IM writing this email to make contact with you. I have been searching for days to find any information and today i came across your information.

My story-

On Jan. 3rd I went to use my debit card at a store, and it was declined. I went in right away and discovered a pending charge and 2 completed charges. that I did not do.

I immediately called and cx the card and reported the fraud on the first 2 charges that went through on Jan. 2. 2019 for the total amount of 255.53 cents two different stores h&m and victoria secret in Modesto California. I was then told paperwork would be sent in 3-5 business days. I would also need to call back as soon as the other charge of 5 bucks went through from a Lathrop wash pro in Lathrop California. I was told today that no paperwork has been received and if not by close of day on Jan. 17th I lose my right to provisional credit. for the

122

first two charges. I have emailed and faxed the numbers and contact you have provided.
This has me very stressed out and left so confused.

1/16/19 8:00pm Eastern-received email from Marisa; she got her money back into account. Marisa was paid within a day after contacting me. This proved that Conduent knew they were allowing fraud.

From:	*jbsimms*
Date:	*Wed, Jan 16, 2019, 9:40 am*
To:	*mcintyre619@msn.com*
Cc:	*"Cynthia Clark" "Jackie Lynn"*

Dear Ms. McIntyre,
I am following up on our conversation from yesterday. Hopefully you will be able to get your narrative and copy of bank statement presented to police and give notice to Direct Express that you want a copy of the investigation. There is no reason a withdrawal in Atlanta should not be fraud with you living in Washington. If you can scan the letter they sent you, the claim denial, send that to me in email along with the police report. When you send the demand for the investigation, copy me on the request. I will also make sure other governmental official are aware of this.
It is good that Cynthia referred you to us. She know we will work to get your money.
Jim

From:	*jbsimms*
Date:	*Wed, Jan 16, 2019, 1:20 p.m.*
To:	*"Advocacy US" <advocacy@usdirectexpress.com>*
Cc:	*Jackie Lynn, "jon carnley"*

Cardholder Jon Carnley reported fraud upon his account yesterday. This is the second incident of fraud within the last few months.
Mr. Carnley has no active debit card, his provisional credit has not been deposited, and no new card has been sent. Mr. Carnley will be en route to another state for medical treatment in 3 days. He has been calling your office and the office of Susan Schmidt of Comerica Bank, and neither offices answer his call.
You can reach Mr. Carnley at . The Customer Advocacy people who work for Conduent, using the names Brandon and Alisha, are not receiving telephone calls.
I will be making note of this for future litigation purposes.
Sincerely, J.B. Simms

From:	*jbsimms*
Date:	*Wed, Jan 16, 2019 2:26 pm*
To:	*"Carol Gilmer", "Advocacy - US DirectExpress" <advocacy@usdirectexpress.com>, "Jackie Lynn"*
Cc:	*Sarah Lizama (SSA OIG), Walter Bayer (SSA OIG), Nora Arpin (Comerica Bank), Wendy Bridges (Comerica Bank)*

Dear Ms. Gilmer and Customer Advocacy (Direct Express/Conduent),
I am in receipt of the copy of the email below. For those who are unaware, Ms. Gilmore's account was fraudulently compromised in June 2017 in the amount of $584 dollars, and the Conduent/Direct Express people never sent an copy of an investigation to Ms. Gilmer. There is no indication of any investigation or rationale for allowing this fraud.
Subsequent to this, Ms. Gilmore attempted to use her new card and the card was declined. Upon reporting this, a call center person advised Ms. Gilmore that there appeared to be suspicious activity on her card so the card was blocked. Direct Express/Conduent employee then stated they attempted to reach Ms. Gilmore by telephone five (5) times and was not able to make contact. This assertion is based in a lie; Ms. Gilmore's telephone number has not changed in many years.
Below you will see confirmation from an Advocacy employee that a copy of the investigation of June 2017 was being sent to Ms. Gilmore. The report of the investigation has not been received since the assertion on Jan 2, 2019. It is now two weeks (not considering the one and a half years since the fraud was reported) and no report has been received.
This is consistent with the constant violations of various sections of Reg E, and the cavalier attitude exhibited by Conduent, at the direction of Comerica Bank. J.B. Simms

From: jbsimms
Date: Wed, Jan 16, 2019 3:01 pm
To: "Advocacy US" <advocacy@usdirectexpress.com>
Cc: Jackie Lynn, Sarah Lizama (SSA OIG), "jon carnley", Nora Arpin (Comerica Bank)
Dear Brandon,
I just heard from the lady named Lisa who called on behalf of the victim, and cancer patient, Jon Carnley. I heard you refused to give provisional credit to Jon's account, and that you were sending this to the Fraud Unit, which we all know are people who have no knowledge of banking law (nor do you) or fraud.
Jon has to leave the state on Saturday (3 days) for treatment. Along with violating banking law, you people will be exposed as probably the most illiterate and incompetent person who were put into jobs for which you are not qualified. Your lack of understanding is not your fault, it is in your genetics.
We are not done. We are exposing all of you, and those who hired you. Eventually one of you will be testifying on behalf of the victims. Choose your sides carefully. J.B. Simms

Thursday, January 17, 2019

From: jbsimms
Date: Thu, Jan 17, 2019 12:40 pm
To: "Advocacy US" advocacy@usdirectexpress.com
Cc: "Jackie Lynn" "jon carnley", Sarah Lizama (SSA OIG), Walter Bayer (SSA OIG), Sonja Scott (OIG Treasury), Wendy Bridges (Comerica Bank)
You people at Conduent are digging yourselves a hole from which you will never escape.
The person using the name "Brandon" has told Mr. Jon Carnley that the authority to credit his Direct Express account with regard to the fraud on his account is now the responsibility of Mastercard. Mastercard ?
Conduent employees have been making the decision to credit fraudulent charges and no mention of Mastercard has been made until today.
I spoke with Ms. Lizama of Social Security moments ago. This behavior of Conduent, promoted by Comerica Bank, is not going unnoticed.
I now see willful violation of law, and now I see malice. You people at Conduent, posing as Direct Express employees, advocates, fraud investigators, and call center persons, have now changed your responses with respect to the authority to credit the fraud on Mr. Carnley's account.
We will be in touch.
J. B. Simms

From: jbsimms
Date: Thu, Jan 17, 2019, 3:04 pm
To: Wendy Bridges (Comerica Bank)
Cc: "Advocacy US" <advocacy@usdirectexpress.com>, Franklin Lemond (Plaintiff's Attorney), Jackie Lynn, "jon carnley"
Dear Ms. Bridges,
I was optimistic when I learned you had a conversation with Mr. Carnley concerning the violations of federal banking regulations by your subcontractor, Conduent. It appears the Advocacy unit and the Fraud unit of Conduent, working on behalf of Comerica/Direct Express, not only have violated banking regulations with respect to Regulation E, the Advocacy unit, by way of a person using the name Brandon, has exhibited a reluctance to adhere to the said regulations because he feels no repercussion. The fact that this "Brandon" has unilaterally made the decision to bypass law and refuse provisional credit, when, in the face of the evidence presented by law enforcement and merchant, the reasonable deduction is fraud occurred, is the clearly an act of vengeance and malice against Mr. Carnley.
Many other victims who have contacted me have had their fraudulent activity presented to the Advocacy unit and after acknowledging the error of analyzing the error, credit was given. "Brandon" tried to bypass his authority and responsibility by telling Mr. Carnley, with an audible witness present, that he refused to grant the credit and that Mr. Carnley would have to take up the matter with MasterCard.
We do plan to bring MasterCard into this equation, but for now, I hope you can reign in your subcontractor and put measures into place to attempt to divert some liability from Comerica Bank.
Mr. Carnley and his caretaker will be meeting with counsel tomorrow. I will be part of that meeting.
Sincerely, J.B. Simms

124

Friday, January 18, 2019

The first hours of the day were spent reviewing and updating notes.

I had to find someone at Mastercard who would acknowledge that Comerica Bank had violated the terms of the agreement with Mastercard. I found the following person:

Daniel W Rose- Pub Sector Payments- Business Development- M/Card

1138am Carnley called- he got his money. He talked to a person at the Social Security Administration- Darrell- who said he was an investigator.

For now, my job was done for Jon Carnley. There would be others.

Monday, January 21, 2019

I did a bit of research on Conduent:

Christine Landry- Conduent Spokeswoman

The telephone number for Conduent (210) 932-0059 is registered to ACS State and Local Solutions, 485 Quentin Roosevelt Blvd, Building 171, Suite 95, San Antonio, TX 78226

Xerox acquired Affiliated Computer Services on 9/28/09. Xerox then began operating a customer service center.

Victim Number 55: James- Honolulu, Hawaii
Fraud Date: 1/10/2019
Fraud reported: 1/10/19 BJS Wholesale, Valley Stream, NY
1/10 BJ's Wholesale, Valley Stream, NY
1952:03 $879.95
19:56:11 67.38
19:54:10 1,12.50
Tot $1,959.81
Subject: My Dad's Direct Express Account
From: Stefany Tengan
Date: Mon, Jan 21, 2019 6:37 pm
To: jbsimms
Hello,
I saw your name on Facebook regarding Direct Express. Recently my 84-year-old father was a victim of fraudulent charges on his debit card. My father is upset. I took off of work early to assist him. They let over $1900 be charged from his account in Ny. We live in Hawaii. They state that they will stop any suspicious charges, but they didn't. He charged something in Hawaii that very day. So, I called and they stated they would send a form to him for provisional money. We only have 10 days. It's been 6 and no form was received. I tried calling and all I get is, your new card is coming. Goodbye. It's frustrating because of his age, and he has bold and rent to pay that I can't cover all of it. Are you able to assist in anyway?
Thank you,
Stefany Tengan
For James Tengan.

I called Stefany and gave her the Customer Advocacy contact information for Conduent. She sent an email to advocacy and copied me.

Tuesday, January 22, 2019

I was awake at 3am thinking about the call from Stephany a few hours before. I had to get this email out on behalf of Stefany's father.
From: jbsimms
Date: Tue, Jan 22, 2019 4:52 am
To: "Advocacy US" Wendy Bridges (Comerica Bank), Nora Arpin (Comerica Bank), Sarah Lizama (SSA OIG), Walter Bayer (SSA OIG), Sonja Scott (OIG Treasury), "Jackie Lynn"
Cc: "Stefany Tengan"
Dear All,
Ms. Stefany Tengan reached me via email yesterday, and she told me the story of how the Direct Express cardholder account of her 85 year old father was breached. Mr. Tengan lives in Hawaii; the fraud occurred in

the state of New York.

The Conduent/Direct Express/Comerica Bank "Fraud Unit" announced to Mr. Tengan they a "fraud packet" was being sent to him and he had to fill this out and return within 10 days or Conduent would not give him is provisional credit. The fraud packet has yet to arrive, and the Ms. Tengan was directed to fulfill the prerequisite of the fraud packet and send the narrative attached to this email.

There are a few issues which need to be addressed:

1. There is no fraud unit. There are people who are said to look at spending history to try to determine fraud. No one at Conduent will be calling law enforcement or any merchant. No one at Conduent, working on behalf of Comerica Bank, has the understanding that and investigation is more than spending habits.

2. If the spending history is the only parameter of fraud being inspected, a third grader can see that the cardholder is in Hawaii, the fraud occurred in New York, and this matter should have been found to be fraud upon the initial call to the call center.

3. Conduent/Comerica Bank employees are trying to shield themselves from liability for failing to "investigate" this matter by (1) failing to send the investigative packet/questionnaire in a timely manner and (2) using the expiration of the time of receipt of the completed questionnaire to deny the payment of the provisional credit. If/when the questionnaire is returned (with Conduent/Comerica Bank failing to timely send) within the arbitrary timeline established by Conduent/Comerica Bank employees, and the Conduent/Comerica Bank "fraud investigator" decides the time has expired, the cardholder, Mr. Tengan, will be given no option. This is the manner in which Conduent/Comerica Bank tries to hide their ineptness and overt violation of many areas of Regulation E, 15USC1693.

4. There are no security/alert parameters inherent with the Direct Express card which will advise a cardholder of any activity outside any time zone or geographic area. Security parameters such as these are available for Comerica Bank proprietary customers, and most other debit card account holders, but Comerica Bank decided to forgo cardholder safety than spend the money paid to them by Fiscal Services, and line their pockets after paying gratuities.

During the ongoing investigation of Conduent/Comerica Bank by multiple governmental agencies, Mr. Tengan has become another victim of fraud and of unnecessary victimization by Conduent/Comerica Bank.

I suggested that Ms. Tengan call Ms. Lizama immediately today, from Hawaii, and that having an informed and intelligent conversation with a Conduent employee was a waste of time.

I look forward to hearing of a quick resolution to this matter, and of course, this will be submitted to our legal team for examination.

Sincerely,

J.B. Simms

Another victim gets their money returned

The email below which I received made all the work worthwhile.

Subject: Re: filing police report
From: Stefany Tengan
Date: Tue, January 22, 2019, 8:18 pm
To: jbsimms
Hello Jim!
My dad received his money today. I wanted to thank you. We did not file a police report. But I'd like to continue to help in any way I can. Just because we got our money, doesn't mean others were so lucky. We're awaiting the new card and was told by Alisha to contact her by Thursday if it doesn't arrive. She'll expedite and waive the fees.
Thank you so much!!!
Regards,
Stefany

From: jbsimms
Date: Tue, Jan 22, 2019 8:41 pm
To: "Stefany Tengan"
Cc: Jackie Lynn, Nora Arpin (Comerica Bank), Wendy Bridges (Comerica Bank), "Advocacy US"
Dear Stefany,
Tell your father that I am happy for him. It was worth waking up at 3am, finding your email, and having to

126

confront Comerica Bank and Conduent on behalf of you and your father.
This harassment by Conduent, trained by Comerica Bank, is their way of trying to keep victim cardholders from trying to make them accountable to the law. There was no reason to hold your father's money hostage while Conduent employees try to connect dots.
Hopefully your father will receive a message via phone or email apologizing for what they did to your father. A man of his age, or any age, should not be subjected to ignorance, and malice with the ignorance is revealed. I will talk to you in a little while. This has to sink in with me. I have had over 50 persons contact me, and I will fight for all of them.
Of course, Jackie Densmore is the other side to helping, and most times she is more polite than me, sometimes. Comerica and Conduent know they will hear my name again, until they no longer have this contract.
Jim Simms

Tengan got his money the same day I sent the 4:52am nasty-gram and he got his money 14 hours later.
I decided to contact BJ's Wholesale regarding Tengan's fraud. I did not know this was not going to be the last time I had to contact them.

Below is the contact information I found:
BJ's Wholesale- Valley Stream, Long Island
A telephone call was made to (516) 837-4106 10:19; no answer was received.
I found a "chat" box on the website and sent a message. Then found Jeff Desroches-EVP Operations- Emailed and left message for Mr. Desroches to give me a call.

Wednesday, January 23, 2019

Subject: Re: Test and happy getting money back from Direct Express
From: paris
Date: Wed, Jan 23, 2019 12:31 pm
To: jbsimms
Yes, and the money that was stolen from me was a total of 603.00. It was at an ATM at 930 military trail, west palm beach Florida. That is a CHASE BANK ATM. On Jan.4.19, I have been getting the run around all month until I received help from you and named dropped your name... I truly appreciate all you do for people like me and do not ask for a dime. Thank you from my family to yours.
This would be a day I would never forget. This is a victim you will never forget.

The saddest of stories; a victim dies

Victim Number 56 -Latoya: Mississippi
812am- I received a call from Latoya Gillum, was living in Mississippi. Latoya was calling me from a hospital where she was receiving blood treatments as treatment for cancer. She found my phone number on the internet.
Ms. Gillum was a retired US Army E-8, Master Sergeant. She received DDA $960 (VA disability) and SSA disability of $1630 for her disabled child who was in wheelchair.
On 1/4/19 she attempted a purchase at a Family Dollar Story; the purchase was declined.
She called Direct Express (the Conduent call center) 20 times; could not get an answer. She put in a different Social Security number, got thru (they must see the SSN entered and not answer phone). She reported that a purchase was denied. Direct Express was to send her a fraud packet to fill out and return.
The fraud packet did not arrive until 10 days later on January 14. The fraud packet was completed and faxed to Direct Express.
Latoya viewed transaction details on PayPal. It was learned that Ms. Gillum's Direct Express account had been hacked. Purchases on 12/1/18 for $399.00 in Pennsylvania and 1/4/2019 for $400.00 in Mississippi were not made by Ms. Gillum. The payments looked like an auto loan payment; two diff accounts, same address.
Ms. Gillum called and talked to the Mississippi Attorney General office.
She reported the theft to her local sheriff. The suspect was identified as Ralonda Brown. Arrested, not in juvenile detention.
Conduent and Comerica were ignoring her.
I told Latoya I would act on her behalf.

From: *jbsimms*
Date: *Wed, Jan 23, 2019 5:41 pm*
To: *"Advocacy US" <advocacy@usdirectexpress.com>, Wendy Bridges (Comerica Bank), Nora Arpin (Comerica Bank), Jackie Lynn, Kate Berry (American Banker), "Jennifer Kreegar", Sarah Lizama (SSA OIG), Walter Bayer (SSA OIG)*

Again, I received a telephone call from a victim of Comerica Bank/Conduent with regard to the illegal an unconscionable handling of the Direct Express program.

The victim is a disabled veteran. Her name is Latoya Gillum. She lives in Biloxi, Mississippi. Ms. Gillum deserves the respect and admiration of everyone, after having served combat tours in the middle east. Ms. Gillum is a retired E-8, a Master Sgt. for those of you who have no idea the rank and the respect this person deserves.

Ms. Gillum talked to me quite a while. She took my email address, and was going to email me, but she has cancer, fell ill, and her husband texted me that she was receiving blood. Her son is wheelchair bound and disabled. Ms. Gillum receives disability from the VA and Social Security. On January 4, 2019, Ms. Gillum's Direct Express card was declined at a Family Dollar Store. She called at least 20 times. Calls were dropped, no answer, and disconnected. When she put in her Social Security Number, calls were dropped. She finally got someone on the phone by using a different Social Security Number.

Ms. Gillum reported the fraud and was told that she was to be sent the "fraud packet" to fill out and return, and if the form was not returned within 10 days, she would not be getting her money. The packet did not arrive until January 14, 2019.

While researching the internet, Ms. Gillum found information I posted which included a fax number. She used this fax number to send information to the Advocacy Unit of Comerica, and beat the arbitrary deadline created by the Conduent person with whom she spoke on January 4, 2019.

No word has been received from Conduent.

It was determined that Ms. Gillum suffered the following fraud:

12/1/2018 $399 from Pennsylvania
1/4/2019 $400 from Mississippi

As a result of her investigative skills, Ms. Gillum determine who fraudulently took her money in Mississippi, and that person is now incarcerated. The person who committed the fraud in Pennsylvania is probably associate with the Mississippi defendant.

When I have contact from Ms. Gillum, I will be forwarding more information. Until that time, let's see if there is an honorable person employed with Conduent or Comerica and contact this victim at (228) 209-1195, apologize to this veteran, and return her money. I have spoken to over 50 victims, and this case really exposes the vile underbelly of the manner in which unskilled, unschooled, disrespectful, and previously unchallenged Conduent workers, hired by Comerica Bank, treat American veterans.

All of you know who I am, and most of you know who I know. This could be the case that immediately ends the career of some persons at Comerica Bank and Conduent. You people did this to another veteran, who is copied on this email, and I encourage that veteran to make contact with Ms. Gillum.

Personally, I have never been so disgusted with the ignorance and contempt suffered by Ms. Gillum. She knows many people. Comerica Bank (Mr. Babb, Ms. Arpin, Ms. Bridges, and Susan Schmidt) will be hearing from someone soon.

Until then, you know what you need to do.
Sincerely,
J.B. Simms

Victim Number 57- Jamia: Louisville, KY
9:25am-Jamia called me.
She was out to lunch on January 2, 2019, and her card was declined, so she checked the app on her phone.
A withdrawal was made at an ATM located at 963 Military Trail, West Palm Beach, FL at 3am, just 6 hours earlier: two withdrawals- total $603. She called and talked to Direct Express Level 2 person and reported the fraud. The attendant said, "…[t]his is your fault. You are to withdraw the money from an ATM when it is deposited. We are not a real bank."
She was referred to Melissa (in Detroit).
A fraud packet was received 1/11(8 days after reporting the fraud) and was completed and mailed to the Direct Express (Conduent) address on January 14.

Jamia called Comerica Bank (210) 334-6673 Veronica not there and talked to Susan (did not know if was Schmidt or Rutledge). Jamia was told she would get $ back before 1:30pm on this date.

10:44am Jamia called me- she received a call from a person named Shauna and was told the money was on her account.

Later in the day I received email below from Jamia; she got her money.

On Wed, Jan 23, 2019, 2:04 PM jbsimms wrote:
Jamia,
Glad you got your money. I need to see the exact monies taken from your account and the location. We will use this against them being stupid.
Jim Simms

Friday, January 25, 2019

I texted Latoya Gillum to determine if she had received any feedback regarding the email I sent on her behalf. At 3:07pm her husband replied to the text using Latoya's phone, "Latoya passed yesterday." She contacted Conduent on Thursday January 24 at 7am and was waiting for a letter from Alisha at the Customer Advocacy Department.

I wanted to cry and scream.

Mr. Gillum gave me his email address.

Gillum's death and my response

From: jbsimms
Date: Fri, Jan 25, 2019, 2:13 pm
To: "Advocacy US" <advocacy@usdirectexpress.com>, Wendy Bridges (Comerica Bank), Nora Arpin (Comerica Bank), "Jackie Lynn", Kate Berry (American Banker), , Sarah Lizama (SSA OIG), Walter Bayer (SSA OIG)
Friday January 25, 2019
I received a text a hour ago from the husband of Latoya Gillum, the lady with whom I spoke two days ago, Wednesday January 23, 2019.
Latoya Gillum, the US Army Master Sergeant, war veteran, mother, and wife, died yesterday. One of her last acts was to call me and have the money for her family returned by the person at Conduent/Comerica Bank who ignored her.
Ms. Gillum, according to a text from her husband, called and made contact (probably with Alisha in Advocacy, but I gave her a number of people to call), they said they got here paperwork. Ms. Gillum called twenty times or more to to customer service, she called Conduent on January 4, and it was not until I gave her direct numbers to call that anyone admitted having her paperwork.
Twenty-one days passed. Conduent and Comerica Bank added to her stress. If she had not called me, Conduent and Comerica Bank would have sat on the approximately $800 and deprived her wheelchair bound son his care.
You see above that Austin Gillum, Latoya's husband, who is making funeral arrangements as I type, is being copied on this email.
I was a private investigator, now a writer/author, but I cannot find an adjective bad enough to refer to you people at Conduent and Comerica Bank. You think you can play hide and seek with laws and regulations, toying with persons lives. This lady sacrificed her life for all of you, whether you are American citizens or not, working at Conduent. I watched my son leave in 2003, not knowing if he would return. You people disrespect our veterans with your games. You will be made accountable, on behalf of MSgt. Gillum, and others.
J.B. Simms

Jackie was now going after MasterCard. She had contacted Seth Eisen of Mastercard, but the "zero-liability" claim of Mastercard was not supported. Mastercard never investigated Comerica Bank, probably because the Direct Express program was a federally funded program, and no one would make Comerica Bank or Conduent accountable.

Monday, January 28, 2019

From: jbsimms
Date: Mon, Jan 28, 2019, 5:02 pm
To: "Stefany Tengan"
Dear Stephany,
Again, I am happy your dad got his money. I have nothing good to say about these people.
BJ's corporate people were not helpful, at first, but I became quite convincing. There have been two more
victims at BJ's since your case. One person filed a police report, and I forwarded this to the BJ's corporate guy
because he supposedly could not do anything without a police report. I will get the other victim to do the same.
If you could, write the narrative (which you have done) and print out a copy of your statement showing the
fraud (which you have done) and tell the Honolulu police you need to file a report for identity theft. This will be
a simple procedure, check some boxes and fill in name and address. In the blank area of the report, simply
write "see attachments" and make sure these two items are included.
Get a copy of the incident report, scan it and send me a copy. I will forward it to the BJ's place. I have a feeling
we will see more victims, but the hoop jump is necessary to maybe catch the criminals. Wouldn't it be
interesting if this was traced back to Conduent?
This would be a great help. I hate to put your dad through this, and I tried to make it as easy as possible. Jim

I had to talk to the security people at BJ's store.

From: jbsimms
Date: Mon, Jan 28, 2019, 1:55 pm
To: pnewsham@bjs.com
Cc: "Jackie Lynn"
Dear Mr. Newsham,
Thank you for being receptive to this matter. I am certain you will do your due diligence to validate my identity
and background.
As I stated, one of the victims lives in Hawaii, and I was able to "convince" the Conduent call center persons to
credit the victim's account after exposing how ridiculous it was not to validate a fraud claim when four hours
before the fraudulent charges were made, the victim made a purchase in Honolulu. For your amusement, I am
attaching a copy of this statement.
There were two other victims who called me today. I will hopefully get copies of police reports for you.
Sincerely,
J.B. Simms

Below is the email to the daughter of the victim. The fraud was in NY, they live in Hawaii.

Subject: Incident report: Deborah Davis
From: jbsimms
Date: Mon, Jan 28, 2019, 2:20 pm
To: pnewsham@bjs.com
Dear Mr. Newsham,
Attached please find a copy of a police report filed by a fraud victim. This fraudulent transaction occurred in
College Point, NY on what appears to be January 18, 2019, at 9:13am and 9:16am in the amounts of $1,027.45
and $116.37, respectively.
While the narrative does not specify the exact date, the words "this morning" caused me to assume that the
fraud occurred on the date of the filing of the incident report. If I have any definitive information to clarify this,
I will forward this to you.
Sincerely,
J.B. Simms

Jody McIntyre called- she got her money today at noon. Another satisfied victim.

Jackie was on the tail of Rep. Keating and continued to contact Michael Jackman.

Jackie Lynn
Mon, Jan 28, 2019, 1:53 PM
to Michael, me
Hello Mr. Jackman,
Thank you for taking my call today, as discussed since my social security number was compromised in Aug 2018 I have two attempts of fraudulent purchases one on my chase credit card in Dec. 2018 and one more recent on my discover card. Both attempts were caught by my credit cards security and declined. I had put more security features on these cards once I knew my social security number was stolen from Direct Express.
I have never had a problem of identity theft since Direct Express which leads me to believe my information might have been sold around the time of Aug 2018. Since I filed a claim with direct express I have no information on the investigation that supposedly took place in order to get Derek's Funds back all I know is that the money was issued back onto the card but as far as the investigation no clue. I have asked Direct Express numerous times and every time they tell me supervisors will contact me. As of today's date, I have not received a phone call or paperwork pertaining to my claim or what was investigated.
The only thing I know is Comerica claims: (in American Banker)
This is what Comerica VP Nora Arpin told reporter Kate Berry (American Banker) about the cardless benefit program and how my information was breached, but what happened to that employee?

Jackie had developed a rapport with Mr. Jackman, the staffer for Rep. Keating of Massachusetts.

Victim 58: Deborah- CO
Deborah was paying a bill for a storage unit.
"I tried it again while I was on the phone; again, the charge was declined. I hung up and immediately checked my account online, which I had checked at 8:30 AM MT in the morning; at that time the funds I expected to be there were."
"After Tracy tried my debit card it didn't work. I checked my account again; it was just after 11:00AM MT; my account was empty with two pending charges from BJ's Wholesale Company in College Point, NY."
One charge is $1,027.45 at 9:13:58 AM ET and the other charge is for $116.37 at 9:16:38 AM ET; these charges interestingly completely wiped out every cent I had to the exact penny.
January 28, 2019: Received email from Deborah.
I sent an email to Advocacy on her behalf.
9:25am text- Deborah talked to Susan Rutledge (Comerica). Rutledge was to get onto this now.
1/28/2019- evening, Davis gets email from Alisha (Conduent). Alishia stated the investigation was going on. Later that evening, the funds were paid back.

I had to call BJ Warehouse and let them know what is going on. That was the second victim at BJ Wholesale. Another victim would soon appear.

It was time for me to contact BJ Warehouse's security.
1111am T (774) 512-7400 for Desroches- sent to Paul Newsham. Left message with Jessie.

Victim Number 59-Peter Jackson: Tennessee, Fraud discovered: January 13, 2019
Fraud reported: January 13, 2019, Credit paid: February $1,2019
Nature of Fraud: BJ's Warehouse, Brooklyn, NY $664

I contacted many people in the same email on behalf of victims. It worked for Jennifer Kreeger and others. People in Washington, D.C. needed to know what Comerica Bank was doing. Actually, they did not care.

Conduent fraud unit investigates "nothing"

From: jbsimms
Date: Mon, Jan 28, 2019, 12:56 pm
To: "PETER JACKSON"
Cc: "Jackie Lynn", Sonja Scott (OIG Treasury), Walter Bayer (SSA OIG), Nora Arpin (Comerica Bank), Wendy Bridges (Comerica Bank), "Advocacy US" <advocacy@usdirectexpress.com>
Dear Mr. Jackson,

As was discovered months ago, the "Fraud Unit" of Conduent, having been contracted by Comerica Bank to handle fraud claims by cardholders, investigates nothing.

While it is apparent that your victimization is blatantly evident and acknowledged by Conduent personnel, there is no reason for you to be held hostage by the Conduent call center persons.

You are the third victim of fraudsters using BJ's Wholesale who have call me within the last week. I now have direct contact with their corporate office. They request a police report before acting, but I can still send them information that they can use to "check into" things.

Alisha, I believe you people in the Customer Advocacy office of Conduent should have a meeting with the Fraud Unit (I know these are a homogeneous bunch, having no lines of demarcation) and start giving the victims immediate credit for obvious fraud. You people need intelligent people who know how to converse with law enforcement to stop these crimes, unless there is a reason the Conduent employees are avoiding reporting crimes for their benefit. You know my background, and this theory was not created in a vacuum.

J.B. Simms

Subject: FRAUD against our Veterans
From: PETER JACKSON
Date: Mon, January 28, 2019, 12:02 pm
To: <ntarpin@comerica.com>
Cc: jbsimms
Dear "Alisha",

On or about the 13th of this month a withdrawal from my Direct Express account for a little more than $700. This withdrawal or "charge" was in the exact amount of the remaining balance of my account. I just happened to notice this transaction the morning it was made and called your customer service to file a report of the theft. Your customer service agent immediately informed me that it had already been noted as "fraud" and that these charges from BJ's Wholesale Warehouse were well known as being fraudulent.

This agent then told me that my card, (which I rely on exclusively for all of my money) has to be destroyed and I would have to wait for a new card to arrive. My account was then charged $13.50 for the mailing of this card which left my account with a negative balance of $13.50. She then tells me that I would have to wait for another package in the mail with paperwork that I must fill out and send in detailing the account of fraud and that I could possibly receive my money in 3 to 6 months!!!

I don't know about you, but I live on that $1000 disability compensation payment. It is all I have. I served this country proudly and take great comfort in knowing that it would take an act of congress to change my payment. It has been nearly 3 weeks and my account balance is negative $13.50

It would seem to me that if you knew it was a fraudulent charge before I ever called you that you would have stopped payment immediately. Having not done so, one might assume that you either don't care about fraud or are complicit in the fraud itself.

Having now done some research on this matter I have found that there are many veterans that have experience this exact same fraud!! WAIT!! HOW CAN THIS BE??

I would like my money returned to me and the charges for the new card rescinded immediately. Furthermore, I would appreciate a full accounting of the actions that you take on my behalf.

These crimes are horrific! I can only imagine the pain that all of these veterans have had to endure without the funds they need to survive and it is my sincere intent to see that several people spend a very long time in prison for either theft, negligence, or conversion!

Quite sincerely, Captain Peter Jackson

On February 2 a text from Peter Jackson was received; he got paid $664 plus fee of $13.50.

The three victims whose money was spent at BJ Wholesale were repaid in a short period of time, only after they contacted me. I was glad to have helped the victims.

Victim Number 60-Jessica: CA

"I went to withdraw money on 11/05/2018 and all my money was gone Immediately filed a claim for fraudulent charges with direct Express I then filled out the paperwork and immediately fax it to them they gave me a transitional credit and then they denied my claim and didn't want to hear from the merchants cuz they told me to get up at the merchant but the merchant said was obviously an apparently fraud and they gave me a reference number to give to direct Express direct Express was not hearing anything else of it I have contacted several people and they all think it's funny."

Jackie got draft of letter signed by Schmidt acknowledging identity theft through merchants.

Jackie Lynn
Mon, Jan 28, 2019, 9:56 PM
to Delmar, Michael, me, Direct, Nora, Walter, Sonja, Sarah, Michael
I agree with JB two victims contacted you about fraud at bjs and now this posting?!?! What is being done about this it's not a coincidence!
Sonja, can you investigate these claims since they are all linked to Bjs? I bet there are more as well in this state. Hope you are all taking notes JB has had over 61 victims come forward and only one victim which was me was due to cardless program which means what is causing all this fraud and leaks?!?!
61 guys!!! Staggering numbers considering his info is only on the Internet imagine how many more victims out there?!?
Social security I am shocked you are not warning cardholders. I will remind all agencies you have put on notice 61 victims.
Jackie

Jackie was getting wound up. I kept her informed as to the number of victims that had contacted me, and the number at this point was sixty-one.

Sonja Scott (OIG Treasury)
Jan 29, 2019, 4:52 AM
to Richard, Michael, Jackie, me, Direct, Nora, Walter, Sarah, Michael
Jackie - the BJ's association has and is being investigated. Sonja

We got their attention, but we never knew if OIG Treasury ever investigated anything.

Tuesday, January 29, 2019

From: Sonja Scott (OIG Treasury)
Date: January 29, 2019 at 8:04:46 AM EST
To: 'Jackie Lynn'
Subject: RE: More
Just learned about it recently from Comerica. Despite what you may think, Comerica is being proactive with this BJ's matter. I have no idea how many affected at this time. Sonja

Comerica Bank and OIG Treasury were reactive, not proactive

J B Simms
Tue, Jan 29, 2019, 8:20 AM
to Sonja, Jackie
Dear Jackie and Ms. Scott,
I am no grammarian, but the reply from Ms. Scott to Jackie, stating that Comerica is being "proactive" is a misnomer; the correct word is "reactive."
With all due respect, Comerica chose not to be proactive in protecting the security of cardholders by pocketing the money from Fiscal Services which was to be used to implement security measures, the least of which are offered to the propriety customers of Comerica Bank.
Jim Simms

Jackie got Susan Schmidt's email address. Jackie then called Sonja Scott- Nora Arpin talked to Sonja about BJ's fraud. Arpin was worthless and cared nothing about the victims; she cared only about herself.

Three people got hit at BJ Warehouse. One was in Hawaii, Colorado, and Tennessee.
Comerica was not proactive. I talked to the security guy myself. It was all BS from Comerica and Nora.

Seth Eisen of Mastercard replied to Jackie. He stated he would pass along her concerns.
Yeah, right.

Ben Dupre and Ronald Wilcox were attorneys in California representing a client suing Comerica in California courts. Dupre asked Jackie and me to help by submitting an affidavit. I also got Marteshia McPhail to submit one as well.

Ben Dupré <bendupre@gmail.com>
Tue, Jan 29, 2019, 12:12 PM
to Ronald, me
Hi JB
Will get a draft of your declaration to you via e-mail by tomorrow.
Could you tell me your full name and street address? I would want to add it to the declaration.
Thank you,
Ben

From: Amicia Mattox
Date: Tue, Jan 29, 2019 3:41 pm
To: jbsimms
Dear Mr. Simms,
Thanks so much for your help.
My son did finally receive his card. I've been moving into a new place, sorry for the delay.
I was able to give my co-worker your email address. Her dad was going through the same issue. If I'm not mistaken he had been waiting for approximately 4 months so far. Unfortunately I don't have his name on hand. Thanks again!!!
Mrs. Amicia Mattox

Wednesday, January 30, 2019

Victim Number 61-Amber:
I saw your email online and was hoping you may be able to tell me what is fraud suspension? My 4-year-old daughter receives ssi on a direct express card every month and now it says card status=fraud suspension

I sent her an email asking for info 1/31/19 sent another email day later.

Victim Number 62-Kaaren-NY
Fraud detected: 12/31/2018.
Fraud reported: 12/31/2018.
Verizon Wireless 2:02am $770.00
Received Provisional credit: 1/18/2019.
Provisional credit reversed: 1/28/2019.
Hi, I have been having one heck of a time getting my money back from DE after a fraud was done online on my account. This is my only income, and they are of no help. I called hours after the fraud took place and they cancelled my card immediately which left me with no way to access my account. Then they sent me to a level 2 Representative named Alexis. she took all info and said she would send me a form to fill out. I received the form 5 days later, filled out and went directly back to Post Office same day and returned with priority 2 day mail with receipt requested. I guess I should tell you the fraud was done at 2:02am 12/31/19 by Verizon, 2 hours after my S.S. check was deposited. Total taken out $770.00. I called my local Police and they wouldn't make a report because it was from another state and online. said they had no way to investigate this. Received a credit adjustment of $770.00 on 1/18/19 and then a reversal debt for the same amount on 1/28/19. They said I made the purchase!!!!!! If you study my banking history you can see this is not true and why would I go thru all this if I was guilty. This is my only income and on the first of march they will have my SS check and I can do nothing!!!!! I need your help PLEASE....
1/30/19 got info. Money was taken in Ft. Mill, SC. She lives in NY.
1/31/19 sent group email to advocacy and other for Kaaren.
1/31/19 Kaaren email- she to call Alisha tomorrow.
2/7/19 sent email for clarification.
2/22/19 Paid $700 of $774.00 and charge was reversed.
It took a month, but she got her money.

Victim Number 63-Kerri-: Mishawaka, Indiana

Fraud detected: 1/1/19

Fraud reported: 1/1/19

On January 1, 2019, at 6:30pm, $134.95 taken at Champs store in Valley Stream, NY. She lives in Indiana.
$134.00 She sent texts.

1/31/19 I sent emails with copy of screenshot to advocacy and others.

2/7/19 sent email asking for update.

2/12/2019 got copy of police report

2/13/19 IM- she called today and had sent copy to Advocacy. I emailed Conduent Advocacy for her.

Multiple fraud at two retailers

From: *jbsimms*

Date: *Wed, Jan 30, 2019, 9:03 pm*

To: *"Advocacy US" <advocacy@usdirectexpress.com>, Susan Schmidt (Comerica Bank), Wendy Bridges (Comerica Bank), Sonja Scott (OIG Treasury), Sarah Lizama (SSA OIG), "Jackie Lynn", Nora Arpin (Comerica Bank)*

Here is a screenshot of the fraud on Kerri Uchiha's account.

She faxed this information on 1/10/19 to Direct Express. She also filed a police report.

This lady lives in Mishawaka, Indiana; the transaction was in NY, Long Island.

Are you actually trying to convince me it takes 20 days to see this is fraud, at 4:44pm, in NY? Comerica Bank knows I have over 60 victims at this time, and more coming every day. Comerica Bank cannot train Conduent workers to see what is obviously in front of their faces, and Comerica Bank, including Ms. Arpin, Schmidt, and Bridges, have done nothing to change this abhorrent behavior.

It will be too late to save Comerica Bank's contract with Fiscal Services and those within the bank from being liable, but you would think they would make a gesture to abide by the law while they are on their way out.

The fraud was at Champs store in Valley Stream, NY. We just had a case of fraud on Direct Express cardholders at BJ's at Valley Stream a week or so ago.

This is another reason Comerica is going to be sorry they hired Conduent in order to save money and victimize the cardholders. Ms. Uchiha sent in the information 20 days ago and these Conduent people are still sitting on this lady's money?

J.B. Simms

Note from Kerri Uchiha, Wednesday February 14, 2019:

I just wanted to say thank you. I spoke to Alisha & she said it was on her desk & she would handle it & she apologized. I finally got my credit this morning! Not even after 24 hours of speaking to her. I really appreciate all the work you do!

Kerri Uchiha got the entire $134.95 credited to her account.

Jackie and I are back and forth with Sonja Scott almost daily. Jackie is very cordial but trusts Sonja less than I do. She seemed willing to talk to Carnley (whose story was all over the map).
I had to deal with Carnley's caretaker girlfriend. That was another story.

Thursday, January 31, 2019

From: *jbsimms*

Date: *Thu, Jan 31, 2019 12:56 pm*

To: *Abby Webber (Aide to Sen Eliz Warren)*

Cc: *"Jackie Lynn"*

Dear Ms. Webber,

I received a note from Ms. Densmore that you would consider revisiting our request that the General Accounting Office (GAO) be involved in this investigation. Ms. Densmore stated you might need "refreshing" regarding addressing the self-serving and protective answers submitted to Senator Warren by Ralph Babb. Please re-read this attachment as I proofed the proposed letter to be issued by Senator Warren.

Let me be clear again about the need for the involvement of the GAO:

1) Senator Warren and Senator Hatch were the persons requesting the initial report, GAO 17-176. The report was a scathing rebuke of Fiscal Services and lack of transparency, which involves Comerica Bank.
2) Evidence in the Treasury OIG reports (17-034 and 14-0-31) reveals Comerica Bank submitted false and incomplete information to Fiscal Services to gain the Fiscal Agent contract.
3) Fiscal Services and Social Security have a vested interest in self-preservation, and this agenda carries forth to the OIG of each agency. Although the OIG appears to be independent, they are not. I have experience in this arena.
4) A follow-up request by Senator Warren to the GAO would be the most logical step to take to eliminate the possibility of conflict of interest with OIG office of other agencies.
I do hope this helps.
J.B. Simms

All we needed was one person from Congress to endorse the follow-up investigation. Just one. The GAO would expose OIG Treasury and Bureau of Fiscal Service for their negligence and complicity.

Paul Lawrence, head of the VAB (Veteran Affairs Benefits) joined my LinkedIn internet page today. I had been sending messages to him regarding the Direct Express program and how the VA was ignoring the veterans. Lawrence never replied to me but was reading my posts and messages. All Paul Lawrence was interested in doing was looking for a "photo-op" and act as though he was working on behalf of the veterans. My input showed he had not been doing his job.

I would have to find another way to get the attention of the Veterans Administration.

Today I followed up on a number of victims, sending emails and calling for updates. This was an everyday thing.

Another dying victim and massive fraud

Victim Number 64: James-Florida
James Sims, of Florida, was a victim and his story is very sad.
Rebecca Newton (daughter)- en route to hospital
Fraud Detected: Jan 2019
Fraud Reported: Jan 2019
Fraud amounts: $7,043.61
March 2018 - $606.37
April 2018 - $2,555.14
May 2018 - $1,202.31
June 2018 - $638.14
July 2018 - $1,224.30
August 2018 - $817.35
Grand Total - $7,043.61

The fraudsters were buying pizzas and other food items (along with other items) in Savannah, GA. Mr. Sims was in central Georgia and Tampa, Florida. Comerica Bank and Conduent ignored the fraud complaint.

Subject: US Direct Express Fraud for James Sims
From: "rebeccamnewton@aol.com"
Date: Thu, January 31, 2019, 1:19 pm
To: jbsimms
Dear Mr. Simms,
Attached are the US Direct Express Statements from March 2018 - August 2018 for my Dad, James Edward Sims Jr.
My name is Rebecca Newton. On January 9th of this year, I had my Dad moved to a skilled nursing facility near me in Tampa, FL called Rehabilitation & Healthcare of Tampa. Before this he was in a skilled nursing facility in Macon, GA called Cherry Blossom from September 2018 until January 9, 2019. Before he was at Cherry Blossom his Social Security checks were going to his US Direct Express Card, which he is still in possession of. From March 2018 - August 2018 every charge on his card which is shown on the statements is Fradulent. He never made or authorized any of them. My Dad is diabetic, a double amputee below the knees, has had a stroke

previously, a pacemaker and has had triple bypass and has been in end stage renal failure for 2 years. Every facility he has been in his wallet has been locked in a safe at the facility.

Currently my dad is in ICU at St. Joseph's Hospital in Tampa. He has pneumonia, the flu, bed sores that are infected, a Urinary Tract infection, a blood infection (sepsis), high fevers, low blood pressure, high blood sugar, he is on a ventilator and currently sedated, his platelet count is extremely low. He has already had a blood transfusion and 3 platelet transfusions in the last five days. The Cardiologist is wanting to do a TEE because they think there is infection in the valves in his heart, but they can't do that until is platelet count is at least 60000 and his current count is 17000.

When my Dad first came down here he asked me to help him with all these fraudulent charges on his account. I have called and talked to many people at Customer Service. All they do is give me the run around or say they can't help me. I have called at least 10 times between January 10th and January 26th.

I am hoping that you will be able to help me with this.

My contact information is:

Rebecca Newton

I look forward to hearing from you soon.

Sincerely,

Rebecca Newton

P.S. - Currently my Dad has given me his wallet to hold on too.

1/31/19 Talked to Rebecca- she would be sending an email. I sent one on behalf of her father.

From: jbsimms
Date: Thu, Jan 31, 2019, 2:12 pm
To: Jackie Lynn, Abby Webber (Aide to Sen Eliz Warren), "Advocacy US"
<advocacy@usdirectexpress.com>, Susan Schmidt (Comerica Bank), Sonja Scott (OIG Treasury)
Cc: rebeccamnewton@aol.com
This was sent to me, and I have spoken with Ms. Newton.
She received terrible service from the Conduent call center, which is normal.
She contacted me, and now you all know.
Ms. Newton is going to be sending an email to Advocacy and following up with "Alisha" and Ms. Schmidt. Let's see what happens.
Hopefully the office of Senator Warren can see that is regular behavior of Direct Express/Conduent to ignore fraud when it is obvious.
J. B. Simms

2/1/19 Rebecca talked to Susan Rutledge of Comerica- Rutledge was receptive. She sent info Alisha (Conduent). Alisha (Conduent) denied liability. Rebecca Newton sent email to Alisha with pics of dad. JBS sent email as well.

Rebecca called Alisha- read my email with the federal statutes. Alisha said she would send to management and make an exception.

2/8/2018 Dad died. Mr. Sims knew the work that Rebecca and I were doing. His last words to Rebecca were, "I'm sorry.'

The only way to get the money repaid was through probate court.

Friday, February 1, 2019

From: jbsimms
Date: Fri, Feb 01, 2019, 4:17 pm
To: "Advocacy US" <advocacy@usdirectexpress.com>, Walter Bayer (SSA OIG), Sarah Lizama (SSA OIG), Sonja Scott (OIG Treasury), Jackie Lynn, Kate Berry (American Banker), rebeccamnewton@aol.com, Susan Schmidt (Comerica Bank)
I just got a call from Rebecca Newton of Lutz, Florida. He father, James Sims Jr., was the victim of fraud. This was reported to Conduent/Direct Express on January 10, 2019. The daughter of Mr. Sims, Rebecca Newton, just got off the phone with "Alisha" and "Alisha" had no knowledge that the fraud had been reported. Now Mr Sims is on a respirator.

Regulation E, 15USC1693, mandates that the investigation begin upon notice, and if the investigation takes more than 10 days, the cardholder is to receive the entire amount as provisional credit.

No one at Conduent adheres to the law. Ms. Newton talked to Ms. Rutledge in the office this morning and Ms. Rutledge.

There is nothing to keep the people at Conduent from crediting the the account, regardless if "Alisha" thinks she needs something in writing. Credit the account.

Comerica knows that there never will be an investigation. The fraud unit is a sham, and I have proven this. Conduent is protecting the criminals within their organization, and Comerica is complicit.

I am very comfortable in a courtroom. Comerica and Conduent employees will be a bit more nervous after I testify.

J.B. Simms

I had many open cases of victims I was working on at the same time. I continued to write emails and make phone calls for them.

From: jbsimms
Date: Fri, Feb 01, 2019, 5:07 pm
To: "Advocacy US" <advocacy@usdirectexpress.com>
Cc: Susan Schmidt (Comerica Bank), Nora Arpin (Comerica Bank), Wendy Bridges (Comerica Bank), Sonja Scott (OIG Treasury), Sarah Lizama (SSA OIG), Walter Bayer (SSA OIG), "Carol Gilmer" ,"Jackie Lynn"

Dear Advocacy,

Again, you people are in violation of Regulation E for not giving provisional credit, then you based your decision to deny this claim made by Ms. Gilmer upon the intelligence of persons working for Conduent. No one read a police report. No one saw a surveillance video.

Remember, the burden is upon you to determine that fraud did not occur.

It will be determined within legal proceedings where you people were trained, but I will be glad to come to your office and read the law, 15USC1693, to you in English. Those of you who do not speak English will need an interpreter.

This will over pretty soon. I suggest the persons assigned to Direct Express update their visas or be exposed. J. B. Simms

Peter Jackson 250pm- Texted me- Alisha (Conduent) called Peter- Got $664 back plus $13.50 from BJ's Wholesale, Brooklyn.

Saturday, February 2, 2019

From: jbsimms
Date: Sat, Feb 02, 2019, 9:46 am
To: "Lori Matherne"
Lori,
I am glad you got your money. I will document this and prove they can fix things if they want.
Send me your address so I can complete the info. Jim
Subject: Re: update on Direct Express issue
From: Lori Matherne <lmatherne1960@gmail.com>
Date: Fri, February 01, 2019 11:23 pm
To: jbsimms
Yes Jim I immediately got a credit back on my account after I spoke to Ms. Cherry. Then I received a letter about a month later stating that it was the ATM machine that kept my money. I thank you for your assistance on this matter. You helped me out extremely.
Lori Matherne

Jackie wrote emails on behalf of the victims.

from: Jackie Lynn
to: Sonja Scott (OIG Treasury
cc: Richard Delmar (OIG Treasury),
date: Feb 2, 2019, 5:38 PM
Jackie Lynn
Attachments
Feb 2, 2019, 5:38 PM
to Sonja Scott (OIG Treasury), DelmarR, me, rebeccamnewton
Sonja,

I spoke to Ms. Newton this evening who was in tears tonight from having to take care of her father and his failing health conditions.

She has spoken to Susan Rutledge and Susan assured her that she would have this investigated as well as contact the Advocacy group. Ms. Newton had already spoken to that dept from Jim Simms giving her that number.

The advocacy (Alisha) has refused to send Ms. Newton a fraud packet or an explanation of how the fraud occurred instead her account is now locked and in suspension.

Her story is below as well as evidence of her father's failing health. How can anyone in their right mind say it was him who made those purchases.

I am beyond sick with what's being done about this, please contact her. Ms. Newton's attention needs to be focused on her dad and not dealing with the complete incompetence of Conduent and advocacy group. Sonja I really do t know how these people can sleep at night. We are at victim 64 and I know you are doing your best, but this man was saving money so that his daughter wouldn't have the burden of paying for his Cremation when the time came. Please I can't tell you how many pieces my heart broke into when I heard her tell me that. Sonja, please do everything you can for her including reaching out to her.
Thank you.
Jackie

Victim 65 Erika-OH

Fraud Detected: 2/1/19, Fraud Reported 2/1/19

Fraud activity: Son's DE account was hacked 2/1/19 at 00:12:59.

2/4/19- talked to Erika- (303) 334-0135. She went to the Cleveland Police- they said they need affidavit of fraud from DE. See that ATM is located at 1899 Biscayne Blvd, Aventura FL Erika called Fraud, was disconnected. Sent emails to Conduent.

Erika Kirts- account hacked 2/1/2019 00:12:59 (twelve minutes after midnight), $803.00. Address of ATM was 1899 Biscayne Blvd, Aventura FL

I sent an email to Conduent on behalf of Ms. Erika.

Subject: Direct express fraud victim
From: Erika Kirts
Date: Sat, February 02, 2019, 4:07 pm
To: jbsimms
Good afternoon, my name is Erika Kirts and my son's direct express account was hacked on February 1, 2019 at 12:59 a.m. in Aventura, Florida. It showed that an atm cash withdrawal was made in the amount of $803 dollars. I called direct express numerous times to let them know that we are victims of fraudulent activity before they've decided to answer, and the representatives didn't seem that concerned and told me it could take up to 45 to 90 days and there wouldn't be any guarantee that he would receive any of his money back. I have called the treasury department and filed a complaint and even went to the closest social security building, and they told me there was nothing they could do and this matter was between me and direct express and I don't think it is fair and right when we are victims of fraud when it is plain to see.I am seeking help with this matter and I was led to you by my mom. If there is any way that you could help, please call me at 330-344-0136 or by email. Thank you!

A couple hours were spent updating information (addresses, telephone numbers, etc.). This was very important. The information about the victims had to be communicated and I had to be on top of all the information.

Sunday February 3, 2019

On Wed, Feb 6, 2019, at 2:37 PM, Advocacy - US Direct Express
<advocacy@usdirectexpress.com> wrote:
Hello Ms. Kirts, your claim was closed approved yesterday, are you still requiring assistance?
Thank you,
Alisha

From: jbsimms
Date: Sun, Feb 03, 2019, 9:54 pm
To: "Advocacy US" <advocacy@usdirectexpress.com>, avion1005@yahoo.com
Cc: "Jackie Lynn"
First, your email is being forwarded to Conduent, which is the subcontractor for Comerica Bank which administers the Direct Express card.
They have to start their "investigation immediately, as per Regulation E. They cannot take the 45-90 days that the call center people told you.
You must be credited with the provisional credit within 10 days of the notice, which was fulfilled by me sending this email.
I want you to file an incident report with your local police, and safe a copy of the report.
Send a copy to me and to advocacy@usdirectexpress.com.
I will call you tomorrow for more instructions and explain more about legal claims against Conduent, and how their company violates banking laws.
J.B. Simms

Monday, February 4, 2019

I had been in constant contact with Rebecca Newton regarding her dad. Conduent was ignoring her. The fraud was evident, and both Comerica Bank and Conduent were violating Reg E. Her dad was dying.
Subject: My Dad, James Sims
From: Rebecca Newton
Date: Mon, February 04, 2019 6:58 am
To: Jackie Lynn, jbsimms
jbsimms
He is getting worse. I know fraud cases can take a while, but time is not his friend right now. His blood pressure is dangerously low today and the ventilator is back on.
Rebecca Newton

From: Jackie Lynn
Sent: Monday, February 4, 2019, 7:47 AM
To: Sonja Scott (OIG Treasury)
Subject: Direct express fraud victim: another victim Erika Kirts.
Good morning, Sonja,
just sending over yet another victim. Please look into this and add to list.
Also wanted to let you know I have spoken to McPhail ($30,000) victim and they have not heard a word nor have had their money returned. The special agent assigned called her that one time, never met with them. And that is the last time she heard anything about things.
Same with my case I spoke to that one guy but nothing since. If they think they can just check in once and call it a day, they are wrong we have a right to know what's going on.
Also, I wanted to see if you would reach to Rebecca Newton today. I sent you over her contact info this weekend. One last thing can you tell me if you have had any reports other than mine of fraud from people in Massachusetts?
Thanks
Jackie

J B Simms
Mon, Feb 4, 2019, 7:59 AM
to jbsimms, Jackie, Sarah, Sonja, Nora, Direct, Franklin
Below is the summation by Rebecca Newton of her talk with Susan Rutledge today.
Are we now to belie that Conduent is in control of Comerica Bank?
This opens a new issue:
"I talked to Susan Rutledge. She said even though Conduent is contracted through them that she cannot tell them how to do their jobs. She said all she could do for me is call them right now and tell them to escalate my dad's claim and have them reach out to me as soon as possible. It is so aggravating at this point. There is no way now for me to get a POA from my dad because he can't even sign being back on the ventilator. In my email this morning when I said time is not his friend I wasn't kidding. I was told this morning by three different doctors that he may last days, possibly a week maybe two if he's lucky. I'm still at the hospital if I come downstairs cuz I'm so upset. Jackie just called me to give me Franklin's number see if we could figure something else out but I'm just trying to get my head cleared and on the right page before I call anybody else cuz I'm just emotionally torn and upset at this point. I have called Alisha at least six times this morning but of course it rings"
Comerica cannot control their contractor, as cardholders are continually victimized.
JB Simms

From: jbsimms
Date: Mon, Feb 04, 2019 8:10 am
To: "Advocacy US" <advocacy@usdirectexpress.com>, Sonja Scott (OIG Treasury), Sarah Lizama (SSA OIG), Jackie Lynn, Wendy Bridges (Comerica Bank), Susan Schmidt (Comerica Bank)
Cc: rebeccamnewton@aol.com
Below you will see an email I received from Rebecca Newton.
If ever Ms. Scott wants to bring up an issue with Bureau of Fiscal Services pertaining to the ignorance, vengeance, and malfeasance on the part of Comerica Bank by hiring Conduent as a subcontractor, look at this case.
Mr. Sims' account was used all through south and mid Georgia while he was in a nursing facility, and the fraudsters bought $95+ worth of pizza, along with other items, totaling over $7,000.
It makes no difference if Mr. Sims gave authority to his daughter, Ms. Newton, to access his account while his is disabled. Comerica Bank must credit Mr. Sims' account regardless who he gave access.
Conduent hired non-US citizens to try to make logical decisions. This cost saving adventure by Comerica Bank will result in great scrutiny and consequences.
J.B. Simms

Many times, Jackie would find a source and ask that I create an email for her. Jackie was tenacious as she found sources. Jackie was recruiting another senator for assistance.

From: Jackie Lynn
Date: February 4, 2019 at 8:59:29 PM EST
To: Matt.brass@senate.ga.gov
Cc: Joe Almon
Subject: Direct express / proof a GAO in needed
The need for a GAO investigation subsequent to GAO 17-176
Tuesday, December 11, 2018
Preface
Subsequent to and concurrent with the filing of two US Treasury OIG reports (14-031 and 17-034), citing numerous violations of the Fiscal Agent Agreement entered into by Comerica Bank with Bureau of Fiscal Services (Department of Treasury) and also citing a lack of prudent oversight by the commissioner(s) of Fiscal Services, it has been learned by an official with the General Accounting Office that US Senator Orin Hatch and US Senator Elizabeth Warren requested that the General Accounting Office conduct and independent investigation into the workings of Fiscal Services and the Fiscal Agent Agreements.
The findings of this GAO investigation were published in January 2107 as GAO 17-176. This report mainly addressed the issue of lack of transparency by Fiscal Services, but the author, Mr. Michael Clements, was not aware of the victimization of Direct Express debit card holders being perpetrated by Comerica Bank officials.

The "lack of transparency" at Fiscal Services hid the truth about the contract negotiations which awarded the contract to Comerica Bank.

One of the Fiscal Agents of the Bureau Fiscal Services is Comerica Bank, which disburses funds from many governmental agencies. Comerica Bank is one of eight (8) fiscal agents who have contracted with Fiscal Services.

A victim of identity fraud read the two OIG reports and determined that Comerica Bank, as the overseer of Direct Express (the debit card created by Fiscal Services) had not only violated the Fiscal Service agreement with Fiscal Services, but was violating banking law, namely Regulation E (15USC1693) on a regular basis after cardholders were victimized by identity theft. Thus, cardholders were being victimized twice.

In February 2018, this victim, J.B. Simms, announced the revelation to an official of Treasury OIG, both orally and in writing. Treasury OIG commissioned an investigation which is ongoing based upon facts presented by Mr. Simms.

Another victim, Jackie Lynn Densmore, was also a victim of identity theft, and experience similar subsequent victimization by Comerica Bank and the call center personnel masquerading as Direct Express employees. These call center personnel work for Conduent.

After hundreds of reports of victimization have been unearthed at the Consumer Financial Protection Bureau, and dozens more victims having been assisted by the two victims, J.B. Simms and Jackie Lynn Densmore, and in conjunction with media revelations by Kate Berry of American Banker and Tamara Christian of KOVR TV of Sacramento (CA), it became evident that a follow-up investigation by the GAO be commissioned.

The person who signed off on GAO Report 17-176, Michael Clements, has been briefed on the facts surrounding lack of compliance by Comerica Bank, lack of oversight by Fiscal Services, and the egregious and immoral behavior sanctioned by Comerica Bank officers toward identity theft victims, and depriving the victims the protection of Regulation E by using outsourced untrained and uninformed call center persons to communicate with persons reporting a loss due to fraud.

Mr. Clements has agreed that a follow-up report is necessary and will be independent of any investigation of any OIG division of any governmental office. Mr. Clements stated to Mr. Simms on numerous occasions orally and in writing that he only needed a letter of request be submitted by a member of Congress, hopefully from Senator Hatch and/or Senator Warren, who originally requested the GAO conduct an investigation which resulted in GAO 17-176.

Senator Warren, through one of her aides, communicated that Senator Warren would be satisfied with the report from OIG of Treasury and was not "interested" in having a follow-up investigation by the GAO. It is apparent that the GAO would present the most objective of investigations.

Senator Warren requested the GAO in 2106. Her motive for not engaging the GAO to request a follow-up investigation, while her aides are aware of abuse by Comerica Bank, to be concurrent with any OIG investigation, is indefensible.

The GAO official admittedly is waiting for Senator Warren, or any person from Congress, to request the follow-up investigation. The case laid out to the GAO by Mr. Simms was clear, concise, factual, and convincing.

This report proves the necessity of a follow-up GAO report. A synopsis of the GAO report published in January2017 is below, along with interspersed comments.

From: jbsimms
Date: February 3, 2019 at 11:54:19 PM EST
To: "Advocacy US" <advocacy@usdirectexpress.com>,
Cc: "Jackie Lynn"
Subject: RE: Direct express fraud victim
First, your email is being forwarded to Conduent, which is the subcontractor for Comerica Bank which administers the Direct Express card.

They have to start their "investigation immediately, as per Regulation E. They cannot take the 45-90 days that the call center people told you.

You must be credited with the provisional credit within 10 days of the notice, which was fulfilled by me sending this email.

I want you to file an incident report with your local police, and safe a copy of the report.

Send a copy to me and to advocacy@usdirectexpress.com.

I will call you tomorrow for more instructions and explain more about legal claims against Conduent, and how their company violates banking laws.

J.B. Simms

Victim Number 66-Shirley: Arlington, Texas
Resident state of victim: Texas
Date Fraud was discovered: February 4, 2019
Date Fraud was reported: February 4, 2019
Dates of fraud: $129.00 minus card fee, $94.69
Nature of fraud: Kohls and Family Dollar in Miramar, Florida
Amount of fraud: $129.00 minus card fee, $94.69
Date account was credited: February 14, 2019
Amount account was credited: $129.00 minus card fee, $94.69
Source of Monthly payment (Soc Sec, SSI, VA, etc):
Notes/Interaction:
Shirley had been locked out of her account. When she called, she was told that 80-90 dollars were at a Kohls store, $20 somewhere else, and other charges pending. Fraud was on 2/4 (Kohls) and 2/5 (Family Dollar). Crime was in Miramar, FL.

Peter Jackson- he contacted Blackburn. Tt Dana Magneson (731) 660-3971
832am- I called Magneson and talked to her. We to get constituents to call her

Tuesday, February 5, 2019

Rebecca Newton texted me: Dad dying.
I sent the text to everyone and sent the following email.
From: jbsimms
Date: Tue, Feb 05, 2019 8:54 am
To: Nora Arpin (Comerica Bank), Susan Schmidt (Comerica Bank), Wendy Bridges (Comerica Bank), "Advocacy US" <advocacy@usdirectexpress.com>
Cc: Sonja Scott (OIG Treasury), Sarah Lizama (SSA OIG), Richard Delmar (OIG Treasury), Kate Berry (American Banker), Jackie Lynn, Michael Clements (US Gen Acct Office) Franklin Lemond (Plaintiff's Attorney)

James E. Sims, a Direct Express cardholder whose daughter Rebecca Newton has submitted documents validating the fraud claim of over $7,000 on his account, is dying. Rebecca was given notice of the DNR this morning. I believe Mr. Sims is in Tampa General Hospital, Tampa, Florida.

During the spring of 2018, Mr. Sims' account was fraudulently accessed while he was a resident in a nursing facility. The fraudsters spent money all over mid an eastern Georgia, buying items such as $95.00 worth of pizza while Mr. Sims lay in a nursing facility bed.

Conduent got the fraud information and did not give the provisional credit as mandated in Reg E. I have proven that members of the Fraud Unit at Conduent, the subcontractor for Comerica, have no idea of the laws to which they are to abide.

Regardless of the fact that Mr. Sims had given access to his account to Ms. Newton, his daughter, Conduent has the duty to see this report as fraud and return the money to the account. Conduent not only refused to return the money, they locked the account so if the money were to be returned, Ms. Newton would not have access to the account to use the money for the burial of her father.

This exposure of Comerica Bank, Conduent, and lack of oversight by the Bureau of Fiscal Services has caused their employees who have knowledge of this case to act in a malicious manner, intentionally inflicting pain and suffering upon this family.

Words cannot express my disgust for you people as humans, as adults, and as persons of responsibility. When Ms. Newton tell this story to a jury, I will be there to see the faces of the defendants. Hopefully some of your family members will be there to learn how you treated others and failed to abide by law and benefited from your greed. You thought you were protected, which empowered you.

I am waiting for the call from Ms. Newton. You who are holding a dying man hostage for your own personal agenda have the power to abide by the law, replenish the funds, unlock the card account, and allow this man to be buried with honor.
J.B. Simms

It became necessary that I address the Conduent Fraud Unit and their violations of Regulation E regarding Mr. Sims. Shantelle Johnson was head of the Fraud Unit and evidently not familiar with banking law.
Date: Tue, Feb 05, 2019 12:40 pm

To: shantelle.johnosn@conduent.com
Cc: Kate Berry (American Banker), Jackie Lynn, Sonja Scott (OIG Treasury), Sarah Lizama (SSA OIG), Richard Delmar (OIG Treasury), Nora Arpin (Comerica Bank), Susan Schmidt (Comerica Bank), Walter Bayer (SSA OIG), Wendy Bridges (Comerica Bank), rebeccamnewton@aol.com, Franklin Lemond (Plaintiff's Attorney)

Dear Shantelle,

I just got off the phone with Rebecca Newton, the daughter of James E. Sims. This is the dying man whose Direct Express debit card account was hacked while he was in nursing facility, allowing the fraudsters to buy hundreds of dollars of pizza and other items destined for "the hood."

You people have no Fraud Unit. No one who is assigned to the Fraud Unit contacts merchants or law enforcement to confirm the fraud. The burden of proof is upon the financial institution, not the cardholder, to establish fraud. I do not expect you to be able to read and understand this, but I will print it for the others to explain to you.

§1693g. Consumer liability

(b) Burden of proof

In any action which involves a consumer's liability for an unauthorized electronic fund transfer, the burden of proof is upon the financial institution to show that the electronic fund transfer was authorized or, if the electronic fund transfer was unauthorized, then the burden of proof is upon the financial institution to establish that the conditions of liability set forth in subsection (a) have been met, and, if the transfer was initiated after the effective date of section 1693c of this title, that the disclosures required to be made to the consumer under section 1693c(a)(1) and (2) of this title were in fact made in accordance with such section.

Mr. Delmar and Mr. Lemond are attorneys. Comerica Bank has attorneys on staff. They understand the liability Conduent has for violation of federal statutes.

You lied to Ms. Newton. This matter is to be handled in your area of Conduent. Your people did not prove this was not fraud. Any person having an IQ over 70 can see this is fraud.

It makes no difference who has access to the account of Mr. Sims. You have a duty to credit his account, and open his account, regardless whether he will be taken off life support today or if he is on the moon. It is none of your business if Mr. Sims gave permission to his daughter to have access to his account in order to have the funds to bury him.

You want to send this to your "legal" section? Your legal section will be shaking when they see what you and your people have done to Mr. Sims. and you know that I know he is not the only victim Conduent and Comerica have abused. If you have the courage to forward this to your legal section, ask them to contact me. I have proved that call center people like you have no knowledge of the law, nor do you care.

You just made a big mistake.

Sincerely,

J.B. Simms

Below is the email sent from Rebecca Newton, daughter of James Sims, to Richard Delmar, head of OIG Treasury. I sent a copy of this to Jackie.

From: jbsimms
Date: Tue, Feb 05, 2019 6:17 pm
To: "Jackie Lynn"
Subject: James Edward Sims Jr.
From: Rebecca Newton Rebecca Newton
Date: Tue, February 05, 2019, 3:13 pm
To: Richard Delmar (OIG Treasury)

Mr. Delmar,

Per our phone conversation this afternoon attached please find the Direct Express Card statements from March 2018 through August 2018. When you look at each statement none of those charges should be there they are all fraudulent. The total amount due back to my dad is $7,043.61. I have also spoken with Susan Rutledge at Comerica; I have also spoken with Shantelle Johnson at Conduent and Alicia at Conduent. None of them are willing to help me unless I have something signed by my dad saying I'm allowed to handle this for him and in his current condition he is unable to do that. As we speak I am in an ICU room with him worthy of just taking him off all of machines and making him comfortable so that he may pass peacefully. Not only was my father *victimized when his money was stolen but now he's being victimized again by Conduent and Comerica. If the direct express call center employees that my dad and I spoke to an early January add father to document the fact my father told them repeatedly that he wanted me to handle this for him I don't believe that my dad and I would be in this situation. Like I said previously my father was saving that money on his card so that when something like this did happen to him it wouldn't put me in such a financial burden. And now here I am this is still unresolved and my father is about to pass and I have absolutely no way financially to take care of him once he does pass. I am truly hoping that you can help me and at least bring some peace for me and my dad.*

Also when speaking to Conduent Last Friday they put a non-suspension fraud hold on my dad's Direct Express Card. So even if the money did get back to us somehow, I don't even know how we would get the money. So I'm hoping you can help with that as well please.

Rebecca Newton

From: jbsimms
Date: February 5, 2019 at 10:55:00 AM EST
To: Nora Arpin <ntarpin@comerica.com>, Susan Schmidt (Comerica Bank), Wendy Bridges <wwbridges@comerica.com>, Advocacy US <advocacy@usdirectexpress.com>
Cc: Sonja Scott Sonja Scott (OIG Treasury), Sarah Lizama (SSA OIG), Richard Delmar (OIG Treasury), Kate Berry <Kate Berry (American Banker)@sourcemedia.com>, Jackie Lynn, Michael Clements <ClementsM@gao.gov>, Franklin Lemond <Franklin Lemond (Plaintiff's Attorney)@webbllc.com>
Subject: Violation of law, and intentional infliction of pain by vengeance, James E. Sims

James E. Sims, a Direct Express cardholder whose daughter Rebecca Newton has submitted documents validating the fraud claim of over $7,000 on his account, is dying. Rebecca was given notice of the DNR this morning. I believe Mr. Sims is in Tampa General Hospital, Tampa, Florida.

During the spring of 2018, Mr. Sims' account was fraudulently accessed while he was a resident in a nursing facility. The fraudsters spent money all over mid an eastern Georgia, buying items such as $95.00 worth of pizza while Mr. Sims lay in a nursing facility bed.

Conduent got the fraud information and did not give the provisional credit as mandated in Reg E. I have proven that members of the Fraud Unit at Conduent, the subcontractor for Comerica, have no idea of the laws to which they are to abide.

Regardless of the fact that Mr. Sims had given access to his account to Ms. Newton, his daughter, Conduent has the duty to see this report as fraud and return the money to the account. Conduent not only refused to return the money, they locked the account so if the money were to be returned, Ms. Newton would not have access to the account to use the money for the burial of her father.

This exposure of Comerica Bank, Conduent, and lack of oversight by the Bureau of Fiscal Services has caused their employees who have knowledge of this case to act in a malicious manner, intentionally inflicting pain and suffering upon this family.

Words cannot express my disgust for you people as humans, as adults, and as persons of responsibility. When Ms. Newton tell this story to a jury, I will be there to see the faces of the defendants. Hopefully some of your family members will be there to learn how you treated others and failed to abide by law and benefited from your greed. You thought you were protected, which empowered you.

I am waiting for the call from Ms. Newton. You who are holding a dying man hostage for your own personal agenda have the power to abide by the law, replenish the funds, unlock the card account, and allow this man to be buried with honor.

J.B. Simms

From: Delmar, Richard K.
Date: Tue, Feb 5, 2019 11:32 PM
To: Rebecca Newton
Subject: RE: James Edward Sims Jr.
BFS's chief security officer advises that he's working to get this reviewed and resolved. I'll keep after it and keep you advised.

Delmar responded to Rebecca Newton. Our confidence in Delmar was never consistent. We tried being objective or personal. When a government official receives a complaint, all they want to do is get you off the phone and hope you grow weary and disappear.

Wednesday, February 6, 2019

A victim who pushed back, and won

Victim Number 67-Carroll: Galion, OH
Reported by caretaker (Karen Faye):
Date Fraud Detected: February 1, 2019
Date Fraud Reported: February 1, 2019 to FTC as well.
Nature of fraud: lost 771.00 my whole check, Direct Express sent the check to 1161 S Park Rd Apt 211 Hollywood Florida 33201 the phone number was 941 883 8175 no longer in service looked up the address belongs to a 65 year old Hispanic lady.
Date of Credit and amount: Monday February 11, 2019 $736.00 charged for overdraft by fraud

Subject: DIRECT EXPRESS/FRAUD]
From: Carroll
Date: Thu, February 07, 2019 1:17 pm
To: jbsimms
I lost 771.00 my whole check, Direct Express sent the check to 1161 S Park Rd Apt 211 Hollywood Florida 33201 the phone number was 941 883 8175 no longer in service looked up the address belongs to a 65 year old Hispanic lady. No except for talking to that lady last night no one else has called.

Karen told me they used the ATM @ Wells Fargo North Miami 12700 Biscayne Rd.

Thursday February 7, 2019- I talked to Karen- girl friend of Carroll (Craig). She talked to Schmidt last Friday for an hour. Got Schmidt info online. Found my info on Facebook. Schmidt apologized. Also talked to Alisha (thought she was in Arizona) and Calvin (both from Conduent). Calvin was to change email addresses, then realized he sent email to previous address. Calvin never changed the info. Karen sent a complaint to FTC. We have a copy. She is expecting to get new card and money very soon.

Monday February 11, 2019: $771.00 PAID. A five-day turnaround was pretty good.

Thursday, February 7, 2019

From: Rebecca Newton
Date: Thu, Feb 7, 2019, 4:42 PM
To: Delmar, Richard K.
Subject: James Edward Sims Jr.
I know you said you would get back to me as soon as you heard something, and I truly appreciate that. However, I am currently sitting bedside next to my Dad while he is slowly slipping away. I just want to be able to tell him that everything got resolved and he got all his money back. That money is for my Dad's burial. I don't have the financial means to take care of him after he passes. I'm sure this process does take a little time but I'm not sure how much time my Dad has left. I'm honestly not trying to bug you or get on your nerves about this but doesn't my Dad deserve a nice burial like anyone else?
Sorry if I seem overbearing or pushy. I hope to hear from you soon.
Thank you,
Rebecca Newton

Updated contact and payment information for at least ten victims. So many and so much to do some info is overlooked. Some were communicating on Facebook.

Friday, February 8, 2019

James Sims dies; OIG Treasury betrayed him and his daughter

From: jbsimms
Date: Fri, Feb 08, 2019 7:04 am
To: Richard Delmar (OIG Treasury), scscchmidt@comerica.com, shantelle.johnson@conduent.com
Cc: "Jackie Lynn", Kate Berry (American Banker)

James E. Sims, Jr. died approximately 90 minutes ago.

Comerica Bank, along with Conduent employees, attempted to ignore the rational and evidence-based pleadings of the surviving daughter, Rebecca Newton, to acknowledge the blatant fraud on the account of this dying man, and subject Ms. Newton to anguish upon burial and other expenses.

Mr. Sims had been disabled for a long time and was in nursing homes. Rebecca attended to his finances and was given access to his Direct Express account. Since the fraud was reported, and even with pleas for rational thought to Richard Delmar, Ms. Newton's pleas were passed around with no person at Conduent taking responsibility.

The charade which is the "Fraud Unit" is stocked with persons who list banking experience on their resume, as does Ms. Johnson. I fail to see this experience or intellect carried over in her position at Conduent. Mr. Delmar appeared sympathetic to Ms. Newton on the telephone but was impotent with regard to Comerica Bank operation although Delmar is charged with the oversight of Comerica. Susan Schmidt freely talked last Friday and acted on behalf of the significant other whose account was defrauded, and has been proactive, but she has ignored the same scenario for Ms. Newton. This has not escaped me.

Ms. Newton has been asking that the fraud totaling over $7,000 be reinstated on the debit card and the account reopened so she can bury her father with dignity.

You people know that I see your behavior, it is documented, and one day we will all meet before a Senate subcommittee, or in a courtroom, which is a place of which I am all too familiar. The time has come to rid the Direct Express cardholders of Conduent involvement and Comerica's complicity of this inhumane behavior. That is my goal.

J.B. Simms

James Sims died. Rebecca Newton sent me the following text and I sent it out to the others.

The following persons received a copy of the above email:

Subject: [FWD: Last words]
From: jbsimms
Date: Fri, February 08, 2019 7:16 am
To: Richard Delmar (OIG Treasury), Susan Schmidt (Comerica Bank),
shantelle.johnson@conduent.com, "Advocacy US"
<advocacy@usdirectexpress.com>, Nora Arpin (Comerica Bank)
Cc: "Jackie Lynn", "Kate Berry"
<Kate Berry (American Banker)@sourcemedia.com>, "Franklin Lemond" Franklin Lemond (Plaintiff's Attorney)
The last thing he said to me was I love you and I'm sorry. He had no reason to be sorry. It's just absolutely breaks my heart. I have no idea how I'm going to pay to have my father cremated because these bastards are so stupid and wouldn't give him back his money. I haven't checked my email yet but thank you for sending out the email.

Now that Mr. Sims had died, Conduent and Comerica Bank would keep the $7,000 stolen from the account of Mr. Sims. The burden placed upon Mr. Sims, feeling he had to apologize to his daughter for the transgressions of others, was terrible.

Jackie wrote to Delmar and Treasury;
This again could have been avoided if Comerica Bank was stopped and had not been awarded the contract.
I'm beyond heartbroken for this family, this man died knowing the burden he was leaving his daughter with and all involved did nothing !
I hope she sees all of you in court and sues you for everything you have.
You all have known about the fraud for years and your time is up.
I will as well as others make it a mission in life to hold you accountable for your actions.
Sincerely disgusted,
Jackie Densmore

Text message sent to J B Simms from Rebecca Newton
Feb 8, 2019, 3:18 PM
to jbsimms
Still angry, depressed. Found out the County will cremate my Dad at no charge but that means I can't even afford a proper funeral for him. 😕 They said I will get his ashes back in a little wooden box in a few weeks.

From: jbsimms
Date: Fri, Feb 08, 2019 1:02 pm
To: "Martha Best" <shellyandbensmom@hotmail.com>
Cc: Sonja Scott (OIG Treasury), "Susan Schmidt" <Susan Schmidt (Comerica Bank)>, Nora Arpin (Comerica Bank), Sarah Lizama (SSA OIG), Walter Bayer (SSA OIG), shantelle.johnson@conduent.com, Richard Delmar (OIG Treasury)
Dear Ms. Best:
Attention to all:
We know of 4 other victims at BJ's Warehouse. All of you are aware. There is no reason for this cardholder to wait one minute longer.
I recommend that this account be made hole quickly.
Sincerely,
J.B. Simms

Saturday, January 9, 2019

Victims of BJ's Warehouse

Victim Number 68 Donald-GA
Date Fraud Detected: January 9, 2019
Date Fraud Reported: January 10, 2019
Nature of Fraud: January 9, 2019 BJ's Warehouse $523.88, NY
Date of Credit and amount: February 11, 2019 $523.88
Agency source of funds:

Subject: Fw: Fraud on my card
From: Martha Best
Date: Fri, February 08, 2019 12:37 pm
To: "advocacy@usdirectexpress.com" <advocacy@usdirectexpress.com>
Cc: jbsimms
From: Martha Best
Sent: Saturday, February 2, 2019 9:10 AM
To: advocacy@usdirectexpress.com
Subject: Fraud on my card
On Jan.10th, 2019 I called and informed you that a charge of $523.88 made on the 9th was not made by me and that it was still pending. It was made at a BJ's wholesale club in New York for the exact amount that I had on my card (how does that happen). I was told that the charge could not be stopped and to call back in 5 days. I was also told to contact BJ's. BJ's said there was nothing they could do without the member number and of course I didn't have that. I called your company back and after several days was finally able to talk to someone about the fraud. Because I don't hear well and have been very ill with bladder cancer and prostate cancer I asked them to talk with my wife. No problem they said okay after I was able to answer the security questions. My wife was transferred to a very rude woman that said she had to talk only to me (my wife has my Power of Attorney). My wife told her I didn't hear well and that she would have to talk louder to me. Your employee told my wife she couldn't talk any louder and my wife handed me the phone and we were suddenly disconnected. I would like to have my money returned to my account right away. I understand that this should be done on a provision basis. I would also like a copy of this investigation. I have been in touch with a number of people about this situation including my Congressman and I would like to be able to tell him you refunded my money. This is not a fix on your part. My card ends with 6097.
Thank you,
Donald Roy Best

Donald Roy Best received $523.88 Monday February 11, 2019, three days after he contacted me.

Victim Number 69-Donna: OR
Claim filed January 2019.
Residence state of victim: Oregon
Date Credit was placed on account: February 2019 Source of Funds: SSI
Email Saturday February 9, 2019
Dear JB Simms
My name is Donna Friton
I'm a Direct Express cardholder. I receive monthly SSI payments.
In January I filed a claim for unauthorized charges on my account. I filled out & returned paperwork as instructed. I also received a new card. The new card does not work, it is declined (I did activate it)
It declines also when I try to use it at ATM.
I've tried calling customer service countless times and get automated answering and hung up on I'm now borrowing money to pay rent & truck payment.
I did some reading & found you. I called Susan Schimdt & she was supposed to get back to me but hasn't I tried calling her again & she's in a meeting. I called Nora & got her voicemail & left her a message.
Thank you for listening to my story. I'm not sure what to do now but I need my money ASAP and would appreciate your input on this matter.
Thankyou,
Donna Friton

From: Donna Friton
Date: Sat, February 09, 2019 12:25 pm
To: jbsimms
I had to drive from Eugene Oregon to Seattle yesterday so I apologize for not getting back to you. I did hear back from Susan though - probably because of your input. Thankyou
I checked my balance online & I was credited back the money from the claim.
Because of you I believe these dishonest people are realizing that they better straighten up & they can't continue to lie & get away with it.
Sincerely,
Donna Friton

From: jbsimms
Date: Sat, Feb 09, 2019 11:06 pm
To: "Donna Friton" Cc: "Jackie Lynn"
You know I am happy for you. They know they are wrong and busted.
Again, Jackie and I are very happy.
Jim

Victim Number 70- Zechariah: OR
Veteran US Army VA benefits $7,181.31 missing questioned. The number of items purchased was 114 items from March 2018 thru January 2019.
Zechariah was sent a Direct Express card. He was made to believe it was mandatory. He is a disabled veteran suffering from severe PTSD and had previously been receiving a check. He could not remember what he charged. Was evicted and was living in car. Suicidal. I had to talk to police and his VA counselor.
Jackie Densmore sent money to Zechariah so he could eat. Jackie is a wonderful and caring person, and a joy to work with.
A friend helped him fill out the fraud form. Conduent never investigated the case.
Many emails, texts, and telephone calls were made between Zechariah, Jackie, and me. Zechariah was talking about suicide. I talk to the police, who were familiar with Zechariah.
I talked to a VA counselor to confirm the PTSD. Zechariah should never have been made to use the Direct Express debit card.
(February 13, 2019- I called Zechariah; his VA counselor helped and he now getting paper checks).
Carol Gilmer emailed me; she received an email. She got the investigative report from Conduent. She not pleased. I called Carol. She told me the investigative report was simply a filled-out form. No information was included in the "investigation."

149

More cases at BJ's- Donna Friton and Donald Roy Best (Martha's husband) were added to the fraud experienced by Tegan and Jackson as victims of BJ's Warehouse fraud.

Sunday, February 10, 2019

215pm. Peter DeGrandis got a letter from Alisha (Conduent) and shared it with me. The investigation was opened twice, cannot prove fraud. Peter called DE- was told do not call again. Conduent never looked at the video of the person(s) who stole his money at the ATM.

2:50pm Rebecca Newton called. Delmar said he had seen "lots of complaints against Comerica" (Tuesday Feb 5) and she "is not the first." I know how it feels, my mom passed recently."

It was hard for me to have any sympathy for Delmar losing his mother when he was neglecting Rebecca Newton.

Monday, February 11, 2019

Alishia got her money

Date: Mon, February 11, 2019 1:32 pm
To: Advocacy US <advocacy@usdirectexpress.com>, jbsimms
Hello, I have just received the card with the full amount of $841.72. I have already taken the money and I would like to cancel this card and my account with your company. Thanks!
Alisha

Monday February 11, 2019, Alisha go her card and full refund $841.72 She was paid within 10 days of contacting me. Conduent had closed her fraud complaint before she contacted me. These were some very unscrupulous people.

Sandra Chapman- television interview
Sandra Chapman <sandra.chapman@wthr.com>
Mon, Feb 11, 2019, 11:56 AM
to me
You were great...thank you. Looking forward to getting this story on the air!
I'll be in touch.
Sandra Chapman, 13 Investigates Reporter

I had a long talk with Sonja Scott (OIG Treasury Investigative Office today. I got her fax number: (202) 927-5404. Many subjects were discussed concerning the failure of OIG Treasury to thoroughly investigate Comerica and Conduent. The bidding process for the new contract was taking place at BFS and Jackie Densmore and I wanted BFS to know what we know. The rampant violations of Reg E by Conduent should be recognized in the investigation which will be submitted to be included in the audit.

This is the feeling of all fraud victims of the Direct Express program. The victims are glad to be rid of Comerica, Conduent, and Treasury.

Tuesday, February 12, 2019

Marteshia McPhail texted me; Marteshia gave me permission to talk to the police/sheriff department regarding her case.
I sent LinkedIn message to Dr. Paul Lawrence, VA Benefits area. He never responded.

From: jbsimms
Date: Tue, Feb 12, 2019 10:23 am
To: Jackie Lynn, Franklin Lemond (Plaintiff's Attorney)
I believe this is updated.
3 got paid yesterday.
Jim

Three victims got paid yesterday. This is progress. I had to share this with Jackie. She knew how hard I had been working on this.

I began work on McPhail. There is no reason why the police and FBI had not arrested anyone. Conduent had the records and would not reveal anything to the McPhail family. I would now have to be involved in the criminal investigation.
Incident report 201807-0410
Deputy Lori L. Newman 7/23/2018
Investigator Caroline A Kinney 7/25/2018
Sgt William K Sumner- signed off 7/28/2018

12:19pm T (843) 398-4501 Darlington Co Sheriff Department, for Caroline Kinney-talked to Briana. Kinney-Kinney is at the academy for training. Left message for Lt Cusak. He to call tomorrow. I want to know what has been done to investigate the $30,000 stolen from Mr. McPhail.
Shirley England- she texted- got her money today- $129.00 and $94.69 crime in Miramar Florida.
Kerri Uchina- got police report. Got paid 2/14/2019 she to email police report to Conduent Customer Advocacy.

615pm Jackie Densmore called- Zech Allen bad off. She talked to him. He is suicidal.
T (541) 693-6911 Redmond, Oregon Police-Talked to dispatcher.
Zech Allen called- he is living in a Ford Edge. There is at rest stop, cliff side, Hwy 97. Thrift Market was 5 miles away. He has tt Kevin at Conduent (retarded). Refused to listen.
Josh Power- Redmond Police- called. He was familiar with Zech Allen. Advised Allen is homeless and might be in need of assistance.

Wednesday, February 13, 2019

From: jbsimms
Date: Wed, Feb 13, 2019 4:22 pm
To: "Sharita Williams" <akingslady@gmail.com>
Shirita,
Since you got a denial on the fraud, you can demand a copy of the investigation.
Email these two email addresses and request a copy of both investigations. Make sure you copy me in the request so they know that I am involved.
advocacy@usdirectexpress.com
shantelle.johnson@conduent.com
In the meantime, see if the cop will get you a copy of the photo. If there is no record of the Conduent people contacting law enforcement, considering you emailed them the police report, we will really go after them.
Jim Simms

Subject: A thought, and maybe a proactive approach to problem solving
From: jbsimms
Date: Wed, Feb 13, 2019, 7:20 pm
To: Richard Delmar (OIG Treasury)
Cc: Sonja Scott (OIG Treasury), Walter Bayer (SSA OIG), Sarah Lizama (SSA OIG), Jackie Lynn, Kate Berry (American Banker)
Bcc: "Michael Clements" <ClementsM@gao.gov>
Dear Mr. Delmar,
Based upon the last 7 months of me receiving at total of 70 Direct Express cardholder complaints of being defrauded and subsequently victimized by Comerica Bank and Conduent (which was not exposed in the previous OIG "audits" I read over a year ago), along with the blatant malfeasance and violation of federal law, it occurred to me that you and/or Mr. Thorsen could withhold any payments made to Comerica Bank until the publication of the investigation by your office.
You know I know most of the issues which I would gladly present to you and Mr. Thorsen, or an interested member of congress. It is obvious that dozens of persons have received rightful credits to their accounts since the involvement of Ms. Densmore, Ms. Berry, and me. There is no proactive behavior from Treasury OIG, even though hundreds of complaints are logged at the CFPB, BBB, and various websites. The disclaimer by

Comerica Bank is that these numbers are a minuscule percentage of customer complaints, but a vast majority of the complaints are not solely complaints; these complaints have been revealed to be violations of law, and malfeasance on the part of Comerica Bank hiring a subcontractor to conduct banking "financial" operations when Conduent is not a "financial institution" and will attempt to avoid liability as such. Violations of the Fiscal Agency Agreement, noted in the two OIG audits, were never enforced.

Willful transparency on the part of Fiscal Services was requested and suggested and documented in the GAO Report 17-176, dated January 25, 2017. The GAO was ignored, as evidenced by OIG 17-034, published the day before the GAO report.

I feel I can speak for the known and unknown victims of Comerica Bank when I ask that you and Mr. Thorsen seriously consider immediately withholding disbursement of any funds to Comerica Bank until a full investigation is completed, accountability is made, and penalties imposed.

Sincerely,

J.B. Simms

Thursday, February 14, 2019

Big Day: suit was filed against Comerica Bank and Conduent

Today was a big day: Franklin filed suit against Comerica Bank and Conduent. We had nine plaintiffs. One would drop out years later. Franklin sent me the complaint to review.

The Direct Express contract with BFS was open for bids

The new contract bidding was ongoing and the announcement of the bank receiving the Fiscal Agent contract for the Direct Express program was to be announced in May 2019. Jackie and I had a plan to be involved in the process.

Instant Message (IM) was sent to me from Kerri Uchiha- she got her reimbursement of $135.34.

Another victory, but the fact Conduent and Comerica Bank continue to victimize cardholders was keeping me very busy.

In the email below, I wanted Shantelle Johnson, of Conduent, to know who she was up against. She knew my name and so did her boss Mitch Raymond.

From: jbsimms
Date: Thu, Feb 14, 2019, 12:39 pm
To: Shantelle Johnson (Conduent), Nora Arpin (Comerica Bank), "Advocacy US"
<advocacy@usdirectexpress.com>
Cc: "Lisa Mena" <lisamena73@yahoo.com>, "Jackie Lynn", Sarah Lizama (SSA OIG), Walter Bayer
(SSA OIG), Richard Delmar (OIG Treasury)
I have been involved in more at least 70 cases involving neglect, malfeasance, cruelty, and ignorance on behalf of many people, but as I revisit this case, this was one of the worst.

Lisa Mena was evicted from her apartment, an apartment in which she needed a caregiver to assist her. Her card was used without her authority at times when she had thought she had the card in her possession. The fraudulent charges are listed and easily discernible.

No person at Conduent made any effort to reach out to any merchant or find any surveillance to validate the claim that this disabled lady falsely reported fraud on her account. The amount was less than $264.78. This amount o of money caused her to be evicted from her apartment and live in motels and vehicles.

This happened because the "fraud unit" at Conduent conducts no investigation and uniformly never has any informative basis, outside their limited scope, for denying a claim. The damages we hope to recover for Ms. Mena, and other victims, will be exponentially greater than the $264.78 she lost.

I suggest this matter be revisited.

Either do an investigation, review surveillance footage, or return the money claimed. Damages against you people will be determined at a later date.

Below is the story for you to read again.

J.B. Simms

As was written, the number of people who cases I had worked had reached 70. My phone rang constantly. Sonja Scott, US Treasury, emailed me and asked for the list of 70+ victims whose cases I had been assisted. It was as though she was challenging my honesty. I sent he the list.

Friday, February 15, 2019

From: jbsimms
Date: Fri, Feb 15, 2019, 3:15 pm
To: "Michael Clements" <ClementsM@gao.gov>
Cc: "Jackie Lynn", Kate Berry (American Banker)
Dear Mr. Clements,
The problem now is this: since Sen Warren has delayed/refused to do this[endorse the GAO investigation), the bidding process will have passed us by before any investigation done by your office could be considered.
I do not know if any work by your office could be completed and considered before the final bid in awarded, but we will take any suggestion you might give.
Thanks,
Jim

Victim Number 71- Debra Smith-WI
Date Fraud was discovered: February 1, 2019
Date Fraud was reported: February 1, 2019
Dates of fraud: February 1, 2019
Nature of fraud: Today's Health (877)8435966 ($94.99) Health Cleanse (888)3579855 ($93.95)
Both were pending transactions.
Amount of fraud: $94.99 and $93.95
Date account was credited: February 22, 2019
Amount account was credited: $94.99 and $93.95.

Below is Debbie Smith's email.
Subject: Direct Express Fraud
From: Debbie Smith
Date: Fri, February 15, 2019, 4:49 pm
To: "advocacy@usdirectexpress.com" <advocacy@usdirectexpress.com>
Cc: jbsimms
"Sarah Lizama (SSA OIG)" <Sarah Lizama (SSA OIG)>, " ntarpin@comerica.com"
<ntarpin@comerica.com>, "Sonja Scott (OIG Treasury)@oig.treas.gov" Sonja Scott (OIG Treasury)
My name is Debra Smith. On February 1st,2019 I checked my balance on my account and noticed 2 pending transactions which I did not make. The first one was for 94.99 on Feb. 1st 2019 at13:48:46. The next one was 2 seconds later for 93.95. {13:48:48} also on Feb. 1,2019. The first one was todayhealth,8778435966. The 2nd one was healthclnse,8883579855. I called Direct express right away and the man knew right away which ones they were. He even said they were fraudulent. He told me to call back in 3-4 days to see if it was still pending. He said he could not stop the payment from going through. At midnight the same night it was no longer pending. I called the numbers on my statement and it rang once and went right to the same "HOLD" music that I hear every time I'm put on hold when I call DE. I called both numbers numerous times. No one ever answered. Just music. I called DE back and was put on hold for about 48 minutes. Then the person I talked to transferred me to someone else. She put me on hold and after a few minutes the call was disconnected. I had to call back again and was put on hold for about 58 min. just to be told it could take 45-90 days to get my money back. She said she would send some paperwork and I should get it in I believe she said 7-10 days. I have not received the paperwork as of yet. I had to take the little bit of money I had and cancel my card and request a new one, which I have received. I am stressed out. I needed that money to pay my gas and light bills. They will disconnect me, and I am on oxygen. There is a rule where I live that I can be evicted for failure to keep up on my utilities. Aug. 29th 2018 I was in the hospital in a coma for a few weeks, then a nursing home. I did not authorize the transactions. Why couldn't they stop them before they were paid out? The woman I talked to said these peple first started charging my card on Jan. 20th 2019 but the funds were not on there. I don't make transactions when I don't have the money on my card. I never saw any pending transactions from them before Feb.!2019 I am looking forward to hearing from you soon. Thank You and have a nice evening.

From: jbsimms
Date: Fri, Feb 15, 2019 5:20 pm
To: "Debbie Smith, "advocacy@usdirectexpress.com" <advocacy@usdirectexpress.com>
Cc: "Sarah Lizama (SSA OIG)" <Sarah Lizama (SSA OIG)>, "ntarpin@comerica.com"
<ntarpin@comerica.com>, "Sonja Scott (OIG Treasury),"Jackie Lynn"
Dear Ms. Smith,

Thankfully you are resourceful enough to find the posted information and have contacted the right persons. Your first contact with Direct Express is notification. The "investigation" that is to be conducted is done by persons working for Conduent, which is a subcontractor for Comerica, and is not a financial institution.

As per Reg E, 15USC1693, your funds are to be returned to you as full provisional credit within 10 days after notification of the fraud. Since Comerica Bank outsourced all their call center, customer advocacy, and fraud unit functions to Conduent, not a financial institution, Conduent has regularly violated laws which apply to financial institutions, leaving Direct Express cardholders no recourse, until now. I will explain our recourse when we talk on the phone.

The fraudulent transaction could have been stopped. I will explain this to you also.

The fraud investigation unit is a sham, and a scam. The persons employed by Conduent as fraud investigators have varying degrees of banking experience, some none. There is no evidence that any person within the fraud unit has called any law enforcement agency, merchant, or bank where fraudulent ATM activity occurred. The exposure of culpable Conduent employees as a result of an "investigation" deters an actual investigation.

The email you sent to Advocacy will suffice with respect to any written narrative necessary for Conduent to read. The fraud packet is full of invasive and intrusive questions which give the Conduent employees more information than necessary, thus continuing to be jeopardizing your funds.

You can call me at (803) 309-6850. I have banking experience and you can google me to confirm my experience as private investigator. I thought I had retired as a PI until my account was hacked, but my experience has allowed me to assist dozens of victims.
J.B. Simms

Victim Number 72- Terri: FL
Date Fraud was reported: February 4, 2019
Dates of fraud: 2/1/2019
Nature of fraud: Verizon Wireless transaction in Ft. Mill, SC $1,104.09
Amount of fraud: $1,104.09

Tuesday February 19, 2019 Email to Calvin:

Hello, Calvin. I realize yesterday was our first contact, but I have been in contact with Direct Express since Monday morning, February 4, 2019 wherein I notified DE that a fraudulent transaction had all but drained my account taking my entire February Social Security Disability check. I left you a message a little after 1:00 today regarding this.

I am writing this to put you on notice that your company, Direct Express, has already violated the deadline for a provisional refund to be given to me by 5 days as of today. It has now been 19 days since you were notified of the fraud that was perpetrated on me via Direct Express.

I am forwarding all previous information I have regarding this claim, together with any documentation from this date forward to Jim Simms to be included together with any other victims of Direct Express.

Thank you for your attention to this matter. I am sure that I will hear from you by close of business today, as you promised me yesterday. Have a good afternoon,
Terri Moran
cc: jbsimms

Saturday, February 16, 2019

Gwen Grant- stolen money
1227pm she called office-talked to FTC Special Crime Unit (Charles) at 1pm yesterday.
After call, got back $131.00 just now.
FTC center stated has many calls.

Brian Shelly called- Brian got his money. This is always good news. I recovered hundreds of thousands of dollars.

Sunday, February 17, 2019

Subject: meeting
From: jbsimms
Date: Sun, Feb 17, 2019 6:23 pm
To: Sonja Scott (OIG Treasury), Richard Delmar (OIG Treasury)
Cc: "Jackie Lynn", Kate Berry (American Banker)
Dear Ms. Scott and Mr. Delmar,
It has occurred to me there are two issues about the Treasury OIG which cause concern with respect to this matter with Comerica Bank, Fiscal Services, and Conduent:
1) Even with recommendations made in the first two "audits" there was no enforcement of Fiscal Services or Comerica Bank to adhere to the FAA
2) The exclusion of cardholders with respect to suggestions for implementation of safeguards encourages the same decision makers who developed the FAA to offer the same impotent agreement, inviting corruption, graft, dereliction of duty, taking improper gratuities, and various criminal offenses.
If you want to appear to have the best interest of veterans and other cardholders, allow a select group of cardholders to meet you across a table and let you see the suffering, face to face. Then listen to them. No GS level title claim to have common sense and humanity within its prerequisites.
If this matter is not open to representatives of the cardholders, no one will trust you to do your job, or to protect veterans and other cardholders. If you think meeting with cardholders is an admission of guilt, just remember that the cardholders do not trust you, so this might be a way to gain favor.
If/when the cardholders appear and testify at a public forum, you might want them to say that Fiscal Services did their job, rather than what they are ready to say.
Feel free to share this with Mr. Thorsen.
J.B. Simms

Victim Number 73- Samantha: PA
Date Fraud was discovered: Feb 6, 2019
Date Fraud was reported: February 6, 2019
Dates of fraud: 2/6
Nature of fraud: International purchase fee: $1.58 Cash purchase: 52.76
Amount of fraud: $1.58 and $52.76

Below is part of email I sent to Sonja and Delmar, and cc Samantha Cardinal.
This been reported to Conduent, the contractor for Comerica Bank, which is charged in the administration of the Direct Express program.
It is my understanding that this fraud has been reported and, as is a pattern of Conduent, ignored.
This noticed, given by a person having proprietary knowledge of the fraud, pursuant to Regulation E, am putting Conduent and Comerica Bank on notice of the fraud.
Quoting from Ms. Cardinal:
"I could not cancel those myself because when I googled that place it came up something in a different language!!
So I just needed those to be cancelled and put back. Because whatever that is was from the internet.!!"
It appears Conduent/Comerica Bank is in violation of giving provisional credit to Ms. Cardinal, in violation of Regulation E, which Ms. Arpin has stated (an is recorded) that Comerica Bank adheres to this legal obligation. Comerica Bank and Comerica have now been given notice on behalf of Ms. Cardinal.
J.B. Simms

Monday, February 18, 2019

J B Simms
Mon, Feb 18, 2019, 8:55 AM
to Jackie, Kate, Sandra,
Bids are being received.
Fiscal Services thinks they can fix the problem they created (stopping payoffs, etc).

The Treasury OIG report will be published soon.
Will the Treasury OIG findings be published before the decision is made to grant the bid?
How can Fiscal Services create a list of parameters, which they screwed up in the beginning, when they have not considered the OIG report?
Maybe OIG gave advance copy to Fiscal Services.
We do not know if Comerica is bidding.
My suggestion is to break out all VA payments and create a new fiscal agent, strictly for veterans.
As Michael Clements wrote in GAO 17-176, there is no transparency at Fiscal Services.

If Comerica Bank, as the incumbent Fiscal Agent, submits another bid, we want to be involved.

Malfeasance by Bureau of Fiscal Services, Comerica Bank, and Conduent

Below is a submission I made to many legislators in an attempt to commission a new GAO investigative audit.

Monday, February 18, 2019

The need for a follow-up to GAO Report 17-176

The US Bureau of Fiscal Services, a division of the US Department of Treasury, was created to electronically disburse federal funds to a number of different classes of recipients. Recipients supposedly were given the option of having funds electronically deposited into a bank, credit union, or the Direct Express debit card. The truth is many veterans have had their disability payments unwillingly sent to them via the Direct Express card. Some veterans received paper checks for years and involuntarily received the Direct Express debit card. The recipient classes include but are not limited to Social Security, Social Security Disability (SSI), Veteran Compensation and Pension, Veteran Health Administration (Disability Income), Veteran Reserve Education Assistance, and other classes of recipients. The entire list of recipients can be found at:
https://www.usdirectexpress.com/faq.html
Comerica Bank bid twice and was twice selected to administer the Direct Express program. The bidding process for the third cycle began in November 2018 and the bidding ends in March 2019. The awarding of the third contract will be determined by the Director of Fiscal Services, counsel, and other designated persons.
In February 2018, J.B.Simms, after having twice been the victim of financial identity fraud as a Direct Express cardholder, examined two Treasury OIG reports pertaining to the performance of Comerica Bank and Fiscal Services:
 Treasury OIG 14-031, published March 26, 2014
Treasury OIG 17-034 published January 24, 2017
Simms found both reports to be deficient in substance. Treasury OIG was advised that both reports failed to provide any enforcement of recommendations, and failed to investigate the advocacy, customer service, and fraud units of Conduent, which served the Direct Express card holders. Also indicated was the lack of any investigations being performed by the fraud unit of Conduent, which is under the charge of Comerica Bank. Based upon this revelation to a chief auditor of Treasury OIG, an "investigation" versus an audit, was commissioned.
This information of victimization of Social Security recipients convinced the Social Security Administration OIG to commission an investigation of the victimization of Social Security recipients by Conduent, and Comerica Bank.
In 2016, Senators Orrin Hatch and Senator Elizabeth Warren requested an investigation of Fiscal Services by the General Accounting Office. The GAO is independent, works for Congress, not for any agency.
 The result of this investigation is found at:
https://www.gao.gov/assets/690/682274.pdf
GAO 17-176: Revenue Collections and Payments
Treasury Has Used Financial Agents In Evolving Ways but Could Improve Transparency
"GAO was asked to review Treasury's use of financial agent. "
The lack of transparency by Fiscal Services by failing to reveal payments by Fiscal Agents, as well as a revelation of incomplete documentation submitted by bidders, was noted in the report.

This report, GAO 17-176, was submitted to Senators Hatch and Warren by Michael E. Clements, Acting Director, Financial Markets and Community Investment.

Mr. Simms contacted Mr. Clements in October 2018. Mr. Clements stated the recommendations for transparency did not generate any change since the publication of GAO 17-176 in January 2017.

Mr. Clements was briefed that Comerica Bank enabled dozens of victims of identity and financial fraud, to including veterans, within the Direct Express program. The following issues were addressed:

1. The Direct Express program is endorsed and encouraged by Fiscal Services, Social Security, and Comerica Bank.

2. The Direct Express cardholders are exposed to a program in which Comerica Bank offers no security parameters, but security parameters are available for proprietary customers of Comerica Bank.

3. Comerica Bank had hired a subcontractor, Conduent, to handle all call center, customer relation (Customer Advocacy), and fraud investigations.

4. Upon examining the activity of the Conduent fraud unit, it was discovered that fraud claim workers, employed by Conduent, never contacted law enforcement, merchants, or other banks which owed ATM, to see surveillance footage or verify the fraud claim submission.

5. Decisions to deny fraud claims were performed by inexperienced persons who admittedly were not familiar with Regulation E (15USC1693) and, using a cursory glance at previous statements as the litmus test for fraud.

6. Many fraudulent transactions that were denied were consummated in geographic regions far away from the cardholder, some outside the United States, or nearly simultaneous with transactions by cardholders.

7. Comerica Bank officials defer all questions to a non-banking institution, which has exempted itself from banking regulations.

The result of fraud perpetrated upon veterans and other victims has resulted in failure to obtain medication, food, being evicted from housing, hopelessness, and frustration.

Mr. Clements stated, based upon information supplied to him, he would commission a new GAO report as a follow up to GAO 17-176. This would be a more objective report than from Treasury OIG or Social Security OIG. All Mr. Clements needed was a letter from a senator (preferably on the Finance Committee) or a representative specifically asking for a follow up investigation.

It is imperative that we engage the GAO in this matter.

Comerica Bank violations, the hiring of a non-banking subcontractor (Conduent) and the lack of oversight by Fiscal Services, needs to be investigated by the GAO.

Tuesday, February 19, 2019

Michael Clements, at the GAO, told me he needs a member of congress to begin inquiry. Warren will not authorize it. Senator Warren was covering up for Comerica Bank because Senator Warren was a declared candidate for the Democrat Party nomination to become President and was counting on contributions from the banking industry.

Thursday, February 21, 2019

Victim 72, Terri from Florida, called. She talked to Calvin at Conduent Customer Advocacy. Funds were being put back into her account. Told her this is what it takes; expose and confront.

Victim Number 74: Keith-CA
Date Fraud was reported: February 3, 2019.
Dates of fraud: February 1, 2019.
Nature of fraud: Two transactions: Card Purchases Feb 1, 2019
SINGLCHANGEMAK $89.79 SUPEREXTRACTXR MANGO $93.23
Amount of fraud: $183.02
I reported the fraud on February 3rd,2019 because we couldn't get in touch with them for the first two days. Once we received the dispute papers, we sent them back and when calling yesterday (February 20,2019) to check the status, my husband was told he didn't have enough information and we needed to provide a receipt even though the money was stolen. They were very rude and showed no concern of his money being stolen. February 26, 2019 emailed sent to Shantelle for copy of investigation.

Monday March 4, 2019- I gave phone numbers for him to call Schmidt and Rutledge.

Friday, February 22, 2019

Victim 71, Deb Smith, called- she talked to Susan Schmidt at Comerica (I gave her the contact numbers). Both charges of fraud, $94.99 and $93.95, were refunded.

Monday, February 25, 2019

Victim Number 75: Kathy-IL
I've attached the transaction I'll be referring to in this email.
I made a transfer on 2/20 to my regular bank acct. From my direct express card. As of this morning, it's not gone thru. Direct express says they no longer allow transfers but it allowed mine. Now they are saying it's in dispute and can take up to 90 days and I might not even get my money back. How's that possible when my bank confirmed the $200 was not received? I get less than $700 a month. Why is direct express doing this when they gave me a transfer confirmation # and they won't check to see if it went to a wrong account...is this a scam? Social security recommends this card...shame on them.. None of the reps know what they are talking about. I've been told the money is there, that my bank, Chase bank is telling lies, I'm told it's a Mastercard so the bank won't accept the transfer. Chase said it doesn't matter as the transfer is done as a direct deposit. Today I was told Direct Express is not a bank and will not cancel transfers...lie after lie. Chase bank has been wonderful with trying to help me but since the transfer has not been received, it's up to Direct Express. With what's left on my card, after I pay rent, I'll be left with less than $20 until the 3rd Wednesday in March unless I get my $200 back. Can you help? A poster left your email, stating you may be writing a story on this....

I replied to her email and forwarded email to Comerica , Conduent, and others.

Tuesday, February 26, 2019

I went to LinkedIn- found Joe Plenzler, Director, Wounded Warrior Project, Public Affairs, and I sent him a message. Joe Plenzler would become a great ally to help in the cause to help victimized veterans.
Kathy (Victim 75) called today; she got her money. When she called Conduent, they told her "we are not a bank, we don't do that."

LaTashia Woods had to contact Shantelle Johnson, the manager of the Fraud Unit of Conduent on behalf of her husband, Victim 74 Keith Woods. The email is below.

Date: Tue, Feb 26, 2019 at 1:32 PM
Subject: To: <shantelle.johnson@conduent.com>
Hello Shantelle Johnson, My name is LaTashia Woods and I am emailing you on behalf of my husband Keith Woods, he has been a victim of fraud in the amount $183.02 and has been told he cannot receive a refund for the funds stolen from him. I am well aware of the class action suit and according to regulation E he's entitled to a copy of the investigation and would like to receive a copy. I have tried to contact you and have not received a call in return. I feel my husbands money shouldn't be kept away from him due to fraud, and I have talked to Jim Simms and I plan to take further action because direct express is not doing their job to please their customers. Down below you will find a copy of the letter that was sent to my husband. If you have any questions please feel free to contact me at any time

Subject: RE: [FWD: Direct Express Card]
From: Kathleen Cerrito
Date: Tue, February 26, 2019 5:21 am
To: jbsimms
I just checked my card and the money, including their transfer fee has been returned to my card. I'm taking every penny out today. Thank God my social security goes into my bank account starting March.
Thank You. I believe it's been returned because of your action. Keep doing this work!
Kathy Cerrito

Subject: The bid
From: jbsimms
Date: Tue, Feb 26, 2019 8:46 am
To: Sonja Scott (OIG Treasury)
Cc: Richard Delmar (OIG Treasury)
Dear Ms. Scott,
How can I find out which banks are bidding for the Fiscal Agent slot now occupied by Comerica?
Have you seen the interview aired on the NBC affiliate in Indianapolis yesterday?
We will be suggesting that Fiscal Services create a new fiscal agent specifically for veterans. I know the suggestions made in this last two audits were ignored and no enforcement of the FAA was evident. Hopefully that will not happen again. If you and/or Mr. Delmar could forward this link to Mr. Thorsen, hopefully he will see a need to protect the veterans, who are mostly former enlisted and do not deserve this abuse.
Jim Simms

Wednesday, February 27, 2019

I sent an email to Marteshia and advised her I had been contacting the Darlington County Sheriff's Department about the $30,000 fraud on her dad's Direct Express card. Below are excerpts of that email:

Incident report 201807-0410
Deputy Lori L. Newman 7/23/2018- Incident report filed
Investigator Caroline A Kinney 7/25/2018- Date of submission of report
Sgt William K Sumner- signed off 7/28/2018- Date of review of investigation
In September 2018 you contacted me. I assisted you in attempting to get some clarification of the denial of fraud claim from Direct Express, which we determined is actually Conduent.
This matter was brought to the attention of Sonja Scott and Richard Delmar of Treasury OIG. My understanding is that months ago you were contacted by someone from Treasury, your father was not contacted, and that was the end of the investigation.
Within the past few weeks, I attempted to determine the status of the investigation at the Darlington County Sheriff Department. I called to talk to Investigator Caroline Kinney and learned that she was in training at the SC Law Enforcement Academy. Messages were left for her superior, Lt, Cusak, who never returned a call. A call was made to Major Yarborough, who did speak to me on Thursday, February 21, 2019. Major Yarborough insured me he would look into the matter and call me the following day. No call was received.
Today, Wednesday, February 27, 2019, I called and left a message for Major Yarborough. The call was returned by Deputy Epps. Deputy Epps was not as familiar with the case as I would have expected. We discussed the fact that nowhere in the report is there a record of Inv Kinney making any calls, especially to the motel where your brother and his mother stayed, and we discussed the fact that the first fraudulent charge was 3 hours before the payment of the motel room.
Epps confirmed that there was nothing in the file to state that an investigation had occurred, or that, since there was no evidence that the crime was committed in Darlington County, that the case was turned over to a federal agency. Oddly, there should have been clarification in the file that the case was sent to Treasury OIG or the US Attorney office in Florence, SC (that office would authorize the FBI to look into the case).

Friday, March 1, 2019

I continued to use LinkedIn to send messages. I discovered Pamela Powers, who was the Acting Chief of Staff (and a retired USAF colonel). Since Paul Lawrence, who was the head of the Veteran Benefits, was ignoring my messages, I was pleased that Ms. Powers would communicate a bit with me. Below is the response I received from her: "I will look into this at the VA".
I sent a message to Laurine Carson- Dep Exec Dir (SES) VA- 30 years.She replied she would forward my concern to Office of Finance Management

Victim Number 76-Dale:MI
Date Fraud was discovered: January 28, 2019
Date Fraud was reported: January 28, 2019
Dates of fraud: January 28, 2019

Nature of fraud: Version Wireless, South Carolina
January 28, 2019 $905.98 at 01:01:13 and $905.98 at 11:48:49
Amount of fraud: $1,994.98
Date account was credited: March 11, 2019.
Notes: March 11, 2019 email: Calvin has had DE issue me a $905.98 credit for one of the fraudulent charges made against my account. Verizon Wireless refunded the other $905.98 charge.
Fraud occurred twice at Verizon Wireless in SC. Claim was accepted, then retracted. One claim was retracted.
Victim 76 is retired Homeland Security employee.
Below is the email sent by Dale, Victim 76:

Attached are jpeg files of my letters to you showing I was defrauded of $1,828.46. Two charges of $905.98 each were debitted from my account on 1-28-19, 1st was at 01:01:13 and 2nd was at 11:48:49. Both were to Verizon Wireless in South Carolina. I have never had a Verizon account and have never lived in South Carolina! I was at my home in Michigan with my debit card in my wallet when these charges were made against my account. I reported the fraud on the evening of the same day, because I could not get through on your phone number to cancel the card any sooner. I did transfer my balance from my account to prevent further fraud when I could not get through to cancel the card. I was charged $1.50 fir the balance transfer even though it was necessary because of your phone "service" being unavailable! I was also charged $15 for expedited service of the replacement card even though I told the service agent I would not pay for expedited service!! On 2-4-19 Verizon returned $890.39 to my account. On 2-14-19 $905.98 a reversal credit was added to my account. On 2-28-19 at 22:48 the reversal credit was taken from my account. Therefore, you still have $938.07 of my money. I demand IMMEDIATE return of all stolen funds plus fees charged to my account because of your negligence in approving these charges! Contact me no later than 17:00 on 3-4-19 or I will be pursue this matter in the courts.

Part of the big lie by Conduent was when a fraud victim was ignored by Conduent, the fraud victim might go to the merchant. Technically the Investigation Unit of Conduent is supposed to be contacting the merchant or giving immediate credit. This email confirmed that Conduent would falsify their records to make it appear they were giving provisional credit when in fact the money was being returned by the merchant.

Monday, March 11, 2019

10:24am Email to me from Victim 76-Dale Liikala:
Hello Erik. Calvin has had DE issue me a $905.98 credit for one of the fraudulent charges made against my account. Verizon Wireless refunded the other $905.98 charge. Calvin also had DE refund the $13.50 expedited shipping charge for my new card. I am still fighting for them to refund me for the $1.50 balance transfer fee that would not have been necessary if I could have reached their "customer service" number to have the card cancelled to prevent any further fraud from taking place. I hope this time the $905.98 credit will not be reversed as the last one was but I will keep you informed. Thanks for all your help. I probably would still be hitting a brick wall if you hadn't provided the contact information needed to get their attention. Keep up the good work and let me know if I can provide any more information that may help you proceed against Direct Express for their complicity and gross negligence that allows debit card fraud to occur so easily.
Regards,

It was comical that since my email address is jbslmms, some thought my name was Erik. Erik was my dog.

Saturday, March 2, 2019

Victim Number 77-Sandra: OH
Fraud: March 1, 2019 Walmart: Stockbridge, GA 0745, $103.49 $62.52 Advance Auto: Decatur, GA $.85 and $803.00
She contacted DE
Total: $1,771.01
Fraud 3/1 Walmart in GA, 103.49 and 61.52. Advance Auto .85 and $803.00.
My name is Sandra Green. I was told to contact you concerning fraud on my direct express card I went to pay my bills and my card was declined. My account was wiped out of 1,771.01 dollars. Now I cant pay my house payment, health insurancr, homeowners insurance, buy my medicine and other expenses. Im so upset. This happened on 3/1. I live in Ohio. I have possesion of my.card. The first charges were on 3/1 at walmart store

160

0745 Stockbridge, Georgia. One for $103.49 and another charge for $61.52. The other charges were dine at Advance Auto Parts on 4794 Flat Shoals Parkway, Decatur, Georgia. One charge was for 85 cents and the other charge was for $803. I called Direct Express fraud department to report the fraudulent charges. They took the report then transferred me to their Dispute Department which completed the report. The Dispute Department is supposed to send me documents to complete. Then they will investigate and it can take 45 to 90 days after they receive the completed report. I cant pay my bills and buy food. The people that used my card number and made these charges somehow got into Direct Expresses system and changed my address. I had hard time convincing Direct express that im the owner of the card because they didnt have record of my address. Ive lived here 14 years. Please help me.

There were times I submitted fraud claims for victims, which I was entitled to do.

From: jbsimms
Date: Sat, Mar 02, 2019 7:35 pm
To: "Advocacy US" <advocacy@usdirectexpress.com>, Shantelle Johnson (Conduent), "Susan Schmidt" <Susan Schmidt (Comerica Bank)>
Cc: Walter Bayer (SSA OIG), Sarah Lizama (SSA OIG), Sonja Scott (OIG Treasury)
Attached is notice of fraud which will supersede any fraud packet Conduent portends to send to Ms. Green. Pursuant to Regulation E, 15USC1693, notice of fraud can be communicated by any third party having proprietary information about such fraud.
Ms. Green stated she called and reported the fraud. Again, pursuant to Regulation E, the investigation is to begin immediately upon notice, and fully accessible provisional credit is to be afforded the victim/cardholder, Ms. Green.
Ms. Green, if you do not have this matter resolved before noon on Monday March 4, 2019, contact me via email and I will put you in touch with the persons responsible for adhering to these federal regulations whether or not these persons are familiar with laws which govern them and protect cardholders.
I do ask that an investigator at Treasury OIG be assigned to this matter. Conduent refuses to communicate with law enforcement.
Sincerely,
J.B. Simms

Below is the resolution performed by Victim 77:
Saturday March 2, 2019- Sandra sent email to Customer Advocacy and demanded provisional credit.
Monday March 4, 2019 Sandra sent an email info to Shantelle Johnson (Conduent Fraud Unit)
Friday March 8, 2019- I received an email from Sandra. She got paid.

Sunday, March 3, 2019

Below is a case of a mother of who suffering from Multiple Sclerosis.

Victim Number 78: Paula-CA
Date Fraud was discovered: January 4, 2019
Date Fraud was reported: January 4, 2019
Dates of fraud: January 3 and January 4, 2019
Nature of fraud: ATM withdrawals in Lincoln, RI
Amount of fraud: $1,555.00

Paula had Multiple Sclerosis. 22 calls were made to connect with Direct Express Laura said would get prov credit if fraud packet received within 10 days. Letter stating conflicting info:
I am a single mother of two who is on Disability because I have Multiple Sclerosis.
I have had horrible experiences with Direct Express since utilizing the Direct Deposit Card. I had 3 large sums of money withdrawn from my card in January of 2019, while I was in Saunderstown, Rhode Island caring for my terminally ill Boyfriend, who had been diagnosed with a rare form of Colon Cancer just after Thanksgiving. I receive a deposit for both myself and I my Daughter each month to the Direct Express card. I was paid on January 3, 2019. I woke up the following morning and found a low balance alert was sent to me in the early hours on the 4th, while I was sleeping. I have a text come once my balance is under $75.00. I panicked and quickly went online to pull up my Direct Express account. I was horrified to find that very late on the third and

into the early hours of the 4th of January 3 transactions had been made at an ATM in a town called Lincoln, RI quite a way from where I was staying.

I am in a very desperate situation and I can not afford them to ignore me yet again. My total loss was $1,555.00 in addition they charged me $13.50 for receiving a new card.

The" conflicting" information" reply is standard for Conduent. Nothing was ever investigated. The "conflicting information" was the standard reply from the Conduent Fraud Unit.

Victim Number 79: Jamie- Brown Summit, NC
Date Fraud was discovered: March 3, 2019.
Date Fraud was reported: March 3, 2019.
Dates of fraud: March 1, 2019
Nature of fraud: ATM accessed in Nebraska
Amount of fraud: $563
Mother of disabled child, 6-year-old daughter

Hi, I am writing as a customer of direct express. I went to use my card today to be denied. I called and discovered an atm withdrawal in the amount of 563 dollars was taken in the state of Nebraska. I reside and use this card only in North Carolina. I filed a complaint to direct express and am waiting for paperwork to sign. I'm not sure who I need to speak to but would like the provisional credit while they do their investigation. I am a mother to a disabled child and was not expecting this financial burden. Anything you can do to help is very much appreciated. Thank you.

Jamie

Hi, just wanted to make sure I email you this info tonight as I set to go full force in morning. So I currently live in Brown Summit NC and receive SSI for my 6 year old daughter who was born with a major heart defect. On Sunday March 3rd 2019 I discovered on the 1st of March there was an ATM withdrawal from my account for $563 from a machine in Nebraska. I opened up my case with Direct Express in the evening of Sunday March 3rd. I need to get my case number again and will forward it to you tomorrow.

On the following day, Monday March 4, 2019, Jamie sent emails to Conduent and others.

Monday, March 4, 2019

Victim Number 80: Toya-PA
$349 Fraud occurred in GA. Victim lives in Pennsylvania; obvious fraud.
The victim was on hold for an hour with Conduent then Conduent hung up.

Tuesday, March 5, 2019

Victim Number 81-Anita: MD
The email below was sent on behalf of the above victim. The narrative of her email to me in within this email.
From: jbsimms
Date: Tue, Mar 05, 2019 11:46 am
To: Richard Delmar (OIG Treasury), Sonja Scott (OIG Treasury)
Cc: Nora Arpin (Comerica Bank), "Susan Schmidt" Susan Schmidt (Comerica Bank) Bcc: Franklin Lemond (Plaintiff's Attorney)
Dear Mr. Delmar and Ms. Scott,
I am aware that the bidding process for the Fiscal Agent to administer the Direct Express program is ongoing. Here is another example of why Comerica Bank should not be considered as a Fiscal Agent, and the FBI (not the Treasury OIG) be brought in to investigate malfeasance on the part of all parties.
Below is the text of an Instant Message which I received this morning. I have spoken to the wife of John, a Vietnam War veteran, and a victim of Comerica Bank, Conduent, and your office.
"My husband received VA disability checks monthly.VA talked him into this direct express card and it was hacked last month to the tune of $500. I was able to get $65 of it refunded by calling ITunes which was one of the places the funds were spent, but there are about $30 more that need to be refunded back from I Tunes and there is $380 that needs to be given back from a Verizon Wireless store. I called the store it stated it was charged from and they said they had several calls like mine that day and that nothing was charged at their store. So these are obviously overseas hackers. My husband depends on his income and to just throw that away is not an option. Makes me sick that he was getting checks for so many years and the VA talked him into this

card. I have called and called for days now and cannot get through to this Direct Express. I see you have been able to assist. Can you help us as well."

You and Mr. Thorsen, who I assumed would be sympathetic to veterans, are accountable. Neither of you would engage me in dialogue to fix this problem, so we will do what is necessary.

As for Comerica Bank and Conduent, the work I began a year ago has resulted in the class action suit against both entities.

Our goal is to remove Comerica Bank as a fiscal agent, establish a ninth fiscal agent solely for VA Benefit, and allow veterans to continue to use paper checks.

You know how to reach me.

Sincerely,

J.B. Simms

I was not getting much cooperation from the VA and no communication form VA Secretary Wilkie. The following was a bit of background on Wilkie and his staff:

Sr ADV US Senate-2015-present (must be mid 2018)
Sworn in as Sec of VA 7/30/2018
Acting sec 3/28/18-5/29/18
Pamela Powers, Chief of Staff VA, sworn in 8/18/2018
James Byrne Gen Counsel
It appeared Wilkie brought Powers onboard when he was confirmed.

Tuesday, March 6, 2019

Subject: big connection I need to tell you, very important and will make you angry
From: jbsimms
Date: Wed, Mar 06, 2019 1:37 am
To: "Jackie Lynn"
Before confirmation as VA Secretary, Mr. Wilkie served Secretary James Mattis as his Under Secretary of Defense for Personnel and Readiness—the principal advisor to the Secretary and Deputy Secretary of Defense for Total Force Management as it relates to readiness, National Guard and Reserve component affairs, health affairs, training, and personnel requirements and management, including equal opportunity, morale, welfare, recreation, and the quality of life for military families.
The son of an Army artillery commander, Mr. Wilkie spent his youth at Fort Bragg. Today, he is an officer in the United States Air Force Reserve assigned to the Office of the Chief of Staff. Before joining the Air Force, he served in the United States Navy Reserve with the Joint Forces Intelligence Command, Naval Special Warfare Group Two, and the Office of Naval Intelligence.
Wilkie is a member of the US Air Force Reserve.
You see the date he became Sec of VA? Sworn in on July 30, 2018.
Powers knows more than she is letting on. The letter sent by Warren to Wilkie was shared with Powers and Byrne, and she is playing a game here. I am getting ready to drop on her and tell her we know she is aware of Warren's letter, and she has not addressed this matter with Dr. Lawrence, head of the Veteran Affairs Benefit. She knows the cards are being forced upon the vets. She knows everything and has chosen to run game on me.

We found out later that secret meetings were being held with SSA, BFS, Comerica, and the VA. Powers would not share that information. I was indebted to her for becoming involved, but if she had told me the "truth" of what was happen, things would have been different.

Wednesday, March 7, 2019

Pamela Powers sent me the following message on LinkedIn:
JB. As I mentioned, I have a 380k organization to run and this is not the only issue we are working. I reached out to you, which I didn't have to do. I asked for your patience and said we are working it and looking into it, which we are. Your attacks are not helpful.

Not helpful? Attacks? The VA was ignorant as to the victimization of veterans, I point it out, look for accountability, and I an attacking her?

Research code- Immediate investigation.

12CFR205.6 (b) (5) Notice to Financial Institution

Must begin investigation upon receipt of notice

12CFR205.11(b)(2)

2. *Investigation pending receipt of information. <u>While a financial institution may request a written, signed statement from the consumer relating to a notice of error, it may not delay initiating or completing an investigation pending receipt of the statement.</u>*

This meant that the investigation is to begin immediately.

I posted this on the Legislative Network, CFPB, and my LinkedIn sites.

"The day of reckoning, accountability and exposure is here: A secret office within the Bureau of Fiscal Services (Treasury) is receiving oral presentations from bidding applicants, and incumbent, to administer the corrupt and inefficient disbursement of funds to veterans and social security recipients from a debit card, Direct Express. This secret office within Fiscal Services has denied any of the over 500 victims of fraud to have a voice in this process, ignoring said victims, while enabling and rewarding Comerica Bank (currently a defendant in 3 lawsuits, one being a class action suit) as the current Fiscal Agent. Treasury OIG is too timid to become involved. If any of you at Fiscal Services or Treasury have a conscience, you can forward information which will lead to the identity of this secret group and immediate and direct communication with the oversight chairperson to jbsimms, or (803) 309-6850. You can shield your identity if need be; we just want access to the wizard behind the curtain. The media is knocking on my door."

Subject: Notice of fraud: Kenneth Tillman, Direct Express card ending 5645
 From: jbsimms
Date: Thu, Mar 07, 2019 5:50 pm
To: "Advocacy US" <advocacy@usdirectexpress.com>, Shantelle Johnson (Conduent), Nora Arpin (Comerica Bank), "Susan Schmidt" <Susan Schmidt (Comerica Bank)>, Richard Delmar (OIG Treasury)
I received a telephone call this afternoon from a customer, Kenneth Tillman, a Direct Express MasterCard cardholder, whose card end with "5645," telling me that his debit card had been hacked, again. The first time was approximately 6 months ago. Mr. Tillman was stranded at a gasoline station, unable to purchase fuel for a return trip home. His intention was to find a pawn shop and pawn his ring and/or watch.
Mr. Tillman's balance was zero. He called the call center and was told his money was spent at a Dick's Sporting Goods store in Haywood, CA and another place. The Conduent call center person told Mr. Tillman he would be receiving a fraud packet to fill out, return, and an investigation would begin, then he could expect the investigation to last upwards of 60 days, with no provisional credit during the "investigation."
 A fellow victim of Comerica Bank/Conduent came to his aid and sent money to Mr. Tillman.
Pursuant to FDIC Regulation 12CFR205.6, derived from 15USC1693 (Regulation E), I am putting Comerica Bank/Conduent on notice as a person having proprietary knowledge of the fraud and of the victim of the fraud. This notice, in conjunction with the verbal notice, satisfies the statute with regard to notification and the fact that the investigation is to begin immediately upon notification
"Notice may be considered constructively given" when the fraud is reported to the call center.
12CFR205.6(b)(5)(iii)
Also see in Section 205.11:
"Written confirmation of oral notice. A financial institution must begin its investigation promptly upon receipt of an oral notice. It may not delay until it has received a written confirmation."
12CFR205.11(c)(2)
I am not a lawyer; I just happen to be literate.
If the full amount of the fraud is not credited upon the account of Mr. Tillman before 8:00 am on Friday March 8, 2019, I will be giving telephone numbers to the above recipients for Mr. Tillman to call. To my knowledge, Mr. Tillman is not at this time a plaintiff on the class action suit, which was brought forth weeks ago, nor am I at this time a plaintiff in this action.
Sincerely,
J.B. Simms

Friday, March 8, 2019

Subject: FYI: I have the information about the bidding process
From: jbsimms
Date: Mon, Apr 08, 2019 10:03 am
To: Sonja Scott (OIG Treasury)
It appears that a person at Fiscal Services named Brett Smith is the person involved with the oral presentations, according to an inside source.
His telephone number is (222) 874-6666 (easy to remember).
He has[not] returned my call.
Maybe you can get his attention, investigate his office's complicity in this matter, and get me to the committee.
Jim

It was learned that Brett Smith not only refused to return calls to me, but my telephone number was also flagged at his office. Two attendants asked if I were Mr. Simms before asking my name.

Sue Martin got a refund from Conduent. I told her to get the money out before they changed their minds. She did. Conduent wanted to debit her card again.

Subject: RE: status
From: Sue Martin
Date: Fri, March 08, 2019 3:31 pm
To: jbsimms
$1771 on 3/7 as a credit adjustment
Then on 3/8 $17.50 (refund of expedite fee and card replacement fee for charges made on my account to send card to thieves). I took all these monies out of the account and the account is zero. On 3/7 is when I received the new card and I logged onto my account and saw the 1771. I immediately went to town it was in evening, so I drove to the first bank and activated the card and withdrew 800 from the atm then I drove to another nearby bank atm and withdrew 800. Then I went to Walmart and spent 139.94 for some food and $100 cash back. Then I spent the remaining money on food 29.74 that left 46 cents on the card. Today 3/8 I received a call from Conduent, he said Alisha told him to call me to find out the status of my claim. I told him I took all the money that was credited back to me on 3/7 out of the account. I asked him can you please refund the card replacement fee of $4 and the expedited mailing fee of 13.50 to my account he put me on hold and got the approval to refund that money immediately. I spent it right away so now my account is zero. Yesterday I went to social security office and my April social security will go to my bank. I told him what happened to my direct express account, and he suggested to lock down my social security account so that it can not be accessed by phone or internet. If I want changes I have to into social security office and show id. I told yes please lock down my account. If you need more info let me know.

Saturday, March 9, 2019

Another admission of investigations being conducted, and no results

From: Jackie Lynn
Date: Sat, Mar 9, 2019 at 7:23 AM
Subject: Delmar admitting investigation
To: jbsimms
On Fri, Sep 14, 2018 at 11:11 AM Delmar, Richard K. Richard Delmar (OIG Treasury)) wrote:
Treasury OIG has been reviewing how BFS and Comerica have executed the Direct Express program for several years and has identified problems and recommended corrections in that execution.
We continue to conduct those reviews, as well as actively investigating allegations of misconduct involving the program. To clarify, our previous Direct Express work was focused on BFS' efforts to award the FAAs and not on the details of fraud monitoring and customer service. Our new audit and investigative work focus on issues raised by Mr. Simms and Ms. Densmore. Mr. Simms's criticism to the contrary, our prior work, as all our work, complied with all GAO and CIGIE standards, and is objective and independent, as the Inspector General Act requires. Rich Delmar, Counsel to the Inspector General, Department of the Treasury

Jackie and I knew there were ongoing secret deliberations regarding the consideration of the bids which bank submitted in an attempt to gain the Fiscal Agent Contract. I wanted to address the committee or group making these deliberations. Jackie agreed and stated she would go with me to Washington DC and address any group concerning Comerica Bank and the Direct Express program.

Subject: the identity of the Director of Electronic Fund Transfer
From: jbsimms
Date: Tue, Apr 09, 2019 1:24 pm
To: Sonja Scott (OIG Treasury), Richard Delmar (OIG Treasury)
Cc: "Jackie Lynn"
Dear Ms. Scott and Mr. Delmar,
In an attempt to determine the identity of the group which is receiving the oral presentations, I came upon a person who would be privy to or involved with this decision making.
The person is Brent D. Smith, Director of Electronic Fund Transfer at Fiscal Services. His telephone number is (202) 874-6666.
Since Mr. Delmar stated that Fiscal Services would not be obligated to schedule me in to make an oral presentation, and that both of you are somewhat sympathetic to the victims, and supposedly having knowledge of the malfeasance, I would assume either or both of you would make a benevolent gesture on behalf of the victims by contacting Mr. Smith and asking him to return my telephone calls.
He might not want to answer my questions, but he will certainly not want to answer the questions presented by the person who comes behind me.
This is the issue Mr. Clements wrote of in GAO 17-176, lack of transparency.
I look forward to the results of your inquiry to Mr. Smith.
Jim Simms

Secret meetings were held

From: jbsimms
Date: Tue, Apr 09, 2019 5:36 pm
To: FMVision@fiscal.treasury.gov
Cc: Jackie Lynn, Richard Delmar (OIG Treasury), Sonja Scott (OIG Treasury),
I would like to talk to the person(s) receiving oral presentations for the bids to administer the Direct Express program.
Please feel free to consult with Mr. Delmar and/or Ms. Scott with respect to this request.
J.B. Simms

Pamela Powers sent a message on LinkedIn. The fact she responded was amazing.
"We are working with Treasury to find the extent of the problem."

Jackie got this email from Sonja Scott at Treasury:

Jackie Lynn
Mar 9, 2019, 7:33 AM
to me
Jackie – We met with the Bureau of Fiscal Service today who oversees Direct Express and discussed many of these issues. I will send these to their rep also. Sonja

Where is the result of this meeting? We were getting nothing.

Subject: Exchange with Pamela Powers on LinkedIn. Notice she made contact today. See Delmar email at end.
From: jbsimms
Date: Sat, Mar 09, 2019 9:12 am
To: Joe Plenzler (Wounded Warriors),
Pamela Powers is sending messages on a Saturday morning. Her "working" with Treasury is like the US govt "working" with the Diem regime in the early sixties while Diem's brother and wife were making the US look bad. It got them both killed. The email from Delmar, dated September 14, 2018, validates all I am telling you. A month later, Powers and Wilkie got the letter from Sen Warren.

Sunday, March 10, 2019

Subject: something to add to the amended complaint- Shaw v US SCOTUS 15-5991.
This case involved bank fraud and Franklin needed to know about it.
"In the case heard before the SCOTUS, Shaw v. US, 15-5991, the defendant raised the defense that the "fraud" he perpetrated against his victims was intended only to target the victim. The Court ruled that the bank was also victimized, and the bank can and should bring charges of bank fraud against the defendant."
As a pedestrian civilian, not an attorney, I respectfully suggest this case of Shaw v US be cited in the amended complaint and blast Comerica out of the water.
My mind goes to odd places.

Today I sent a message to Pamela Powers and cited Shaw vs. US 15-5991 Bank Fraud. This explains why all fraudsters can be arrested.

Victim Number 82- Linda: GA
January 3 and 4, 2019- four charges $451.50
Jan (?) - $100 credited, no explanation
 Feb 7, 2019- received letter- prov credit $351.50.
Linda Ray
Sat, Feb 23, 2019, 10:12 AM
to me
After filing a fraud report in January, my account was inexplicably credited with a $100 fraudulent charge. Next, I received a provisional credit for the remainder of $351.50 in February. Yesterday, I checked my balance as I've been doing regularly since getting ripped off and found that one of the charges was deducted from my account, a "reversal debit."
After no success of getting through yesterday I finally made contact today. All I got for my efforts was rudeness and the runaround from the rep and an alleged supervisor.
I am angry.
Linda Ray

Victim Number 83 -William-CT
Date Fraud was discovered: March 1, 2019
Date Fraud was reported: March 1, 2019
Dates of fraud: March 1, 2019
HAD MY SOCIAL SECURITY AND VETERANS DISABILITY STOLEN ON 3/01/2019.
 I looked on my Direct Express app on my cell phone about 1:15 am that Am and saw a bunch of withdrawals were done and someone took all my money out. i have my card in my possession. i called the Police to do a report, i then tried calling direct express and it would not recognize the card number, then my social security. i eventually tried Comerica bank who then transferred me to direct express that morning. They said they would send me a new card with paperwork. i got my card on 3/08/19 and the paperwork on 3/09/19 Saturday).

Monday, March 11, 2019

I wanted to see the Fiscal Agent Agreements made between Comerica Bank and Bureau of Fiscal Service. Sonja Scott agreed to help, and this is what she received:
Subject: RE: Fiscal Agency Agreements
From: Sonja Scott (OIG Treasury)
Date: Thu, April 11, 2019 5:49 am
To: "jbsimms
This is what I got from the BFS:
 "We do not publish our FAAs publicly, but they are FOIA-able with redactions."

Bureau of Fiscal Service did not want us knowing the parameters of the deal made with Comerica Bank.
I sent emails, venting, t to Michael Clements at the General Accounting Office describing the issues we were having getting a GAO report commissioned. Mr. Clements wanted to help, but his hands were tied. No legislator would help us, and Santaniello was blocking us.

After sending emails to Michael Clements, I sent the following email to Treasury to try to find out more information about this bidding process to become a Fiscal Agent.

Subject: Transparency
From: jbsimms
To: Richard Delmar (OIG Treasury)
Cc: Franklin Lemond (Plaintiff's Attorney)
Date: Mon, Mar 11, 2019 9:12 am
To: Sonja Scott (OIG Treasury),
Dear Ms. Scott and Mr. Delmar,
In the spirit of transparency, as stated is lacking and necessary at Fiscal Services by Michael Clements in GAO 17-176, I have a couple questions for you:
What financial institutions have placed bids for the renewal of the Direct Express program?
Has Comerica Bank submitted a bid?
How can Comerica Bank be considered when the results of the ongoing Treasury OIG report have not been published?
J.B. Simms

Subject: Direct Ex
From: Dale
Date: Mon, March 11, 2019 10:24 am
To: jbsimms
Calvin has had DE issue me a $905.98 credit for one of the fraudulent charges made against my account. Verizon Wireless refunded the other $905.98 charge. Calvin also had DE refund the $13.50 expedited shipping charge for my new card. I am still fighting for them to refund me for the $1.50 balance transfer fee that would not have been necessary if I could have reached their "customer service" number to have the card cancelled to prevent any further fraud from taking place. I hope this time the $905.98 credit will not be reversed as the last one was but I will keep you informed. Thanks for all your help. I probably would still be hitting a brick wall if you hadn't provided the contact information needed to get their attention. Keep up the good work and let me know if I can provide any more information that may help you proceed against Direct Express for their complicity and gross negligence that allows debit card fraud to occur so easily.
Regards,
Dale

It was now time to go directly to the person who is the designated cover-up person for Bureau of Fiscal Service at US Treasury, Thomas Santaniello. This was our attempt to attend the bidding process and testify against Comerica Bank.

Subject: RE: The Direct Express® program and the Bureau of the Fiscal Service
From: jbsimms
Date: Fri, Apr 12, 2019 1:25 pm
To: "Thomas E. Santaniello" <Thomas.Santaniello@fiscal.treasury.gov>
Dear Mr. Santaniello,
After having experienced the reluctance and refusal of Fiscal Service employees to answer a question, answer an email, or answer a telephone call, it was refreshing to receive your email.
I would like to address the committee which is entertaining oral presentations by the bidding financial institutions. It is only fair that since the committee is listening to bidders give an presentation, the cardholder victims of the Direct Express program have a right to be heard as well.
It is apparent that the two Treasury OIG reports (14-031 and 17-034) were ignored by the "Business Process Owner" which is charge of implementing and enforcing the Treasury OIG recommendations. The GAO report 17-176 also casts Fiscal Services in a bad light with respect to lack of transparency. The decision awarding the Direct Express contract to Comerica Bank was a big mistake, and I and hundreds of others, probably more, have suffered as a result of lack of insight and intellect of banking laws by Fiscal Services.
I will arrive in Washington, D.C. to speak in person if necessary. Those persons involved in the class action suit, including the attorney, as well as those at Treasury OIG, know that I am very conversant with the issues and I have pierced the veil of secrecy between Comerica Bank and Fiscal Services.

My telephone number is (803) 309-6850. If you want to Skype a presentation, I will do that. My presentation will also involve a question-and-answer session with the committee which accepting oral presentations. You may call me at any time.
Sincerely,
J.B. Simms

Below is the reply from Santaniello.

Subject: The Direct Express® program and the Bureau of the Fiscal Service
From: "Thomas E. Santaniello" <Thomas.Santaniello@fiscal.treasury.gov>
Date: Fri, April 12, 2019 11:30 am
To: jbsimms
Mr. Simms - Thank you for your interest in the Direct Express® program. The Treasury Office of the Inspector General has referred your inquiry about the process we use to select a financial agent to the Bureau of the Fiscal Service. I am also responding to other inquiries you have made about this process to Fiscal Service offices.

As you may be aware, the Direct Express® card program serves more than 4.5 million individuals who receive their social security, veterans, and other benefit payments electronically. For the past 10 years, the program has consistently maintained a very high customer satisfaction rating of 94%. We believe this high success rate is due in part to the care we take in listening to our customers, and in responding appropriately to their concerns. In particular, we are aware of the concerns you have raised over the past year and have discussed them with our financial agent.

We are currently reviewing applications from financial institutions to operate the Direct Express® program as our agent. We use many criteria in our evaluation, including customer satisfaction, compliance with applicable law, and fraud management experience and expertise, and base our evaluation on information provided by the applicants as well as other information available to us. Our evaluation process does not include an opportunity for public comment or for direct public contact with the evaluation team. However, customer service capability has always been critical to the success of the program and the evaluation of customer satisfaction and fraud management as factors in the selection process furthers long-standing program goals.

Please direct any further communication concerning the Direct Express® program to me, Thomas E. Santaniello, Office of Legislative and Public Affairs. Thank you.

Santaniello was blowing us off. The deal was done with Comerica Bank and persons at Bureau of Fiscal Service. The bidding process was a sham. We would find out later that our work did make Comerica Bank engage a new partner as a new call center.

Here is more validation to attack Comerica Bank and Bureau of Fiscal Service and show a necessity for Jackie and me to address the Bureau of Fiscal Service.
This email was sent to Sonja Scott of US Treasury.

From: jbsimms
Date: Fri, Apr 12, 2019 3:35 pm
To: Sonja Scott (OIG Treasury)
Cc: "Jackie Lynn"
I basically defended your office to Fiscal Services. They ignored the two OIG audits and the recommendations. They renewed the contract after OIG reported in 14-031, Pages 5 and 6, stating:
Documentation should have been more complete.
Oversight needs to be improved.
OIG could not support selecting Comerica: Comerica did not provide lowest cost/high quality service.
FS did not document its evaluation of Comerica Bank for full technical capabilities.
Amended the FAA on 3/31/11 to give compensation to Comerica (was to be a no pay contract).
On Page 9:
Paragraph 1- OIG 14-131 stated that the FAA did not stipulate that Comerica notifiy OIG of violations of fed criminal laws (like bank fraud, as legislated in Supreme Court case 15-5991 Shaw v US). So, who was Comerica going to notify? No one, because the finger would be pointed at them, and Conduent.
Page 33:

OIG is concerned with FS administration of the Direct Express program an [lack of] enforcement of terms of the FAA.

Oddly, I did not see 15USC1693 mentioned in `14-031.

I do appreciate you for replying to my email after hours.

I will be your best advocate if I get in front of the committee. While the genesis of this matter was my discontent with the actual OIG reports (audits, not investigations), Fiscal Services' failures as pointed out in the OIG reports should have made every person in OIG livid.

There is a person having the title of "Business Process Owner" who supposedly accepts your reports. That is one person we want to identify.

If you can email Santaniello and vouch for me to make an oral presentation, you will not regret it.

Jim

Below is the email I sent to Thomas Santaniello which basically let him know that Jackie and I know the game that is being played by not allowing Jackie and me to be present to address the "Evaluation Team" which gave the contract to Comerica Bank. Santaniello was covering up for Comerica Bank and the failure of BFS.

Santaniello kept Jackie and me from making a presentation: more secrets

From: jbsimms

Date: Fri, Apr 12, 2019 10:43 pm

To: "Thomas E. Santaniello" <Thomas.Santaniello@fiscal.treasury.gov>

Cc: Richard Delmar (OIG Treasury), Sonja Scott (OIG Treasury), Joe Plenzler (Wounded Warriors), "Jackie Lynn", Kate Berry (American Banker)

Dear Mr. Santaniello,

I want to make one point very clear to you: just because you state "Our evaluation process does not include an opportunity for public comment or for direct public contact with the evaluation team" does not mean it cannot happen.

The "evaluation team" used to convey the contract to Comerica Bank ignored two Treasury OIG reports and a GAO report. No one on the evaluation team was intelligent enough to see that there were no security parameters on the card. None. If your evaluation team is afraid to listen to what I know, and to admit what "swayed" the evaluation team to give the contract to Comerica Bank, then let them admit it.

Maybe you and your evaluation team will answer to someone else since I cannot exact consequences upon them. Lack of consequences is what enabled Comerica Bank to violate 15USC1693 in a cavalier manner, thinking no one would figure out how they got the contract and who would cover for them. Your due diligence of me will give you an idea of the origin of my insights.

You can reach me at (803) 309-6850. Feel free to reach me over the weekend.

J.B. Simms

Wednesday, March 13, 2019

A victim named Lisa Tower sent me an email; she got her money in 2 days after consulting with me.

On this day I spent hours updating 10 victims, sending emails requesting information to complete contact. All this was time consuming, but I had to have all information ready for Treasury and for Franklin Lemond.

Defendants change attorneys; bring in the "big guns."

Franklin sent us (Jackie and me) an email telling us that the defendants have brought in bigger law firm. Comerica and Conduent have decided to bring in King & Spalding to handle this case. This is the biggest firm in Atlanta. The main two attorneys handling the file are going to be David L. Balser & Jonathan R. Chally.

Victim Number 84-Kendall:MN

Date Fraud was discovered: Feb 1, 2019

Date Fraud was reported: February 2, 2019

Dates of fraud: Feb 1, 2019

Nature of fraud: Fraud in Miramar, Florida

Amount of fraud: $673.00

My card never left my possession and I never provided anyone with my PIN number. My T-Mobile phone records show that the fraudulent call originated from direct express. My direct express statement shows that at

7:07 am on 1/29/19 I used my card at caribou coffee in St. Paul. I live 40 minutes from there and went straight home. My phone records show I was home. Minnesota was experiencing life threatening cold and my phone records will show I never left my house. It is ridiculous to state that I somehow got to Florida and back when I can prove I never left my home. I still have my card so my card wasn't stolen, only the numbers which I am guessing were used to create a duplicate card and change my PIN number using the direct express system

Thursday, March 14, 2019

I worked on Vera Lyn Best's Excel spreadsheet to identify all the times her car was used on the West Coast while she lived in New Jersey. Vera lost thousands of dollars and the Lyft company refused to cooperate.

Friday March 15, 2019

Victim 60 Jessica Renee Martinez texted me- she got her money. She was going to find the documents and email me. This was another victim who recovered their money after having been denied by Conduent.

Comerica Bank/BFS lies to a US senator

Someone at the Bureau of Fiscal Service, the agency that awarded the contract to Comerica Bank, sent this to the aide of Senator Marsha Blackburn. More federal propaganda.

March 15, 2019
From: Bureau of Fiscal Affairs, US Treasury
"Dear Ms. Magneson,
This is in response to your email dated March 5, 2019, to the Department of the Treasury on behalf of your constituent Peter Jackson. Mr. Peter Jackson wrote concerning his account being breached of his personal data and how Comerica intends to safeguard his privacy in the future.
The Department of Treasury's Bureau of the Fiscal Service provides centralized disbursing services to most Federal agencies. These services include disbursing both electronic and Treasury check payments. We disburse payments based on instructions/certifications from Federal agencies such as the Veterans Administration (VA).
Upon receipt of your email we contacted Comerica Bank, for assistance with Mr. Jackson's concerns. According to Comerica Mr. Jackson's Social Security number has not been compromised via the Direct Express program. While Mr. Jackson did experience fraud on his Direct Express card, that fraud was due to a data breach at an unknown merchant.

This was a big lie: Comerica blamed this upon the merchants. Conduent employees have access to victim information and can easily sell it on the black market. That makes more sense that the lie being pedaled by Bureau of Fiscal Service of Treasury. More work was done to finish file updates.

Saturday, March 16, 2019

I worked on files all day. I create profiles for prospective plaintiffs to send to Franklin. The profiles had to have current contact information and narratives which could be understood.

Sunday March 17, 2019

The work on the files continued through today. This has to be done. All data had to be updated and formatted.

Monday, March 18, 2019

Jackie and I emailed each other many times a day. We talked 2-3 times on most days. I would give her my thoughts and we exchanged views. We were the best team.

Comerica Bank lies to Senator Warren: fraud notification calls do not exist

Subject: issues
From: jbsimms
Date: Mon, Mar 18, 2019 10:00 pm
To: "Jackie Lynn"
Comerica Bank has no security notification alerts on the cards.

The allegation by Babb, repeated by Warren, that calls are made to cardholders, is a lie.
Warren and Hatch requested the GAO investigate in 2016, after the 2014 Treasury OIG report 14-031
The GAO report is GAO 17-176
Both Treasury OIG reports state problems with Comerica and Fiscal Services.
Warren sent letters to all parties involved in the mishandling of accounts, refusing to reveal responses.
Warren refuses to request a follow up investigation by GAO
Again, the only office to give a clear investigation will be the GAO

Tuesday, March 19, 2019

From: jbsimms
Sent: Tuesday, March 19, 2019 8:28 PM
To: Joe Plenzler (Wounded Warriors)
Subject: A misstep of Pamela Powers
On February 28, 2019, I engaged Pamela Powers, VA COS, on LinkedIn messaging. After mentioning the matter of the Direct Express program with Ms. Powers here were two responses:
Feb 28, 2019:
"Hi JB. I Am unaware of this issue but will forward the matter on to Dr Lawrence."
March 6, 2019
"JB, with a 370k member organization that supports 20 million veterans, as you can imagine, we have a lot going on. I am looking into it. I am aware of the Warren letter, and it will take some time to find out the full measure of the issue."
Gentlemen, the "Warren letter" was sent to VA Sec Wilkie on October 16, 2018, and the letter has been answered.
I that Ms. Powers was aware of this letter on or about October 16, 2018, and that Ms. Powers and Dr. Lawrence could be named in the response. Senator Warren is not giving up that response, nor is the giving up the response from Ralph Babb or Social Security.
Powers stated she was unaware of the issue on Feb 28, then admitted having knowledge of the October 16 letter.
Paul Lawrence is not responding.
Jim Simms

Wednesday, March 20, 2019

Subject: VAB and the end run
From: jbsimms
Date: Wed, Mar 20, 2019 11:29 am
To: Michael Clements (Gen Acct Office)
Dear Mr. Clements,
Paul Lawrence, who heads up the VA Benefits office, is making a full-frontal media blitz touting the "accomplishments" of the VAB. He has received a handful of requests from me to address the matter of VAB endorsing and forcing veterans to use the Direct Express card, which we know is fraught with corruption and lack of security.
Pamela Powers, COS at VA, responded to me, first stating she was unaware of the issue of security with the debit card (and Fiscal Services), then less than a week later admitting she was aware of the letter dated 16 Oct 2018 from Senator Warren to Sec Wilkie. That letter asked for Sec Wilkie to respond, and I will bet you that Power saw that letter, in October, prior to Wilkie.
Lawrence is posting "newsy" items on LinkedIn, and now stating he is meeting with the General "Accountability" Office to discuss VA issues.
Are aware of these meetings? This announcement by Lawrence, and the actual meetings appear to be an attempt at an "end run" to avoid inspection by your office when/if we get your office to commission a follow-up to GAO 17-176. Your office is the only avenue for honestly investigating this matter. Each time a person of the group under suspicion makes a comment, it is usually found to have contradicted a previous statement or deflected attention away from themselves.
Thank you.
Jim

Jackie Lynn
Wed, Mar 20, 2019, 4:41 PM
to Abby, Ashley_Woolheater, Cate
Hello Staffers of Sen. Warren,
I would like to point out to you that in your findings ~Comerica claims no security breach occurred however Nora Arpin VP of Comerica Bank claims differently even going as far as stating an employee was fired over the breach in the article by American Banker, Kate Berry in August of 2018. It is clear to me as well as others that your office failed to properly investigate this instead you took the word of this corrupt bank and choose to be satisfied with the lies they told you and perhaps this is why you are refusing to request a GAO? Like all corruption it will be uncovered.
I think it's very disgraceful to act like your office cares during elections but chooses to ignore the ongoing issues into these cards now. Votes count and so do people who except these benefits it's wrong what your office is doing and frankly I'm beyond disgusted.
Do the right thing!
Sincerely
Jackie Densmore

Joe Plenzler called- we had a long talk. His attention to his as the PR person at Wounded Warriors Project was very important to me. He had been very helpful, and I was grateful.

Senator Warren was not responding.

Victim Number 85: Jason-WA

"Fraud was posted to my account and deducted from my balance. I went through all the normal routine dispute steps and they issued a provisional credit of the amount I disputed.
The ATM that used was inside of a Walgreens and the entire transaction was videotaped. Very cut and dry. A week later Direct Express reversed the provisional credit and in one of two letters that they issued on the same date, regarding the same dispute; one letter advised me that no errors were found and hence they were reversing the provisional credit. The very same day they issued a second letter stating that they were going to let me keep 20.00 of the 320.00 provisional credit but would not say anything more about the now closed investigation.
The bottom line is I've since moved my business to a real bank however I know for a fact that there had to be an error found if they truly had the owner and operator of the ATM machine complete the normal audit procedures.
I just want my money back and I'm not interested in getting anything more out of them. I wouldn't waste my time or anyone else's time claiming something happened when it didn't.
If you're able to provide me with a name or number of who I might be able to assist me with this I'd be grateful. Very sincerely,"

Victim Number 87: Noel- MD

Date Fraud discovered: March 2, 2019
Date Fraud reported: March 4, 2019
Dates of fraud: August 4, 2018 $489.00
August 23, 2018 $388.90 December 6, 2018 $740.00
Tuesday March 19, 2019- Noel called me- money taken. Not clear when, don't have statement handy. Fraud appears to have been done in Arkansas. She is only one who knows the pin.
Her husband, Isaac Daniel Robertson did 2 tours in Vietnam. Died 1973 as a result of Agent Orange.
Below is the first indication that Conduent stopped taking fraud reports. Victims had been sending emails and faxes of narratives to Conduent and Comerica employees (mostly Susan Schmidt) and now the Advocacy Office responded with an email.

Conduent Fraud Unit stops taking fraud complaints

Subject: Receipt of letters dated 12/6/2018, 8/23/2018, 8/4/2018, Card ending 9303
From: jbsimms
Date: Wed, Mar 20, 2019 4:56 pm
To: "Jackie Lynn", Franklin Lemond (Plaintiff's Attorney)
Look at this.

The Advocacy office has stopped taking fraud info.
The more I do, the more they mess up.
This is huge. They blinked. Now they want to place a hardship on the persons who have experienced fraud.
The statute does not restrict where the reporting of the error must be made. Believe me, there are other email addresses to be used to satisfy the statue, and I have them.
They think they are being smart and slick. Make a note that this happened today to as a form of harassment.
Call centers do not answer phones. This places an undue burden on cardholders.
The more they fight, the more flaws they expose.

Subject: Developments at Conduent, and Dr. Paul Lawrence, head of VA Benefits
From: jbsimms
Date: Wed, Mar 20, 2019 10:51 pm
To: "Jackie Lynn"
Cc: Sonja Scott (OIG Treasury), Richard Delmar (OIG Treasury), Walter Bayer (SSA OIG), Nora Arpin (Comerica Bank), "Susan Schmidt" <Susan Schmidt (Comerica Bank)>, Joe Plenzler (Wounded Warriors), Kate Berry (American Banker)

The following message was sent to Dr. Paul Lawrence, head of Veteran Affairs Benefits. After receiving a promise two weeks ago from Pamela Powers, COS of VA, that she would have someone reach out to two veteran victims, Ms. Powers has yet to honor her word, or "Integrity First."

"Wednesday March 20, 2019
J B Simms 10:40 PM
It was learned today that Conduent, the outsourced customer service arm of Conduent Bank, disabled the email address to Customer Advocacy which enabled veterans to expeditiously transmit narratives and documents proving fraud on their Direct Express cardholder accounts. Conduent is trying to enforce the sending of a "fraud packet" as a substitute for a narrative submitted by the veteran, which is allowable as stated in Regulation E. This is another ploy to have cardholders' submissions miss an arbitrary 10 day limit to return tangible information, then denying the claim. If you want to discuss culpability of VAB, I can do that, with ease. If you want to discuss how this can be fixed, I can do that, too. The goal is to have Comerica Bank no longer be a fiscal agent of Treasury, and have a separate fiscal agent created specifically for VA Benefits. VAB should cease endorsing and promoting the Direct Express program until the corrective measures are met. Your office has not been avoid the truth; you have been avoiding the truth being exposed. Ms. Powers knows exactly what I am saying. I am ready to talk when you are."

Thursday, March 21, 2019

Victim Number 88-Caroll: Washington, DC
Date Fraud was discovered: Feb 27 2019
Date Fraud was reported: Feb 27 2019
Dates of fraud: Feb 27 2019
Nature of fraud: ATM withdrawal
Amount of fraud: $1003.00

Subject: Victim of fraud
From: Caroll Thompson
Date: Thu, March 21, 2019 3:48 pm
To: jbsimms
On the 27th of February $1000.00 of my SSI funds was stolen off of my Direct Express card. Today I stumbled across your article on the lawsuit with Direct Express.
I have reported my card stolen that morning when I realized my balance.
In a nutshell, I have been denied reimbursement of my funds. The call center informed me today that my statement form was received by them om 3/15/2019 and processed and denied on 3/15/2019.
How can this be? They also told me that I could not appeal the decision, it was final. There was no one in the fraud dept. that I could talk to about my situation.
I wish I would have known of your article before I filed my claim. However, I know they are in the wrong. It is

no way they could have conducted a thorough investigation in just a matter of a couple of hours. I am very eager to hear back from you. Thank you in advance.

I immediately responded and gave Carroll the script to email Comerica and Conduent:

First, send an email to the following email addresses, and state, "Pursuant to Regulation E, I am requesting, as of the date of this transmission, a full and complete copy of the investigation which was conducted, resulting in the denial of my fraud claim, number _____."

I listed the email addresses of people at Comerica and Conduent.

Friday, March 22, 2019

Victim Number 89: Timntami-

I am emailing you because I reported my card damaged and it was shipped on March the 15 2019 is March the 22 2019 and still no card I have over a 1000$ on my card and need it so bad me n my family have not paid our bills and are getting throwed out today I just need my new card number so I can call activate it n pay my bills online but no one will help someone has my card number please can you help me

Saturday, March 23, 2019

I emailed Jackie continually to update her on developments, victims, and developments.

Comerica Bank protects their customers, not Direct Express cardholders

From: jbsimms
Date: Sat, Mar 23, 2019 5:22 pm
To: "Jackie Lynn"

Comerica Bank won two bids to get a contract from Fiscal Services to run the Direct Express debit card program.

This contract allowed Comerica Bank to disburse funds from Veteran Affairs, Social Security, Railroad retirement, and other programs.

The bid from Comerica offered no options for security parameters, except for a customized low balance alert.

Comerica bank offers a three tier level of security alerts for customers of Comerica Bank, not offered to Direct Express cardholders.

Over 400 claims through Feb 2018 were made against Comerica Bank to the Consumer Financial Protection Bureau, which never enforced Regulation E.

Veteran Affairs, Social Security and Fiscal Services ignored all complaints until February 2018, and now a class action suit has been filed.

Veterans and others are being deprived of monthly income, food, medicine, housing, and privacy with all their confidential information being exposed.

The Conduent fraud department denies fraud claims never contacts merchants, law enforcement, or banks where ATM fraud occurs.

The Conduent fraud department ignores all police reports, which keeps Conduent employees from being questioned.

Bring a copy of the letters and the GAO report. Both will show the name of Warren, and show she is hiding something.

Maybe it would be good that you send the letters to the reporter/producer now, and that way they might ask questions about your interaction with the Warren people.

Victim 90 Crystal-NM

Crystal – NM inquired as victim.

Hi I was directed to you through a friend of a friend. How do I go about getting my money back to me if a agency scammed me and won't stop charging my card without my permission. I've had to replace my card several times already.

Sunday, March 24, 2019

Below is a victim who said the vendor would reveal the fraudster to the police.

Social Security attendant admits much Direct Express fraud

Victim Number 91-Tracii:

Tracii Taylor- Conduent admit know a fraudster.

I got suuuuuper, super lucky. Victoria's Secret was able to stop the carrier from shipping the $500+ fraudulent order so they treated it as if I ordered it & refunded me. Whew! May I ask for opinions about online banks or other cards here?

Tracii Taylor to Jim Simms: they told me that they could tell the police the name of the person but could not tell me so I'm curious as to what is on the police statement when I pick it up. I know I'm going & opening a bank account this week.

Friday March 29, 2019 -I still have to pick the police report up. My health hasn't been great so that got in the way but I at least got to social security today & direct Express will not be handling my money anymore. The woman there said she hears A LOT of complaints about Direct Express.

Thursday, March 28, 2019

From: jbsimms
Date: Thu, Mar 28, 2019 9:29 am
To: Sonja Scott (OIG Treasury)
Cc: Jackie Lynn, Franklin Lemond (Plaintiff's Attorney)

For some reason I was waiting for this request from you, as I was wondering how Norma Arpin was justifying the malfeasance and banking law violation by Comerica.

I have been added as a plaintiff in this matter, which excludes my information from discovery. We decided that in order to protect selected information which will be used at any specific time, a shield from discovery would be necessary. While I intend no offense to you, I cannot be assured that the names of the people I forward to you would not be communicated to the defendants.

This does not prohibit me from assisting more victims, but I will have to confer with Mr. Lemond if the updated roster of victims can be sent to you. Many have been referred to your office in an attempt to prompt action, and those referrals would seem to have established a pattern on my behalf.

Your request will be presented to Mr. Lemond, and I will reply immediately.

Your request is not interpreted as a challenge to the truthfulness of any statement I made to you, as if to say, "Is this guy for real?"

You mentioned my professional history in passing. I am not "somebody" but I do have a bit of investigative experience (prob about 30 years), banking, and an understanding of an OIG (as documented in my latest book). Hopefully someone on your staff will do some due diligence before we have the conference on Tuesday. There is plenty to find on the internet.

If you have a list of issues or questions you wish to send me prior to our conference, please feel free to do so. There are many issues which I would like to present, and I will forward those to you. I"f you have a specific format in mind, I can accommodate. If I would be able to give you and those present an "opening statement" as such, maybe 5-10 minutes, I would be grateful.

For the record, I have 4 goals in this matter:

1) compensation for victims

2) fines, both personally and for Comerica and Conduent

3) Comerica Bank not be eligible to retain the FAA now or in the future

4) a ninth Fiscal Agent be established solely for VA disbursements

Thank you again for returning my call yesterday. If you have any immediate questions pertaining to your interview with Ms. Arpin that I might counter, call me anytime.

Jim

Treasury, Sonja Scott, asks to see victim list

Subject: List
From: Sonja Scott (OIG Treasury)
Date: Thu, March 28, 2019 8:30 am
To: "'jbsimms
Mr. Simms – You mentioned yesterday that you have list now of 90 victims. Can you forward me the new list?
Thanks. Sonja

Subject: RE: List
From: Sonja Scott (OIG Treasury)
Date: Thu, March 28, 2019 10:38 am
To: "'jbsimms'
Yes, there is a difference. However, during this conversation, we will be asking more programmatic questions.
Sonja

From: jbsimms
Sent: Thursday, March 28, 2019 1:27 PM
To: Sonja Scott (OIG Treasury)
Subject: RE: List
I can be reached at (803) 309-6850.
As was agreed during my conversation with Paulette Battle a year ago, I see s difference between an audit and an investigation, where the results of each are forwarded, and the jurisdiction and authority to impose sanctions and/or consequences. As was observed in the previous Treas OIG audits (14-031 and 17-034) concerns and violations were noted, no corrective action was taken, and veterans and civilians suffered. We are looking for a government entity which has teeth and has not conflict of interest or conscience.

Fiscal Services played the role of the "substitute teacher" allowing Comerica Bank to misbehave in the classroom.

From: jbsimms
Sent: Thursday, March 28, 2019 2:35 PM
To: Scott, Sonja L. Sonja Scott (OIG Treasury)
Cc: Jackie Lynn
Subject: RE: List
Would you and your associates be asking my perception of how many specific agencies failed to perform their mandate, or are you interested in "hearing" my suggestions of how this problem could have been fixed, and what can be done to insure this never happens again?
I ask that you indulge me for 5-10 minutes at the beginning of the conference to allow me to give your colleagues a summation of matters I have brought forth to you over the past months. Also, I would like to be given the courtesy of having the opportunity to ask questions.
Hopefully this matter will be aired in another venue, and addressing issues presented by me will be a great deal more comfortable than if presented by someone of authority who can levy consequences.
I know we understand one another. Maybe Mr. Thorson and/or Mr. Delmar would like to be present.
Jim

Friday, March 29, 2019

An admission of open investigations

On Mar 29, 2019, at 7:19 AM, Scott, Sonja L. Sonja Scott (OIG Treasury) wrote:
I believe there are 3-4 open investigations. I have no idea when they will be completed as I am not the case agents. We also have an audit on Comerica/Conduent. Yes, Sen. Waren's office has contacted our office.
Sonja

Here Ms. Scott admits the existence of 3-4 investigations. Months later, Richard Delmar and Loren Sciurba would deny that any "investigations" were ongoing. I submitted a Freedom of Information request in order to obtain the results of the investigations but was denied all documents.

From: Jackie Lynn
Sent: Friday, March 29, 2019 7:53 AM
To: Sonja Scott (OIG Treasury)
Subject: Re: Questions on when your reports will be coming out
Strange how there is only 3-4 cases on this forgive me I'm not too educated on how these investigations go ,
could you please explain .
Are you saying 3-4 small investigations or 3-4 big investigations , covering multiple states . Do you know out of
any of these investigations any arrests? The criminal who stole my brothers money is still at large.
Also can you tell me what parts of Comerica and Conduent you are doing an audit on and when will that take
place and will your findings be public record?
Sorry for all the important questions but I'm just trying to figure out how this process works Jackie

Below are the procedures for selecting the Fiscal Agent by Bureau of Fiscal Service:
3/29 Notify finalist of Fiscal Agent selection.
4/1-5-10 Financial Agreement sent- Oral Presentations are permitted.
5/17 Fiscal Services Selects Fiscal Agent.
6/3 Implementation of the selected Fiscal Agent.
1/3/2020 Services of the selected Fiscal Agent begins.

Below is a message I sent email to BFS website FSInternet@fiscal.tresury.gov:

This inquiry was submitted through the BFS Web site and has been routed to the appropriate program office. A copy has also been forwarded to the sender. If you believe this message has been misdirected, please forward to FSInternet@fiscal.treasury.gov.	
NAME:	'J. B. Simms' - jbsimms
COMMENTS:	According to the Q and A published by Fiscal Services, the bidding process for the contract to administer the Direct Express program will result in the finalist for the bid to be notified Friday March 29, 2019. I want a list of the finalists.
ROUTED TO:	Direct.Express@fiscal.treasury.gov

J B Simms
Fri, Mar 29, 2019, 5:37 PM
to Sonja, Jackie
Now do you wonder why Pamela Powers and Paul Lawrence at VA won't talk to me?
The VA is still endorsing this corrupt program.
Here are questions for your investigators: How many claims were denied, monies never returned to the
cardholder, and the funds converted to the use of Comerica Bank?
How much money did Comerica pay to Conduent to deny claims and confiscate cardholder funds?
Look forward to the interview.
Jim

Victim Tracii Taylor instant message:
I still have to pick the police report up. My health hasn't been great so that got in the way but I at least got to
social security today & direct Express will not be handling my money anymore. The woman there said she
here's A LOT of complaints about direct Express.

Jackie continues to involve elected officials

From: Jackie Lynn
Sent: Friday, March 29, 2019 5:51 AM
To: Jackman, Michael
Subject: Questions
Good Morning Mr. Jackman
I am again following up with you to see if you had any answers as to if Comerica put a bid in and just how many fraud cases have been reported that OIG Treasury and OIG social security are and have been investigating. I would like to know the number of cases of the entire program not just the cardless benefit program. I would also like the amount stolen from when Comerica received the original contract to present. I just did an interview with channel 7 and have a few more set up with other media outlets.
Social security, Veterans Affairs, Direct Express and Comerica Bank feel no need to alert cardholders so I will use my voice to get the message out .
As of today's date JB Simms has had over 90 victims contact him , and that's just through the internet so we are hoping we can reach more through the tv and would like for your office to be part of it in a positive way not a negative way .
I look forward to speaking with you soon and ask that you forward my questions to the appropriate agencies for answers.
Jackie Densmore

Conduent Refuses to Allow Narratives to be Emailed

Saturday, March 30, 2019

Subject: Do you guys have any idea what I feel when I see things like this?]
From: jbsimms
Date: Sat, Mar 30, 2019 9:07 am
To: "Jackie Lynn", Franklin Lemond (Plaintiff's Attorney)
Shantelle Johnson has now put this as an automatic reply to people sending fraud information.
The more they struggle to get out of the noose, the tighter the noose becomes.

Conduent was blocking fraud victims from sending their narratives directly to the Fraud Unit. This would cause more time delay for victims to get their money returned. Conduent is full of evil people who relish victimizing people.

Subject: Automatic reply: Do you guys have any idea what I feel when I
see things like this?
From: "Johnson, Shantelle" <Shantelle.Johnson@conduent.com>
Date: Sat, March 30, 2019 12:21 am
To: jbsimms
If you think an error has occurred in connection with your electronic transactions, call us at the Customer Service number, (888)741-1118 as soon as you can; or write us at Payment Processing Services, P.O. Box 245998, San Antonio, Texas 78224- 5998. Your dispute or question regarding your electronic transaction errors must be received through one of these two reporting methods – disputes or errors for card transactions will not be processed from an email.

Conduent fraud department blocked all incoming emails. All fraud complaint forms were to be mailed, further delaying the reimbursement. Conduent proved their Fraud Unit was inept, investigating nothing. This was a direct violation of Regulation E by limiting the legal options victims could use to report a fraudulent transaction.

Monday, April 1, 2019

Victim Number 92-Susan:CA
Monday April 1, 2019
Text from Susan- then talked to Susan- she sent email to Schmidt on Sunday March 31. Monday April 1, 2019- Brandon called Hauser. Putting money back Hauser sent BBB report.

Victim Number 93 Jeffrey- CA

My name is Jeffrey Harding, I am writing you concerning Direct Express. (DX) In doing research online for how to get my father's money back my mom found on FB and LinkedIn that you have helped many people get their money back from Direct Express and other places., such as the VA etc. I know you are busy man and I want to get on this bandwagon with DX. I am a USAF Disabled Veteran and my Father is a USN veteran. This is concerning my father's account with DX, he is 75 years old and on social security. Up until Feb, 2019 he was living in a nursing home in Edna, Tx. I picked him up and brought him to Yuba City, Ca just north of Sacramento on HWY 99. His mail would be opened before receiving it in the nursing home and he had to get a 2nd card this past year because the first one would not activate because someone else tried to activate it from the wrong number on file. He had a surplus of funds on his card because of being in the home and not having access to his card/account for months because of being unable to get to the Social Security office.

Several times on the trip from TX to CA and since arriving his card would not work and he had to call. I did not witness all of the calls or get involved until I realized what had happened on the 13th of Mar,2019. He has over $2000.00 in fraudulent charges made to his account. He called DX on the 19Mar2019 and the rep was not friendly because my father was a little upset and she told him "Ok sir...thank you for validating the charges your card is now active have a nice day." His memory is not too well as far as phone calls etc. He did not want to deal with it and even told the lady he was authorizing them to speak to me and they refused to speak with me...said they could only speak with the cardholder.

Still have been unable to get a detailed transaction history, and DX is claiming that it is only 1933.00 approximately when it is in fact 2285.86.

I had a telephone conversation with Jeff Harding. Jeff told me that his wife worked at Conduent and she hated it. If Conduent employees had too much personal debt, their work was restricted. Claims get denied then fraud packets arrive. No investigation began until the packet arrived.

Victim 94 Melanie-TX

When I attempt to get an assistant from the bank regarding direct express I am hung up on. I lost $ 25,000 over a four-month period of time... and I would call attempting to get assistance from any one there... I was unable to access online statement and I was losing an average of $ 2,000 to 3000 per month. I attempted to get assistance from these people, and I was not believed in the beginning and then I was told I had to contact each business to report the fraud. I even had one ass in the fraud department tell me because the money was being stolen in the town, I lived in... I must be responsible.... I fall to mention I was losing money to companies I had never heard of before and if I got through to speak to someone I was never called back or told that the company did not have a fraud department... I have made a police report

BFS refuses to reveal applicants for the Direct Express program

Reply from Fiscal Services
Mon April 1, 2019 10:12am
Thank you for your request for information regarding the Direct Express® Financial Agent selection process. The deadline for submitting applications was March 8, 2019. We are now in the process of evaluating applications. In order to maintain integrity in the process, Fiscal Service does not disclose information about applicants during the evaluation and deliberation period. You may resubmit your question(s) once we have publicly announced results from the evaluation process. Please note, information in the applications is generally considered to be confidential and proprietary business information, which we may not be allowed to publicly disclose. Thank you once again for your inquiry.

Tuesday, April 2, 2019

Subject: RE: List
From: Sonja Scott (OIG Treasury)
Date: Tue, April 02, 2019 8:11 am
To: "jbsimms
Are we still on for 1 PM EST?
We will be asking about you- a brief bio, your personal issues with Direct Express and your work with victims, and what you see the problem is and solutions. Of course, you may ask questions. Sonja

Subject: RE: List
From: Sonja Scott (OIG Treasury)
Date: Tue, April 02, 2019 8:40 am
To: "jbsimms
We always start our interviews with a quick bio. Your background is important because it helps show your ability to identify issues and conduct research as an investigator. The mtg will be attended by several auditors and they will give you their names at the beginning. Sonja

Sonja Scott (Treasury) admits investigations take place: Delmar lied

Sonja Scott- Interview 1pm Eastern
Scott stated there is a difference between the investigation and audit. I stated I would be wanting a copy of any investigation. Scott stated this would be available via FOI.

Scott would be interviewing Nora Arpin today.

Jackie discovers the "inserts" endorsing Direct Express

Jackie's brother in-law (Derek) had been receiving VA benefit and Social Security in the form of a check for both entitlements. Jackie had noticed there was an insert in both individual envelopes advising veterans and Social Security recipients to stop using checks and enroll in the Direct Express program.
This enraged Jackie. How could the VA and Social Security endorse a corrupt program such as Direct Express? This issue became one of the points I would make to Pamela Powers as she communicated with me on LinkedIn. Ms. Powers seemed to be attentive to my concerns of veterans being victimized by the VA but she was not offering me any information regarding what she was doing. I would not learn anything until December 16, 2019, eight months later, that I would learn that Ms. Powers had requested meetings with VA, Social Security, Comerica Bank, BFS, and Treasury to address my concerns.

Jackie Lynn
Apr 2, 2019, 9:40 AM
to me
The VA and social security use the same envelopes!
Big deal: VA and SSA are endorsing BFS. Who is in charge?

Subject: RE: List
From: jbsimms
Date: Tue, Apr 02, 2019 9:47 am
To: Sonja Scott (OIG Treasury)
Here is what is on the back of the envelopes of VA and Soc Sec recipients of paper checks.
This "fraud" number is a call center for Conduent.
I will tell you how they work.

I told Sonja Scott that the VA and Social Security were endorsing the Direct Express program by using inserts placed into envelopes of persons receiving checks, as well as printing promotional data on the back of the envelopes.
After the interview with Sonja Scott on April 2, 2019, I sent a list of topics we discussed with Jackie and Joe Plenzler.

Highlights of Interview with Sonja Scott (OIG Treasury) April 2, 2019

From: jbsimms
Date: Tue, Apr 02, 2019 11:48 am
To: "Joe Plenzler" <plenzlerjm@gmail.com>, Jackie
Here are the outtakes from the interview:
There were 6 persons in the interview, including Sonja Scott.
The interview lasted over an hour and 15 minutes. I did most of the talking for the first hour. Scott asked some questions, and only 2 or so others asked questions.

181

I challenged them with the fact that over the past year, all the transgressions have taken place, and not changes have been made. I told them that VA, Soc Sec, Treasury, and Comerica still endorse this program online and with check inserts. The reply from Scott was "We are doing something."

I questioned if the bidding process continues past the investigation, how can you give Comerica the bid? The answer was " amend the FAA based upon the investigation." We know the bid will be awarded in 45 days. Comerica could conceivably get the bid and "make changes" after the fact. They have not made any changes in the past year (other than disbanding a card-less benefit program). No changes in customer service, fraud, or advocacy.

The same issue arose with respect to the investigation, and request to interview persons who have been victimized. OIG will never be done in time to affect the bidding process.

No one knew if Comerica was bidding for the contract. They stated they did not know who knew. I told them that I bet they could find out faster than I could.

OIG is a reporting group, not the enforcement group. I reminded them of Andrew Jackson's quote after he violated a court order allowing Indians to live in north Florida after having been given ownership to their land. He shipped the Indians to Oklahoma and as for violation of the law, Jackson said, "you have your law, now try to enforce it." I told OIG they have no input with respect to enforcement, and they are quite impotent. I told them "you can work hard to present a report, but no one cares. That cannot be very self-fulfilling." Delmar and Thorson are not listening, although they say, "we work together."

The referred to Delmar as "Rich" and that they would be talking to Rich about our conference. They all work in same office.

I got a pic of the back of the envelope that Jackie sent me, showing that VA and Soc Sec are still recruiting persons to use Direct Express.

I told them that Conduent employees work on a "call-number" basis, and their pay is determined by their call volume. They regularly drop calls.

As for why/how I became a spokesman, I answered that I did this for a living, and I find out things. It angered me to see vets and others be victimized emotionally and financially with no recourse.

Comerica has been aware of this from me for over a year and have made no changes to adhering to Reg E or access to a fraud unit. It is all Conduent, a non-banking call center.

Bottom line, everyone has ignored this for the past year. Everyone was on notice.

They asked for my suggestions:

1) Eliminate Comerica and Conduent from all involvement with Fiscal Services.

2) Separate VA benefits from the Direct Express program and create a ninth fiscal agent for VA benefits.

3) Regulation E must be enforced.

I stated that in the next few weeks, financial institutions are bidding to get the contract. I submitted that the victims of Comerica Bank have the opportunity to stand before the same panel and make a case to prohibit Comerica Bank from getting the bid. That is to be researched. I will pursue that.

I stated that in the next few weeks, financial institutions are bidding to get the contract. I submitted that the victims of Comerica Bank have the opportunity to stand before the same panel and make a case to prohibit Comerica Bank from getting the bid. That is to be researched. I will pursue that.

Hope you can contact Ms. Scott to follow up on this conference and see how Delmar and Thorson drop the ball.

Jim

From: jbsimms
Date: Tue, Apr 02, 2019 5:02 pm
To: Richard Delmar (OIG Treasury)
Cc: Sonja Scott (OIG Treasury), Jackie Lynn, Kate Berry (American Banker), Joe Plenzler (Wounded Warriors), "Michael Clements" <ClementsM@gao.gov>
Dear Mr. Delmar,

It is certain you are aware that a conference was held today with six Treasury OIG employees. Ms. Sonja Scott was the moderator, and she should be commended. While many of the transgressions by Fiscal Services were detailed, the fact that both OIG reports (14-031 and 17-034) were basically ignored by Fiscal Services. As was stated to the group, citing President Andrew Jackson concerning Supreme Court Justice Marshall and the ruling in favor of the Cherokee Indians, "[J]ohn Marshall has made his decision; let him enforce it now if he can." You can submit all the reports you wish, and it is apparent that your office has no power to enforce and corrective action suggestions or enact consequences for fault that was found.

The GAO report 17-176 (attached) was correct; Fiscal Services lacks transparency. But, we now see more than we were supposed to see.

Treasury OIG can conduct audits (the first two were ignored and faulty, which is why you were contacted a year ago) and investigations, but if the results are ignored by Fiscal Services, or people are "motivated" to turn their heads as corruption and malfeasance exists, Treasury OIG is wasting their time.

It is reasonable to assume there are conscientious and honorable persons within both Fiscal Services and Treas OIG, and the Direct Express cardholders are entitled to see evidence of these traits among any of the employees of these offices.

While it was learned that the identity of the financial institutions who have "qualified" to be considered will not be published, we as cardholders do not know if Comerica Bank submitted a bid. One goal is to exclude Comerica Bank and Conduent from any association with Fiscal Services by virtue of their planned lack of security against fraud, and other issues of malfeasance. The remaining bidders are now making their "pitch" to obtain the bid. The Direct Express cardholders have a right to be heard and be protected against being continually subjugated by Comerica Bank as Comerica Bank, validated by Fiscal Services, violate Regulation E 15USC1693 with impunity and glee; the glee is experienced by the officers of Comerica Bank knowing they will suffer no consequences as long as they have the backing of those in authority at Fiscal Services.

Please respond with a date certain when the committee assigned to hear presentations will be available to hear a presentation in opposition to Comerica Bank receiving this bid. Better yet, forward this to the members of the committee, individually, so to be identified, and the chairperson can reply.
Sincerely,
J.B. Simms

Wednesday, April 3, 2019

Subject: RE: Follow up
From: Sonja Scott (OIG Treasury)
Date: Wed, April 03, 2019 5:27 am
To: "jbsimms
Thanks for speaking with us. I will send your request to our BFS liaison, but never heard of a process for the public to provide opinions re a contract bid/award. Sonja

Ms. Scott knew that Jackie and I wanted to address this sham of a group which was entertaining presentations (the dog and pony show) from banks vying for the contract. This "Evaluation Team" needed to know the truth of the Direct Express program and the truth was their own people allowed people to be victimized by awarding the Fiscal Agent contract to Comerica Bank. Santaniello was the gate-keeper, protecting others and himself.

Thursday, April 4, 2019

Subject: the level playing field, and the request to make presentment to
the committee
From: "Delmar, Richard K." Richard Delmar (OIG Treasury))
Date: Thu, April 04, 2019 5:17 am
To: jbsimms Cc: Sonja Scott (OIG Treasury), "'jackiedenzz@yahoo.com'", "'Kate Berry (American Banker)@sourcemedia.com'"
, "'ben.kesling@wsj.com'", "'jplenzer@woundedwarriorproject.org'"
, "'ClementsM@gao.gov'"
Mr. Simms – thanks for your input. To reiterate what our auditors and investigator told you, we have on-going audit and investigative work underway that addresses concerns about the integrity and customer service practices of the program.

We've had discussions with BFS and Comerica officials, and are reaching out, consistent with the requirements of the Right to Financial Privacy Act, to affected Direct Express benefit recipients to identify and pursue instances of benefit theft.

We cannot direct BFS to invite you to participate in their financial agent selection process. We are using all of our authorities under the Inspector General Act to pursue problems with the administration of this program.
Rich Delmar
Counsel to the Inspector General
Department of the Treasury

I was trying everything I could to get Jackie and me into a meeting with BFS. BFS was a paranoid bunch, and Jackie and I had nailed them.

Subject: RE: the level playing field, and the request to make presentment to the committee
 From: jbsimms
Date: Thu, Apr 04, 2019 7:54 am
To: Richard Delmar (OIG Treasury))
Cc: Sonja Scott (OIG Treasury), "'jackiedenzz@yahoo.com'", Kate Berry (American Banker) , "
<jplenzer@woundedwarriorproject.org>, <ClementsM@gao.gov>, "Jackie Lynn"
Dear Mr. Delmar,
Thank you for your reply.
I understand that you cannot direct BFS to include me or any person to address any group involved in the selection of the fiscal/financial agent. This is consistent with the fact that BFS was not obligated to consider OIG 14-013, OIG 17-34, or GAO 17-176. This fact must be a very disconcerting those at Treasury OIG, even though, as you state, you are using all of your authority to pursue problems considering the fact that the first two OIG audits did not expose the problems which victimize veterans and others.

Although BFS is not obligated to involve any non-applicant to address the group receiving the oral presentations, I ask that you forward me contact information of this BFS decision making group. If they refuse, that will tell another story, but I will pursue this.
Sincerely,
J.B. Simms

Mr. Delmar was marginally polite and respectful, but he knew the truth about the corruption. It would be refreshing for Jackie and me to have received a "thank you" but these government employees were and are so caught up in their egos that they will not admit to any mistakes.

Subject: RE: Bounced email
 From: jbsimms
Date: Thu, Apr 04, 2019 10:51 am
To: Sonja Scott (OIG Treasury)
I forwarded your telephone number to Rebecca Newton. Her father died while Conduent refused to discuss the fraud with her as her father requested.
Hopefully this story will touch you. No one should be subjected to the emotional stress as she and her father endured. He mentioned this matter as he was dying. Conduent kept the $7,000 of fraudulent transactions. Now she has to establish a probate case in Hillsborough County, Florida. I had to get her a lawyer to talk to her as I am from that area and know attorneys there. Even if BFS is not obligated to listen to me, maybe you can knock on their door and convince them to listen to us.
Jim

I was trying to get Ms. Scott to take a step to make BFS listen to Rebecca Newton. Her father was dead, and took the burden placed upon him by Conduent, Comerica Bank, and BFS with him into death.
Jackie followed up with Jackman, the aide to Rep. Keating:
From: "Jackman, Michael" <Michael Jackman (Aide to Rep Keating)>
Date: April 4, 2019 at 4:17:41 PM EDT
To: Jackie Lynn
Subject: RE: Questions
Jackie - I got your message. I know you are impatient, but we moved our office on Monday, so I have not been able to follow up on those questions. I have reached out to staff for the Oversight Committee in DC, there may be some interest there.
I will keep you posted on any and all information I am able to gather.
--Mike Jackman

From: Jackman, Michael (Aide to Rep Keating)]
Sent: Thursday, April 4, 2019 4:43 PM
To: Delmar, Richard K. Richard Delmar (OIG Treasury))
Subject: RE: Treasury Direct Express - Inspector General action
Mr. Delmar—
It has come to my attention that Treasury's contract with Comerica for providing federal benefits to beneficiaries who are not able to receive direct deposits. Given the widespread fraud that has been reported anecdotally to this office, I wanted to ask a few follow up questions:
To your knowledge, how many federal beneficiaries receive benefits through a Direct Express card?
How many reports of fraud involving Direct Express is the Office of Inspector General aware of? How many fraud investigations involving Direct Express cards are currently underway by the OIG?
How many investigations of fraud involving the Direct Express program has the OIG completed? Of those, how many investigations found that fraud had been committed? Without identifying any individual employees, what consequences resulted from those productive investigations?
What is the current status of the Dept. of Treasury's contract with Comerica to implement the Direct Express program?
If the contract was recently renewed, was the incidence of fraud in the Direct Express program, and Comerica's ability or lack thereof to address it considered when deciding to renew this contract? Were any additional fraud safeguards written into the contract?
Thank you for your attention to this email. I look forward to your response.
Michael Jackman, District Director
Office of Congressman Keating (MA-09)

Jackie had gotten Jackman's attention. We were hoping this email to Mr. Delmar would help our cause.

From: Jackie Lynn
Date: April 4, 2019 at 12:06:41 PM EDT
To: Richard Delmar (OIG Treasury)
Hello Mr., Delmar,
I was emailing you regarding your pending investigation with Direct Express and what the status was meaning when we could expect the reports? I am also looking for information on my case. I have heard absolutely nothing on it in fact because the bank refuses to communicate with the Hollywood Police Department my case has been closed, we have a woman on tape pretending to be me and she is still at large? I mean this case couldn't be more easier to solve. It is my understanding that not a single criminal in any of these complaints we have sent your office has been arrested. It is concerning that victims are left in the dark as to their investigations but then again, we are at the mercy of the government agencies that put us in this spot in the first place.
I would like a detailed report on my case please, also I would like to know where else my case has been referred to (meaning other agencies like FBI or other law).
It is unfortunate that the beneficiaries have no right to know who is bidding in the new contract, if people are being forced into electronic payments then they should be given the information as to which banks are involved in applying for the contract. Once again leaving people feeling hopeless and forced by Government who failed all of us in the first place. I am shocked that not one warning to cardholders have gone out or that government agencies neglect to notify people that is going on and what to look out for to protect themselves. As I am sure you are aware Victims come forward almost daily, none of which were part of the cardless benefit program and that is why those numbers received by Sen. Warren's office are fabricated. Comerica Bank Lied to Sen. Warrens office. We hope that with your investigation the truth comes out, hopefully you can shed some light on my case as this is causing my family and I extreme stress.
Thank you for your time,
Jackie Densmore

Here Delmar replies to my questioning Santaniello from blocking Jackie and me from appearing at BFS.

Friday, April 5, 2019

Victim Number 95-Anthony: AR

On 4-3-19 I noticed my direct express card was hacked on 4-1-19and used until my bank account was empty. There were 3 charges out of California I myself live in Arkansas. My card was not lost or stolen. I called and reported the fraud. They said I'd have to wait for the purchases to go through before I could call and dispute the charges. They acted as if this was an everyday thing with cardholders. They cancelled my existing card and said they'd send me a new one in the mail. I called back the next day 4-3-19 after I seen the charges had went thru and they said they'd send me a letter in the mail and I'd have to write down the charges I was disputing. I'm a single father living off of a disability check. My rents past due my bills still need to be paid meanwhile I'm sitting here waiting for a letter to fill out to dispute the charges which could take weeks. Every other bank has this stuff settled within 10 days. It's ridiculous that I'm expected to wait weeks. I'd like this matter settled as soon as. I'm attaching a screenshot of my account history for April. The last 3 charges are the fraudulent ones they are based out of California. One is at JC Penney's another at Burlington stores and another at advantage laundry. They are all fraudulent and not made by me the card holder. The purchases in Arkansas are the ones I made as I live in Arkansas. I look forward to hearing from you soon with a resolution to this issue.

Subject: RE: Delmar's admission of BFS not obligated to hear my
presentation
From: Joe Plenzler
Date: Fri, April 05, 2019 6:37 am
To: jbsimms
Another reporter wants to speak to you. He is an investigative journalist by the name of Jasper Craven. He's very good. With your permission, I'll pass him your phone number.

Joe Plenzler believed in our case and how we were trying to protect veterans. Joe had forwarded a number of reporter contacts to me, most of whom never followed up.

Subject: Oral presentation for bid submission: Direct Express program
From: jbsimms
Date: Fri, Apr 05, 2019 11:17 am
To: Media.Relations@fiscal.treasury.gov
Cc: "Jackie Lynn"
I am looking for the persons/committee which is receiving oral presentations for the banking institutions which have submitted bids to administer the Direct Express programPlease call me as soon as possible.
Sincerely,
J.B. Simms

Jackie and I tried everything to get to talk to BFS. They knew they were corrupt, and the deal was done to give the contract again to Comerica.

Sunday, April 7, 2019

Victim Number-96: Aturo

Apr 7, 2019, 2:58 AM
to me
hi my name is artur.. i have been on social security for about 8 years most of those getting my money from directexpress commercia bank. i am not mobile and live on a limited income so most of my bills get paid online. in the 8 years since ive had direct express i can prove there has not been one month where unauthorized money was taken from my acct i have filed over 6 unauthorized claims with direct express and not once have they ever ruled in my favor never giving me a reason and refusing to give me any info regarding their corporate offices over the years and after countless days and hours on the phone with them . i came to the conclusion i was to ill to deal with them and just let it happen. a week ago on the first of april 2019 i went to attempt to take all my money out before it could happen again i decided to buy a prepaid card i paid 500 dollars and the card was not activated. direct express then put my money on a pending hold and for six long days refused to return it. i have never in 7 years paid my rent late and i am on housing i was almost evicted because they would not release my

money. after 5 days of calling being hung up on and being harrassed they released my money i had to pay late fees and my light was late they gave no explaination. i am writing in hopes that what is happening to me somehow my story will help it not to happen to anyone else. this month there is over 150 dollars of unauthorized amounts taken from my acct and i am now awaiting 10 days to get paperwork from them to file a claim to see if i can get my money. please if you cannot help me use this to help anyone dealing with commercia bank direct express we are elder sick human beings who should not be having to go through this because of some fraudalant company put in charge of our money thank you

Monday, April 8, 2019

Victim 97 Charles-OH
Hello

My name is Charles and I am a disabled individual. My April sis check was deposited to my direct Express account on Apr 1st. I paid my phone bill and one other bill online that day but was extremely I'll with flu so I didn't leave my apt the rest of day. I went next morning to purchase money order for rent and a monthly cota pass and was informed my card was declined. Upon checking balance I was told I had only 3.85 cents on my card.

I and my case mgr both has been trying to contact company about this but with no success or to even get a live person. I need help please as i suffer from mental illness and I'm facing losing my housing over this as well as being out over 700 dollars which i cant afford to lose.

Can someone please guide me how to proceed in this

April 16, 2019 (email sent to me)

Nobody has replied at all Jim. My mental health case mgr going to talk to them today and I feel she can get things straightened out. When i 1st contacted Alisha and received paperwork via email on apr8th she stated 23rd but when i found out case already closed how does this timeframe work. In emails I stated I wanted case reopened and my credit given but I've not heard one thing since. I just finally received the actual papers to fill out for dispute yesterday and still no letter of denial but was informed when I called the 11th I was denied. Please help me as I'm losing my sanity over this and while my case manager good lady dont know much about things like this.

Thank you

I called Charles. He been homeless 4 years. No money to buy food. Has money for cell phone.
He got email from Alisha at Conduent on 4/9. Fraud was not confirmed, claim denied.

From: "Alison B." <alison@pissedconsumer.com>
Date: Mon, Apr 08, 2019 2:49 am
To: jbsimms
Hi JB,, We have published your video interview in our social networks.

Tuesday, April 9, 2019

Delmar admits to investigations.

Notice he said they cannot provide info about "ongoing" investigations.
That means they CAN provide info about "closed" investigations.

More admission of investigations with no results

from: Delmar, Richard K. Richard Delmar (OIG Treasury))
to: Jackie Lynn
cc: "jb.simms10@gmail.com"
date: Apr 9, 2019, 7:55 AM
subject: RE: RE: waiting for updates as usual
mailed-by: oig.treas.gov

Ms. Densmore - What I can tell you is that we're actively working the matter in both our Audit and Investigations offices. We're seeking records from the entities and working directly with identified victims. We're doing all we can do under the IG Act, and the procedural requirements of the Right to Financial Privacy Act. We cannot provide more information about open investigations.

Fiscal Services was hiding the presentations by the bidders.

I believed I had located the persons involved. They are not answering phones.

Call Brett Smith at (202) 874-6666, Director of Electronic fund transfer, or Edita Rickard (202) 874-7165, Analysts Disbursement (202) 874-6790.

The disbursement number is now on voice mail after my calls.

Brett Smith was the Director of Electronic Fund Transfer. He was the person to whom I had left messages. He was too cowardly to return my calls.

Wednesday, April 10, 2019

A real human with a real story

Victim Number 98-Sandra-CA

Thank you, do you still think I should wait to file anything? There is so much more they have done, I have phone records showing my calling them 26 times where I was auto transferred to recording intentionally. S. Schmidt claimed in her CFPB response she personally as well as other reps had attempted to contact me, all untrue. I received a letter in January claiming they had just reviewed my case again and found there had been no errors in processing under Regulation E which refers to not cancelling access by the violator (crazy). If they had reviewed my account they would have seen my 20 requests for information used in deciding my case as well as my request for transaction codes that I can't pursue collection without. Banks readily make this information available within an online account, DE doesn't and then refuses to provide. This entire company is unethical and against our Country's sick and disabled. I still to date have not recovered financially from this loss and the stress involved has caused anxiety and depression which I am being treated and have two visits a week in trying to cope with the frustration of being victimized again by the bank following the unauthorized transactions.

I have attached the complaint and response from CFPB and Susan Schmidt stated my claim did not follow normal fraud activity as I had my card throughout the theft. This is because the person was staying with me and taking my card and putting it back. The charges he did are not anything I do. I do not know anyone from jail to receive collect calls, I don't have multiple cell phones which there are 2 bills paid, I do not go to McDonalds much less spend $67 and $53 nor do I have a playstation account or frequent a casino. These charges are easily proven not to be mine yet I am refused the transaction codes to prove it. Again, I have a police report on hold waiting for transaction codes which to date I do not have.

I haven't done anything wrong yet I am suffering on top of the theft that is still very emotional. I need my claim resolved as my benefits are my only income. My car insurance is cancelling in 2 days, I have had my water shut off land other utilities are scheduled for next week. I have requested my transaction codes repeatedly and get no response. I have almost 3 months of benefits involved in the claim and my benefits are my only income. I am facing a foreclosure auction that was postponed from November 29th and have to buy medicine for my dog with cushings disease and other necessary items I need. My Thanksgiving was not with my family because I had no gas or insurance and now Christmas will be ruined as well. Federal guidelines are not a suggestion they are law. Regulation E reads consumers are protected and my rights in several instances have been violated. Please review the attached letter of appeal I wrote following the complaint to CFPB which will provide more specific information.

This email above was forwarded to OIG Treasury and others.

Victim 99 Craig (Kathlene Paglia)-NC

Craig Houser- Wife's mom (mom on law) victim

2 transactions at ATM $800 and $120, then Burger King

April 29, 2019 I found out that his mother in law, Kathleen Paglia, had contacted Franklin Lemond and had been added as a Plaintiff to the Complaint as a Plaintiff.

702am T Brett Smith (202) 874-6666 Dir Electronic money transfer FS- Left Message on voicemail.

706am t Edita Richard (202) 874-7165 BFS Left message voicemail

Jackie got a letter today telling her that her case has been closed in Florida. Jackie was livid. The Treasury Agent and local police never contacted the Walmart store where the black woman took the money from Jackie's account. We knew the address of the woman; it was the same woman who was involved in Paul Katynski's fraud.

Jackie and I knew we were battling this all by ourselves.

Thursday, April 11, 2019

1050am T Brett D Smith- (202) 874-6666 FS Director-transferred-Left message voicemail
1050am T Edita Richard (202) 874-7165 FS Distribution Analyst- Left message voicemail
1057am T (202) 874-6790 FS Payment Management Left message voicemail

Friday, April 12, 2019

954am T Brett Smith BFS- (202) 874-6666 Left message voicemail
957am T BFS Disbursements- (202) 874-6790 Left message voicemail
959am T Edita Rickard BFS (202) 874-7165 Left message voicemail
1011am T Tracie Middleton BFS Dir Fin Mgt (202) 874-6950 Left message voicemail
T (304) 480-7777 BFS It Service-Tammy Breeden. She in Parkersburg, WV.
She was in the same office as Brett Smith and sees Brett Smith on the phone. Sent him message on Skype.
Brett Smith such a coward he would not take my messages and return my calls. The corruption within this
agency was widespread.

From: Sonja Scott (OIG Treasury)
Date: Fri, Apr 12, 2019 2:28 pm
To: jbsimms
Cc: "jackiedenzz@yahoo.com" <jackiedenzz@yahoo.com>
I have informed our BFS liaison. I can also inform Santaniello, but you already have and I do not know him.
Sorry for any lack of communication from me. I was in training most of the week and will be on warrants out of
town most of next week. Sonja

From: jbsimms
Sent: Apr 12, 2019 4:38 PM
To: Sonja Scott (OIG Treasury)
Cc: Jackie Lynn
Subject: [FWD: RE: The Direct Express® program and the Bureau of the Fiscal Service]
If you can contact Santaniello and tell him I am serious about making a presentation, regardless if they feel
obliged to do so, that gesture would be greatly appreciated by me, as well as Ms. Densmore.
Jim

Saturday, April 13, 2019

Santaniello was not found on LinkedIn.

Jackie sees Santaniello quoted in Kate's article, sends email to get Santaniello contact info.

From: Cyn C
Date: Sat, Apr 13, 2019 4:22 am
To: Thomas.Santaniello@fiscal.treasury.gov
Dear Mr. Santaniello,
In November of last year $1500+ were fraudulently removed from my account. The money was taken as soon as
my SS payment was made .
I live in Georgia but my card was charged in California, New Jersey, and Michigan. By contacting DE I quickly
discovered that
1. The best time to reach them is after midnight. 2. They don't have a special fraud department.
3. DE does not investigate cases of fraud. I have my closed case copies which shows that the only information is
the evidence that I had provided. 4. It took DE over 20 days to issue me a provisional credit.
I was fortunate enough to recoup my monies but I had to work for it.
I called the merchants and reported the fraudulent charges, Direct Express did not.
Please consider another fiscal agent for our SS payments.
Thank you for your time.
Respectfully, Cynthia Clark

Sunday April 14, 2019

Jackie lays into Santaniello:

Jackie Lynn
Sun, Apr 14, 2019, 3:11 PM
to me

Dear Mr. Santaniello,

Let me take a moment to introduce myself, my name is Jackie Densmore and I am a victim of Direct Express fraud that is issued by Comerica Bank, You know the one your agency awarded the contract to that has an F rating with the Better Business Bureau.

Words can not describe what fiscal Services has done to my family as well as thousands of other victims by awarding such a corrupt bank not only one contract but a second. Not to mention the lies they told people who were owed these benefits by Fiscal Services. These cards are not safe , or backed by Mastercard's zero liability or safer than a paper check and should have never been recommended by the US Treasury Department. People also had the right to request a paper check by simply filing out a waiver that Fiscal service as well as other agencies failed to tell the public instead, they used scare tactics by enclosing documents in these beneficiaries monthly checks saying they were in volition of the law if they do not switch to electronic payments. I I will as well as so many do whatever it takes to take the" blinders" off and expose what this bank has done and continues to do to these innocent beneficiaries as well as their families. I have reached out to many Senators including my Senator Elizabeth Warren who has exposed only a fraction of corruption that has been displayed by Comerica Bank and the third-party Call. That fraction of corruption was the cardless benefit program that I know you are aware of from your statement in the American Banker Article dated August 2018 by Kate Berry for your memory please see link.

https://www.americanbanker.com/news/comerica-scrambles-to-address-fraud-in-prepaid-benefits-program
The Bureau of the Fiscal Service is working with the Treasury Office of Inspector General, Comerica and its partners to effectively address bank card fraud and other consumer concerns and protect the more than 4.5 million Direct Express benefit recipients who rely on this program for their monthly federal benefits," said Thomas Santaniello, a spokesman for Treasury's Bureau of the Fiscal Service.
As I will also point out to you that Comerica's stories have changed from first saying :
Comerica said that it believes the Direct Express fraud is limited to the cardless service, and that one employee at a Direct Express call center has been fired over the security breach. Comerica has oversight of the Direct Express program but outsources the main call center function to Conduent, a publicly traded conglomerate in Florham Park, N.J.
Then the claim in the second article by American Banker dated Jan 2018:
https://www.americanbanker.com/news/warren-comerica-fraud-shows-need-for-security-fix-in-prepaid-program
Comerica had claimed that accounts were not compromised through a cybersecurity breach of the bank, but rather that beneficiaries likely had their private identifiable information stolen from third parties, according to briefings Warren received from Comerica and Treasury's OIG.
Strange how they go as far a saying an employee was fired over then breach then quickly change the story when Sen Warren asks. I will tell you that we have senators that because of their constituents contacting us we have been working close with them to grant a GAO! The truth will be uncovered, this fraud has not just been limited to the cardless program, this call center and bank is linked to extreme cases of fraud both from Federal and State programs known as the Eppicards.
Please do not try to convince us these cards are safe and what your bogus satisfaction ratings are. We know too much and are requesting to be invited to address the committee so that they do not make the same mistake again by awarding a unqualified bank and call center that offers no security.
Fiscal Services ignored two OIG reports and the GAO report.
Fiscal Services had no one smart enough see that this debit card has no security parameters.
The low balance alert does no good if a person is hit 5 times between midnight and 6am and never reaches the low balance alert figure.
There have been over 400 complaints at Consumer Financial Protection Bureau in the spring of 2018 and no one at Fiscal Services acknowledged this.
Comerica Bank is enabling Conduent to violate Regulation E in many ways:
1) not acknowledging that "notice" is effective when the call centers gets a call

2) not giving full provisional credit within 10 days of notice.
3) not giving the copy of the investigation to the cardholder
4) telling the cardholder that the burden of proof is on the cardholder (specifically stated in Reg E that this is the burden of the financial institution)
The fraud unit puts the burden of contacting merchants and bank atm location on the cardholder. Not to mention that we as well as many others have seen the" fraud" department denial letters. The letters are all signed the" fraud" Department funny how the number for the fraud department is the same number as the customer service number. They don't enclose the real number so that cardholders will not meet the 10 day reporting time frame on purpose instantly denying them their much needed funds. I am very familiar with the issues of malfeasance, deceit, and the dispensing of misinformation done by this bank as well as call center employees. So, I can without a doubt tell, you these cards are not safe and neither is your personal information. I will also tell you that the bank as well as other agencies have refused to notify cardholders that over a half of millions of dollars has been reported stolen either on their websites or by mail. I have not received one letter explaining the fraud or the investigation and neither has any of the other victims which I find disgusting! I am outraged that no notification has gone out alerting the public, my feeling is that if notification went out thousands more victims would come out and damage the bogus satisfactory ratings and hold people accountable.
Maybe after all the lawsuits are filed Fiscal Services as we.l as other agencies will realize how much damage they have caused by awarding an unqualified bank and putting millions of people's lives in jeopardy.
Monies kept from cardholders is put onto bogus unused accounts, to be used later by fraudsters.
Do not lie to us and tell us Fiscal Services did their job. People at Fiscal Services turned a blind eye to all the violations by Comerica Bank, and we want to know what "motivated $$$" persons at Fiscal Services to ignore Comerica violations of Reg E, and to give them the contract renewal.
I am very familiar with the issues of malfeasance, deceit, and the dispensing of misinformation as am I.
As I know that your office has received applications for a new contract perhaps educate yourselves before making a third mistake
Below are some helpful links:
Just a few we can address with the committee to ensure that no one is paid off when they choose which bank will get the award hopefully after all the information I as well as many others have provided your office with Fiscal Sevices will actually choose a bank that deserves it and how follows the law according so that innocent people are not victimized. Also perhaps Fiscal Services will stop lying to people saying they have only two options in receiving their benefits through direct deposit or Direct express which clearly people can and are receiving paper checks!
I would like to address the committee which is entertaining oral presentations by the bidding financial institutions. It is only fair that since the committee is listening to bidders give an presentation, the cardholder victims of the Direct Express program have a right to be heard as well.
Sincerely,
Jackie Densmore

Monday, April 15, 2019

Sandy emailed me. I did not edit this. I want you to understand the emotion as she is typing this and looking for help. SS benefits not coming through.

Santaniello and the government workers made up the rules to suit their conscience

I stated the following to Santaniello:

Convince me why "[O]ur evaluation process does not include an opportunity for public comment or for direct public contact with the evaluation team."

A victim calls Conduent 26 times

Victim Number 100-Sandy:CA
My name is Tracy and Im Payee for my Aunt Sandy Childs who recieves ssi benefiets and is paid monthly to direct express card that she recieved by the ssi dept. My Aunt sandy has yet to recieve her monthly pay for the

month of april.Ive phoned direct express to find out where i should begin the process to get my aunts money..The d.e.customer service ssid its not there problem .So i then call ssi dept. Who referred me back to direct express as the payment was sent to a other card but inactive and so the new card was recieved and im still waiting for the direct express agency to put monirs on my new card from the old card..Im getting the run around and about to be evicted utilities shut off no food..Please HELP as im not knowing what recourse to take..

From: Sandra Willson
Date: Mon, Apr 15, 2019 2:12 pm
To: jbsimms

Thank you, do you still think I should wait to file anything? There is so much more they have done, I have phone records showing my calling them 26 times where I was auto transferred to recording intentionally. S. Schmidt claimed in her CFPB response she personally as well as other reps had attempted to contact me, all untrue. I received a letter in January claiming they had just reviewed my case again and found there had been no errors in processing under Regulation E which refers to not cancelling access by the violator (crazy). If they had reviewed my account they would have seen my 20 requests for information used in deciding my case as well as my request for transaction codes that I can't pursue collection without. Banks readily make this information available within an online account, DE doesn't and then refuses to provide. This entire company is unethical and against our Country's sick and disabled. I still to date have not recovered financially from this loss and the stress involved has caused anxiety and depression which I am being treated and have two visits a week in trying to cope with the frustration of being victimized again by the bank following the unauthorized transactions. I am very upset as much as when it happened and will do anything requested in pursuit of justice. Susan Schmidt, Brandon Garcia and Alisha? all need to be fired!
Sandra Willson

Tuesday, April 16, 2019

From: jbsimms
Date: Tue, Apr 16, 2019 1:07 pm
To: <Thomas.Santaniello@fiscal.treasury.gov>
Cc: Jackie Lynn, <Walter Bayer (SSA OIG)@ssa.gov>, Richard Delmar (OIG Treasury)), " Sonja Scott (OIG Treasury),

Dear Mr. Santaniello,
Do you people have any idea what is like to be homeless for 4 years, get an apartment, experience fraud, and be ignored by the bank that told you your funds were secure?
I talked to Chuck today. The call that was answered was at Susan Schmidt's office. All the Conduent numbers are going to voicemail.
This man is receiving SSI, disabilty. He probably receives less than one thousand dollars a month, much less than your house payment. There only buttons to push to get attention from Fiscal Services are logic and compassion. We know those don't work. You want to send Mr. Westfall some cash ? His email is attached below.
One lady in Florida watched her father die, and in his last words he apologized for the pain she was enduring because Comerica denied a fraud claim of $7,000, performed while the dying man was in hospital care. The fraudsters bought hundreds of dollars of pizza, 100 miles from where the man was lying, and the claim was denied. Comerica has now converted this money to their own use while the lady had to take charity to have her father cremated. Fewer than 2 months later, this lady's mother died. Some of you have experienced a mother dying, I was 14 years old when I experienced that.
These are the stories you wish to hide from this evaluation team because it was the failure of Fiscal Services to supervise Comerica Bank which led us to where we are.
Do you want to talk to some victims? Sitting you and others at Fiscal Services in a chair, having to listen to what you have done by allowing Comerica to do these things will be like the scene from Clockwork Orange, where the eyes of the perpetrators were clipped open and they could not avoid seeing the pain they caused others.
It might be up to the government workers copied here to get to Ms. McCoy and get a response and have our voices heard. Her complicity will dictate her response.

Wednesday, April 17, 2019

The beginning of the day was spent working on Terms and Conditions of the Direct Express program, technically the legal insert which accompanied the debit card received by cardholders. Within the Terms and Conditions, it was read the financial institution would adhere to state and federal regulations, this meaning Regulation E. We knew this was not happening, which is why this mess started.

Thursday, April 18, 2019

805am T Brett Smith- BFS (202) 874-6666 BFS left message voicemail
806am T Disbursements- BFS (202) 874-6790- Left message voicemail
808am T Edita Rickard BFS (202) 874-7165 Left message voicemail
828am T (202) 874-6850 –"to access mailbox…" hit # and pressed Brett Smith #, Left message voicemail
842 TT Melanie Clevenger (806) 500-5718; She is contacting Senator Cornyn's office.
12:34 Eastern
I called (202) 874-6650. A gentleman identifying himself as Christopher Thompson answered. I told him I was trying to reach Brett Smith and Edita Rickard. I stated, "This is Jim Simms" and his reply was "J.B. Simms?" Thompson was sucking wind. He said he was going to forward my number to his supervisor. I asked him the name of his supervisor. He stated "...[w]e have a few supervisors here. I will tell them this is very important. They will want to talk with you. "
Since speaking with Mr. Thompson, I have made 3-4 calls to him. One was made moments ago. His calls went straight to voicemail, as do calls to Brett Smith and Edita Rickard.
Mr. Santaniello has yet to respond to discuss this matter, other than stating that he would forward my concerns to the evaluation team. What a comfort that was to hear.
This is what I always referred to as "a pattern of deceit." Maybe Mark Felt said it best, "Follow the money."
Brett D. Smith- (202) 874-6666 Director of Electronic Transfer (Treasury)
Edita Rickard- (202) 874-7165 Disbursements (Treasury)
Messages have been left with these persons. No response has been received.

Victim 101 Kelly-TX
Discovered funds missing: April 4, 2019 Reported funds missing: April 4, 2019
She is contacting Mason at Sen Cornyn office (972) 239-1316
Friday April 19, 2019 Hi Mr. Simms.
I did speak with Cornyn's office. They are mailing the form to me. Once I fill it out I will fax it back. Jackie said I should email what I have to you. The only thing I have is screenshots of the "fraud packet" Direct Express sent me. I mailed it back to them on the 17th.
Wanted to let you know that I haven't hear back from Calvin.
Another email: I did call the 800 Disability # today to have it noted in my acct that my $ was stolen. The local San Antonio office told me I should do that. I'm just covering every base I can.
1222pm Kelly Chambers – DE victim- 8/4 balance was zero. Called DE- took 7 days to get packet.

Saturday, April 20, 2019

Subject: A document to send to your evaluation team. Fiscal Services cover-up for Comerica Bank
From: jbsimms
Date: Sat, Apr 20, 2019 11:22 am
To: <Thomas.Santaniello@fiscal.treasury.gov>
Cc: <jplenzler@woundedwarriorproject.org>, ", Richard Delmar (OIG Treasury)), " Sonja Scott (OIG Treasury), " <Walter Bayer (SSA OIG)@ssa.gov>
Dear Mr. Santaniello,
Since you have taken it upon yourself to be the point-person for the "evaluation team" which is entertaining bidder oral presentations by financial institutions vying for to be the Fiscal Agent for the Direct Express program, let me take this opportunity to "hold up a mirror" to your group. Treasury or Fiscal Services never responded to Senator Collins (see attached letter) but I can assure you that her office is being reminded at this very moment. A new administration might see this matter a bit differently.
You and your group, however high ranking the matter ascends, might not feel it necessary to answer to me, but as they say, "You will be very impressed with who I send."
Let me know when you want to talk. J.B. Simms

From: jbsimms
Date: Saturday, Apr 20, 2019, 2:02 PM
To: Scott, Sonja L. Sonja Scott (OIG Treasury),. Richard Delmar (OIG Treasury)
Cc:, Franklin Lemond <Franklin Lemond (Plaintiff's Attorney)@webbllc.com>, Jackie Lynn, Michael Clements <ClementsM@gao.gov>
The bidding process is happening, and Fiscal Services is refusing to allow us to address the "evaluation team."
I will be glad to discuss this with either you at any time.
J.B. Simms

Monday, April 22, 2019

From: jbsimms
Date: Mon, Apr 22, 2019 8:40 am
To: Sonja Scott (OIG Treasury)
Cc: "Jackie Lynn"
Dear Ms. Scott,
After receiving no return calls from messages left for Fiscal Service employees (Brett Smith, Edita Richard and others), it the lack of transparency (as quoted from GAO 17-176) appears appropriate.
A source revealed to me that the actual enforcement of recommendations made by Treasury OIG in 14-031 and 17-034 is the duty of a person having the designation as the "Business Process Owner." This person(s) is responsible for implementing the recommendations made by Treasury OIG audits and making certain the Fiscal Agent (Comerica Bank) remains in compliance with the FAA and federal law. Please advise me if the above information is correct, and the identity of such person (or office) at Fiscal Service.
As was stated to me, the Business Process Owner was charged with reviewing Treasury OIG 14-031. There was no reference to this enforcement or lack thereof in Treasury OIG 17-034. It would seem appropriate that the second audit would point out that the first audit was ignored, which would have been an honest conclusion based upon the subsequent audit.
I am requesting confirmation of and identity of the Business Process Owner at Fiscal Services which (who) is charged with implementing audit finding recommendations, plus oversight and enforcement of Comerica Bank. Feel free to call me.
Sincerely,
Jim

From: Sonja Scott (OIG Treasury)
Date: Mon, Apr 22, 2019 10:10 am
To: "'jbsimms'" <jbsimms>
Cc: Jackie Lynn
According to our Office of Audit, the "Business Process Owner" would be the BFS Commissioner. However, the current Commissioner was not in that position when the audits were conducted. Sonja

It looked like the head of Bureau of Fiscal Service was the "Business Owner" and responsible for the contract with Comerica Bank. That made sense.

We continued to request a meeting with the selection committee

Subject: RE: verifying source information re: Fiscal Services
 From: jbsimms
Date: Mon, Apr 22, 2019 10:48 am
To: Sonja Scott (OIG Treasury)
Cc: "Jackie Lynn"
My source was adamant that this person behind the curtain is the "Business Process Owner" and that person receives the Treas OIG report/audit.
I am not being combative when I say that there is a difference between an audit and and investigation. I would think an "investigator" would use the audit as a tool, and the audit is not the desired end result.
I can save your Office of Audit a little time in searching for what has changed or not changed:

(1) CFPB continues to receive complaints about Comerica Bank violating Regulation E by not giving provisional credit within 10 days of having received notice.

(2) Comerica Bank has violated Regulation E by not furnishing copies of investigations to all cardholders which received denials of fraud claims.

(3) The denial letters sent by Conduent expressly state that the cardholder did not prove a fraud was perpetrated, when Regulation E states the burden of proof is on the financial institution. There is no evidence of any investigation being conducted by Conduent other than a cursory glance at cardholder statements in order to "establish a pattern" of sorts. Well, when the fraud occurs thousands of miles from the home address of the cardholder, that is a clue that the fraud claim is valid.

(4) Comerica Bank has not placed any security measures on the Direct Express program, exposing cardholders to fraud which proprietary Comerica Bank customers are not exposed.

(5) Fiscal Services, US Treasury, Veteran Affairs, and Social Security continue to endorse the Direct Express program, knowing full well of the malfeasance and corruption therein.

(6) There are no enforcement policies in place to mandate that the fiscal agent, Comerica Bank, adhere to any FAA or 15USC1693, or any federal regulation interpretation by any agency of government (Fed Reserve or FDIC).

(7) The Terms of Agreement sent to cardholders state that Comerica Bank was to follow all state and federal law. The federal law 15USC1693 has been violated on a regular basis through Conduent, and Comerica Bank is well aware, and enables the violation.

(8) The Bureau of Fiscal Services does not give a damn about any report, audit, or revelation made by Treasury OIG, specifically David A. Lebryk, Sheryl Morrow (retired), and Kim McCoy. Treasury OIG is the tattle-tail who tells a teacher that the teacher' pet did something wrong or got into a fight with the teacher's pet. You know how that ends up. (Yes, I have personally done that, and did not care of the consequences, and there were consequences which I gladly accepted. It was worth the fight.)

I will stop at this point. I did not refer to my notes while writing this email.

I ask that you please determine the following:

1) Ask your Audit Team to look into this matter of the Business Process Owner at BFS.

2) Arrange for victims to give oral presentations to the secretive "evaluation team" at BFS. We should be given at least one week's notice for travel. The presentation should be open to the public, media, and Treasury OIG. If we get scheduled to make an oral presentation, I suggest you get your popcorn early. You will not want to miss anything.

Jim

The identity of the "Business Owner" at BFS is exposed and named

Subject: RE: verifying source information re: Fiscal Services
From: jbsimms
Date: Mon, Apr 22, 2019 11:00 am
To: Sonja Scott (OIG Treasury)
Cc: "Jackie Lynn"

The BFS commissioner, David Leybryk, was commissioner on March 26, 2014 (the date of Treas OIG 14-031). Leybryk still works for BFS. Kim McCoy was not the commissioner during either audit, but was with BFS during that time, and has full knowledge of this issue.

If McCoy is charged with overseeing and enforcing FAA and fed law, and she is the "Business Process Owner" then she might need not to be interviewed but interrogated.

Tuesday April 23, 2019

An email was received from Sonja Scott- "this program not being ignored by this office." This made me laugh.

Subject: RE: The Business Process Owner, and Santaniello
From: Sonja Scott (OIG Treasury)
Date: Tue, April 23, 2019 6:35 am
To: "jbsimms
Cc: Richard Delmar (OIG Treasury), "Thorson, Eric M"<ThorsonE@oig.treas.gov>
Jim – As I have said before, our Office of Audit is reviewing their former audits and the current status of the Direct Express Program through a Corrective Action Verification. They are also working closely with the

Office of Investigations regarding complaints we have received regarding the program. This program is not being ignored by this office. Sonja

From: jbsimms
Date: Tue, April 23, 2019 11:46 am
To: Kate Berry
Jackie called, and I am forwarding this to you.
Santaniello is the guard dog for the Evaluation Team at Fiscal Services. We know the evaluation team is receiving oral presentations, and just because outsiders might have never made a presentation against a bidder, we want in.
Sonja Scott and Richard Delmar are making gestures as though they might be listening.
If you get with Santaniello and ask him what the hell is going on, and why are victims being blocked from the "Wizard of Oz" operation.
Jim

Wednesday, April 24, 2019

From: jbsimms
Date: Wed, Apr 24, 2019 10:11 pm
To: " Richard Delmar (OIG Treasury), Sonja Scott (OIG Treasury), Walter Bayer (SSA OIG)@ssa.gov
Cc: <Thomas.Santaniello@fiscal.treasury.gov>, "Jackie Lynn", "Jeff Harding"
James Harding is a 75-year-old USN veteran. His son, Jeff, is a disabled USAF veteran, and cares for his father.
I believe I have forwarded information about this case to you. The elder Harding fraudulently lost $1,933.70 while he was in a nursing home.
Attached is a copy of the denial letter from a Conduent worker using the name "Sonia."
Please focus on a couple items:
Paragraph Two, Line Two: "...[w]e cannot confirm that fraud occurred. Our investigation indicates that you entered into an agreement with the merchant [unnamed], and the transaction was processed in accordance with that agreement."
Conduent placed the burden of proof upon Mr. Harding (violation of 15USC1693g(b) and also failed to explain their "investigation" and their proof Mr. Harding (lying on his back in a nursing home) entered into any agreement with any merchant.
We want to address the "evaluation team" and let them know the truth. The need to hear it from a credible source.
J.B. Simms

From: Zechariah Allen <therealbearjew420@gmail.com>
Date: April 24, 2019 at 10:16:14 AM EDT
To: jackiedenzz@yahoo.com
Subject: Hello
Hello Jackie this is zech I hope all is well, I wanted you to be the first to know I'm smooth sailing again I've gotten 2 checks now and life has been moving up pretty quickly still got quite a work load a head but it's moving up, gotten all my accounts that we're hacked deleted and new number as well now. I'll never forget you and Jim Simms if it wasn't for the two of you I don't think I would have made it and for that I am more than greatfull I hope to be able to meet in person some day!!!
Best regards, Zechariah

Comerica began blocking victims from sending email fraud narratives.
Thomas Santaniello of Fiscal Services was protecting the evaluation team, denying us from making a presentation.

Friday, April 25, 2019

Subject: Kelly Chambers
From: jbsimms
Date: Thu, Apr 25, 2019 6:56 am
To: Sonja Scott (OIG Treasury)
Dear Ms. Scott,
My day starts early with the victims.
I received a text from Kelly Chambers, telling me she talked to you and described you as "super nice lady."
Thank you for speaking with her.
I am interested in exactly what "buttons" you think you can push to make something happen. If you wish to call me, please do.
If there is any feedback from BFS you can share, I am all ears.
Jim

Friday, April 26, 2019

I always questioned why the Fraud Department of Conduent never interacted with law enforcement. This issue was addressed with Sonja Scott at Treasury.

Subject: one question on one subject
From: jbsimms
Date: Fri, Apr 26, 2019 6:48 am
To: Sonja Scott (OIG Treasury)
Cc: Richard Delmar (OIG Treasury), Jackie Lynn, Franklin Lemond (Plaintiff's Attorney)
It is evident that Conduent does not report fraud to law enforcement. There is a reason. Could the reason be that the fraudsters are inhouse?
If contacts with Conduent and Comerica are privy to proprietary information, passed on by Conduent and Comerica employees, knowing that there are no safeguards on the cards, no reporting, and no diligence, and no repercussions or penalty, there is no reason no to commit the crime. Many of the fraud reports smack of inside work.
Jim

Monday, April 29, 2019

Subject: any comment on Conduent refusing to be acknowledging fraud narratives?
* From: jbsimms*
Date: Mon, Apr 29, 2019 10:01 am
To: Sonja Scott (OIG Treasury), Richard Delmar (OIG Treasury))
Cc: "Jackie Lynn", "Cyn C"
Dear Ms. Scott,
In light of Conduent refusing to accept fraud narratives at the email addresses of Customer Advocacy (advocacy@usdirectexpress.com) and Conduent Fraud Unit (Shantelle Johnson, shantelle.johnson@conduent.com), which began approximately April 1, 2019, and inconsideration that fraud narratives had been accepted and solicited to these Conduent email addresses, it appears that the recipients at these email addresses have taken it upon themselves act with vengeance to avoid giving timely attention to losses by the cardholders.
While me, not being a lawyer and being in need of an explanation, this change in "policy" by Conduent, authorized by Comerica, appears to be in violation of the following:
Title 15USC1693f(a) Error Resolution-Notification to financial institution of error
"If a financial institution, within sixty days after having transmitted to a consumer documentation pursuant to 1693(a),(c), or (d)...receives oral or written notice in which the consumer...(3) sets forth the reasons for the consumer's belief (where applicable) than an error has occurred, ..."
Looks to me like the call to the call center satisfies this prerequisite for notice.
Written notice to Advocacy and Fraud have been blocked.
Conduent wants to funnel all complaints to a post office box number to avoid having to be confronted by cardholders.

With Comerica Bank being regulated by the FDIC, the following seems applicable:

FDIC Regs 6500-1005.6 Liability of Consumers for Unauthorized Transfers

(5) Notice to financial institution. (i) Notice to a financial institution is given when a consumer takes steps reasonably necessary to provide the institution with the pertinent information, whether or not a particular employee or agent of the institution actually receives the information.

(ii) The consumer may notify the institution in person, by telephone, or in writing.

(iii) Written notice is considered given at the time the consumer mails the notice or delivers it for transmission to the institution by any other usual means. Notice may be considered constructively given when the institution becomes aware of circumstances leading to the reasonable belief that an unauthorized transfer to or from the consumer's account has been or may be made.

Again, notice is not regulated to a post office box in this passsage.

This decision by Comerica Bank intentionally put a burden in cardholders who experience fraud. Add in the fact that no fraud investigations are conducted, and you have the recipe for criminal activity at Conduent. Hopefully this matter will be part of the Treasury OIG investigative report. Someone made the edict that the automatic email responses, refusing to accept fraud narratives, was to be sent to all persons sending fraud narratives to Conduent email addresses.

Who was that person?

I would like to discuss this matter with you.

J.B. Simms

1012am T Christopher Thompson (Fiscal Services) (202) 874-6650 Left message voicemail
1019am T Brent Smith (Fiscal Services) (202) 876-6666 Left message voicemail
1021am T Edita Rickard (Fiscal Services) (202) 874-7165 Left message voicemail

Franklin Lemond sent me a copy of the Amended Complaint to be proofed. Jackie and I were hoping Franklin Lemond would be as aggressive as we had been.

I had told Treasury, and Sonja Scott in particular, that Conduent was no longer receiving fraud narratives. Victims were being held hostage by the delivery time of the fraud packets. Sonja Scott did make an effort to investigate this matter.

Sonja Scott determined Conduent blocked all victim fraud complaints

Subject: RE: any comment on Conduent refusing to be acknowledging fraud narratives?

From: " Sonja Scott (OIG Treasury)

Date: Mon, April 29, 2019 10:14 am

To: jbsimms,

Richard Delmar (OIG Treasury))

Cc: Jackie Lynn , Cyn C

Jim – I tried the email and got the following response.

If you think an error has occurred in connection with your electronic transactions, call us at the Customer Service number, (888)741-1118 as soon as you can; or write us at Payment Processing Services, P.O. Box 245998, San Antonio, Texas 78224- 5998. Your dispute or question regarding your electronic transaction errors must be received through one of these two reporting methods – disputes or errors for card transactions will not be processed from an email.

I informed our Office of Audit. Sonja

I was hoping Sonja would see how Conduent was treating fraud victims.

Tuesday, April 30, 2019

Candy Childs called; her electricity had been turned off. I sent her to Sonja Scott.

This is another heartbreaking example of being victimized by BFS and Comerica Bank.

From: Candy Childs
Date: Tue, Apr 30, 2019 11:28 am
To: jbsimms
Sir the amount is $931.72 and im in desperate need of help im being evicted now please please help

Wednesday, May 1, 2019

My phone number has been identified and no one at Fiscal Services will take my call.

Monday, May 6, 2019

Emails sent to Sonja Scott. This is the list of the 103 victims

Subject: Confidential
From: jbsimms
Date: Mon, May 06, 2019 8:04 am
To: Sonja Scott (OIG Treasury)
Cc: "Jackie Lynn", Richard Delmar (OIG Treasury))
Dear Ms. Scott,
Here is the list.
I am also sending you the narratives, which is a separate document.
I would like to discuss how you think the best way for victims to be able to justify their claims or have an "advocate" to assist them. Schmidt is not answering calls. Conduent is not taking email notification for fraud; they stopped that weeks ago, leaving disabled persons (and others) without a way to report the claim in a timely manner. This is more than cruel.
On my end, my telephone number has been flagged by Fiscal Services. I believe I related to you that I made a call a few weeks ago to a number at Fiscal Services and upon giving the name "Jim Simms" the persons replied, "J.B. Simms?" There are those at Fiscal Services, OIG Treasury, and Comerica who have chosen not to talk to me, and here we are. As they say, you cannot make this up.
What I have attached is the master list, the master list of profiles, and two submissions of victims which qualify as plaintiffs in the class action suit as a result of blatant violations of different parts of Reg E. Our attorney, Mr. Lemond, chose only a few.
This information is to be strictly held by OIG Treasury.
I am fearful and in anticipation that unless enforcement is brought upon Comerica Bank and Conduent quickly, more victims will appear.
Jim

Since Rob Ferry asked me to be an administrator of the Direct Express Cardholder Victims page on Facebook, the number of members was increasing daily. Santaniello needed to see the victims' stories and face. He was responsible for protecting the criminals.

Direct Express victims Facebook page increases with more victims

Subject: Facebook link
From: jbsimms
Date: Mon, May 06, 2019 9:46 am
To: <Thomas.Santaniello@fiscal.treasury.gov>
Cc: " Richard Delmar (OIG Treasury)), thorsone@oig.treas.gov, "Jackie Lynn", Sonja Scott (OIG Treasury), <ClementsM@gao.gov>
Dear Mr. Santaniello,
Below is a link to a Facebook page which has 710 members. This group is of Direct Express (SSI) victims. You want to guard the evaluation team from hearing an oral presentation by the victims. Since my telephone number has been flagged by your agency, maybe the evaluation team would like to hear from Ms. Densmore and Ms. Clark. They are well briefed and know how Comerica Bank actually got the contract.
Give a copy of this attached amended complaint to the evaluation team you are protecting. Get an attorney to explain to them what will happen when discovery begins, and protection ends.
We will be waiting for your reply.
J.B. Simms

The number of members of the Direct Express Cardholder Victims increased daily.

Spies on the Facebook page

I found Mitch Raymond (Conduent) and other spies as members of the Factbook page. I had to change the membership parameters. While I applauded the ingenuity to infiltrate the ranks of the enemy, Conduent and Comerica Bank, along with Santaniello and BFS, had no conscience.

On March 29, 2019, Nora Arpin communicated by email with Brett Smith (Bureau of Fiscal Service) regarding a post I made on the Direct Express Cardholder Victims page on Facebook. Within the email, Arpin cited a document I posted and warned Brett Smith that he/BFS should be aware of the document and the "[s]alient" points I made in case inquiries are made.

Subject: Contact with the VA, lack of response
From: jbsimms
Date: Mon, May 06, 2019 11:54 am
To: Sonja Scott (OIG Treasury)
Cc: Richard Delmar (OIG Treasury)), Jackie Lynn,
 Below is the last chat I received from Pamela Powers, Chief of Staff of the VA on March 9, 2019. She has not made any contact since.
To what extent is this statement from Pamela Powers true?
Pamela Powers, SES 6:03 AM March 9, 2019
"We are working with Treasury to find the extent of the problem."
From LinkedIn
Jim

We found out a year later that Pamela Powers (Veterans Administration) was holding secret meetings with BFS, Comerica, OIG Treasury, and SSA.

Subject: Facebook link
From: jbsimms
Date: Mon, May 06, 2019 9:46 am
To: "Thomas Santaniello" <Thomas.Santaniello@fiscal.treasury.gov>
Cc: Richard Delmar (OIG Treasury), thorsone@oig.treas.gov, Jackie "Cynthia Clark" , Sonja Scott (OIG Treasury), "Michael Clements" <ClementsM@gao.gov>
Dear Mr. Santaniello,
Below is a link to a Facebook page which has 710 members. This group is of Direct Express (SSI) victims.
Since Fiscal Services ignored the two OIG Treasury audit (14-031 and 17-034) and used questionable ethical and legal criteria to award the Fiscal Agent contract to Comerica Bank, the credibility of the designated "evaluation team" continues to be suspect.
As is the tenor of the political atmosphere in Washington DC these days, it is time for the investigators to be investigated, and your evaluation team should be "evaluated."
The behavior of lack of transparency was duly noted by Michael Clements at GAO upon the publication of GAO 17-176 which was published one day from OIG Treasury 17-034. Fiscal Services ignored both of these reports and continued "business as usual" by awarding Comerica Bank the Fiscal Agent contract.
You want to guard the evaluation team from hearing an oral presentation by the victims. Since my telephone number has been flagged by your agency, maybe the evaluation team would like to hear from Ms. Densmore and Ms. Clark. They are well briefed, and know how Comerica Bank actually got the contract.
Give a copy of this attached amended complaint to the evaluation team you are protecting. Get an attorney to explain to them what will happen when discovery begins, and protection ends.
We will be waiting for your reply.
J.B. Simms

Tuesday, May 7, 2019

Subject: *Addressing the Evaluation Team*
From: jbsimms
Date: *Tue, May 07, 2019 9:54 am*
To: *<Thomas.Santaniello@fiscal.treasury.gov>*
Cc: *Richard Delmar (OIG Treasury)), Sonja Scott (OIG Treasury), Walter Bayer (SSA OIG), Jackie Lynn, Franklin Lemond (Plaintiff's Attorney)*
Dear Mr. Santaniello,
After having been excluded from having any communication with those at the Bureau of Fiscal Services charged with responsibility for disbursement of funds through the Direct Express program, I continue to wish to be afforded the opportunity to address the "evaluation team" which is considering bidders for said Direct Express program.
You know this evaluation team will not want to hear what I have to say, be it fact or editorial comment, nor do they want to answer my questions.
I continue to ask for this opportunity for victims to draw back the curtain and address this group.
J.B. Simms

Santaniello would not reply.

Wednesday, May 8, 2019

Now we know that Santaniello DOES communicate with Comerica Bank.
Read this.
From: Chuck Westfall
Sent: Wednesday, May 8, 2019 9:52 AM
To: Thomas E. Santaniello <Thomas.Santaniello@fiscal.treasury.gov>
Subject: Direct Express
Good morning
My name is Charles Westfall and I've been involved in a dispute with Direct Express since April.
I just received my 2nd denial letter and copy of my so-called investigation report which only contains info supplied by me.
This was closed reopened and denied twice with no kind of explanation except conflicting information.
I've almost lost my housing due to this situation. The only thing that kept my housing was my property mgr knows day these charges occurred I was in bed ill.
Ive had to make up a whole month back rent and had to borrow money all of April just to eat and pay necessary bills.
Now may is here and I'm still having to continuously borrow money as paying extra rent took my whole check and I'm surviving on soups and hotdogs.
Every person I've contacted has never even bothered to return one phone call or email.
To make matters worse on May1st when I went to use my card it had fraud block on it. After 24 phone calls i finally got that fixed.
My investigation was opened April 8th and there no date when reopened but closed again may1st which was definitely more than 10 business days so I am demanding my provisional credit that by law I'm entitled to.
The reason my card was blocked May1st due to fraudulent activity which further substantiates my earlier dispute so why is this constantly being denied.
This company needs to abide by law and pay credits or at least do proper investigations as their own notes and paperwork shows that fraud has occurred but they are unwilling to return on phone call or email and give me proper answers as I did not make these withdrawals and I feel company knows that but unwilling to honor their agreement and abide by law.
I would love to speak with you sometime.
Sincerely
Charles Westfall

On Wed, May 8, 2019, 10:03 AM Thomas E. Santaniello <Thomas.Santaniello@fiscal.treasury.gov> wrote:
Mr. Westfall, I am sorry to hear about your troubles with the Direct Express card. I have received your emails and voice mail and have asked our staff overseeing the Direct Express program to promptly work with Comerica to address your dispute and the problems you have experienced. Thanks you for bringing this to my attention.

Santaniello could not ignore us or the victims. Santaniello's email was a hollow gesture. There was no evidence that Santaniello did anything to help the victims he helped create.

From: Chuck Westfall
Sent: Wednesday, May 8, 2019 12:32 PM
To: Thomas E. Santaniello <Thomas.Santaniello@fiscal.treasury.gov>
Subject: Re: Direct Express
Thank you for your assistance. My case mgr and I both have had nothing but problems dealing with this situation and I'm at with end dealing with this company.

On Wed, May 8, 2019, 1:11 PM Thomas E. Santaniello <Thomas.Santaniello@fiscal.treasury.gov> wrote:
Comerica is going to reach out to you. Thank you

This exchange between Santaniello and Westfall is an indictment of Santaniello. He admitted or asserted having input with Comerica Bank but endorsed the failed program and shielded those within BFS from accountability.
From: Chuck Westfall
Date: Wed, May 8, 2019, 2:29 PM
Subject: Re: Direct Express
To: Thomas E. Santaniello <Thomas.Santaniello@fiscal.treasury.gov>
Thank you! I do appreciate this. I almost lost 1st apt I've had in 4yrs due to this and having struggles ever since this happened.

This proved connection between Santaniello and Comerica.

Thursday, May 9, 2019

Below is the email I sent to Charles Westfall.
Subject: Direct Express
From: jbsimms
Date: Thu, May 09, 2019 9:12 am
To: "Chuck Westfall"
Cc: Jackie Lynn, "Cyn C"
Mr. Westfall,
The fact that you got an email from Santaniello is huge.
I want you to email him and ask him to clarify his statement that his is reaching out to "Direct Express." We do not know who he is referring to; was he talking about Comerica or Conduent.
Remember: there is no Direct Express company. Direct Express is a program, not a company. Santaniello just needs to explain exactly WHO he is communicating with.
This email is larger than you think. Glad you reached out to him.
Jim

This victim's email put Santaniello in his place

Subject: No contact yet
From: Chuck Westfall
Date: Thu, May 09, 2019 2:05 pm
To: Thomas Santaniello <Thomas.Santaniello@fiscal.treasury.gov>
Cc: jbsimms
Hi Tom
I've been waiting all day for someone from Comerica to contact me. This is just like everytime someone passes on word to contact me. I never hear anything. I've had Sonja Scott from treasury do same thing as you say you

done and NEVER hear from anyone who can give me answers or provide my provisional credit as required by law.

I'm tired of eating soups and lunch meats because every agency or organization allows Comerica and Conduent to break law and cheat disabled persons when ripped off.

By notes in Direct Express system my card was blocked in May due to someone having my information and called in, plus my investigation filed April 8th was reopened and not closed till May1st but of course their papers sent to me didn't include date case reopened and since this case has been handled so poorly and fraudulently on Conduent and Comerica side I demand that my provisional credit be awarded immediately as I'm sure that 10 business days has passed which by law this is my right.

The negilience exhibited by every person that allows this organization to continue to defraud and keep persons money from them when entitled to credits or refunds is sickening.

I wish to know who you passed my case to so I can contact them directly as this group of individuals are just running scared and stalling for time while our funds are making them more money.

Everyday more and more persons are suffering from exactly same treatment I'm receiving and when Comerica loses contract which up soon are just going to walk away scott free while disabled Americans are being robbed by system supposed to be helping them.

Please send me contact information for whoever you contact at bank as my case mgr csn also verify for 6days my access to my transaction records was locked out as we both tried.

We couldn't even report this fraud till Jim Simms contacted advocacy on my behalf and Alisha sent me dispute papers on April 8th.

If this transaction record was legitimate why couldn't we access my records so I dont even believe that these withdrawals were actually done but my acct drained and records fabricated.

My case manager is furious at this as we have done everything possible to rectify this situation and only thing we accomplished is still being ignored and if we are lucky enough to contact someone they do same thing as you said pass our info to someone else who ignores us.

I want answers and my credit as law states I'm entitled to so I may live like normal poor person again.

691.50 not lot of money to you but it a fortune to someone who pay bills and lives on 771.00 a month.

Tom step up and have this bamking scam stop and all persons that lost money recover what they are entitled to and get rid of Cometica bank handling direct Express but before they lose contract pay all disputes as so many already closed like mine with automatic denials.

I would like you to send me contact info for someone at Conerica who I can actually speak to and get real answers and explanations.

Also send me your fax number and I'll fax you copy of my so called investigation and you can see for yourself how fake this is.

Thank you
Charles Westfall

This was an amazing email.

A heartwarming thank you

Subject: Re: Hey Jim
From: Missy Witt <cnr720@icloud.com>
Date: Thu, May 09, 2019 1:01 pm
To: jbsimms
A MILLION THANKS FOR TRYING TO "HELP" ME! YOU ALWAYS BELIEVE ME! I NEVER LIED OR MISLEAD ANYONE BUT THERE IS NO "JUSTICE "FOR ME !!!!!!!!!!!!!!!!!!!!!
THE LAWYER DOESNT WANT TO ADD ME! BASED ON FACT IT WAS MY LATE SISTER!
I JUST HUNG UP ON HIM I SO SICK OF BEING TREATED LIKE THAT!!
Charity

Tuesday, May 14, 2019

Subject: Consumer Financial Protection Bureau Escalation Carol Gilmer
 From: jbsimms
Date: Tue, May 14, 2019 10:26 pm
To: Sonja Scott (OIG Treasury)

Cc: "*Thomas.Santaniello@fiscal.treasury.gov*" *<Thomas.Santaniello@fiscal.treasury.gov>, , Richard Delmar (OIG Treasury), Walter Bayer (SSA OIG), "Jackie Lynn"*
Dear Ms. Scott,
My understanding of the investigation being performed by OIG Treasury and your charge is to audit and investigate the Bureau of Fiscal Services.
The Bureau of Fiscal Services flatly ignored and failed to implement both Treasury OIG 14-031 and Treasury OIG 17-034. The dismissal of both OIG reports by Mr. Lebryk and Ms. Morrow was evident to me, and validated by the fact that my submission to OIG Treasury in February 2018 has resulted in the current investigation. With all due respect, there is no investigation of the Direct Express program or Comerica Bank as Fiscal Agent without an concurrent investigation into the motives (personal or professional) of those persons at Bureau of Fiscal Services who endorsed, enabled, and empowered Comerica Bank to violate federal banking law 15USC1693 at will, while ignoring veterans, disabled persons, the elderly, and children who Comerica Bank knew would not have the ability to challenge Comerica Bank nor make it accountable.
Mr. Santaniello has proven that he has been designated to be the person to shield the "evaluation team" receiving oral presentations from financial institutions vying to be the Fiscal Agent for the Direct Express program. Victims of Comerica Bank and Bureau of Fiscal Services have something to say, but this deliberative conclave will not want to hear what we have to say and will not want to answer our questions.
It would be logical that many "dots" would need to be connected in order for the OIG Treasury report to be complete and comprehensive, which leads back to Mr. Santaniello, which is why I choose to respectfully challenge your assertion that Santaniello is not being investigated. Giving you an analogy, Robert Mueller targeted those around President Trump and charged (and convicted) them with "process crimes" in an attempt to validate claims against President Trump. Those persons charged and convicted were, as they say, "low hanging fruit." Being a bit vertically challenged myself, Santaniello is accessible, as he protects Ms. McCoy and others.
Thank you for being receptive to the victims I have sent your way. It appears the path you would take to address the victimization of my referrals would be to the Bureau of Fiscal Services. This has the appearance of having come "full circle" back to the designated target of your investigation. Regardless whether Bureau of Fiscal Services "files away" your new investigation as they did the previous two, it will be used in further proceedings.
Sincerely,
J.B. Simms

In the email below, it appears Sonja Scott was getting a little defensive. OIG Treasury was now protecting BFS employees, and particularly Santaniello.

Subject: RE: Consumer Financial Protection Bureau Escalation Carol Gilmer
From: Sonja Scott (OIG Treasury)
Date: Tue, May 14, 2019 5:41 pm
To: jbsimms
"loracgilmer.60@gmail.com" <loracgilmer.60@gmail.com>
Cc: "Thomas.Santaniello@fiscal.treasury.gov"
<Thomas.Santaniello@fiscal.treasury.gov>
We are not investigating Mr. Santaniello. We are investigating incidents of fraud involving individuals scamming and stealing from Direct Express card holders. Sonja
OIG Treasury should have been investigating Santaniello, but he was too close for them to name him as a suspect.

Santaniello should have been investigated.

Thursday, May 16, 2019

I wanted Sonja Scott to confirm the VA had been in touch with OIG Treasury. The games continued. (We found out a year later of secret meetings).

Subject: would like confirmation on statement made by VA
From: jbsimms
Date: Thu, May 16, 2019 9:10 pm
To: Sonja Scott (OIG Treasury)
Dear Ms. Scott,
Some weeks ago, Pamela Power, COS of VA, made a comment to me via LinkedIn, stating that the VA (probably VA Benefits) has been in touch with your office concerning this matter of malfeasance of Comerica Bank and violations of Regulation E.
Dr. Paul Lawrence, head of VA Benefits, has received communication from me and has refused to reply. Ms. Powers replied a few times and halted after being a bit uncomfortable with my questions. Although she and Mr. Thorson are both alumni of USAFA, it appears she has forgotten the motto.
Can you tell me the scope of the VA participation in this investigation and/or if/when your investigators have reached out to the VA for information concerning VA benefits passing through the Direct Express program?
Jim

Friday, May 17, 2019

LinkedIn message to Pamela Powers were written.

J B Simms 8:11 PM

Had hour+ chat with congressional liaison of SSA. Since this issue involves 3 diff agencies (Treasury, VA, SSA) the GAO should be involved for transparency and complete investigation. The author of GAO 17-176 is Michael Clements, with whom I have had numerous conversations and emails. Mr. Clements is awaiting a request from a congressperson or a rep from agencies to do follow up. You can reach him at **clementsm@gao.gov** , (202) 512-7763, and I suggest you read GAO 17-176. Mr. Clements has been emailed today with details of my chat with SSA official, Walter Bayer, formerly of GAO. I will be talking to Mr. Clements on Monday.

Subject Identity fraud, my identity, and failure of SSA to respond
From: jbsimms
Date: Fri, May 17, 2019 8:04 pm
To: "Bayer, Walter Office of the Inspector General" <Walter Bayer (SSA OIG
thanks for the call.
I will pursue the angle of asking OIG of Treasury (if you can put in a request for SSA) to have GAO do follow up because this is an inter-agency issue.
Thanks also for forwarding my personal experience to someone who will answer the question of the genesis of communication to SSA that changed my address.
Jim

Monday, May 20, 2019

Subject: Status of the bidding for the Direct Express program
From: jbsimms
Date: Mon, May 20, 2019 9:02 am
To: "Thomas Santaniello" <Thomas.Santaniello@fiscal.treasury.gov>
Cc: Walter Bayer (SSA OIG), Richard Delmar (OIG Treasury), Sonja Scott (OIG Treasury), Jackie Lynn, , "Michael Clements" <ClementsM@gao.gov>
Dear Mr. Santaniello,
Since you have been able to temporarily shield Fiscal Services from accountability as well as victims of Comerica Bank and deny victims of the Direct Express program from this bidding process, I want to know the status of the process, and which financial institution will be receiving the bid. The need for transparency, as was the title of Mr. Clements report in GAO 17-176, was ignored by Fiscal Services, as were both OIG Treasury reports.
Hopefully OIG Treasury will investigate this matter (as is their mandate) and find the genesis of the corruption. Other investigative agencies are to be involved, and the exposure is forthcoming.
An offer of a bit of candor would be welcomed.
Sincerely, J.B. Simms

From: jbsimms
Date: Mon, May 20, 2019 9:43 am
To: "The Light" <light4ever1212@gmail.com>
Cc: Sonja Scott (OIG Treasury), Walter Bayer (SSA OIG), "Thomas Santaniello"
<Thomas.Santaniello@fiscal.treasury.gov>, "Jackie Lynn"
Dear NC,
If you go onto the Facebook page of Direct Express Cardholder Victims, you will see postings of telephone numbers to call.
I could give you a 90 minute talk of how bad this situation is.
There are two persons who you can call directly, and both communicate with me weekly if not daily:
Walter Bayer, Soc Sec Congressional Liaison (202) 358-6319 Walter Bayer (SSA OIG)@ssa.gov
Sonja Scott, OIG Treasury, (202) 927-5874 Sonja Scott (OIG Treasury)@oig.treas.gov
Thomas Santaniello, (202) 874-6773 Thomas.Santaniello@fiscal.treasury.gov
Write a narrative of your experience. Email this to the above two people. You can copy me in the email.
After sending the email, wait a day, then call both Mr. Bayer and Ms. Scott. Comerica Bank operates the Direct Express program, but the day-to-day matters are run by Conduent, a subcontractor of Comerica Bank.
Santaniello is the person assigned to be the doorkeeper for Fiscal Services, hiding the identity of those who have allowed this program to be operated by Comerica Bank. He serves no useful purpose to any citizen other than those who dictate to him, but, his lack of involvement to cure the problem indicts him and those around him.
Procedural matters (motions) are scheduled in the class action suit, and we are waiting for the hearings before moving forward. The attorney will be deciding to add more plaintiffs, then we will load the "subpoena cannon" and aim it toward the appropriate target(s).
It is better to write the story before discussing the matter with anyone; people read faster than others talk. They can make notes and references to written pages.
If you need to make one phone call immediately, call Ms. Scott. Calling Comerica and Conduent is a waste of time.
J.B. Simms

The saddest and most horrific engagement with a Direct Express victim would occur beginning May 20, 2019. The death of a person victimized by Conduent, and Comerica Bank, left me feeling so terribly sad.

Subject: Direct Express
From: The Light <light4ever1212@gmail.com>
Date: Mon, May 20, 2019 8:57 am
To: jbsimms
Hi Jim,
I saw a post on a forum about the current class action lawsuit against Direct Express that is gaining momentum.
Your name and contact info was included as someone to contact and who seemed to have inside information about this.
My issue with DE began two plus weeks ago when I went on a information gathering extended vacation to Mexico.
When I called DE to tell them I would be in Mexico the rep took my information and assured me I had international status for several months and could extend that time if I wanted and everything was in place so my card would be accepted anywhere in Mexico that accepted Mastercard.
Long story short, my card allowed me to purchase any products I wanted to buy in Mexico but refused my cash back transactions repeated from numerous different sources here in this area of Mexico.
I have spent many days and countless hours on the phone (which was my friend's magic jack phone because my cell phone is unable to get through to their 888 number no matter what I do).
The reps have given me such a run around it is insane and here I am a solo, senior female who is physically challenged, who does not have a vehicle, has no money and has no way to pay my bills here in Mexico that I must pay to survive here like people must do everywhere.
I finally was able to make a western union transfer of the funds left on my card to a Mexican friend here after I responded to Western Union's email to me requesting I call them.

Western Union wanted to verify my identity before authorizing the transfer which I fully cooperated with and there was no problem.

The transfer went through and as soon as it did Direct Express put a fraud suspension on my account.

Now what? I hear very scary things are going on with DE and their fraud investigations and meanwhile I am here in Mexico and have no one who is in a financial position to help me out should I be stuck without funds for months.

I am going to call DE'S 333 number as this number will go through on my phone but I am not terribly hopeful of getting any good news.

I would like to be included in the lawsuit if possible, now that my case is technically a fraud case and I would appreciate any guidance you can provide me in how I can best do this.

Thank you Jim,

Sincerely, NC

"NC" was Nona Clarke. Her story will be continued over the next few days.

From: The Light <light4ever1212@gmail.com>
Date: Mon, May 20, 2019 3:41 pm
To: jbsimms

Thank you so much JB,

I saw your Facebook page and the video you put on Facebook.

What has been going on is really atrocious and I don't really have a hard time believing how corrupt things are but it just makes my soul feel sick.

Since I did not initiate the fraud alert I don't really understand what was going on when they were allowing me to purchase products but not get any cash back. Then initiating the fraud suspension when I Western Unioned the remainder of my money to a friend here in Mexico so I could pay my rent and not end up on the streets of a foreign country.

I have begun my description of the events and I will try to call all the people on your list but my phone is not letting me make calls to the US even though I have a Telcel chip and an unlimited telcel phone packette.

I tried to call you today and it rang a number of times then stopped ringing but no one answered.

If you got a call from Mexico or a 334-374-3628, it was me.

What concerns me the most about this is will I get my money on June 3rd. If I don't I don't know what I am going to do but I will have been out of the country for 30 days and I saw that I have to change my address while in the states if I am going to stay in Mexico longer then 30 days.

I signed up for the FB group but my facebook name is Jenny Brown.

Thank you for all you are doing for us JB.

I will cc you on the description of my ordeal with DE when I email it.

NC

On Mon, May 20, 2019, 11:44 AM <jbsimms> wrote:

Dear NC,

If you go onto the Facebook page of Direct Express Cardholder Victims, you will see postings of telephone numbers to call.

I could give you a 90 minute talk of how bad this situation is.

There are two persons who you can call directly, and both communicate with me weekly if not daily:

Walter Bayer, Soc Sec Congressional Liaison (202) 358-6319 Walter Bayer (SSA OIG)@ssa.gov

Sonja Scott, OIG Treasury, (202) 927-5874 Sonja Scott (OIG Treasury)@oig.treas.gov

Thomas Santaniello, (202) 874-6773 Thomas.Santaniello@fiscal.treasury.gov

Write a narrative of your experience. Email this to the above two persons. You can copy me in the email.

After sending the email, wait a day, then call both Mr. Bayer and Ms. Scott. Comerica Bank operates the Direct Express program, but the day to day matters are run by Conduent, a subcontractor of Comerica Bank. Santaniello is the person assigned to be the doorkeeper for Fiscal Services, hiding the identity of those who have allowed this program to be operated by Comerica Bank. He serves no useful purpose to any citizen other than those who dictate to him, but, his lack of involvement to cure the problem indicts him and those around him.

Procedural matters (motions) are scheduled in the class action suit, and we are waiting for the hearings before moving forward. The attorney will be deciding to add more plaintiffs, then we will load the "subpoena cannon" and aim it toward the appropriate target(s).

It is better to write the story before discussing the matter with anyone; people read faster than others talk. They can make notes and references to written pages.

If you need to make one phone call immediately, call Ms. Scott. Calling Comerica and Conduent is a waste of time.

J.B. Simms

Tuesday, May 21, 2019

Subject: McCoy is out
From: jbsimms
Date: Tue, May 21, 2019 7:40 am
To: Sonja Scott (OIG Treasury), Richard Delmar (OIG Treasury)
Cc: Jackie "Anita Bobetich", "Cynthia Clark",
Dear Ms. Scott and Mr. Delmar,
Looks like Ms. McCoy is out at Fiscal Services. The interesting part of this article is the fact that David Leybryk gave McCoy such a glowing sendoff, and it was Leybryk who began this relationship between Comerica Bank and Fiscal Services.

"This might be something you might want to include in your report."

Subject: The delay of the selection process
From: jbsimms
Date: Tue, May 21, 2019 1:02 pm
To: "Thomas Santaniello" <Thomas.Santaniello@fiscal.treasury.gov>
Cc: Richard Delmar (OIG Treasury), Sonja Scott (OIG Treasury), Jackie Lynn, "Cynthia Clark"
Dear Mr. Santaniello,
It has come to my attention that the selection process for the Fiscal Agent for the Direct Express program has been delayed. The selection was supposedly to be made on May 17, 2019.

I would hope Mr. Gribben is aware of the issues involved in this matter. If you would forward this email to him, I would be grateful. He can reach me at (803) 309-6850.

If during this delay, the "evaluation team" has reconsidered their denial of receiving oral presentations from victims of Fiscal Services and Comerica Bank as having oversight of the Direct Express program, I am certain there are those of us who will stand before any person or group of authority and tell what we know. It might be good that we condition our appearance with the presence of person(s) from OIG Treasury.

Since you seem reluctant to engage us on this matter, I again request you forward this to Mr. Gribben. I am sure he did not expect to see this on his first day at work.

Sincerely,
J.B. Simms

From: jbsimms
Date: Tue, May 21, 2019 7:37 pm
To: "Thomas Santaniello" <Thomas.Santaniello@fiscal.treasury.gov>
Cc: Richard Delmar (OIG Treasury), thorsone@oig.treas.gov, Sonja Scott (OIG Treasury), Walter Bayer (SSA OIG), Franklin Lemond (Plaintiff's Attorney), Jackie Lynn, Michael Clements (US Gen Acct Office), Kate Berry (American Banker), James_Erwin@aging.senate.gov
Dear Mr. Santaniello,
Mr. Michael Clements of GAO signed off on GAO 17-176 which was published January 25, 2017. This report, entitled "Treasury Has Used Financial Agents in Evolving Ways but Could Improve Transparency."
Below you will find links to a forum of the Data Coalition, September 23, 2015. One of the speakers on the panel was David Lebryk, the first Commissioner of the Bureau of Fiscal Services, who, along with counsel, approved and endorsed Comerica Bank to become the Fiscal Agent for the Direct Express program. It was Mr. Lebryk who authorized Comerica Bank to be paid millions after the original contract was a no-pay contract.
My notes are in sentence fragments, but I bet you can figure them out. I will transcribe my notes to a more eloquent form when necessary during litigation.

This talk was given 16 months before the publication of Mr. Clements report. While I am not certain how long the research had been ongoing before the publication of GAO 17-176, it appears the "transparency" which Mr. Lebryk was touting sounded good at the time, but was never implemented.
The denial by you of our request to address the "evaluation team" is part and parcel of the pattern of deceit. Where is the transparency purported by Mr. Lebryk forty four (44) months ago? Nothing changed, and Comerica Bank is still the wonder-kin of BFS.
Give my telephone number to Mr. Lebryk. I would like to ask him a few questions about transparency.
J.B. Simms

Jackie and I wanted to know what was going on with the secretive bidding process of the Direct Express contract. See her email below.

Jackie Lynn
Tue, May 21, 2019, 5:50 AM
to Michael, me
Mr. Jackman
I am following up with you on the request I made to you concerning this document,
I am requesting information on ~
(1) who the winner is as well as other finalists
(2) a date when all investigations will be completed as well as when reports will be published
(3) the number in total of fraud investigations they have ongoing and closed since Direct Express's original contract.
(4) how much money over that time period has been approximately stolen
I urge you to ask these questions since reading this document shows lack of transparency, why would they refuse to announce the winner until the investigations were complete unless they wanted to leave room to change or coverup their original decision?
I will remind everyone ~ this affects the most vulnerable people as well as tax payers dollars.
I will look forward to your responses
Thank you
Jackie Densmore

Fiscal Service Welcomes New Commissioner (BFS website)

May 13, 2019

The U.S. Department of the Treasury's Bureau of the Fiscal Service (Fiscal Service) has announced a change in the key leadership with the retirement of Commissioner Kim McCoy and the appointment of Tim Gribben as the next commissioner, effective May 13.

Mr. Gribben comes to the Fiscal Service from the Small Business Administration (SBA), where he served as the chief financial officer (CFO) and was responsible for all aspects of SBA's financial management, performance management and program evaluation. Prior to joining SBA in 2009, Mr. Gribben was a manager at the U.S. Postal Service. Mr. Gribben also spent more than five years at a privately-held technology firm as director of a business unit and two years with J.P. Morgan. Mr. Gribben graduated from the College of William & Mary with a bachelor's degree in accounting, and earned an MBA from Duke University.

"Tim is a respected senior executive in the federal CFO community with more than 20 years of transformational leadership experience," said Assistant Secretary David A. Lebryk. "He is an innovative and forward-thinking leader with proven expertise in using data to measure and improve program performance. As commissioner he will leverage this background and lend his knowledge as a former customer of Fiscal Service's financial management services to shape strategic priorities and drive customer-centric solutions that will benefit the public we serve."

"In my previous role as CFO at SBA, I have been impressed by the talent and energy of Fiscal Service employees and their dedication to improving federal financial management," said Mr. Gribben. "I am both humbled and excited by the opportunity to lead a bureau whose mission impacts every American."

Mr. Gribben succeeds Kim McCoy, who began serving as Fiscal Service Commissioner on May 2, 2018. Prior to this role, she served as the deputy commissioner for the offices of fiscal accounting and shared services, including oversight for the bureau's Administrative Resource Center (ARC). Ms.

McCoy joined the Treasury Department in 1992 as a computer specialist. She was appointed to the Senior Executive Service in 2007, serving as the chief information officer.

"Kim has been a leading force in developing a 10-year vision, refining and refocusing the bureau's strategic priorities, and ensuring continued operational excellence," said Mr. Lebryk. "Kim's drive and commitment strengthened the bureau's operations, promoted innovation, and advanced federal financial management across the U.S. government. She will be greatly missed."

The Fiscal Service is responsible for annually issuing trillions of dollars in Treasury securities to finance government operations and account for the resulting public debt; disbursing essential benefit payments including social security and veterans' payments; collecting trillions in federal revenue, including taxes; operating a central debt collection operation; providing government-wide accounting and reporting including the daily and monthly Treasury statements; and providing administrative and information technology services to Federal agencies through shared services.

For more information about the Fiscal Service, please visit www.fiscal.treasury.gov

Last modified 05/13/19

McCoy was out as the head of BFS. They were all running so as not to be found to be culpable.

Nona Clarke sent me another email, and I forwarded her email. Nona was in Mexico and could not get her money. See below:

The narrative from Nona Clarke. Suicide was her escape from pain inflicted by Comerica Bank

Subject: Nona Clarke's Ordeal with Conduent Employees at the Direct Express Call Center.
From: jbsimms
Date: Tue, May 21, 2019 9:11 am
To: "Jackie Lynn"
another victim
Subject: Narrative of Nona Clarke's Ordeal with Conduent Employees at
the Direct Express Call Center.
From: The Light <light4ever1212@gmail.com>
Date: Tue, May 21, 2019 8:54 am
To: Walter Bayer (SSA OIG)@ssa.gov, Sonja Scott (OIG Treasury)@oig.treas.gov,
Thomas.Santaniello@fiscal.treasury.gov, scschmidt@comercia.com,
advocacy@usdirectexpress.com, jbsimms
To All Concerned,
My ordeal with the Direct Express call center began on Saturday, May 4, 2019, when I arrived in Mexico for an investigative vacation.
The issue began with my debit card being declined for any cash back transactions in Mexico even though I had international status and has now escalated to a fraud suspension without my having initiated a fraud claim or having authorized a fraud claim.
The call center reps have lied to me repeatedly, withheld information from me and wasted so much of my time and energy that I do not have the energy left to continue perusing what has only been a waste of time for me.
I have been in Mexico since May 4, 2019 without a penny to my name and have been relying on the kindness of virtual strangers here.
If this fraud suspension interferes with my June benefits or my ability to access my benefits fully, I will be overstaying social security's thirty day guideline for being outside the US, because of the unprofessionalism of the numerous individuals at the Direct Express call center whom I have tried to deal with and whom virtually have the welfare of a US citizen (me) in their hands but are completely indifferent to the situation they have created for me.
Thank God for the kindness of the Mexican people I have met here who have shown me the kindness and concern my own people have refused me by deliberately withholding my funds for no valid reason other then because they can.
I appreciate your time and attention to this matter and apologize for the length of the narrative I have prepared. Please keep in mind that this situation is dire and has been going on for eighteen days now and involves numerous call center employees and numerous calls over the span of many days.
Sincerely, Nona Clarke

Nona died soon thereafter, killing herself in the restroom of a food shop after her Direct Express debit card failed her again, My name and phone number were on a piece of paper found in one of her pockets. I got the first call. Her blood is on the hands of Comerica Bank, Conduent, Bureau of Fiscal Service, OIG Treasury, and the Social Security Administration.

From: jbsimms
Date: Wed, May 22, 2019 6:23 pm
To: DirectExpress@fiscal.treasury.gov
Cc: "Thomas Santaniello" <Thomas.Santaniello@fiscal.treasury.gov>, Jackie Lynn, "Cynthia Clark, "Anita Bobetich"
There has been a delay in naming the fiscal agent which will take over the Direct Express program. We are aware that Fiscal Services is under investigation by OIG Treasury with respect to the administration of this program.
Is the delay in the announcement because OIG Treasury has not publicized their findings?
The cardholder victims of the Direct Express program were excluded from communicating with the "evaluation team" which was receiving oral presentations given by candidate financial institutions vying for the contract. Thomas Santaniello refused to allow us communication with the decision-making body, which is consistent behavior with the lack of oversight of the fiscal agent, Comerica Bank, by those persons at the Bureau of Fiscal Services.
As was stated by David Lebryk in September 2015, Treasury (and Fiscal Services) were to become "citizen centric." That never happened; Santaniello saw to that.
Although Santaniello and others at Fiscal Services have chosen not to be "citizen-centric," we continue to ask for transparency. Tim Gribben might cause this to happen, and we hope the culture created by Lebryk, Morrow, and McCoy will continue to be exposed and repercussions observed by the citizenry.
We remain wanting to know the status of the selection and announcement of the new fiscal agent for the Direct Express program. Hopefully the program was divided, for veterans to have a separate program and fiscal agent.
We would love to brief Mr. Gribben on the history of this Direct Express program.
Sincerely,
J.B. Simms

Monday, May 27, 2019

Below is proof Comerica Bank offered security measures for their customers which they did not offer to Direct Express customers.
Subject: Proof that Comerica offers text alerts for ATM and other other withdrawals, but not to Direct Express customers
From: jbsimms
Date: Mon, May 27, 2019 11:03 am
To: Sonja Scott (OIG Treasury), Richard Delmar (OIG Treasury), "Thomas Santaniello" <Thomas.Santaniello@fiscal.treasury.gov>
Cc: Jackie Lynn, "Cynthia Clark", Franklin Lemond (Plaintiff's Attorney), "Anita Bobetich"
Dear Mr. Delmar and Ms. Scott,
I am looking forward to your OIG Treasury investigation of Fiscal Services. There are many issues which I have brought forward to you during the past year with regard to Fiscal Services ignoring your reports and the lack of honesty and transparency at Fiscal Services. My telephone number has been flagged, so no one at Fiscal Services will engage me in conversation.
Below is a link to a page from the Comerica Bank website:
https://www.comerica.com/personal-finance/banking/online-services/mobile-banking.html
You will see that Comerica Bank offers text alerts to their proprietary customers, texts which if had been available to Direct Express customers, would have avoided much fraud, in that the customers would have been notified immediately of withdrawals to their accounts and pending fraudulent purchases.
An easy alert to avoid fraudulent ATM withdrawal would be an immediate alert to a telephone to advise of a withdrawal, and an option to approve the transaction.
I would like to know to whom the OIG Treasury report is going to be addressed. Since Ms. McCoy left, we assume it will be the new commissioner, Mr. Gribben. Maybe Mr. Santaniello can arrange for a meeting

between Mr. Gribben and a few Direct Express cardholder victims so Mr. Gribben will not be victimized by a sanitized report from any government entity.

Mr. Santaniello, if you have nothing to lose, make the request from us to Mr. Gribben. I look forward to us having direct access rather than having to tolerate "Winkie Guards" protecting those at Fiscal Services who have allowed and encouraged Comerica Bank to administer such a faulty program.

Are the recipients of funds via Direct Express less entitled to fraud protection than proprietary Comerica Bank customers? Many of these recipients are elderly, disabled civilians, and disabled veterans. On this Memorial Day, I would think that Mr. Thorson (OIG Treasury) and Ms. Pamela Powers (VA), both USAFA graduates, would hold Fiscal Services and Comerica Bank accountable. The sad thing is the only accountability will be exposure via the class action suit, unless some federal employee shows the integrity necessary to rid Fiscal Services of the bad actors.

Integrity, First.

Sincerely,

J.B. Simms

Tuesday, May 28, 2019

BFS was supposed to announce the new Fiscal Agent. It did not happen. Santaniello is not talking.

We need to know what is going on. Much is happening with us: Franklin is suing, Jackie is pursuing Warren, and I am going after Santaniello and BFS.

Chapter Seven
Comerica Bank: No Contract, No Rules, No Problem

Friday, May 31, 2019

Below is a post that was made on LinkedIn. Mr. Gribben had been appointed as Commissioner of the Bureau of Fiscal Service. Mr. Gribben had no idea about the corruption within the disbursements area, including Brett Smith and Thomas Santaniello, regarding the contract that was to be renewed with Comerica Bank.

J B Simms   Publisher, National Award-winning Author, Screenwriter, and Investigative and Publishing Consultant:
Mr. Gribben walked into BFS as a yearlong investigation by OIG Treasury was being conducted. BFS personnel prohibited victims of a corrupt and flawed Direct Express program from making presentations to a secret group who is selecting a new fiscal agent, or renewing the incumbent, for the program. The announcement of the secret selection has been postponed for 2 weeks. Mr. Gribben, you walked into a cesspool of citizen victimization, lack of accountability, absence of transparency, and a charade of trust. The responsible BFS employees do not return calls to victims because they know they will not like our questions. There is no accountability where there are no consequences.

Saturday, June 2, 2019

Subject: Narratives of victims
From: jbsimms
Date: Sun, Jun 02, 2019, 8:26 am
To: Sonja Scott (OIG Treasury), Richard Delmar (OIG Treasury), Eric Thorson (OIG Treasury)
I sent the list of the victims who have contacted me. Attached is the compilation of narratives from the victims. I made only one insertion of a description of one victim since I sent the list.
These persons lost parents and suffered unbelievable hardship as a result of Fiscal Service's "connection" with Comerica Bank.
Please give me an acknowledgement of receipt of this compilation. Hopefully this will give you a bit more insight into the pain suffered.
There were hundreds of emails. I cut and pasted some and inserted them into this compilation. The format is not "book ready" but you will get the idea.
When I got to about number 70, I had recovered funds for about 50 persons. If you see the word "PAID" in the narrative, the monies were returned, but only because of my involvement, which does not make me a hero but exposes Fiscal Services and Comerica Bank (and Conduent) as the culprits. I confronted the culprits on behalf of the victims and exposed the malfeasance. J.B. Simms

Tuesday, June 4, 2019

Ms. Densmore – we are conducting audit work on the program's operation, which we expect to be wrapped up by early fall. Our report will be on our website.
We are also conducting investigations of specific instances of theft. Investigations are not posted on our website but may be obtained by FOIA request.
They will be completed as soon as possible, consistent with their complexity and resource constraints.
Rich Delmar

Subject: Re: US Direct Express - Fraud (Comerica Bank)
From: Kate Berry (American Banker)
Date: Tue, Jun 04, 2019, 11:06 am
To: "Jackie, J B Simms,
Hi Jackie, JB -
Wanted to check in with you two -- my two favorite sources -- who are the most incredible stalwart people to go after a company that I have ever encountered!! I've received a couple of new emails from folks defrauded by Direct Express who found my story. I am forwarding them to you.
Sorry, I'm so overwhelmed with stories, I still have not done a follow. Wanted to know if you've heard anything.
best, kate

Kate's kind words were encouraging. We needed Kate to print the truth for us.

Subject: A layman's interpretation of "fraud proceeds theft" in financial theft RE SCOTUS 15-5991
From: jbsimms
Date: Tue, Jun 04, 2019, 7:48 pm
To: Richard Delmar (OIG Treasury)
Cc: Sonja Scott (OIG Treasury). "Jackie Lynn", Kate Berry (American Banker), Franklin Lemond
(Plaintiff's Attorney)
Dear Mr. Delmar,
With me not being an attorney but rotating my head in wonder at some email I read, I felt it necessary to respond to a statement you made in an email to Ms. Densmore, here reply, and my "take" on the issue. Ms. Densmore and I have had discussions about the fact that in matter of the Direct Express program, fraud always proceeds theft. If a person who is authorized to perform designated transactions on behalf of a cardholder, and performs transactions outside the bounds of the directive, the fraud is then perpetrated against the cardholder. If a person assumes the identity of a cardholder and steals money from the cardholder, the cardholder has experienced fraud and theft.
If the criminal fraudulently assumes the identity of the cardholder in order to steal money from the cardholder, there is no bank account from which the criminal is to steal; the repository from which the funds are stolen through fraud is the US Treasury.
Of the 103 persons who personally contacted me for assistance, over 70 percent were reimbursed after I and the victim pursued Conduent and Comerica Bank for violating various sections of Regulation E. When this reimbursement was made, from where did the money appear for the reimbursement? The cardholder was reimbursed (not considering the cost of the delay, emotional and psychological damage) but the fraudster/thief, maybe thinking that "no harm/no foul" drifted away. Conduent never stopped a pending transaction discovered by a cardholder, so in each transaction involving merchandise, the transaction was allowed to be processed, to the glee of the fraudster.
Back to the point of which entity lost money and was defrauded (prior to theft). Even if Conduent had stopped a transaction, the attempt at fraud was made. This takes us to SCOTUS 15-5991 (Shaw v US) in which Lawrence Eugene Shaw made the case that forged check funds that were reimbursed to customers caused no harm to the customers, so there was no crime. The Supreme Court ruled that Shaw had defrauded the financial institution. Thus, all fraudulent transactions should be considered a fraud against the US Treasury and should be prosecuted as such.
The lack of insight by Fiscal Services allowed this to happen. I assert that there are persons working at BFS who have more formal education than me, but they never thought that the motivation of a select few who allowed this flawed program would be discovered and published. No person would turn their head to allow the Direct Express program to be awarded to Comerica Bank unless they were "motivated."
The message from BFS to the fraudsters, be they from Conduent, Comerica Bank, or elsewhere, was this: There is no security on the Direct Express card, so, when you steal from a recipient, we will never pursue you or hold you accountable, and will never interrupt or deny any pending purchase.
That is what Lawrence Shaw thought, and he went to prison. I hope this investigation will reveal the people at BFS who are responsible for this. Some have retired in order to escape scrutiny.
Sincerely,
J.B. Simms

Tuesday, June 5, 2019

Subject: Direct Express Fraudulent Charges
From: Melissa Farmer
Date: Wed, Jun 05, 2019, 3:54 am
To: jbsimms
Jim,
Thank you so much for the email. I put a call into you yesterday, referred by Jackie Densmore.
I was driven to homelessness because I was evicted for not paying rent after a $4400.00 fraudulent charge for which Direct Express would not reimburse me. Resulting from homelessness were, among other serious problems, Attorney's fees and the cost of renting a storage unit. I was homeless for 8 months.
I typed to advocacy@Direct Express but received an auto-response indicating the accepted means to address my issues are via mail or fax and not via email.

I have relied on faxing Direct Express over the years, but this only once elicited a response (a phone call from Alicia).

I emailed Ms. Scott, who responded that the age of my two claims may be a disadvantage. This is alarming, because I have tried continually through the years (as documented) to pursue this with Direct Express' alleged Fraud Department.

Any further light you may shed on this issue, generally or specifically, would be greatly appreciated. Thank you.

Sincerely,
Melissa Farmer

Wednesday, June 5, 2019

Jackie Lynn
Jun 5, 2019, 6:45 PM
to ScottS, Richard Delmar (OIG Treasury), Walter.Bayer, Thomas, Sarah Lizama (OIG Social Security), ClementsM, Michael, me

I want you all to read these messages, this victim found Kate Berry's story on American Banker and reached out to her asking her for help because his account was drained and had nowhere to turn after the run around from Conduent and Comerica Bank. Kate then reached out to me and Jim to see if we could help. It's absolutely disgusting that people who elected to choose such an unqualified bank pretend that this is not really happening and continue to tell people their money and their personal information is safe with this bank when we all know how untrue that is.

I want to know why these programs were never monitored by proper agencies. Federal money just getting stolen from a bank by whom you all selected. A bank you all pushed on people by saying it's safe in fact safer than a paper check! It should be your job to follow up on these things. I want to know how a congressman can make one call and the money is returned immediately. I guess it all depends on who you are in this world but believe me when I tell you I will be calling this congressman first thing tomorrow morning because apparently he's the only one who can do a job correctly. Get ready guys I just piled more work on your desks!

Sincerely,
Jackie Densmore

Email from Delmar, admitting that the investigation/audit will be finished in fall of 2019.

Below is the email I sent to everyone today:
Subject: RE: Facebook and Fiscal Agent
From: jbsimms
Date: Wed, June 05, 2019, 10:55 am
To: Sonja Scott (OIG Treasury)
Cc: Jackie, Richard Delmar (OIG Treasury),
Thomas Santaniello (Bureau of Fiscal Service), Walter Bayer (SSI OIG), >, Michael Clements (Gen Acct Office)
Dear Ms. Scott,
Thank you for your reply.
As I conveyed to you during our 75-minute interview (or better said, my monologue) The Facebook page I referenced, Direct Express Cardholder Victims was created by Rob Ferry. A contact of Mr. Ferry asked that I become a moderator, and I complied. This Facebook page is dynamic; it is ever-changing and new victims join regularly looking for answers.

As you know, another victim, who is caring for his dying mother, contacted me this morning. The story is the same; fraud and theft. Someone created a new card and used it in another state, draining his monthly social security payment.

You and others might be waving off emails from me, as Treasury officials have flagged my telephone number (confirmed by a Fiscal Service employee), and might be tired of me beating you over the head with facts and observations, but indulge me a moment to give you one fact that I find very disturbing:

Since my contact with Paulette Battle of OIG Treasury in February 2018, and the revelation made to her of malfeasance of BFS by lack of oversight and compliance with Comerica Bank in the awarding of the contract and the flawed product that is Direct Express and the admission of an investigation by Mr. Delmar of OIG

Treasury, I see no changes in the administration of the program other than the fact that you and Mr. Bayer personally will accept communication from victims.

Conduent has blocked all transmission of fraud narratives to Customer Advocacy and to the Fraud department. Comerica Bank, namely Susan Schmidt and Nora Arpin, direct victims to Conduent, knowing full well that Conduent, acting as a quasi-financial institution, has regularly violated Regulation E. They never thought we would confront them, or any government agency.

The Conduent call center person continues to read the script which avoids communication with Conduent employees in the Customer Advocacy and Fraud units. Both of these divisions of Conduent are useless, admittedly have no knowledge of Regulation E (15USC1693), and some of the Conduent employees post previous banking experience on their LinkedIn pages.

Comerica Bank and Conduent, as well as BFS, are in a box. If they make any changes, that is an admission that we (the victims) are validated. If they make no changes, and continue business as usual, there will be continued victims but no repercussion or accountability. No one at BFS will go to Comerica Bank and point out the flaws in the program because it was the "evaluation team" of BFS which awarded the contract to Comerica Bank, twice. Now, Mr. Santaniello wants to shield this "evaluation team" from scrutiny, both the present and former members of this deliberative group. It does not seem logical that members of this group would be so inept as to allow a debit card program to funnel money to millions of persons and the card would have no security parameters. The awarding of this contract is no different than the awarding of a concrete pouring contract in NYC before 1990. There was motivation to award this contract, and it is my hope that the genesis of this matter, dating back to 2008, will be reported in the next OIG Treasury report.

I respectfully suggest you have someone create a Facebook page and ask to join the group. A false narrative can be created and submitted, and you will see persons/victims attending to each other's problems.

Let me see some changes, and I will know progress is being done.

Jim

Thursday, June 6, 2019

I mailed my book, Friendly Fire at the Veterans Hospital, to Pamela Powers, Vermont Ave, Washington, DC.

I sent remarks to the BFS LinkedIn page:
J B Simms, Publisher, National Award-winning Author,
Screenwriter, and Investigative and Publishing Consultant
A group of victims of one of the disbursement programs, Direct Express, were blocked from giving oral presentations to the "group" approving the new contract for the Fiscal Agent. A year-long investigation of BFS and the Direct Express debit card program is to conclude in the fall of 2019. BFS has delayed the announcement of the new (hopefully) Fiscal Agent (a financial institution government contractor). Comerica Bank has been the contractor since the beginning of this program. We would like to brief Mr. Gribben on matters of malfeasance within BFS which he will not hear from his subordinates.

Friday, June 7, 2019

Shocking that Conduent did not refund McPhail's fraud claim

Subject: Re: Harrold McPhail
From: Kate Berry (American Banker)
Date: Fri, Jun 07, 2019, 9:43 am
To: jbsimms
Cc: Sonja Scott <Sonja Scott (OIG Treasury)>, "Richard K. Delmar", Jackie Lynn
McPhail didn't get his money back? I did not know that. Why? How?

I was contacted by another recipient last week who lost $5G. I don't understand how they could be investigating and not resolve these frauds -- unless they expect a certain amount of fraud is baked into the program.

There clearly needs to be more oversight, if there is any, of Conduent. I don't even know what Comerica's role really is, other than having an executive in charge.

Sorry to say I'm buried under better, even more inflammatory, stories than this one, but will try to get to a follow.

Kb

On Fri, Jun 7, 2019, at 12:31 PM jbsimms wrote:
Dear Ms. Scott,
I communicated with Marteshia McPhail yesterday. She told me her father has had no communication from anyone on the $30,000 fraud he experienced last year. He received one call from a person identifying himself as a Treasury agent, and the matter was shelved.
I believe I told you that I personally spoke with Mr. McPhail. Marteshia handed the telephone to him as she was sitting in his home. Mr. McPhail explicitly told me he wanted to pursue this matter, which is evidenced by the fact that he filed a police report, which I have read and forwarded to you.
Please excuse my assumption, but if you or your agent thinks Mr. McPhail filed a false police report or is in some way culpable for a crime, why has he not been charged? We all know the Green Dot connection, and that Comerica Bank asserted that the fraudster used Mr. McPhail's address, but Comerica Bank is withholding information that would identify the fraudster, which we all know.
The challenge to your office is to either effect the arrest of Mr. McPhail or expose and arrest the fraudster, who might be affiliated with Comerica Bank and/or Conduent. It will be unfortunate that discovery in the civil proceeding would be necessary when a simple bit of communication with Mr. McPhail and his family would be easy to do.
I was involved in this case since last September, and know it well, and am aware you cannot discuss this matter with me. The concern is that Mr. McPhail is an older gentleman, a Vietnam veteran, and he possibly could pass away before this matter is finalized, putting an additional undue burden upon his family. There are other victims whose family members have died and are having to open a probate file in order to get money being held by Conduent.
Please contact Mr. McPhail and let him know your intentions. Ms. Marteshia McPhail is copied in this email; you can see her email address above.
Sincerely,
Jim

Sunday, June 9, 2019

Subject: Direct express fraud
From: Kol Stuf
Date: Sun, Jun 09, 2019 8:14 pm
To: jbsimms
Hi my name is Karen Jorgensen and I'm emailing because my direct express children's account is missing a lot of money I'm disputing all the transactions made in the month of September 2017 because around the 14th Direct Express froze our card ending in 8771 which had a balance of $6,217.74 on it which was on the card for June July August up until September 14th with no transactions of spending it also Social Security said there should have been another deposit of $4,021 around that time also well on the 14th of September Direct Express put a freeze on that card I have no idea why and sent out another card ending in 2518 without transferring my balance with it I have been dealing with Direct Express about this matter for at least 8 months straight talk to about 16 Direct Express employees and at least six of their supervisors who all agreed and seen this balance on the first card and not on the second , but still nothing has been done about it I've asked them to send me OD fraud packet but I still have not received it I doubt that they're even sending it but I'm still trying from all my printouts from Direct Express I figured they all my children around $16,000 all together they have been taking balances adding my kids benefits and then debiting the whole amount back to zero and there's more than 2 adding errors were they added up the charges or debits wrong and this has happened over and over without them even acknowledging that they are to blame I've called them and called them just to be put on hold for numerous hours or to be hung up on or to be told that this is a system error and not their fault but still nothing's been done and we need our money back I also have an account with Direct Express and I have the print-outs but I haven't had a chance to really look over those because this large amount of money that is missing has given me anxiety and blood pressure so high I should be hospitalized and we very much need your help .
Thank you
Karen Jorgensen.

Sonja Scott replied. She offered to forward my email to BFS. Ms. Scott seemed to believe in what I was doing but could not agree publicly.

217

Monday, June 10, 2019

I sent an email to Sonja Scott and others about Jorgensen.
I gave Jorgensen telephone numbers for Susan Schmidt and Susan Rutledge at Comerica Bank.

The outrage continued. Mr. Harding cannot get anyone in Washington, DC to help.

From: J B Simms
Date: Monday, June 10, 2019
Subject: The POA outrage
To: Sonja Scott <Sonja Scott (OIG Treasury)>
Cc: Jackie, Franklin Lemond (Plaintiff's Attorney)>, Eric Thorsen (OIG Treasury), Richard Delmar (OIG Treasury), Thomas Santaniello (Bureau of Fiscal Service)
I cannot get a signal for my Kindle in this restaurant, but this cannot wait.
Jeff Harding, in CA, has a legit POA and submitted it to our friends(?) at Conduent.
Conduent refused to acknowledge this POA. Conduent refused to discuss the fraud matter with Jeff when the elder Harding handed the telephone to Jeff while in mid-conversation with a Conduent employee. The letter states the POA was not accepted by government agencies. My military intel revealed this is not true.
The elder Mr. Harding is a USN veteran, disabled, and hardly communicative.
Jeff is sending you a copy of the letter from Conduent. These cowards take their ethical cues from BFS by trying to hide their identities.
The next sound you will hear will the churning of water when the rats run off the ship. Babb was one. There will be more before we are done.
Jim

Tuesday, June 11, 2019

Below is another installment of the tragedy in the life and death of Nona Clarke.
Nona Clarke's email to me was sent to Sonja on June 11, 2019.

Subject: Narrative of experience with Direct Express call center employees
From: "Kitty's korner" <nonaclarkeemail@gmail.com>
Date: Tue, Jun 11, 2019 2:43 pm
To: Sonja Scott (OIG Treasury)
Cc: jbsimms
Dear Ms. Scott,
I am a member of the Facebook group "Direct Express Victims" and Jim Simms gave me your email address and phone number.
On this Facebook group I use the name Anna Clark to try to remain anonymous because Direct Express employees have come to this page.   I fear possible further retribution if my involvement in this Facebook group becomes apparent to Conduent employees and I want to minimize the possibility of that happening.
After reading my attached narrative I hope the reasons I fear further retribution from Conduent becomes clear.
I only recently have been able to make purchases again using my Direct Express card after having Conduent employees place a fraud suspension on my card after I used Western Union to transfer money from my DE account to a person I know so I could pay my rent.
I did this after numerous phone calls to the DE call center from Mexico where I have been since May 4, 2019 and have not been able to access cash back this entire time.
I was told numerous times in the beginning, by various call center employees that they could see no reason for my card to not allow my cash back transaction and these Conduent employees told me it must be a problem inside Mexico.   A number of store managers and bank managers have approved my cash back transactions so Conduent employees can no longer say this is a problem on Mexico's end.
I will call you at the phone number Jim Simms gave me for you in a few days to answer any questions you may have.
Thank you for taking the time to read my narrative.
Sincerely, Nona Clarke

I had spoken to Nona several times, beginning when she was in Atlanta, before going to Mexico. Her story is heartbreaking. Sonja Scott at OIG Treasury was being kept informed of the developments.

Meanwhile, Jeffrey Harding continued to try to help his father as they battled against Conduent.

Subject: Direct Express/POA
From: Jeffrey Harding
Date: Tue, Jun 11, 2019, 4:44 pm
To: "Sonja Scott (OIG Treasury)" <Sonja Scott (OIG Treasury)>
Cc: "Richard Delmar (OIG Treasury " jbsimms, Thomas Santaniello (Bureau of Fiscal Service)
Ms. Scott,
My name is Jeffrey Harding. I believe you have been copied on previous e-mails concerning Direct Express for my father. We completed a Power of Attorney giving me authority over his account and to deal with Direct Express. I received the attached letter from them recently stating that they did not have to comply with the POA because of the funds were from a Federal source and that the federal government does not recognize aPOA. When I was on active duty Air Force spouses were given POAs all the time during our deployments.
I have been working with Jim Simms since March on getting funds that were used fraudulently when he had his social security check deposited to a Direct Express account. Direct Express denied the fraud claim before even receiving the police report or details. How can an investigation be completed before it has even started?
I know that I am not the only one going through issues with Direct Express. My question is what is being done about it? They are not even following their own protocols and procedures that they have in place. Please let me know if there is any more information that you need from me.
Jeffrey L Harding

Sonja Scott accepts 103 victim narratives

Sonja Scott agreed to accept the 103 narratives of the victims. We were grateful she accepted these. The document was well over 200 pages.

From: jbsimms
Date: Tue, Jun 11, 2019, 7:54 am
To: Sonja Scott (OIG Treasury)
Cc: "Jackie Lynn"
Dear Ms. Scott,
While I am encouraged by you being receptive to the narratives of victims of fraud at the hands of Comerica Bank, Conduent, and Fiscal Services, I am very concerned with the admission that you (and maybe those working with you) are referring the victims of the egregiously illegal, and emotionally and financially traumatic behavior by Comerica Bank and Conduent to the agency which condoned and rewarded the perpetrators.
I would think there are agents within OIG Treasury who would be able to investigate these matters (if I can understand the issues, I assume many at your agency can do the same) and confront employees of Conduent and Comerica Bank and conduct a criminal investigation of the instances of fraud. If Conduent employees are found to have communicated information to the physical perpetrators of the fraud, this will be easy to determine. The victims did not cause this victimization and should not be turned over to the same associated perpetrators to solve a problem which was caused by Bureau of Fiscal Services.
This being said, I respectfully request that if/when you or someone from your office refers a victim to BFS, the name and contact information of the BFS employee be given to the victim so the victim can communicate directly with the BFS employee, and ultimately hold the BFS employee to a degree of accountability to which no BFS employee or member of the administration of BFS has previously experienced.
The only analogy to which I can conjure to having Direct Express victim inquires received by your office being forwarded to unnamed BFS employees is the same as having a prison warden appoint convicted child molesters operate a day care facility. Blindly forwarding the inquiry subjects the victim to further emotional and financial horrors.
Please forward my concern to the person from whom you received your directive. If you can from this point identify the person(s) to whom you refer the victims, that would be a comfort to the victims.
Sincerely,
J.B. Simms

Tuesday, June 18, 2019

Below is evidence that the Treasury was monitoring the Facebook page of Direct Express Cardholder Victims.

Subject: social media
From: Sonja Scott (OIG Treasury)
Date: Tue, Jun 18, 2019, 9:37 am
To: jbsimms
Cc: Jackie Lynn
I have seen the FB posts. Sonja

Wednesday, June 19, 2019

Subject: a continuation of the pattern of theft by Conduent, with knowledge by Comerica
From: jbsimms
Date: Wed, Jun 19, 2019, 10:49 am
To: "Sonja Scott", "Richard K. Delmar"
Cc: "Jackie Lynn", "Franklin Lemond"
Bcc: "Melissa Farmer"
I just got off the phone with a victim who lost $4,000. Susan Schmidt called her last night (8pm Schmidt time) to schedule a chat.
They talked today. Schmidt denied knowing anything about the delay of announcement of new Fiscal Agent. Schmidt stated the money from the victim's account was deposited into another account (the victim was not able to write the last four digits) and that the money withdrawal was made from a US Bank in Los Angeles. Comerica ignored all attempts of the victim to prove she did not commit the fraud.
The new account was created, a person having the new card presented the card at the bank and got $4,000. Neither Comerica nor Conduent conducted any investigation, but "someone" created the new card and new account and took the money. Only people at Conduent had that information. Even Scooby Doo can figure this out; arrest one person and watch what happens.
This scam at Conduent has happened many times; new account, new card, money transferred, no one arrested. On this same account, the fraudster made a $500.00+ purchase from a Wal Mart store. The victim stated she has a letter from Wal Mart stating they have no record of a transaction in her name. The victim states she never has entered the doors of a Wal Mart (most of us wish we never had).
I know Ms. Scott is overwhelmed with victims.
By the way, at the end of the conversation with the victim, Schmidt stated she was going to call "Calvin" at Conduent (Customer Advocacy). If Schmidt was so secure in her assertion that the victim's fraud claim was not valid (after years of calls trying to be reimbursed), why would she waste her time calling Calvin at Conduent, and then offer to make a return call to the victim?
Am I missing something?
Jim

Thursday, June 20, 2019

Jackie was getting frustrated with Richard Delmar, OIG Commissioner.

Jackie Lynn
Thu, Jun 20, 2019, 7:13 AM
To: Richard Delmar (OIG Treasury), me
Mr. Delmar
It has come to my attention that your office has not responded to the questions that Mr. Jackman has forwarded over to your office on June 10, 2019. These questions were pertaining to the delay on the announcement of the new Direct Express Contract for 2020.
As your office is "actively "investigating all of these claims you would think you would also want to know why there is a delay. The American people who depend on this money deserve to know what's going on. For people who are withholding information, shame on them. These people are at the mercy of a corrupt bank and agencies that have failed to protect them. I will ask again ~ why is there a delay and who has bids in for this contract?

It is extremely alarming to me that as your office is conducting investigations and not one person has been arrested.
Sincerely
Jackie Densmore

Kelly Chambers called. Her money was taken from her again by Conduent. The provisional credit was given. Conduent sent a letter, telling her that the investigation revealed she purchased items from the merchant (Walmart) and Western Union. No copy of the investigation was included in the letter.
She did not know her money had been withdrawn until a friend used the card to get food for Kelly and the card had a negative balance.
I sent info to Sonja, who replied. I sent Sonja all of Kelly's documents.
Kelly had been a quadriplegic for years as a result of a traffic accident.

Friday, June 21, 2019

The fraud experienced by Kelly Chambers and being ignored by Conduent and Comerica Bank was horrific.

From: jbsimms
Date: Fri, Jun 21, 2019, 9:41 am
To: Sonja Scott (OIG Treasury)
Cc: "Kelly Chambers, "Jackie Lynn"
Ms. Scott,
I received a call from a weeping Kelly Chambers. She was a victim of fraud and theft, having fraudsters steal money from her Direct Express account via Western Union ($600) and (I believe) Walmart ($200+- more). Ms. Chambers was to email you or call you today, but having seen no copy for me, I decided to contact you myself on her behalf.
Ms. Chambers is paralyzed as a result of an automobile accident and is highly intelligent.
After contacting me, she received her provisional credit. Recently, she sent a person to buy food (using the card), and the card was refused. Ms. Chambers received a letter a few days later, advising her that their "investigation" revealed that the interaction with the merchant and Western Union (money transfer to places unknown) was performed with the permission of Ms. Chambers. Conduent dropped the ball into the lap of Ms. Chambers, telling her to deal with the merchants, and if Ms. Chambers wanted to see the investigation, she had to make a request to Conduent.
There are a few issues here. Blindsiding Ms. Chambers by taking her money with no notice, or no interview with her, was unconscionable, as well as not including the investigation in the letter/notification. No one knows the destination of the money that was transferred from the account of Ms. Chambers, and no one will divulge this information.
I know you are tired of hearing the stories, my mantra, and my advice as to how to find the criminals, but my advice was not created in a vacuum or from watching movies. Treating victims as second-class citizens, and exalting Comerica and BFS as bastions of honesty and credibility will not solve this problem. These are some very dirty people, they know I know, but are counting on people like Santaniello to shield them from accountability and consequences.
Hopefully, Ms. Chambers will be able to talk to you soon.
Jim

I called and talked to Kelly. She was such a pleasant person. I hated this for her as with all other victims of Conduent and Comerica Bank. Kelly told me she talked to Sonja Scott at Treasury.

Political Contributions Made by Conduent

Friday, June 21, 2019

If there was any question that Conduent was gaining political favor and avoiding liability, here was part of the evidence. Conduent contributed $5,000 to the Democrat National Committee and $10,000 to Cory Booker.

Federal Election Commission
Conduent 2017-2018 $5000 to Democrat National Committee
Cory Booker- $10,000

Monday, June 24, 2019

We continued to request for copies of the investigations used to create audits from Delmar and Scott

From: *Richard Delmar (OIG Treasury)*
Date: *Mon, Jun 24, 2019, 2:43 pm*
To: *jbsimms, Sonja Scott (OIG Treasury)*
Cc: *Jackie Lynn, Walter Bayer (SSA OIG)*
Treasury OIG expects its audit report to be final and posted on our website by the end of August.
Recommend you contact BFS regarding its schedule for the selection process.

From: *jbsimms*
Date: *Mon, Jun 24, 2019, 3:07 pm*
To: *Richard Delmar (OIG Treasury)*
Cc: *Jackie Lynn, Sonja Scott (OIG Treasury)*
Dear Mr. Delmar,
If you can suggest an effective manner in which, or a person, we could make contact with in BFS, we would be grateful.
Persons working in the area of electronic transfer of funds have their Voip Skype telephones on automatic voicemail (I know this because I had a worker send an immediate message to Brett Smith- (202) 874-6666 (Director of Electronic Money Transfer) while Smith was simultaneously on the telephone. This was performed after Smith refused to answer or return calls). You are aware Santaniello is guarding the "evaluation team" from victim input.
Other BFS workers have refused to discuss this matter with either myself or Ms. Densmore.
If you by chance have a communicative relationship with any person at BFS who is knowledgeable of the Direct Express program, or maybe the new director, please pass along the wish of myself and Ms. Densmore that we would like an audience with the director. I would gladly defer to Ms. Densmore if the preference would be for a BFS employee to speak with Ms. Densmore rather than me.
It you could arrange this meeting/conference, we would be grateful.
Jim

Tuesday, June 25, 2019

Subject: posted on LinkedIn on the page of the Bureau of Fiscal Services
From: *jbsimms*
Date: *Tue, Jun 25, 2019, 3:13 pm*
To: *"Jackie Lynn"*
J B Simms   Publisher, National Award-winning Author, Screenwriter, and Investigative and Publishing Consultant
In the spirit of "transparency," at BFS, as requested by the GAO in report 17-176, BFS is withholding information from victims of the ill-fated Direct Express program. A designated "guard dog" has been appointed to shield the decision makers from feedback from victims of their decisions, the announcement of the new contract has been delayed for a month because BFS is being investigated, and the new commissioner has yet to be briefed on the severity of the matter. There is no transparency at BFS; maybe that will change with the new commissioner, and those guilty of malfeasance will be held accountable. I am easy to find.

Wednesday, June 26, 2019

I was active on behalf of all victims as I contacted their congressional representatives.
Below is an email I sent on behalf of Texas victims. Some identifying information was redacted.
From: *jbsimms*
Date: *Wed, Jun 26, 2019, 3:14 pm*
To: *"Office, Dallas (Cornyn)" <Dallas_Office@cornyn.senate.gov>*
Cc: *"Jackie Lynn"*

Dear Senator Cornyn,

Thank you very much for your attention to this matter and your reply. I respectfully disagree with your assertion that this issue is outside the bounds of your jurisdiction, in that the prerequisite for requesting a follow-up investigation to GAO 17-176, as stated by Michael Cements, whose name is on GAO 17-176, is simply a request by a senator or congressperson. We have presented the case to your office in detail, along with a number of victims from your state.

Mr. Clements stated he is convinced this matter is substantive, evidenced by the fact that OIG Treasury began their third OIG audit/investigation as a result of the evidence I presented. Our point is, with no disrespect to OIG Treasury, an independent investigation, such as one to be conducted by the GAO, is preferable than being spoon-fed an agenda as a result of a unilateral inquiry.

If you or any of your staff would like to discuss our plea, I would be glad to make our case. Malfeasance on the part of Bureau of Fiscal Services has resulted in the enabling of Comerica Bank and its cohort, Conduent, to violate federal banking law Regulation E, and regulations of the FDIC and Federal Reserve. A class action suit is progressing.

Below is a list of some of the victims from Texas. Some of these victims have contacted your office:

1. Melanie Halley Clevenger Monday April 1, (94)

2. Shirley England- Monday January 4, 2019 (66)

3. Lisa Tower-December 3, 2018

Emailed her with directions: she made calls to Nora.

12/5- $783.00 Was paid within 2 days.

4. Carol Gilmer December 2, Appealing a 2017 fraud at ATM at gas station. All done on June 9, 2017 at Racetrack $584.00 (34)

5. Debra Savage- September 18, 2018 (646) 251-0034 card stolen, used while in hospital $1,103. Text November 13, 2018

6. Kelly Chambers April, 2019

I look forward to communicating with you or your staff at a time available to you.

Sincerely,

J.B. Simms

Thursday, July 4, 2019

I sent *Don't Get Arrested in South Carolina* and *Friendly Fire at the Veterans Hospital*, to Sonja Scott.

Subject: RE: This is why I wrote the book. This is what was ignored by OIG VA

From: Sonja Scott (OIG Treasury)

Date: Thu, Jul 04, 2019 3:52 pm

To: jbsimms

Thank you. Got the books. Happy 4th!

Sent with BlackBerry Work (www.blackberry.com)

From: jbsimms

Sent: Jul 4, 2019 2:40 PM

To: Sonja Scott (OIG Treasury)

Subject: This is why I wrote the book. This is what was ignored by OIG VA

OIG VA was given these pics. OIG VA asked for documentation of malfeasance. OIG VA whitewashed the entire matter, and never held anyone accountable.

The doctors allowed rogue techs to do this and covered it up. The administration aided in the cover-up.

This happened to many veterans. OIG VA went to the chief tech to get info, privately, then OIG VA exposed the source, betraying the source. It cost the source her job, and physical and mental health. These pics are in the book, which has been delivered (interesting story there, but I got a manager to take the books).

Enjoy your day off.

It was a day off for Sonja Scott, but not a day off for me.

Sunday, July 7, 2019

Subject: The review of two OIG Treas reports, notes and remarks

From: jbsimms

Date: Sun, Jul 07, 2019, 2:05 pm

To: Sonja Scott (OIG Treasury), Richard Delmar (OIG Treasury), Eric Thorsen (OIG Treasury)

It is not for my perception that you are bored that I send this critique to you. You might have seen this within the numbers of attachments I have sent.

I was cleaning up hard drive files, putting errant files into folders as I listed to a baseball game, when I happened upon this. Without casting personal attack and being familiar with a compromised OIG investigation (outlined in my book), you will understand why I studied the OIG reports submitted in 2014 and 2017 to find a similar attitude of trepidation with a seasoning of bovine reconstitution.

There are hundreds of documents in these files which have been compiled since my chat with Ms. Battle, and a bit overwhelming at times.

We want to trust that OIG Treasury will recommend that BFS do what is necessary and expel Comerica Bank as a Fiscal Agent. I would hope you will challenge the accepted principle that there is no accountability or consequences for public sector employees. Private sector citizens not only are accountable to public sector employees, but the reverse, having a public sector employee accountable to a private citizen, would be welcomed.

Monday, July 8, 2019

Jackie was working as hard as me.

From: "Erwin, James (Aging)"
Date: July 8, 2019, at 3:39:10 PM EDT
To: Jackie Lynn
Subject: RE:
Dear Ms. Densmore,

I wanted to shoot you a quick update on our conversations with SSA. We were able to talk to them about the issues with Direct Express. They are not able to disclose any information on the bidding process per SSA regulations and We are not able to influence the process. This regulation is meant to safeguard its integrity and independence. It seems as though that is all the information we will get out of them.

Please let me know if you have further questions.
James Erwin
Staff Assistant
U.S. Senate Special Committee on Aging
Susan M. Collins, Chairman
(202) 224-5364

Thursday, July 11, 2019

Subject: RE: Direct Express Fraud
From: Sonja Scott (OIG Treasury)
Date: Thu, Jul 11, 2019, 7:04 am
To: 'Medic 45' <medic3245p@gmail.com>, Richard Delmar (OIG Treasury), "jbsimms"
Mr. Rogers – We have your complaint in our system and will reach out to the Bureau of Fiscal Service on your behalf. Sonja

From: Medic 45
Sent: Thursday, July 11, 2019, 9:30 AM
To: Sonja Scott (OIG Treasury); Richard Delmar (OIG Treasury); jbsimms
Subject: Direct Express Fraud
Dear Ms. Scott and Mr. Delmar
Jim Simms has asked that I contact you all in reference to a situation that I am having with Direct Express. On June 20, 2019 in the evening I was checking my account balance and had noticed that it was lower then it should be. I started looking over the transactions and noted 2 that I did not make.
1, June 11, 2019 at Footlocker Store #07446 for 201.40
2, June 11, 2019 at Rue21 Store # 1487 for 43.96
These appear to be from New Jersey area but I am unsure.
I immediately contacted Direct Express, after sitting on hold for a little over 45 minutes I was able to talk to a Human. I explained the situation to them. They cancelled my card and Issued a new one. And said they would be sending out some paperwork for me to fill out and that they would open an investigation. As of today July

11,2019, I have yet to receive any paperwork from them. I did however receive my new Card on June 26th. On June 26th when the card came and I still had no paper work I started calling them again. I was never able to reach a human in their office. I kept getting a message stating that they were busy and to try back again later and then it hangs up on you. On some days I would call several times and try different automated options to contact someone but still got the same message, just trying to get a Human on the line. I do not know the exact times but here are the dates that I called Direct Express using Number 1-888-741-1115
June 27, 2019
June 28, 2019
July 1, 2019
July 3, 2019
July 5, 2019
July 8, 2019
July 9, 2019
I have since took all the money off of the card so this doesn't happen again. This money was my Income from SSA, who I also contacted on Friday June 21,2019 and had all future payments stopped to this account and to be sent by paper check from here on out.
I sure hope that you can help me get my funds back.
Thank you
Brian Rogers
606-872-9054

Monday, July 15, 2019

Another email was received from Nona Clarke while she was in Mexico struggling with Conduent.

Subject: Information pertaining to our conversation earlier today.
From: The Light <light4ever1212@gmail.com>
Date: Mon, Jul 15, 2019, 11:01 am
To: jbsimms
Hey Jim,
It was so nice to talk with you today. I feel like a huge weight has been lifted from my shoulders just talking about this.
I am going to call Sonja again today and I will be sure to tell her you are not Charles Manson so she knows you and I talked.
So, this is the information I told you about. I actually had to create an email account to join the subscriber's list for Derek Rake's Shogun Method email list so I could get the messed up emails he sends to his client base.
He showcases certain emails to use as selling points to potential buyers. The most recent email claims to be from an attorney who says this Shogun Method really works and he is going to try it on juries next.
The guy in Atlanta who schmoozed me couldn't help bragging on himself and how well this method worked for him. He also claimed to be getting ongoing advice from the membership forum on what to do when I got uppidy and in his face.
When you have time please give me a call again. I really feel for your lady friend. Been there done that but thank God I have a zero tolerance for hateful bullshit directed at me or anyone else.
The tremendous effort made to keep me financially destitute is to try to make me financialky dependent on someone else so I can't leave bullshit situations I find myself in.
If your lady friend is interested, I can guide her to information she will probably find helpful for her recovery. If she is interested and would like to talk that would be cool too.
Talking to someone who knows what you are going through and have been through can be so helpful and healing.
Talk with you soon.

No one knew how badly this was going to end.

Thursday, July 18, 2019

Subject: Letter to S. Scott
From: K C <kchambers222@gmail.com>
Date: Thu, Jul 18, 2019 7:52 am
To: jbsimms
Hello Mrs. Scott.

I hope you are doing well. I've put off emailing you because I was waiting to see if I was ever going to receive the paperwork I requested from Direct Express. They ruled against my fraud claim, stating that the merchants involved are saying that I authorized the use of my debit card. The 2 merchants they are speaking of is Western Union & Cricket Wireless. I can assure you that I never authorized any of the transactions. Once I thought my card was misplaced, I changed the pin # to be safe. There were several other transactions the month before that Direct Express never even addressed. All of the transactions occurred after I changed the pin #. The only reason I didn't cancel the card and order a new one is because I thought I had just misplaced it. I didn't want to cancel it only to find it and then have to wait 10 days for a new card to come in the mail. I will email you all of the original paperwork again. Direct Express put the Provisional amount Into my account, I had already spoke with you and discussed it with you that they were saying I didn't get the paperwork in in time and I wasn't eligible for the provisional amount. Even though the paperwork was postmarked within the 10 business days they gave me. So 1st, Direct Express said I wasn't eligible and then they just decided to deposit the money. I'm assuming this happened after you became involved. Then all of a sudden my bank account was negative $218 when I had $400 left in my bank account the last I had checked. I called them after being on the hold for over 2 hours, I finally hung up and called them again the next day. The representative I got was extremely rude to me. That is when they informed me that it was the provisional amount of money and I shouldn't have spent it. If you can't spend it on bills then why do they give it to you? Then they said that the merchants involved said that I authorized the transactions on my card and they decided to take their money back. However, I had no phone call from them and I got a letter in the mail several days after they took the money telling me that they were taking the money. So they took $400 plus a negative $218 amount. When my disability check came July 3rd, they automatically got $218 of it plus $4 for a new card. I'm really depressed over all of this & it has turned my life upside down. It is hard enough to live life with a disability. Adding to that disability, never knowing when somebody's going to take your money, its just too overwhelming. It is far from easy to live on a disability check. I truly believe that they did not mail out a letter to me telling me they were going to take that money until after they had already taken the money. Thank Goodness, this time I had paid my rent and my water. I wasn't able to play my electric bill before the money was gone. I am still behind on my bills due to this whole nightmare. It basically has just caused a snowball effect in my life. I'm having a hard time catching up on my bills and buying my groceries. Mentally I am exhausted over all of this, as it has affected my life in negative ways since April 2019. They said I can contact the fraud department in Austin to ask for a copy of the paper work of why they decided not to honor the fraud case. I don't understand why they didn't automatically send that information. Of course, I want to see the paperwork. On June 25, 2019 I called the number Direct Express provided me(twice) to ask for a copy of the case. All I was able to do was leave a voicemail. When the number rings it immediately goes to voicemail. I left my information in the message & I have yet to receive anything from them. I don't believe I will receive anything from them. I feel Direct Express has allowed all of this to happen. Basically, I truly believe I have been robbed by Direct Express. I really don't know where to turn anymore.

I know that you had social security contact me and I appreciate that. However, they would not allow me to transfer my disability check to my Credit Union account. For the 3rd time since I started using Direct Express, I had to Find a ride to social security and fill out the paperwork again. I have a hard enough time finding a ride to the grocery store much less social security 3 times for the same problem. Supposedly, the issue has been fixed & on August 3rd my disability check will be deposited in my Credit Union Account. I'm curious to see if this will actually occur. Each and everytime I pay a bill now I get anxiety because I'm worried my money is gone again. It causes definite anxiety because not only have I seen my check disappear but the last incident gave me a -$218(negative balance).

I appreciate the time that you are taking to investigate these cases. It all has taken its toll on me and I have since started seeing a psychiatrist. I'm having problems sleeping at night because I am in fear that I will eventually lose the roof over my head due to the negligence of Direct Express.

I'm sending you attachments of all of the paperwork between myself and Direct Express. I would like to point out that they only addressed the check that was missing from Western Union & Cricket Wireless. There were several other charges to my card, transactions that occurred after I changed my pin # the month before.

Absolutely none of the transactions I wrote to them about were authorized by me in any way, shape or form. Once again, I thank you for your time and I look forward to hearing from you.
Sincerely,
Kelly Chambers

Below is an email from Nona Clarke, and the next is the reply email she had received from me.

Subject: Re: Information pertaining to our conversation earlier today.
From: Only the Truth <light4ever1212@gmail.com>
Date: Thu, Jul 18, 2019 10:08 am
To: jbsimms
Hi Jim, I just saw this email, sorry. I agree with you. I still maintain all this is connected, every part of it. Unethical people don't care who they climb into bed with as long as whoever that is plays nice with them. I've heard rabid black activists who refer to white people as those white devils claim they have met a few white guys that are ok. These ok white guys they were referring to were rabid neo nazi's. The hate is mind-blowing to me. Anyway, take care.

On Tue, Jul 16, 2019, 6:39 AM jbsimms wrote:
Glad you got her attention.
Mixed feelings; they are part of the cya system, and I see no resolution when she refers the problem to BFS, and will not tell us who is supposed to address the issue.
"Tell me who at BFS you called and I might trust you a bit more."

Nona was talking to Sonja Scott, but Sonja seemed to "believe in" the credibility of BFS.

Sunday, July 21, 2019

Subject: Lack of news and accountability
From: jbsimms
Date: Sun, Jul 21, 2019, 12:04 am
To: Sonja Scott (OIG Treasury), Richard Delmar (OIG Treasury), "Eric Thorson" <Eric Thorson (OIG Treasury)>
Cc: "Jackie Lynn"
Why has there been no announcement of any arrests of fraudsters in the BFS/Comerica/Conduent investigation?
Are you people afraid of embarrassing fellow Treasury Department employees? I would think a bit of integrity would have surfaced by now.
We (I and other victims) gave more than enough information to you to find the criminals and expose corrupt Treasury employees.
To whom do you answer?

Monday, July 22, 2019

Jackie was still going after Jackman, the staffer for Rep. Keating.
Jackie Lynn
Attachments
Mon, Jul 22, 2019, 7:58 AM
to Michael, me
Very upset you have not responded to this nor have any answers on this.
Good morning, Mr. Jackman,
As I was looking over all of my emails and information I came across this letter from Sen. Collins, I believe I sent it to you months ago. I have reached out to Sen. Collins office several times and was told by James Irwin that they know about the DE situation and are looking into doing a press release after they speak with Treasury. This was several months ago. I have heard nothing back including my request to see if they ever received answers to this letter.

227

I was wondering if you would be able to reach out to her office for the answers, unfortunately with all these issues it is extremely difficult to get any answers by myself. I know this issue is not easy and it is taking up a lot of your time but I feel that it is so important given how many innocent people it effects.

According to this letter she raised a lot of concerns one in particular, listed as schedule "c" listed as #1 Identify each Treasury employee who at any time was or is an employee of Comerica Bank. Now this raises some red flags to me, why would she ask this question and was it ever answered? Perhaps maybe your office could find this out. My thought is that all of these concerns should be sent to BFS along with Sen. Warren's questions and answers so that they can make a decision when they have all of their facts. If this card is US Treasury recommended, then they should have no objection on having these answers / questions outlined.

I am asking your office to

1) review this document

2) write to Sen. Collins office requesting information on this document including any and all answers received on DE (if she ever did get a response)

3) ask Mr. Delmar if this document can be included with the OIG report, also wondering if he knew of this document

As always Mr. Jackman, thank you for your dedication to this ongoing issue.

Jackie

Tuesday, July 23, 2019

Subject: The future of victims
From: Richard Delmar (OIG Treasury)
Date: Tue, Jul 23, 2019, 1:25 pm
To: jbsimms, Jackie Lynn
Cc: Sonja Scott (OIG Treasury)
Mr. Simms – as we've previously explained, we are doing both audit and investigative work related to the Direct Express program, and aspects of how BFS administers it and Comerica carries out its responsibilities as a financial agent. When problems are brought to our attention, by you and by others, we review them critically and take appropriate action, including incorporation in our audit and investigative work and, where appropriate, coordination with BFS and to Comerica for attention and resolution.

We are doing what we can within our scope of jurisdiction under the Inspector General Act. When our audit work is completed, it will be available on our website. When our investigative work is completed, it can be requested via FOIA. Until such time, we cannot discuss matters under review by this Office. We appreciate your interest and assistance and will reach out to you if we need further information.

Rich Delmar
Acting Inspector General
Department of the Treasury

Wednesday, July 31, 2019

Subject: The FOI for the investigative report
From: jbsimms
Date: Wed, Jul 31, 2019, 8:10 am
To: Richard Delmar (OIG Treasury), Sonja Scott (OIG Treasury)
Cc: Jackie Lynn, Franklin Lemond (Plaintiff's Attorney)
Dear Mr. Delmar and Ms. Scott,

I am certain you have become weary with respect to this matter of BFS, Comerica, and Conduent, and the victims as well. The victims are weary of this fight for other reasons, and you are weary of my questions.

It is important to impress upon you that having to use an FOI request to get a copy of investigative information associated with any OIG Treasury report seems a bit odd. You know I will read the report and have questions that the investigative report might answer.

You are aware that Ms. Densmore submitted an FOI request to Treasury in September 2018. This request was ignored. Ms. Densmore has no recourse, other than file suit as many media agencies do (such as Judicial Watch), and Treasury knows there will be no suit (not from her personally) to get the requested FOI information. Treasury seems to be operating as the VA did before President Trump allowed VA workers to be fired for cause, the absence of that policy lead to the circumstances detailed in the book I sent you.

The point is this: having evidence of failure to perform by the FOI section, your investigative notes will, in effect, be "off limits" to us because the FOI section will ignore this request again. I am requesting that someone from your office "make a call" to confirm this request is handled in the manner in which it was intended. You will have the information at your fingertips, and I fail to see the necessity for an FOI request.
I want the investigative report (notes, etc) at the same time the OIG Treasury report is published. I hope you can make this happen. Your office does have oversight of the FOI section.
Jim

Thursday, Aug 1, 2019

After months of one-way communication with Pamela Powers of the VA, she told me she was communicating with Treasury and Comerica Bank. While I did not expect her to give me a report of the meetings, it would have been nice to have had some confirmation.

Subject: VAB interaction
From: jbsimms
Date: Thu, Aug 01, 2019, 2:02 pm
To: Richard Delmar (OIG Treasury), Sonja Scott (OIG Treasury)
Cc: Jackie Lynn, Franklin Lemond (Plaintiff's Attorney)
I received a message from Pamela Powers, COS of VA. Ms. Powers stated her office has been communicating with OIG Treasury on this investigation of BFS and Comerica Bank.
I would like confirmation of the statement made by Ms. Powers, and the scope of the involvement of the VA in this investigation.
I see that Ms. Scott is not accessible at this time, and I look forward to her reply at her leisure.
Jim

Sunday, August 4, 2019

Nona Clarke's saga continued.
Subject: Re: Important concerns regarding SSDI recipient.
From: "Youdon't Say" <youdontsay211@gmail.com>
Date: Sun, Aug 04, 2019, 4:12 pm
To: jbsimms
On Sun, Aug 4, 2019, 17:19 Youdon't Say <youdontsay211@gmail.com> wrote:
Dear Ms. Lizaman,
My name is Nona Clarke and Jim Simms recommended I contact you immediately.
I have been in Santa María Hualtuco México since May 4, 2019, when my Direct Express card unexpectedly would not allow me to get cash back under any circumstances but, I was able to buy anyting I wanted as long as I had enough money on my card.
Direct Express knew I would be in México, I notified them of when and for how long.   But when I arrived here in Hualtuco and tried to get cash back to pay my rent it was imposible.
I spent countless hours talking with the service center reps to no avail despite explaining my situation. Much of that time I spent on hold or calling back because I was hung up on repeatedly.
My situation was precarious in Mexico to say the least, for over two months I was in a foreign country where I do not speak the language and had no cash in a country where cash is king.
The man I have been renting from claimed to not be able to take electronic payments for my rent but had me make payments on air conditioner units for his apartment units in the amount of my rent.
This seemed very kind of him to do until he would act as if he didn't undertand me when I asked for a receipt. I had to demand receipts for the rent I paid him, even after the cash back began working again on my Direct Express card and I was able to pay him cash.
One of this man's acquaintances informed me that a) I could be arrested for failing to pay even one peso I owe my landlord and that in Mexico it only takes two Mexican citizens to go before a judge to say a person is crazy and tell the judge you need to be cared for to loose all your freedoms un México. This person claims this is true even for Americans here in México.
Strange things are taking place here and I know when people are gaslighting me and intentionally trying to provoke me to make a scene, but I have been keeping to myself and have not taken the bait.
I am terrified these people are setting me up so they can have a judge make me their ward which will give them control of my social security money.

I have a plane ticket to México City on the 8th of August and maybe enough money to flyer to Texas or somewhere very inexpensive after that, but then I will be broke and homeless after going through this ordeal. I have chronic CPTSD and it is a miracle I have held it together during this ordeal as Wells as I have. Direct Express's failure to do right by me made the situation here so much worse then it needed to be. I stayed locked into this situation here much longer then I wanted because of how carelessly and callously my situation was handled by Comerica.
I appreciate your time reading this and I hope you can help me somehow.
Regards, Nona Clarke

Nona was reaching out. Sonja seemed as though she cared, but no one was making Comerica and Conduent accountable.

Tuesday, August 6, 2019

From: Shanna Miller <shannaerrn@gmail.com>
Date: Tue, Aug 06, 2019, 5:06 am
To: jbsimms
Hi Jim, my name is Shanna Miller. I have a direct express card and have for years for my children's death benefits from their father. On August 4, 2019, I was a victim of fraudulent transactions. Date and location of fraud:
1st fraudulent transaction was a successful ATM withdrawal at 0908 am on 8/4/2019 for the amount of $683.00 at 3300 N Miami Avenue Miami, FL 33127. This address links to a Citibank in Miami, FL
There was an attempt for an ATM withdrawal on 8/5/2019 at 0622 am for 63.00 at 18235 Biscayne Blvd North Miami FL that did not go through at according to Direct Express because I did not have enough money in the account. However, this is not true there was still 75.08 in my account when this transaction took place. This address links to a Chase Bank. In Miami, FL.
My address is 61 Lee Rd 215 Phenix City, AL 36870. My phone number is 334-614-2306.
I became aware of the fraud on 8/5/2019 at about 0800 am.
I reported the fraud immediately on 8/5/2019 to Direct Express but I was on hold for about an hour and a half. I also filed a police report with Phenix City Police Dept in Alabama while on hold with Direct Express on 8/5/2019.
I have not currently sent any information in but a packet for investigation is supposed to arrive in 3-5 BUISNESS days.
I spoke to the lawyer handling the class action lawsuit yesterday and he states that the judge has yet to sign off on it as a class action lawsuit and this could take up to a year as direct express ha files motions on some of the claims filed against the company. He did tell me that if anything happens of importance, he will contact me. Please help me if possible

From: Sonja Scott (OIG Treasury)
Date: Tue, Aug 06, 2019, 9:12 am
To: jbsimms, Shanna Miller <shannaerrn@gmail.com>
Cc: Jackie Lynn, Richard Delmar (OIG Treasury), Sarah Lizama (SSA OIG), Walter Bayer (SSA OIG)
Ms. Joyner – we will request that the Bureau of Fiscal Service look into the matter. We will also add this matter to our complaint system. Sonja
From: Sonja Scott (OIG Treasury)
Date: Tue, Aug 06, 2019, 9:48 am
To: jbsimms
Cc: Jackie Lynn
Our office is, and will remain, a means for the public to make complaints about Treasury related programs, including BFS. Just because an investigation and/or audit are released, does not terminate our work. Sonja

From: jbsimms
Date: Tue, Aug 06, 2019, 10:36 am
To: "Teri" <trowe0511@gmail.com>
Cc: Sonja Scott (OIG Treasury), Richard Delmar (OIG Treasury), Sarah Lizama (SSA OIG), Walter Bayer (SSI OIG), Jackie, Franklin Lemond (Plaintiff's Attorney)
Dear Teri,

I am forwarding this to fed employees, and Ms. Scott has assured me she will receive and work on your case.
Comerica Bank and Conduent (the call center subcontractor) routinely violate Reg E by delaying your immediate provisional credit. Based upon your email, Direct Express aka Conduent (Conduent, there is no company named Direct Express, it is a program, not a company) admitted their liability to you.
It is not unusual for Conduent employees to compromise personal data. Ms. Scott, of OIG Treasury, has assured me her office is investigating this matter. It has happened many times.
You have to cover yourself. Conduent is going to tell you that they are sending out a "fraud packet" but Conduent will use the timeframe of sending out the packet and its return by you to exclude you from your money.
The original call to the call center is "proper notice." The fact that I am forwarding this to the above-named people is also proper notice.
Conduent is trying to avoid liability in paying you back your money.
Make a copy of your statement from your computer, or a screenshot off your phone. Print out the statement/screenshot, and fax it to (512) 298-3461, (512) 298-3461, and (512) 671-2298. Then call (210) 334-6673, which is the number for Shantelle Johnson, head of "investigations" at Conduent.
I am sorry you have to be doubly victimized by having to do this.
Also, write a detailed version (a narrative) of your loss, what you were told, etc. Send this to Sonja Scott whose address is above. Copy me in that email.
Jim Simms

Nona Clarke commits suicide because of Conduent

Subject: Message from Paige Clarke
From: J B Simms
Date: Fri, Aug 09, 2019, 11:51 am
To: jbsimms
Thank you, JB. For forwarding your communication with my mom and for your kind words.
My sister spoke with the investigator and the doctor who performed the autopsy.
I'm not sure why Anna told you it was a traffic accident; I think she felt uncomfortable telling you information without being her next of kin.
She was found in the bathroom of a grocery store with a sharp object. They were looking into foul play, but they thought that it was suicide. They asked several questions about her mental health, relationships with family and if she had any sleep problems. All of that combined with stress around not being able to have access to her funds and being in physical pain could have led to her taking her own life.
I really appreciate you having supported her through this tough time, I'm sure your kindness and connection meant a lot to her.
Warmly,
Paige

Subject: hold your hats
From: jbsimms
Date: Thu, Aug 08, 2019 10:15 am
To: Franklin Lemond (Plaintiff's Attorney), "Jackie Lynn"
The new head of Bureau of Fiscal Services, Gribben, was head of the Small Business Administration.
Eric Thorson, who retired as head of OIG Treasury, was head of OIG for Small Business Administration before coming to OIG Treasury.
There seems to be a small gene pool of people from which to choose to head agencies.
I wonder what the OIG Treasury report will reveal.

Friday, August 9, 2019

The situation with Nona Clarke being in Mexico and not having access to her funds had become more strenuous for Nona.

I received a telephone call that would change everything.

11:37am Anna Martinez +52 928 117 0851 Huatulco, Mex, she called my office.
Called to say Nona Clarke had been in an auto accident.

Did not know of relatives.

Anna works for the government (in the town where Nona died).

She found my name and number as the first contact.

My heart sank. I was furious and sad. Connections were made with these victims. Nona was a great lady.

Subject: kind of a mercy request; victim in Mexico in an accident and I have limited background info
From: jbsimms
Date: Tue, Aug 06, 2019, 12:10 pm
To: Sonja Scott (OIG Treasury)
I just got a call from Anna Martinez, who speaks a bit of broken English.
the connection was poor.
She got my number from Nona Clarke, who is the DE victim living in Mexico.Clarke has been in bad auto accident.My number was in her book to call in case of an emergency.I do not know her dob, or her age (I will guess 50 or so).
She lived in Atlanta and Washington state.If I can get a hit on her dob, my database guy can run with this.
If you can get BFS to get her dob, you can get passport info.
Anna Martinez number is +52 (958) 117-0851
If you speak Spanish, this might help. I reviewed emails from Clarke; she stated you lived in Mexico City.
this is a shot.
She must have family somewhere.
I will do my thing until I hear from you.
Jim

The next email went to the American Consul in Mexico City.

Subject: Nona Clarke, American in Huatulco, auto accident
From: jbsimms
Date: Tue, Aug 06, 2019, 12:42 pm
To: conagencyoaxaca@state.gov
Cc: Sonja Scott (OIG Treasury)
Dear Sirs,
I received a telephone call from a lady named Anna Martinez, who works for the government of Huatulco. She got my number from a piece of paper in the possession of a lady named Nona Clarke, an American. Ms Martinez told me that Nona Clarke had been in an auto accident and my number was given as the first contact.
I have had limited contact with Ms. Clarke and know no relatives of Ms. Clarke.
The number used by Ms. Martinez is +52 (958) 117-0851. She is in Huatulco.
I am copying Sonja Scott of OIG Treasury, who has had contact with Mr. Clarke with regard to banking issues in Mexico.
Hopefully you can reach Ms. Martinez, and research information on Ms. Clarke to determine her next of kin. She lived in Atlanta and supposedly Washington State.
Sincerely,
J.B. Simms

Subject: RE: kind of a mercy request; victim in Mexico in accident and I have limited background info
From: jbsimms
Date: Tue, Aug 06, 2019, 12:49 pm
To: Sonja Scott (OIG Treasury)
phone she used was (334) 384-3628
Prob a throw away phone
i sent email to consulate in the state of Oaxaca where Huatulco is located.
I would have to connect a few dots to get a dob, but she must have passport and US info.
the lady who call me was Anna Martinez, +52 (958) 117 0851
looked like the email to consulate went into a rat hole.

Subject: Nona Clarke had died
From: jbsimms
Date: Tue, Aug 06, 2019, 1:14 pm
To: Sonja Scott (OIG Treasury)
I just got off phone with Paul Mastin, US Embassy in Mex City.
He conveyed that they found the daughter of Nona Clarke.
Nona had died as a result of the traffic accident. That is all that is known.

12:52 T (844) 528-6611 US Embassy
Transferred to Acapulco, then to Mexico City
Talked to Paul Mastin- adv Nona Clarke had died.
Mastin stated a daughter has been notified. Believe the daughter is Amy.
I gave the phone number of Anna Martinez to Mastin.
Nona had emailed a narrative to Sonja Scott, Scott replied, also to Sarah Lizama.
Huatulco Mexico is in the state of Oaxaca.
I sent email to consulate at Oaxaca.
They emailed me with phone number (844) 528-6611.

Subject: RE: kind of a mercy request; victim in Mexico in accident and I have limited background info
From: Sonja Scott (OIG Treasury)
Date: Tue, Aug 06, 2019, 12:26 pm
To: jbsimms
Jim. I am confused. Do you want me to check on Nona Clarke? I do have her email, but not sure about a tel #.
My Spanish is poor. I lived there as a child when my father was teaching at the University of Mexico. Sonja

From: jbsimms
Sent: Tuesday, August 6, 2019, 3:10 PM
To: Sonja Scott (OIG Treasury)
Subject: kind of a mercy request; victim in Mexico in accident and I have limited background info
I just got a call from Anna Martinez, who speaks a bit of broken English. The connection was poor. She got my number from Nona Clarke, who is the DE victim living in Mexico.
Clarke has been in bad auto accident. My number was in her book to call in case of emergency.
I do not know her dob, or her age (I will guess 50 or so).
She lived in Atlanta and Washington state.
If I can get a hit on her dob, my database guy can run with this. If you can get BFS to get her dob, you can get passport info.
Anna Martinez number is +52 (958) 117-0851
If you speak Spanish, this might help. I reviewed emails from Clarke; she stated you lived in Mexico City. This is a shot. She must have family somewhere.
I will go my thing until I hear from you. Jim

Tuesday, August 7, 2019

From: jbsimms
Sent: Wednesday, August 7, 2019, 12:09 PM
To: Sonja Scott (OIG Treasury)
Subject: RE: Conduent Fraud Investigation
(512) 298-3461 Alisha and Brandon
(512) 671-2298 Calvin
These were the numbers I have for the above named Conduent workers. According to the attachments, these numbers are not working. This is not happening in a vacuum.
Jim

Sonja Scott replied and thanked me.

Thursday, August 8, 2019

From: jbsimms
Sent: Aug 8, 2019, 12:22 PM
To: Sonja Scott (OIG Treasury)
Cc: Jackie Lynn; Franklin Lemond (Plaintiff's Attorney)
Subject: [FWD: Re: Conduent Fraud Investigation]
Dear Ms. Scott,
I just got off the phone with Teri Miller/Rowe.
Oddly enough, after a bit of pushing, she received an email from the Advocacy group at Conduent.
The Advocacy person, Calvin, gave her a phone number and fax number to contact him.
The fax number is the same one that was not operational.
BFS is not going to make Conduent accountable. Calvin was emailing the fraud packet to Teri. This is a change in procedure for Conduent. Calvin stated he would opt out as a rep for her if she was a part of the class action suit.
Teri made it clear that she would be part of the suit when available.
Calvin is trying to make the provisional credit contingent upon receipt of the "fraud packet" which is less comprehensive than the narrative written by Teri.
Teri has 5 children. Her husband died as a direct result of PTSD that developed from military service.
Run this story past Mr. Thorson to get his reaction.
Jim

Sonja Scott had sent me the email below which I evidently missed seeing before I sent the above email:

From: Sonja Scott (OIG Treasury)
Date: Thu, Aug 08, 2019, 9:31 am
To: jbsimms
Cc: Jackie, Franklin Lemond (Plaintiff's Attorney)
Thank you for the update. Just FYI, Thorson has retired. Counsel Delmar is the acting IG. Sonja

Paige Clarke called me: Page is the daughter of Nona Clarke.
I told Paige that her mom, Nona, had died in Mexico.
Gave her the number for Anna Martinez
Paige had learned mom died in the bathroom of a store. Appeared to be suicide. Wrists cut.

Another satisfied victim; got her money

Subject: Re: Conduent Fraud Investigation
From: Teri <trowe0511@gmail.com>
Date: Fri, Aug 09, 2019, 3:07 pm
To: jbsimms
They credited me the full balance today!!!!
Thank you and thank you again for your help on this...God Bless you!!!!!

Wednesday, August 14, 2019

Jackie sent me an email; she found OIG Report 19-041 and Delmar had not told us it had been published. The report was dated July 29, 2019. Katherine Johnson wrote the report, and it was identified as an interim report. A copy had been sent to Gribben, the new Commissioner of the Bureau of Fiscal Service. In fact, the report was directed to him. The number given was (202) 927-8783 to reach Katherine Johnson.
Jackie found OIG 19-041 at oversight.gov.
Sonja and Delmar did not tell us that the audit report had been issued.

I reviewed the audit report and responded within a few days with insertions. I sent my edits to Delmar and Sonja Scott.

From: jbsimms
Date: Wed, Aug 14, 2019, 11:22 pm
To: Sonja Scott (OIG Treasury)
Cc: Jackie Lynn, Franklin Lemond (Plaintiff's Attorney)
Dear Ms. Scott,
Ms. Densmore discovered OIG 19-041 and sent it to me tonight.
I wish I had known of this sooner. Maybe you were restricted from making me or Ms. Densmore aware of this document.
Convey my gratitude to Ms. Johnson.
The revelation that Comerica Bank "co-mingled" data in order to skew performance percentages might be the genesis of a pattern of deceit. Comerica certainly did not count on us to light this fire, and BFS's lack of oversight (willful) resulted in no reduction of compensation.
All this plays to the fact that Santaniello blocked us from addressing the "evaluation team."
I assume Mr. Lemond will know the best place to take this report.
My exposure to OIG reports with respect to the VA gave me good insight to the language used by an OIG and in-house subject of the investigation. Ms. Johnson could have been more direct, but we hope the final audit, and the investigation of BFS, Comerica, Conduent, and this Direct Express program will expose who might be living beyond their means. BFS is in a box regardless of whether Comerica get the contract or not.
I hope to see the investigative report as well as the audit.
Jim

Thursday, August 15, 2019

From: Jackie Lynn
Date: August 15, 2019, at 8:16:41 AM EDT
To: Richard Delmar (OIG Treasury)
Subject: Status reports
Good morning Mr. Delmar,
I can't seem to think this information somehow got lost and perhaps you may have been bogged down with new work from your promotion, so I won't hold it against you. It's a good thing we are so interested in this investigation and your findings. someone who may not have been so passionate would not have even looked. So moving forward I would hope that you would inform myself and Mr. Simms in a timely manner of any upcoming release dates and also information on identifying investigations that Ms. Scott is referring to in this email.
I hope to hear from you soon,
Jackie Densmore

Subject: RE: OIG 19-041
From: Sonja Scott (OIG Treasury)
Date: Thu, August 15, 2019, 4:00 am
To: jbsimms
I thought Mr. Delmar sent it to you. Unlike an audit, there is not one investigation, but several. These are not public and must be obtained by a Freedom of Information Act request through Mr. Delmar. Sonja

Jackie's long-lost FOI Request: It came a year late

Jackie received a letter from OIG Treasury acknowledging FOI request of September 18, 2018. This letter was received August 15, 2019. They said they lost it. It was lost for eleven months.
Email from Sonja- she thought Delmar sent the report to us, and more than one investigation is taking place. Delmar would later deny any investigations were conducted.

From: jbsimms
Date: Thu, Aug 15, 2019, 10:00 am
To: Sonja Scott (OIG Treasury)
Cc: Jackie Lynn, Richard Delmar (OIG Treasury), Franklin Lemond (Plaintiff's Attorney)
Since I have not received a reply, I left a voice message for Ms. Johnson who signed off on OIG 19-041.
Maybe she can help identify the reference numbers for the investigations which we want.
I assume Mr. Delmar has a few more duties to perform and hope he will be justly rewarded.

With all due respect, if someone would reply with a direct answer it would not be necessary for me to circumvent inquiries within OIG Treasury and save me a bit of time and continued anguish. I see no reason for withholding the information of completed investigations and the report number.
I assume Ms. Johnson relied upon said investigations in order to have the information to submit to Gribben, and I also assume Mr. Delmar, you also have that information, which should not be proprietary.
Jim

Subject: a review of the preliminary OIG report
From: jbsimms
Date: Thu, Aug 15, 2019, 10:53 pm
To: Sonja Scott (OIG Treasury), Richard Delmar (OIG Treasury)
Cc: Jackie Lynn, Franklin Lemond (Plaintiff's Attorney)
Dear Ms. Scott and Mr. Delmar.
Attached please find my review of the preliminary OIG 19-041 report.
If you would be so kind as to send a copy to Ms. Katherine Johnson, I would be grateful.

Friday, August 16, 2019

From: jbsimms
Date: Fri, Aug 16, 2019, 8:37 am
To: Sonja Scott (OIG Treasury), Richard Delmar (OIG Treasury)
Cc: "Jackie Lynn"
As you know, this is the attitude of the victims. I hope the victims eventually trust federal workers to do their jobs. Paul and Jackie Densmore were both victimized in Miramar, Fl and the agent did nothing.
Cardholders are victimized twice.
I hope the cardholders eventually trust OIG Treasury.

Friday, August 16, 2019

Sonja Scott agreed to send the 103 narratives to Katherine Johnson, who was the person creating the audit.

Was OIG Treasury taking these issues seriously?

Subject: RE: Not rhetorical question
From: Sonja Scott (OIG Treasury)
Date: Fri, Aug 16, 2019, 10:33 am
To: jbsimms
Jim – As I have said before, Treasury OIG takes these issues seriously, but is a small office and does not have the resources to investigate every loss. We are referring these matters to be reviewed by the BFS who has a team that reviews losses and other issues related to Direct Express. This team then reports back to the OIG.
Sonja

From: jbsimms
Sent: Friday, August 16, 2019, 1:54 AM
To: Sonja Scott (OIG Treasury); Richard Delmar (OIG Treasury)
Cc: Jackie Lynn ; Franklin Lemond
Subject: a review of the preliminary OIG report
Dear Ms Scott and Mr. Delmar.
Attached please find my review of the preliminary OIG 19-041 report.
If you would be so kind as to send a copy to Ms. Katherine Johnson, I would be grateful.

After I critiqued OIG Audit 19-041, Delmar sent me an email claiming I had made assertions.

Subject: RE: a review of the preliminary OIG report
From: Richard Delmar (OIG Treasury)
Date: Fri, August 16, 2019, 12:25 pm
To: jbsimms
Mr. Simms – We appreciate your interest in our audit work regarding BFS's administration of the Direct Express program. However, the standards and protocols that govern our work do not contemplate consideration or incorporation of unverified assertions and comments.
As we have previously explained, in both our audit and investigative work, we are doing all we can within the scope of our jurisdiction.
In the future, please address your concerns about Treasury programs and operations to our Hotline, at https://www.treasury.gov/about/organizational-structure/ig/Pages/OigOnlineHotlineForm.aspx, where they will be evaluated, and assigned as appropriate.
Rich Delmar
Acting Inspector General
Department of the Treasury

Delmar was blowing me off. He did not want to hear any more Direct Express victim stories.

From: jbsimms
Date: Fri, Aug 16, 2019 5:20 pm
To: Richard Delmar (OIG Treasury)
Cc: Jackie Lynn, Sonja Scott (OIG Treasury), Franklin Lemond (Plaintiff's Attorney)
Thank you for your email. I assume anything I have represented to you is unverified and unsubstantiated until someone from Treasury decides to make the effort to do so. My assertions and evidence can very well be ignored by your office if and when you choose, and your report can be skewed in any manner you wish. I have made assertions, and no one has challenged or found my assertions not to be valid. Your office is the gatekeeper of your truth, but not the whole truth.
Your is not my first interaction with government or law enforcement, and your due diligence will bear that out. If you want me to list assertions for you and have you assign a specific agent to validate or investigate my claim and have that agent report back to me with a chronological narrative report of the calls and field calls made which support the report, I will be glad to review and validate the claim made by your agent.
Sonja Scott told us that she thought you had informed us of the publication of OIG 19-041, when in fact, we received nothing from you. I would ask if you actually said you would (or did) send this to any of the victims. Luckily, Ms. Densmore found this. I hope it is not necessary for me to explain to you how important this document is, and by shielding us from this document, you have in effect harmed other victims and might have allowed the same malfeasance to occur which has affected veterans, disabled children, retirees, and other Social Security recipients.
Your hotline is a joke and referring me to this hotline is your attempt to be arrogantly dismissive.
You take my "assertions" and forward them to the hotline if you wish, or wherever you wish to send them. I am asking you for the report numbers of all the investigations associated with this matter. I will determine from these investigations if my assertions were investigated and not verified.
I do not mind having an intelligent conversation. Your office is under scrutiny as is all others.
J.B. Simms

Mr. Delmar was getting a bit testy. He knew his office failed to audit and investigate BFS and the Direct Express program. He would be trying to protect his people and his agency. I was having none of it.

Saturday, August 17, 2019

I replied to Delmar again. I told him his office was the first target.
Subject: RE: a review of the preliminary OIG report
From: jbsimms
Date: Sat, Aug 17, 2019, 10:42 am
To: Richard Delmar (OIG Treasury)
Cc: Jackie Lynn, Franklin Lemond (Plaintiff's Attorney), Sonja Scott (OIG Treasury)
Mr. Delmar,

I would prefer direct, honest, and adult communication with you. In summary of the attached email, you are now referring me to the OIG Treasury Hotline to send my "allegations."

If I had sent my "allegations" to this Hotline in February 2018 my "allegations" concerning the scope and effectiveness of OIG Treasury, reports 14-013 and 17-034 would have gone down the Black Hole and never have seen the light of day. I went to the source, Ms. Battle, who succeeded the author of 17-034, and to her credit realized that I had the evidence to prove my allegations of faulty OIG Treasury reports. This was on February 26, 2018.

OIG Treasury was my first target to expose this victimization. I knew that there was no way Comerica Bank would be able to victimize citizens without an enabler, and the original enabler was OIG Treasury. OIG Treasury enabled BFS, which used lack of consequence to name Comerica Bank as a Fiscal Agent, knowing the product was dangerous to the citizens and below par with other debit card programs. BFS also was guilty of lack of supervision, as has been echoed and confirmed by your office. I was correct in my conclusion that the said OIG Treasury reports were inadequate, which branded me within your office and at BFS.

OIG Treasury was busted.

The current investigation is a result of areas of concern exposed by me, not by any post-investigative meeting among your associates. This was your "oh yeah" moment.

My allegations concerning BFS, Comerica Bank and Conduent have been proven true as a result of over 100 case files I have delivered to your office. When I told one of your agents that I had over 50 files, I was asked to confirm the allegation. I sent the files to OIG Treasury. When I later told the same agent I had over 100 files of victims, my veracity was again challenged, and I produced the evidence.

If I make false assertions, these assertions would not affect only my reputation, but the reputation and testimony of all victims. This is no burden; this is a privilege to advocate for persons who cannot speak for themselves against pompous public sector employees who hold envious disdain for those in the private sector.

You can choose to work with us or against us. The fact that we have no vehicle to exact direct repercussions against you, OIG Treasury, and BFS other than abject shame, will not deter us from exposing the truth. Shame, as a motivating factor for the aforementioned agencies, is an impotent choice of motivator.

We can begin a new and adult dialogue when OIG Treasury "owns" what they did and performs their job as expected. The "you can't make me" attitude at OIG Treasury is the same I saw from my then teen-aged son, of whom you might be familiar by now.

I ask that you get with Ms. Katherine Johnson and review the proposed publication of the final report. I also ask that all investigations used to create this report be identified by number so the reports may be immediately accessible.

J.B. Simms

More from Nona Clarke's family

From: jbsimms
Date: Sat, Aug 17, 2019 2:50 pm
To: "Paige Clarke"
I just got this software, and you mom's messages were the first I saved.
we had good chats.
she had lots to tell.
she had much stress with the Direct Express matter. Hopefully you will be able to get the real story.
Jim

Nona's death hurt in many ways. We did have great talks. She introduced me to the issue of the "Red Pill" and other social issues.

I had voicemail messages from Nona which I wanted to share with her family. They had not heard from her for a while, and I was the person trying to help her get her money.

Subject: Re: recordings of voicemails
From: Paige Clarke
Date: Sat, August 17, 2019, 2:08 pm
To: jbsimms
They came through. Thank you for these Jim, it's so wonderful to hear her voice. And even through all of her struggles the tone in her voice sounded like she was doing well.

Sunday, August 18, 2019

Subject: a review of the preliminary OIG report
From: jbsimms
Date: Sun, Aug 18, 2019, 11:45 am
To: Michael Clements (Gen Acct Office), Walter Bayer (SSI OIG)

Dear Mr. Clements and Mr. Bayer,

I appreciate your receptiveness with respect to this struggle. While we battle with senator staffers to understand the gravity of this matter (and present to their boss) we still have to battle with OIG Treasury, which after having had a change of command have assumed am more arrogant and dismissive attitude.

The OIG Treasury report 19-041 was published, and Jackie Densmore just happened upon it. Delmar told Sonja Scott he would advise us this report was available but did not. Delmar anticipated exactly what he got, my response to the preliminary report.

I am attaching these emails and the referenced reports (OIG Treasury 19-041 and my response) for you to read. The behavior of Delmar is consistent with GAO 17-176 which was signed off by you, Mr. Clements, which exposed the lack of transparency at BFS. This lack of transparency has either expanded to OIG Treasury or originated at OIG Treasury.

I bring your attention to the gesture by Delmar asking me to refer "assertions" to the Hotline. OIG Treasury has been the beneficiary of information sent directly to them, at their request. Delmar does not appreciate someone critiquing work published from OIG Treasury. I do not need "transparency" to see the truth and know who is accountable for malfeasance.

Mr. Clements, again I appreciate our chats, and I can only be disappointed that we could not meet your prerequisites to generate another investigation. The revelation of this attitude by Mr. Delmar is certainly consistent with your report.

Jim Simms

Monday, August 19, 2019

Jackie sent a shot across the bow to Delmar.

I needed to look at the response I made to 19-041 and edit out to print.

Jackie Lynn
Attachments
Mon, Aug 19, 2019, 9:47 PM
to Richard Delmar (OIG Treasury), ScottS, Kate Berry (American Banker), Franklin Lemond (Plaintiff's Attorney), me

Dear Mr. Delmar,

I am sending you a copy of this PDF I just got from Treasury FOI area. Since whoever sent it to me did not have the guts or honesty to sign their name, and since your office is supposed to investigate all parts of the Treasury, you can begin an investigation of this FOI request and the lies and cover-up which are all over this. Then the letter gives an address to send my reply. Do I trust that my reply won't get lost for another year? I think not.

The person who sent this email to me did not read OIG Treasury 19-141. There in that report lack of oversight was stated in that report, but the FOI person lied and stated the report showed no lack of oversight and wants to charge me for copying fees. I want the name of the person who sent this to me.

First, I sent the request to the address and the fax number that is on the Treasury website. There is no way this was not received until a few weeks ago, almost a year. My request was not found hiding under a stack of papers. My request was stuck away until your OIG report was about to come out so BFS would not be embarrassed, and when your office found out in February 2018 that BFS ignored your first report, and the second report, and you did nothing about it, you did not want to be exposed. Well, you are now.

Do you think that the FOI area contacted BFS when they go my request? Do you think that someone at BFS told someone at FOI to hold off on the FOI? You got onto Mr. Simms about making claims (which ended up being right) so now I am making a claim of conspiracy between BFS and FOI sections to lie about losing my request. This email is my official request for an investigation into this matter. I want to see the communication between FOI and BFS. I want to see who found my FOI request, and where was it.

I have been told the cover up is usually worse than the crime.

I do not know how stupid you think I am. Do you not think I cannot talk to you, or that I am not talking to other people? This whole thing began with you hanging up on me, but it will end in a different way.
Your lack of response to my emails is disappointing, but then again not surprising. I would not get too comfortable in your new position. I have a feeling a demotion is in your future.
Sincerely
Jacqueline Densmore

I sent a copy of the email of my interaction with Delmar to Kate Berry. Kate would be able to get more conversation from Delmar than I had.
Jackie received an email from the Treasury regarding her FOI request of Sept 18, 2018. The email stated that her FOI request had been lost. If she does not pay for copying costs, they will close the inquiry.
I drafted a response for Jackie, and she would be sending this to Treasury. The truth was Treasury did not lose the FOI request. The request was mailed and faxed to the addresses on the Treasury website. The corruption at Treasury was evident.

Tuesday, August 20, 2019

On Tue, Aug 20, 2019, at 12:53 PM jbsimms wrote:
Dear Kate,
I just got off the phone with Jackie.
She read my response to OIG 19-041, outlined in red.
I know you have to be more diplomatic than me in your writing.
Here are the points that jump out at me:
1) The email Jackie just got telling her that her FOI request of Sept 18, 2018 was "lost" cannot be true. This failure to divulge info coincides with the timing of the publication of the OIG report.
2) Delmar's email to me, telling me that OIG Treasury is not in the business of fielding "allegations" and that if I had any concerns, to send my concerns to the Hotline, was his attempt to make me go away.
OIG Treasury is in denial; they are the first group to be held accountable for not doing their job.
BFS is corrupt as hell. Comerica knows how to "pay to play." No one is accountable, and no consequences exist. Reporters and members of congress have been scared off.
If you want to interview a former OIG auditor, whose name is on one of the reports, I will share that person's info with you.
Jim

Kate Berry believed in what Jackie, and I were doing.

Monday, September 24, 2019

OIG- US House of Representatives
Christen Stevenson-Auditor
(202) 226-1250 1100am(pst)
A brief conversation was conducted with Ms. Stevenson. It was learned that an "investigative" side of Treasury OIG exists, independent of the Audits. The OIG Hotline was given as an option, but Ms. Stevenson was told that this investigation had involved Richard Delmar, and a different perspective was necessary.
Ms. Stevenson had worked for a long time in OIG Treasury and left Treasury to work for the House of Representatives.

Wednesday, August 21, 2019

Jackie Lynn
Wed, Aug 21, 2019, 2:40 PM
to me, Sonja, Shannon
Another victim helped by you JB perhaps people should be taking notes, you could do their jobs with your eyes closed. I hope this victim will now request a paper check!

In the above email, Jackie was referring to a victim who was a veteran and did not know an option was available to receive paper checks. BFS and SSA were lying to the public by denying the option of receiving a paper check for their federal payments.

240

Thursday, August 22, 2019

Based upon the email Jackie had received, stating her FOI request submitted in September 2018 had been "lost." I felt it necessary to let Treasury and others know exactly how I felt.

I emailed Delmar and Scott. We wanted an investigation into the "lost" FOI request.

Subject: Request for OIG Treasury investigation, and effects on subsequent requests
From: jbsimms
Date: Thu, Aug 22, 2019, 10:13 am
To: Richard Delmar (OIG Treasury)
Cc: Jackie Lynn, Franklin Lemond (Plaintiff's Attorney), Kate Berry (American Banker), Sonja Scott (OIG Treasury)
Dear Mr. Delmar,

I was shocked at the hubris exhibited by the Treasury FOI office which asserted to Ms. Densmore that her FOI request (mailed and faxed using information on the Treasury FOI website) submitted in September 2018 had been "lost," which is the reason for the 11-month delay in response.

I assert to you that Ms. Densmore is fully capable of speaking for herself in this manner, but in consideration of the fact that she has a full-time job, is caring for her brother in-law who is a disabled veteran, and has a family of her own, I thought it more timely and effective to email you on her behalf.

This response also coincides with the anticipated publication of the report, hereto referred to as OIG Treasury 19-041, the final report said to be published soon. The interim report has been published, and you have received my review of this document.

The timing of the communication to Ms. Densmore from Treasury FOI can only be defined in criminal parlance; it is suspect. There is no mystery that this behavior of treachery by Treasury FOI coincides with the publication of OIG Treasury 19-041. Again, I am requesting a formal investigation into the matter of the failure of Treasury FOI officers to communicate and furnish the requested information to Ms. Densmore as is statutorily mandated.

This brings up the issue of obtaining the investigative report used in the creation of OIG Treasury 19-041. You stated that the record of the investigation could only be obtained via an FOI request. This request will be made, as you have directed, and I do not want to see the same behavior from the Treasury FOI office as has been the experience of Ms. Densmore.

As Director of OIG Treasury, you have the authority to comply with my requests. As an attorney, I assume you will not need to confer with a legal staff to understand the legitimacy of my requests and can make honest and unilateral directives.
Sincerely,
J.B. Simms

From: Michael Jackman (Aide to Rep. Keating)
Date: August 22, 2019 at 2:39:51 PM EDT
To: Jackie Lynn
Subject: RE: Email from James Erwin

I spoke with James Erwin. Senator Collins sent a letter to the Treasury back in 2014 when she was chair of the Aging Committee. James was not working in the office at that time. He asked one of his colleagues who was about the Treasury's response - he said the response did address some technical issues that the Treasury hoped to resolve. James put it, the fact that frauds have continued indicates that not all of the technical and other issues have been addressed.

James also mentioned that they have asked the Treasury's office about the current contractor selection process but have not received much information.

In the email you sent me, James refers to complaint he has filed. He tells me that his role with the Committee on Aging is to run the fraud hotline, so he often forwards scam/fraud complaints to the Federal Trade Commission. He does not know what the status of those complaints are.

Finally - I asked Richard Delmar about the vendor selection process and he says the vendor has not yet been chosen.

The FOI office of US Treasury was going to make Jackie pay for the FOI information they lost. Jackie was running into a deadline, and she sent the following to Delmar.

241

Subject: Re: Request for OIG Treasury investigation, and effects on subsequent requests
From: Jackie Lynn
Date: Thu, Aug 22, 2019, 10:49 am
To: jbsimms
Cc: Richard Delmar (OIG Treasury), Franklin Lemond (Plaintiff's Attorney)>, Kate Berry (American Banker), Sonja Scott <Sonja Scott (OIG Treasury)>
I also may add I have left numerous messages on the number provided in the email asking how to send my payment in order to receive these documents of course they have not returned my call almost as if they are trying make sure I miss the deadline date like how they lost my request the first time.
I find this sort of deception very alarming to say the least!
I do not give up,
Jackie

Friday, August 23, 2019

BFS Merges Three Cards

I had put a Google Alert on my email and received a link (see in the email below) that BFS had merged some Navy benefit debit cards and was then to be serviced by one Fiscal Agent. This was a good idea.

Subject: Suggestions?
From: jbsimms
Date: Fri, Aug 23, 2019, 3:50 am
To: Jackie Lynn, Franklin Lemond (Plaintiff's Attorney)
Cc: Richard Delmar (OIG Treasury), Sonja Scott (OIG Treasury), Thomas Santaniello (Bureau of Fiscal Service)
This is a good idea, merging 3 fiscal agents
Why doesn't the VA take benefits and put them into the same program?
When Ms. Scott asked me for a suggestion, I suggested take all veteran benefits from the Direct Express program and put in a separate program. So, why not have the same Fiscal Agent handle all benefits for all active military and inactive?
The reason victims were blocked from addressing the so-called "evaluation team" was some might see problems at BFS.
https://www.dvidshub.net/news/336578/new-eaglecash-consolidates-dods-stored-value-cards

From: jbsimms
Date: Fri, Aug 23, 2019, 2:21 pm
To: Richard Delmar (OIG Treasury), Sonja Scott (OIG Treasury)
Cc: Franklin Lemond (Plaintiff's Attorney),Jackie Kate Berry (American Banker), , "Thomas Santaniello"
Over the past 18 months, and after having made the initial call to Ms. Battle at OIG Treasury in February 2018, I can only draw one analogy of the role of OIG Treasury with respect to Bureau of Fiscal Services: appeasement. The four OIG Treasury reports, beginning with OIG Treasury 14-031, point out violations in the same fashion as Neville Chamberlain did 80 years ago to a country which had infiltrated Chamberlain's country by invitation, succession, and association. It is as if someone at OIG Treasury does not want to step on the toes of other "civil servants" for fear their own foibles will be exposed.
My father and the fathers of my friends faced the enemy which Chamberlain was afraid to face. I learned that lesson of integrity from my father.
I hope with a changing of the guard at OIG Treasury you might find your Churchill.
J.B. Simms

From: Kate Berry (American Banker)
Date: August 23, 2019 at 9:55:38 AM EDT
To: Kate Berry (American Banker)
Subject: American Banker: IG to Treasury: Don't whitewash lapses in Comerica benefits program

Kate emailed us the following story she wrote regarding OIG Treasury.

IG to Treasury: Don't whitewash lapses in the Comerica benefits program.

Below is the story written by Kate Berry.

By Kate Berry

Published August 22 2019, 9:00pm EDT

Comerica Bank or a different bank tasked with managing a government prepaid benefits program in the future should have to lose compensation for customer service blunders, according to a watchdog report.

The recent findings suggest Comerica could face more consequences over how the Texas bank handled fraud cases last year tied to the Direct Express program, which allows beneficiaries to access benefits payments through prepaid cards.

With the Treasury Department's Bureau of Fiscal Service set to decide soon whether Comerica will keep the Direct Express contract, Treasury's Office of the Inspector General released a report saying the bank's past compensation should have been cut for poor customer service. Going forward, the bureau should strengthen oversight, the IG said.

"As Treasury's financial agent, Comerica is acting as a fiduciary of the Government and as such should be encouraged to further the administration's agenda related to customer service, including compliance with Regulation E," the report said.

Comerica Bank

Comerica won the first government contract to oversee Direct Express in 2008 and the contract was renewed in 2014 despite some criticism by the Treasury OIG in prior audits over how the program was being run.

Bloomberg News

The IG is recommending that future contracts tie compensation more directly to improved customer service metrics and compliance with consumer protection law. Direct Express serves 4.5 million Social seniors, veterans and others who get federal benefits.

Several fraud victims claimed that Comerica was slow to reimburse them and, in some cases, suspended accounts and charged some cardholders fees to reissue and activate new cards, in violation of Regulation E.

"Improving the customer experience and compliance with Regulation E will increase the public trust in Direct Express and Fiscal Service," the report said. "As part of our audit, we plan to review Comerica's compliance with the Regulation E cardholder protections including the reimbursement of Direct Express cardholders' stolen benefits, including related fees."

The report, which was addressed to Bureau of Fiscal Service Commissioner Timothy E. Gribben, was released as Comerica's contract is up for renewal. The bureau plans to announce the next Direct Express agent later this summer.

Last August, the $70.6 billion-asset Comerica said it had shut down a service allowing cardholders to withdraw funds if they lost their card — even when they were away from their home state. Comerica acknowledged that fraudsters had exploited security flaws in its Cardless Benefit Access Service. The bank said one employee of Conduent, the outsourced call center operator for Direct Express, had been fired as a result of the fraud.

The IG report showed for the first time that Comerica and Conduent received poor ratings for several activities including customer service response times and compliance with regulations related to chargeback, dispute processing and dispute resolution. Direct Express uses monthly scorecards with "service level requirements."

The OIG reviewed monthly performance scorecards from early 2015 to 2018 and found that "Comerica's compensation was never reduced despite poor ratings in some categories."

"In our review of the 47 Direct Express SLR Monthly Scorecards, we noted 4 SLRs related to customer service representative response times, representing a total of 188 Final Ratings. Comerica/Conduent received the lowest possible Final Rating in 79 out of 188 instances, or 42 percent of the ratings," the report said.

Further, the report, which was released on July 29, found that the scoring system grouped Comerica's performance results in a manner where higher scores for certain activities offset lower scores for other activities, essentially skewing the results.

"We believe the co-mingling of all SLR scores does not provide an incentive or disincentive to achieve a high standard in all areas, including chargeback and dispute processing and customer service representative response times," the report said.

At one point, the report takes the bureau's management to task for inaccurately claiming that Comerica had met certain target performance goals 100% of the time.

Comerica won the first government contract to oversee Direct Express in 2008 and the contract was renewed in 2014 despite some criticism by the Treasury OIG in prior audits over how the program was being run.

"We believe that under this financial agent selection process, the SLR and target performance for the various activities need to be reviewed and revised with an emphasis on providing better customer service related to the call center and compliance with regulations related to chargeback and dispute processing," the report said. Comerica declined to comment. Conduent, a Florsheim Park, N.J., conglomerate that operates many federal benefits programs, did not respond to a request for comment.

Beneficiaries who were defrauded of funds said they were surprised that the report did not explain how — or even if — Comerica and Conduent were investigating and combating fraud.
"They should be investigating the fraud that is occurring in the call centers," said Jackie Densmore, a caregiver for her brother-in-law, Derek Densmore, a disabled Marine in Bourne, Mass., His $814 in disability payments got routed last year by fraudsters to a Walmart in Hollywood, Fla. "Fraud still continues and more victims have come forward," Jackie Densmore said.
She also faulted Comerica, the Bureau of Fiscal Service, and other government agencies including the Social Security Administration and the Department of Veterans Affairs, for urging beneficiaries to sign up for the prepaid debit cards while failing to explain that they could still receive paper checks as an alternative.
Because of privacy issues, Comerica cannot provide information to Treasury's inspector general or the Bureau of Fiscal Service on individual fraud cases. The Bureau of Fiscal Service only receives aggregate fraud data on Direct Express. The OIG said in the report that it did not have the data necessary to conduct an audit or investigation.
Instead, the OIG said it had created an authorization form that when signed by a cardholder will allow Comerica to disclose information "for the purposes of identifying and tracking unauthorized and/or fraudulent uses."
The IG report made three recommendations. First, compensation for the next Direct Express agent must be tied to performance metrics to ensure that the company is "incentivized to provide excellent service."
Second, the Bureau of Fiscal Service must request access to Reg E compliance reviews conducted by other banking regulators and use the reviews to improve oversight and the performance of the program.
Finally, the OIG said the bureau should coordinate with the agent on developing regular reports "on potential violations of federal criminal laws, including internal and external fraud relating to Direct Express."
In a letter to the OIG, Gribben agreed with all three recommendations.
"Since the inception of Direct Express in 2008, customer service and fraud protection have been a top priority," he said in the July 16 letter. "We work closely with the Direct Express financial agent and federal agencies to quickly address customer service challenges for cardholders who rely on the program to receive critical payments."
Under the government's agreement with the Direct Express agent, Treasury's IG must be notified "of any instance of a possible violation of federal criminal laws regarding fraud, conflict of interest, bribery, or illegal gratuities."
The OIG report disputed an interpretation by Bureau of Fiscal Service staff that that agreement with Comerica applies only to "insider crimes such as fraud, bribery or embezzlement by Comerica employees or its subcontractors." The OIG said the agreement "does not distinguish between internal and external violations."

The OIG also said that it had verified only four corrective actions taken by the Bureau of Fiscal Service out of 14 total recommendations made in past reports in 2014 and 2017 on Comerica and the Direct Express program. It is unclear whether the bureau is still working on the 10 outstanding recommendations.
"This is all about fraud and how cardholders are treated so poorly when they report a fraud, and how the fraud has not been investigated," Densmore said. "They are validating that they have a problem, but corrections haven't happened and there have been no repercussions for Comerica or Conduent."
Kate Berry covers the Consumer Financial Protection Bureau for American Banker.

Federal Court allows our case to be heard

Franklin Lemond, our attorney, called. We obtained a ruling on the violation of Regulation E from the federal judge in Atlanta. Jackie and I were excited, but then I had to do the research and read the ruling.

Sunday, August 25, 2019

I found the ruling from the judge and the Answer that had been filed. I found this on Pacer. The ruling also stated that only the defendants from Georgia were to be admitted in the Georgia federal district; all others must be admitted in another jurisdiction.
We would have to get an attorney in Texas to domesticate the case in Texas, and file there.
I had to confront Franklin, our attorney, for not divulging this to us.

Monday, August 26, 2019

I sent an email challenging Franklin that the ruling had been issued weeks before and he admitted sitting on the ruling. Franklin told Jackie and me he did not want to upset us.
We were not children, and this would not be the last time we had and issue with Franklin Lemond regarding withholding information from us.
Jackie and I sent a list of subpoenas to Franklin to follow up. Making his follow-up on the subpoenas was something Jackie and I had to do because Franklin just was not aggressive; he wanted to be friendly and cordial. Jackie and I were having none of that.
Franklin called- he had found an attorney in Texas and was ready to file this new summons and complaint in the Northern Texas District of federal court.
10:26am Sonja Scott called- the caller was listed as "unknown."
The audit is not done. Sonja was sure Comerica put in a bid to remain at the Fiscal Agent. She did not know why the Bureau of Fiscal Service had not announced the winner of bid. I advised her that if I had not come along, the bid would be a slam dunk.
Sonja office sent out questionnaires to a select number of people. Now waiting for responses.
We discussed debit card parameters, no offer of security as with proprietary customers for Comerica Bank, the Warren letters, and the inept Conduent fraud unit.

Sonja Scott appeared to be sympathetic to the plight of the victims, but she seemed to have no authority to be proactive in any manner. We needed someone with the guts to make something happen.

Tuesday, August 27, 2019

J B Simms
Tue, Aug 27, 2019, 11:04 AM
to Franklin, Jackie
I am a tactician. I see vulnerabilities in everyone and failure to perform. That is how the target is created.
Jackie is resourceful and asks for accountability from everyone.
Franklin supplies the law, targeted toward the person who is most vulnerable and will help us the most.
If I don't have the law as a final weapon, after I confirm the target, the target laughs at us.
If either of you read my first book, you will see to what extent I will go to win, regardless of who is keeping me from the goal.
I know the people in the cast of characters.

Thursday, August 29, 2019

We checked the OIG website. There was no listing of OIG report or of BFS having listed their new fiscal agent.
Jackie talked to Franklin. Emails from Franklin state he will be ready for subpoenas and depositions.
Wilcox talked to Jackie. Said will be tough getting fair trial in TX, home office of Comerica. Wilcox sent me a dismissive email. Wilcox forgot Jackie and I were gracious enough to submit an affidavit to help his client and he was rude and arrogant. We helped him and he was blowing us off.

From: jbsimms
Sent: Thursday, August 29, 2019, 11:43 AM
To: Sonja Scott (OIG Treasury); Richard Delmar (OIG Treasury)
Cc: Jackie Lynn
Subject: publication of the report
Dear Ms. Scott and Mr. Delmar,

Might either of you, as a courtesy, email Ms. Densmore or me to advise us of the publication of the final report on 19-041? That gesture would be greatly appreciated.
Jim

I went to the Treasury website:
I found the following notation of an OIG report:
BFS   12/14/2018
OIG-19-024 Financial Management: Management Report for the Audit of the Department of the Treasury's Consolidated Financial Statements for Fiscal Years 2018 and 2017 is Sensitive But Unclassified. To obtain a copy of this report, please contact the OIG Office of Audit at (202) 927-5400.
Another run-around from Treasury. The report is to be public not "Sensitive" or categorized in a covert fashion.

Friday, August 30, 2019

From: Richard Delmar (OIG Treasury)
Date: Fri, Aug 30, 2019, 5:00 am
To: jbsimms, Sonja Scott (OIG Treasury)
Cc: Jackie Lynn
We will send you a copy when it's published.

Delmar will send us the OIG report when ready.
He will treat my request for OIG 19-024 as an FOI and will forward it to me. Good; now if I were to believe him that would be different.

Sunday, September 1, 2019

Jackie Lynn
Sun, Sep 1, 2019, 9:37 AM
to Franklin Lemond (Plaintiff's Attorney), me
Franklin,
Given the fact the ruling from the judge came out Aug 9 2019 and you did not notify us until Aug 23 because you felt you needed a game plan before you told us. I am very dissatisfied that in 23 days you still have not locked in an attorney to represent the additional 5 plaintiffs. As you can see this does not look good for all involved.
You had mentioned an attorney that you have been trying to contact but neglected to release her name so I am asking for that name today, I would like to do some homework on this. I also would like to set a deadline of September 5, 2019 for you to lock in an attorney to represent the 5 plaintiffs. If this is not done on or before this date the victims of direct express will need to find other representation. They are prepared to do so. We believe you have had more than enough time to get this done actually you would have had exactly 27 days.
I hope to hear good news from you in the coming days or please prepare release forms for all victims as they will be requesting them.
Thank you
Jackie
The fact that Franklin Lemond withheld the fact that the ruling had been published and that the ruling was bifurcated was the inkling that we needed to stay on top of Franklin to have more up to date information.

Tuesday, September 3, 2019

From: Michael Jackman (Aide to Rep. Keating)
Date: September 3, 2019, at 1:53:51 PM EDT
To: Jackie Lynn
Subject: RE: Follow up on your last email
Jackie – I think the memorandum from Auditor Katherine Johnson says that finalists were invited to make oral presentations. That is the only reference to a hearing or oral presentation that I saw in Katherine Johnson's memo.
The memo is very interesting. It notes the difficulty that Treasury faces in reviewing individual cases of fraud, as well as some deficiencies that Comerica has demonstrated in customer service. The changes that Fiscal Services will be making to the Financial agency agreement will make some improvements, but I am wondering

if they will share info on individual cases of fraud with Congressional offices that have obtained a similar privacy release. I will follow up with Richard Delmar on that issue.
--Mike Jackman

Wednesday, September 4, 2019

After I discovered that the case was to be filed in Texas, Jackie received the following email from Franklin Lemond, our attorney.

From: Franklin Lemond (Plaintiff's Attorney)
Date: September 4, 2019 at 4:49:43 PM EST
To: Jackie Lynn
Subject: Direct Express
Jackie,
Hope your travels to Jamaica went smoothly. Just wanted to let you know that the Texas attorney from Baron & Budd that we discussed yesterday, Allen Vaught, is fully on board with the case and will be filing the complaint tomorrow. Enjoy your trip and if you have any questions, feel free to give me a call or send me an email.
Franklin

It was apparent that Jackie and I would have to follow up and challenge much of the performance of Mr. Lemond. This will become more apparent when we begin having subpoenas served and mandating federal offices to abide by the subpoenas.

Thursday, September 5, 2019

From: Franklin Lemond (Plaintiff's Attorney)>
Date: September 5, 2019, at 5:47:40 PM EST
To: Jackie Lynn
Subject: Activity in Case 5:19-cv-01075 Carnley et al v. Conduent Business Services, LLC et al Complaint
Jackie,
See below. The case has been re-filed today in Texas.

The case was filed in Texas, Case 5:19-cv-01075.

Monday, September 9, 2019

I looked up case *5:19-cv-01075* on the Pacer website. This site allowed me to access the federal case. It was observed that the suit was filed on Sept 5, 2019

Case 5:19-cv-01075

Atty: Allen R. Vaught, Vaught Law Firm, (214) 675-8603, allen@vaughtfirm.com
News article
From: "Danner, Patrick"
Date: Mon, Sep 09, 2019, 9:59 am
To: jbsimms
Lawsuit: Direct Express users defrauded; Cardholders getting federal benefits say company failed to protect them
Publication date: 9/7/2019 Page: B001 Section: Edition: State
Byline: Patrick Danner
A San Antonio federal lawsuit alleges thousands of retirees, veterans and disabled people who receive federal benefits through Direct Express prepaid debit cards were fraud victims whose claims were routinely denied.
The publication of this article above would be helpful in exposing the violations of banking law Regulation E by Comerica Bank and the administrator of the Direct Express cardholders, Conduent.

Monday, September 16, 2019

Bank card flaws and Santaniello blocking access to BFS

Subject: More obvious flaws pushed by Comerica and BFS
From: jbsimms
Date: Mon, Sep 16, 2019, 7:51 am
To: Sonja Scott (OIG Treasury), Richard Delmar (OIG Treasury)
Cc: Jackie Lynn, Franklin Lemond (Plaintiff's Attorney), , Thomas Santaniello (Bureau of Fiscal Service)
Dear Ms. Scott and Mr. Delmar,
We have communicated many times over the past year, and I have exposed many issues to you with respect to the lack of integrity and ignorance of BFS by empowering and endorsing Comerica Bank as the Fiscal Agent of the Direct Express program. Allow me to point out the following two issues as we wait for the final OIG Treasury 19-041 report.
1. Comerica Bank does not allow fund transfers from the Direct Express card. You must withdraw funds via ATM or use merchant purchase (or draft) to access funds.
2. Remember that Thomas Santaniello, posing as the guard dog for BFS, refused to allow victims of the decision of BFS to become the Fiscal Agent of the Direct Express program to address the "Evaluation Team" (the self-appointed decision-making panel) and question the actual motivation to award this obviously flawed product. Let's hope these issues are addressed in the final report, as other issues were ignored in the two previous OIG Treasury reports.
J.B. Simms

Wednesday, September 18, 2019

Franklin sent us drafts of subpoenas. Jackie and I filled out the information we were to request in the subpoenas. Jackie and I had more knowledge of who was participating in the case and Franklin needed us to send him the names of people as well as documents to be requested. We filled out the subpoenas and sent the narratives back to Franklin.

A victim evicted from her apartment; Comerica and Conduent to blame

Subject: the adversary
From: jbsimms
Date: Thu, Sep 19, 2019 8:48 pm
To: Franklin Lemond (Plaintiff's Attorney
Cc: "Jackie Lynn"
During the last 18 months, I have experienced the attempts of Comerica, Conduent, BFS, CFPB, OIG Treasury to dismiss my advocacy for the victims as someone who will become weary and fade away. The vast majority of the victims have become weary, as evidenced by Lisa Mena.
Lisa contacted me almost a year ago when her caretaker took her Direct Express debit card and used it without the knowledge or permission of Lisa. Lisa could not pay her rent. I contacted Conduent and Lisa's landlord on her behalf. Lisa was evicted during the Thanksgiving holiday last year. Lisa continued to contact me, and I continued to make her case with Conduent and Susan Schmidt of Comerica. There was no basis for the denial; charges were made at odd hours of the night by the caretaker for items Lisa would never use.
The reason Conduent denied the charges was the debate whether there was permissive use. There is no permissive use when you allow a person to use your debit card knowing the result would be that you, as a disabled person, would live in your car.
After attending to 105 victims, I began referring the victims to OIG Treasury, Sonja Scott. Ms. Scott was receptive to the victims, but she referred the matter of the victims to BFS and Comerica to be investigated. There is the joke; Comerica/Conduent and BFS caused the problem. Their goal in life was CYA, not accountability. Ms. Scott never revealed any person to whom she referred cases.
Today I received an email from Lisa. She had communicated with Sonja Scott. Ms. Scott revealed to Lisa that Comerica's stance was the funds were taken as a result of theft, not fraud. As a layman, let me give you the logical theory of the definition of what happened.

I was on the phone with the landlord and with Lisa many times. Comerica Bank and Conduent ignored Lisa, as were many other victims using the Direct Express debit card.

Thursday, September 19, 2019

Jackie called me. She told me Franklin just noted he just found the two OIG reports from 2014 and 2017. Jackie and I laughed at his jubilation because I had accessed the read the same reports in February 2018, 19 months prior.

This was too funny.

Michael Jackman, the staffer for Representative Keating, had been acting on behalf of Jackie Densmore. Mr. Jackman agreed to act on behalf of Jackie, who was a constituent of Representative Keating. Below is an email sent to Mr. Jackman by a person named "Tom" who might have been Thomas Santaniello of BFS.

From: Jackman, Michael
Sent: Thursday, September 20, 2018 10:47 AM
To: 'Jackie Lynn'
Subject: Direct Express Card Program and Densmore Fraud Issue
Jackie—here are the responses we received from Bureau of Fiscal Services. I have forwarded questions 5 and 6 directly to Richard Delmar. —Mike Jackman
Mr. Jackman, thank you for your questions concerning the Direct Express card program and your constituents the Densmore family. The following are responses to your questions. Thanks Tom

Q1. How much federal funding has been diverted due to fraud committed against the Cardless Benefit Program that Comerica recently suspended? Please provide a breakdown by agency (ie Social Security, VA, etc.)
A1. No federal funds are diverted in the case of fraud on a Direct Express card. All fraud losses for the Direct Express program are losses to Comerica— not to Treasury or Direct Express cardholders.
Q2. In an instance such as Ms. Densmore's case, when Comerica has disbursed funds to a fraudulent recipient, who funds the "make-whole" payment to the rightful recipient—Comerica or the Treasury?
A2. The "make-whole" payment to the rightful recipient is funded by Comerica.
Q3. How much is Treasury currently paying to Comerica to manage each Direct Express Account? (I have heard $5 and $2—which is accurate?) Also was this fee written into the original Fiscal Agent Agreement between Comerica and the Treasury?
A3. The exact fees paid to Financial Agents are confidential commercial information and/or trade secrets of the Financial Agent and therefore not for public dissemination.
Q4. How much has Treasury paid to Comerica to maintain "unused accounts"? What is the purpose of maintaining these unused accounts, especially given that the OIG reports that their existence could make the Direct Express program more vulnerable to fraud? What is Treasury's current position on maintaining an inventory of unused accounts?
A4. Treasury does not pay Comerica to maintain unused accounts. Following the IG's 2017 report, Fiscal Service re-assessed the treatment of unused accounts in the Direct Express program. Fiscal Service concluded that the treatment of unused accounts is appropriate and does not create or heighten fraud risks.
Q5. I understand that, as part of its auditing, the Office of the Inspector General of the Dept of the Treasury now requires Comerica to report all suspected cases of criminal fraud to OIG. How many cases of fraud have been reported since this requirement was put into place? What is the success rate in prosecuting these cases of fraud? What is OIG's role in investigating these reports of fraud?
A5. This question has been forwarded to OIG for their response.
Q6. Please describe what OIG and/or Comerica have done in the case of fraud perpetrated upon the Densmore family. Have either OIG or Comerica made contact with any local law enforcement officials in support of investigative efforts?
A6. The Densmore family case concerning the Direct Express card is considered private financial information and cannot be disclosed without an appropriate Privacy Act release. As you are aware, this case has been resolved. Treasury OIG has advised that it has been in contact with a representative of the Densmore family, and is actively taking appropriate steps regarding their allegations and concerns.
Q7. What is the status of the Dept of Treasury's agreement with Comerica/Direct Express to provide this service? If this is the subject of a contract, when does the contract expire? Are there efforts underway to extend or renew this contract? What anti-fraud provisions are written into the current agreement between Comerica and the Treasury?

A7. Comerica operates the Direct Express program as Treasury's Financial Agent under a Financial Agency Agreement that expires on January 2, 2020. Financial Agents are designated under statutory authority to provide banking and other services to Treasury. See, for example, 12 USC 90.
The current Financial Agency Agreement provides that Comerica must extend Regulation E protections to cardholders. Regulation E is the primary consumer protection rule covering bank accounts, pursuant to which cardholders are protected from losses for unauthorized transactions to their accounts. The Financial Agency Agreement provides that Comerica is liable for any loss or claim arising under Regulation E. Comerica is subject to fraud and risk management control audits and examinations with respect to the Direct Express program by its prudential regulators, which include the Federal Reserve Bank of Dallas, the FDIC and the Texas Department of Banking.
Oddly, I contacted most of these regulators and none admitted having supervisory responsibility.

Bureau of Fiscal Service (BFS) was telling Mr. Jackman that the Fiscal Agent (Comerica Bank), "must extend Regulation E protection to cardholders." We knew this was a lie and our federal lawsuit was based upon this lie. BFS was not monitoring Comerica Bank or Conduent.

Friday, September 20, 2019

Jackie's FOI request was ignored, and OIG reports delayed.

From: Jackie Lynn
Date: Fri, Sep 20, 2019, 3:09 pm
To: jbsimms
Cc: Richard Delmar (OIG Treasury), Franklin Lemond (Plaintiff's Attorney)>, Allen Vaught <allen@vaughtfirm.com>
Mr. Delmar
I'm not sure why you neglect to follow up on my FOIA REQUEST as it has been over a year and still no answers. I am starting to feel that I am being treated differently and my requests have been ignored by you and your office, perhaps because I am a woman? I have followed all protocols and yet no answers or documents, this is quite concerning. I see that you are willing to post the whole report on Mr. Simms request however you fail to list a date this report will be coming out.
I also was told the OIG report on Direct express would Be published at the end of summer perhaps you should look at your calendar considering it's fall already! When is this report going to be released?
thank you for your time,
Jackie Densmore

Wednesday, September 25, 2019

Jackie Lynn
Wed, Sep 25, 2019, 11:11 AM
to Richard Delmar (OIG Treasury), Walter.Bayer, me, Michael, ScottS, Franklin Lemond (Plaintiff's Attorney)
Good Afternoon,
Upon doing some research to find out when the OIG report was going to be issued I came across this link I wanna point out to all of you the date August 7, 2019!
I see they are still claiming these cards are safe and easy to use which we all know was a lie.
Why would they be releasing this information if Comerica bank was not the chosen fiscal agent???   Do they know something we don't know?
https://secure.ssa.gov/poms.nsf/lnx/0202402007

This link was to a promotion by Social Security (see SSA in the link) which promoted the Direct Express Debit Card, stating it was a safe and secure manner in which to receive Social Security payments.
As Jackie said, this was a lie, and we were proving it was a lie. We did not know why SSA was so attached to this program. We also knew that the VA was promoting the Direct Express cards, but our battle with the VA (my battle) would bear fruit in a few months.

Subject: sharing of information with BFS
From: jbsimms
Date: Wed, Sep 25, 2019, 7:12 am
To: Richard Delmar (OIG Treasury), Sonja Scott (OIG Treasury)
Cc: Jackie Lynn, Franklin Lemond (Plaintiff's Attorney), "Allen Vaught" <allen@vaughtfirm.com>
Dear Mr. Delmar and Ms. Scott,

While the lack of comprehensive investigations of BFS by OIG Treasury brought us to this point, I am interested in knowing the interaction and sharing of agenda by OIG Treasury with BFS with regard to OIG Treasury 19-041. It is no coincidence that BFS has delayed the announcement of the Fiscal Agent for the Direct Express program (which was to be May 19, 2019) and I am interested to know what communication is there between OIG Treasury and BFS with regard to naming this (hopefully) new Fiscal Agent.

We know the circumstances surrounding the naming of Comerica Bank as Fiscal Agent on two previous occasions are suspect. OIG Treasury reports did note incomplete and erroneous information within Comerica Bank application information but there was no recourse against BFS for allowing these transgressions.

It is apparent that BFS is waiting for the publication of OIG Treasury 19-041 before making their announcement so as to not conflict with the results of the upcoming report. This delay might be interpreted as if this current investigation is a bit more thorough that the past investigations, which we hope is the case. Hopefully, BFS dare not appear as a petulant child and rename Comerica Bank as the Fiscal Agent "because they can."

My concern is the communication and collaboration between OIG Treasury and BFS, and what information is shared or leaked to BFS during the "investigation" that gives BFS the opportunity for damage control versus accountability, sanctions, penalties, and public exposure of malfeasance by officials at BFS. You are aware BFS refused to allow Direct Express cardholder victims the opportunity to address the "evaluation team" as the deliberation was being made to award the contract as Fiscal Agent for the Direct Express program. Santaniello did his job as the buffer between the cardholders and that faux deliberative body which he identified as the evaluation team.

This investigation by OIG Treasury (19-041) is supposedly being conducted as any investigation, with the subject of the investigation not being privy to information being gathered by the investigator. Our attorneys might be able to couch a direct question to your office in a more eloquent manner, but the question remains, "What information/communication is being shared/conducted by OIG Treasury agents with BFS (Gribbens or Santaniello) with respect to the ongoing investigation (19-041)?"
Sincerely,
J.B. Simms

No Fiscal Agent announced; still questioning the VA

Subject: Leaking of proprietary information
From: jbsimms
Date: Wed, Sep 25, 2019, 11:44 am
To: Richard Delmar (OIG Treasury), Sonja Scott (OIG Treasury)
Cc: Sarah Lizama (SSA OIG), Jackie, Pamela Powers (Chief of Staff, VA)
Dear Mr. Delmar and Ms. Scott,

It appears that leaking of proprietary information in Washington is not limited to House committees.
The following link was forwarded to me:
https://secure.ssa.gov/poms.nsf/lnx/0202402007
This is the updated version, August 2019, of the Social Security website. You will see that the Social Security Administration is touting the benefits of the Direct Express program, and the fact that Comerica Bank is securely managing this program.

Does the Social Security Administration have access to information from OIG Treasury (or BFS) that the rest of us do not have?

Although OIG Treasury has not published the final report of OIG Treasury 91-041, and BFS has not announced which bank has been awarded the new BFS Fiscal Agent contract, I find it quite odd that Soc Sec Admin would continue to advertise and promote Comerica Bank as the continuing Fiscal Agent.

I have not checked the VA website, but have had brief communication with Ms. Powers, COS of VA. She has stated she is aware of the issues with the Fiscal Agent (Comerica Bank) but there is no evidence of any acknowledgement from Paul Lawrence, who heads up VAB.

If during your investigation one of your agents is illegally sharing information with BFS or the VA, I assume you would want to know this. No law enforcement agency confers with a suspect to share info, and BFS, Comerica Bank, and Conduent are your suspects.
Jim

Thursday, September 26, 2019

Subject: info needed and might need a favor
From: jbsimms
Date: Thu, Sep 26, 2019, 3:27 pm
To: Sonja Scott (OIG Treasury)
Cc: "Jackie Lynn"
Who is the agent of service for US Treasury? I am going to assume it would be the Office of General Counsel at OIG, which is the position vacated by Mr. Delmar. Someone is sitting in his old spot.
Can you enlighten me?
I have an issue to discuss with the FBI. I visited their office in Fresno on Tuesday, Sept 24 and was given a cutout piece of paper with websites to access and phone number to call to "get an appointment" in their office. Of course, the telephone number is a national number that leads a person through a maze that does not allow a person any resolution.
I am going to return to this office and tape the cutout to the door of the office, noting that I adhered to the directions, and attach a business card that has my name and telephone number. This matter possibly involves the matter in which we are involved. If I can politely get past the Quantico attitude and give a reference as to who I am and what is happening, I might have to drop your name, and maybe that of Mr. Delmar.
There are other references I can use, but as I stated, this might involve our issues.
Jim

From: Michael Jackman (Aide to Rep. Keating)
Date: September 26, 2019 at 4:28:43 PM EDT
To: Jackie Lynn
Subject: RE: Follow up
Today I sent another request asking Richard Delmar for:
--final decision on vendor selection
--list of finalists
--copy of sample Financial Agent Agreement
These are all items I have been requesting for several months.
In addition, I asked that the Dept give your FOIA request its full and fair consideration.
--Mike Jackman

Friday, September 27, 2019

Jackie Lynn
Fri, Sep 27, 2019, 12:00 PM
to Franklin Lemond (Plaintiff's Attorney), me, Allen
Hi Franklin I received a call from Senator Warren's office from Jessica Wong regarding my case a couple of things she touched upon was she wants me to fill out a privacy release for my FOIA request she's very unhappy with the fact that it's taking as long as it has so going to her office will definitely speed this process up she also said that the letters that Senator Warren received from Ralph Babb ,Social Security Administration and Veterans Affairs -they are not willing to release so she said that a subpoena would be needed in order to get those letters because without them we will not be receiving them as far as the 2020 contract and the OIG report she has reached out to both Departments neither one of them have given them a definitive answer on any dates in fact she relayed to me that the bureau of fiscal service is still in the selection process and do not know who the fiscal agent will be at this time.
I pointed out the timeframe that they have until the 2020 contract and let her know it would be absolutely impossible to reroute cards in the short period of time that they have so that they should be putting some pressure on BFS to make that announcement sooner than later however she was reluctant to do that in fear by rushing the selection process they don't want to be responsible for making any mistakes in that process. 😊

I'm going to reach out to some media outlets and see if I can get people to hold these agencies accountable for missing deadline dates.

I know in your last email you stated that you did not want to send subpoenas to the Senators office only as a last resort however I feel this is the only way we are going to get them and feel we should act quickly on it now.

Do you think you can send them out by Monday? If not, can you please explain reason as to why Thanks. Jim

Monday, September 30, 2019

From: Jackie Lynn
Sent: Monday, September 30, 2019, 11:09 AM
To: jbsimms
Cc: Richard Delmar (OIG Treasury); Sonja Scott (OIG Treasury)
Subject: Re: promises, promises FOI requests and 19-024
Jim,
Thank you for always stepping up to the plate. I can assure Rich and Sonja that withholding my documents as requested will only prove the corruption that goes on in these organizations. I have never Shied away from media and this is top on their list. You both with be hearing from very big news reporters in the coming weeks. I can only hope I will see both of you in court soon uncovering all the stuff you both have brushed under the rug What you did to allow my request to be ignored is disgusting, I have rights and I intend to use them .
Jackie

From: Richard Delmar (OIG Treasury)
Date: September 30, 2019 at 3:05:30 PM EDT
To: 'Jackie Lynn', jbsimms
Cc: Sonja Scott (OIG Treasury)
Subject: RE: promises, promises FOI requests and 19-024
Ms. Densmore and Mr. Simms – thanks for your input. Here's what I advised Rep. Keating's staff person last week:
I've asked BFS's Chief Counsel to track the status of Ms. Densmore's FOIA request.
The last action of which I'm aware is BFS's 8/15/19 reply to Ms. Densmore.
I have followed up with our Office of Audit to assure that report OIG-19-024 is posted on our web site.
I have also inquired of Treasury's central FOIA processing office about Mr. Lemond. They report no record of a request from anyone with that name. Can you provide further information?

Subject: promises, promises FOI requests and 19-024
From: jbsimms
Date: Mon, Sep 30, 2019, 3:54 pm
To: Richard Delmar (OIG Treasury)
Cc: Sonja Scott (OIG Treasury), Franklin Lemond (Plaintiff's Attorney), "Jackie Lynn"
It is my understanding that Ms. Densmore submitted her FOI request on September 18, 2018. She not only submitted the FOI in mailing on that date and faxed the same document to the telephone number given on the website.
If Mr. Keating is in the FOI section, then he might be the person responsible for receiving this, but I am not certain who is ultimately responsible. I seem to remember reading that Chief Counsel of OIG is responsible for overseeing the FOI procedure.
The statement made by the FOI office that Densmore's request was sent to the wrong address is not true. She also faxed this to them. I can go through my emails and confirm this.
I am aware of the FOI because I was heavily involved in the creation of this document. If Mr. Lemond is motivated to use Discovery to expose the chain of command of this request, we certainly have the supporting documents to prove my assertion that the procedures spelled out on the Treasury website were followed to the letter.
Please advise me of the agent of service for the Department of Treasury so we may have pleadings served in an effective manner, and not have to experience the withholding of documents and veracity as with the FOI office.
I hope you are as tired of this as I am. We both have multiple witness malfeasance on the part of BFS and the OIG office. You did step up and commission 19-041 as a result of my bidding. Things work differently in the private sector. People get called out. People get fired. People are more accountable. I wish we felt that complete candor would be possible.

253

Please let us know when the questions submitted by Ms. Densmore in her FOI request of September 18, 2018 is ready, and the agent of process for Treasury.
Jim

Tuesday, October 2, 2019

Jackie sent a copy of article printed by Sandra Chapman about Kreegar.
The Watchdog agency created a new tracking option for Direct Express fraud victims.
Jennifer Kreegar's benefits were stolen from her account. (Photo: WTHR)

SANDRA CHAPMAN
PUBLISHED: SEP 26TH, 2019 - 8:12PM (EDT)
UPDATED: SEP 27TH, 2019 - 12:59AM (EDT)
INDIANAPOLIS (WTHR) - A government watchdog agency says it was in the dark about half a million dollars stolen from retiree and disability accounts.
The money was snatched right out of Direct Express bank accounts without alerts to the U.S. Treasury. In fact, thieves siphoned cash from one Indiana veteran.
13 Investigates has learned the company handling the payments for 4 million people will now face new oversight.
The Office of the Inspector General is stepping in to track the fraud and to provide help to victims.
An investigation conducted by the Office of Senator Elizabeth Warren discovered 480 people had their money virtually disappear out of their government accounts last year.
Now 13 Investigates has learned the Inspector General of the U.S. Treasury didn't know about the widespread fraud because the company contracted to administer the Direct Express program failed to report it. A treasury memo shows there was confusion over reporting requirements. The Treasury Inspector General issued recommendations to change that.
•RELATED: Consumer alert: Thieves are stealing VA and social security benefits from retirees, disabled
13 Investigates first learned about thieves stealing retirement and disability benefits when an Indianapolis veteran came forward to say it happened to her.
Jennifer Kreegar said one minute her monthly VA disability check was there, and the next, it was gone.
Someone had gotten into Kreegar's account and changed her address without her knowledge. Then, almost three weeks later, the thieves canceled her card and had a new one expedited to Georgia. She never got a single alert about the changes until the end of the month, and by then it was too late.
By the time she discovered the fraud, all but $10 had been swiped.

When she went to put in her social security number, she discovered her information no longer matched the records Direct Express had in its system. She was, in effect, locked out of her own account. She recalls the panic that flushed over her.
"You're trying frantically to get through on the line, but you can't talk to a person," she told 13 Investigates.
The Inspector General of the Treasury said victims like Kreegar weren't the only ones caught off guard and unaware of what to do.
In a memo to the Commissioner of the U.S. Bureau of Fiscal Services, the Audit Director, Katherine Johnson, said the Office of the Inspector General of the Treasury was supposed to be alerted within one week of "any instance of a possible violation of federal criminal laws." And that alert should have come related to the fraud in the Direct Express Program.
But Fiscal Services said due to the Right to Financial Privacy Act (RFPA), Comerica, the bank with the Direct Express contract, only reported "insider crimes" of fraud, bribery or embezzlement by its employees or subcontractors.
The OIG said that interpretation is inaccurate and that the limited information Comerica provided about fraud in the Direct Express program was not enough to launch an audit or investigation. That is why the Inspector General's Office said it was unaware of the extent of the fraud involving nearly 500 victims nationwide, including Kreegar.
Fiscal Services maintained that Comerica would need a subpoena or signed authorization to release more-detailed information about the fraud cases reported.
In order to close the reporting gap, the Inspector General recommended Comerica Bank provide a means of authorization for Direct Express cardholders.

254

It means victims will get to choose to have their fraud cases investigated by the Inspector General's office and tracked for three months to ensure the cases are resolved appropriately. It will also give the Treasury better oversight of the entire benefits program.

Franklin email response:

Jim,
I'm happy to explain the status of discovery. When discovery opened on September 23, I served counsel for Defendants with the Interrogatories and Requests for Production of documents that I had shared with you and Jackie prior to that date. That same day, I also sent opposing counsel copies of the affidavits that I had previously circulated, which I am required to do by rule prior to having the third parties formally served with the subpoenas. Subsequently, I sent the subpoenas to the private process server so that they can personally serve the subpoenas. The process server owes me an update on whether the subpoenas have been formally served. Once the subpoenas are formally served, I will receive an affidavit of service and will file the same with the Court. I hope that clears things up.
Franklin

Wednesday, October 2, 2019

From: *Franklin Lemond (Plaintiff's Attorney)*
Date: *Wed, Oct 02, 2019, 2:01 pm*
To: *Jbsimms*
Cc: *Jackie Lynn*
Jim,
I'm confident that Nora is or will become aware of the interrogatories and requests for production. She is responsible for managing the Direct Express program, so I don't see how Comerica could legitimately respond to the discovery requests we have served without her participation. Plus, they already identified her as a potential witness in the Defendants' Initial Disclosures (attached).
Franklin

Thursday, October 3, 2019

Curtis Farmer replaces Ralph Babb as CEO of Comerica

Curtis C. Farmer Named Comerica's Chief Executive Officer; Ralph W. Babb Jr. Assumes Title of Executive Chairman

Subject: RE: Veteran victimized by Comerica Bank/Conduent, failing to report fraud, allows more fraud
From: *jbsimms*
Date: *Wed, Oct 02, 2019, 1:15 pm*
To: *Richard Delmar (OIG Treasury), Sonja Scott (OIG Treasury), Pamela Powers (Chief of Staff, VA),, Sarah Lizama (SSA OIG) Cc:"Jackie Lynn"*
I wanted to thank you at OIG Treasury for being receptive to this matter and continue to receive fraud complaints. Months ago Ms. Scott opened the door to receive complaints, and victims have told me of their interaction with Ms. Scott, and the results. The fact that veterans such as Ms. Kreegar now have a remedy to the failed security parameters of the Direct Express program, and lack of oversight (as well as unexplained enabling) by BFS gives us a bit of comfort.
Veterans, and others, do not deserve to be treated as second class citizens. Hopefully those guilty of this malfeasance will be held accountable.
Jim

Friday, October 4, 2019

Franklin acknowledged subpoenas were served.
Mastercard was served on 10/3/19.
BFS was served 10/4/19.
OIG Treasury and VA have to be served.

From: Franklin Lemond (Plaintiff's Attorney)>
Date: Fri, Oct 04, 2019 1:24 pm
To: Jackie Lynn, jbsimms
JB & Jackie,
See below. BFS has been served with the subpoena. As soon as I get the affidavit of service, I will file it with the court.
Franklin

Subject: subpoenas
From: jbsimms
Date: Fri, Oct 04, 2019, 4:25 pm
To: Sonja Scott (OIG Treasury)
Cc: "Jackie Lynn"
Dear Ms. Scott,
I just got notice that BFS was served a subpoena (I think I was sent a copy, but I don't remember, but will look). I do hope Mr. Delmar can light a fire under FOI to reply to Ms. Densmore's request of Sept 2018 without more litigation and procrastination.
Jim

Monday, October 7, 2019

Kate Berry
Mon, Oct 7, 2019, 11:51 AM
to jbsimms, me, Jackiedenzz@yahoo.com
Hi Jackie, J.B. --
I got a call from a woman, Sandra Galvez, who thinks she accidentally left her DirectExpress card at a Wal-Mart and someone found it, used it, and used up her remaining monthly benefits of roughly $560.
I just got off the phone with her. She had left a sad VM for me in which she started crying about being unable to pay her bills. It just breaks my heart.
I gave her the link to file a complaint with the CFPB, and also to call Nora Arpin and Wendy Bridges at Comerica.
But you guys are the cavalry --- is there anything else we can do?
DirectExpress gave her the run-around, told her to file a police report (she did,) then said only the policy could look at Wal-Mart video to try to find the person but the police wouldn't do anything.
Hope you guys are both doing well.
kate

Sent copy of the DE twitter notice to JD, FL, and OIG (RD and SS.)
Looked at DE website. Someone said it was a new site.
I did not know who created it.
 Here is what was posted:
9. The U.S. Department of the Treasury encourages recipients to consider the Direct Express® Card
9.1 Will the U.S. Department of the Treasury mandate the use of this card for benefit recipients who currently use paper checks and don't have a checking or savings account?
The U.S. Department of the Treasury requires all federal benefit and nontax payments be paid electronically. Anyone applying for benefits, must choose an electronic payment method at the time they apply for the benefit. Those already receiving federal benefits by paper check must contact their paying agency to switch to an electronic payment method. Benefit recipients can choose to receive their payments by direct deposit to the bank or credit union account of their choice or to a Direct Express® Debit MasterCard® card account. For more information, please visit www.GoDirect.gov.

More bull.

Franklin Lemond (Plaintiff's Attorney)
Attachments
Oct 7, 2019, 2:18 PM
to Jackie, me
Jackie,
Attached are the 5 subpoenas that are out for service - keep in mind that the MasterCard and the initial BFS subpoenas have already been served.
I am trying to finalize the subpoena that we discussed on Friday.
Franklin

The five subpoenas were to OIG Treasury, Mastercard, BFS Treasury (2), and OIG SSA

Tuesday, October 8, 2019

From: Jackie Lynn
Date: October 8, 2019, at 5:06:03 PM EDT
To: FOIA <FOIA@fiscal.treasury.gov>
Cc: Richard Delmar (OIG Treasury), Michael Jackman <michael.jackman@mail.house.gov>
Subject: Re: 2019-08-012 FOIA Clarification Request
Here is the clarification you are looking for; I would greatly appreciate a time frame when to expect the cost as well as these documents. For any other questions or clarification needed please reach out to me. Any more delay in this time sensitive information is not needed and can easily be resolved with a quick phone call.
AS YOU MAY HAVE NOTICED I HAVE COPIED RICHARD DELMAR OF OIG TREASURY IN THESE EMAILS AND MICHEAL JACKMAN OF CONGRESSMEN KEATINGS OFFICE. HOPEFULLY THERE WILL BE NO MORE UNNECESSARY DELAYS IN THIS PROCESS
Inquiry #1
The "original offering" refers to the original application and any documents submitted by Comerica Bank prior to naming Comerica Bank as the original fiscal agent.
Inquiry #3
I am requesting all submissions of all bidding banks for each of the first two appointments as Fiscal Agent of the Direct Express program. This will include forms completed, letters, and email communication between employees of Bureau of Fiscal Service and Comerica Bank.
Inquiry #6
I am requesting copies of all communication between Comerica Bank and Bureau of Fiscal Service beginning with the date Comerica Bank was named as the original Fiscal Agent, and the alteration of the terms of agreement of the original contract by Bureau of Fiscal Service.
Inquiry #7
This inquiry might seem to overlap Inquiry #6, but for clarification, I am specifically requesting all correspondence from any Bureau of Fiscal Service employee prior to the alteration of the original FAA, including but not limited to Nora Arpin and Ralph Babb of Comerica Bank.
Inquiry #9
This inquiry requests copies of communication of Bureau of Fiscal Service with any members of the Board of Directors of Comerica Bank from the time of the naming of Comerica Bank as Fiscal Agent of the Direct Express program.
Inquiry #10
This inquiry requests communication between current and former Bureau of Fiscal Service and Comerica Bank subsequent to Comerica Bank being named the original Fiscal Agent and prior to the establishment of the amended FAA. The clarification on this request includes former employees.
Inquiry #12
The interpretation of the inquiry is correct: All invoices and payments made to Comerica Bank with regard to the Direct Express FAA is requested.
Inquiry #22
I will limit this inquiry to include any inquiry made by the FBI or US Treasury OIG (or any Treasury Agent) with respect to reports of fraud reported by Direct Express cardholders.

On Oct 8, 2019, at 4:40 PM, Jackie Lynn wrote:

FOIA Disclosure Office
Bureau of Fiscal Service
RE: FOIA #2019-08-012
Dear Sir/Madam,

I have received your email, dated October 8, 2019 in reference to my FOIA request which, in Paragraph 3 of your email, you acknowledged was received by your office on September 18, 2018. Thus, your response violated federal statutes, and we will proceed at this point.

Paragraph 3 of your email also acknowledged that there were 31 inquiries, of which your office needed clarification on inquiries number 1, 3, 6, 7, 9, 10, 12, and 22, being eight (8) total clarification requests. If my math serves me correctly, that leave 23 inquiries which of which you need no clarification and could have forwarded to me, but you did not. I consider this a continued lack of good faith and continued violation of the federal FOIA statute.

I request you forward me the answers to the 23 inquires immediately. I will email you the clarification of the eight inquiries today.

Please include a telephone number and identification of the FOIA officer who has been assigned this inquiry, and who sent me the referenced email.

Sincerely
Jacqueline Densmore

On Oct 8, 2019, at 11:05 AM, FOIA <FOIA@fiscal.treasury.gov> wrote:

Ms. Densmore:
Please see the attached letter concerning the above-mentioned FOIA request.
Sincerely,
****

FOIA Disclosure Office
Office of Legislative & Public Affairs
Bureau of the Fiscal Service
U.S. Department of the Treasury

Monday, October 7, 2019

Subject: Misleading and erroneous information
From: jbsimms
Date: Mon, Oct 07, 2019, 3:03 pm
To: Richard Delmar (OIG Treasury), Sonja Scott (OIG Treasury), "Thomas Santaniello" Thomas Santaniello (Bureau of Fiscal Service)
Cc: Jackie Lynn, "Franklin Lemond
Dear Mr. Delmar et al.,

After learning that Comerica Bank revived the cash advance program at Walmart (of which there were no security parameters) after the program was suspended in Aug 2018, We are searching for the reason and the authority given which allowed this to occur. We assume since Mr. Santaniello has been chosen to be the point person on this matter, I would like a direct answer from him.

I looked at the website for Direct Express, and evidently some entity, we assume is BFS that controls this website, is touting a new and improved website. Upon making a passing glance at the website, it was discovered that misleading and erroneous information was posted on the website. If BFS maintains the website, they are responsible for posting such misinformation. Whatever entity controls this site (and I will make that determination) is responsible for the malfeasance.

This site is recruiting recipients to use the Direct Express card. Evidently the use of this card benefits someone, and if BFS is being used as the carnival barker for Comerica Bank, there must be some remuneration to officials at BFS to spew this to the unknowing.

Read this from the website:
9. The U.S. Department of the Treasury encourages recipients to consider the Direct Express® Card
9.1 Will the U.S. Department of the Treasury mandate the use of this card for benefit recipients who currently use paper checks and don't have a checking or savings account?
The U.S. Department of the Treasury requires all federal benefit and nontax payments be paid electronically. Anyone applying for benefits, must choose an electronic payment method at the time they apply for the

benefit. Those already receiving federal benefits by paper check must contact their paying agency to switch to an electronic payment method. Benefit recipients can choose to receive their payments by direct deposit to the bank or credit union account of their choice or to a Direct Express® Debit MasterCard® card account. For more information, please visit www.GoDirect.gov.

BFS was implicating the entire US Treasury, including OIG Treasury, to validate this flawed and circumspect program? I would assume that Mr. Delmar would want to know who authorized the maker of this website to usurp his endorsement after having commissioned an investigation of BFS and Comerica over 16 months ago. If BFS thinks that Ms. Densmore and I do not see the obvious sham being presented to future recipients, they are sadly mistaken, and your day will come hopefully in our presence.
J.B. Simms

The secret BFS Mentoring Program

The Bureau of Fiscal Service secretly created a "mentor program" for banks that want to participate as fiscal agents of Treasury, as is Comerica Bank.

Subject: US Bank Mentoring program
 From: jbsimms
Date: Wed, Oct 09, 2019, 12:08 am
To: susan.beatty@usbank.com
Cc: Jackie Lynn, Kate Berry (American Banker)
Dear Ms. Beatty,

I, along with Ms. Denmore, have been the moving force that has resulted in the filing of several federal lawsuits against one of the Fiscal Agents designated by Bureau of Fiscal Service. On May 19, 2019, Bureau of Fiscal Services was to have appointed the new (or incumbent) Fiscal Agent for the Direct Express debit card program. This appointment has been delayed and not fulfilled.

Documents, affidavits, and narratives of over 100 victims detailing the failure of the current Fiscal Agent, Comerica Bank, have been presented to the Office of Inspector General, and we are in constant, almost daily, contact with the Acting Director of OIG Treasury Richard Delmar and US Treasury Agent Sonja Scott. Ms. Densmore and I have been out front on this matter, leaving the attorneys to use the information we supply to create their pleadings.

My allegation made in February 2018 of malfeasance, failure to protect cardholders, and violation(s) of Regulation E (15USC1693) by Fiscal Agent Comerica Bank was the genesis for the much-anticipated report, OIG Treasury 19-041. The preliminary report was published July 29, 2019, and after receiving my critique of said report, we await the final report.

A federal judge in the North District of GA recently ruled Comerica Bank did violate Regulation E with regard to the Direct Express card holders. Bureau of Fiscal Services blocked cardholders from making inquiries, which led me to go directly to the Office of Inspector General of Treasury.

After reading the article published in Business Wire (October 2, 2019) which announced US Bank would be mentoring First Independence Bank, it leads me to believe that my assertion that the supervisory capability of Bureau of Fiscal Service, which I called into question and is a focal point of the investigation by OIG Treasury, has been validated. I can only wish Comerica Bank had a mentor instead of cardholders being victimized both by fraudsters and the bank controlling their welfare and livelihood.

It would be good that First Independence Bank take over the Direct Express program under the direction and supervision of US Bank.

I would like to schedule a conference with you, Ms. Densmore, and myself. We both were victims of the Direct Express program and will take this matter to the end. I certainly look forward to your reply.
Sincerely,
J.B. Simms

Subject: News from BFS that has not been discussed re US Bank
 From: jbsimms
Date: Wed, Oct 09, 2019 12:19 am
To: Richard Delmar (OIG Treasury), Sonja Scott (OIG Treasury)
Cc: "Jackie Lynn"
I assume both of you have heard about this. [website stating US Bank in Mentoring Program]
You think First Independence Bank could do a better job, having US Bank as a mentor, than Comerica Bank having Bureau of Fiscal Service's "oversight" and direction?

The need for a mentor validates my "assertion" that BFS failed in its mandate to oversee Comerica Bank and the Direct Express program. I hope this validation is entered into the final 19-041 report. Even a federal judge concurred with my assertion.

If you can let us know if First Independence Bank is in the running to be the next Fiscal Agent, or comment on the news article, I am certain we both would love to hear from either or both of you.

Jim

Thursday, October 10, 2019

Jackie Lynn
Oct 10, 2019, 6:46 AM
to Bernice, ScottS, Sarah. Lizama, me
Bernice ,
Thank you for sending me this email and for reaching out the first contact I want to give you is Sonya Scott of OIG treasury they are actively investigating the direct express fraud she will also be copied in this email but her direct line is 202-927-5874. if she is not at her desk be sure to leave her a detailed message any dates would be super helpful as well and your contact information name and address she'll need. Moving forward I also want to let you know that because fraud is so rampant on these direct express cards you should get a paper check through the Social Security office to further protect you against any fraud that may occur after the fact. Unfortunately, once a criminal has your information they can attack your card more than once we've seen this way too many times with other victims.
The second person I want you to contact is Sara Lizama she is office of Inspector General for the Social Security office her contact number is 410-966-8685 she will be able to put protection on your Social Security number as well as getting you started in a paper check she is also CCed in this email.
I recommend calling them as well as emailing them both with all of your information and keeping good notes of dates and times when you could have been contacted by them.
Lastly, I would send an email to Nora Arpin she is the senior Vp of Comerica bank her email is Ntarpin@Comerica.com
Be sure to enclose all that you have endured since your money was stolen and your contact info.
Jackie

On Oct 10, 2019, at 9:18 AM, Bernice Johnson <bernicejohnson1990@gmail.com> wrote:
Yes I was trying to pay my light bill with demco electric company in Greensburg Louisiana they had swiped my card to try to get the money off and it was like that they couldn't get the money off so it was another electric company from Texas had took $195.70 off my card a company I had never even heard from or heard about until that day so when I try to call a company about getting my money back they was like I had to call the card holder I've been calling, calling calling but haven't nobody been trying to take my calls about getting my money back I'm trying to see if you can Investigate so y'all can put my transaction back on my card so I can pay my light bill before it get disconnected thank you

Sonja Scott (OIG Treasury)
Oct 10, 2019, 6:49 AM
to Jackie, Bernice johnson, Sarah Lizama (OIG Social Security)@ssa.gov, me
Thank you. This will be entered in our system and reviewed. I am at a meeting with Comerica today. Sonja

Friday, October 11, 2019

to Sonja, jackie
Did the meeting with Comerica take place?
Was the meeting in DC?
Can you relate who was at the meeting and the nature of the agenda?
When can we expect a report on this meeting?
I am watching the sun rise in central Utah on my train ride to meet with the USAF Major in Denver to discuss recommending the USAF suggest all USAF Reserve retirees not receive retirement benefits via BFS. BFS has proven to be inept and corrupt. Maybe Gribben can make a change, but the die is cast.
Believe me that I have the ear of the Major.
Jim

From: Jackie Lynn
Date: October 11, 2019, at 8:49:34 AM EDT
To: Jessica_Wong@warren.senate.gov
Subject: Please answer question 6
Good Morning Sen .Warren and Staffers

As you know my family and I became victims of DE fraud over a year ago now and unfortunately have more unanswered questions now then I had when we became victims.

One question in particular I had was number 6 and the response to this question presented by Sen. Warren. I have yet to understand why your office has declined to publish the answers to these questions knowing very well that the information I presented to your office was valid, in fact that it was a much bigger problem than the bank and other agencies wanted to admit.

Here we are over a year later and these agencies still dodge any repercussions in the fact they have so grossly delayed the deadline on the announcement of the new fiscal agent. May I remind your office this affects MILLIONS of our most vulnerable citizens, delaying how they are going to receive their benefits could lead to devastating effects.

I ask your office to hold these agencies accountable for failing to meet deadlines and for improperly running these programs, if these agencies we're doing their jobs in the first place by monitoring this bank and following up on the Requirements issued in the GAO report (OIG-17-34) perhaps so many would have become victims. The fact that these agencies have failed to alert these cardholders of the potential risk of fraud on these cards is so concerning. Even your office after having all of the information still will not release a press release on the dangers of these cards and what the delaying of the announcement of new fiscal agent is as well as the FULL OIG report and the affects it has on the American people both beneficiaries and tax payers.

These agencies were put in place to help people not hurt them. I so kindly ask your office to release a statement on the victims behalf as well as the taxpayers demanding answers. I also urge your office to follow up on my requested FOIA request.
Thank you,
Jackie Densmore

Saturday, October 12, 2019

from: Jackie Lynn
to: Richard Delmar (OIG Treasury)
cc: Sonja Scott (OIG Treasury),
Michael Jackman (Aide to Rep. Keating) Jessica Wong@warren.senate.gov,
Abby Webber <Abby_Webber@warren.senate.gov>,Kate Berry (American Banker),
Franklin Lemond (Plaintiff's Attorney) , Steve Tellier <stellier@whdh.com>,
Thomas Santaniello (Bureau of Fiscal Service),Sarah Lizama (OIG Social Security)@ssa.gov
date: Oct 12, 2019, 5:37 PM
Attn : all listed in this email

This was sent to me by a victim who had their money stolen from them and now have been receiving paper checks for his social security benefits. After his money was stolen he contacted me and I put him in contact with Walter Bayer of social security who helped in getting him paper checks for now on.

Scared that he was going to have no other choice in how he was going to receive his benefits then to go to the bank who allowed his money to be stolen from him in the first place he contacted me. Now he is receiving these threatening letters in with his monthly checks.

Now we all know this is a Lie considering based on his disability he would qualify for a paper check with the waiver below that government failed to notify beneficiaries about!!!!!!! Instead, they send him this almost causing this man an anxiety attack and raising his blood pressure.

What is being done to these poor people is an outrage, and I will not stand for it. I am making it a mission to stop the scare tactics and the misleading information about how they can get their benefits. I encourage every victim to seek legal action on this for each and every agency who has lied to them. You all fail to alert the public that fraud is occurring on these cards instead they are misled into thinking they have no other options. I am so disgusted in how our most vulnerable Americans are being treated. This will not be swept under the rug.
Jackie Densmore

Wednesday, October 16, 2019

Subject: Subpoena being served
From: jbsimms
Date: Wed, Oct 16, 2019 1:46 pm
To: Richard Delmar (OIG Treasury), Sonja Scott (OIG Treasury)
Cc: "Jackie Lynn"
Dear Mr. Delmar and Ms. Scott,
A process service company was met by a security guard at your building and interrupted the legal execution of the service of a subpoena. Please address this matter with your security company. Please send me the name of the agent of process in your office, address, email address, and telephone number. This cannot happen again. Sincerely, J.B. Simms

Subpoenas had been served upon Treasury. The subpoenas were being ignored. I was raising hell with Franklin about enforcing the subpoenas.

From: Treadwell, Trish (USAGAN) <Trish.Treadwell@usdoj.gov>
Date: Wed, Oct 16, 2019 at 2:45 PM
Subject: Almon v. Conduent and Comerica Bank -- FS/Treasury Subpoena
To: franklin@webbllc.com <franklin@webbllc.com>
Cc: adam@webbllc.com <adam@webbllc.com>, matt@webbllc.com <matt@webbllc.com>
Franklin:
I am hoping to set up a call this week or early next week regarding the Subpoenas that Plaintiffs served on the Bureau of Fiscal Services in this matter. I am the N.D. Ga. AUSA who will be handling any filed responses or litigation, although I am hopeful that we can discuss a solution that allows for the production of some subset of documents that will obviate the need for any motion to quash or to compel.
Please let me know if there is a time tomorrow or next week that you all are available to discuss. (I will be in meetings out of the office all day on Friday.)
Trish Treadwell

from: J B Simms
to: "Kevin A. Guishard" <guishardk@oig.treas.gov>
cc: Jackie Densmore,
Sonja Scott <Sonja Scott (OIG Treasury)>,
Richard Delmar (OIG Treasury)
date: Oct 16, 2019, 10:06 AM
Mr. Guishard,
Attached is the Ruling with the finding that Comerica Bank violated Reg E. Please share this with Ms. Katherine Johnson.
If the release you are sending would have been sent two weeks ago, I would have been in California to receive it. I will be in SC in a few days and be technically unavailable until 10/27. My friend is having surgery on 10/30, and I am looking at least a two-week recovery period.
Let me think how you can get documents to me.
I leave 10/22 to visit old friends, return to SC on 10/27, then care for another.
Ms. Johnson, Mr. Delmar, and Ms. Scott have my response to prelim to 19-041.
BFS is up to their necks in corruption by allowing Comerica Bank to have the contracts, and "people" benefited.
Let me think what address to use.Jim

Guishard, Kevin A. <GuishardK@oig.treas.gov>
Oct 16, 2019, 10:30 AM
to Katherine, me
Mr. Simms,
Thank you for the ruling. I have passed the information on to Ms. Johnson as well.
As we will begin sending out the documents by certified mail next week, please provide the best address to reach you at for the week of October 21st-27th.Thanks,Kevin

Wednesday, October 16, 2019

From: Franklin Lemond (Plaintiff's Attorney)>
Date: Wed, Oct 16, 2019, 1:03 pm
To: Jackie Lynn, Jbsimms
Guys,
See below. OIG Treasury continues to try to evade service of the subpoena.
Franklin

I sent the following email to Richard Delmar:

From: jbsimms
Sent: Wednesday, October 16, 2019, 4:47 PM
To: Richard Delmar (OIG Treasury); Sonja Scott (OIG Treasury)
Cc: Jackie Lynn
Subject: Subpoena being served
Dear Mr. Delmar and Ms. Scott,
A process service company was met by a security guard at your building and interrupted the legal execution of the service of a subpoena.
Please address this matter with your security company.
Please send me the name of the agent of process in your office, address, email address, and telephone number. This cannot happen again.
Sincerely,
J.B. Simms

Delmar responded. The subpoenas got served. The following email was Delmar's response.

From: Richard Delmar (OIG Treasury)
Date: Thu, Oct 17, 2019, 8:49 am
To: jbsimms
Mr. Simms:
To what address did your courier come? Had you called or written beforehand, we could have advised you of the standard Treasury procedure for service of process.
The General Counsel of the Department of the Treasury is the Department's designated agent for service of process.
The Department's courier service receives "Service of Process" documents at 701 Madison Place, NW., Washington, D.C. This building is between H Street and Pennsylvania Ave., N.W., on the eastern edge of Lafayette Square. Upon arrival at this address please have the courier call 202-622-1650 to arrange for a representative of the Office of General Counsel to pick up the document.

Oh, hell no. The process server could not get into the building. What an amateur.

Saturday, October 19, 2019

Jackie found this insert in the Social Security check for her brother-in-law.

Jackie Lynn
Sat, Oct 19, 2019, 8:20 PM
to Walter.Bayer, me
Dear Mr.Bayer ,
I am following up on the Letter addressed to Sen Warrens office from the OIG dated December 19, 2018. In this email Gail Stallworth says they do not currently have any work ongoing related to the security of the Direct Express program, however, they will include a review in the fiscal year 2019 audit work plan that will identify potential vulnerabilities of Social Security payments deposited to pre-paid debit card, such as the Direct Express debit card.
First of all I find this extremely hard to believe that Social Security had no idea the severity of the fraud, especially when it had $460,000 stolen from cardholders in just one year . I also find it concerning that Social Security Administration continues to endorse Direct Express cards and that SSA has not alerted the public about the risks associated with Direct Express instead they keep our most vulnerable Americans in the dark .The fact that routine audits and investigations are not done on federal programs such as the direct express card is probably the most concerning to me as well as the public , this is taxpayers money and it supports disabled Americans. No wonder why criminals have a field day stealing from cardholders. There are no investigations no arrests and no consequences.
I would like to know if Social Security has launched any investigation what so ever since the date of Dec. 19 2018 . I would also like to be informed when and if your audit work plan has been published and where I could find it.
I have enclosed the judge's ruling on the class action lawsuit filed against the bank ~The judge has ruled in our favor that the bank is guilty of violating Reg E laws. Subpoenas have already been filed and I have confidence in our case that agencies that ignored these complaints with be held accountable.
I look forward to your response into this important matter. Jacqueline Densmore

264

Monday, October 21, 2019

Two Social Security audits planned, none were published

From: "Bayer, Walter Office of the Inspector General" Walter Bayer (SSI OIG)
Date: October 21, 2019 at 2:20:48 PM EDT
To: Jackie Lynn
Cc: "Lizama, Sarah Office of the Inspector General" <Sarah Lizama (OIG Social Security)@ssa.gov>
Subject: 20181220095901286.pdf direct express
Ms. Densmore,
We have two planned audits related to Direct Express in our recently released FY 2020 Audit Work Plan (see https://oig.ssa.gov/sites/default/files/audit/full/pdf/FY%202020%20Work%20Plan.pdf), but I believe this one would be closest to the one we discussed:
Beneficiaries Who Receive Payments Deposited to Prepaid Debit Cards (A-09-18-50699)
All SSA beneficiaries and SSI recipients' payments must be delivered via direct deposit, a Direct Express debit card, or an Electronic Transfer Account unless an exemption to the electronic payment requirement is met. SSA accepts pre-paid debit card accounts for direct deposits, such as Green Dot, GoBank, and Comerica. Our review will identify potential vulnerabilities of payments deposited to pre-paid debit cards and determine whether there was indication that payments were made to potentially fraudulent accounts.
The Audit Work Plan describes reviews we plan to begin in FY 2020.
I hope you find this to be helpful.
Thanks
Walt
Walter E. Bayer, Jr.
SSA-OIG Congressional and
 Intragovernmental Liaison

Kate Berry (American Banker)
Mon, Oct 21, 2019, 12:18 PM
to Jackie,, jbsimms
I agree, interesting there is an audit; interesting that someone at Social Security is interested.
but we don't know if they awarded the contract back to Comerica!kb

Can't anyone serve a simple subpoena?

From: Franklin Lemond
Date: Monday, October 21, 2019
Subject: Walter Bayer's response
To: J B Simms
Cc: Jackie Lynn
JB,
The subpoena to SSA already seeks complaints regarding fraud (see attached).
Below is a summary of the service attempts on OIG Treasury:
Attempt 1: 10/04/2019 at 10:41   246999 1500 Pennsylvania Ave., NW
Washington, DC 20220   Attempt An employee explained to me that this is the wrong address for service on OIG. She directed me to 717 14th St. NW, #500, Washington, DC 20005.
Attempt 2: Date: 10/16/2019 at 15:58 Address: 717 14th St. NW, #500 Washington DC 20005
Event: UPON ARRIVAL, I WAS GREETED BY SECURITY WHO INSTRUCTED ME TO CALL (202)727-2540; I CALLED MULTIPLE TIMES AND GOT NO RESPONSE;
WE ARE CONTINUING TO ATTEMPT SERVICE
Attempt 3: We went back again today and found the following:
Fri 10/18/2019 15:12   Attempt 717 14th St., NW, #500 Washington DC 20005   NO   When I arrived at the address provided, I was asked by security to call \"my contact\" so I called (202)727-2540. A woman answered and said someone would be right down. The Deputy Inspector General for Business Management came down and introduced herself as Jainey Arussi. She said that she cannot accept the documents because documents addressed to the Office of Inspector General, U.S. Department of Treasury, need to go to Treasury Office of

Inspector General located at 1401 H St., NW, Suite 469, Washington, DC, 20005. No further information was provided.
An additional attempt is being made today at this new address.
Additionally, I spoke with the AUSA today regarding the BFS subpoenas, we are going to speak again later this week. Documents will be forthcoming, but they need some additional time and want to discuss some limitations. I tried to call Wilcox again today - his voicemail is full and not accepting messages. I sent him an email as well. If I hear anything I will let you know.
Franklin

J B Simms
Mon, Oct 21, 2019, 12:53 PM
to Franklin, Jackie
It is always better to be proactive than reactive.
Need to subpoena ssa for complaints, and subpoena Green Dot (Bayer opened the door with his email, circumventing our complaint in Texas.
Need to know if those amateurs in Washington severed the subpoena to treasury.
Franklin, if those idiots did not know how to serve a subpoena, there are plenty of people to do it. Not my first rodeo.
Jim

From: Jackie Lynn
Date: October 21, 2019 at 6:16:20 PM EDT
To: Walter.Bayer@ssa.gov
Subject: Audit work (A-09-18-50699) direct express
Mr.Bayer,
Thank you for the quick response on my last email to you in regard to the upcoming audit work on Direct Express. I thank you very much for sending the link. It was very helpful although I did have some questions. Upon reading through it 2 things jumped out at me that I was hoping you could answer for me.
On page 10 ▭does this mean you have had reports of Direct Express not returning money to SSA and not freezing deceased cardholders accounts? What has prompted your agency to add this into your audit?
Reclamations of Social Security Administration Payments to Direct Express Debit Cards
A-04-18-50637
The Department of the Treasury contracted with Comerica Bank to establish the Direct Express debit card program, which allows beneficiaries, recipients, and individual representative payees who do not have bank accounts to have their federal payments direct deposited into a debit card account. When a cardholder dies, SSA informs Comerica Bank through the Death Notification Entry process. Once notified of the cardholder's death, Comerica freezes the debit card account and returns to SSA any payments posted to the account after the date of death. This review will determine whether the payments made to the Direct Express debit cards after the death of SSI recipients are appropriately returned to SSA.
The second question I had has to do with page 39~does this mean that people collecting Social Security benefits can have monthly benefits deposited onto a green dot card or GoBank card instead of using Comerica or their own bank account? Does bureau of fiscal services have a contract with either one of these prepaid cards?
Beneficiaries Who Receive Payments Deposited to Prepaid Debit Cards
A-09-18-50699
All SSA beneficiaries and SSI recipients' payments must be delivered via direct deposit, a Direct Express debit card, or an Electronic Transfer Account unless an exemption to the electronic payment requirement is met. SSA accepts pre-paid debit card accounts for direct deposits, such as Green Dot, GoBank, and Comerica. Our review will identify potential vulnerabilities of payments deposited to pre-paid debit cards and determine whether there was indication that payments were made to potentially fraudulent accounts.
Thank you for your time and dedication into this ongoing problem , as you may know bureau of fiscal services has delayed the announcement of the new contract and now with less than four months of its deadline date which is January 2, 2020 we were hoping to have some answers by now perhaps you could send an email requesting information on the new contract considering it's going to affect the Social Security administration office as well as the card holders. Could you please inform me when to expect the audit report to be finalized through the Social Security administration office on Direct Express so that I may look out for it.
Sincerely,Jackie Densmore

Subject: Subpoenas, again
From: jbsimms
Date: Mon, Oct 21, 2019, 4:36 pm
To: Richard Delmar (OIG Treasury), Sonja Scott (OIG Treasury)
Cc: "Jackie Lynn"
Dear Mr. Delmar and Ms. Scott,
Below please see the report from the process service company. While I am certain the Capitol Police are following a protocol of their making, they appear to be woefully unaware of civil procedure.
MLG Attorney Services submitted this report to attorney Franklin Lemond of Atlanta.
I do not know which of the two (MLG or Capitol Police) is culpable in this "snafu", but I have every confidence one of you can remedy this.
Neither you nor I have time or tolerate such inept behavior. I apologize for having to send this to you. One day this will end.
Jim

Tuesday, October 22, 2019

Kate Berry (American Banker)
Tue, Oct 22, 2019, 9:54 AM
to me, Jackiedenzz@yahoo.com
There are many, many talented, brilliant attorneys, analysts, rulemaking experts and researchers at the CFPB. I do not think a lot of these folks, many of them quite young, are punching the clock until retirement, though they are more highly paid than other federal employees.
They have a lot on their plate right now in additional the Supreme Court case in which the director refused to defend the CFPB's constitutionality, they are working on the payday rule, debt collection and other mortgage rules, plus HMDA.
We do not know if the bureau has opened an investigation into Comerica and DirectExpress. But we do know they are interested in going after fraud --- but perhaps not in a government program. That doesn't look politically very attractive for them to pursue publicly.
kb

J B Simms
Tue, Oct 22, 2019, 11:06 AM
to Kate, Jackiedenzz@yahoo.com
If you can find the appropriate and receptive person at cfpb who can interpret the Ruling as a violation (😊🍌) maybe, they will now attend to their mandate and enforce federal law as I told them 20 months ago.
Fed Reserve OIG is supposed to investigate cfpb, and I had sent emails to two officials who ignored all and never responded.
If anyone at cfpb proves to have the character and integrity of which you give them, here is their chance to admit to their failures and do their jobs.
These people have allowed this to happen. I have not one scintilla of sympathy for any of them.
Cfpb was given a cap, a uniform, cleats, and a bat, then refused to swing the bat. No one knows to which team they have allegiance. 😖
If you find us the person a person at cfpb who is willing to read the Ruling, please forward to them and tell them we are coming. Thank you for all you have done.
Jim

I found out the name of the process service company whose employee failed to serve the subpoena to Treasury. This is the email they got from me.

Subject: Failure to serve subpoenas to OIG Treasury for Franklin Lemond
From: jbsimms
Date: Tue, Oct 22, 2019 10:33 pm
To: orders@mlqattorneyservices.com
Cc: "Jackie Lynn"

Our attorney, Franklin Lemond, has advised us that representative from your company has not been able to serve subpoenas to OIG Treasury, and that a guard stopped your process server. Having decades of experience in civil and criminal investigation, fugitive apprehension, and the service of hundreds of civil filings, I cannot understand the problem. The confrontation by a security guard, and lack of knowing the protocol to effectively serve the subpoena has been brought to the attention of Richard Delmar, former Chief Counsel and Acting Commissioner of OIG Treasury. Mr. Delmar replied immediately via email, giving me the protocol and the agent of service. This information was forwarded to Mr. Lemond, and I assume Mr. Lemond forwarded the directive.

OIG Treasury has been waiting for this subpoena for quite some time, and your employees just cannot figure out how to get this done. This failure affects many people, including me.

I will forward directions to you if necessary. I will be in direct contact with OIG Treasury in a few hours to determine if the task was fulfilled.

Sincerely,
J.B. Simms

Wednesday, October 23, 2019

From: "Bayer, Walter, Office of the Inspector General" Walter Bayer (SSI OIG)
Date: October 23, 2019 at 2:39:47 PM EDT
To: Jackie Lynn
Subject: Audit work (A-09-18-50699) direct express
Ms. Densmore,
At this time I can only share what is publicly available regarding our planned audits, and I expect the auditors still have more information to gather and review as they initiate this work. As far as the scheduled issuance of these reports, at this time we are only committing to starting these reviews this fiscal year. In general, we issue our audit reports within 12-months of officially starting them with the Agency.
Thanks,
Walt
On Wed, Oct 23, 2019 at 8:00 AM Jackie Lynn wrote:
Good Morning Franklin,
Hopefully, some of your time has been freed up so that we can have some questions answered.
The First question I have is have you put together a subpoena together for my FOIA request? This is very, very important to me and I have to admit I'm very frustrated over
 The subpoena for the information you requested from BFS vis FOIA was served on BFS on October 7 - see attached affidavit of service. When I spoke with Trish earlier this week, she acknowledged receipt of both subpoenas and was aware of the similarity between your FOIA and the second subpoena. I thought I had made it clear that the subpoena regarding your FOIA had gone out.
 The second question I have is again pertaining to a subpoena to Elizabeth Warren?
  I have prepared the subpoena to Senator Warren's office but have not sent it to opposing counsel yet prior to service. I plan to do that this week.
The third question I have is pertaining to the subpoena -OIG treasury has that been served yet successfully? If not, can we look into getting a different person to get the job done?
 Per my email from earlier today, that subpoena was served earlier this week.
 The fourth question I have is where are you with the eppi card lawsuit I believe last time we spoke on this you were receiving discovery information do you think any of that discovery information can help us in our case what are you finding? Do you feel the bank is more likely to settle? Which case in your opinion is stronger? Can this case be found on the pacer?
  There is certainly information from my EPPICard case that will be useful or helpful in our case, but as I indicated previously, the documents produced in that case are for use in that case only and not for use in your case. I will certainly make sure we obtain the same documents in the GA and TX cases now that I am aware of them, but due to the confidentiality order in the other case, they cannot be shared. I plan on making a settlement offer in that case soon, but I am not sure what their interest in settlement is. In my opinion, the defendants' exposure is much smaller in the EPPICard case.
 Has there been any new developments in our case?
  In the Texas case, the Defendants' response to the complaint is due tomorrow.
  In the Georgia case, Defendants asked for an extra week to serve their discovery responses, which I agreed to give them. Their written responses are now due on October 30. I have also been negotiating a

268

confidentiality agreement and an ESI agreement that will govern the production of computer files and emails in this case.

Have you set up the telephone conference with the woman named Trish?

Yes. As I indicated in my email to JB on Monday, I spoke with AUSA Trish Treadwell on Monday regarding the two BFS subpoenas. She asked for some additional information, which she claims I must provide pursuant to 31 CFR 1.11, before they can produce the documents requested by the subpoena. I am in the process of finishing up what she requested and plan to provide that to her tomorrow.

Subject: IOG - Treasury has been served
From: Franklin Lemond (Plaintiff's Attorney)>
Date: Wed, Oct 23, 2019, 6:56 am
To: Jbsimms, Jackie Lynn
See the attached affidavit re: service on OIG Treasury.
Comerica's and Conduent's response(s) to the TX complaint are due tomorrow.
Subject: Observation and recommendation
From: jbsimms
Date: Thu, Oct 24, 2019, 5:19 am
To: Richard Delmar (OIG Treasury), Sonja Scott (OIG Treasury)
Cc: "Jackie Lynn"
With all the litigation happening, delayed appointments, delayed reports, Ruling validating my claim of violation of Feb E by Comerica, and other drama which is the product of BFS/Comerica malfeasance, the following appeared to me:

1) BFS cannot handle banking matter involving adherence to federal banking regulations

2) All federal agencies dispensing funds should cease endorsing the Direct Express program.

3) All federal agencies dispensing funds should manage all dispensing of their funds, not involving BFS. These agencies should publish to their recipients that each person can use any debit card, only needing to open a debit card account and obtain the routing number of the supporting bank, the obtain their proprietary account number. These two variables will be communicated to the federal agency. This eliminates the need for BFS.

4) All Direct Express recipients will be given one year to transfer their Direct Express accounts to a different debit card.

5) All agencies cease endorsing the Direct Express program, as they give instructions how to use generic debit cards.

These suggestions relieve BFS from overseeing multiple areas of dispensing, which they clearly have been proven to be inept.I do appreciate that you have become more receptive to Jackie and me after a contentious beginning. Accountability is key. Jim

Monday, October 28, 2019

Susan Beatty, US Bank
Gmail Subject: Inclusion of the Mentor Program in the OIG Treas rpt 19-41
From: jbsimms
Date: Mon, Oct 28, 2019, 9:11 am
To: Richard Delmar (OIG Treasury), Sonja Scott (OIG Treasury)
Cc: "Jackie Lynn"
Dear Mr. Delmar and Ms. Scott,
Below is the final paragraph of the article I forwarded to you earlier today:
https://www.blackenterprise.com/first-independence-bank-teams-up-with-u-s-bank-in-u-s-treasury-protege-program/
In May 2019, two other black banks — The Harbor Bank of Maryland and Liberty Bank and Trust Co.—were chosen to work with JPMorgan Chase & Co. as part of The Financial Agent Mentor Protégé Program sponsored by the U.S. Department of the Treasury. Both Liberty Bank and the Harbor Bank of Maryland are also on the BE Banks list of the nation's largest black-owned banks.
This decision to implement this program is a direct result of work by Ms. Densmore and me. The fact that the minority banks were chosen in May 2019, at the same time the appointment of the new/incumbent Fiscal Agent, did not escape me, and I hope you and Ms. Johnson realize that BFS is making changes because of our "assertions."
The implementation of this mentor program by BFS should be noted in no small manner within 19-041. Jim

From: jbsimms
Date: Mon, Oct 28, 2019, 10:20 am
To: "Susan Beatty" <susan.beatty@usbank.com>
Cc: "Jackie Lynn"
Dear Ms. Beatty,
Below please find an email I sent to you almost 3 weeks ago.
I would like to have a reply and conversation with you. If you prefer to have your compliance or legal office contact me, I will fine with that. You allowed your name to be published as the contact person with regards to the mentor program with BFS, so I assume you are prepared to discuss the matter.
Your immediate reply would be appreciated.

Wednesday, October 30, 2019

Franklin agreed to the conference on Tuesday. I want to talk about the Mentor Program
Sonja knew nothing about this. Wow!

Notice of Electronic Filing
The following transaction was entered on 10/28/2019 at 4:19 PM CDT and filed on 10/28/2019
Case Name: Carnley et al v. Conduent Business Services, LLC et al
Case Number: 5:19-cv-01075-XR
Filer:
Document Number: 17
Docket Text: Order and Advisory (Proposed Scheduling Order due by 11/25/2019,), Notice of right to consent to disposition of a civil case by a U.S. Magistrate Judge. Signed by Judge Xavier Rodriguez. (rf)
5:19-cv-01075-XR Notice has been electronically mailed to:
Allen R. Vaught - allen@vaughtfirm.com, allenvaught@hotmail.com
E. Adam Webb - adam@webbllc.com, franklin@webbllc.com, matt@webbllc.com
G. Franklin Lemond - Franklin Lemond (Plaintiff's Attorney)
Henry B. Gonzalez , III - hbg@gcaklaw.com, ebroussard@gcaklaw.com, lpriolo@gcaklaw.com

Our federal case was moved to Texas where Comerica's home office was located.

Jackie Lynn
Wed, Oct 30, 2019, 7:05 AM
to Franklin Lemond (Plaintiff's Attorney), me
Development in case Jb uncovered, we should move quickly on this
Franklin:
JB outed the Mentor Program, which was shielded by BFS since May 2019. You see Sonja Scott admitted she knew nothing about it.(I believe you were copied in those emails with the links on the mentor program this week)
We have to subpoena BFS to get all records about the program, the beginning of it, who is in charge at BFS and US Bank, and we need this now. They are hiding this for some reason.
BFS blindsided OIG Treasury and us.(see below Sonja's response)
Santaniello has to be involved.
Please update us with your thoughts
Thanks
Jackie

On Oct 30, 2019, at 8:59 AM, Sonja Scott (OIG Treasury) wrote:
Jim - I actually do not know anything about the BFS Mentor Program but looking into it. Sonja

Sonja Scott knew nothing about BFS mentor program

Unbelievable. Sonja knew nothing about the Mentor Program created at BFS.

From: J B Simms
Sent: Wednesday, October 30, 2019, 8:54 AM
To: Sonja Scott (OIG Treasury)
Cc: Jackie Densmore
Subject: BFS Mentor Program and OIG knowledge
Sonja,

I am sitting in SC waiting for a former employee to emerge from cervical disc replacement (C3-C7). She worked for me beginning in 1986 and asked for me to attend. Yes, she has known me that long and still talks to me, go figure.

I am having to use my phone to send this email. The matter of BFS, the Mentor Program, and Santaniello shielding us from this information is a big issue. While I understand OIG Treasury, you, and Mr. Delmar do not "offer" us anything, we can assume you were aware of this program.

I would like to discuss the genesis of this program, your knowledge of this, the BFS employees involved, if Comerica is being mentored, and hopefully an honest assertion that this program was created to protect rather than punish Comerica.

As a victim of the Direct Express program, I would hope OIG Treasury would willing to discuss these matters with victims, be accountable, fall on your sword as a result of the two previous audits, and try to convince victims/taxpayers that you see what we see.

I sincerely applaud you for being receptive to victims.

I never wanted a contentious relationship; I did expect a bit of withholding, but I also expected OIG Treasury to understand that Jackie and I understand more than enough which makes the dishonest persons at Treasury defensive.

I want to discuss this Mentor Program with you. If you can arrange a call from a conference room, patch in Jackie, I promise it "...will be a perfect call." Jim

Jackie Lynn
Wed, Oct 30, 2019, 8:03 AM
to Franklin Lemond (Plaintiff's Attorney), me
Franklin: felicity got in touch with me today regarding these letters apparently OIG treasury department is subpoenaing her records from Comerica bank based on her account that was fraudulently hacked,
This could be good, the fact they are also Sending subpoenas on their own!
Jb knows more on this victim let's set up a conference call early next week?
Thanks
Jackie

Subject: Re: Parameters for OIG Treas subpoenas
From: Sonja Scott (OIG Treasury)
Date: Wed, Oct 30, 2019, 9:58 am
To: jbsimms
Cc: Jackie Lynn
Yes. I spoke with Ms. Palma.
Subject: Parameters for OIG Treas subpoenas

From: jbsimms
Date: Wed, Oct 30, 2019, 9:07 am
To: Sonja Scott (OIG Treasury)
Cc: "Jackie Lynn"
Sonja,
Paulette Battle sent a form/release for Felicity Palma to obtain the info from Conduent. This is very encouraging. I will get Felicity to return documents to Ms. Battle asap.
I was sent a packet as well. I should receive it today.
Question is this: which victims are being singled out to have records subpoenaed? I would think Jackie and McPhail would also be included.
Your thoughts?
Thanks. This will end, we do need your help. Jim

Subject: RE: Parameters for OIG Treas subpoenas
From: jbsimms
Date: Wed, Oct 30, 2019, 11:55 am
To: Sonja Scott (OIG Treasury)
Cc: "Jackie Lynn"
Thank you for speaking her Felicity.
She has been brow-beaten by Conduent. Sad.
Is OIG Treasury sending out more releases to be used to subpoena Conduent and Comerica?
I hope you get to the bottom of the "Mentor Program" and US Bank. The PR lady at US Bank named in two of the articles has been sent 2 emails and has yet to respond. No surprise there.
Maybe she will respond to one of your people.

J B Simms
Wed, Oct 30, 2019, 7:18 AM
to Franklin, Jackie, Sonja, Richard
The dots have been connected.
The reason Santaniello blocked Jackie and me from giving an oral presentation to the so-called "BFS Evaluation Team" was he knew if Jackie or I questioned them, we would have found out about the Mentor Program, which was put into place in May 2019.
BFS hid this from OIG Treasury and us and did not make this program public until months later. This was Santaniello blocking us from getting to the Evaluation Team, and the attempt to act accountable (even after two OIG Treasury reports).
I look forward to the result of Ms. Scott's inquiry.
Jim

J B Simms
Wed, Oct 30, 2019, 7:24 AM
to Franklin, Jackie
Weeks ago, Sonja Scott interviewed Nora Arpin. Sonja said there was no report generated from the interview. That response was less than honest; we all know Sonja had to submit a report to someone.
We need the results of that interview to craft Interrogatories are to be sent to Nora.
I can continue to go after Sonja, but I thought a nice communication from an attorney (maybe to Delmar) might get the report.
We all know a report of Nora's interview exists.

Thursday, October 31, 2019

Jackie Lynn
Thu, Oct 31, 2019, 7:34 AM
to ScottS, me
Good Morning Sonja,
After much discussion with Mr. Simms and many of the victims of DE fraud we have some questions and Mr. Simms, and I were hoping to set up a conference call with you to go over them. I believe this will be most beneficial for your report.
Would you have time next week to discuss?
Both Mr. Simms and I will be available for you at your convenience.
Thank you for your time.
Jackie Densmore

Subject: Very confusing mailing from Altemus
From: jbsimms
Date: Thu, Oct 31, 2019, 11:26 am
To: guishardk@oig.treas.oig
Cc: Delmar@erikpublishing.com, Sonja Scott (OIG Treasury), "Jackie Lynn"
Mr. Guishard,
I received the release which was mailed to me via Jackie Densmore. The mailing is very confusing to me, and the directions are not clear. This is a recipe for failure.

The telephone number given by Mr. Altemus is routed to an answering service, not to the desk of Mr. Altemus. Those persons having less experience with legal proceedings will be lost. I hope this snafu was not intentionally done to dissuade victims from filing complaints.
Sincerely,
JB Simms

Friday, November 1, 2019

Sonja Scott (OIG Treasury)
Fri, Nov 1, 2019, 4:34 AM
to Jackie, me
I spoke to our Audit group who would benefit from this call. They would like to take part. Let's work on a date next week. Sonja

BFS would not give out information about the Mentor Program

Subject: The Mentor Program at BFS
From: jbsimms
Date: Fri, Nov 01, 2019 11:36 am
To: Mark.Stromer@fiscal.treasury.gov, Evelyn.Daval@fiscal.treasury.gov,
Timothy.Walters@fiscal.treasury.gov
Cc: "Jackie Lynn"
Dear Mr. Stromer, Ms.Daval, and Mr. Walters,
I found the PDF published by BFS which noted the Mentor Program at BFS. Other sources reveal this program was instituted as far back as May 2019, and US Bank was designated as the mentor bank to minority banks in the Detroit area.
We have a number of questions for your agency concerning not only the inception of this program, but the genesis of such. We are aware the naming of a Fiscal Agent for the Direct Express program was to have been named in mid-May 2019 and the announcement of the Fiscal Agent has yet to be announced.
Please furnish us with the names of all mentor banks, all applicants to the mentor program, and if you three are the contact persons on this matter.
It is interesting that the Mentor Program began (as cited in two published accounts) in May, 2019 which is the same time as the projected naming of the Fiscal Agent for the Direct Express program. Is this mentor program supposed to oversee a new Fiscal Agent for this program because BFS failed to oversee Comerica Bank?
Many at BFS are familiar with Ms. Densmore and myself. If you would like to forward this request to Mr. Gribben, that might be a good thing to do.
You can reach me via telephone at (803) 309-6850.
Sincerely,
J.B. Simms

Subject: the mentor pamphlet
From: jbsimms
Date: Fri, Nov 01, 2019, 12:16 pm
To: Sonja Scott (OIG Treasury)
Cc: "Jackie Lynn"
here it is, the Mentor program pamphlet.
https://fiscal.treasury.gov/files/fampp/FAMPPFlyer.pdf
The wording of this "voluntary" program seems a bit different from the three news articles I sent you.
At this point, who knows what they are doing at BFS?

Subject: VERY Important letter from Treasury, need instructions
From: jbsimms
Date: Fri, Nov 01, 2019, 4:00 pm
To: "joe almon" <harveymushman170@yahoo.com>, "jon carnley", "Cynthia Clark", "Paul Katynski" <designnmind@yahoo.com>, "Jennifer Kreegar", "Marteshia McPhail" <MardeeMack@hotmail.com>, "Kenneth Tillman", "Jackie Lynn"
Hello fellow plaintiffs,

This is important. I just got off the phone with Jackie, so this will save her a little time.

I received a packet of stuff from OIG Treasury. You might have gotten the same thing. The packet is a release form to allow OIG Treasury to look at the fraud on your case. By law, Comerica does not have to reveal bank info, and Comerica is trying to use this law.

The release is a one-page document. All you have to do is sign the release and mail it to the address listed on the page with the heading CUSTOMER'S MOTION TO CHALLENGE GOVERNMENT ACCESS

Let me explain the other documents, which you can ignore. If the government subpoenas the bank for your records, you have the right to protest the government getting your records. That right to "protest" had to be put into the packet because Comerica does not want Treasury to find out they violated Reg E and did no investigation. All that CUSTOMER'S MOTION TO CHALLENGE GOVERNMENT ACCESS is there to protect government intrusion, but that does not involve us. Comerica refused the subpoenas and will not allow OIG into the accounts without the release.

Let me know if you got a packet. Just fill out the release and sent back to:

A.J. Altemus

Counsel to the Inspector General/OIG Treasury

875 15th Street NW, Suite 4052, Washington, DC 20005

Jackie and I are busting our tails to protect us all.

Jim

Email from Sonja Scott- we to get conference with Audit group.

Sonja Scott (OIG Treasury)
Nov 1, 2019, 6:55 AM
to Jackie, me
They would like to do this Wednesday, Nov 6th. All I have so far that day is a meeting from 9-10. Would 11 AM EST work for you? Sonja

Jackie Lynn
Fri, Nov 1, 2019, 7:07 AM
to Sonja, me
Yes that works perfect!
Thank you Sonja

This was huge. We were getting a conference.

Monday, November 4, 2019

Worked on the syllabus of notes for the conference.

Jackie Lynn
Mon, Nov 4, 2019, 7:12 PM
to Walter.Bayer, me, Franklin Lemond (Plaintiff's Attorney), ScottS, Thomas, Jessica_Wong
Walter ,
I'm wondering if you could perhaps include this in your upcoming audit, clearly the fraud with DIRECT EXPRESS was so bad your agency had to create a site to centralize direct Express reclamation cases . Your agency even created a policy ~only ACCEPTABLE prepaid cards are allowed to receive Social security benefits (section GN 02403030E of SSA PROGRAM OPERATIONS MANUAL)
How many cases in October 2011 did the office of Inspector General track of allegations of unauthorized changes to direct express information and redirected beneficiary payments to other accounts? Where can I locate this information? I find this extremely interesting and would like some more information on it please. I would also like to know the different options of pre-paid cards that Beneficiaries can choose in addition to the direct express card as listed in the fourth paragraph.
Best,
Jackie Densmore

Subject: conference notes and remedy to end Direct Express
From: jbsimms
Date: Mon, Nov 04, 2019, 6:11 pm
To: "Jackie Lynn"
Here are the notes for the conference, along with how I would reorganize the dispensing of funds to persons who used the Direct Express program.
I did this in a hurry, but you will see the gist of my point.

Below is the syllabus I sent to Sonja Scott for our meeting:

Conference with OIG Treasury, November 6, 2019

Issues for the conference with Sonja Scott:
OIG sending subpoenas to 30 victims, release sent to victims- make directions more user friendly.
Jackie's FOI request, and the one-year delay
The mentor program- BFS hid this from the Audit group. Mentor program proves BFS could not monitor DE program, allowing Comerica to violate Reg E. Need to know the origin of this program, dates, names.
BFS, specifically Thomas Santaniello, blocked all victims from communicating with BFS "Evaluation Team." Who at OIG Treasury has had contact with Santaniello? Does Gribben know Santaniello blocked victims from addressing BFS?
Note: Fed judge ruling that Reg E was violated by Comerica
DE can be dismantled: all agencies promote the use of debit cards for their recipients. Eliminates Conduent, Comerica, Conduent, BBB, CFPB.
We need the letter from Babb: Warren marked the letter as confidential.
We need the letters from Treasury and VA
BFS consolidated other programs under Fiscal Agent. EZ Pay merge with Navy Cash and Eagle Cash; Fed Reserve now running the program.
Since FRB endorsed the merging of DOD SVC's and FRB OIG is supposed to audit CFPB, persons at FRB are ignoring their responsibility.
Survivors of deceased cardholders do not have access to funds.
Refusal of Conduent or Comerica to engage with designated persons having POA.
Mastercard: ignored our inquiries, no zero liability, no accountability with Comerica.
BFS still not announced Fiscal Agent of DE Program
Who is the person at VA who has been the contact person with the investigation being conducted by OIG Treasury?
Personally: my identity was hacked at Social Security on June 19, 2018, in addition to having had my Direct Express account hacked in Jan 2017 and Dec 2017. Social Security is refusing to reveal how the fraudster got into my Social Security account. This information possibly was compromised via Conduent.
Jackie Densmore's identity was compromised by a person in Florida. A treasury agent dropped the investigation, as well as parallel investigations within the same geographic region for at least two more victims. We want to know the results of all investigations on these matters in Miramar, Florida, and the identity of the supervisor of the assigned agent.
Brief in Support of Elimination of Direct Express program, and remedy.
1.   Comerica Bank was granted status as Fiscal Agent of the Direct Express program even though it was documented that Bureau of Fiscal Service ignored the fact Comerica Bank submitted false and incomplete information in order to obtain the contract.
2.   Both OIG Treasury reports, 14-031 and 17-034, revealed the failure of OIG Treasury to fully investigate Bureau of Fiscal Services, Comerica Bank, and Conduent.
3.   It was only after the failure of OIG Treasury to sufficiently investigate the Direct Express program, to include Bureau of Fiscal Services, Comerica Bank, and Conduent, was exposed in February 2018 that a new investigation was commissioned.
4.   Bureau of Fiscal Services has ignored violations of federal banking laws, specifically Regulation E (15USC1693) and is continually in denial of their malfeasance.
5.   Over 425 complaints were made to the CFPB about Comerica Bank as of February 2018. All complaints were forwarded directly to Susan Schmidt, SVP of Comerica Bank, who forwarded the complaint to Customer Advocacy of Conduent.
6.   *Customer Service of Conduent is staffed with persons ill equipped to handle banking matters.*

275

7.   The Investigative Division of Conduent, while having hired some persons having banking experience, regularly denied fraud claim losses by Direct Express card holders having use suspicious and unprofessional means to determine the validity of the fraud claim.

8.   A federal judge has made a ruling that Comerica Bank, in conjunction with Conduent, violated Regulation E with regard to Direct Express cardholders.

9.   Bureau of Fiscal Services has proved to be inadequate and maybe complacent with regard to managing the Direct Express program.

10.   Bureau of Fiscal Services, VA, Social Security, and US Treasury websites endorse the failed program which each agency knows of victims.

11.   The Direct Express program should be eliminated, with the following plan implemented to serve the recipient:

(a)   Each government agency which distributes funds will distribute funds to recipients either by debit card, bank account, or paper check.

(b)   Each agency will publish an announcement that the Direct Express program will end in one year.

(c)   A new temporary Fiscal Agent will be appointed and monitored heavily by US Treasury.

(d)   It will be the job of each agency to determine the individual recipients using the Direct Express program, help recipients to convert away from Direct Express, and created a new advertising and instructive webpage for recipients.

(e)   Each recipient will be notified that the Direct Express program will be ending. New recipients will be directed to obtain accounts with their personally preferred card.

(f)   Recipients who do not qualify for a paper check will have their monies electronically deposited to a bank account or debit card.

(g)   If a debit card is preferred, the recipient will furnish the bank routing number and account number associated with the card to the dispensing agency.

(h)   Most debit card holders do not know that all debit cards are associated with a bank, and each individual debit card has an account number associated with the routing number, as can be seen on the bottom left corner of a personal check.

(i)   No dispensing agency will not endorse any bank nor any debit card. The dispensing agency will simply give directions to recipients to contact the office of the debit card to obtain the necessary routing and account numbers.

(j)   If fraud occurs, the recipient will communicate directly with the debit card company and also with the dispensing agency. The dispensing agency will create an advocacy division to be actively involved with the recipient to guarantee the debit card company (or bank if a bank account is used) adheres to all federal banking regulations, a complete investigation is conducted, and all valid fraud claims are forwarded to law enforcement. All cases forwarded to law enforcement will be monitored on a continual basis.

(k)   This plan eliminates the Bureau of Fiscal Service, Comerica Bank, Conduent, Better Business Bureau, and Consumer Financial Protection Bureau; none of which were responsive, proactive, or effective in addressing matters of financial fraud. CFPB never used their authority to investigate or prosecute, BBB simply forwarded all complaints to Susan Schmidt (as did CFPB), Comerica Bank forwarded all fraud matters to Conduent, and Conduent employees were inept (and Comerica Bank knew this, as did I).

Subject: conference notes and remedy to end Direct Express
From: jbsimms
Date: Mon, Nov 04, 2019 7:10 pm
To: Franklin Lemond (Plaintiff's Attorney)
Cc: "Jackie Lynn"
Franklin,
Here is an email I sent to Jackie this evening. We talked a while after she read the attachment.
Here is where we need your input: Jackie and I have a conference scheduled with Sonja Scott and a room full of Treasury agents. We will be sending Sonja a list of issues (attached) and she has agreed for us to address our concerns. Hopefully she will answer questions.
We want you to look over our list of issues and give us an issue or a question we have not mentioned. You probably will know of a point to be made that will help our case against Comerica.
We have pelted OIG Treasury to the point that they are listening. Hopefully their report will help our case.
Jim

Tuesday, November 5, 2019

J B Simms
Nov 5, 2019, 5:22 AM
to Jackie, Franklin, Sonja, Kevin, Katherine, Michael
I assumed this list would not be published or released. I am interested in the parameters used to select the persons who received the packets. If Ms. Battle could create a sanitized version of the parameters, I would be interested in receiving a copy.
I applaud your office for pursuing accountability of BFS, Comerica, and Conduent.
Ms. Densmore and I are scheduled to confer with Ms. Scott and her associates tomorrow at 11:00am.
Many issues are to be addressed. Hopefully Ms. Battle and Ms. Johnson can be present during the conference.
Jim

Subject: Overstepping authority
From: jbsimms
Date: Tue, Nov 05, 2019, 6:04 am
To: Thomas Santaniello (Bureau of Fiscal Service)
Cc: Sonja Scott (OIG Treasury), Jackie, Richard Delmar (OIG Treasury), Franklin@erikpublishing.com, Franklin Lemond (Plaintiff's Attorney)
Dear Mr. Santaniello,
In conjunction with the investigation which will result in the publication of OIG Treasury 19-041, it has been reported to Treasury authorities that you assumed the authority to block Ms. Densmore and me from addressing a group designated as an "Evaluation Team" which was entertaining oral presentations from prospective Fiscal Agents for the Direct Express program.
My sources reveal you to be a congressional liaison employee and not authorized to act as a gatekeeper for any division of group at the Bureau of Fiscal Service, or Treasury.
I am asking you to produce the authority granted to you which validated your act of concealment of this Evaluation Team and the prohibition of victims of malfeasance within your department to present evidence and ask for accountability.
Sincerely, JB Simms

Subject: Synopsis for conference tomorrow: OIG Treas
From: jbsimms
Date: Tue, Nov 05, 2019 7:39 am
To: Katherine Johnson (OIG Treasury), Sonja Scott (OIG Treasury), Richard Delmar (OIG Treasury),Jackie Franklin Lemond (Plaintiff's Attorney)
Please see a draft of topics which Jackie Densmore and I would like to address during our conference scheduled for tomorrow at 11am.
Ms. Densmore will probably be adding to this list of issues.
I also submitted a brief in support of dismantling the Direct Express program. The plan I submit will save millions of dollars, eliminate outsourcing, encourage accountability, and help recipients cut through red tape when they become victims of fraud.
I am certain that persons attending the conference will have response and input to my brief. I do not have to have all the answers; I just need to know enough to be able to generate questions. Hopefully my submission will be taken seriously and used as a template for accountability and effective government. J.B.Simms

Subject: A roster of attendees to the phone conference
From: jbsimms
Date: Tue, Nov 05, 2019 9:12 am
To: Sonja Scott (OIG Treasury)
Cc: "Jackie Lynn"
Sonja,
Can you forward us a list of persons who will be attending the phone conference tomorrow ?
This will be easier than having them yell their names across the table.
Maybe we can confirm the list with you when the conference begins.
Jim

Subject: OIG Treasury Conference syllabus
From: jbsimms
Date: Tue, Nov 05, 2019 1:52 pm
To: Pamela Powers (Chief of Staff, VA)
Cc: "Jackie Lynn"
Dear Ms. Powers,
Thank you for reaching out to respond to my message on LinkedIn. Again, I do look forward to any person at the Dept of Veteran Affairs contacting me.
Attached is a draft/synopsis of the topics being presented by Ms. Densmore and me. Ms. Densmore is the caretaker for her brother in law, who is disabled as a result of military service.
Please acknowledge receipt of this email and attachment. Hopefully this will bring a bit more insight to the matter than what you have been told by those within the VA.
Sincerely,
Jim Simms

Amy Altemus cancels our conference OIG Treasury; paranoia was evident

Subject: RE: conference cancellation
From: Richard Delmar (OIG Treasury)
Date: Tue, Nov 05, 2019, 3:50 pm
To: jbsimms, Sonja Scott (OIG Treasury)
Cc: Jackie Lynn
Mr. Simms – sorry for the mistake in email addressing. Here's what Acting Counsel Altemus sent.
Ms. Altemus has a full understanding of this matter, and of the scope of this office's authority. She has my full confidence, as do our offices of Audit and Investigations.
Rich Delmar
Dear Mr. Sims, Ms. Densmore:
I'm writing to cancel the meeting I understand had previously been scheduled for tomorrow. Upon review, it appears the agenda you have submitted is beyond the scope of our work and our jurisdiction. However, if you feel you have additional material for our review that documents specific problems and deficiencies in how BFS and its current financial agent are operating the Direct Express program, we would appreciate your providing that information in writing or electronically. All such submissions will be reviewed, applied as appropriate to our investigative and audit work, and made part of our records. You may submit such information to the Office of Counsel at OIGCounsel@oig.treas.gov, or to the Office of Inspector General at the address below. While we surely appreciate your investment in this matter, our mandate is to provide impartial and dispassionate review of the programs and whatever issues it faces, and ensuring that the process is seen as such, including the avoidance of any potential appearance of impropriety or partiality in our work and ensuring that the work is completed timely and with all necessary attention and expertise on the issues and findings.
My apologies for the late notice, and thank you for your understanding and assistance-
Sincerely,
Amy
A. J. Altemus, Attorney-Advisor, Office of the Inspector General
U.S. Department of the Treasury

Amy Altemus got involved, cancelled our interview with Treasury, and would become quite an annoyance in this matter. Altemus is an attorney who worked for Delmar. OIG Treasury was exposed. The coward(s) who decided to cancel our meeting would be identified.

From: jbsimms
Sent: Tuesday, November 5, 2019, 5:30 PM
To: Sonja Scott (OIG Treasury)
Cc: Jackie Lynn; Richard Delmar (OIG Treasury)
Subject: conference cancellation
Sonja,
Jackie just got an email from Amy Altemus, telling her the conference was being cancelled. I did not get the email. Ms. Altemus referenced the issues I presented. I assume you have seen this email.

While the assertion that Ms. Altemus made, stating some of the matters I presented were outside the scope of work, that did not prohibit the matters to be addressed. If the matters were outside the scope of work, direct me to the area which is responsible.

It is clear that Ms. Altemus does not have an understanding of this matter, and she would have nothing to offer. It appears the cake is baked, and the persons accountable for the malfeasance will be allowed to conduct business as usual. What an incestuous bunch I see; not being able to hold BFS accountable.

The email was condescending, arrogant, and uninformed. I have not received my copy because it appears my name was misspelled. This is as polite as I can be at this time. While I am disappointed, I am not surprised. This reply from me is probably expected.

Jim

Kevin A. Guishard, the auditor, refused to tell me the parameters of the 30 chosen and would not identify the persons receiving releases.

4:48 AM

J B Simms
Tue, Nov 5, 2019, 1:17 PM
to Joe
Pamela Powers is talking to me again. This was a reply from a LinkedIn message I left, telling her of the conference tomorrow.
Got to keep on them. Cant wait for a rep from the VA to contact me.

This came from LinkedIn
Pamela Powers 12:18 PM
Thanks JB. I have been tracking from my end. Our VBA has a good way forward and I know they will be reaching out to you to discuss.

We needed to get the messages from Powers. If she is referring to VBA persons reaching out to me, maybe she was talking about Lepper, (who did not contact me until a month later).
I checked my email and found this.
I had sent syllabus to Sonja. Need to find that.
The reason I had not seen the email is because Altemus misspelled my last name and the email was never delivered.

Jackie Lynn
Tue, Nov 5, 2019, 3:18 PM
to ScottS, OIG Counsel, me
Sonja ,
As I am sure you have been briefed before the cancellation of our meeting tomorrow I did have some pretty important things to discuss. ~hopefully you can pass along the information
Today I received information that another victim from Massachusetts has fallen victim to direct express fraud his name is Isaac Garcia his contact number is 508 685 4115 . He is a resident of New Bedford . After speaking with Mr. Garcia I could feel his pain, not being able to buy food or pay his mortgage is devastating!
He informed me that he had filed a Police report with the New Bedford South division and that the detective had told him he has had multiple reports of direct express fraud .
I felt compelled to call the police station and speak with him . Sargent Jones @ 508 991 6355 extension 79502 took my call . I explained how I was a victim and asked if he had had any reports come in he stated ~ multiple . He stated to me that most of the fraud is occurring in FLORIDA AND NEW JERSEY. No surprise there .
He told me that he is unclear how to help these people considering it's a federal program and wait times when calling DE exceed over a hour . I hope you don't mind that I gave him your contact info , I hope that you will contact him and offer your assistance and include your findings in your report .
Because this happened to another Massachusetts's resident I also contacted Sen. Warrens office and Congressman's Keating office as well as Boston's investigative reporters .
I DO HOPE MY FOIA WILL BE RELEASED TO ME AS A CITIZEN WHO HAS THE RIGHT TO THIS INFORMATION. I HAVE ASKED FOR OVER A YEAR NOW . Perhaps 'Amy ' from oig counsel can follow up on that as she states - While we surely appreciate your investment in this matter, our mandate is to provide

impartial and dispassionate review of the programs and whatever issues it faces, and ensuring that the process is seen as such, including the avoidance of any potential appearance of impropriety or partiality in our work and ensuring that the work is completed timely and with all necessary attention and expertise on the issues and findings.

I also have spoken with a source from SSA who states that in the upcoming audits they are investigating the death of beneficiaries accounts and if the bank follows procedures on closing accounts and returning money BK to SSA. This is not the banks money this is taxpayers and you may recall the article I sent to your office of the woman who stole $86,000 using her deceased mothers DE CARD BECAUSE THE BANK FAILED TO REPORT IT TO SSA. Mr. Simms assisted with multiple victims that were forwarded to your office regarding death accounts. I do hope this is added in your audit report.

I did want to discuss the intern report with you and the findings .It is my understanding that it was uncovered that the bank fabricated the ratings that they received however it did not state that the bank was to pay back the money that they were paid on for the ratings ? As a taxpayer I find this very concerning. I thought this program was to save money not waste it ? Hopefully the attorney~advisor can make a memo on this fact .

I wanted to discuss your plans with the new contract . I have been told a fiscal agent has not been awarded as of yet. I find this hard to believe but ok I'll play along .

How is BFS going to reissue new cards and accounts if Comerica is not chosen (by the way I was given information that indeed Comerica did bid) in less then 58 days !

My I remind your team that this effects millions of people and they are at the mercy of the people who put them in this Predicament in the first place . Are you going to extend Comericas contract until your report is finalized ,and what is it going to cost the American people ?

I would like to know what if ANY Penalties BFS will need to pay considering they have missed their announcement deadline with no follow up information provided? Your attorney ~advisor AMY TALKS ABOUT COMPLETING WORK ON A TIMELY MANNER , I BELIEVE MAY 2, 2019 IS GROSSLY UNACCEPTABLE. I THINK THAT NEEDS TO BE INCLUDED IN YOUR REPORT .

lastly I encourage your office to contact Sen Collins office regarding the direct express program . They had concerns years before this came to a head .Your office should ask for the responses to the letter dated July 13,2015 .

Some very intriguing questions she asked ;

Identify each treasury employee who at any time was or is an employee of Comerica from 2007 to present. For each person so identified state the date on which day commenced concluded service for each discretes position held within the treasury and Comerica respectively.

I point this out because it should be investigated by your office. If your counsel is trying to remain impartial you need to look within your circle .

I thank you for your time ,
Jackie Densmore

Sent LinkedIn mail to Pamela Powers about telephone meeting tomorrow.

Pamela Powers 12:18 PM
Thanks JB. I have been tracking from my end. Our VBA has a good way forward and I know they will be reaching out to you to discuss.

No one from the VBA reached out to me. Paul Lawrence did not have the courage to engagee me.

Wednesday, November 6, 2019

Delmar email: apologized for my name being misspelled. It proved Amy Altemus was not up to speed on the issues. Delmar certainly knew how to spell my name.
Subject: Fines and remuneration
From: jbsimms
Date: Wed, Nov 06, 2019, 9:01 am
To: Sonja Scott (OIG Treasury)
Dear Sonja,

I am quite disappointed we could not have the conference and I am certain my response was anticipated. The justification presented by Ms. Altemus was creatively vague.

My question today is this: In reference to the passage in the preliminary 19-041 report, it appears OIG Treasury can levy fines and request refunding of monies from Comerica Bank for violating the Fiscal Agent Agreement and misuse of funds. If, as a result of the investigation, Comerica Bank is found to have misused funds and/or violated the FAA, can and will your office or a different authority within Treasury levy the financial penalties?

Again, I was encouraged that you would schedule a conference only to have it cancelled. I was looking forward to expressing my views. It appears there are many cooks in the kitchen.
Jim

Subject: RE: Fines and remuneration
From: jbsimms
Date: Wed, Nov 06, 2019, 2:56 pm
To: Sonja Scott (OIG Treasury)
Jackie sent me prelim 19-041 submitted by Ms. Johnson.
I did not have the doc handy.
Page 5 addressed monies paid to Comerica, stating "Comerica's compensation was never reduced..."
Ms. Johnson was questioning why compensation was not reduced in light of violations.
So, can Comerica be fined or have to return compensation.

Saturday, November 9, 2019

J B Simms
Sat, Nov 9, 2019, 3:16 PM
to Kevin, Jackie, Sonja, Hope
Mr. Guishard,
As predicted, one of the persons who received the package from Ms Altemus (Hope Gearhart) contacted me for clarification. As I told Ms Altemus directly, the package was confusing.
Remember, I was the person these people called from the beginning to tell of their fraud experience, and I was able to recover the money for prob 70 percent of them. Ms Densmore is familiar with the issues and has also been a source for victims.
Remind Ms Altemus that just because many of the 30 persons she authorized the releases be sent received reimbursement, Comerica ignored complaints, and Conduent violated Reg E with regularity by refusing to give full provisional credit within 10 days of notice.
Please have a bit of patience with the victims; they will not have the professional or educational sophistication of some Treasury employees, but their integrity is above reproach, and will challenge anyone at Treasury.

Sunday, November 10, 2019

Chat with Jackie about fraud reporting issues by Comerica and Conduent.
Email Sonja, Delmar, Katherine Johnson: Want to address just the reporting of the fraud.

Subject: A conference; connecting dots on Comerica failure reporting fraud, FAA violation, financial penalties/fines, and Arpin admission
From: jbsimms
Date: Sun, Nov 10, 2019 10:12 am
To: Sonja Scott (OIG Treasury), Richard Delmar (OIG Treasury), Katherine Johnson (OIG Treasury)
Cc: "Jackie Lynn"
Dear All, and good Sunday morning,
While Ms. Densmore and I are disappointed that the conference was cancelled, I can see that the issues I presented were overwhelming. This morning Ms Densmore and I discussed the issue of the failure of fraud reporting by Comerica/Conduent, the unacceptable justification, and the reference to the issue by Nora Arpin reported by Kate Berry in American Banker published August 2018.

Whereas Arpin laid the blame on so-called organized fraud rings that were said to have been known to the Conduent call centers, this admission by Arpin generated a veiled reference in the preliminary 19-041 report submitted by Ms. Johnson.

Ms. Densmore would like to discuss this matter with Ms. Scott, Ms. Johnson, and if Ms. Altemus would be interested in participating, her as well.

Many questions surface which we would like to address, and we will limit our agenda to fraud reporting/fraud prevention in order to allow you to be able to focus on one issue and the inherent tentacles rather than the syllabus of issues I submitted last week prior to the cancelled conference.

The preliminary report referenced "confusion" on the part of Comerica /Conduent with respect to reporting internal or external fraud. As evidenced by Ms. Arpin's admission to Ms. Berry, Ms. Arpin was keenly aware her interpretation of external fraud, but this interpretation was never validated or challenged by BFS or OIG Treasury. The assertion that external fraud was the culprit, excluding infernal fraud, fails on two fronts:

(1) neither categories were reported to FinCen or BFS

(2) examination of persons committing external fraud by law enforcement never occurred to expose the connection to internal fraud

Another issue is failure of BFS to levy fines, reduce payments, or demand repayment of monies paid to Comerica as a result of documented violation of the FAA and, as reported in an OIG Treasury report, the revelation that Comerica submitted incomplete and false information to BFS in order to obtain and retain Fiscal Agent status.

We would like an open and transparent discussion on this matter and would like the investigation by OIG Treasury and the audit headed by Ms. Johnson address the matters I referenced above.

Sincerely,

JB Simms

Thursday, November 14, 2019

From: Sonja Scott (OIG Treasury)
Date: Thu, Nov 14, 2019 11:06 am
To: jbsimms
Cc: Jackie Lynn

Jim – I can see the FB page. I communicate regularly with the DE victims as they contact me, and review the FB page occasionally. Sonja

November, 18, 2019

US Bank- Susan Beatty (612) 303-9229
952am T (612) 303-9229 lmvm
Had emailed on 10/9, 10/28,

From: jbsimms
Date: Mon, Nov 18, 2019, 8:22 am
To: "Jackie Lynn"
Cc: "Joe Plenzler" <jplenzler@woundedwarriorproject.org>

This was sent to Pamela Powers at the VA. She sent me a message stating that someone from the VA would be contacting me. Paul Lawrence is afraid of the truth, as he trots around having photo ops.

Joe, I thank you for forwarding our story to members of the media, and reporters. The writer from the WSJ was evidently told to stand down, as was Jasper Craven. The only person brave enough to write stories is Kate Berry of American Banker. If you have any suggestions, we are all ears.

J B Simms 7:17 AM to Pamela Powers, COS of VA (via LinkedIn)

I look forward to discussing the Direct Express program with the person you assign, and addressing the endorsement given by the VA. The dots I see to be connected, and the unanswered questions, are baffling to those who understand the culture of keeping citizens in the dark. BFS started a mentor program at the same time as the Fiscal Agent for Direct Express program was to be announced, but BFS failed to name the new Fiscal Agent (May, 2019). BFS prohibited victims of the Direct Express program from addressing the group at BFS which was to announce the new FA. OIG Treas report, 19-041, was published in preliminary form, and after my critique was received, the final has not been published. The VA continues to endorse this flawed program. OIG Treasury has now shied away from conferring with Ms. Densmore and me, after scheduling a conference. Now, after you are offering of a VA official contacting me, that too has not happened. The fact that we see the corruption and malfeasance makes people uncomfortable and bolsters their attitude of no accountability. I am ready for a chat.

Tuesday, November 19, 2019

1201pm I called US Bank at (612) 303-9229 to get information about the Mentor Program. I left a message on my voice mail.

These people at US Bank were not going to talk to me. They knew the creation of this program was a direct indictment of BFS and the failure to enforce regulations on other fiscal agents, namely, Comerica Bank. Web-fiscal.treasury.gov/training/financial-agent-mentor-protégé-program.html

A Treasury Mentor program link was discovered: www.treasury.gov/resource-center/sb-programs
(202) 622-1499 Brian.Watson@treasury.gov

An email was sent to Treasury to get information regarding the Mentor Program.
Subject: Mentor Program webinar
From: jbsimms
Date: Tue, Nov 19, 2019, 10:08 am
To: arm@fiscal.treasury.gov
Cc: "Jackie Lynn"
Dear Sirs,
Ms. Densmore and I would like you to furnish us with the link or portal for us to view the webinar for training and explanation of the Mentor program which was held on September 12, 2019. We have questions concerning this program.
Sincerely,
J.B. Simms

Subject: Lack of Transparency, Mentor Program BFS
From: jbsimms
Date: Tue, Nov 19, 2019 10:21 am
To: Sonja Scott (OIG Treasury), Richard Delmar (OIG Treasury)
Cc: "Jackie Lynn"
https://www.kansascityfed.org/events/2018/financial-agent-mentor-protege-program-summit-091118
https://www.fiscal.treasury.gov/training/financial-agent-mentor-protege-program.html
Ms. Scott,
Since I was the person to bring the BFS Mentor program to your attention a month or so ago, a program that began in May 2019, I thought you might want to know that there have been meetings and seminars detailing this program. The program which was to have been available on September 12, 2019 was publicized as being available to all federal employees, but this announcement seemed to have been missed by your office.
Lack of transparency by BFS seems to be working very well. BFS is covering for their malfeasance, and we are the ones to bring this to you attention. I would take this as a personal affront as BFS dances around your audits and investigation. Gribben seems to be no different than Lebryk, Morrow, or McCoy.Jim

From: jbsimms
Date: Tue, Nov 19, 2019, 6:08 pm
To: Brian.watson@treasury.gov
Cc: "Jackie Lynn"
Dear Mr. Watson,
Having been made aware that the Mentor Program began in May 2019, I and others have questions about this program. Today I found this site:
https://www.treasury.gov/resource-center/sb-programs/Pages/dcfo-osdbu-mentor-protege-index.aspx
I would like to arrange for a conference call between us and Ms. Jackie Densmore at your earliest possible convenience.
Please email us and advise me a time we can talk.
Sincerely,, J.B. Simms

Wednesday, November 20, 2019

From: *jbsimms*
Date: *Wed, Nov 20, 2019, 8:38 am*
To: *Brian.Watson@treasury.gov*
Cc: *"Jackie Lynn"*
Thank you for your reply.
I will pursue this matter via the link you supplied.
If you would allow me to ask a question and connect a few dots, that would be helpful.
My understanding is that the Mentor Program was initiated in May 2019. Ms. McCoy resigned, and Mr. Gribben took over BFS after May. Your reference to the fact that the Mentor Program is being operated by SBA indicates to me that Mr. Gribben was known to be the new commissioner, and that Mr. Gribben was, to his credit, was involved in the initiation of this program.
I am privy to more than four or more internet articles stating the Mentor Program began in May 2019, at the same time BFS was to have announced the new or renewal of the Fiscal Agent contract.
As a spokesperson to US Treasury, can you give me a definitive date of your understanding of the initiation of this Mentor Program?
Thank you very much.
JB Simms

Subject: Connecting a few more dots
From: *jbsimms*
Date: *Wed, Nov 20, 2019 12:10 pm*
To: *Sonja Scott (OIG Treasury)*
Cc: *"Jackie Lynn"*
Sonja,
I assume you are as tired of our emails as we are of being ignored.
This Mentor Program of which you had no knowledge was well underway, according to other Treasury offices, in May, 2019. Oddly, this was just before Gribben took over from McCoy. Gribben must have been the person to originate the Mentor Program at BFS because it did not exist before his being named commissioner.
This is the same Mentor Program to which Brian Watson referred me in the attached email.
The interesting connection is that the BFS Mentor Program originated at the same time BFS delayed the naming of the Fiscal Agent for 2020.
While I applaud Gribben for getting this implemented, it is quite obvious the program is a CYA for BFS, and it kinda didn't work; we kinda see through it.
One of the disturbing things is you claimed no knowledge of this until I brought it to your attention.
We still want to talk with you.Jim

From: jbsimms
Sent: Tuesday, November 19, 2019 8:09 PM
To: Watson, Brian <Brian.Watson@treasury.gov>
Cc: Jackie Lynn
Subject: https://www.treasury.gov/resource-center/sb-programs/Pages/dcfo-osdbu-mentor-protege-index.aspx
Dear Mr. Watson,
Having been made aware that the Mentor Program began in May 2019, I and others have questions about this program. Today I found this site:
https://www.treasury.gov/resource-center/sb-programs/Pages/dcfo-osdbu-mentor-protege-index.aspx
I would like to arrange for a conference call between us and Ms. Jackie Densmore at your earliest possible convenience.
My telephone number is (803) 309-6850. Please email us and advise me a time we can talk.
Sincerely,J.B. Simms

Friday, November 22, 2019

From: *jbsimms*
Date: *Fri, Nov 22, 2019 7:54 am*
To: *"Susan Beatty" <susan.beatty@usbank.com>*

Cc: "Jackie Lynn"
Bcc: Kate Berry (American Banker)
Dear Ms. Beatty,
Your name is listed as the contact person in numerous web articles, including a release by your employer US Bank, with respect to the involvement of US Bank and Bureau of Fiscal Service in the Mentor Program. This email is the third email I have sent you over the past six weeks and I have yet to receive a reply. Two telephone calls have been made, messages left, and also ignored.
If your agenda is to avoid accountability, it is apparent that a more honest person would have deferred this responsibility to an employee who would fulfill the prerequisite of the position and title conferred upon you. If you would simply respond and advise me of your intentions, I will take it from there.
JB Simms

From: jbsimms
Date: Mon, Nov 25, 2019, 10:27 am
To: Sonja Scott (OIG Treasury), Richard Delmar (OIG Treasury)
Cc: "Susan Beatty" <susan.beatty@usbank.com>, "Jackie Lynn"
Dear Mr. Delmar and Ms. Scott,
After discovering the Mentor Program implemented by BFS in May, 2019, it was noted that a person named Susan Beatty of US Bank had her name listed on a number of media announcements as the contact person for US Bank who would respond to inquiries concerning said Mentor Program.
Over the past 6+weeks, emails and telephone messages have been sent and left for Ms. Beatty. No response has been received. I have not reached out to her boss but decided instead to ask for your assistance. If you determine that Ms. Beatty is going to continue her behavior of non-compliance with regard to transparency with citizens, albeit consistent with the history with BFS, I will ask that you intervene on behalf of the taxpaying citizens.
You are well aware we are privy to the "mushroom cultivation" attitude of BFS with respect to transparency and accountability to citizens as well as to your office. This attitude appears to have gravitated to US Bank. If either of you could contact Ms. Beatty, or her supervisor, on behalf of the citizens, I would be grateful.
Sincerely, J.B. Simms

Sunday, December 1, 2019

Jackie sent questions to Delmar. 4 pages.

Tuesday, December 3, 2019

US Bank- No response from Susan Beatty
LinkedIn- Davin Palombi- EP, Pub Affairs US Bank- message sent.
Article – Rebekah Fawcett, US Bank Pub Affairs and communications
Rebekah.fawcette@usbank.com
(612) 303-9986
1007am T Rebekah Fawcett (612) 303-9986 Left message on voicemail
Sent email to Fawcett.

Subject: Contact with Susan Beatty, and the Mentor Program
From: jbsimms
Date: Tue, Dec 03, 2019 8:24 am
To: Rebekah.fawcett@usbank.com
Cc: "Jackie Lynn"
Dear Ms. Fawcett,
We are trying to reach the contact person with US Bank with regard to the Mentor Program which US Bank partnered with Bureau of Fiscal Service in May, 2019. There were a number of publications which named Ms. Beatty as the contact person from whom to obtain information about this program.
Emails were sent to Ms. Beatty on October 9 and October 28, 2019. No response has been received. Two telephone calls were made to Ms. Beatty in November 2019, neither of which were returned after voice messages were left.

Please forward this to the appropriate supervisor of Ms. Beatty, and we ask that you confirm receipt of this inquiry.

If you are aware of a the identity of the person to whom Ms. Beatty is to report, please furnish this to us so we can further pursue this matter.

Sincerely,

J.B. Simms

Subject: RE: FW: Mentor Program, and failure to communicate
From: jbsimms
Date: Tue, Dec 03, 2019 2:21 pm
To: "Leamon, Cheryl U" <cheryl.leamon@usbank.com>
Cc: Jackie Lynn, Kate Berry (American Banker)

Dear Ms. Leamon,

After having read the articles published by your employer (US Bank) where Susan Beatty was listed as the person to whom inquiries were to be submitted, I fail to understand why Ms. Beatty refused to acknowledge my inquiries and why, since you are admitting you are in possession of said communication with Ms. Beatty and have knowledge of the two voice messages, it took two months for someone from US Bank to respond to my email inquiry.

Unless you are referring all inquiries submitted to Ms. Beatty to Bureau of Fiscal Service, I will pursue this matter further to obtain definitive justification for your behavior and that of Ms. Berry.

Since this is a program using taxpayer dollars, we would assume a bit of transparency would be in order. If you prefer a different person, make the inquiry, that can be arranged.

Pass this along to your staff attorneys and have one of them contact me.

Sincerely,

J.B. Simms

The mentor program is hidden

Subject: FW: Mentor Program, and failure to communicate
From: "Leamon, Cheryl U" <cheryl.leamon@usbank.com>
Date: Tue, Dec 03, 2019 12:38 pm
To: jbsimms

Mr. Simms—we have received your email regarding the Bureau of the Fiscal Service Mentor Protégé program. We respectfully refer you to the Bureau of the Fiscal Service, Office of Legislative and Public Affairs at media.relations@fiscal.treasury.gov on this matter.

Thank you,

Cheryl

Cheryl U Leamon
Senior Vice President | Public Affairs and Communications
p. 651.435.7460 | cheryl.leamon@usbank.com

Wednesday, December 4, 2019

US Bank refuses to respond regarding the BFS Mentor Program

Subject: RE: RE: FW: Mentor Program, and failure to communicate
From: "Leamon, Cheryl U" <cheryl.leamon@usbank.com>
Date: Wed, December 04, 2019, 3:08 pm
To: jbsimms

Mr. Simms—I encourage you to contact the Bureau of the Fiscal Service, Office of Legislative and Public Affairs at media.relations@fiscal.treasury.gov on this matter. U.S. Bank will not respond to additional requests for information.

Thank you.

Cheryl

From: jbsimms
Date: Wed, Dec 04, 2019, 7:41 pm
To: "Leamon, Cheryl U" <cheryl.leamon@usbank.com>
Cc: Richard Delmar (OIG Treasury), Sonja Scott (OIG Treasury), Katherine Johnson (OIG Treasury),Jackie Kate Berry (American Banker), Franklin Lemond (Plaintiff's Attorney)

Dear Ms. Leamon,

While your response and failure to forward my inquiry to your staff attorneys does not surprise me, it is incumbent upon me to let you know that Bureau of Fiscal Service is being investigated and the preliminary audit was published July 29, 2019. Malfeasance and failure to properly administer a fiscal agent by Bureau of Fiscal Service is the subject of this investigation, and Thomas Santaniello of the Office of Legislative and Public Affairs (BFS) prohibited victims of malfeasance to address Bureau of Fiscal Service.

It would be an exercise in futility for anyone to request information about the Mentor Program from Bureau of Fiscal Service. This matter with US Bank and Bureau of Fiscal Service, along with the investigation and audit of Bureau of Fiscal Service, has become the "tar baby" for everyone, both individually and collectively. Your failure to pass this to your counsel rather than give a directive to send inquiries to the subject of an investigation attaches you to the matter in a manner penned by Aesop.

You have an option.

Sincerely,

J.B. Simms

From: jbsimms
Sent: Monday, November 25, 2019 11:27 AM
To: Sonja Scott <Sonja Scott (OIG Treasury)>; Richard Delmar (OIG Treasury)
Cc: Beatty, Susan L <susan.beatty@usbank.com>; Jackie Lynn
Subject: Mentor Program, and failure to communicate

Dear Mr. Delmar and Ms. Scott,

After discovering the Mentor Program implemented by BFS in May 2019, it was noted that a person named Susan Beatty of US Bank had her name listed on a number of media announcements as the contact person for US Bank who would respond to inquiries concerning said Mentor Program.

Over the past 6+weeks, emails and telephone messages have been sent and left for Ms. Beatty. No response has been received. I have not reached out to her boss but decided instead to ask for your assistance. If you determine that Ms. Beatty is going to continue her behavior of non-compliance with regard to transparency with citizens, albeit consistent with the history with BFS, I will ask that you intervene on behalf of the taxpaying citizens.

You are well aware we are privy to the "mushroom cultivation" attitude of BFS with respect to transparency and accountability to citizens as well as to your office. This attitude appears to have gravitated to US Bank. If either of you could contact Ms. Beatty, or her supervisor, on behalf of the citizens, I would be grateful.

Sincerely,

J.B. Simms

Wednesday, December 4, 2019

From: Sonja Scott (OIG Treasury)
Date: December 4, 2019, at 10:19:22 AM EST
To: jbsimms
Cc: Jackie Lynn
Subject: RE: Acknowledgement of emails

My office would like me to have our counsel respond to all requests for information and FOIA. I am, however, still communicating with victims as I handle incoming complaints. Sonja

From: jbsimms
Sent: Wednesday, December 4, 2019 9:24 AM
To: Sonja Scott (OIG Treasury)
Cc: Jackie Lynn
Subject: Acknowledgement of emails
Dear Sonja,
Jackie and I have been discussing the fact that we do not receive confirmation of emails we send. The fact that the conference was cancelled reinforces my point to Jackie that "They just don't want to have a conversation with us."
It is apparent that the attitude at Treasury is that "...we do not work for these people, and we do not answer to them." The fact is we have exposed issues, beginning with my initial chat with Ms. Battle in February 2018, that OIG Treasury was not aware, and was never printed in an OIG Treasury report.
US Bank will not discuss the Mentor Program, and they referred us to Santaniello. Jackie's FOI request, which was submitted over a year ago, has not been addressed, and person(s) at the FOI section lied about not receiving it and having a wrong address; it was mailed and faxed to the destination printed on the website.
Jackie has not received a copy of the investigation of the theft on her case which happened at the WalMart in Florida. These are a few of the issues which Treasury ignores.
We cannot be criticized for continuing to connect dots of malfeasance on the part of different divisions of Treasury; dots which have been ignored or brought to light by us. It appears some take our revelations and our inquiries as a personal affront.
Can you simply acknowledge the information sent to you about the questionable BFS activity of the Mentor Program, and send the FOI request information to Ms. Densmore ?
Can you also give us a reason why the conference was cancelled and why all communication from your office has stopped ?
Jim

Jackie Lynn
Wed, Dec 4, 2019, 5:44 AM
to Cate, Franklin Lemond (Plaintiff's Attorney), ScottS, Richard Delmar (OIG Treasury), me
OIG TREASURY - will not respond to me about the fact the bank was paid money they did not deserve, my FOIA request and my packet into my investigation
They are refusing to Answer me on any of this, they are not responding to me

From: Michael Jackman (Aide to Rep. Keating)
Date: December 4, 2019 at 12:26:34 PM EST
To: Jackie Lynn
Subject: FW: Questions re: Direct Express program
Richard Delmar at OIG asked that these questions be put directly to BFS. I sent this email this morning.
--Mike Jackman

From: Jackman, Michael
Sent: Wednesday, December 4, 2019 9:44 AM
To: Thomas.Santaniello@fiscal.treasury.gov
Subject: Questions re: Direct Express program
Hello,
It is our understanding that the Bureau of Fiscal Services is in the process of re-bidding the Financial Agent for its Direct Express program.
Our office is interested in the BFS's process and the ongoing Direct Express program as run by Comerica. Richard Delmar of the Office of the Inspector General has referred me to BFS to obtain answers to the following questions:
Can you provide a copy of the sample Financial Agent Agreement that was sent to the finalists for the DE program? Referred to in the attached memo.
Can you provide a list of the finalists?
Has the vendor for the DE program been chosen? If so, who was the successful candidate? If not, what is the timeline for selection?

Our constituent Jacqueline Densmore has submitted a Freedom of Information Act request to the BFS regarding Comerica and the Direct Express program. What is the status of her request?
Thank you for any information you can provide.
Michael Jackman, District Director, Office of Congressman Keating (MA-09)

Kate Berry (American Banker)
Wed, Dec 4, 2019, 10:51 AM
to me
Hi JB - Hope you had a great Thanksgiving!
I have no idea whether the CFPB has done any investigation of Comerica, but if they have, they are keeping it under the auspices of "supervision," rather than enforcement. I'm hearing that many of their actions are now being done as supervisory matters that allow banks not be taken to task publicly, and to resolve issues in private (something all businesses prefer, but that the former administration tended to make public.)
But who knows??
I will see what I can get from a FOIA.
best,
kate
Kate Berry
Reporter American Banker

I had traveled to St. Petersburg, Florida to assist a friend with her new business. I kept working on this case.

J B Simms
Wed, Dec 4, 2019, 11:43 AM
to Jackie, Kate
Thanks so much.
I am in St Pete, Florida. Might be here through spring training. My fastball is not what it used to be 😔.No one at CFPB or OIG Treasury wants to go after BFS or Comerica.
OIG Treasury is now referring our inquiries to Thomas Santaniello, the Legislative liaison. He is the one who blocked Jackie and me from personally addressing BFS. Now OIG Treasury is in bed with Santaniello. I equate Santaniello as the "Whitey Bulger" of BFS; he has dirt on everyone and uses the leverage to deflect our inquiries.
Being from a family of Boston lawyers, Santaniello knows exactly what being "Bulger" means. OIG Treasury is supposed to be investigating BFS and Santaniello, not forwarding our inquiries to BFS.
The more they delay the OIG Treasury report 19-041 and BFS delays naming the Fiscal Agent, and US Bank refuses to answer questions, the deeper we go.
These are some very (fill in the blank) people.
We appreciate your help and your input.
Now I gotta work on my fastball 🤚
Jim

Subject: RE: RE: FW: Mentor Program, and failure to communicate
From: "Leamon, Cheryl U" <cheryl.leamon@usbank.com>
Date: Wed, Dec 04, 2019 3:08 pm
To: jbsimms
Mr. Simms—I encourage you to contact the Bureau of the Fiscal Service, Office of Legislative and Public Affairs at media.relations@fiscal.treasury.gov on this matter. U.S. Bank will not respond to additional requests for information.
Thank you.
Cheryl

BFS was hiding information about the Mentor Program

Secret meetings were being held regarding Conduent. OIG Treasury was not happy with Conduent, but the meetings were not public. The Mentor Program was a direct result of the failure of Conduent and Comerica Bank.

From: jbsimms
Sent: Tuesday, December 3, 2019, 3:21 PM
To: Leamon, Cheryl U <cheryl.leamon@usbank.com>
Cc: Jackie Lynn ; Kate Berry (American Banker)
Subject: Mentor Program, and failure to communicate
Dear Ms. Leamon,
After having read the articles published by your employer (US Bank) where Susan Beatty was listed as the person to whom inquiries were to be submitted, I fail to understand why Ms. Beatty refused to acknowledge my inquiries and why, since you are admitting you are in possession of said communication with Ms. Beatty and have knowledge of the two voice messages, it took two months for someone from US Bank to respond to my email inquiry.
Unless you are referring all inquiries submitted to Ms. Beatty to Bureau of Fiscal Service, I will pursue this matter further to obtain definitive justification for your behavior and that of Ms. Berry.
Since this is a program using taxpayer dollars, we would assume a bit of transparency would be in order. If you prefer a different person make the inquiry, that can be arranged.
Pass this along to your staff attorneys and have one of them contact me.
Sincerely,
J.B. Simms

Subject: The investigation of my fraud experience.
From: "Guishard, Kevin A." <GuishardK@oig.treas.gov>
Date: Thu, Dec 05, 2019 10:32 am
To: jbsimms
Cc: "'jackiedenzz@yahoo.com'" , "Johnson, Katherine E." <JohnsonK@oig.treas.gov>, "Levin, Michael A." <LevinM@oig.treas.gov>
Mr. Simms,
We have received your signed release and I will forward your narrative along to Ms. Altemus.
Thanks,
Kevin

Friday, December 6, 2019

Franklin Lemond
Fri, Dec 6, 2019, 6:32 AM
to Jackie, me
Jackie,
Thanks for your email. The opposition to the motion to dismiss the Texas case is due today. Attached is our current draft, that will be filed by COB today.
The Jan. 9 hearing that was scheduled by the Texas Judge earlier this week will be oral argument on the motion to dismiss.
More subpoenas are definitely needed. We are also in discussions with the Defendants about consolidating all the cases back together. They seem open to the idea, but I want to make sure everything is handled appropriately.
In addition to this brief being filed today, I have another filing due today and two more on Monday. After I get past Monday let's schedule a call.
Franklin

Subject: concerns
From: jbsimms
Date: Tue, Dec 10, 2019, 7:15 am
To: Sonja Scott (OIG Treasury)
Cc: Jackie Lynn, Richard Delmar (OIG Treasury), Katherine Johnson (OIG Treasury)
Sonja,
We know that since our conference was canceled that OIG Treasury has effectively shut down communication with us. You do not want to hear our comments, our insight, our conclusions, or revelations of contradictions or "head-shaking" decisions made by OIG Treasury or BFS. Based upon what we have seen, and the decisions of

BFS to ignore your two OIG reports, the motivation of particular persons at BFS is clear, and the logo for BFS should be changed to BF$.

OIG Treasury Report 19-041 cannot be completed until Ms. Altemus completes her audit of the 30 verified victims taken from the list of 105 I presented you. Direct contact with Comerica Bank and Conduent employees was not evident in the preliminary report.

OIG Treasury Report 19-024 has not been forwarded to me, as was promised by Mr. Delmar.

BFS's (Santaniello) decision to block us from addressing their agency has not been explained, nor their motive. BFS has not named the successor (or incumbent) at the expiration of this last Direct Express contract. We suggested, in brief detail, how and why the Direct Express program should be eliminated (taking BFS out of the cookie jar).

The FOI request submitted by Ms. Delmar has been languishing within the halls of OIG Treasury for over a year. There are no consequences where there are no penalties.

Treasury has many balls in the air before 19-041 can be published. We know that.

We want to have faith in the process and that your office will act on behalf of citizens rather than perpetuating the careers of incompetent and unscrupulous federal employees.

We still want the conference.

Jim

Wednesday, December 11, 2019

From: Jackie Lynn
to: Michael Jackman <michael.jackman@mail.house.gov>
cc: Thomas Santaniello (Bureau of Fiscal Service),
date: Dec 11, 2019, 12:13 PM
subject: Fwd: FOIA # 2019-08-012 (Densmore)
Good Afternoon Mr. Jackman and Mr. Santaniello

I would like to discuss how a request for my FOIA was sent over a year ago and according to this email I received on AUGUST 27 2019 they state that they are calculating the fees . It has been over 106 days since I received this email. In no way should this be taking this long regardless of the scope of my questions.

As far as the deadline of announcing the new fiscal agent of 2020 on Jan 2nd, do you think Mr. Santaniello that your office will meet that deadline or grant an extension of the current contract with Comerica? I would think since you are the one running the show you would know this answer. I did not see anything on the BFS website that the deadline will be missed however I find it incredibly difficult that you will be able to notify over 4.1 million Americans that a new fiscal agent has been selected in less than 22 DAYS. Beneficiaries accounts will be in limbo during the beginning of the month when monthly deposits will be going into direct express accounts issued by Comerica Bank .

I do hope you see the concerns that I have and I would like an answer on these questions please ~ will your office be announcing the new fiscal agent on or before January 2, 2020 ? Are you still in the selection process or not?

I have asked two direct questions Mr. Santaniello both which you should be able to answer.

I look forward to your responses and hope there is no more delays as this effects millions of people nationwide, Mr. Santaniello. I have emailed you several times, every single one unanswered ,I do hope with Mr. Jackman attached in this email that you respond to me .

Thank you for your time,
Jackie Densmore

On Wed, Dec 11, 2019 at 11:24 PM Jackie Lynn wrote:
Franklin I agree with Jim, it's time to take off the gloves and handle this situation .
You had promised me a phone call 2 days ago, I would like these answered before we speak.
Before you call us I want to know you have done these things -
1- my subpoena /freedom of information act update, have they responded to you and have they exceeded the amount of time on their response ? Did you send it and the date please?
2- information on Sen Warrens subpoena and have they exceeded the amount of time for their response?
3- detailed information on your next round of subpoenas who will be getting them and what will you be asking for
4- update on the video from Walmart in Hollywood FL, have you received this or even asked for it ?

5- have you secured any documentation from Sen Collins and retired oig Social Security Administration Patrick O'Carroll

6- with the new evidence that Jim and I have sent to you on the mentor program and also the call center that treasury opened a mile away from Comerica bank what are you planning to ask for with these new findings . Jim and I both are very interested in these findings and feel that you should move quickly on this.

7- I would also ask you to include requests to social security on why they are doing an audit on death benefit accounts, it is my understanding that there is a program in place . This is meant for Comerica to return money and close accounts once a cardholder passes away. I believe Comerica is not doing this and keeping the money why else would SSA be investigating this.

8- I also want representation on whistleblower for the overpayment of taxpayers' dollars to Comerica bank according to the oig report findings .

9- when treasury opened the call center for Comerica and ran it they put procedures in place for fraud since they reports kept coming in what were these procedures and why was it documented in any of the reports or audits.

10- Card suspension is purely for the cardholder," she said. "If we identify the fraud through our scanning systems, then we reimburse the cardholder within 10 days. When fraud is identified before the cardholder calls us, we'll make an outbound call. If we can't reach the cardholder, we'll temporarily suspend their card." What scanning system is Arpin talking about in this article????

They stated they never make outbound calls and this is why the fraud happened on Derek's account because they did not call us.

11-I would like to know how many reports of fraud has been documented through social security and through the VA

These numbers I'm sure will be higher then what the bank gave you .

Please answer each question and send back to me and please enclose a date for a conference call I believe that is overdue.

Thank you. , Jackie

Subject: Message sent to Chief of Staff of VA today December 10, 2019
From: jbsimms
Date: Wed, Dec 11, 2019 8:49 am
To: Jackie Lynn, Sonja Scott (OIG Treasury), Franklin Lemond (Plaintiff's Attorney), Richard Delmar (OIG Treasury), "Joe Plenzler" <jplenzler@woundedwarriorproject.org>, Kate Berry (American Banker)
Ms. Powers offered to have a rep from VBA contact me. This offer was over a month ago. During one exchange, Powers stated her office was communicating with OIG Treasury on this matter. No confirmation of this has been received. OIG Treasury is operating in stealth mode, refusing to answer questions or address matters which affect veterans and civilians as victims of this ill-conceived program. The motivation of Bureau of Fiscal Service not only to grant the contract to Comerica Bank, but to refuse cardholders access to those who grant the contract, is more than a bit suspicious. A GAO report 17-176, published almost 3 years ago, laid out transgressions of BFS and lack of transparency.
Kate Berry has been vigilant in reporting on this matter. Mr. Plenzler had been gracious enough to refer us to other media outlets, who, after being anxious to print the story, shied away from the story.

Subject: A fear of OIG Treasury 19-041 being parallel to the FISA application by FBI
From: jbsimms
Date: Wed, Dec 11, 2019 11:57 am
To: Richard Delmar (OIG Treasury)
Cc: Jackie Lynn, Franklin Lemond (Plaintiff's Attorney), Sonja Scott (OIG Treasury), Katherine Johnson (OIG Treasury), Kate Berry (American Banker)
Dear Mr. Delmar,
My concern with the content of the upcoming publication of OIG Treasury 19-041 was validated with the preliminary report published on July 29, 2019. After you received my rebuttal of this preliminary, and challenged the evidence I presented as "assertions," I see a parallel mentality with OIG Treasury reports and the recent and ongoing public debate of the FISA application(s) submitted by the FBI; exculpatory, incomplete, and inaccurate information was presented by the FBI, and I found the same to be true of the preliminary report OIG Treasury 19-041. When I challenged these shortcomings of 19-041, you appeared to be defensive and

surprised that a common citizen could dissect this report and/or the fact I would have the gall to present my findings to a person of your stature.

Ms. Johnson (OIG Treasury 19-041), as was David Lebryk (OIG Treasury 14-031) and Sheryl Morrow (OIG Treasury 17-034) would not have been able to publish any OIG Treasury report without the approval of the director of OIG Treasury. Lebryk and Morrow obtained approval from Mr. Thorson, who retired 6 months ago. Mr. Thorson refused to be questioned with respect to the veracity of the reports which he approved, but when I challenged these reports, it was apparent that suspicions arose and a new investigation was commissioned, as was confirmed by you to a reporter, Kate Berry, of American Banker.

While my understanding and knowledge of evidence of malfeasance and corruption by Bureau of Fiscal Service might be dismissed by you inadequate and not arising to your level of intellect, my knowledge of proprietary information of the behavior of Treasury personnel along with direct and personal interaction with victims of this malfeasance gives me a more objective and complete view of the problem than would be of an investigator or auditor of OIG Treasury, who drinks from the same trough as the entity/personnel under investigation.

I pray, for the victims who have been subjected to this malfeasance from every corner of Treasury, that the changing of the guard at OIG Treasury and BFS, that you and Mr. Gribben will honestly clean out the swamp in both of your offices.

Ms. Densmore and I stand firm in our request to address you and anyone in your office. An anonymous person cancelled our conference 6 weeks ago, with no explanation. We have questions which might make some uncomfortable, but we know how the cake was baked. Hopefully we can have this conference before the publishing of 19-041. We will need no attorney to prep us.
Sincerely, , J.B. Simms

Looking for honesty regarding the Mentor Program

Subject: RE: RE: FW: Mentor Program, and failure to communicate
From: jbsimms
Date: Wed, Dec 11, 2019 2:42 pm
To: "Leamon, Cheryl U" <cheryl.leamon@usbank.com>, "Thomas Santaniello" Thomas Santaniello (Bureau of Fiscal Service)
Cc: Jackie Lynn, Richard Delmar (OIG Treasury), Sonja Scott (OIG Treasury), Katherine Johnson (OIG Treasury), dana.ripley@usbank.com, "Michael Jackman" <michael.jackman@mail.house.gov>, Franklin Lemond (Plaintiff's Attorney) Kate Berry (American Banker)
Dear Ms. Leamon,

Since receiving the email from you (see below) an email was sent to Mr. Ripley Chief Communications Officer at US Bank. Mr. Ripley was asked to forward our query to Mr. Chosy, General Counsel of US Bank.

Questions concerning Fiscal Agents at Bureau of Fiscal Service have been directed to Thomas Santaniello, who has positioned himself as the deflector of all inquiries submitted to Fiscal Services, other than a reply from a staff member of a member of the House of Representatives (Keating), Mr. Jackman. Mr. Jackman made an inquiry on behalf of a constituent, Jackie Densmore, concerning failure of Bureau of Fiscal Service to respond to an FOI request made over a year prior. This is the behavior of Bureau of Fiscal Service that is consistent with their failure to monitor or question malfeasance by another Fiscal Agent.

The fact that US Bank and Bureau of Fiscal Service would refuse to answer questions about a government program which, observed in multiple publications began in May 2019, is consistent with my motivation to question OIG Treasury 14-031 and 17-034 which led to the current investigation of Bureau of Fiscal Service, 19-041. GAO 17-176 was published one day after US Treasury 17-034 and exposed Bureau of Fiscal Service as having a lack of transparency, among other transgressions. Nothing has changed. Bureau of Fiscal Service, using Mr. Santaniello as the mouthpiece, has been consistent in his attempt to disguise facts and shield other workers at Bureau of Fiscal Service of any accountability or scrutiny of a number of highly questionable ethic violations.

We assume you were told "...[j]ust send Simms an email and tell him to send inquiries to Fiscal Services." Evidently you did what you were told to do, and now you are in the chain of communication, and justification for your email to me will be part of the new inquiry.

Mr. Santaniello, we ask that you submit a brief, or have a clerk compose such, which will detail the origin of the Mentor Program, the selection process, the payments being made to US Bank, and the identity of the persons at Bureau of Fiscal Service who are responsible for overseeing this program. We will be happy to refer all our inquiries through Mr. Jackman since you choose not to communicate with private citizens.

A brief from Mr. Chosy would also be welcomed. Sincerely, J.B. Simms

Thursday, December 12, 2019

Delmar gave me a number for the subpoena to be served.

(202) 622-1650 336pm T (202) 622-165 0 Left message on voicemail.
Delmar was to send me information on where to send the subpoena.

From: Franklin Lemond (Plaintiff's Attorney)>
Date: Thu, Dec 12, 2019 10:01 am
To: Jim Simms
Cc: Jackie Lynn ,
Jim,
Thanks for your email and your continued efforts. I will see about a subpoena to Santaniello personally, that might be a good idea. I would like nothing more than to be a grinch to those in charge of Direct Express. I am fighting off some grinches who are trying to spoil my Christmas currently but will be sure to focus on these important subpoenas soon.
Franklin

From: Richard Delmar (OIG Treasury)
Date: Thu, Dec 12, 2019 1:47 pm
To: jbsimms Cc: Jackie Lynn
I believe so but am checking with Treasury OGC for any changes. Stand by.

From: J B Simms
Sent: Thursday, December 12, 2019 2:04 PM
To: Guishard, Kevin A. <GuishardK@oig.treas.gov>
Cc: Jackie Densmore
Subject: Investigation status
Mr. Guishard,
As I sit at lunch, and after having to deal with other OIG Treasury matters as well as Thomas Santaniello of BFS making false statements to the aide of a member of Congress, it occurred to me that I have not received a copy of the investigation of the fraud I experienced on my Direct Express account.
I will bring to your attention that in addition to the fact the Better Business Bureau and the Consumer Financial Protection Bureau simply refer complaints to Susan Schmidt (I have a letter from Schmidt admitting receiving my complaint from CFPB), my initial call to Schmidt was ignored. Schmidt stated voicemail messages to her office were monitored and returned, and when my call was never returned, I challenged Schmidt to research the call. I gave her the date and time.
My account was hacked earlier that year, January 2017, and I contacted merchants, with no interaction from Comerica or Conduent, to "convince them" to return my money.
This might seem trivial to you and Ms. Altemus, but there are disabled persons who have experienced the same exclusion and rejection, and who do not have the luxury (or burden) of my experience or focus. Please send me a copy of the audit of my account including the summary narrative.
J.B. Simms

From: J B Simms
Sent: Thursday, December 12, 2019, 2:59 PM
To: Guishard, Kevin A. <GuishardK@oig.treas.gov>
Cc: Jackie Lynn
Subject: Re: Investigation status
Thank you for your prompt response.
I signed a release, at your request, enabling you to obtain and audit the fraud claim upon my account with Comerica Bank. This was sent to you at the end of October/first of November. You have confirmed having received the said release. Your office was to request documents from Comerica Bank, validate the fraud claim, and determine if proper protocol (Regulation E 15USC1693) was followed. It is my understanding that 30 persons were selected from the list of 105 which I submitted to Sonja Scott.

I assumed that the subpoena, to which my release would be attached, has been served upon Comerica Bank within the month since you received my release.
I am asking (1) when was the subpoena served upon Comerica Bank (2) where is the copy of response by Comerica (3) where is the narrative from your office with regard to this matter?
Jim

On Thu, Dec 12, 2019 at 11:19 AM Guishard, Kevin A. <GuishardK@oig.treas.gov> wrote:
Mr. Simms,
Other than the documents you sent to me last week. The Office of Audit has not received nor are we in possession of any audit of your account.
Thanks,
Kevin

What a lie. I sent documents to them in October, and signed releases for them to get my bank records.

From: jbsimms
Sent: Thursday, December 12, 2019, 3:44 PM
To: Richard Delmar (OIG Treasury)
Cc: Jackie Lynn
Subject: RE: Subpoena being served
Dear Mr. Delmar,
We will be in need of having subpoenas served upon officials at Bureau of Fiscal Service.
Are the directions stated in the attached email below to be followed for subpoenas being served upon Bureau of Fiscal Service?
I remain grateful for your assistance in facilitating the service of the previous subpoenas.
Sincerely,
Jim Simms

Friday, December 13, 2019

Delmar sent an email- gave address where to send the subpoena, a kind gesture on his part.

From: Richard Delmar (OIG Treasury)
Date: Fri, Dec 13, 2019 11:20 am
To: jbsimms
The process has been simplified a bit; you can leave the material with the courier office: The General Counsel of the Department of the Treasury is the Department's designated agent for service of process.
The Department's courier service receives "Service of Process" documents at 701 Madison Place, NW., Washington, D.C. This building is between H Street and Pennsylvania Ave., N.W., on the eastern edge of Lafayette Square. When you or your agent deliver the material, the courier service will have a representative of the Office of General Counsel pick up the document and complete the acceptance process.

From: Richard Delmar (OIG Treasury)
Date: Fri, Dec 13, 2019 3:05 pm
To: jbsimms
Another change; third time's the charm:
The Department receives "Service of Process" documents at 701 Madison Place, NW., Washington, D.C. This building is between H Street and Pennsylvania Ave., N.W., on the eastern edge of Lafayette Square. Upon arrival at this address, you or your agent should call 202-622-1650 to arrange for a representative of the Department's mailroom/courier service to pick up the document. The Department's mailroom employee will complete the acceptance process and then deliver the document to the Department's Office of General Counsel.

From: Franklin Lemond (Plaintiff's Attorney)
Date: Fri, Dec 13, 2019 4:13 pm
To: Jbsimms
Cc: Jackie Lynn
Thanks. I'll update the subpoena with this new address and circulate a draft on Monday.
Franklin

Subject: subpoena for Santaniello
From: jbsimms
Date: Fri, Dec 13, 2019 11:26 am
To: Franklin Lemond (Plaintiff's Attorney)
Cc: "Jackie Lynn"
Franklin,
I got an email from Delmar, stating he would get me the agent of service for Santaniello at Bureau of Fiscal Service. The info below came from their website.
Thomas Santaniello
Legislative and Public Affairs Specialist at Department of Treasury, Bureau of Fiscal Service
Department of the Treasury, Bureau of the Fiscal Service
3201 Pennsy Drive, Building E, Landover, MD 20785
Office of Legislative and Public Affairs
202-504-3502

Subject: Subpoena being served]
From: jbsimms
Date: Fri, Dec 13, 2019 11:30 am
To: Franklin Lemond (Plaintiff's Attorney)
Cc: "Jackie Lynn"
From the horse's mouth, here is where the subpoena goes.
I can't wait to write this book.

Saturday, December 14, 2019

J B Simms
Dec 14, 2019, 5:25 AM
to Franklin, Jackie
Santaniello does not want us to know the changes that have been enacted as a result of our action with OIG Treasury.
The issue with Mentor Program is BFS realized they screwed up and could not supervise the program, and Comerica violated Reg E and BFS had no one who cared or understood (or $ to ignore stuff).
The Mentor Program plays into our hands.
The Conduent fraud unit is inept. I have proven that. They used their interpretation of transaction history as a basis to deny claims.
They never called merchants. There was no record of calls to merchants, law enforcement, or other banks.
Conduent fraud unit could not connect dots to detect or prevent fraud (see serial fraud at diff places.
Conduent fraud unit cannot find an elephant in a phone booth, or a submarine in a small pond.
Period

Monday, December 16, 2019

This was the big day. Jackie got FOI information from Treasury. Tons was redacted.

From: Altemus, Amy J. <AltemusA@oig.treas.gov>
Date: Mon, Dec 16, 2019 at 7:05 AM
Subject: RE: Investigation status
To:
Cc: Guishard, Kevin A. <GuishardK@oig.treas.gov>, Johnson, Katherine E. <JohnsonK@oig.treas.gov>
Dear Mr. Simms:

As Mr. Guishard has noted, our audit pertains to Comerica Bank and the administration of the entire Direct Express program rather than any individual account holders. We thank you for your participation in this process, but we cannot release information regarding ongoing audits or investigations. Should you wish to request official documents when the matter is complete, you may submit a FOIA request at https://www.treasury.gov/foia/pages/gofoia.aspx. At all times, however, you are free to request account documents pertaining to your own account directly from Comerica.
Sincerely,
AJ Altemus
Acting Counsel to the Inspector General
Office of Counsel

The VA was defeated; new program was created

Subject: Direct Express Program
From: Steven Lepper (Military Banks of America)
Date: Mon, December 16, 2019 11:30 am
To: jbsimms
Mr. Simms,
I have been told that you are a vocal critic of the Direct Express program, especially as it is employed as a payment mechanism for VA monetary benefits. As a veteran who receives monetary benefits and the CEO of a trade association of "military banks" — banks that serve the military and veteran communities — I also have concerns about various aspects of the DE program.
I'm writing today to inform you of a new effort in which my organization, the Association of Military Banks of America (AMBA), is collaborating with the Veterans Benefits Administration to educate and inform veterans of their option to have their benefits directly deposited into bank checking or savings accounts. This program, which we're calling the Veterans Benefits Banking Program, will simply offer veterans currently receiving their benefits via DE or paper checks an opportunity to connect with banks that have experience dealing with the unique financial challenges of service members, veterans, and their families. Several banks have volunteered to make the connection and to offer a fresh start to veterans who may have had bad experiences with banks in the past. We hope that by taking a new look at banks, qualified veterans will open accounts and avoid the high fees, poor customer service, and inefficient fraud response endemic in the DE program.
Our plan is to launch the program on 20 December. AMBA will host a website that will serve as a bridge between VBA's benefits website and the participating banks' web portals. We will also initially offer some basic financial education to help veterans compare the programs currently available so they can make informed choices. As time goes on and in partnership with VBA, we hope to populate our website with more financial education for our veterans and their families.
Thanks for caring about the financial health of our veterans. Please let me know if you have any question.
All the best,
Steve

This was the first acknowledgement that my work against the VA was being addressed. Mr. Lepper would become a huge player in this battle.

On Dec 16, 2019, at 2:45 PM, jbsimms wrote:
Dear Mr. Lepper,
Thank you very much for your email, which was a great comfort to receive. Veterans using the Direct Express program need protection that Comerica Bank (and Conduent) along with VBA (under the direction of Paul Lawrence) has not afforded veterans. It was my exposure of the inadequacies of OIG Treasury reports in Feb 2018 that initiated the current investigation(s) into Comerica Bank, Conduent, and Bureau of Fiscal Service. It would be a pleasure and honor for me to give you a briefing of what is happening. Your involvement could make the difference for veterans whose benefits are interrupted by malfeasance on the part of the parties involved. My telephone number is (803) 309-6850. Let me know when you can speak, and I will make myself available.
Sincerely,
Jim Simms

From: Steven Lepper (Military Banks of America)
Date: Mon, Dec 16, 2019 1:20 pm
To: jbsimms
Cc: Jackie Lynn, Joe Plenzler <jplenzler@woundedwarriorproject.org>
Jim,
I'm glad you identified the problems that exist in the DE program. I know many veterans don't like banks.
Some may have had bad experiences in the past; others may believe their financial condition prevents them
from opening a bank account. This program we're developing with VBA is intended to address these problems.
It should interest you to know that our new program was VBA's idea. Dr. Lawrence and his staff have been
leaning forward to address the problems you and many veterans have identified with DE and paper checks.
They really do want to protect our veterans from financial products and services that don't meet their needs or
that might cause them financial injury. In fact, they've been flogging us to meet a 20 December launch date.
I'm available this afternoon for a quick call. My only schedule conflict is at 1630. Otherwise, I won't be
available again until 23 December.
Wishing you a happy holiday season.
Steve

Subject: I talked to General Steven Lepper and we need to talk
From: jbsimms
Date: Mon, Dec 16, 2019 2:17 pm
To: Franklin Lemond (Plaintiff's Attorney), "Jackie Lynn"
I just got off phone with Lepper.
VA is making changes to their website. We win. The VA does not necessarily like me, but I got their attention.
Lepper thinks (?) Comerica was only bidder for the contract.
We need to talk.
Lepper wants copies of documents to validate claim. Lepper was JAG officer and now involved in banking. I am
available anytime.
Jim

Subject: Re: OIG Treasury 19-041 and my review of 19-041
From: Steven Lepper (Military Banks of America)
Date: Mon, Dec 16, 2019 5:20 pm
To: jbsimms
Jim,
Thanks for sending these. It was great to talk with you today. Stay tuned for our program launch on 20
December. As I told you during our conversation, I'd appreciate your feedback.
Happy Holidays!
Steve

On Dec 16, 2019, at 6:07 PM, jbsimms wrote:
Dear Mr. Lepper,
Attached is the interim report from OIG Treasury and my reply, which was not well received.
I will be sending you a breakdown of the violations of Reg E by Comerica and Conduent as soon as I can find
the document.
Jim

Email from BFS and FOI stuff for Jackie Densmore- terrible- all redacted.

New secrets regarding the selection process of the fiscal agent

Subject: putting an assertion into perspective
From: jbsimms
Date: Mon, Dec 16, 2019 7:35 pm
To: Franklin Lemond (Plaintiff's Attorney), "Jackie Lynn"
Mr. Lepper implied to me that Comerica Bank was the only bank that submitted an application to be the new
Fiscal Agent.

What might that mean?

The Evaluation Team was never assembled.
The mention of the Evaluation Team was a hoax.
Blocking Jackie and me from making a presentation to the evaluation team was a ruse.
If Comerica was the only applicant, the other banks knew they could not get the contract; the cake was baked.
All this chatter with Santaniello was a joke.
This makes me think of adding another question about the Evaluation Team.

Tuesday, December 17, 2019

Jackie thanks Steven Lepper for helping our case against the VA

Jackie Lynn
Tue, Dec 17, 2019, 7:07 AM
to Steven, me
Dear Mr. Lepper,
Thank you for reaching out to Mr. Simms yesterday. I became involved in this Direct Express issue in August 2018 when my brother-in-law, Derek Densmore, a disabled veteran, had his benefits stolen through the Direct Express program.
I found Mr. Simms at that time, and we have been fighting the VA, SSA, BFS, and OIG Treasury ever since. The VA never addressed the issue that they continue to endorse the Direct Express program while they knew it was not safe. Mr. Simms told them many times and only got LinkedIn messages from Pamela Powers implying that he was annoying her. Promises were made, and no one from the VA ever contacted us. They wouldn't discuss the matter with us. This is why we are so glad you made contact.
I have personally talked to veterans who have been victimized by this program. One talked of suicide to me because Comerica and Conduent ignored him.
We have gone to senators including Senator Warrens office who uncovered half a million dollars were stolen from cardholders including Veterans yet nobody had the courage to make the first step and refuse to endorse these cards until now. I am so grateful you have reached out to Mr. . Simms. After hearing the heartbreaking stories of so many people this gives us hope that people will not fall victims of this flawed and unsafe program. They threatened our Veterans and the American people into thinking they had no other options which is why your program will help so many .
Even BFS has blocked us from communicating with them. BFS never withheld funds or fined Comerica for violating their agreement and Reg E. They never decreased the banks compensation despite their poor ratings in the OIG report. The bank owes millions back to the government and taxpayers, but again they refuse to take the first step.
Thank you again. Hopefully your help and your association will stop this and make someone accountable. Too many people are hurting because of this corrupt bank.
My family thanks you for your dedicated service to our country and your continued work on this ongoing issue.
Sincerely
Jackie And Derek Densmore

Steven Lepper (Military Banks of America)
Dec 17, 2019, 7:28 AM
to Jackie, me
Ms. Densmore,
Thanks for your note and your story. I'm so sorry that your brother-in-law experienced this unnecessary financial difficulty with the Direct Express program.
As I told Mr. Simms yesterday, my organization has partnered with VBA to create a program that will hopefully encourage veterans who currently receive their benefits through the DE program to open bank accounts instead. Our website, which should launch in the next couple of days, contains links to banks that have volunteered to provide these veterans assistance in opening accounts. It will also include information we hope will compel these veterans to seek assistance from these banks or any other bank with which they feel comfortable. Our ultimate objective is to maximize the number of veterans who move from DE to more responsible, regulated, and safe banking products.

As I told Mr. Simms yesterday, once we launch this program, we hope you and other veterans, beneficiaries, or caregivers will provide us feedback. We want this program to be helpful, not confusing, to our veterans.
Happy holidays to you and your family!
All the best,
Steve

Steven Lepper (Military Banks of America)
Attachments
Tue, Dec 17, 2019, 4:39 PM
to me, Jackie
Jim,
As promised and three days before scheduled, here is the press release announcing our new program with VBA. Hope this helps resolve all the problems you and others have experienced with the DE program.
Happy holidays,
Steve

Subject: FOI request from Ms. Densmore, forwarded a year after the request/redactions
From: jbsimms
Date: Tue, Dec 17, 2019 2:02 pm
To: Richard Delmar (OIG Treasury), Amy Altemus (OIG Treasury), Katherine Johnson (OIG Treasury), Sonja Scott (OIG Treasury)
Cc: Jackie Lynn, Kate Berry (American Banker)
Dear All,
It appears my characterization of BFS, having shown to be consistent with that of Mr. Clements of GAO, continues to be validated by BFS.
"[L]ack of transparency..." as stated by Mr. Clements in GAO 17-176 is a bit of an understatement as I review the 4+ documents supplied by BFS after a year-long wait by Ms. Densmore. While I see that BFS is attempting to charge an exorbitant fee to Ms. Densmore, I also see that the charge for the time it took for BFS officials to redact some documents was time charged for redaction that occurred in 2017. That required an explanation.
That apparent lack of integrity at BFS notwithstanding in "double billing," the redaction of the names of the persons at Comerica Bank and BFS who were instrumental in the creation and operation of the Direct Express program were uniformly redacted. BFS had not basis for this redaction other than to inhibit accountability of persons who betrayed the trust of American citizens and turned the requested documents into a document resembling a Rorschach test developed by a person dropping acid.
I assume none of you (a few being attorneys) have reviewed these redacted documents. If you had, I also assume you anticipated this email.
Hopefully, before the beginning of the holiday, you will be able to contact Mr. Gribben and Mr. Santaniello, as well as your FOI section and get a few answers to the issues I have presented.
You can reach me at any time. Happy Holidays to you all.
J.B. Simms

Subject: Direct Express Program
From: jbsimms
Date: Tue, Dec 17, 2019 2:13 pm
To: "Bayer, Walter Office of the Inspector General" Walter Bayer (SSI OIG)
Cc: "Jackie Lynn"
Thanks so much.
BFS is so dirty. They sent documents to Jackie this week that were requested through FOI and the redaction was outrageous. I had a 30-minute chat with Gen Lepper. Great chat. He got my name from Sec Wilkie and COS Powers of VA. I assume they have grown weary my messages and input.
Lepper agreed we need to get VA and SSA to stop endorsing the Direct Express program on the websites and steer recipients to other financial options. BFS has proved it cannot ethically monitor that program, and the truth of how things got done is just coming to light.
SSA can direct anyone who is a veteran to the AMBA for options, and others (retirees, mothers with dependent children, disabled persons) can be advised they can get their benefits sent to any debit card of their choice.

Most of them already use debit cards. Simply instruct them to determine the routing number and account number of their card, take that info to an SSA office, and they transfer will be done.
Thank you again for your help.
I still have had no feedback on my person identity hack, but I will pursue that later.
Jim

Subject: yep, we did it
From: jbsimms
Date: Tue, Dec 17, 2019 6:26 pm
To: Kate Berry (American Banker)
uh, the VA now is not endorsing Direct Express.
How you like those apples ?

Lepper pushed this press release ahead a bit. This was another win for us.

FOR IMMEDIATE RELEASE

Dec. 17, 2019
VA introduces new direct deposit options for Veterans, beneficiaries.
Partners with Association of Military Banks of America
WASHINGTON – The U.S. Department of Veterans Affairs (VA), in partnership with the Association of Military Banks of America (AMBA), launched the Veterans Benefits Banking Program (VBBP), available starting Dec. 20.
The program will provide Veterans and their beneficiaries the chance to safely, reliably, and inexpensively receive and manage their VA monetary benefits through financial services at participating banks.

"VBBP offers another way to simplify banking choices to help eligible Veterans select
the right bank for themselves and their families," said VA Secretary Robert Wilke. "The VA and AMBA are proud to provide this opportunity to connect veterans with banks that understand their needs."
VA's collaboration with AMBA will leverage its consortium of military-friendly financial institutions that cater to service members. AMBA is the only trade association representing banking institutions specializing in providing services for military personnel, Veterans, and their families around the world. VBBP leverages participating AMBA institutions and banks operating within the gates of installations of all branches of service and National Guard and Reserve components.
"AMBA and its member banks welcome the opportunity to provide our nation's Veterans additional financial services options to help them achieve greater financial independence, resiliency, and literacy," said AMBA president and Air Force Veteran Steve Lepper. "We hope that as Veterans recognize the benefits of working with the banks to achieve financial stability, more Veterans, banks and credit unions will join this effort."
The current available banking options include direct deposit into an existing bank account, electronic funds transfer into a Direct Express pre-paid debit card and mailing of a paper check for pre-approved beneficiaries. VBBP introduces new financial resources to Veterans and their beneficiaries.
The program is an effort to address the problems some Veterans experience using these payment methods. VBBP offers these VA beneficiaries – including many who have been unable to open bank accounts in the past – the opportunity to deposit their benefit funds directly into existing or new bank accounts offered by participating AMBA member banks.
Neither VA nor AMBA is endorsing any particular bank or requiring Veterans and other beneficiaries to use them. It does not require Veterans who are satisfied with their current financial situation to change how they receive their VA monetary benefits.
All Veterans and other beneficiaries – who currently receive more than $118 billion in financial benefits through VA – are eligible to access this program. There are approximately 250,000 Veterans and beneficiaries who receive their VA benefits through a pre-paid debit card or paper check who may not have a bank account.
VA's Veterans Banking Benefits and AMBA's Veterans Benefits Banking Program websites have details for identifying participating banks.

To have your federal benefits electronically transferred to a Veteran's designated financial institution (e.g. bank), VA beneficiaries interested in changing direct deposit options can also call 1-800-827-1000 with their relevant banking information.

VA financial literacy information is an additional resource available to Veterans and VA beneficiaries.

Wednesday December 18, 2019

Wrote blog, copied FB and LinkedIn

Subject: VA introduces new direct deposit options for Veterans, beneficiaries
From: Joe Plenzler <jplenzler@woundedwarriorproject.org>
Date: Wed, Dec 18, 2019 11:40 am
To: "jbsimms"
JB, I know you have been campaigning against the Direct Express card. Looks like you got VA to move…see attached.
JOE PLENZLER, APR
communications director
Wounded Warrior Project

From: Emmet, Bronwyn <Bronwyn.Emmet@va.gov>
Sent: Wednesday, December 18, 2019 12:38 PM
Cc: Curtin, Joseph G. <Joseph.Curtin@va.gov>
Subject: FW: NEWS RELEASE: VA introduces new direct deposit options for Veterans, beneficiaries
CAUTION: This email originated from outside of the organization. Do not click links or open attachments unless you recognize the sender and know the content is safe.
Good afternoon,
This news release, attached and cut and pasted below, will be posted on VA's news releases webpage. Please make appropriate notifications.
Best,
Bronwyn

The news release obtained the day before was attached to this email.
We were pleased. Franklin filed the subpoena for Santaniello.

Wednesday, December 18, 2019

A former client sends congratulations to me

Jim Bigham
Wed, Dec 18, 2019, 2:41 PM
Jim.
I am really proud of what you have been able to accomplish by staying tenacious and persistent. I am certain that a lot of people will benefit from your hard work. It is unfortunate that you will not receive the recognition you deserve for all of your efforts.
God bless you and I hope you have a Merry Christmas!
Jim Bigham, Captain, A320, JFK

Monday, December 30, 2019

Subject: meeting with persons at SSA OIG
From: jbsimms
Date: Mon, Dec 30, 2019, 9:58 am
To: Walter Bayer (SSI OIG)
Cc: Jackie Lynn, Sonja Scott (OIG Treasury), Katherine Johnson (OIG Treasury, Franklin Lemond (Plaintiff's Attorney)
Dear Walt,
Seasons greeting, of course.
Back to work.

In our last exchange, I had forwarded you an email I received from Mr. Lepper, CEO of the Association of Military Banks of America. Since no person at the VA (Wilkie, Powers, Lawrence, et al) would engage me in conversation, they left it up to Mr. Lepper to advise me that the VA was changing their policy of endorsing the corrupt Direct Express program whereby VA recipients received money. I am interested to know the discussions which took place which resulted in the change that was made.

We are hoping that the rationale presented by "whomever" at the VA (and we know the genesis of the information they had to make their decision) during their meetings will be passed along to you as you hopefully use the same talking points to SSA OIG which will result in the Social Security Administration to cease recommending the Direct Card to receive benefits. Below are a few options:

1) All SSA benefit recipients having served on active duty and are a veteran qualify to be directed to Mr. Lepper's organization, the Association of Military Banks of America. This group will counsel veteran recipients (and maybe their spouses and dependents) as to a best financial institution for funds to be directed.

2) SSA recipients should be told that all debit cards are associated with a bank. Each card has a bank routing and account number. Many persons using the Direct Express debit card use other debit cards. SSA should be aware by now that Comerica Bank put no security parameters on the Direct Express debit card; no daily balance notification, no transaction notice, and no way to cancel fraudulent transactions upon discovery by the cardholder and/or notification given to the Conduent call center. Many other cards have these features at no cost, and the SSA has a duty to educate the recipients (I will be glad to write the copy for SSA).

If you would like, I invite you to contact Mr. Lepper directly. He was cordial and helpful. It would be nice if persons at the VA could take a cue from Mr. Lepper. He might give you more insight into the workings of the decision that was made.

Another point to be made is the transparency of the SSA with recipients with regard to fraud. We know (and I personally) that some of the fraud is conducted by persons calling the SSA to change addresses, then having Conduent issue a new card to the fraudulent address. SSA has refused to reveal to victimized recipients when the fraudulent call (or access to the online account) was made and the address where the card was sent. This happened to me in June 2018 and SSA has yet to comply with my inquiry. This policy allows fraudsters within Conduent and SSA to have free reign over accounts with no accountability.

Thank you for indulging me; there are so many transgressions that when I start listing them I just can't stop. Lastly, please advise us when you plan to meet with the SSA OIG. Maybe you can invite Ms. Scott of OIG Treasury (I believe she knows my name) and Ms. Katherine Johnson (Auditor of proposed OIG Treasury 19-041) to share their findings and maybe validate my claims. Ms. Scott might be taking time off, but hopefully she will get this email.

Sincerely,

Jim

Sonja Scott took a transfer from the post at OIG Treasury soon thereafter.

Tuesday, December 31, 2019

Posted on Direct Express Cardholder Facebook

Katherine Ward The direct express program should have ended a long time ago when this stuff started happening but no social security keeps using them well I think Social Security most likes that people are getting frauded by Direct Express. I don't take it too kind when a social security worker acts like an ass about fraud oh no we can't help you sick of social security and Direct Express in the bank Comerica Bank. To know that this bank could care less if they fraud you. This so sick of it done everything I could and I feel that every direction I went in was a brick wall it may be I can contact one person and we'll see what he says about it maybe I'll get the help maybe someone to listen maybe we need to move this into the airwaves of the news.

Jackie sent copies of inserts to Lepper and me. Derek got inserts in his VA and SSA check. All hell broke loose.

J B Simms
Tue, Dec 31, 2019, 5:42 AM
to Steven, Jackie
Jackie,
Thank you for doing the research and forwarding this to me, and to Mr. Lepper. It is encouraging that Mr. Lepper has communicated with us in a respectful manner, and we feel he understands the issues, albeit limited from VA briefings, which have been presented to him. His genuine concern for former military personnel is helpful to us in our attempt to make persons in Washington accountable for perpetuating this inept and corrupt

program. The attitude toward us of those in Washington is a result of fear and guilt; fear we will expose (and have) those who have failed to do their jobs, compromised their morals, have a humane concern for others, and their guilt for endorsing and allowing the Direct Express program to be defined by closed door meetings and "blind eye" decisions.

This issue affects not only veterans but persons who did not serve, retirees, children, disabled persons, and others. This is why we are hoping that Walt Bayer of SSA OIG will, as he suggested, take a cue from the VA and direct the SSA to disassociate themselves from endorsing this failed program.

While we are being kept in the shadows of the "decision making" and no one will actively say that they "want" to hear what we say, I continue to wish to know how the VA came to their decision and what info they used to do so.

We thank you again, Mr. Lepper, and I hope to be able to come across the bay to meet with you and thank you personally at time and place convenient to you. I am certain you know my version of events and encounters with VA officials and others will be different from the briefings you have received.

Jim

J B Simms
Tue, Dec 31, 2019, 6:20 AM
to Jackie, Steven

I apologize for sending additional emails, but I want to validate my claim that the briefings received by Mr. Lepper were quite sanitized. We had stories of elder veterans whose designated caregivers were ignored by Conduent and Comerica Bank, allowing perpetual fraud to occur.

Also, to show the benevolence of Ms. Densmore, I had communicated with a veteran who was suffering with PTS. He lived in Washington State. The VA made him use the Direct Express program after he had been using paper checks. He was so confused by this program, and ignored, that he lost so much money that he lost his apartment and was living in his car. He was prone to outbursts, and the local police were aware of him (I communicated with the police to calm the situation). The veteran, after talking with me for hours and reviewing months of his account paperwork, Jackie (Densmore) had a phone conversation with this veteran. He was overtly suicidal. Jackie sent her own money to this veteran so he could eat.

When I told OIG Treasury that I had narrative accounts of 70+ victims, they challenged me. I sent the narratives to OIG Treasury. When I stopped directly taking calls from victims, the number of victims totaled 105, of which at least 70 percent of the victims received full refunds after I interceded on their behalf with Comerica Bank and Conduent. Many of these victims were prior service military receiving Social Security, some having served in Vietnam. OIG Treasury assured me they would take the complaints from victims (Sonja Scott was the designated OIG Treasury person) but the VA refused to accept any documentation or discuss the matter.

The VA took the attitude that they would respond by dressing up the issue in order to divert eyes from themselves and take credit for helping the Veterans. Their intel came from others in Washington (who got their info from Jackie and me), who, among their cabal, rehearsed and coordinated their responses to avoid any complicity or acts of omission which would point a finger at anyone personally or collectively. We trust none of them, and with good cause.

The progress made could not have been done without Ms. Densmore. She and I have communicated almost daily since early August 2018 (16 months) and you cannot imagine what we have encountered. We thank you, Mr. Lepper, for your involvement.

Jim

From: Steven Lepper (Military Banks of America)
Date: December 31, 2019 at 6:37:13 AM EST
To: Jackie Lynn
Cc: Andia Dinesen <Andia.dinesen@ambahq.org>
Subject: Re: Top 128 Reviews about Direct Express
Jackie,

Thanks so much for sending these. I will forward them to the banks that are and are considering participating in the Veterans Benefits Banking Program to let them know how important bank accounts would be for these people. Most of the problems described here would be either prevented or much more easily resolved if these people had their government benefits direct deposited into a savings or checking account.

Wishing you a very Happy New Year.Steve

Steven Lepper (Military Banks of America)
8:16 AM (48 minutes ago)
to Andia, me, Jackie
Mr. Simms, Ms. Densmore,
Thanks for the notes and for continuing your engagement with the government agencies still participating in the Express Direct program. The stories Ms. Densmore sent me this morning, and which I forwarded to my banks, are truly astounding. For veterans and social security recipients to be treated this way is shameful. Although I haven't yet started my social security payments, I do receive VA disability. I'm fortunate that my disability check isn't the only income I receive, but I'm very aware that a great number of veterans rely on theirs for most if not all of their income. My bankers — most of whom are also veterans — also understand.
Let me ask you both a hypothetical question: As you probably know, each military recruit must have a bank or credit union account before reporting to MEPS so that their paychecks can be directly deposited into their accounts. During their military service, each service member must maintain a bank account to receive their military pay. What would you think if VA and Social Security adopted this approach for the recipients of their monetary benefits? I realize that some of our veterans and retirees simply don't like banks and prefer prepaid cards or paper checks. Would the community you support be offended if VA and Social Security finally ended the Direct Express program and simply required all benefits be deposited in a regulated, insured financial institution? I ask because I believe this may be the only way to eliminate the rampant fraud, excessive fees, and shoddy customer service inherent in the DE program. I'd appreciate your thoughts.
Wishing you and Ms. Densmore a very Happy New Year. I hope we'll get an opportunity to meet in 2020.
All the best,
Steve

From: Steven Lepper (Military Banks of America)
Date: Tue, Dec 31, 2019 at 11:56 AM
Subject: Re: Top 128 Reviews about Direct Express
To: J B Simms
Cc: Jackie Lynn , Andia Dinesen <Andia.dinesen@ambahq.org>
Mr. Simms,
Thanks for your quick reply. When I met with Secretary Lawrence several weeks ago, I recommended that VA consider adopting DoD's approach and require all VA monetary benefits recipients to have bank accounts. I'm glad you agree with that approach. Based on the feedback I've received from VBA, I do believe they see its wisdom. Despite your less-than-satisfying interactions with them and other government agencies, Dr. Lawrence, himself a veteran, seems truly motivated to fix all these problems with the Direct Express program. That's why he originally reached out to my organization for assistance.
After we launched our website on 22 December, I reached out to several of my members to ask them to join this effort. I won't list the banks here; they are all small-to-medium sized banks across the Nation that have focused on serving military and veteran communities for decades. They all responded positively to my request, and I expect they will join us in the next couple of weeks. I mention this because I believe our veterans — and, ultimately, our Social Security benefits recipients — should have banking choices. The more, the better. I'm glad you agree.
I commend you for your determination to end the shameful treatment the Direct Express recipients listed in these reviews have experienced. I'm proud to join your efforts by encouraging all veterans enrolled in the DE program to join banks that understand their unique financial challenges. I hope 2020 will the year we can achieve these objectives.
All the best,
Steve

What a year this had been.
Pamela Powers of the VA responded on LinkedIn. Paul Lawrence hides from me.
Altemus denies investigations at OIG Treasury.
BFS creates a Mentor Program but will not discuss the program.
Subpoenas are served upon OIG Treasury and Santaniello.
Steven Lepper is designated by the VA to contact me after a new program was created.
Next year will have just as much drama.

Make life easier. Go digital.

Whether you are receiving this paper check on behalf of someone or for yourself, save time and hassle by switching to direct deposit or a Direct Express® card.

Chapter Eight
The VA Change, Inserts, FOI Hell

As the year began, Jackie and I became more frustrated with government agencies failing to do their jobs and ignoring not only the veterans but all disadvantaged citizens using the Direct Express Debit Cars.

Wednesday, January 1, 2020

From: Jackie Lynn
Attachments
Wed, Jan 1, 7:33 PM
To: Franklin Lemond, Sonia Scott, Michael Jackman, Walter Bayer, me, Steven Lepper, Katherine, Kate Berry, Richard Delmar
Hello all and Happy New Year,
I would like to point out that BFS has yet to update their website on the status of their Direct Express contract according to this information the contract expires tomorrow-~JAN 2 2020. Once again, the American people have no answers, I would like to know if any penalties or fines will be enforced for BFS 1) neglecting to notify cardholders 2) missing deadlines 3) how much more money are they paying Comerica to extend this Jan 2 expiration date? Taxpayers have the right to how much money is being spent now that BFS has allowed the contract to expire.

The contract with Comerica Bank to administer the Direct Express program was set to expire and no announcement had been made regarding who got the bid for the contract. The bidding for the contract ended before June, but the meetings requested by Pamela Powers coincided with the bidding process. Something was happening to keep BFS from postponing the announcement.

Derek Densmore gets an "insert" into his check.

Jackie was hot mad. The insert that the SSA put into Derek's check endorsed the Direct Express debit card program and encouraged those getting their payment by check to use the Direct Express card. The battle against the inserts was just beginning. Jackie would have me write emails for her. Jackie was brilliant, but not at writing. I wrote an email for her on January 16, 2020, found later in this chapter.

Thursday, January 2, 2020

The hell of the inserts begins

From: J B Simms
Thu, Jan 2, 12:23 PM
to Steven Lepper, Jackie
Dear Mr. Lepper,
We will do all we can to direct traffic to your organization. I have not listened to the recording, but Jackie tells me options are now being given. This is the first step in reducing Direct Express cardholder numbers.
Of course, all this is being done behind closed doors. These people feel no accountability to veterans or other recipients, and "have heard enough" from Jackie and me.
Our goal is for all persons with military service, spouses and dependents, to contact your organization.
This will cut out maybe 20-25 percent of fees paid to Comerica bank, at the outset, maybe more.
At least I feel we got someone's attention.
Jim

From: JB Simms
Thu, Jan 2, 12:32 PM
to Walter Bayer, Jackie
Walt,
Jackie's brother-in-law got this insert with his check. This implies the Direct Express program is safe. Whoever created this did a bad thing.
Can you explain this to us? Jim

I developed Walter Bayer as a contact with Social Security OIG. I thought Bayer was going to help us. He betrayed us sometime later. The issue here was Social Security endorsing the Direct Express program and we could not find out who was creating the inserts.

From: J B Simms
Thu, Jan 2, 12:57 PM
to Steven Lepper, Jackie
I am sorry you had to be the recipient of my vitriol. I will be away from the phone for an hour or so, and after talking to Jackie, here are the points:
The VA threw us a bone, but they endorsed the Direct Express program not only in the body of the insert but also in the words "safe and secure" at the bottom next to the Direct Express logo.
I want to know who created this and who approved this.
Your organization [Association of Military Banks of America] should be listed on this insert.
[Paul] Lawrence [at the VA] has some explaining to do.
Jim

From: Steven Lepper (CEO-Military Banks of America)
Thu, Jan 2, 1:58 PM
to Andia, me, Jackie
Thanks for forwarding this. I have no idea what prompted this mailing, but I will certainly try to find out. I can tell you that VBA does not like the DE program, so I'm surprised that this went to any veterans. I'll let you know what I learn.
Best,
Steve

We had faith that Mr. Lepper believed in us and would help. He did get the VA to acknowledge my work. Jackie wrote this to Mr. Lepper begging for his help.

From: Jackie Lynn
Thu, Jan 2, 2:39 PM
to Steven Lepper, me
April 2019 - old marketing they used to make people switch over Vs What they are using now see below.
Mr. Lepper,
Today in both my brother in laws VA and Social Security checks we received this so both agencies are still endorsing this bank, they are even still using the same phone number 😳 just changed their marketing. Whoever is allowing this needs to be held accountable.
Try calling the number they are still encouraging our Veterans that this program is safe even going as far as having the recording calling this- The US treasury electronic solution program.
They had months before their marketing went out to change their forms and make a whole new recording which shows me they had no intention of another bank being awarded or alerting anyone of what was truly happening. I do hope with your help we can get to the bottom of this,
Thank you.
Jackie

From: J B Simms
Thu, Jan 2, 5:34 PM
to Jackie, Steven Lepper
Jackie,
You see I am copying Mr. Lepper. Truth is our work exposing the VA and Paul Lawrence put Mr. Lepper and his association into the equation for referrals, and for that I am grateful. Our veterans, be they disabled or having served, deserve our protection from the VA.
It befuddles me that the VA, after making the press release on Dec 17, 2019, would not include the AMBA on this insert, and publish the phone number of the AMBA. Instead, it lists Direct Express as an option with the words "safe and secure" next to the Direct Express logo. Did Paul Lawrence, Pamela Powers, and others forget that the press release stated the VA was endorsing the AMBA, then create a flyer ignoring the press release?

Even the telephone number given directs the person to the Direct Express program with no mention of the AMBA.

I guess it is up to Mr. Lepper to find out who authorized this insert and who decided to exclude AMBA. Mr. Lepper, in his email response to me, stated he would look into this

This event [the inserts] reinforces my disdain for those who take advantage of people because they can. I am on this.

Jim

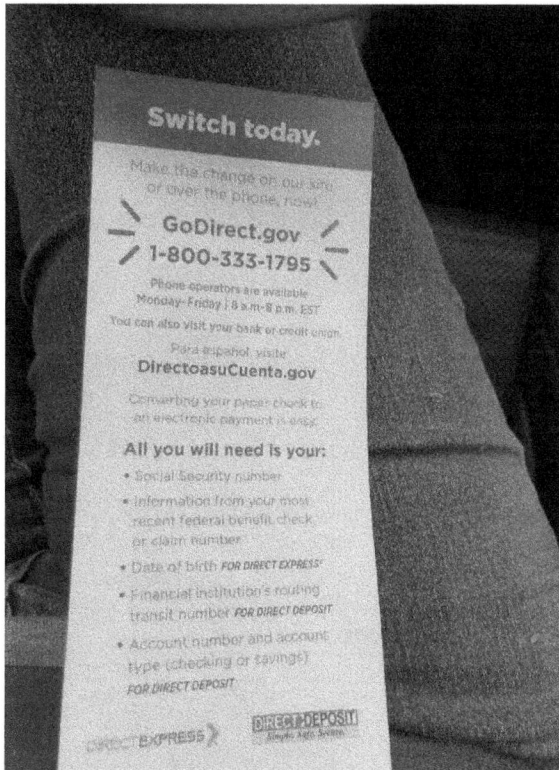

Friday, January 3, 2020

From: Steven Lepper (CEO-Military Banks of America)
Fri, Jan 3, 5:26 AM
to Andia, me, Jackie
Mr. Simms,
I'm still checking to see how this flyer was included with VA and SSA checks this month. I suspect Treasury did this since I think they actually issue checks for all these programs. I'll let you know when I find out for sure. You sent me the VBA newsletter yesterday. Thanks. I also receive those newsletters myself since I receive VA disability benefits. I sent the newsletter to all our currently participating banks as well as our banks who are hoping to join the program. I also receive the newsletter, along with an "attaboy" from the CEO of the Wounded Warrior Foundation. He's also pleased that we're moving in this direction.
I'll keep you posted on our progress. In the meantime, I hope you have a great weekend.
Best,
Steve

Note the times of these emails. My day always started early. I was spending 8-10 hour a day on this case.

Subject: insert in the VA check for Jackie's brother-in-law
From: jbsimms
Date: Fri, Jan 03, 2020, 5:47 am
To: Joe Plenzler (Wounded Warriors)
Cc: Jackie Lynn
Good morning, Joe,
Attached are the inserts found in the VA benefits check for Jackie's brother-in-law.
They are still touting the Direct Express program and did not mention Mr. Lepper's group, the Association of Military Banks of America. The VA had their press release on Dec 17 stating they were working with the AMBA but did not put them on the insert. Then, in the VA Benefits Newsletter, they endorse the AMBA.
Send this contradiction to the reporter at Stars and Stripes and tell them I can fill in the back story. We have made progress, but this type of stuff is not acceptable.
Thanks for your support of this project to protect the benefits of the veterans.
Jim

We needed publicity. The feds were hiding reports (OIG Treasury) and the SSA was stalling.

Subject: Paul Lawrence's Webcast for Jan 30
From: jbsimms
Date: Fri, Jan 03, 2020, 6:30 am
To: Jackie Lynn; Joe Plenzler (Wounded Warriors), Steven Lepper <(CEO-Military Banks of America), Jennifer Kreegar
Good morning to all,
The VA News newsletter has a notice for a newscast given by Paul Lawrence to share "the accomplishments and challenges" from the first quarter of 2020.
I will register and see what Mr. Lawrence has to say about the endorsement and partnership with the AMBA.
Joe, if you have a place in your newsletter, I hope you can make reference to this new alliance and direct the disabled veterans to Mr. Lepper's organization.
Mr. Lawrence, and the VA, just didn't want to admit overlooking this matter until we exposed this. We are looking for a clean break and having the VA ceasing to mention the Direct Express program.
I thank everyone. Jackie and I will continue to work to end this program.
Jim

Paul Lawrence was a useless person. He refused to engage me, knowing he and his office were at fault. His "flag-waving" photo opportunities were a charade. Lawrence was all about himself.

Subject: "A Treasury recommended debit card?
From: jbsimms
Date: Fri, Jan 03, 2020, 6:54 am
To: Richard K. Delmar, Sonja Scott, Steven Lepper
Cc: Jackie Lynn; Jennifer Kreegar
Good morning.
After seeing the inserts received by Derek Densmore, Jackie's brother-in-law (attached) I started clicking links to the Go-Direct program. There was a little surprise.
Not only was the VA not mentioning the partnership with the Association of Military Banks of America (Mr. Lepper's organization) but this link states the Treasury recommended the Direct Express debit card for veterans to deposit their benefits.
Mr. Lepper was made aware of the inserts yesterday and has the ear of Paul Lawrence at the VA. I just thought it necessary for Mr. Delmar to know that Treasury was noted as endorsing the Direct Express program. Maybe Mr. Delmar would want to look into this matter as well.
J.B. Simms

Delmar did not care about the "appearance" of OIG Treasury. He was now in charge.

Subject: the website directed to by the VA insert
From: jbsimms
Date: Fri, Jan 03, 2020, 7:26 am
To: Sonja Scott (OIG Treasury), Richard Delmar (OIG Treasury), Steven Lepper (CEO-Military Banks of America), Joe Plenzler (Wounded Warriors), Walter Bayer (SSA OIG)
Cc: Jackie Lynn, Jennifer Kreegar
Here we go again.
Here is the link to the Direct Express site, the link was attached to the VA site at the Go-Direct site.
The Direct Express website states this is the "new" Direct Express card, a joke, right? Look at the bottom of the Direct Express page. They are still saying it is "safe" while still stating this is endorsed by the Treasury (technically it is endorsed by the Bureau of Fiscal Service, a division of Treasury, but we know the contract "deal" between BFA officials and Comerica Bank is questionable). Someone needs to have a sit-down with Mr. Gribben of BFS. Maybe Mr. Delmar might want to do that.
Mr. Gribben [the new head of Bureau of Fiscal Services) needs to know the VA is endorsing the AMBA in its newsletter and press release of December 17, 2019. All veterans need be directed to the AMBA.
The Go-Direct site did not mention, nor did they put a link to the Association of Military Banks of America, which, on the VA newsletter, was announced as a partner with the VA to assist veterans.
We all know that the BFS failed to protect all recipients. The real connection between Comerica Bank employees and employees at BFS has not been exposed.
Jim

Unknown to us at this time was the fact that Comerica recruited a different administrator, i2c, (instead of Conduent) to handle the operation of the Direct Express Debit Card. This revelation would come about a year later.

Monday, January 6, 2020

Paul Lawrence would not reply. I found his boss, Pamela Powers, Assistant Secretary of Veteran Affairs.

Subject: VA failed to change printing on inserts
From: jbsimms
Date: Mon, Jan 06, 2020, 7:22 am
To: Pamela Powers (VA-Chief of Staff)
Cc: Jackie Lynn
Ms. Powers,
Since the VA published the news release on Dec 17, I assumed the VA would have alerted the IT people to remove the endorsement of the Direct Express program from the insert sent to disabled veterans and to direct them to the AMBA. The telephone number given tells veterans to get a bank account or enroll in the Direct Express program. I seem to be the only person who noticed this. Do you think you can get this revelation to Paul Lawrence so the veterans will not be confused with the mixed message being sent? Mr. Lepper has been briefed on this matter. Lawrence evidently will communicate with Mr. Lepper, if with no other. If you want to see the inserts, I have copies sent to me from Ms. Densmore.
Jim Simms

Ms. Powers' contact information was found on LinkedIn. Katherine Johnson was the person who signed off on audit 19-041, and the updated version was long past due.

Now back to Amy Altemus. Altemus did all she could to derail our case against Comerica.

Subject: Conference, the investigation of the 30 victims, and the BFS Mentor program
From: jbsimms
Date: Mon, Jan 06, 2020, 9:42 am
To: Amy Altemus (OIG Treasury)
Cc: Jackie Lynn, Sonja Scott (OIG Treasury), Katherine Johnson (OIG Treasury)
Dear Ms. Altemus,

When will the results of the "investigation" into the victimization of the 30 persons by Comerica Bank, dba Direct Express, be concluded and published? My case(s) were included in the group of thirty.

Jackie Densmore and I continue to wish to address OIG Treasury. You are aware our scheduled conference was canceled fewer than 24 hours before our conference of a couple of months ago was to take place. You appear to have had some input with regard to this cancellation, and we would like clarification for said cancellation.

Lastly, for now, is the issue of the Mentor Program which was launched by BFS in May 2019. This timing coincided with the failure of BFS to announce the grantee of the contract to administer the Direct Express program. US Bank is refusing to comment on the program and referred all inquiries to BFS. BFS, through Santaniello, also refuses to comment on the creation and operation of said Mentor Program. While Commissioner Gribben, as head of the SBA, administered a Mentor Program at the SBA, it seems likely that this program was recommended by Mr. Gribben before the resignation of Ms. McCoy.

As Mr. Clements stated in his report GAO 17-176, the culture of BFS is that of a lack of transparency. The more we know, the more we understand why this culture existed and why it continues. It is unfortunate that a taxpayer has to hire an attorney to have a subpoena served upon a subject within a federal agency in order to have a simple question answered.

These issues stated above should also be addressed by Ms. Scott and Ms. Johnson as Ms. Johnson composes OIG Treasury 19-041. I am certain Ms. Densmore and I have raised issues and exposed malfeasance which did not appear in any investigation to be copied and pasted into the published audit.

A dialogue would be preferable to the secondary abuse we continue to experience at the hands of the agency to which we reported the initial abuse.

Sincerely,

J.B. Simms

Tuesday, January 7, 2020

BFS awards Direct Express to Comerica Bank, again

Subject: False statements in the press release by Thomas Santaniello
From: jbsimms
Date: Tue, Jan 07, 2020, 9:59 am
To: Media.Relations@fiscal.treasury.gov
Cc: Steven Lepper (CEO-Military Banks of America), Joe Plenzler (Wounded Warriors), Walter Bayer (SSA OIG), "Kate Berry", Sonja Scott (OIG Treasury), Katherine Johnson (OIG Treasury), Amy Altemus (OIG Treasury), Thomas Santaniello (Bureau of Fiscal Service)

I received a copy of the press release dated today in which the Bureau of Fiscal Service granted the contract to be the Fiscal Agent for the Direct Express program for the next five years.

The assertion of customer satisfaction is a lie, an overt lie. It has been proven that Comerica Bank used in-house skewed surveys which resulted in the numbers you published.

There is no evidence of any competitive selection process. In fact, Thomas Santaniello prohibited Direct Express victims from addressing the sham "Evaluation Team" in order to hide the process in which Comerica Bank and certain employees of the Bureau of Fiscal Service privately benefited.

The Bureau of Fiscal Service was so inept and corrupt that it allowed Comerica Bank and its unqualified subcontractor Conduent to fail to implement or offer any security measures or fraud notifications.

Veterans and civilians receiving benefits from VAB and Social Security have been victimized by the corruption at the Bureau of Fiscal Service which has been exposed to all. Every veteran employed at the Bureau of Fiscal Service should be ashamed of themselves for not confronting Santaniello, McCoy, Morrow, Lebryk, and now Mr. Gribben and be willing to protect fellow veterans. You bring dishonor to the uniform for not defending fellow veterans, each of you.

No one at the Bureau of Fiscal Service had the integrity or the courage to engage me, Ms. Jackie Densmore, or any other victim of this program. While those the at Bureau of Fiscal Service.

Sincerely,

J.B. Simms

This email from Santaniello was a direct slap in our face

From: Thomas Santaniello (Bureau of Fiscal Service)
Sent: Tuesday, January 7, 2020, 10:25 AM
To: Michael Jackman (Legislative Aide, Massachusetts)
Subject: Fiscal Service Direct Express Selection Announcement

Good morning, I wanted to share with you today's announcement regarding our selection of Comerica bank to continue as our Direct Express debit card financial agent under a new agreement for five years, beginning in January 2020.

As promised, we are available to brief you on the selection at your convenience.   Thank you, Tom
Thomas Santaniello, Legislative & Public Affairs, Bureau of the Fiscal Service

Did Santaniello, BFS, and OIG Treasury delay the publication of investigations?

Subject: Did Santaniello get a "heads-up" on investigations and unpublished reports?
From: jbsimms
Date: Tue, Jan 07, 2020, 10:26 am
To: Sonja Scott (OIG Treasury), Amy Altemus (OIG Treasury), Katherine Johnson (OIG Treasury)
Cc: Jackie Lynn; "Kate Berry" (American Banker)
Dear Ms. Scott, Altemus, and Johnson,
In consideration of the press release today by the Bureau of Fiscal Service, stating they renewed the Fiscal Agent Agreement of Direct Express, one can only assume that BFS and Mr. Santaniello were briefed and/or given copies of your investigations which have not been published. BFS would not have awarded this contract without knowing what was to be published from any or all of your offices.
Mr. Santaniello had some sway in the decision to cancel our conference a month or so ago.
J.B. Simms

Subject: Re: Did Santaniello get a "heads-up" on investigations and
unpublished reports?
From: Kate Berry (American Banker)
Date: Tue, January 07, 2020, 10:37 am
To: jbsimms
You crack me up, JB. You pull no punches. Always coming out swinging!
You remind me a little of Bernie Little, the main character in a mystery book I'm currently reading about a P.I. and his dog.
The book is told from the point of view of the dog, Chet, and it's pretty funny.
Your email made me think that you could be the basis of the Bernie character, a private investigator and former combat veteran, who used to be a police officer. Good stuff with the dog part thrown in.
kb

I loved Kate. She knew me well. She knew what I thought about BFS and Treasury.

Subject: Re: False statements in the press release by Thomas Santaniello
From: Steven Lepper (CEO-Military Banks of America)
Date: Tue, January 07, 2020, 11:15 am
To: jbsimms
Mr. Simms,
I appreciate you remaining engaged in this effort. I received the link announcing Comerica's award of the new DE contract from both Ms. Densmore and VBA today. While I feel your frustration, I doubted the DE program would simply go away at the conclusion of Comerica's original contract. The fact remains that too many veterans and social security annuitants are dependent on the program, despite its many problems.
I think the best way to deal with this situation is to encourage DE enrollees to open bank accounts. Any bank or credit union will work for the Direct Deposit program. The value of the Veterans Benefits Banking Program in which VBA and AMBA have partnered is that it involves banks that currently serve and understand the military and veteran communities.
We are working with VBA to get the word out. On the day that our program was featured in the most recent VNA newsletter— last Friday— we received almost 10,000 visitors on the VBBP website. What we'd like to

313

do— and maybe you can help— is to collect some testimonials in support of Direct Deposit or the VBBP, preferably from veterans who previously participated in the DE program. There are lots of testimonials about the DE program's problems that should discourage veterans from continuing to use it. We'd like to see success stories from VBBP participants that will encourage veterans to use it. As the VBBP program matures, we'll collect them.
Have a great week!
Steve

Subject: Did Santaniello get a "heads-up" on investigations and unpublished reports?
From: jbsimms
Date: Tue, Jan 07, 2020, 11:32 am
To: Sonja Scott (OIG Treasury), Amy Altemus (OIG Treasury, Katherine Johnson (OIG Treasury)
Cc: Jackie Lynn, Kate Berry (American Banker), Steven Lepper (CEO-Military Banks of America)
I just hope one of you, or anyone at OIG Treasury, will break from the "Neville Chamberlain" agenda with regard to the Bureau of Fiscal Service and assume the role of Mr. Churchill.
I and other victims, and veterans, put our faith in you. Time will tell if this was a misguided venture on our part.
J.B. Simms

How could these agencies not hold anyone accountable? We thought Walter Bayer of SSA, who appeared to be receptive, would give us a way to directly address the SSA. The information in the inserts was a lie. This is our government, lying to us.

Subject: RE: False statements in the press release by Thomas Santaniello
From: jbsimms
Date: Tue, Jan 07, 2020, 11:56 am
To: Steven Lepper (CEO-Military Banks of America)
Cc: Jackie Lynn
Mr. Lepper,
Thank you for your email. While is a bit of consolation knowing the concerns of mine and Ms. Densmore have been validated and supported by you, we are yet a bit disappointed.
You have been assigned the role of the conduit which VA appears to want to communicate with Ms. Densmore or me. Your communication with Mr. Lawrence was evidently convincing, and the AMBA was able to gain an endorsement. Hopefully, this ill-advised decision by BFS to grant the contract to Direct Express will be interpreted by VA officials for exactly what it is: a lack of accountability and integrity.
If we/you can get the VA to create an accurate insert to accompany paper checks, endorsing your organization, we will continue to use the social media tools at our disposal to direct veterans and spouses/dependents to your organization as well. This might necessitate a PR push with counselors at every VA as well as the orientation from Public Affairs Officers at military bases. I do have a close personal resource from which to glean wisdom from the Public Affairs angle, as I know you do.
The other issue is SSA, and hopefully, Mr. Bayer will convey our facts and concerns to his OIG SSA associates. Mr. Bayer did send me an encouraging email, stating that he would present the matter. If we get the SSA to endorse and promote the AMBA, that will be a victory. If you have the inclination to contact Mr. Bayer, he can be reached at Walter Bayer (SSA OIG) (202) 358-6319.
The more we work to dissuade persons from using the Direct Express program, the less money Comerica Bank will make, and that would be pleasing.
I am glad you got the responses you did with respect to the first press release, and we hope to keep your office busy for a while.
J.B. Simms

On Tue, Jan 7, 2020, at 12:27 PM jbsimms wrote:
Dear Ms. Scott, Altemus, and Johnson,
In consideration of the press release today by the Bureau of Fiscal Service, stating they renewed the Fiscal Agent Agreement of Direct Express, one can only assume that BFS and Mr. Santaniello were briefed and/or given copies of your investigations which have not been published. If the reports from your offices were to be accurate and complete, the reports would confirm allegations of malfeasance and corruption on the part of Santaniello and others at BFS.

BFS would not have awarded this contract without knowing what was to be published from any or all of your offices.

Did Mr. Santaniello had some sway in the decision to cancel our conference a month or so ago?.

Have any of you forwarded any preliminary report to Santaniello or any of his assigns, personally, through Mr. Delmar, or any other person?

J.B. Simms

Subject: RE: Did Santaniello get a "heads-up" on investigations and unpublished reports?
From: jbsimms
Date: Tue, Jan 07, 2020, 1:12 pm
To: "Kate Berry" (American Banker)
Cc: Jackie Lynn
Jackie knows more about the Walmart thing than me.
You know if changes were made, this is a penalty for doing something wrong.
We need to see the OIG Treasury report[19-041] and see what they are willing to publish.
OIG Treasury does not want to validate Jackie or me, and they ignore our emails. I copy others just to confirm that they got what I sent. Get what you can. You know what we need. 😎
Jackie and I had not been able to get BFS to answer us, but Santaniello answered Jackman.

We had sent emails to Santaniello and no response.
Below is an email from a plaintiff in our lawsuit who is a disabled veteran.

Subject: Direct Express
From: Jennifer Kreegar
Date: Tue, Jan 07, 2020, 2:14 pm
To: Media.Relations@fiscal.treasury.gov, Thomas Santaniello (Bureau of Fiscal Service)
Recently Comerica Bank was again awarded the contract by the US Treasury Dept under false pretenses. I was one of the hundreds of victims that were systematically robbed of my benefits. This is an ongoing problem, because of fraudulent records provided by Comerica and Conduent/Direct Express. I promise you I will diligently work to squeeze the life out of the corruption that runs rampant in the bureaucracy and government that prays upon innocent people. And continue to help expose those that receive under-the-table payments that keep the corruption going. Their time is coming to be exposed.
Sincerely,
Jennifer Kreegar

Spineless people at Comerica and Treasury

J B Simms
Tue, Jan 7, 3:02 PM
to Richard, Sonja, Katherine, Amy Altemus, Jackie, Franklin, bcc: Kate Berry
As I sit in a moving car away from my computer and using personal email, I am quite disappointed that you people allowed BFS to not only not be accountable, letting Santaniello tell you to postpone your reports until after the press release, you did not have the integrity to keep him from controlling the narrative.
It does not matter what I say to you.
Either you people are spineless and lack the courage to be an advocate of the citizens who pay you or you are as corrupt as Santaniello. It is either A or B.
There is no need for me to repeat the incidences of disrespect and apathy.
You can block me as BFS has done, but there is no evidence you have listened to anything I said. You were more focused on the cover-up than you were on hearing the truth.
Sadly, you have reinforced the stereotype of a government worker.
I am not done with Santaniello, and I will also have questions for each of you. You wasted our time, presenting us with a false agenda. You lied from the beginning.
I will travel to DC to meet any or all of you. You know how to reach me, or ping my phone if you wish.
J. B. Simms
Sent from my iPhone.

I was tired of the lies and the lack of integrity in Washington, D.C.

Subject: Re: False statements in the press release by Thomas Santaniello
From: Steven Lepper (CEO-Military Banks of America)
Date: Tue, January 07, 2020, 3:32 pm
To: "jbsimms Cc: Jackie Lynn
Mr. Simms,
I truly believe VBA is committed to fixing this problem. It was they who contacted me to set up this program. I know from my direct engagement with him that Dr. Lawrence, a veteran himself, doesn't like what's going on with the Direct Express program and is making every effort to "bank" veterans who are receiving their monetary benefits on DE's prepaid card and by paper checks. I know your experience with the federal government has been less than satisfactory; however, I'm convinced that VBA is doing everything it can right now to encourage DE participants and paper check recipients to sign up for bank accounts. VBA is not the enemy. If I thought they were, I'd be right there with you flogging them.
I will be meeting with my VBA partner on Friday in DC. We're going to deliver a talk about this program to a gathering of MSOs & VSOs that have veteran and military financial education as part of their missions. I'm hoping that our message can also be delivered by them to their networks so we can finally get these veterans off of DE and into mainstream banking.
Social Security is the next hill to take. Thanks for sending Mr. Bayer's contact info. I'll keep you posted on our progress.
All the best,
Steve

On Jan 7, 2020, at 11:09 PM, jbsimms:
Thank you. We have charged up the hill, and we need a few reinforcements. We are very grateful.
I know you feel my passion, and that of Ms. Densmore. We were the ones fielding the calls. I did this for over a year, and SSA not only gave minimal lip service to the problems, but they also refused to tell anyone, including me, how our identities were compromised at the SSA.
This could happen to any veteran receiving SSA, which is a heads up for you because if you direct a person to an AMBA bank, and SSA funds are received, SSA security is lax and no one there will reveal how it happened.
Mr. Bayer is aware of the identity fraud on my account. Luckily, I was at the SSA office a few days after the fraudulent interaction and corrected the change of address.
You might have to intercede on behalf of a client/veteran depositor. If someone from SSA tells you or another victim, as they did me, that they cannot reveal how the fraud was perpetrated, you would be as incensed as I was. A person at SSA did this.
We know that Conduent personnel has access to all info on Direct Express accounts. We both know how this information is leaked.
Santaniello must have quite a bit of leverage for him to be able to control the narrative and have this press release BEFORE the three reports from OIG Treasury (Ms. Altemus at Office of Chief Counsel(investigating 30 of the 105 victim narratives I supplied), Ms. Scott at OIG Treasury (investigation of fraud and violation of Reg E), and Ms. Katherine Johnson (the chief auditor charged with publishing OIG Treasury 19-041).
Remember, Katherine Johnson's audit has to have a signed document from BFS Commissioner Gribben before publication.
Attached is the preliminary audit report, published July 29, 2019, along with my edits in red. I had quite a back-and-forth with Mr. Delmar after he received my reply.
My apologies for the length of this reply. I see you have a grasp of the matter.
Thank you again,
Jim

January 7 was a busy day. There was a huge backstory that Jackie and I did not know. Comerica had made a deal with the devil to keep the contract. No one was going to tell us. It took another year to find out the truth.

Wednesday, January 8, 2020

Mr. Lepper had sent me a link to an article printed by Kate Berry of The American Banker. We valued Mr. Lepper's help. He sent this on his own.

Subject: RE: False statements in the press release by Thomas Santaniello
From: jbsimms
Date: Wed, Jan 08, 2020, 5:39 am
To: Steven Lepper (CEO-Military Banks of America), Cc: Jackie Lynn
Mr. Lepper,
Thank you.
Kate Berry has been quite the advocate for us and has printed a number of articles at our request. She jumped on this yesterday within minutes. We know Kate has to be more diplomatic than I would be I (or I can be) but she did pepper the article with controversy as she quoted BFS in their self-serving validation dance. Kate also asked pointed questions to Wendy Bridges, the PR person, to whom Nora Arpin directed the foray of questions from Jackie and me. Bridges was way over her head in this and simply gave boilerplate cut-and-paste answers. When we reduce the income to Comerica Bank by diverting recipients to your organization, maybe Kate can write another story touting the AMBA as the preferred alternative to the Bureau of Fiscal Service.
Sincerely,
Jim

Subject: The hits just keep on coming, and BFS is running the show
From: jbsimms
Date: Wed, Jan 08, 2020, 6:02 pm
To: Amy Altemus (OIG Treasury), Katherine Johnson (OIG Treasury), Richard Delmar (OIG Treasury)
Cc: Jackie Lynn; Kate Berry (American Banker) Steven Lepper (CEO-Military Banks of America), Walter Bayer (SSA OIG)
Bcc: Franklin Lemond (Plaintiff's Attorney)
Dear Mr. Delmar and Ms. Scott, Altemus, and Johnson,
Below is pasted a copy of a post on the Facebook page of almost 375 people who has joined to help victims. While I find it interesting that BFS was able to convey the contract to Comerica Bank before the reports from Ms. Scott, Altemus, and Johnson were published (the investigative report would come from Ms. Scott, the investigation of 30 victims from Ms. Altemus, and the audit report 19-041 from Ms. Johnson), I assume there was conversation/concession with Commissioner Gribben that the anticipated reports, upon publication, would not report findings which would appear to cast BFS in a bad light. That was "[T]he Art of the Deal," and Santaniello has the leverage.
Read this and tell me if Ms. Johnson and Ms. Scott might want to make a few more phone calls.
"Paul Scott to Direct Express Cardholder Victims
"For the last 30 days my card has not been working at my local bank to withdraw money. They told me to call the cardholder. I've tried for the last 30 days and they just hang up never get a person this is crazy. So today I went to the bank to see if my card would work nope and there's a sign on the ATM that reads Direct Express card holders' cards do not work at this ATM and if your account holder we cannot take money off your card to put in your account. The problem is I live in a small town 40 miles from anywhere we have one Bank. So I drove to the next town to my surprise there was a sign on their ATM that read the same thing so evidently, this is a way bigger problem than I thought. Not only me but nobody can draw money out of an ATM but you can buy stuff online and it's a grocery store, but you just can't get cash. Does anybody know what's going on because no matter how many times I call today I called 40 times it always says high call volume try later 30 days in a row if I can ever get this straightened out I will open an account at the bank and get rid of my card but they are truly holding m,e hostage?. Being a disabled American, this is got to be against the law. Thank you for letting me blow off my Steam".
I got this today. You can go online and find it. Paul Scott has been directed to call Ms. Scott.
I went after Comerica on behalf of 105 victims. Ms. Scott has the narratives. I will be in touch with this victim to see if anyone in Washington will do anything about this.
Sincerely,
J.B. Simms

Mr. Lepper did reach out to Kate Berry for an interview.

Thursday, January 9, 2020

Subject: The sign refusing Direct Express cardholder service at ATM
From: jbsimms
Date: Thu, Jan 09, 2020, 7:39 am
To: Thomas Santaniello (Bureau of Fiscal Service)
Cc: Richard Delmar (OIG Treasury), Sonja Scott (OIG Treasury), Katherine Johnson (OIG Treasury),
Walter Bayer (SSA OIG), Jackie Lynn; Kate Berry (American Banker) Steven Lepper (CEO-Military Banks of
America)
Mr. Santaniello,
This cardholder could not get his money. Read the sign.
Until we learn the leverage you have over persons at Treasury, resulting in skewed in incomplete investigations,
you will continue to be responsible for this. The persons at Treasury who allow you to continue your "punkish"
behavior are culpable for ignoring the real connection between you and officials at Comerica Bank.
I am requesting a copy of the recent full and complete Fiscal Agent Agreement between Bureau of Fiscal
Service and Comerica Bank.
I wish to sit across a table with you and hear you defend or justify this decision. Bring whomever you wish to
the meeting. I can handle this solo.
J.B. Simms

From: Cat Pekins
Date: Thu, January 09, 2020, 2:26 pm
To: jbsimms
Hi Mr. Simms,
I am at a loss as to where to have my Direct Express statements mailed to me and to my SSI case manager. The
case Manager has said if I do not have these statements in two weeks I could lose my Income. I have called
Direct Express customer service and Comerica trying to obtain statements from 2017 to now. I have not
succeeded. I have gotten in touch with Direct Express complaint line and was told the Direct Express advocacy
group would be contacting me in 48-72 business hours. I have Legal Aid involved and I read your name on a
webpage stating that you could help as well. Please let me know if you have any suggestions-
Thank you,
Catherine Perkins

Saturday, January 11, 2020

J B Simms
Sat, Jan 11, 5:41 AM
to Sonja, Amy, Katherine, Jackie
Jackie,
They put the responsibility for fraud monitoring on Mastercard. MC needs to know this as they dodge the
subpoena.
There still appears to be no transaction alert.
Reg E violation is the cornerstone of our case. I have detailed many overt violations, and for DE to advertise
compliance is a bit disingenuous (10-day reimbursement, using the fraud packet to hold cardholders hostage
for reimbursement, non-existent fraud department and failure to investigate or report investigations).
I had scores of people who were denied a claim, only to be reimbursed fully after my involvement. Sonja Scott
cannot ignore the 105 narratives I sent to her. It is quite arrogant for those in Treasury to feign concern for
victims and want you to think they are doing their jobs when those in Treasury had to approve the FAA with
Comerica. They were working on this for months, telling us nothing, and ignoring us.
There is no way BFS could get approval for the terms of this contract unless private personal deals were done
between Comerica Bank and employees of Treasury. he only way Comerica got the deal was to get OIG
Treasury to "ramp down" investigative reports to make Comerica Bank appear to be less culpable.
To those at Treasury, reveal the reports from Altemus, Scott, and Johnson and prove me wrong. It was my
"assertion" (a word used by Delmar to attack me) that OIG Treasury failed in two previous OIG Treasury
reports to fulfill their responsibility. Send me a copy of the new agreement and let me see what you approved,
then let me see your investigations. Jim

Regulation E Protection from the Consumer Financial Protection Bureau never existed

The same consumer protections for fraud, loss, and errors that are provided to traditional bank account holders under the Consumer Financial Protection Bureau's (CFPB) "Regulation E", are provided to Direct Express® cardholders. Regulation E establishes a basic framework of the rights, liabilities, and responsibilities of participants in the electronic fund and remittance transfer systems. Indeed, in making cardholders whole, Direct Express® often goes further than what is required by Reg E.

The Consumer Financial Protection Bureau (CFPB) talks a big game but enforced little.

Sunday, January 12, 2020

Subject: Sad commentary, but more victims agree this is inside job and feds refuse to investigate
From: jbsimms
Date: Sun, Jan 12, 2020, 10:14 am
To: Richard Delmar (OIG Treasury), Thomas Santaniello (Bureau of Fiscal Service)
Cc: Sonja Scott (OIG Treasury), Amy Altemus (OIG Treasury, Katherine Johnson (OIG Treasury), Jackie Lynn; Walter Bayer (SSA OIG), Steven Lepper (CEO-Military Banks of America)
Mr. Delmar and Mr. Santaniello,
I did not expect to have to email you on a Sunday, but this post on the Facebook page at Direct Express Cardholder Victims was made today. I replied.
You, people, think all this is funny. Most of these victims do not have the education nor the suffix's after their name as you do, but they see exactly what I have been saying for two years; the corruption begins with Santaniello protecting Comerica Bank's malfeasance (his motivation is yet to be exposed), Conduent protects the criminals within their midst, Social Security ignores inquiries and avoids accountability to victims of identity theft, and OIG Treasury is too timid to conduct a thorough investigation into any of the aforementioned criminal acts.
Victims know this is tightly woven inside job. Santaniello hid the decision-making process from the public and awarded the contract to Comerica Bank BEFORE three reports of investigations from OIG Treasury were published. OIG Treasury reviewed this decision by Santaniello before the announcement after Santaniello was assured OIG Treasury was going to "go easy" on the Bureau of Fiscal Service, so when the reports are published, Santaniello will bask in the glow of validation from OIG Treasury. Santaniello must have taken some compromising photographs at a Treasury Christmas party.
Here is the post from the victim:

On Jan 12, 2020, at 12:43 PM, jbsimms wrote:
Mike Miller to Direct Express Cardholder Victims
Thanks for adding me. Im on social security & get my check on a direct express card. Someone got my card info & made a bunch of online purchases without my knowledge & i have called direct express several times to speak to someone about these purchases that i did not make & last night sat on hold for 1 hour 42 minutes & 19 seconds only for it to disconnect me . I called again this morning & the man that answered told me he would have a supervisor call me in 30 minutes & im still waiting. Im now homeless with my little Chihuahua Spankey which is a registered emotional support animal because of all of this .

The email below touched my heart. This man was living in his car. Mr. Lepper was focused on helping us. He understood my fight with the VA, telling me, "…[t]he VA is not your enemy anymore." BFS, OIG Treasury, and SSA remained my enemy.

Date: Sun, Jan 12, 2020 4:54 pm
To: jbsimms
This truly is depressing. I just copied you on a note I sent Jackie. We're totally focused on making DE irrelevant. I hope that this gentleman will realize that the safest way to receive his Social Security benefits is to have them deposited into a checking or savings account. Perhaps you can recommend that to him and send him to our website. Even though he's not a veteran, I'm sure most or all of the banks participating in our program would be willing to help him.
Best, Steve

Monday, January 13, 2020

Below is an email from an attorney who worked with Delmar. For some reason, this attorney was coming to the defense of Santaniello of BFS. First, this attorney (Sciurba) admitted that "investigations" took place at OIG Treasury, then denied the investigations were conducted when faced with an FOI request. These were, and are, some career criminals.

Enter Loren Sciurba, attorney, OIG Treasury

Subject: RE: Another victim of Comerica Bank and BFS
From: Loren Sciurba (OIG Treasury)
Date: Mon, Jan 13, 2020, 9:00 am
To: jbsimms
Cc: Richard Delmar (OIG Treasury)), Sonja Scott (OIG Treasury), Amy Altemus (OIG Treasury)
Mr. Simms:

As you are aware, the Office of Inspector General for the US Department of the Treasury was established to conduct and supervise audits and investigations relating to the programs and operations of the Treasury. Your concern for Direct Express beneficiaries is appreciated but demanding that this Office intervene in individual cases is neither legally nor practically possible. We recommend such individuals contact the bank or the Bureau of Consumer Financial Protection for assistance. This Office does not possess the legal mandate or the resources to assist individual customers of financial institutions. Should you have information that contains specific facts sufficient to establish a violation of law, regulation, or policy within the jurisdiction of this Office, you may send such to the Office of Counsel at OIGCounsel@oig.treas.gov, or to the Office of Inspector General Hotline. All such submissions will be reviewed, applied as appropriate to our investigative and audit work, and made part of our records.

Your frequent communications, demanding meetings, personal interviews, and referring individual Direct Express customers here, do not aid our work, and cause a disservice to the customers. We have no authority or power to assist individual consumers and are specifically prohibited from engaging in program operating responsibilities, such as taking action on behalf of a specific constituent. We urge your associate to contact the Bureau of Consumer Financial Protection or Comerica itself to obtain a resolution and redress.

Lastly, we take issue with your repeated defamatory claims regarding Mr. Santaniello. I advise you, again, that Mr. Santaniello had nothing to do with the cancellation of the meeting you requested, nor have we received any evidence that Mr. Santaniello has improperly influenced the audit process in any way. Unsupported assertions of misconduct and bad faith are of no use to this Office and may be actionable by the subjects thereof. Should you have any factual evidence of wrongdoing, we invite you to provide it.

We intend this to be our last communication with you on this matter. When the audit is completed, it will be publicly available on the Treasury Office of Inspector General's website.
Sincerely,
Loren Sciurba
Acting Counsel to the Inspector General

Sciurba was trying to spread his wings. He jumped into the fray way too late to have any credibility. Sciurba used a generic email address from OIG Treasury to identify himself, noting that my reply would go to many people in that office.

Subject: Another victim of Comerica Bank and BFS
From: jbsimms
Date: Mon, Jan 13, 2020, 9:46 am
To: "OIG Counsel" <OIGCounsel@oig.treas.gov>
Cc: Jackie Lynn
Dear Ms. Sciurba,
Thank you for your email.
There are many issues of which you appear to be unaware.
Mr. Santaniello did impede the victims from participating in oral presentations to said "Evaluation Team" before May 2018. Any reference to Mr. Santaniello or characterization of Mr. Santaniello is based on fact, not allegation or supposition. There is no way BFS could give the delayed conveyance of the Direct Express

contract without having proprietary knowledge of the information to be published by either Ms. Altemus, Ms. Scott, or Ms. Johnson.

Mr. Santaniello did not have the integrity to engage me or any victim to defend the position of BFS to grant this contract. I assume the failure of Mr. Santaniello to challenge any of my "assertions" in what you refer to as an "actionable" manner is because someone made him aware of a SCOTUS 376 U.S. 254 (1964) which allows the protection of citizens and restricts the ability of public officials to sue for defamation.

Furthermore, after my veracity was challenged by OIG Treasury to prove that scores (final total being 105) of victims had contacted me for assistance with respect to violations of Reg E on behalf of Comerica Bank, and is endorsed by the Bureau of Fiscal Service, I forwarded the narratives to Ms. Sonja Scott. Ms. Scott then agreed to begin receiving direct communication with victims. You have been misinformed.

Ms. Altemus contacted me as one of a group of 30 victims, all derived from the list of 105 submitted to her by Ms. Scott. The number of victim accounts being investigated, 30, was confirmed by Ms. Altemus. That report has not been published.

The preliminary OIG Treasury 19-041 was published on July 29, 2,019 and the final report has not been published. Oddly, the preliminary report included a signature page noting signed acceptance from Mr. Gribben. After having reviewed this preliminary report and submitting my feedback on the failure(s) to address matters and to correct historical references made in this preliminary report, confirmation was received by Mr. Delmar that my response had been received. The auditor who signed this report was Ms. Katherine Johnson.

We assume this preliminary report was used as the basis for BFS to award the Fiscal Agent contract to Comerica Bank because the preliminary report was found to be quite impotent.

Many months ago, Mr. Delmar promised to publish OIG Treasury 19-024 after I submitted all proper protocols to see this document. This promise has not been fulfilled.

Your suggestion that I refer victims to other federal agencies is the same mantra experienced by other victims and is callous.

It was only after my conversation with Paulette Battle on February 26, 2018, that OIG Treasury was made aware that OIG Treasury needed to be more thorough in the investigation of the Bureau of Fiscal Service and Comerica Bank with regard to the Direct Express program.

After having read OIG Treasury 14-031 and 17-034, and based upon my experience, I acted.

If you wish to communicate directly, the invitation is open to you.

Sincerely,

J.B. Simms

Subject: RE: Another victim of Comerica Bank and BFS

From: OIG Counsel <OIGCounsel@oig.treas.gov>

Date: Mon, Jan 13, 2020, 12:17 pm

To: jbsimms

Cc: Jackie Lynn, Richard Delmar (OIG Treasury)), Amy Altemus (OIG Treasury), Sonja Scott (OIG Treasury)

Mr. Simms,

I am well aware of the situation and everything in my previous email message still stand. When the audit is completed, it will be publicly available on the Treasury Office of Inspector General's website. I have nothing more to say on this matter.

Sincerely,

Loren Sciurba

Acting Counsel to the Inspector General

Sciurba was getting a bit testy. He knew he was hiding information. Notice he did not mention the "investigations" in this email. Sciurba had been in the background but chose this point to poke his head out of the hole.

Below is another tragic story, emailed to me.

"To Someone Who Can Make a Difference,

I have surpassed my 16th call to Direct Express, exceeding 1100 minutes on the phone attempting to access my funds. I can recite the hold quote from memory.

Unfortunately, my health is declining, and undue stress is making my family suffer in ways you can't even imagine.

On December 18th I was unable to login to my Direct Express account. I received no notices or emails indicating that a problem had occurred. They had no issues with my making transfers in the previous three months from here, but now I'm not allowed to do anything!

After speaking with 16 different customer support representatives, 13 supervisors, sending my passport picture, resetting my ID and password twice while on the phone with a supervisor and redoing my security questions.....I can't access my internet account for more than 2 minutes. If I hear the words "Escalated to our fraud department, " I'll scream!

The first call was nothing short of funny. The woman I spoke with was American, yet she was unsuccessful at pronouncing the words on the screen she was reading! I had to help. Next, I was told to call Social Security to have the situation dealt with. I explained to that woman, nicely I might add, why calling Social Security wouldn't help my situation.

But I digress. ... I can't transfer money, buy airline tickets for my husband, children and I to get back to the states or much of anything else. I have notes, recorded calls and more.... but not my money!

Who can I call, what can I do? Any guidance would be greatly appreciated.

Thank you"

Another victim reached out to me. These victims were being ignored, but not by me.

Below is a reply to Sciurba, advising him there were three (3) ongoing investigations taking place. Sciurba claimed to know the issues. Delmar had Sciurba begin replying in hopes Sciurba would intimidate me. What a joke.

Sciurba receives my reply to his involvement

Subject: RE: Another victim of Comerica Bank and BFS
From: jbsimms
Date: Mon, Jan 13, 2020, 8:20 pm
To: "OIG Counsel" <OIGCounsel@oig.treas.gov>
Cc: Jackie Lynn; Richard Delmar (OIG Treasury)), Amy Altemus (OIG Treasury), Sonja Scott (OIG Treasury)

Dear Ms. Sciurba,

With all due respect, and to bring you up to speed, there are three investigations (one termed an audit, by Ms. Johnson) simultaneously being conducted by OIG Treasury. I listed these three in a previous email, but I will be glad to do so again for you:

Sonja Scott- Investigation of Bureau of Fiscal Service/Comerica Bank FAA and violations of Reg E, as well as being receptive to victims after I forwarded the 105 narratives. A copy of this investigation will be requested upon being notified of completion.

Katherine Johnson- Auditor, assigned to receive the investigation from Ms. Scott and fashion into an "audit" OIG Treasury 19-041. A copy of this audit, as you stated, will be viewed as published, as was the preliminary 19-041.

A.J. Altemus is conducting an investigation of 30 victims; the narrative of each victim selected by Ms. Scott and delivered to Ms. Altemus. A copy of the final report by Ms. Altemus will be requested.

Ms. Densmore and I were gleefully anticipating a telephone conference, scheduled by Ms. Scott, a few months ago to be conducted by Ms. Scott. In fewer than 24 hours, we received an email (I do not remember the author/sender of the email) canceling this conference. Discussion topics were solicited by Ms. Scott. I submitted one page of issues to be addressed and one page of the plan to end the Direct Express program. Shortly after I sent the requested syllabus, the meeting was canceled, with no explanation.

Since that date, the attitude of personnel at the US Treasury ceased to be receptive. It was as if "we do not need your input anymore, and we will let the victims flounder, some becoming homeless, as we direct victims to remote agencies which have no record of helping these victims." The CFPB, Comerica Bank, Conduent, and BFS frustrate the victims.

The cancellation of that conference was the turning point. That appears to have been a very questionable decision. Scrutiny, accountability, and revelations by victims were to be expected.

We are still open to having the conference. Ms. Densmore and I are up to speed on the issues.

I will accept your proposition that no employee at BFS had knowledge of the substance or findings of any of the three ongoing investigations. That being said, and if that is, if fact, true, then I interpret the awarding of the contract to Comerica Bank as a "salute" to OIG Treasury. BFS probably assumed OIG Treasury was not going to hold BFS accountable in the administration of the Direct Express program as was the case in the two previous OIG reports, so why not give the contract to Comerica Bank again? Why wait for an OIG Treasury report before making the new deal with Comerica Bank?

When the full contract between BFS and Comerica Bank is examined and is summarized by Ms Johnson, we will have a few answers..

Sincerely,

J.B. Simms

Sciurba was in over his head on this matter. Sciurba's first name was Loren. How was I to know he identified himself as a man?

Wednesday, January 15, 2020

Mike Miller (Direct Express victim) wrote:

"I reported my fraudulent transactions to direct express on January 2nd & had my old card shut off. I received my new card on January 6th. I talked to a man at direct express customer service on January 2nd & he said he was transferring me to the dispute department & i sat on hold for 1 hour 42 minutes & 19 seconds & it hung up on me & i've tried several times to talk to someone in the dispute department but im always put on hold & then it hangs up . Its been well over 10 days & I am really stressed out over this . I can't take much more."

This was another heartbreaking email. Since we filed the lawsuit, I could not directly contact Comerica or Conduent. I had to direct persons to do more on their own.

Thursday, January 16, 2020

Below is the complete email from Jackie to Delmar

Jackie Lynn
Thu, Jan 16, 8:07 AM
to Richard, Cate, Michael, Franklin, me
Dear Mr. Delmar,
Thank you for sending me the report of the investigation on the fraud on the Direct Express account used for my brother-in-law, Derek Densmore.
I found a few things in the report that are inaccurate and would like corrected.
Page 1, First sentence
The report stated OIG Treasury received information from Money Gram and Comerica Bank about fraud in the CBA program. This sentence makes it look like the first time OIG Treasury heard of this was from Money Gram and Comerica Bank. This is not true.
My fraud was first told to Mr. Delmar by Kate Berry of American Banker, not Comerica Bank or Money Gram. I then called Mr. Delmar personally and told him about this before anyone was in touch with Comerica Bank. This investigation began with Kate Berry, and me, not the bank.
Page 3 Line 3
The only reason the fraud was "noticed" was because I brought it to your attention after you were interviewed by Kate Berry of American Banker.
Page 5 line 13
"Comerica Bank proactively terminated the Direct Express CBA program."
This is a lie. Comerica Bank did not "proactively" do anything. Comerica Bank "reacted" to my conversation with Nora Arpin on a Friday evening to communication she received from JB Simms.
Also if the amount of money was documented to be stolen and an email exist from Ms. Scott saying that multiple investigations were happening nationwide then how is that all linked to Florida?
It also does not state anything about Sen Warrens inquires or Michael Jackman's which is strange considering they played a huge part in this investigation.
Conduent and Comerica Bank did not investigate this matter within their own companies. OIG Treasury did not investigate Conduent or Comerica Bank, where the fraud began.

The report failed to state how many victims were included in the $349,819.68 fraud. If the average person gets $1,000 per month, does that mean 349,891 people were defrauded? This fraud did not happen overnight. Comerica Bank and Conduent allowed this to continue until I reported the fraud. Get your story straight. Your report dated July 2019 conflicts with this investigation -so what was the date of the first report of fraud with the card less benefit program? According to the letters sent to Veterans affairs and to Social Security, VA and SSA had no knowledge of fraud because the bank never notified them.
The OIG said the agreement "does not distinguish between internal and external violations."
Jackie Densmore

Jackie might have had a little "help" writing the email. She let him know that she was not being fooled. These were dirty people.

The denial of investigations continued

Below is the response to Senator Warren's staffer about Treasury's answer the o Comerica contract amid investigations

J B Simms
Thu, Jan 16, 12:10 PM
to Jackie, Franklin
Here is a response to Warren's staffer about the contract begin granted to Comerica:
When we found out that Bureau of Fiscal Service granted the Direct Express contract to Comerica Bank, we challenged OIG Treasury with at this announcement and made the following statement and lack of justification: The granting of the contract of the Direct Express program was delayed from May 19, 2019 until January 7, 2020. During this time the following investigations were being conducted:
1. Katherine Johnson, OIG Treasury, Audit of Bureau of Fiscal Service/Comerica Bank/Conduent, began June 2018. Preliminary report was published July 29, 2019 and signed by Commissioner Gribben (Bureau of Fiscal Service) The final report is not completed.
2. Sonja Scott, OIG Treasury, Investigations, investigation began June 2018
3. A.J.(Amy) Altemus, OIG Treasury, Office of Special Counsel, audit of 30 individual fraud cases, began October, 2019
Considering these investigations have not been completed, Bureau of Fiscal Service granted the contract to Comerica Bank, the same bank which is under investigation. The self-appointed person coordinating the awarding process, shielding the process from the public, is Thomas Santaniello.
The fact that you questioned the awarding of the contract to Comerica Bank while Comerica Bank and Bureau of Fiscal Service are the subject of three (3) ongoing and concurrent investigations validates our suspicion. We challenged OIG Treasury, submitting the proposition that Santaniello must have proprietary information about the result of the investigation or is influencing OIG Treasury to tamp down the culpability of Bureau of Fiscal Service for their lack of oversight and malfeasance.
We received a response from Loren J. Sciurba, Acting Chief of OIG Treasury Office of Special Counsel (Sciurba@oig.treas.gov). Mr. Sciurba responded defensively, stating that Santaniello did not have inside information and warned J.B. Simms against defamatory remarks. Mr. Sciurba was reminded of SCOTUS case Sullivan v NY Times regarding statements made about public officials.
Mr. Sciurba was then challenged. We accept his proposition that Santaniello did not have inside information or is/was influencing OIG Treasury investigations.
Santaniello and those at the Bureau of Fiscal Service had no concern of retribution or accountability by awarding the renewed contract to Comerica Bank. The Bureau of Fiscal Service was well aware of two OIG reports published in 2014 and 2017 which criticized the Bureau of Fiscal Service in the administration of the Direct Express program. There were no fines, admonishments, sanctions, or enforcement procedures placed against Bureau of Fiscal Service after those to reports, so why should they be concerned with any other report? OIG Treasury was not going to enforce anything, and since Mr. Santaniello has a person Loren J. Sciurba, Acting Chief Counsel of OIG Treasury defending Santaniello, why should Santaniello or anyone at the Bureau of Fiscal Service care about the results of any investigation?
That is the case in a nutshell.

Friday, January 17, 2020

Mr. Lepper was actively engaged in our project. The VBBA was created, and Mr. Lepper was working behind the scenes.

From: Steven Lepper (CEO-Military Banks of America)
Date: Fri, January 17, 2020, 5:24 am
To: jbsimms Cc: Walter Bayer (Soc Sec), Jackie Lynn
Mr. Simms,
Thanks for the note. I just finished a week in DC, during which I met a couple of times with VBA. Our Veterans Benefits Banking Program is getting up to speed and VBA is fully behind it. In the coming weeks, they will be engaging in more outreach with veterans who still use Direct Express and paper checks to encourage them to migrate to more reliable, less expensive bank accounts. Our VBBP banks are simply some of the choices they can make among banks that understand the financial needs and challenges of veterans.
All the best,
Steve

Mr. Lepper engaged with the persons at the Veterans Benefit Association. This was good. I am certain there were some interesting interactions regarding the work I presented. There would be more to come.

From: jbsimms
Date: Fri, Jan 17, 2020, 5:55 am
To: Steven Lepper Cc: Jackie Lynn
Dear Mr. Lepper,
Thank you from our hearts.
Jackie and I had a conversation yesterday concerning the inserts which were included with paper checks. The inserts from last month noted the Direct Express program, and we questioned that.
Was that subject brought up, the endorsing of the Direct Express program on the inserts? Jackie was thinking these were printed some time ago and simply added to the checks with no mention of AMBA.
As you see there is great controversy with respect to the awarding of this contract by BFS to Comerica Bank. BFS is refusing to reveal the contents of the agreement which would be compared to the old agreement.
Sincerely,
Jim

Subject: Warren press release, and failure to produce responses to letters
From: jbsimms
Date: Fri, Jan 17, 2020, 6:13 am
To: Walter Bayer (SSA OIG)
Cc: Jackie Lynn, Franklin Lemond (Plaintiff's Attorney)
Walt,
I forgot to copy you with our reply.
I hope you make some headway with SSA OIG and see the direction the VA is heading with respect to public information being put out by the SSA.
I hope this change made by the VA is an endorsement of all we have been trying to do. We simply want the SSA to direct any veteran to the AMBA and others to a bank or any debit card without mentioning the Direct Express card.
The controversy surrounding the awarding of the contract continues. As can be predicted, those of us who challenge BFS or OIG Treasury for justification of the awarding of this contract are met with a great defense.
Jim

Walter Bayer had promised to take our concerns to the SSA Office of Investigations. It never happened. We were betrayed, but Bayer continued to communicate with us from time to time.

J B Simms
Fri, Jan 17, 3:07 PM
to Thomas, Richard, Sonja, Katherine, Jackie, AJ, Franklin
Mike is another victim.

325

He lost his apartment because Comerica Bank violated Reg E, gave no provisional credit, and have yet to begin an investigation. The account is right in front of Alisha and the Conduent employees.
This is why Ms. Johnson and Ms. Scott should be in San Antonio and see what really goes on at Conduent.
Think of Mike Miller while you are in your warm house, with food to eat.

ıll CC Network LTE   5:56 PM   73% ▬

‹   **Mike** ›

> Glad you getting response.
> Correct Schmidt anytime
> she uses the words Direct
> Express.
> There is no company named
> Direct Express
> Alisha works for Conduent

Idk . All i know is me &
Spankey are freezing to
death out here on the
streets & its raining &
sleeting here .

> Wish I could bring you in.

I wish someone would until i
get my next check or they
put my money back on my
card cause its cold as hell
out here .

Wednesday, January 22, 2020

Subject: RE: Another victim of Comerica Bank and BFS
From: jbsimms
Date: Wed, Jan 22, 2020, 3:16 pm
To: "OIG Counsel" <OIGCounsel@oig.treas.gov>
Cc: Richard Delmar (OIG Treasury)), Sonja Scott (OIG Treasury), Amy Altemus (OIG Treasury), Loren Sciurba (OIG Treasury)
Dear Mr. Sciurba,
As was reviewing the most recent emails from victims of Comerica Bank/Bureau of Fiscal Service, I glanced over the below email you sent me under the guise of a generic email address. You asked that if I had information concerning malfeasance committed by Mr. Santaniello, that I should present it.
I am not fully privy to your background as a prosecutor either with the Postal Service or Treasury, but you probably know by now that I have presented information to prosecutors and federal law enforcement agencies which have resulted in prosecution and imprisonment, so I do bring something to the table.
1) Santaniello refused to allow Ms. Densmore and me to address a so-called "Evaluation Team" of which Mr. Santaniello became the self-appointed spokesperson. This body was said to have been deliberating between financial institutions vying for the Direct Express contract. The subversion of this deliberation and failure to allow us to address this body raises more questions than it gives answers.

326

2) Santaniello has been complicit with communication with officers of Comerica Bank, and the awarding of previous contracts. While Santaniello appears to have no banking background, or having attended no AIB certified courses, the association of Santaniello within a "banking discussion" is suspect.
I am puzzled at your reaction to immediately offer a defense of Mr. Santaniello if you are in fact privy to the ongoing investigations at your agency.
If, as you say, you are "up to speed" with this matter, I should not have to repeat myself with revelations from within your agency subsequent to my February 26, 2018 conversation with Ms. Battle.
The investigations and the acceptance of victim by Ms. Scott was being conducted in an orderly manner long before you entered into the fray. Concessions and communication were offered by both Mr. Delmar and Ms. Scott and neither revealed they had to confer with you.
If/or when our investigations conclude with violations of the Department of Treasury Ethics Handbook, and if Mr. Delmar or any other person at Treasury approves an investigation of Santaniello in order to establish probable cause, I will present the email you sent me as an exhibit that you are compromised and should recuse yourself from any investigation or prosecution of Santaniello.
If you would like to discuss this matter, I will make myself available.
Sincerely,
J.B. Simms

Sciurba and Amy Altemus knew they were doing the bidding of Richard Delmar and denying the existence of investigations to which they previously had made reference. Neither would talk to me personally. Altemus canceled our conference in October 2018. These are despicable human beings.

Subject: I am glad Mr. Lepper listened
From: jbsimms
Date: Wed, Jan 22, 2020, 7:16 pm
To: Pamela Powers (VA-Chief of Staff)
Dear Ms. Powers,
It is unfortunate that Paul Lawrence and you would not listen to me but granted all the intelligence you obtained which led to the association with Mr. Lepper did originate from my work.
It is good that the change happened.
Sincerely,
Jim Simms

Pamela Powers knew that all the work involving the establishment of the Veterans Benefit Banking Program was a result of my work. She just was too political to admit it. I have to give her credit for reading my communication.

Thursday, January 23, 2020

A subpoena was supposed to have been sent to Santaniello.

Subject: status of subpoena
From: Franklin Lemond (Plaintiff's Attorney)
Date: Thu, Jan 23, 2020, 3:00 pm
To: Jim Simms Cc: Jackie Lynn
I must be on some nationwide process server blacklist.
I'll check in with him.
Franklin

I would have to step in to get Santaniello served.

Friday, January 24, 2020

Steven Lepper told us that the AMBA is developing a VBBP newsletter for our banks, partners, and the VBA. We intend to report new information about the program and any other relevant developments.

I asked Mr. Lepper "What was the genesis of the decision of the VA to address this issue?"

The reason for the question was that Pamela Powers sent me a message some time ago that she (and I believe Dr. Lawrence) was coordinating/communicating with OIG Treasury on this matter. Ms. Powers would not comment on any particular meetings with OIG Treasury or who was involved.

Eric Thorson retired amid this controversy, elevating Richard Delmar as the Direct of OIG Treasury.

I was wondering exactly who Dr. Lawrence and Ms. Powers talked with and what they were told. The information was substantive enough for a decision to create the Veterans Benefit Banking Program to have been made.

Something was going on with Pamela Powers and Paul Lawrence. Powers were not sharing. The bombshell would drop later.

Subject: Re: Communication between VAB and OIG Treasury
From: Steven Lepper (CEO-Military Banks of America)
Date: Fri, Jan 24, 2020, 1:03 pm
To: jbsimms Cc: Jackie Lynn
Mr. Simms,
No worries. I'm glad we connected over this issue. You understand the community of veterans we're trying to help. I appreciate your perspective.
I truly don't know what discussions within VA/VBA specifically or within the federal government generally led to VBA reaching out to my organization to partner in this project. I can tell you that the VBA was concerned about the stories they'd heard about veterans in the DE program losing control of their finances. I suspect the stories you and other veterans shared were instrumental in their thinking.
My view is that it doesn't matter how we got here; the important thing is that we are now focused — together — on improving the financial health and resilience of all our veterans. Although I understand the frustration you endured along the way, I hope you also feel that we have now arrived at a better place and we need not look back except to ensure our veterans are following us. Our challenge now is to convince veterans in the DE and paper check programs to open bank accounts and take control of their financial lives. That's what my focus will be going forward.
Have a great weekend!
Steve

Mr. Lepper knew of our frustration and the battle I had with the Veterans Administration, particularly Paul Lawrence. I was grateful for Mr. Lepper reaching out to me.

Saturday, January 25, 2020

From: Steven Lepper (CEO-Military Banks of America)
Date: Sat, Jan 25, 2020, 5:00 am
To: jbsimms
Cc: Jackie Lynn
Mr. Simms,
I don't know how VBA will organize its long-term efforts. We've been working with a number of its staff in various divisions — communications, legal, and even the Under Secretary's office — to get this program off the ground. There will be no sharing of personnel; nevertheless, it remains a team effort.
The Under Secretary remains very committed to this program and I know he'll provide it the necessary resources on his end. We are very proud of the fact that VBA reached out to us and we'll also do everything we can to make this program work.
Have a great weekend.
Steve

Tuesday, January 28, 2020

For some reason, I trusted Sonja Scott. She believed us. She communicated. But she still was working for Delmar.

More of Loren Sciurba's interference

It appeared Mr. Sciurba put a lid on all communication between OIG Treasury to Ms. Densmore and me. Treasury would not want oversight by us.

Scott was still working on complaints from victims. There was no indication when any of the 3 investigations at the Treasury on this matter would be completed. I was curious how many of these victim cases being attended to by Scott are veterans.

Thursday, January 30, 2020

The email below puts Mr. Bayer and Social Security on notice.

Subject: Presenting evidence to convince SSA to break from the Direct Express program and BFS
From: jbsimms
Date: Thu, Jan 30, 2020, 4:56 am
To: Walter Bayer (SSA OIG)
Cc: Jackie Lynn; Steven Lepper (CEO-Military Banks of America)
Dear Walt,
You are aware the VA has broken ties with BFS by ceasing to endorse the Direct Express program. The VA created a separate division to help veterans with banking issues and is now associated with the AMBA, headed by Steven Lepper.
You mentioned in an email a month or so ago that you would be presenting some of my concerns about the association and endorsement of the SSA with the Direct Express program to others at SSA OIG.
Can you give me some type of update as to whether you have been able to present our case and the results of communication with others at SSA OIG?
You have received dozens of stories of victims and are aware that Social Security recipients have been victimized by the Direct Express program and persons operating it.
There are a number of options:
1) SSA can become affiliated with the AMBA as did the VA, to assist all veterans to have a safe and secure avenue for their monies to be deposited. All veterans and their dependents can be directed to this organization. The integrity of Mr. Lepper and fellow veterans at the AMBA surpasses that of the Bureau of Fiscal Service.
2) SSA can cease naming the Direct Express program and instead direct potential and current recipients to obtain a debit card (if they do not wish to have a formal bank account). Simply explain all debit cards are associated with a bank and each card has a routing number and account number.
3) Create a secure portal, as is now with the Direct Express feature, for recipients to type in the routing number and account number of the bank account or debit card they wish to use.
4) Enact a more rigorous security protocol for SSA with respect to recipients.
5) Allow recipients to be privy to any and all investigations pertaining to their accounts. Remember that my identity was compromised and it was an SSA employee who changed my address and the SSA refused to tell me how it was done. SSA recipients should not be treated in this manner.
Walt, I do appreciate you being receptive, and I do feel our work is valuable to protect SSA recipients. Having been validated by the VA and Mr. Lepper, I hope you can present our case to the SSA to have changes made. I have copied Mr. Lepper and I am certain he will be receptive to any communication from you.
I look forward to hearing about the proceedings.
Sincerely,
Jim

We were hoping Bayer was taking us seriously.

"Making Comerica irrelevant"

Subject: Re: AMBA just got a plug
From: Steven Lepper (CEO-Military Banks of America)
Date: Thu, Jan 30, 2020, 5:51 pm
To: jbsimms
Cc: Jackie Lynn
Hopefully, we can make Comerica irrelevant to this entire discussion by successfully converting DE customers to bank and credit union accounts. Preventing those banks and credit unions from engaging in the practices that you and other veterans have complained about will be the responsibility of the OCC, FDIC, NCUA, and CFPB. Knowing all of those organizations, I can assure you that our VBBP financial institutions will be held to high standards. Best, Steve

This was as aggressive an email as I had received from Mr. Lepper, Making Comerica "[i]rrelevant" was our goal.

Friday, January 31, 2020

Subject: The Association of Military Banks of America
From: Steven Lepper (CEO-Military Banks of America)
Date: Fri, Jan 31, 2020, 7:58 am
To: jbsimms
Cc: Joe Plenzler (Wounded Warriors), Jackie Lynn
Mr. Simms,
Thanks for the copy. I'm always willing to talk to VSOs [Veteran Service Organizations] like WWP[Wounded Warriors Project] about our efforts to encourage veterans to manage their finances through safe, reliable accounts at banks or credit unions. LTG (Ret.) Mike Linnington, WWP's CEO, happens to be a friend and I would be pleased to help him spread the word to his members.
All the best,
Steve

With Linnington being a friend, this can be a big break with WWP.

Saturday, February 1, 2020

Subject: SSA insert Feb 2020
 From: jbsimms
Date: Sat, Feb 01, 2020, 10:14 pm
To: Walter Bayer (SSA OIG), Steven Lepper (CEO-Military Banks of America)
Cc: Jackie Lynn; "Kate Berry" (American Banker)
Dear Mr. Bayer and Mr. Lepper,
Attached please find copies of inserts that were discovered in the two payments received by Jackie Densmore's brother-in-law, a disabled veteran.
This promotional material was found in both envelopes; one from SSA, another from the VA.
Promotional information was found on the back of both envelopes, touting the Direct Express program.
Mr. Bayer, you have been very gracious as you and I have communicated about this matter with BFS, Comerica Bank, and the Direct Express program. In one our last emails, you stated the matter of Comerica Bank failing to protect cardholders would be presented to OIG SSA. Someone authorized the insert be placed in the envelope.
Mr. Lepper, I assume the VA benefit check received by Derek Densmore was sent by the VA. Announcements made by the VA since December 20, 2019, confirmed the affiliation of the VA with the AMBA, but now a Direct Express promotional insert was found with a veteran's benefit check.
It is also a concern that veterans who do not receive VA benefits do receive SSA payments, and these veterans are being solicited to be victimized by the Direct Express program. All veterans are eligible to benefit from participating with affiliate banks associated with the AMBA. I am confident and was personally assured by Mr. Lepper that veterans will not be subjected to the same abuses and violations of federal statutes when banking with an AMBA bank.
I respectfully ask that, if SSA continues to place promotional inserts with checks, an insert be placed directing veterans to the AMBA for assistance in obtaining a bank account. The Direct Express insert can be replaced with an insert to recipients stating they can use a bank or any debit card to receive their benefits. Simply give the routing number and account number from the card or bank account to a person at the local SSA office. If the SSA has a secure feature allowing persons to do this online, that would be good. Direct Express is not the only option, nor is it safe.
I also respectfully ask that Mr. Lepper to determine how a Direct Express promotion was found with a VA check.
Thank you both for supporting veterans and other citizens in this matter.
Sincerely,
Jim

Sunday, February 2, 2020

Treasury was creating the inserts

Now we knew that the VA is not stuffing envelopes; it was Treasury.

Subject: Re: SSA insert Feb 2020
From: Steven Lepper (CEO-Military Banks of America)
Date: Sun, Feb 02, 2020, 1:24 am
To: jbsimms
Cc: Walter Bayer (Soc Sec), Jackie Lynn, Kate Berry (American Banker)
Mr. Simms,
The short ... and only ... answer to your question is that the inserts are placed by Treasury. All paper checks are issued by the Department of Treasury; VA does not issue checks. I do know that VA and Treasury will be meeting soon to discuss our new VBBP program. Hopefully, it will result in more message coordination between the two agencies.
All the best,
Steve

Tuesday, February 4, 2020

Subject: Inserts and VA/VBBP meeting with Treasury
From: Steven Lepper (CEO-Military Banks of America)
Date: Tue, Feb 04, 2020, 7:26 am
To: jbsimms
Cc: Jackie Lynn
Mr. Simms,
I understand your concerns. I believe the VBA-Treasury meeting is scheduled for this week, but I do not know the scheduling details.
I can assure you that the VBA officials who will be meeting with Treasury are very concerned about the stories Ms. Densmore forwarded to me this morning. In fact, the VBBP was their idea and has always been intended as a response to the fraud, high fees, and poor customer service described by these DE customers. I don't know what the insert will say or whether it will be sent only to veterans, but I do know that our "push" has been and will continue to be to move DE and paper check recipients to responsible, regulated, and responsive banks and credit unions.
I know that these horror stories will continue and that we should not be satisfied until they end. We're working very hard to make the VBBP the preferred option for all our veterans and other government benefits recipients to receive and manage their money. This morning, for example, we added Armed Forces Bank — the bank with the largest number of branches on military installations across the country — into the VBBP. Check out the VBBP website!
Best,
Steve
I appreciated Joe Plenzler's help at Wounded Warriors. Joe understood the politics I was battling.

Wednesday, February 5, 2020

Validation and the suggestion of me using "honey" with the VA.

Subject: LinkedIn Post
From: Steven Lepper (CEO-Military Banks of America)
Date: Wed, Feb 05, 2020, 7:41 am
To: jbsimms
Mr. Simms,
I hope your day in Tampa is starting as nice as the one here in Merritt Island.
I'm writing you today to let you know that I heard from VBA this morning about their plans to "tag" you in their LinkedIn post tomorrow. The Under Secretary will be posting on LinkedIn about the VBBP and he intends to credit your efforts among the reasons why it was created.

Let me offer my "two cents:" For this to work, I strongly recommend you use "honey" instead of "vinegar" if you choose to respond. As we've discussed, this program has the potential to be a game-changer for our veterans currently enrolled in the DE and paper check programs, not to mention our Social Security benefits recipients when the program is ultimately extended to them. I know you've earned a lot of scar tissue in your fights with the federal government in general and with Treasury in particular. VBA is really trying to do the right thing here and a positive message reinforcing its efforts would help the program take root in the veteran community. It would also really help in its discussions with Treasury.

Additionally, I know you've corresponded with VA's Chief of Staff, Pam Powers, about the disastrous DE program. She embraced your messages and was an influential, internal VA voice in getting VBA to start the VBBP. I think it would also be a gracious and appropriate gesture for you to send her a private note acknowledging the good work VA and VBA is trying to do here. I guarantee that a little positive feedback will energize her and VBA as it girds to do battle with Treasury.

Just a couple of thoughts from the peanut gallery. Happy to discuss further at your convenience.

Have a great Florida day!

Steve

Pamela Powers did not like what was happening under her watch. She had Paul Lawrence to deal with. I was pleased she listened to me.

Thursday, February 6, 2020

from: Jackie Lynn
to: Thomas Santaniello (Bureau of Fiscal Service)
cc: J B Simms Steven Lepper (CEO-Military Banks of America),
Walter Bayer (SSA OIG), Richard Delmar (OIG Treasury), Pamela Powers (VA Chief of Staff)
Date: Feb 6, 2020, 5:30 AM
subject: Inserts of monthly checks
Dear Mr. Santaniello,

My brother-in-law, Derek Densmore, received inserts with his paper VA check for the past two months. These inserts directed him to open an account with the Direct Express program instead of using paper checks.

You know the VA broke from the Direct Express program after they were told about the abuses. Money for Derek was stolen because of the Direct Express program does not monitor the Fiscal Agent and no one at BFS knows a thing about federal banking regulations because they don't make the Fiscal Agent follow federal law. We are glad the VA came together with the AMBA and Mr. Lepper.

We also know the Social Security checks had inserts. Many of the people getting these checks are veterans and you and those at BFS are harming more veterans by sending them to the Direct Express program.

I suggest you either stop with the inserts or let me draft an insert for you to ask people getting checks to go to the AMBA for veterans or any debit card for others and do not mention Direct Express. All you have to tell them is to get the routing number and account number and give that to Social Security.

Do yourself a favor and read the heartbreaking stories - people that fought for this country your freedom and you ignore them.

Sincerely

Jackie Densmore

Santaniello was no match for Jackie.

A posting from another victim. The post was taken from Facebook.

First, I want to thank Jim Simms. I did EVERYTHING he outlined in the
Direct Express Fraud Victim Procedure File.
On Tuesday I spoke with Susan Schmidt, I was told she was going to escalate to (someone) and If I didn't get a call by the end of the day to call her first thing in the morning. I didn't get a call and I called her and left a voicemail. IN that voice mail I was polite but also stressed that it was my understanding that LEGALLY they were to have ALL of my money returned to me within 10 days of filing my dispute and that it had been over 2 weeks now. I was super polite during all my dealings with her and thanked her for her help, etc. but I was also forward about my expectation. I also called and spoke to Sonja Scott about the situation and how unhappy I was. SHE as well was going to be making some calls. Later that afternoon I got a call from a woman named

Perla from the "escalation" dept or something like that .. she informed me that by the end of the day my case would be closed and my money returned. and IT WAS!! I got ALL my money back in my account.. they're issuing me ANOTHER new card because the last one never showed up and she acted like they were doing me a "favor" by not charging me to issue it LoL.
Anyways. THANK YOU THANK YOU THANK YOU Jim!!

This posting did make me feel good, but it reminded me of how dirty these people are who ignored the cardholders. The Facebook page was working.

In an email received today, Walter Bayer stated, "[A]s always, I am trying to keep track on what is happening in the public realm and share it internally." There was never any evidence Walter Bayer shared any of this matter to Social Security OIG.

We held out hopes that Bayer was going to get us to SSA OIG and get their attention.

Friday, February 7, 2020

Subject: RE: Victim referrals/SSA conferences
From: Sonja Scott (OIG Treasury)
Date: Fri, Feb 07, 2020, 8:04 am
To: jbsimms
Cc: Jackie Lynn
We have met with SSA and had a telcon with them recently. Our office will continue to take victims' information and work with the BFS to resolve issues. Sonja

Sonja Scott met with the SSA, but we have no report of what was said other than the above email. No one will point a finger at anyone and there is not accountability. When and where did they meet? What was discussed?

From: jbsimms
Sent: Friday, February 7, 2020, 8:43 AM
To: Scott, Sonja L. <ScottS@oig.treas.gov>
Cc: Jackie Lynn
Subject: Victim referrals/SSA conferences
Ms. Scott,
I have received a number of messages from persons noting that they had received replies from you as victims of the Direct Express program and BFS. It is a comfort for them to be able to communicate with an enforcement agency and have faith that their cries for help are heard. My phone continues to ring every day and emails are received from these victims.
The VA has made a break from the Direct Express program. Months ago, VA COS Pamela Powers wrote that the VA was conferring with your office. Ms. Powers was also made privy to knowledge I have about this matter. It was unnerving to hear from Ms. Densmore that her brother-in-law, Derek, a disabled veteran, is receiving inserts from SSA touting the Direct Express program. I would like to know if OIG Treasury is meeting with officials of SSA and the results of discussion of the inserts. Sincerely, Jim
Sonja Scott and others at the VA, Treasury, and Social Security, were being tight-lipped about communication between the agencies. We will find out later what was really going on.

The big lie was submitted to US Federal Court by opposing counsel.

Subject: Your involuntary chuckle for the day
From: jbsimms
Date: Fri, Feb 07, 2020, 8:49 am
To: Sonja Scott (OIG Treasury), Richard Delmar (OIG Treasury)
Cc: Jackie Lynn; Steven Lepper (CEO-Military Banks of America)
Dear Ms. Scott and Mr. Delmar,
Attached please find the Answer to the Complaint filed in the Western District US Fed Court 5: 2019cv01075. This is the case involving Direct Express victims.

Got to page 28. The lawyers for the Defendants claim the Defendants "[c]onducted reasonable investigations..."

No personal offense intended, but regardless of the truth, of which we know, the lawyers will be lawyers and they were paid to say what they think they need to say.

Based upon information we, as victims, have supplied to your office, your reports will be an interesting contrast to this assertion.

We look forward to the reports from Ms. Altemus, Ms. Scott, and Ms. Johnson.

Enjoy your weekend.

Jim

Opposing counsel, Jon Chally, made this assertion, that reasonable investigations had been conducted, when in fact this was not true.

Saturday, February 8, 2020

Subject: Inserts placed into envelopes with Veteran checks and SSA checks
From: jbsimms
Date: Sat, Feb 08, 2020, 8:05 am
To: Thomas Santaniello (Bureau of Fiscal Service)
Cc: Jackie Lynn, Loren Sciurba (OIG Treasury), Sonja Scott (OIG Treasury), Franklin Lemond
Dear Mr. Santaniello,
The two attachments were inserted in the envelopes containing Veteran Benefit checks and Social Security/SSI checks. Inserts were also found in the disbursements from the previous month.
Who at Bureau of Fiscal Service is responsible for authorizing and/or directing the placing of these inserts into the envelopes?
Sincerely,
J.B. Simms

Monday, February 10, 2020

The interaction with Mr. Lepper was very important to us. Looking for a "good news" story would be hard to find.

Paul Lawrence was all about Paul Lawrence. Maybe Mr. Lepper got his attention.

Subject: We all are working on something.
From: jbsimms
Date: Mon, Feb 10, 2020, 5:08 pm
To: "Franklin Lemond
Cc: Jackie Lynn
I am very happy the case is progressing, judge is listening,
The flipping of the VA was no small feat. One of my better ones, if I say so myself. It was not my charm.
I am very concerned about Santaniello's subpoena. The investigations are ongoing at Treasury, and Altemus, Scott, and Johnson have not produced any reports. Santaniello's BFF at Treasury (Sciurba) was too quick to defend him. Altemus works for Sciurba.
The issues now are (1) stopping Social Security from endorsing Direct Express and having SSA announce this online (2) stopping the inserts which validate Direct Express.
We have a good shot at making this happen.
Jim

Santaniello never responded to any subpoena. Franklin never enforced the subpoenas. This issue caused quite a rift between Franklin and me. I never understood why this was not enforced, but Franklin did not have the emotional investment like Jackie and me.

Wednesday, February 12, 2020

The following story made me so angry. I had to share it with Mr. Lepper. A dying veteran was victimized and ignored.

Subject: The horror story you wanted
From: jbsimms
Date: Wed, Feb 12, 2020, 8:23 am
To: Steven Lepper (CEO-Military Banks of America)
Dear Mr. Lepper,
There were so many victims from whom I received telephone calls. Latoya Gillum is one victim who contacted me and for whom I made contact with Conduent to advocate for the victim, enable the victim with information, and make contact with Conduent on her behalf.
Latoya Gillum had monies taken from her account. Conduent ignored her. Latoya stated she is a retired Army E-8 and caring for a disabled son.
As I look back on the case (a year ago) it appears Latoya might have been calling me from a hospital. Her voice was a bit strained; she had cancer.
Ms. Gillum determined who had scammed her Direct Express card; it seems from my recollection there were two suspects. She contacted local authorities, and identified both suspects, one of whom had quite a criminal record. The [law enforcement] authorities validated her report; Conduent would not. Conduent never validated any police reports.
I tried to reach her on the day after she called me. I was not able to reach her. I believe this was a Thursday. On the following day, I received a text from her husband; Latoya Gillum died within a day after we spoke. Her husband did state that after she and I talked, she was reimbursed [after I contacted Conduent on her behalf]. The point is Conduent violated Reg E, and ignored Ms. Gillum, and she reached out to me. I responded. I will never forget that conversation. She died the next day, not knowing if the money stolen from her, which was reported to Conduent, would be recovered for her son.
I was angry, heartbroken, and angry again. I am still angry for Conduent and Comerica Bank disrespecting her.

Sgt. Gillum's story was sad, and the people at Comerica and Conduent should have been ashamed. She called Conduent 20 times, then called me on Tuesday, January 23, 2019. She died two days later.

Conduent would tell fraud victims to report the fraud/identity theft to their local authorities. Conduent never reached out to any law enforcement agency during any fraud investigation, nor did they acknowledge any police reports sent to Conduent to validate a fraud claim.

Thursday, February 13, 2020

Subject: you have got to see this propaganda piece; schmoozing the unlearned and unaware
From: jbsimms
Date: Thu, Feb 13, 2020, 11:52 am
To: Thomas Santaniello (Bureau of Fiscal Service)
Cc: Jackie Lynn, Michael Clements (US Gen Acct Office) Sonja Scott (OIG Treasury), Amy Altemus (OIG Treasury), Katherine Johnson (OIG Treasury), Franklin Lemond (Plaintiff's Attorney), Walter Bayer (SSA OIG), Jennifer Kreegar (plaintiff) , Pamela Powers (VA-Chief of Staff)

Holy Mother of God (thought I would throw in an outrage/shock quip for our friends from the Northeast), either BFS workers are keeping Commissioner Gribben under a rock, or he has bought into the disingenuous goose-stepping exhibited within the administrations of McCoy, Morrow, and Lebryk.
Here is what was posted on Linked in today.
There is a photograph of Commissioner Gribben, standing in front of a wartime patriotic poster. He should have full knowledge that the VA (acting upon my revelation and gentle persuasion) has disassociated itself from the Bureau of Fiscal Service and its inept Direct Express debit card program. Veterans and civilians have been thrown into the lion's den of fraud exposure and the cavalier attitude toward victims by Comerica Bank (the Fiscal Agent of the Direct Express program) and Bureau of Fiscal Service as federal banking laws are ignored. The fight against Bureau of Fiscal Service began 2 years ago. The quip on the post states BFS began changes 2 years ago. The truth is Mr. Santaniello denied Ms. Densmore and me the opportunity to address the secret panel which was deliberating the new contract awardee. No libel here; I have your email.
There has been no change at Bureau of Fiscal Service to protect our citizens. Somehow, the justification still shrouded in secrecy, BFS awarded the new Direct Express contract to Comerica Bank while three (3) independent investigations of BFS and Comerica Bank were in progress.

Does anyone other than those at the VA (Ms. Powers and Dr. Lawrence) have the integrity to divorce themselves from the shameless group at Bureau of Fiscal Service, and act to save veterans and civilians from this corrupt and scandalous Direct Express program?

Hopefully, someone will have the integrity to forward this to Commissioner Gribben, and he will contact me. As they say in Texas, I "will show him how the cow ate the cabbage."

I will be waiting.

Sincerely,

J.B. Simms

Lepper counsels us on the Veterans Benefit Banking Program

Subject: RE: interview tomorrow
From: jbsimms
Date: Thu, Feb 13, 2020, 8:03 pm
To: Steven Lepper (CEO-Military Banks of America)
Cc: Jackie Lynn
Mr. Lepper,

The tedious nature of intertwining the VA with SSA might seem daunting, however, I feel if all veterans receiving any manner of monies from Social Security were directed to the VA (simply check the box if you are a veteran) to confirm or establish a secure banking depository for SSA funds, veterans will be glad to know the VA is involved.

The SSA could direct all veteran applicants having no bank account to the AMBA, as an affiliate of the VA. The SSA can also identify persons using the Direct Express card, contact them, and request they contact the AMBA. This also gives the VA outreach better access to homeless veterans receiving SSA which at this point the VA would have no idea which deserving veterans were sleeping on a sidewalk.

I applaud the work the VA has done to break from the Direct Express program and Bureau of Fiscal Service, and I applaud them for reaching out to you.

I do not have all the answers, but simply a lot of questions. Credit must be given to Jackie Densmore, who is my equal in this journey. We sometimes are pointed in different directions, but we both know more than "they" ever wanted us to know. And, we plan to know more.

We thank you.

Sincerely,

Jim

Friday, February 14, 2020

Subject: VA contact
From: jbsimms
Date: Fri, Feb 14, 2020, 6:30 pm
To: Franklin Lemond
Joe Gurney at VA looks like the guy who found Mr. Lepper. During the interview Gurney admitted finding Lepper to solve the problem.
He might be the person you would gingerly speak with to get a snippet of the back story.
If this promo does not come up, let me know.
Jim

It sounded like Pamela Powers got to Paul Lawrence, and Paul Lawrence handed the problem over to Joe Gurney. Gurney appeared to be the person who involved Mr. Lepper.

Mr. Gurney will play a pivotal role later in the story.

Monday, February 17, 2020

On Feb 17, 2020, at 8:00 PM, jbsimms wrote:
Mr. Lepper,
The day will come when this is behind me. Today is not the day. I am so happy you were contacted by the VA, and that part is done.
Getting Mr. Bayer to come forth and do what he said he would be next. This will help veterans in many ways and is a win/win for SSA knowing the AMBA member banks will be on the front line to protect veterans unlike

BFS's designated, Comerica Bank. If SSA enacts a program to promote AMBA and not the BFS catastrophe, it will be less work for everyone.
Thank you for your confidence in what we are trying to accomplish.
Sincerely,
Jim

Tuesday, February 18, 2020

Subject: Re: Could persons at VA contact Bayer? Could be effective.
From: Steven Lepper (CEO-Military Banks of America)
Date: Tue, February 18, 2020, 5:08 am
To: jbsimms
Cc: Jackie Lynn
Mr. Simms,
The other gentleman who participated in the LinkedIn Live event last week was Joe Gurney, Special Assistant to the Under Secretary. He has spearheaded this entire effort to move veterans from DE and paper checks to bank accounts.
This new program is gaining momentum. We will be onboarding credit unions in the next few weeks, thereby giving veterans even more banking choices. I predict it will be only a matter of time before we extend the program to other groups — e.g., Social Security recipients.
Thanks again for all your efforts. Given everyone's desire to move veterans to mainstream banking, our focus is on educating those who still receive their benefits on prepaid cards and paper checks. We're glad you are part of that effort.
All the best,
Steve

Gurney was our guy. He was at the table with Paul Lawrence in a photo posted on LinkedIn. Paul Lawrence was pushed into action by Pamela Powers, and Gurney made it happen.

Subject: RE: Could persons at VA contact Bayer? Could be effective.
From: jbsimms
Date: Tue, Feb 18, 2020, 5:58 am
To: Steven Lepper (CEO-Military Banks of America)
Cc: Jackie Lynn
I apologize for being too lazy to look back at the promo to identify Mr. Gurney.
I applaud Mr. Gurney for looking outside the VA to find a remedy for the trust they placed in BFS to ensure the Direct Express program was safe and secure for veterans and others. The dilemma I had was that as I was presenting definitive information of corruption and malfeasance to the VA, SSA, and OIG Treasury, their fellow government workers were bombarded with justification and rationalization from BFS. It is incredulous that no one at the VA thought to examine the contract between Comerica Bank and BFS, nor did anyone question the failure of Comerica Bank to offer or deliver security features to the Direct Express card.
Now that the issue of the VA is behind us, SSA is next to admit to having misplaced their trust in BFS and Comerica Bank to furnish a safe manner to receive benefits.
Hopefully, Mr. Bayer will "see" what you and Mr. Gurney have accomplished and direct all future and current veterans to the AMBA.
Sincerely,
Jim

Subject: Taking the lead of the VA
From: jbsimms
Date: Tue, Feb 18, 2020, 6:26 am
To: Walter Bayer (SSA OIG)
Cc: Jackie Lynn, Franklin Lemond
Dear Walt,
Time is drawing near to the first of March, and I hope not to have a spike of adrenaline if the SSA allows BFS to place dangerous inserts into the check envelopes of SSA and VA recipients.

The VA has acknowledged our argument and made changes to protect veterans. The VA no longer endorses or promotes the Direct Express program.

I remember being told that SSA OIG was conducting their own investigation into the matter of BFS and Comerica Bank. You have received volumes of information from me which was unknown and not acknowledged by the SSA. Hopefully what I have sent has been an eye-opener and that those at SSA OIG have a bit more understanding of Reg E.

The violations of Reg E were bad enough, but the refusal of Comerica Bank, with the permission of BFS, to deny Direct Express debit card customers the same financial tools (one of which was instant transaction notification) as is afforded the proprietary customers of Comerica Bank, is appalling. Instant transaction notification alerts card holders of fraud immediately, stopping the transaction, protecting the card holder, and stemming future (serial) fraudulent transactions. Many victims were hit by fraud 2-4 times on the same day (the day of deposit) before they had any idea they had been hit.

Directing future veteran recipients to the AMBA will be just as easy as it is for SSA to direct recipients to the Direct Express program. A simple paragraph, a link, and a phone number would suffice. All veterans have earned the right to use these services.

Steven Lepper of AMBA has been very gracious in accepting and validating our grievances. He, along with Joe Gurney of the VA, made the change to stop endorsing the Direct Express program. It is my prayer the SSA will follow. I will be happy to appear to SSA OIG if necessary.

Sincerely,
Jim

Santaniello confronted with BFS creation of Direct Express inserts

Subject: Inserts being placed into the check envelopes of veterans and civilians receiving VA and SSA payments
From: jbsimms
Date: Tue, Feb 18, 2020, 7:26 am
To: Thomas Santaniello (Bureau of Fiscal Service)
Cc: Loren Sciurba (OIG Treasury), Richard Delmar (OIG Treasury), Sonja Scott (OIG Treasury), Katherine Johnson (OIG Treasury), Amy Altemus (OIG Treasury) , Jackie Lynn; Steven Lepper (CEO-Military Banks of America), Jennifer Kreegar , Walter Bayer (SSA OIG), Franklin Lemond , Kate Berry (American Banker)

Dear Mr. Santaniello,

It has come to my attention that your agency, BFS, is the genesis of the flyer inserts endorsing the Direct Express program being stuffed into the envelopes of veterans and civilian recipients of checks.

While this action by BFS is obviously self-serving considering BFS and your "Evaluation Team" awarded Comerica Bank with a continued contract, the validation of the Direct Express program by BFS was performed in a vacuum.

No other government agency associated with the Direct Express program has validated this program since my exposure of malfeasance at Comerica Bank and at BFS two years ago. The VA, as a result of our exposing harm your agency has caused to veterans, has divorced itself from the program and no longer advertises or endorses the program you tout. The malfeasance on the part of you and BFS is not only exhibited by renewing the Fiscal Agent Agreement with Comerica Bank, but additionally by the arrogance of directing your propaganda laden flyer-inserts accompany the paper check and endorsement of the Direct Express program on your website.

The finger of culpability is pointed at you and BFS. If you wish to present evidence absolving your responsibility for having directed these inserts, be placed into the envelopes, or the fact that BFS created the flyer inserts, I will be glad to retract the allegation.. While you appear to have one ally among the scores of federal workers with whom I have been involved, this ally has yet to furnish any evidence to vouch for your credibility, choosing only to attack me. That did not work out well for your ally.

Since BFS has no viable alternative other than to cease having the inserts being placed into the envelopes, other than directing all veterans to the AMBA or giving civilian recipients bank and debit card options, I request that you forward this email to Mr. Gribben for consideration of ceasing this draconian practice of inserting BFS flyers into the envelopes.

Since you blocked Ms. Densmore and me from addressing your "Evaluation Team" maybe Mr. Gribben, who inherited this "tar-baby" program, would like to hear the truth from us.

Sincerely,
J.B. Simms

Santaniello was associated with Nora Arpin, allowing Comerica to receive the new contract. Santaniello would never engage me or answer questions.

Below is an email I sent to the daughter of a cardholder, Nona Clarke, who killed herself in Mexico because Comerica and Conduent would not respond. This was heartbreaking.

Subject: RE: Direct Express lawsuit-Nona Clarke
From: jbsimms
Date: Tue, Feb 18, 2020, 10:07 am
To: "amy clarke"
Amy,
I just came across the recording your mom left me and was thinking of you.
I am interested in the findings of your mom's death. She and I talked prob 10 times.
Oddly, I was looking for an email from someone and came across this one.
Let me know a convenient time to chat.
Jim

I sent the voice recordings of her mother to Amy. These were messages Nona sent me days before she killed herself in Mexico as a result of financial hardship caused by Conduent. Below is the email Amy sent me.

Subject: Direct Express lawsuit-Nona Clarke
From: amy clarke
Date: Thu, January 23, 2020, 10:29 am
To: flemond@webbllc.com, jbsimms,
paigekirstenclarke@gmail.com
Hello,
My name is Amy Clarke and I'm following up from the voicemail I left you last week. I am interested in speaking with you about our situation and circumstances surrounding our mother's death. JB Simms gave us your contact information and am interested in speaking with you.
Please call me at your earliest convenience.
Thank you,
Amy

A new subpoena for Treasury

Subject: Re: subpoenas
From: Franklin Lemond (Plaintiff's Attorney)
Date: Tue, February 18, 2020, 2:32 pm
To: Jim Simms jbsimms
Cc: Jackie Lynn
The reissued subpoenas (attached) have all been sent for delivery. Franklin
I was happy the subpoenas were being sent. Since the venue of the case had been changed to Texas, new subpoenas had to be issued. Federal agencies ignored the subpoenas.

Thursday, February 20, 2020

Below is an email to another reporter, Abbie Bennett. Note that I mentioned Michael Clements, who worked with the General Accounting Office. Michael agreed to investigate this matter, but he needed two members of Congress to make the request.

Subject   The investigation into violation of REG E at Comerica and Conduent with respect to fraud on my account
From: jbsimms
Date: Thu, Feb 20, 2020, 11:37 am
To: Amy Altemus (OIG Treasury)
Dear Ms. Altemus,

339

In mid-October 2109 (four months ago) a signed document was submitted to your office, at your request, identified as a waiver allowing OIG Treasury to inspect and copy records being held by Comerica Bank with regard to the debit card program (Direct Express) upon which fraud was perpetrated on my account on January 2017 and December 2017. This investigation by your office is being held concurrent with two other investigations/audits in your agency being performed by Sonja Scott and Katherine Johnson, respectively. Not only was your office submit the waiver mentioned above, a detailed narrative of the events of these two instances of fraud was also sent to your office. This narrative fully explained the fraud, the manner in which the fraudulent funds were returned to the account, and the failure of Comerica Bank and Conduent to respond to the fraud in a manner consistent with Reg E, 15USC1693.

Please email a copy of your investigation into the actions, or lack thereof, of Comerica Bank to this email address.

Sincerely,

J.B. Simms

Subject: RE: The investigation into violation of REG E at Comerica and Conduent with respect to fraud on my account

From: Amy Altemus (OIG Treasury)

Date: Thu, Feb 20, 2020 12:51 pm

To: jbsimms

Mr. Simms:

Thank you for your correspondence. As you are aware, requests for any materials contained in Treasury OIG files must be requested via the Freedom of Information Act (FOIA), although completed unclassified audits suitable for publication are published at https://www.treasury.gov/about/organizational-structure/ig/Pages/audit_reports_index.aspx. You may find more information concerning the FOIA process, including how to write a FOIA request, at https://home.treasury.gov/footer/freedom-of-information-act.

Sincerely,

AJ Altemus

Altemus was trying to blow me off. She knew that FOI requests were sent to obtain copies of the investigative report. Altemus and Sciurba then began, as did Delmar, denying the existence of investigations.

I had to file an FOI request to Social Security to get my documents

Subject: The investigation into violation of REG E at Comerica and Conduent with respect to fraud on my account

From: jbsimms

Date: Thu, Feb 20, 2020, 5:34 pm

To: Amy Altemus (OIG Treasury)

Cc: Richard Delmar (OIG Treasury), Jackie Lynn

Ms. Altemus,

I am in need of clarification. The violation of federal statute 15USC1693 by Comerica Bank and its assigned, Conduent, with regard to my personal account, was the premise of the investigative report which I am requesting.

Are you telling me that I have to file an FOI request to be privy to the investigation of which I am the victim? Assuming your staff has completed investigating my case, I respectfully request you immediately forward this email to the FOI section and advise them to use whatever protocol is necessary for me to obtain a copy of this report. I am well aware of the procedure that the FOI section has to reply to the request within a certain number of days (10 I believe), but I do not want to fall into the same trap as did Jackie Densmore when her FOI request was "lost" for a year and then suddenly found.

I do appreciate your prompt reply.

Sincerely, J.B. Simms

Delmar and Altemus would block me from getting a copy of the report, even though I was a victim.

Subject: A victim of the BFS Direct Express program, a Navy veteran, news item over the air
From: jbsimms
Date: Thu, Feb 20, 2020, 6:45 pm
To: Walter Bayer (SSA OIG)
Cc: Steven Lepper (CEO-Military Banks of America), Jackie Lynn; Franklin Lemond (Plaintiff's Attorney), Loren Sciurba (OIG Treasury), Sonja Scott (OIG Treasury), Richard Delmar (OIG Treasury), Katherine Johnson (OIG Treasury), Amy Altemus (OIG Treasury)
Dear Walter,
Attached is a link to a story that came over the wire today. This is another example of why SSA should follow the lead of the VA and cease endorsing the Direct Express program.
If BFS stuffs more flyer inserts into the SSA payments and VA benefit checks at the end of this month, there will be more victims, many of whom are veterans.
You know I have been on this matter for two years. You have seen what Jackie Densmore and I have to endure simply by trying to save veterans and others from being victimized.
I implore you to share this with your SSA OIG. BFS has constantly been pushing this on SSA and the VA. Santaniello over at BFS refused to allow Jackie or me to address their "Evaluation Team" which gave the contract to Comerica Bank, again.
Santaniello has allies who will defend his actions. That will not deter me from trying to protect the victims being created at BFS.
OIG Treasury has 3 ongoing investigations. I was told a long time ago that SSA OIG was conducting their investigation. We have heard nothing from SSA.
Sincerely, Jim

Walter Bayer was privy to all the information I had. There was no reason he or Sarah Lizama did not take the information I gave them and present to SSA OIG.

Friday, February 21, 2020

Amy Altemus and her games

Subject: RE: The investigation into violation of REG E at Comerica and Conduent with respect to fraud on my account
From: Amy Altemus (OIG Treasury)
Date: Fri, February 21, 2020, 6:55 am
To: jbsimms
Cc: Richard Delmar (OIG Treasury)), Jackie Lynn
Dear Mr. Simms:
You may submit your FOIA request electronically via the electronic form at https://www.treasury.gov/foia/pages/gofoia.aspx. Your email does not include information sufficient to submit the request for you. Please remember to identify with as much specificity as possible the information you seek.
Thank you,
AJ Altemus, Office of Counsel
Subject: The investigation into violation of REG E at Comerica and Conduent with respect to fraud on my account
From: jbsimms
Date: Fri, Feb 21, 2020, 9:08 am
To: Amy Altemus (OIG Treasury)
Cc: Jackie Lynn; Richard Delmar (OIG Treasury)
Dear Ms. Altemus,
The FOI request for a copy of the investigative report of Comerica Bank with regard to the account of J.B. Simms had been submitted electronically.
While your statement that the information submitted was not sufficient for a worker at the FOI office to comprehend nature of FOI request the original email was copied and within the "description" field. Non case number or reference number was furnished by OIG Special Counsel office which would identify this investigation, but if one of the FOI persons needs further clarification, you may forward (803) 309-6850 to FOI and clarification will be made.

No report has been received to confirm that the investigation into this matter was concluded. It is assumed the investigation has been concluded based upon deference to an FOI request rather than simply attaching the investigative report to a reply email.

The manner in which this matter is being handled is documented and possibly will be revisited.

Sincerely,

J.B. Simms

Altemus interview requested

From: jbsimms

Date: Fri, Feb 21, 2020, 9:17 am

To: Franklin Lemond (Plaintiff's Attorney)

Franklin,

Here is a continuation of the Treasury FOI shell game.

Altemus investigated 30 victims. I only know of two others; Jackie and Jennifer Kreegar, both of whom are plaintiffs in our case.

I submitted an FOI request electronically. Altemus could have waived this, but she did not.

I think a subpoena for Jackie's and Jennifer's reports from the investigation headed by Amy Altemus might be necessary. My info was requested electronically simply to see if they were going to mess with me, knowing you can have them served with a subpoena for the info.

We ask one time nicely, and then punch them in the mouth. What happened to Jackie should never happen again.

Jim

Saturday, February 22, 2020

Subject Your evidence

From: jbsimms

Date: Sat, Feb 22, 2020, 11:00 am

To: Loren Sciurba (OIG Treasury)

Cc: Richard Delmar (OIG Treasury), Jackie Lynn; Amy Altemus (OIG Treasury) , Steven Lepper (CEO-Military Banks of America), Michael Clements (US Gen Acct Office) Kate Berry (American Banker) Franklin Lemond (Plaintiff's Attorney) , Sonja Scott (OIG Treasury), Walter Bayer (SSA OIG), "Abbie Bennett" <abbie@connectingvets.com>, Joe Plenzler (Wounded Warriors), Pamela Powers (VA-Chief of Staff)

Dear Mr. Sciurba,

The veiled threat you sent me via email with respect to allegations made about your friend Mr. Santaniello, implying slander and/or libel, requested I submit any evidence I have to concur with my supposition. I happened to be placing 600+ documents into specified folders, documents which have been accumulated for over two years in preparation for this project, and came across the attached document. It appears a fellow employee of Mr. Santaniello and I have come to the same conclusion.

If OIG Treasury has any intention of exercising any enforcement authority, I submit to you that you allow an investigation of this allegation by a BFS employee to proceed and that you recuse yourself from any involvement therein. Your email to me exhibits obvious bias in favor of Mr. Santaniello which will exclude you from this matter.

Below is a portion of the attachment.

Sincerely,

J.B. Simms

Below is the response from Santaniello regarding payments to Comerica:

Q3. How much is Treasury currently paying to Comerica to manage each Direct Express Account? (I have heard $5 and $2—which is accurate?) Also was this fee written into the original Fiscal Agent Agreement between Comerica and the Treasury?

A3. The exact fees paid to Financial Agents are confidential commercial information and/or trade secrets of the Financial Agent and therefore not for public dissemination.

Thomas Santaniello Legislative & Public Affairs, Bureau of the Fiscal Service, U.S. Department of the Treasury

The division of our government which approved a bid to oversee the debit card program for Social Security recipients, Veteran benefits, and other disabled persons, will not allow an inspection of disbursements. Where are the payoffs? The person employed at Fiscal Services who responded to the Congressman's inquiry revealed the coverup "is in full swing."

Sunday, February 23, 2020

The development of the Veterans Benefit Banking Program was taking place. Pamela Powers was not going to give any credibility to my arguments, only to communicate with Joe Gurney, and Gurney with Lepper.

Lepper sees my "scars" from battling the Veterans Administration

Subject: Re: Your evidence
From: Steven Lepper (CEO-Military Banks of America)
Date: Sun, February 23, 2020, 5:20 am
To: jbsimms
Mr. Simms,
Thanks for copying me on this note. I won't presume to tell you how to communicate with Treasury; you've been engaged with them over this issue for a long time and I know much scar tissue has developed. I just want to let you know that, despite the concerns you've expressed here, Treasury and VBA are working together to encourage veterans to move from the Direct Express program to having their benefits deposited to bank accounts.
As you know, Dr. Lawrence has spent a lot of time and effort over the past couple of weeks promoting the Veterans Benefits Banking Program. He is deeply committed to eliminating the problems with DE and paper checks you have helped our veterans identify. In short, he wants all veterans to have bank accounts that will provide them safety, good customer service, and access to other financial products and services that will improve their financial lives.
I respectfully suggest that, in addition to or in lieu of your communications to Treasury critical of the DE program, you also tell VA — perhaps Ms. Powers — that you support VBA's efforts. You have become an influential voice in this arena. Encouraging VA and VBA to continue its efforts to promote and further develop the VBBP would go a long way to helping them expand it and, thereby, displace DE.
Have a great week! ,Steve

Subject: RE: Your evidence
From: jbsimms
Date: Sun, Feb 23, 2020 9:36 am
To: Steven Lepper (CEO-Military Banks of America)
Cc: Jackie Lynn
Mr. Lepper,
Thank you for your very early morning email. It is encouraging to hear you tell me that VBA and Treasury are working together, and I assume the division of Treasury to which you refer is only OIG Treasury. Bureau of Fiscal Service appears to be in their own autonomous little world with no fear of consequences, based upon the fact that two OIG Treasury reports, OIG Treasury 14-031 and 17-034, did not cause a ripple of concern by BFS. It was the fact that I reported the two reports were woefully impotent with respect to an investigation or accountability that this whole thing started. If VBA is, in fact, working with Treasury, let us hope VBA will defend veterans against the abuse exhibited by BFS and hold them accountable. Stopping the inserts-flyers would be the first, easiest, and most obvious step, and hopefully Dr. Lawrence can convey this.
You are the only person who will engage or respond to me with regard to VBA. No response has ever been received from Dr. Lawrence, and responses from COS Pamela Powers are boilerplate "...we appreciate your concerns...(sic)" replies. They are not accountable to me, nor will they, and they have let that be known. I have not received any email from Ms. Powers, only messages on LinkedIn. She did state she had received my book, Friendly Fire at the Veterans Hospital, and I encouraged her to read this because some of the same persons named in the book remain employed with the VA, and Ms. Powers needed to know "who she was dealing with." I believe I have expressed my gratitude to Ms. Powers that Mr. Gurney reached out to you. I will reach out to her again. It is a certainty that you will learn of my email to Ms. Powers before I get a response from the VA. Thank you for acknowledging the [my] "scar tissue."
Sincerely, Jim

This email to Ms. Powers spelled out issues that the VA could help eliminate Comerica Bank and the Direct Express program from the VBA and VBBP.

Subject: Acknowledgement
From: jbsimms
Date: Sun, Feb 23, 2020, 9:51 am
To: Pamela Powers (VA-Chief of Staff)
Cc: Jackie Lynn
Dear Ms. Powers,
An email was received from Mr. Lepper today, having been sent at 5:20 am. Mr. Lepper assured me VBA is working with Treasury to address issues I and Ms. Densmore have been promoting for two years. It is unclear if VBA is working with OIG Treasury or Bureau of Fiscal Service (BFS).
I feel I can speak for Ms. Densmore when I express my gratitude for the efforts of VAB to end the relationship with Bureau of Fiscal Service and the Direct Express program.
The final two steps, as I see them, are:
1) stopping BFS from placing inserts/flyers which promote the BFS creation, Direct Express, into envelopes
2) work with SSA to have all veterans receiving any type of SSA benefits via check or Direct Express card to have recipients, and prospective recipients, directed to the AMBA. This is as simple as sending letters to the veteran recipients and adding one question to the SSA questionnaire: Are you a veteran?
We are glad to see the progress. We hope to see more.
If you are inclined to indulge us with any reference to communication or evidence of accomplishment with respect to VBA, VA, BFS, SSA, and OIG Treasury, we would love to see it.
Sincerely,
J.B. Simms

Tuesday, February 25, 2020

FOI Hell

A full day of drama (submissions, releases, identification, etc.) and I finally got my request granted. These people want to wear you down and make you quit. There was no quit in me.
Subject: 2020-02-137_Acknowledgement Letter
From: Cawana Pearson (FOI Treasury)
Date: Tue, February 25, 2020, 8:12 am
To: jbsimms
Good morning Treasury is in receipt of your recently submitted FOIA request.
Thank you, Cawana
Subject: RE: 2020-02-137_Acknowledgement Letter
From: Cawana Pearson (FOI Treasury)
Date: Tue, February 25, 2020 8:58 am
To: jbsimms
Good morning,
Your request has been appropriately assigned.
Thank you,
Cawana

Done. The FOI request was granted.

I submitted an email regarding the Consumer Financial Protection Bureau to Ms. Altemus, and she responded below.

Amy Altemus shifts the blame to CFPB and Fed Res OIG.

Amy Altemus (OIG Treasury)
Feb 25, 2020, 11:37 AM
to Richard, Loren, me, Sonja
Mr. Simms:
I'm glad you asked.

You can suggest she see the Consumer Financial Protection Bureau, or the Federal Reserve Board, both of which have superior jurisdiction to this Office regarding customer complaints from this institution, even where the complaint involves the card contracted by the Bureau of Fiscal Service. The Financial Agency Agreement does not exclude banking and consumer protection agencies from intervention in areas specifically in their jurisdiction, such as banking and finance regulation. While we can and do sympathize, as we have noted, this Office has a remit only to examine the programs and operations of the US Treasury, and it your frustration with this Office may be echoed by ours with the delay occasioned to the victims who should be seeking redress from an agency with the mandate to address it: although you think that agency should be this one, it is not. We are not the regulator of the institution and have no authority to direct the actions of any personnel or programs of a Treasury Bureau or Office. We are, in fact, specifically prohibited from so doing. Our involvement has been to examine the execution of the program vis-à-vis the US Treasury.

The victims of such frauds should be seeking agencies with the legal authority and capability to offer assistance or intervention.

Sincerely,

AJ Altemus

J B Simms
Tue, Feb 25, 12:02 PM
to Amy Altemus

Dear Ms. Altemus,

I have had experience with the CFPB dating back to my first conversation with Ms. Paulette Battle. There were over 400 complaints, covering over 17 screen pages on a lady's computer screen.

I asked if CFPB investigates anything. My complaint went straight from CFPB to the office of Susan Schmidt. CFPB did nothing.

I was told by this lady (I do have time, date, and name if you wish) CFPB cannot investigate individual complaints. I ask the threshold. She had no answer.

The CFPB is not going to investigate a bank involved in a federal program, too close to home.

I will be glad to discuss this with you tomorrow; I have to run. I do have quite a history with CFPB.

Jim

J B Simms
Tue, Feb 25, 3:31 PM
to Amy, jbsimms

Dear Ms. Altemus,

I found an email addressed to a person with whom you might be acquainted. Notice Mr. Bialek, Fed Res OIG? I will find more.

No one from Fed Reserve OIG contacted me. There is a reason no one from Fed Reserve contacted me. I would love to hear your thoughts as to why, having oversight of the CFPB, that no one contacted me. Others at OIG Treasury were well aware of my involvement.

Am I to believe no one at OIG Treasury spoke with Mr. Bialek or Peter Sheridan?

Let me dig a little more and find direct emails to Fed Res OIG.

Sincerely,

J.B. Simms

Altemus underestimated my research skills, but she knew I was not going away

J B Simms
Feb 25, 2020, 3:40 PM
to Amy, jbsimms

Dear Ms. Altemus,

Again you might recognize some of the names of the persons to whom this email was sent. You might notice the names Bialek, Sheridan, and Heist copied in this email. All three have email addresses which identify them as employed by the Federal Reserve. They knew about this, and OIG Treasury knew they knew because Mr. Delmar and others were copied on the same emails.

345

With the evidence pouring into OIG Treasury, would it not seem logical that, since you directed me to the Federal Reserve, that others at OIG Treasury knew 17 months ago that the Federal Reserve knew of this? Your name did not surface until October 2019, but I am sure there were a few rumblings being felt.
Sincerely,
J.B. Simms

Subject: This is Mark Bialek. This is the person to whom you referred me, and the same person who ignored my emails.
From: jbsimms
Date: Tue, Feb 25, 2020, 5:00 pm
To: Amy Altemus (OIG Treasury)
Cc: Jackie Lynn
The Inspector General
Dear Ms. Altemus,
You referred me to the Federal Reserve and Office of Inspector General of CFPB.
Here is the person who ignored emails that were jointly sent to persons at OIG Treasury.
https://oig.federalreserve.gov/the-inspector-general.htm
Bialek knew about this in October 2018. You might ask him why he did not prompt the CFPB to use its investigative and enforcement mandates with respect to Comerica Bank, BFS, and OIG Treasury.
Sincerely,
J.B. Simms

Mark Bialek of the Federal Reserve OIG had ignored my email. Maybe Amy Altemus knew that would happen, but she would never have thought I would have already contacted Bialek. They were all in this together.

Subject: Evidence of conversation with CFPB and complaint numbers.
From: jbsimms
Date: Tue, Feb 25, 2020, 5:20 pm
To: Amy Altemus (OIG Treasury)
Cc: Jackie Lynn
Dear Ms. Altemus,
Hopefully this will be the final email necessary today to validate another claim I made.
As with Ms. Sonja Scott, when she was told I had 70+ victim narratives (ultimately 103), she asked to see them, and I complied.
As with claiming I had information from the CFPB as to complaint numbers, below is a pasting of the reference I made:

Thursday, February 22, 2018
2:01pm
T (877) 275-3342 FDIC
FDIC does not oversea Direct Express
Need talk to Fed Res- (855) 411-2372 CFPB (Consumer Financial Protection Bureau
2:11pm
Federal Reserve, (888) 851-1920
Talked to Andrea. Direct Express is regulated by Comerica. Need to make written complaint on-line, to CFPB at Fed Res website
226pm
T Consumer Financial Protection Bureau (855) 411-2372
Talked to Asha
Direct Express/Comerica has 414 complaints 17 pages.
Need to talk to the CFPB ombudsman (855) 830-7880
Notice the date and time of the call. The call was made Pacific Time. The date is before I called and talked to Paulette Battle, which was Monday February 26, 2018. Our two-year anniversary is tomorrow. Here is the entry for that contact with Ms. Battle.

Researched OIG reports. Found the name of Kieu T. Rubb as an auditor on the latest OIG report. Telephone number of (202) 927-5904 was listed as the telephone number for Ms. Rubb.
915am
T (202) 927-5904 OIG Treasury Audit Director Kieu T. Rubb (signed OIG audit)- VM referred to Paulette Battle, (202) 927-5400 as new auditor
Other names on the final page of the OIG report were:
Michael J. Maloney (202) 927-6512
Christen Stevenson (202) 927-8117
916am
T (202) 927-5400 OIG for Paulette Battle- trans to Battle-gave info
Email Battlep@oig.treasury.gov
958am
Sent email- did not go thru
T (202) 927-5400 question email
T ((202) 597-1819 Paulette Battle- talked more. She to refer to boss. Got correct email.
I believe Ms. Battle was told about my interaction with the CFPB.
Also, after I sent the complaint to the CFPB, instead of investigating the matter, they simply sent my complaint to Susan Schmidt of Comerica Bank. Yes, I have copies of that too.
Now is there any reason why Ms. Densmore or I would feel any level of comfort with any federal worker associated with this case? No personal offense intended, but hope you feel a bit of shame for Treasury for allowing this to happen.
Sincerely,
J.B. Simms

Altemus could and would not reply to this email. She was part of the cabal that wanted to keep us in the dark and bark orders to us.

Friday, February 28, 2020

from: J B Simms
to: Mark Bialek (Federal Reserve Board)
cc: Amy Altemus (OIG Treasury),
Jackie Lynn, Kate Berry, Richard Delmar (OIG Treasury)
date: Feb 28, 2020, 2:40 AM
Subject: Request for investigation by CFPB concerning complaints against Comerica Bank
Dear Mr. Bialek,
Ms. Altemus, copied in this email, as an attorney at Special Counsel OIG Treasury, became involved in the matter I raised two years ago with respect to malfeasance and violations of Reg E by Comerica Bank in its administration of the Direct Express debit card program.
Earlier this week Ms. Altemus, during one of our exchanges as I seek to discover accountability in this matter, Ms. Altemus was told of my conversation with an employee of the CFPB (identified by name, and date of call) who told me of the 400+ complaints against Comerica Bank. Ms. Altemus recommended I contact Fed Reserve OIG which monitors the CFPB. I replied by forwarding copies of emails of which you and one of your associates was copied. There were probably three or four emails that advised you of the issue from this email address. The usual email address I use in this matter is jbsimms.
Copies of these emails were sent to Ms. Altemus to validate my claim that your office ignored my request for an investigation. Research has revealed that the CFPB is mandated to investigate and has enforcement authority. Neither was exercised in this case. The supposition I presented to Ms. Altemus was that since the Direct Express program is a creation of Bureau of Fiscal Service, and the banking law violations and malfeasance point to the failure of Bureau of Fiscal Service to perform their duties, and this being a government entity, that your office would balk at investigating "one of your own."
Since you have chosen not to communicate with me it became necessary to validate my assertion to Ms. Altemus that your office was well aware of the Comerica Bank/Direct Express issue and simply chose not to address the matter.
Maybe you will communicate with Ms. Altemus. If you choose to communicate with me, I can be reached at (803) 309-6850.
Sincerely,
J.B. Simms

I have discussed this matter with a reporter (copied)

Sunday, March 1, 2020

An email was sent to Santaniello asking for the justification for placing the Direct Express promotion insert into the envelopes accompanying the SSA and VA disability checks.

Monday, March 2, 2020

Paul Lawrence and the VA are aware of my "displeasure."

Did Lepper forward my emails to the VA? Read on.

Subject: Re: Back to the issue of the inserts
From: Steven Lepper (CEO-Military Banks of America)
Date: Mon, March 02, 2020, 7:18 am
To: jbsimms
Mr. Simms,
I hope you had a good weekend.
Please be assured that Dr. Lawrence and his staff know about your displeasure with the DE program and your tremendous support of veterans who have experienced difficulties with it. Frankly, that's one of the reasons why they started the VBBP. I keep them apprised of the feedback you give me and they're very appreciative of your outreach to veterans. They are working with Treasury to encourage veterans to transition to bank accounts to deposit their benefits. You should see the results of that collaboration soon. When you do, please let us know what you think.
Also, as you continue keeping your ear to the ground, we'd greatly appreciate any "good news stories" from veterans who have transitioned to bank accounts. We know that many of our veterans are already opening bank accounts; that number should increase as this program continues to gain traction because of encouragement from veteran advocates like you.
Have a great week!
Steve

Mr. Lepper said it all. He knew what I thought of Paul Lawrence and those at the VA who allowed this to happen. I was simply grateful to Mr. Lepper for believing in me.

Tuesday, March 3, 2020

Subject: Proof of ID Requirements
From: Cawana Pearson (FOI Treasury)

Sciurba denial below

Subject: Simms FOIA 2020-02-137
From: Loren Sciurba (OIG Treasury)
Date: Tue, March 03, 2020, 8:01 am
To: jbsimms
Mr. Simms,
I am responding to your FOIA request 2020-02-137 for a copy of a Treasury OIG investigation regarding allegations of fraud perpetrated by Comerica Bank on your Direct Express account in January 2017 and December 2017.
The OIG has no records responsive to this request.
This constitutes a denial of your request, and thus an adverse action under the FOIA.
Sincerely
* Loren J. Sciurba, Counsel to the Inspector General (Acting)*
U.S. Department of the Treasury, Office of Inspector General

Sciurba denied investigations were taking place at OIG Treasury. There is an Office of Investigations within OIG Treasury. Sonja Scott worked there. What do they do in there?

We all knew that Altemus' office was conducting an investigation into 30 of the list of 105 victims I sent to Sonja Scott. I was one of the ones being investigated. Altemus was refusing to reveal the information on my own case, and Sciurba was denying any investigation was taking place.

Subject: Simms FOIA 2020-02-137
From: jbsimms
Date: Tue, Mar 03, 2020, 8:44 am
To: Loren Sciurba (OIG Treasury)
Cc: Amy Altemus (OIG Treasury), Richard Delmar (OIG Treasury), "Jackie Lynn, Steven Lepper (CEO-Military Banks of America), "Abbie Bennett" <abbie@connectingvets.com>, Kate Berry (American Banker) Kevin Guishard (OIG Treasury)
Dear Mr. Sciurba,
Thank you for your reply to my FOI request.
This investigation to which I referred in my FOI request is the investigation having been conducted by your office and specifically A.J. Altemus and her assigns.
The above persons are being copied for your convenience (Ms. Altemus and Mr. Delmar) to confirm the existence of this investigation. I have a string of emails from Ms. Altemus and Kevin A. Guishard which are evidence of the genesis of this investigation. Emails last week from Ms. Altemus also confirmed the existence of said investigation.
The other persons are being copied to confirm this ongoing problem with Treasury FOI submissions. No one would believe me if I conveyed the verbally.
Please confer with Ms. Altemus and confirm that she and Mr. Guishard were in fact investigating 30 victims of the BFS/Comerica Bank/Conduent triumvirate.
Sincerely,
J.B. Simms

Subject: RE: RE: Simms FOIA 2020-02-137
From: Loren Sciurba (OIG Treasury)
Date: Tue, March 03, 2020 9:12 am
To: jbsimms
Cc: Amy Altemus (OIG Treasury), "Delmar, Richard K."
(OIG Treasury)
Mr. Simms,
Your request was processed according to the description you provided. You are welcome to submit a new request that more accurately describes the documents you seek.
Loren J. Sciurba, Counsel to the Inspector General (Acting)
U.S. Department of the Treasury, Office of Inspector General

"Accurately describe requested documents?" This response was a delay tactic and another attempt to stop me.

Subject: RE: Simms FOIA 20 20-02-137
From: jbsimms
Date: Tue, Mar 03, 2020, 10:16 am
To: Loren Sciurba (OIG Treasury)
Cc: Amy Altemus (OIG Treasury), Richard Delmar (OIG Treasury)), Jackie Lynn Kevin Guishard (OIG Treasury), Sonja Scott (OIG Treasury), Steven Lepper (CEO-Military Banks of America), Jennifer Kreegar
Dear Mr. Sciurba,
There is no way I could have been more specific than the narrative which was submitted in the FOI request. If you would have a discussion with Ms. Altemus and Mr. Guishard, it is certain they would tell you of the 30 victims of the Direct Express program, taken from the list of 103 narratives which I submitted to Sonja Scott, whose victimization was documented by me.
The original communication came from Mr. Guishard. A release for me to sign was mailed to the address of Jackie Densmore because I was traveling to SC to attend to a friend who was having surgery. Ms. Densmore forwarded the release information to me in SC, and it was mailed to Mr. Guishard in mid-October 2019.
Ms. Altemus confirmed the existence of said investigation via telephone and email.

I submit to Ms. Altemus that she brings you up to speed to the ongoing investigations as I overlook this oversight or lack of knowledge of all the facets of this matter. It is a lot to comprehend. I have been at this for two (2) years. My notes, timeline, and documentation of this matter are quite complete.

If you wish, I can forward you emails from Mr. Guishard and Ms. Altemus to validate my assertion that Ms. Altemus, Ms. Densmore, and Ms. Kreegar were also part of this investigation.

Sincerely,

J.B. Simms

Sciurba was trying to gaslight me into believing there was no investigation.

Sciurba knew he was going block me.

Subject: Re: An insight into OIG Treasury Special Counsel
From: Steven Lepper (CEO-Military Banks of America)
Date: Tue, Mar 03, 2020, 11:36 am
To: jbsimms
Cc: Jackie Lynn
Mr. Simms,
No apologies necessary. I know from my 3+ decades of service as a judge advocate that the Freedom of Information Act presents significant obstacles for both the public and the government. When the government tells you their hands are tied because of their FOIA processes, they're not lying. Of course, that also doesn't mean that they will provide you the information you're requesting. That is also a crapshoot and often is resolved only when the requestor prevails in a lawsuit.
Best,
Steve

Lepper understood my battle and frustration.

From: jbsimms
Sent: Tuesday, March 3, 2020, 12:34 PM
To: Cawana Pearson (FOI Treasury)
Cc: jackiedenzz@yahoo.com; Amy Altemus (OIG Treasury); Loren Sciurba (OIG Treasury); Delmar, Richard K. (OIG Treasury)
Subject: RE: Proof of ID Requirements
Dear Ms. Pearson,
Thank you for your email.
The parameters for the submission of the FOI request in question were fully met. I submitted the letter which included the narrative of the information requested and the disclaimer "I declare under penalty of perjury that the foregoing is true and correct. Executed on [date]," was included as the last paragraph of the submission.
Oddly enough, an email was received from Mr. Sciurba stating the investigation into my fraud experience with the BFS product, the Direct Express debit card, does not exist.
In the interest of Ms. Altemus, I am not casting dispersions upon you. The fact is I submitted this information a week or so ago, the documentation I requested was acknowledged being available, the submission was authorized by you and Ms. Altemus, and now Mr. Sciurba emails me telling me that the investigation to which I referred does not exist.
I will refrain from making an analogy.
Please review the emails you and Ms. Altemus received and confer with Mr. Sciurba.
You must be aware of the history of Treasury FOI and victims of this matter, specifically Jackie Densmore. Treasury FOI "lost" her request for almost a year. This is very unfortunate.
Sincerely,
J.B. Simms

On Mar 3, 2020, at 12:43 PM, jbsimms wrote:
Dear Mr. Lepper,
I apologize for the fact that I felt it necessary to copy you on emails I received and sent to Treasury with respect to an FOI request submission.

While this is of no direct concern of yours, these exchanges validate all assertions that this matter has exposed the underbelly of this office. This is just a taste of what I and Ms. Densmore have had to tolerate. I cannot imagine how Treasury is denying the investigation being conducted by Ms. Altemus' office.
Gaslighting won't work; we know too much.
I had to be persistent to get the VA to move, and with your help, they did.
Sincerely,
Jim

Subject: RE: RE: Simms FOIA 2020-02-137
From: Loren Sciurba (OIG Treasury)
Date: Tue, Mar 03, 2020, 1:01 pm
To: jbsimms
Cc: Amy Altemus (OIG Treasury), Richard Delmar (OIG Treasury))
Mr. Simms,
Either submit a new FOIA request, or do not. You have also been provided instructions on how to appeal the denial of your request, FOIA 2020-02-137. Those are your options.
Loren J. Sciurba, Counsel to the Inspector General (Acting)
U.S. Department of the Treasury, Office of Inspector General

Subject: RE: Simms FOIA 20 20-02-137
From: jbsimms
Date: Tue, Mar 03, 2020, 8:39 pm
To: Loren Sciurba (OIG Treasury)
Cc: Amy Altemus (OIG Treasury), Richard Delmar (OIG Treasury)), Jackie Lynn; Sonja Scott (OIG Treasury), Katherine Johnson (OIG Treasury), Walter Bayer (SSA OIG), Kevin Guishard (OIG Treasury), "Cawana.Pearson@treasury.gov" Cawana Pearson (FOI Treasury), Steven Lepper (CEO-Military Banks of America)
Mr. Sciurba,
Let me explain something to you; your attempt to gaslight me or any of the other victims is futile. The statement from you that the investigation into the fraud I experience that was being conducted by Ms. Altemus "does not exist" and there is no record of this investigation is garish hubris. I challenge you to walk into the office of Ms. Altemus and tell her that she never directed Kevin Guishard to contact me, that she never talked to me, and that Guishard never sent the release package to me via Jackie Densmore.
It was acknowledged by Ms. Altemus and Ms. Pearson that I satisfied all prerequisites required to submit the FOI request. I have emails that acknowledge my submission was accepted. You, on the other hand, have become involved to simply try to make people believe Ms. Altemus and Mr. Guishard were not involved with investigating the 30 victims.
You scheduled a telephone conference with me, with Mr. Delmar, Ms. Altemus, and Mr. Guishard present, and I will make myself available. I want to hear you deny the work performed by persons in your office, and then maybe you can reveal your true motive for your behavior. If you insist on continuing this charade, I will offer to meet you and the above-named persons personally at the place of your choice.
Your denial of my civil right to submit and FOI request, or deny the existence of the requested documentation, under color of authority, is motivated by something foreign to my nature. If you choose to meet me, you can expose your motive to us all.
Sincerely,
J.B. Simms

Sciurba knew I could do nothing to him. He simply lied and laughed.

Subject: RE: 2020-02-137_Acknowledgement Letter
From: jbsimms
Date: Tue, Mar 03, 2020, 9:04 pm
To: Loren Sciurba (OIG Treasury)
Cc: Richard Delmar (OIG Treasury), Amy Altemus (OIG Treasury), Jackie Lynn; Sonja Scott (OIG Treasury), "Cawana.Pearson@treasury.gov" Cawana Pearson (FOI Treasury)
Dear Mr. Sciurba,

Copied below is validation of my assertion that I satisfied the prerequisites necessary to obtain the requested documents via an FOI request. Ms. Pearson validated my request, and the request was "[a]ppropriately assigned."

You were not involved in this request, nor were you involved in any of the communication between Ms. Altemus, Mr. Guishard, Ms. Pearson, and me.

Even if the person to whom this matter was "assigned" (as stated by Ms. Pearson) told you the information I requested did not exist (as is your stated position), I submit this researcher confer with Ms. Altemus.

This is the same Treasury FOI office which "lost" the FOI request submitted by Ms. Densmore which was mailed and faxed to the address and fax number stated on the Treasury website. Ms. Densmore's FOI request mysteriously appeared approximately a year after the submission. Our faith in the credibility of the FOI section of Treasury was shaken long ago.

Wednesday, March 4, 2020

Subject: your communication regarding Treasury OIG
From: jbsimms
Date: Wed, Mar 04, 2020, 1:15 pm
To: Richard Delmar (OIG Treasury))
Cc: Jackie Lynn; Loren Sciurba (OIG Treasury), Sonja Scott (OIG Treasury), Amy Altemus (OIG Treasury), Kevin Guishard (OIG Treasury), Katherine Johnson (OIG Treasury)
Bcc: Steven Lepper (CEO-Military Banks of America)
Dear Mr. Delmar,

Thank you for your reply and taking the time to address a matter which, although we disagree, has been handled in a very questionable manner.

I forwarded an email from Mr. Guishard which identified this matter as an audit of specific and individual victim accounts. We, as victims, signed a waiver in order for the subpoena served upon Comerica Bank to be effective. You might also be aware that I did have a direct conversation with Ms. Altemus with regard to this matter.

Your characterization of the audit, stating "...[w]e cannot conduct investigations regarding individual payment recipients" is in direct conflict with the fact that I and other victims were asked to sign the waiver so the "individual payment recipient(s)" accounts could be accessed by virtue of the subpoena. Each of 30 persons were contacted by Mr. Guishard and/or Ms. Altemus.

With all due respect, and considering your formal education surpasses mine, refusing to reveal the audit information of my victimization because that information is to be funneled into a larger audit (supposedly that of Ms. Katherine Johnson, 19-041) seems to be an exercise in semantics. This audit/investigation/inquiry needed my signature to enable your inquiry.

I assume you are the court of last resort, so any appeal would be an exercise in futility. Other options must be found. Dialogue is an option, if anyone in your office wants to make that choice.

The fact is that Mr. Sciurba chose to state that the documents that I request did not exist. That documented response by Mr. Sciurba will be analyzed by person much more learned than myself. The motive for Mr. Sciurba to, as I see it, blatantly misrepresent the truth in a cavalier and dismissive manner, has yet to be revealed. As I stated, this denial of civil rights by Mr. Sciurba, under the color of authority, should be explored by you.

It is very unfortunate that you have to take the time to address a matter which could and should have been handled by a subordinate. I share no blame for that.

I will reach out for legal advice and this matter will be revisited. Ms. Densmore and I would prefer a face-to-face meeting with you and the staff attorneys.

I do hope you and those at Treasury are not offended that a citizen might ask for accountability of a federal employee. It is my preference to receive information rather than subjective justification as to why information to which I am entitled is being withheld.

Thank you again for your attention to this matter.
Sincerely,
J.B. Simms

Delmar did not care what happened to the victims. At this point Delmar was sitting on secrets and the coverup. I cold out Sciurba and Altemus all day, but Delmar would not care.

from: J B Simms
to: Loren J Sciurba Loren Sciurba (OIG Treasury)
cc: Kevin Guishard (OIG Treasury),Amy Altemus (OIG Treasury),Jackie Lynn. Richard Delmar (OIG Treasury), jbsimms, Jennifer Kreegar, Walter Bayer Walter Bayer (SSA OIG)
Mar 4, 2020, 4:13 AM
to Loren, Amy, Jackie, Richard, jbsimms, Jennifer, Walter, Kevin
Dear Mr. Sciurba,
Attached below is the email I received from Mr. Guishard regarding the audit/investigation which FOI Treasury and you state does not exist, resulting in your denial of my FOI request. It is my understanding that some of our veterans were also contacted by Mr. Guishard in the same manner. It is unclear why this personal email address was chosen to send the notification of the audit/investigation, but this validates my assertion that the audit does and did exist.
While your agenda and motivation for denying the existence of this audit/investigation is not clear, I will reserve my speculation until more persons will be solicited for their input and evidence.
In the meantime, I respectfully suggest you have a meeting with Mr. Delmar, Ms. Altemus, and Mr. Guishard to be briefed on this matter.
Sincerely,
J.B. Simms

Subject: Sciurba
From: jbsimms
Date: Wed, Mar 04, 2020, 5:47 am
To: Richard Delmar (OIG Treasury)
Cc: Jackie Lynn
Dear Mr. Delmar,
It is evident that you have a real big problem at OIG Treasury, Special Counsel, with Loren Sciurba.
The motivation for his behavior is suspect. His unilateral denial of an audit /investigation within OIG Treasury, denying work being conducted by Ms. Altemus, are part of a recipe for psychological intervention and referral for extended medical leave.
I do hope you can handle the this in quick order. Ms. Densmore and I will be active in this matter for the duration.
Sincerely,
J.B. Simms

Sciurba's denial produced my reply that Sciurba was crazy, but not smart crazy.

Subject: Proof of ID Requirements
 From: Cawana Pearson (FOI Treasury)
Date: Wed, Mar 04, 2020, 6:25 am
To: jbsimms
Cc: Amy Altemus (OIG Treasury) Loren Sciurba (OIG Treasury), (OIG Treasury)
Good morning,
Our office is the liaison between the program offices and the requester with regards to sending the FOIA request where the records most likely exist. You will need to address any concerns to the program office which was assigned your request.

Delmar disagrees that Sciurba is inadequate

Subject: your communication regarding Treasury OIG
From: Richard Delmar (OIG Treasury))
Date: Wed, Mar 04, 2020, 9:21 am
To: jbsimms
Cc: Jackie Lynn, Loren Sciurba (OIG Treasury), Amy Altemus (OIG Treasury)
I have reviewed your complaints regarding Mr. Sciurba and disagree with your assessment. While evidence obtained from Comerica regarding victims of fraud may be used in an audit product, or for an overall evaluation of compliance with laws and regulations regarding the program, search of our investigative database reveals no reports of investigation in which you were named as a victim. The audit work which we

353

are doing related to BFS's management of the Direct Express program, and its supervision of Comerica Bank, its financial agent, is by definition not an investigation. As we've previously explained, we cannot conduct investigations regarding individual payment recipients.

You retain the appeal options Mr. Sciurba has previously explained. Going forward, if you have information relevant to our work, we will of course evaluate it and incorporate it as appropriate. But please cease your unfounded calumny about OIG employees.

Rich Delmar
Deputy Inspector General
Department of the Treasury

My comment about Sciurba was accurate. Delmar was taking up for Sciurba because Delmar could not afford to have Sciurba tell the truth about anything.

Subject: your communication regarding Treasury OIG
From: jbsimms
Date: Wed, Mar 04, 2020, 1:15 pm
To: Richard Delmar (OIG Treasury))
Cc: Jackie Lynn; Loren Sciurba (OIG Treasury), Sonja Scott (OIG Treasury), Amy Altemus (OIG Treasury), Kevin Guishard (OIG Treasury), Katherine Johnson (OIG Treasury)
Bcc: Steven Lepper (CEO-Military Banks of America)

Dear Mr. Delmar,

Thank you for your reply and taking the time to address a matter which, although we disagree, has been handled in a very questionable manner.

I forwarded an email from Mr. Guishard which identified this matter as an audit of specific and individual victim accounts. We, as victims, signed a waiver in order for the subpoena served upon Comerica Bank to be effective. You might also be aware that I did have a direct conversation with Ms. Altemus with regard this matter.

Your characterization of the audit, stating "...[w]e cannot conduct investigations regarding individual payment recipients" is in direct conflict with the fact that I and other victims were asked to sign the waiver so the "individual payment recipient(s)" accounts could be accessed by virtue of the subpoena. Each of the 30 people were contacted by Mr. Guishard and/or Ms. Altemus.

With all due respect, and considering your formal education surpasses mine, refusing to reveal the audit information of my victimization because that information is to be funneled into a larger audit (supposedly that of Ms. Katherine Johnson, 19-041) seems to be an exercise in semantics. This audit/investigation/inquiry needed my signature to enable your inquiry.

I assume you are the court of last resort, so any appeal would be an exercise in futility. Other options must be found. Dialogue is an option, if anyone in your office wants to make that choice.

The fact is that Mr. Sciurba chose to state that the documents that I request did not exist. That documented response by Mr. Sciurba will be analyzed by person much more learned than myself. The motive for Mr. Sciurba to, as I see it, blatantly misrepresent the truth in a cavalier and dismissive manner, has yet to be revealed. As I stated, this denial of civil rights by Mr. Sciurba, under the color of authority, should be explored by you.

It is very unfortunate that you have to take the time to address a matter which could and should have been handled by a subordinate. I share no blame for that.

I will reach out for legal advice and this matter will be revisited. Ms. Densmore and I would prefer a face-to-face meeting with you and the staff attorneys.

I do hope you and those at Treasury are not offended that a citizen might ask for accountability of a federal employee. It is my preference to receive information rather than subjective justification as to why information to which I am entitled is being withheld.

Thank you again for your attention to this matter.
Sincerely,
J.B. Simms

The statement I made in the email above needed an addendum. "*The fact is that Mr. Sciurba chose to state that the documents that I request did not exist*" does not make the statement made by Mr. Sciurba a true statement. Sciurba jumped into the fray long after this started.

Guishard communicated with me, requesting my information, and acknowledging the investigation into my involvement with Conduent and Comerica had been admitted by Guishard. Who was lying? Everyone.

Thursday, March 5, 2020

Subject: RE: Proof of ID Requirements
From: jbsimms
Date: Thu, Mar 05, 2020, 7:06 am
To: Cawana Pearson (FOI Treasury)
Cc: Jackie Lynn, Amy Altemus (OIG Treasury), Loren Sciurba (OIG Treasury), Richard Delmar (OIG Treasury)
Bcc: Franklin Lemond (Plaintiff's Attorney)
Dear Ms. Pearson,
Thank you for your email, defining more of the mechanics of "who does what."
If you can, send me the contact information of the program office to which you are referring with respect to my request and the specific person to whom this matter is being addressed.
We are receiving conflicting information from different persons within OIG Treasury with respect to the existence of said requested documents. First, someone said the documents did not exist, and another suggested I submit another FOI request to obtain the documents. I see no need to make another submission since you did accept the final draft of the letter which met all prerequisites.
I look forward to your reply.
Sincerely, J.B. Simms

Treasury did not want me to see the investigations, even the investigations involved with the OIG report 19-041.

Subject: Proof of ID Requirements
From: Cawana Pearson (FOI Treasury)
Date: Thu, Mar 05, 2020, 7:50 am
To: jbsimms
Cc: Amy Altemus (OIG Treasury), Loren Sciurba (OIG Treasury)
Good morning,
Your request was appropriately assigned to the Office of Inspector General for direct response to you.
Thank you, Cawana
Cawana was always polite. She had to deal with Amy Altemus but could not have been easy.

Subject: Proof of ID Requirements
From: jbsimms
Date: Thu, Mar 05, 2020, 2:00 pm
To: Cawana Pearson (FOI Treasury)
Cc: Jackie Lynn; Richard Delmar (OIG Treasury), Loren Sciurba (OIG Treasury), Steven Lepper (CEO-Military Banks of America)
Dear Ms. Pearson,
Thank you very much for your reply and the direct answer you furnished me.
The I did receive two responses from OIG Treasury; one person at OIG Treasury stated the information I requested did not exist and another person contradicted the first person, stating the information does exist but is not a specified "audit" or "investigation" as I stated in my FOI request.
As a result of these conflicting responses, both of which I contest, OIG Treasury has chosen to withhold this information included in this request.
If there is way I can challenge these decisions to deny my valid FOI, please point me in the direction I must go. Oddly, the persons from whom I received correspondence with respect to the FOI request stated I should resubmit my request. Within this email, you have confirmed that my submission met the necessary prerequisites for submission, so the logic of suggesting I resubmit is a bit suspect.
Again, please forward this to the person in charge of the FOI section of Treasury and ask that they contact me directly. Thank you again.
Sincerely,
J.B. Simms

Sciurba was the one who suggested I resubmit my FOI request. What an idiot. Why would I resubmit my request when it had been denied? I knew they did not want me to see their records.

Subject: RE: Proof of ID Requirements
From: jbsimms
Date: Thu, Mar 05, 2020, 2:22 pm
To: Amy Altemus (OIG Treasury)
Cc: Sonja Scott (OIG Treasury), Katherine Johnson (OIG Treasury), Jackie Lynn, Kevin Guishard (OIG Treasury)
Dear Ms. Altemus,
After the back and forth between you and Ms. Pearson in my attempt to submit an acceptable FOI request for a copy of the investigation (now referred to as an "audit") with regard to your inquiry necessitating a subpoena for information relating to fraud experienced by me in January 2017 and December 2017, I was told that the result of your investigation does not exist.
After being told that the results of your investigation do not exist, I was directed to resubmit my request. Yes, I was told to resubmit a request for something that does not exist.
My assertion is that my FOI request has been validated by Ms. Pearson.
At no time during the exchanges between you and me did you ever state that your work product, of which I was requesting and am entitled, "does not exist" or that I would not be entitled.
I complied with your directive. At no time did you tell me my request was invalid. Hopefully you and others who have entered the fray can sit and compare notes.
Sincerely,
J.B. Simms

Sonja Scott has stated that her "investigation" would be included in the audit, and that I would be entitled to the investigation via an FOI request. Amy Altemus contradicted Sonja Scott, both of whom are in the same office.

Friday, March 6, 2020

The FOI issues are raised.

J B Simms
Fri, Mar 6, 6:09 AM
to Richard, Loren, Amy, Kevin, Jackie, Steven, bcc: Franklin, bcc: jbsimms
* RE: FOI Submission of audit conducted by the office of A.J. Altemus*
Dear Mr. Delmar and Mr. Sciurba,
In reference to the response narratives which I have received from OIG Treasury, indicating that my documents in reference to my FOI request in question either do not exist (Sciurba) or pertains to information to which I am not privy (Delmar), I submit to you the email below which contradict both assertions.
If either of you would like to address this revelation, and immediately validate my request, I feel this would be the honorable thing to do.
You have my telephone number. I can be reached at any time.
Sincerely,
J.B. Simms

Copies of emails from Sonja Scott and Cawana Pearson were attached to the above email. There was no way Delmar, Sciurba, or Altemus would talk to me. These were dirty bureaucrats, as low as it gets, just to coverup the contract with Comerica Bank. It makes you wonder the benefits these people enjoyed regarding this contract.

From: Cawana Pearson (FOI Treasury)
Date: Fri, Mar 06, 2020, 6:34 am
To: jbsimms
Cc: Loren Sciurba (OIG Treasury), (CEO-Military Banks of America)>
Good morning,

I'm not sure of the specifics of what has transpired regarding your FOIA request and the response. I am the liaison between the requester and the program office. OIG is a decentralized program office and responsible for processing their own requests. You should be in communication with their office if you are dissatisfied with their response. I am sure they will be more than happy to assist you.
Thank you,
Cawana

I felt bad for Cawana Pearson. She was a low-level GS employee having to deal work with these unscrupulous people in OIG Treasury.

Subject RE: Proof of ID Requirements
From: jbsimms
Date: Fri, Mar 06, 2020, 2:16 pm
To: "Cawana.Pearson@treasury.gov" Cawana Pearson (FOI Treasury)
Cc: Jackie Lynn
Dear Ms. Pearson,
You and many others have been caught in the crosshairs of an agenda which has yet to be fully exposed. I have definitive emails from Ms. Altemus which state I am entitled to the audit/investigation which her office was conducting.
Mr. Sciurba stated the information I requested did not exist.
Mr. Delmar stated the information does exist, but the information is to be used to supplement another audit/investigation and that I am not entitled to what I requested.
I called the Treasury FOI number yesterday, left a voice-message, and have not received a return call. I called again moments ago and left another message.
The person with whom I need to speak is Ryan Law. As head (as I see it) of FOI Treasury, Mr. Law should be privy to this matter. I have at least three (3) different attorneys giving me different versions of their opinions pertaining to my entitlement to have copies of the documents I requested.
Please forward this to the office of Mr. Law. As the liaison, I am sure you would want to be privy to all incidents of OIG Treasury in which they continue to violate federal law.
I do have your telephone number listed at the end emails, but I did not want to impose by calling. There is too much going on, and I needed you to have tangible evidence of this lawlessness.
If you have the authority to look into this matter, or can refer a person in FOI to do so, I would welcome that. Also, if you can get Mr. Law's office to call me, I would be grateful.
Sincerely,
J.B. Simms

Fri, Mar 6, 2:28 PM
from: Loren Sciurba (OIG Treasury)
to: J B Simms,
Richard Delmar (OIG Treasury))
cc: Amy Altemus (OIG Treasury), Kevin Guishard (OIG Treasury), Jackie Lynn
Steven Lepper (CEO-Military Banks of America), Cawana Pearson (FOI Treasury),
Paul Levitan (Treasury)
Mr. Simms:
You submitted FOIA request 2020-02-137 for a copy of a Treasury OIG investigation regarding allegations of fraud perpetrated by Comerica Bank on your Direct Express account in January 2017 and December 2017. I denied that request because we have no responsive documents. I informed you of your appeal rights and invited you to reframe your inquiry and submit a new FOIA request if, in fact, you were seeking documents other than those you initially described. You have refused to do so, and instead, have fired off a series of emails to a host of Treasury employees insisting that we give you what does not exist and, bizarrely, questioning my sanity.
We have tried on several occasions to explain the work that we are – and are not – doing with regard to Direct Express, and yet you refuse to accept it. Indeed, this is reflected in the messages you attached below to support your argument. Mr. Guishard said quite clearly, "The Office of Audit has not received nor are we in possession of any audit of your account." Ms. Altemus stated, "our audit pertains to Comerica Bank and the administration of the entire Direct Express program rather than any individual account holders." Earlier this week, Mr. Delmar has told you, "While evidence obtained from Comerica regarding victims of fraud may be

used in an audit product, or for an overall evaluation of compliance with laws and regulations regarding the program, a search of our investigative database reveals no reports of investigation in which you were named as a victim." I don't know how else to covey this information in a way that you will accept, but I will try once more: OIG is not conducting an investigation, audit, or inquiry into allegations of fraud on your account. This is a fact. It is not up for debate.

If you want documents other than what you requested, you know what to do. If you are asking for the final audit report on the Direct Express program, you are free to submit that request, but as Ms. Altemus has already explained, we will not release official documents until our work is complete and a report is issued.
That is all.
Loren J. Sciurba, Counsel to the Inspector General (Acting)
U.S. Department of the Treasury, Office of Inspector General

Cawana Pearson could see the contradictions.
A nerve was touched. Sciurba and his lies were exposed. He had Delmar and Altemus to cover for him. It is interesting that Delmar had Sciurba send the email to me. Sciurba must have felt like a big man now.

Saturday, March 7, 2020

J B Simms
Sat, Mar 7, 4:54 AM
To: Loren,
CC; Richard Delmar, Amy Altemus, Kevin Guishard, Jackie Lynn, Steven Lepper,
Cawana.Pearson@treasury.gov, Paul Levitan (Treasury)
Dear Mr. Sciurba,
In my latest email submission, I forwarded a copy of an email from Ms. Altemus which contradicts your assertion that the documents I requested did not exist.
Ms. Altemus plainly stated in her email to me that I would be entitled to this report/investigation/audit and gave me an internet link. I included a copy of that email for you to see. I see no possibility that Ms. Altemus would risk impeachment if questioned directly.
If your intent is to rebuke Ms. Altemus or challenge my veracity, that will be futile.
I submitted an FOI request for a copy of the report submitted by the office of Ms. Altemus with respect to fraud I experienced on my Direct Express account during the months of January 2017 and December 2017.
If you would like to comply with my civil rights with respect to the FOIA, send me a scenario consistent with the admission by Ms. Altemus, and I will be glad to follow your direction. Otherwise, I remain stalwart that my claim that I am entitled to the documents I have requested.
Sincerely,, J.B. Simms
Jackie sent me the email below in which Delmar admitted there were investigations. They denied the existence of the investigations so I would not see their substandard work and how Comerica got the contract.
Altemus refuse to acknowledge the FOI request for investigation into my history with Conduent and Comerica.

Subject: Obvious conflict: FOI request 2020-137
From: jbsimms
Date: Mon, Mar 09, 2020, 7:39 am
To: Amy Altemus (OIG Treasury)
Cc: Jackie Lynn
Dear Ms. Altemus,
After having revealed the copy of your email to me dated December 16, 2019, timed at 7:05am (Eastern), and reading the subsequent denials of the existence of documents referred to in said email, it is obvious this conflict is an internal personnel matter within OIG Treasury and my request simply exposed this conflict.
You certainly felt secure with the fact that I am privy to the documents I requested, or you would not have stated so in your email. The motive for Mr. Sciurba to contradict your assertion is not yet known.
This internal conflict has not only cause me a bit of distress, but has caused me to resort to other options. You stated I was entitled to the information, Ms. Pearson acknowledged I met the prerequisites of a submission of an FOI request, then others come along and try to block me. This puts you and Ms. Pearson in an uncomfortable box. I want that to which I am entitled, and that you acknowledged.
Sincerely, J.B. Simms

Altemus had no scruples. She opened the door to me submitting an FOI, and evidently Delmar and Sciurba convinced her that was a bad idea.

From: jbsimms
Sent: Monday, March 9, 2020, 9:07 PM
To: Cawana Pearson (FOI Treasury)
Cc: Jackie Lynn
Subject: another FOI request
Dear Ms. Pearson,
Attached is a new FOI submission in my attempt to obtain the information which Ms. Altemus stated in her email of December 16, 2019 I was entitled.
I attached emails from Ms. Altemus and Mr. Guishiard, as well as attempted to be more definitive in the wording of my request.
The format and identifying information submitted is identical to the previous submission, 2020-02-137. I pray this submission is acceptable.
Thank you for your attention to this matter.
Sincerely,
J.B. Simms

Subject: FOIA 2020-02-137
From: Cawana Pearson (FOI Treasury)
Date: Mon, Mar 09, 2020, 9:25 am
To: jbsimms:
Good afternoon,
Please provide me with a phone number and I will reach out to you.
Thank you.

Cawana Pearson called me and talked to me while I was riding in Hite Miller's truck in Columbia, SC. I was visiting my friend Hite as I continued this ordeal with OIG Treasury.
I laid it on the line and told her exactly what I thought of OIG Treasury. Ms. Pearson appeared sympathetic, but she had no power over these people.
A person from her office (FOI office) would have to go to OIG Treasury and request the documents. The people at OIG Treasury would state that no records exist, and that would be the end of that.

From: jbsimms
Sent: Monday, March 9, 2020, 10:45 AM
To: Bayer, Walter Office of the Inspector General (Soc Sec)
Cc: Jackie Lynn
Subject: update available?
Dear Walt,
Is there any way you can update Ms. Densmore and me with respect to your presentation to SSA OIG on this BFS/Direct Express matter?
The leaflet/inserts continue to be stuffed into the envelopes for SSA and VA recipients. We were hoping SSA would realize the harm this program is doing to all recipients.
I look forward to hearing from you.
Sincerely,
Jim

Bayer usually responded but we were not sure exactly what he was doing. We never heard from Social Security OIG.

Subject: conversation
From: jbsimms
Date: Mon, Mar 09, 2020, 1:29 pm
To: "Cawana.Pearson@treasury.gov" Cawana Pearson (FOI Treasury)
Cc: Jackie Lynn
Dear Ms. Pearson,

Thank you for calling. The matter of this FOI request is far from over, and you have been helpful and supportive.

As for "appealing" the decision by whomever is the adjudicator, the actual adjudicator has not been identified. Originally, I thought Sciurba was the person making the decision to refuse to address the FOI request, then Mr. Delmar jumped in. Both Sciurba and Delmar contradicted Ms. Altemus. My wish is that Mr. Law and the head of the FOI Treasury office see what is happening and make the decision to show integrity and release the requested documents.

I look forward to bringing this matter to a close.

Sincerely,

Jim Simms

Date: Mon, Mar 9, 2020, at 2:16 PM
Subject: Treasury Office of Inspector General Subpoena, Almon v. Conduent
To: franklin@webbllc.com <franklin@webbllc.com>
Cc: matt@WebbLLC.com <matt@webbllc.com>, adam@webllc.com <adam@webllc.com>, Delmar, Richard K. (OIG Treasury), Loren Sciurba (OIG Treasury)
Dear Mr. Lemond:
We have received your subpoena in the case of Joe Almon et al. v. Conduent Business Services, LLC, Comerica, Inc., and Comerica Bank, in the Western District of Texas, 5:19-cv-01075-XR. Please be advised that requests for testimony or the production of records from a federal agency in a court or other proceeding must be made in compliance with the agency's "Touhy" regulations, so named for United States ex rel. Touhy v. Ragen, 340 U.S. 462. These regulations prohibit the unauthorized release of information by current (and typically former) agency employees and provide a procedure for centralized agency decision-making concerning how the agency will respond to a subpoena or other request for testimony or documents served on a current or former agency employee. Touhy regulations pertaining to the U.S. Department of the Treasury are at 31 Code of Federal Regulations (C.F.R.) § 1.11. Specifically, 31 C.F.R. § 1.11 (d)(3)(i) requires information that does not currently appear to be included in the subpoena. Howbeit, three of the documents you seek are publicly available for download at https://www.treasury.gov/about/organizational-structure/ig/Pages/audit_reports_index.aspx.
Sincerely,
Amy Altemus

Amy Altemus wanted Franklin Lemond to resubmit his subpoenas. Treasury was not going to allow records to be released.

Subject: Treasury Office of Inspector General Subpoena, Almon v. Conduent
From: Franklin Lemond (Plaintiff's Attorney)
Date: Mon, Mar 09, 2020, 4:01 pm
To: jbsimms
Delmar at least knows we have hit them with a subpoena...

It was a bit of a consolation.

Subject*: A reminder with no clarification*
From: jbsimms
Date: Mon, Mar 09, 2020, 6:32 pm
To: Amy Altemus (OIG Treasury)
Cc: Jackie Lynn
Dear Ms. Altemus,
As I researched emails that validate my entitlement to the audit/investigation being conducted by your office (the same audit/investigation denied by Mr. Sciurba) I not only found emails dating from November and December of 2019 using the exact words audit/investigation, but an email dated December 16, 2019 directing me to submit an FOI request for said documents involved in the audit/investigation.
In addition, I found an email from Mr. Delmar, dated November 5, 2019, noting that the misspelling of my name was the reason I had not received the email notice you sent to Ms. Delmar canceling the conference which had

been scheduled for the following day. While your stated reason for canceling the conference was that the proposed syllabus and corrective measures I presented prior to the meeting were outside the purview of OIG Treasury, you never gave us/me the chance to submit these issues into discussion. With all due respect, the reluctance to engage Ms. Densmore and me in dialogue is the same behavior exhibited by Mr. Santaniello as he personally protected the selection process for the Fiscal Agent, Comerica Bank.

You never gave us the courtesy to discuss the issues I presented, which were the issues to be discussed. You wanted to dictate the narrative. We knew the narrative far better than you expected. This reluctance to engage us has led to the place we are now; an atmosphere of total distrust.

We did not create this atmosphere. Attacking us by blocking valid FOI requests, cancelling conferences, and failing to hold fellow Treasury employees accountable for subjecting victims to a similar emotional experience as with the Fiscal Agent, did not help solve the problem.

Personally, I wish persons at Treasury had not behaved in this manner. We are not defeated yet.
Sincerely,
J.B. Simms

Remember the interview/meeting of November 2019 with Jackie and me was cancelled by Altemus because of the syllabus I submitted. Altemus never gave me a chance to submit a syllabus that she would agree with. No one would engage us personally.

From: jbsimms
Sent: Monday, March 9, 2020 9:07 PM
To: Cawana Pearson (FOI Treasury)
Cc: Jackie Lynn
Subject: another FOI request
Dear Ms. Pearson,
Attached is a new FOI submission in my attempt to obtain the information which Ms. Altemus stated in her email of December 16, 2019, I was entitled. I attached emails from Ms. Altemus and Mr. Guishiard, as well as attempted to be more definitive in the wording of my request. The format and identifying information submitted is identical to the previous submission, 2020-02-137. I pray this submission is acceptable.
Thank you for your attention to this matter.
Sincerely,
J.B. Simms

I continued to pelt them with FOI requests. Again, these were some very dirty people.

Tuesday, March 10, 2020

Subject: another FOI request
From: Cawana Pearson (FOI Treasury)
Date: Tue, Mar 10, 2020, 5:25 am
To: jbsimms
Good morning Mr. Simms,
I have submitted your FOIA request to the proper email address which handles new FOIA request. Please note that in the future, you should submit new FOIA requests to FOIA@Treasury.gov.
Thank you,
Cawana

Good. We will see what lame excuse they will have to refuse this FOI request.

From: Cawana Pearson (FOI Treasury)
Date: Tue, Mar 10, 2020, 5:48 am
To: jbsimms Cc: Jackie Lynn
Thank you so much for the notification. No worries at all.

It was interesting that Ms. Pearson continued the dialogue.

From: jbsimms
Sent: Tuesday, March 10, 2020 8:43 AM
To: Cawana Pearson (FOI Treasury) Cc: Jackie Lynn
Subject: New FOI submission
Dear Ms. Pearson,
A new FOI request was submitted in an attempt to get the information with respect to the investigation/audit conducted by the office of Ms. Altemus involving the 30 victims of the Direct Express program.
I will do whatever is necessary.
The Treasury website would not take an online request. The site failed to accept the submission. I had to send the request to you via email. I apologize for that intrusion, but I had no options.
I am still looking forward to receiving a telephone call from Mr. Law or his superior. As you communicate this request to other, please request that when the person calls, and if the person reaches my voice mail, leave a direct callback telephone number.
Thank you for your assistance and your consideration.
Sincerely,
J.B. Simms

J B Simms
Attachments
Mar 10, 2020, 10:10 AM
to Richard, Loren, AJ, Jackie, Kevin
This is what I see daily.

.ıll CC Wi-Fi 🛜   **1:09 PM**   58% 🔋

🔒 facebook.com

| Write something... | 🖼️ Photo |

Timmy J Skaggs ▸ **direct express (ssi) members**   •••
Yesterday at 11:22 AM

Finally it came my mom cried over the stress of this😭😭😭😭😭

👍😢 2   1 Comment

👍 Like   💬 Comment

Timmy J Skaggs ▸ **direct express (ssi) members**   •••
March 6 at 10:12 AM

If I call on a Thursday for fast delivery would I get the card on Saturday or Monday?

👍 1   5 Comments

👍 Like   💬 Comment

Victoria Bolden ▸ **direct express (ssi) members**   •••
22 hrs

362

Sarah Lizama appeared to be helpful from time to time as an employee of the Social Security Administration. Her allegiance would not last long.

Wednesday, March 11, 2020

Subject: 2020-03-042_Acknowledgement Letter
From: Cawana Pearson (FOI Treasury)
Date: Wed, Mar 11, 2020, 4:56 am
To: jbsimms
Good morning,
Treasury is in receipt of your recently submitted FOIA request.
Thank you, Cawana
Subject: update available?
From: Walter Bayer (Soc Sec OIG)
Date: Wed, Mar 11, 2020, 9:57 am
To: jbsimms
Cc: Jackie Lynn
Jim,
I continue to share any incoming information and news stories with the appropriate parties here. I cannot speak to the OIG's work beyond what we have proposed in our Audit Work Plans – see the latest here.
Thanks,
Walt

Walter Bayer was going to propose an audit investigation be conducted. Social Security had been ignoring the Comerica/Conduent issue. It was as if Treasury, specifically Bureau of Fiscal Service, was ramming this program down the throat of Social Security and Social Security was not to contest the issue.

Subject: update available?
From: jbsimms
Date: Wed, Mar 11, 2020, 2:10 pm
To: Walter Bayer (Soc Sec OIG)
Cc: Jackie Lynn; Steven Lepper (CEO-Military Banks of America), Pamela Powers (VA-Chief of Staff)
Dear Walt,
Thank you very much for advocating our work to halt federal dispensing agencies from endorsing BFS and the Direct Express program. It took me bit of effort to gain the attention of the VA, and thankfully they reached out to Mr. Lepper and not only stopped endorsing BFS and the Direct Express program, they created a new program.
Almost daily, I receive requests for assistance from victims of this program. BFS has refused to communicate; revelations of their behavior has made BFS defensive. The majority of the victims are SSA, SSI, and SSD recipients. Many of these person are of a low economic station, and do not have the "tools" to fight a bank or a government agency.
If SSA is intent on changing direction and protecting their recipients, I would hope you and others at SSA OIG would contact BFS (including Thomas Santaniello) and demand that inserts accompanying check be edited to direct recipients to a safe and secure alternatives to a check, or cease the insert program.
We all know I can recite the issues extemporaneously, and I did for a complete hour during an "interview" with OIG Treasury. A year later, an attorney at OIG Treasury canceled a conference with Ms. Densmore and me because they did not like the syllabus I submitted. The truth makes many in Washington very uncomfortable and they refuse to debate the matter. All I can do is present the facts.
Thank you for your attention, and if anyone with whom you confer wish to address this matter with me, I look forward to the exchange.
Sincerely,
Jim

We were trying everything to get Social Security to stop putting the Direct Express inserts into the payment envelopes.

Bayer usually responded but we were not sure of any progress

Subject: RE: FOIA 2020-03-042 Proposed response
From: jbsimms
Date: Wed, March 11, 2020, 2:35 pm
To: Amy Altemus (OIG Treasury)
Cc: Jackie Lynn; Steven Lepper (CEO-Military Banks of America), Richard Delmar (OIG Treasury), Loren Sciurba (OIG Treasury), Kate Berry (American Banker)
Dear Ms. Altemus,
Thank you for your immediate response to my recent FOI submission which is a subsequent submission to FOI request 2020-02-137 requesting results of your audit/investigation of 30 victims of the Direct Express program. I refer you to your email to me dated December 16, 2019 which identifies said independent audit/investigation and your direction to me that I "am" entitled to said audit/investigation. The fact that Mr. Sciurba initiated the denial of my request and to blatantly contradict you, I look forward to presenting this evidence to any person/body to whom you direct me, and others whom I discover have jurisdiction, to expose all motives inherent in the actions of Mr. Sciurba.
Sincerely,
J.B. Simms

Amy Altemus denied the existence of tangible evidence of her lies. Guishard worked for Altemus, and I sent him a release for him to investigate my records. This was crazy town.

Altemus sent me contact information to appeal her decision to deny my FOI requests - 2020-02-137 and 2020-03-042. The first FOI submission, 2020-02-137, was summarily dismissed by Mr. Loren Sciurba.
After reviewing the email of December 16, 2019, from Ms. Altemus to me, which contradicted the assertion of Mr. Sciurba, I decided to submit a subsequent FOI request. After making the submission yesterday, Tuesday March 10, 2020, the reply/denial to abide by the request was received within 24 hours from Ms. Altemus.

Friday, March 13, 2020

I was assured by Ms. Sonja Scott and Mr. Delmar that the results of the investigation to which Ms. Scott was assigned would be revealed to me at the conclusion of her investigation, and that said investigation would be submitted to Ms. Katherine Johnson to be included in her audit report, 19-041.
On July 29, 2019 the preliminary report of Treasury OIG 19-041 was published. This was 7 month ago. After I critiqued the report, and received a response from Mr. Delmar, we all awaited the final report. It is an assumption that the preliminary report has now become the final report, but the issues of accuracy in the preliminary audit report and lack of thoroughness (which were brought to the attention of Ms. Johnson and Mr. Delmar) would make a prudent person think the final report would address issues which were presented.
This is a matter in which persons are not used to or comfortable with oversight from a non-governmental employee.

Monday, March 16, 2020

Subject: Re: subpoenas and my FOI battle
From: Franklin Lemond (Plaintiff's Attorney)
Date: Mon, March 16, 2020 11:53 am
To: Jim Simms Cc: Jackie Lynn
Santaniello has been served

This was the drama regarding the process server trying to get into the building.

We had the affidavit of service on Santaniello, but he would not comply

Subject: FOIA - Treasury OIG - Direct Express
From: Richard Delmar (OIG Treasury))
Date: Mon, March 16, 2020 12:24 pm
To: jbsimms

Mr. Simms – Responding to your FOIA request, Treasury tracking number 2020-03-070, in which you appear to request a Treasury OIG report of investigation (ROI) containing information that was used in the development of Treasury OIG audit report OIG-19-041. This audit report concerns work we've done relating to the Treasury's Direct Express program.

After consultation with our Offices of Audit, Investigations, and Counsel, and research in our investigative data base, I've determined that we have two closed ROIs that relate to the Direct Express program. While these investigations did not inform the cited audit, I am providing them to you so as to interpret and respond to your request as broadly as possible.
Rich Delmar
Deputy Inspector General
Department of the Treasury

Tuesday, March 17, 2020

Subject: subpoenas and my FOI battle
From: jbsimms
Date: Tue, Mar 17, 2020, 5:46 am
To: Franklin Lemond (Plaintiff's Attorney)
Cc: Jackie Lynn
Thank you for this affidavit of service on Santaniello.
I had a 42-minute chat with the head of FOI Treasury yesterday. He admitted his office serves the purpose of "processing" with no oversight or verification. I confirmed with him (Paul Levitan) I would be sending an appeal to both FOI requests which were denied. Two persons at OIG Treasury lied, and I can prove it.
So, the appeal has been sent. I am asking for the investigations which were used to construct the audit; the one by Sonja Scott, and the one by A.J. Altemus.
This is a dirty game.
Jim

Subject: FOIA - Treasury OIG - Direct Express
From: Richard Delmar (OIG Treasury))
Date: Tue, Mar 17, 2020, 7:15 am
To: jbsimms
Mr. Simms – Ms. Altemus did not conduct an investigation. As Acting IG Counsel, she advised the process by which financial records of several Direct Express beneficiaries, including you, were obtained by our administrative subpoena process for use in our audit of the program's administration. And the work of Assistant Special Agent in Charge Scott was to help the victims of the identify theft get assistance from BFS and its financial agent. Please stop making demands and claims which assume otherwise.
Rich Delmar
Deputy Inspector General
Department of the Treasury

The assertion by OIG Treasury that an investigation was not conducted was not true.

Subject: FOIA - Treasury O IG - Direct Express
From: jbsimms
Date: Tue, Mar 17, 2020, 12:02 pm
To: Richard Delmar (OIG Treasury))
Cc: "ogis@nara.gov" <ogis@nara.gov>, FOIA.Public.Liaison@ssa.gov, Jackie Lynn
Bcc: Steven Lepper (CEO-Military Banks of America), Franklin Lemond (Plaintiff's Attorney)
Dear Mr. Delmar,
While I contend that the definition of the action taken by Ms. Altemus is that of an "investigation" and that research of my emails to and from Ms. Altemus and Mr. Guishard will confirm either the verbiage or inference, I welcome an impartial third party to offer their opinion.
As was stated by Ms. Scott and others within OIG Treasury, the audit signed by Ms. Johnson and published on July 29, 2019 (OIG Treasury 10-041) was said to be a preliminary report. As of this date, I have no knowledge that the audit has been revised to become more accurate or thorough, nor has a final audit been published to

include the information with respect to "...[t]he process by which financial by which financial records of several Direct Express beneficiaries, including you, were obtained by our administrative subpoena process for use in our audit of the program's administration."

If information is "[f]or use in our audit of the program's administration" this same information, be it categorized as an investigation, inquiry, or polite suggestion, is discoverable via an FOI request, as I submitted. Both Ms. Scott, in her capacity, and that of Ms. Altemus, told me that their work product (I will refrain from using the word "investigation" to which you object) would be available upon my submission of an FOI request. With all due respect, I would have expected a more accurate and honest reply from you as that OIG Treasury 19-041 had not been published, and the discoverable work product from Ms. Scott and Ms. Altemus would not be available until OIG Treasury 19-041 had been published. That response would have been consistent with my communication with both Ms. Altemus and Ms. Scott and not the response that (1) there is no record of the investigation by Ms. Altemus (from Sciurba) and (2) that there is no investigative report (from Ms. Altemus).

Now that you have defined this work product as a "process" and not an investigation, I will use your definition as the basis for my appeal, which you see above is being forwarded to OGIS for consideration.
Sincerely,
J.B. Simms

Wednesday, March 18, 2020

Date: Wed, Mar 18, 2020, 4:30 am
To: Richard Delmar (OIG Treasury)
Cc: Jackie Lynn; "^FOIA Liaison" <FOIA.Public.Liaison@ssa.gov>, "OGIS@nara.gov"
<OGIS@nara.gov>, Amy Altemus (OIG Treasury) , Sonja Scott (OIG Treasury),
"Cawana.Pearson@treasury.gov" Cawana Pearson (FOI Treasury), Loren Sciurba (OIG Treasury),
"Battlep@oig.treas.gov"
Dear Mr. Delmar,
Your use of the word "process" as being synonymous with or used to replace the word "investigation" contradicts the statements and understanding presented by Ms. Scott and Ms. Altemus. It is clear that you are refusing to release the information I am requesting, and as I have said of Mr. Sciurba, the motive for your actions has yet to be exposed.
Let me be crystal clear with you concerning the "process" being conducted by Ms. Scott and Ms. Altemus.
1) Ms. Scott admitted she was conducting an investigation, differing from the audit. The fact that Ms. Scott is receiving complaints from victims, albeit an altruistic gesture, is true, but Ms. Scott admitted she was investigating this matter long before she was given the list of 103 victims by me. Ms. Scott challenged my veracity long before I ceased receiving direct calls from victims, and my first submission to her was of 70+ narratives. When Ms. Scott offered to receive complaints, I furnished her with the full list of the 103 victims. If I have to find the email to validate this assertion, I will find it. As I questioned Ms. Scott, I was very direct, as was her reply, that she was conducting an investigation which would be forwarded to Ms. Johnson, and that I would be privy to this via and FOI request.
2) After receiving the communication from Mr. Guishard concerning the investigation of the 30 victims (all being generated from the list of 103 narratives I sent to Ms. Scott) I spoke directly with Ms. Altemus on the telephone. I will dig up the date and time of that call if necessary. The assurance given by Ms. Scott was echoed by Ms. Altemus, that I would be privy to her investigation of Comerica Bank and Conduent with respect to general findings, not specific to the other 29 victims.
Also, during the time I was attempting to meet the prerequisites for the FOI submission being laid out by Ms. Cawana Pearson and Ms. Altemus, there was no mention that I was not entitled to said information. There were probably 5 email transmissions and both Ms. Altemus and Ms. Pearson were fully aware if the information I was requesting and Ms. Altemus never indicated, implied, or suggested that I was not entitled to said information. It was not until Mr. Sciurba entered the fray with his statement that "no record existed" of the work I was requesting that was conducted by Ms. Altemus that I had any indication that the information did not exist. That statement by Mr. Sciurba defies explanation and can only be described as an attempt at gaslighting. While Mr. Levitan's office at FOI Treasury only serves as a processing unit, and the Office of Government Information Services appears to serve the same purpose, I see no accountability because I see no consequences for the contradictions and the denial of my FOI requests. I was told the appeals go to you. Presenting a Motion to Reconsider to a judge who has made a ruling against you might seem a bit futile, and only covering bases, but I hope the evidence I will be presenting to you and others will result in an epiphany not yet acknowledged.

This is not just for me; this is for others who cannot speak for themselves and are ignored by the civil servants to whom they reach out to protect them. I just happen to be another victim and their messenger.

You have made it necessary for me to research emails to confirm my assertions (the term you use to identify my statements).

Sincerely,

J.B. Simms

Lepper had sympathy for my battles regarding FOIA submissions

Subject: FOI rejections
From: Steven Lepper (CEO-Military Banks of America)
Date: Wed, Mar 18, 2020, 5:38 am
To: jbsimms
Cc: Jackie Lynn

Mr. Simms,

I hope this note finds you well. Thanks for keeping me apprised of your dialog with Treasury.

Your experience with the Treasury's Freedom of Information Act processes is not unlike the experience others have had dealing with the federal government under FOIA. You are right: The FOIA section of Treasury, like similar sections in other agencies, is only a liaison between the requestor and the offices that maintain the information requested. Some agencies read requests very narrowly and reject them if they don't precisely describe the information in the agency's system of records; other agencies are a bit more liberal. The bottom line is that, in order to maximize success, FOIA requests should describe information as broadly as possible. In your case, it seems your use of the word "investigation" has limited the scope of your request.

Since I know your ultimate objective is to end the Direct Express program or limit it to as narrow a group of beneficiaries as possible, I'm optimistic that our efforts with VBA will help. We're already seeing some movement among DE participants toward opening bank accounts. We obviously need more. We are focusing our efforts on educating and encouraging veterans on the benefits of bank accounts over DE debit cards. I know you support us; it would be great if we could get some "success stories" from veterans who have made the switch.

This health crisis will reveal even more of the benefits of bank accounts over the DE program. As more people confine themselves to their homes, it will become more difficult to continue all their financial activities. I'm convinced having a bank to call will help. If you hear any feedback on the impact of this crisis on veteran financial resiliency, please let me know. I will, in turn, feed that information to VBA, which can take appropriate action.

Wishing you continued good health.

Steve

Mr. Lepper had to be more diplomatic than me. He understood what I was trying to do. Notice the times of the emails. Both Mr. Lepper and I began our daily work early.

Subject: FOI rejections
From: jbsimms
Date: Wed, Mar 18, 2020, 5:56 am
To: Steven Lepper (CEO-Military Banks of America)

Dear Mr. Lepper,

Thank you for your immediate reply.

I am certainly looking for accountability. As for the broad definition of the word "investigation" I submitted to Mr. Delmar a copy of a letter which was to append to a subpoena to Comerica Bank. Mr. Delmar used the words "legitimate law enforcement inquiry" and I replied by forwarding him his letter along with cites from a dictionary and thesaurus which equated the word investigation as an inquiry.

After this appeal process is done, I don't know where to go other than have our lawyer, Mr. Lemond, subpoena the documents. I wanted to get the info via an FOI request. The semantics has become tedious.

As for the virus, in a few days I will be returning to help with a friend of 40+ years who had a double lung transplant 17 years ago. I did many things around his house (plumbing, carpentry, tree trimming, electrical) and he asked that I return to help more before I go to California. I have to be virus free to help him. God knows I would not want to be a carrier.

I continue to monitor a Direct Express victim page on Facebook, and we have almost 400 victim members. I will post an inquiry for stories of vets who have switched their VA benefits.
As for the FOI issue, I am searching for the court of last resort.
I appreciate your attention and your assistance.
Stay virus free.
Sincerely,
Jim

Subject: The audit/investigation/examination
From: jbsimms
Date: Wed, Mar 18, 2020, 3:43 pm
To: Richard Delmar (OIG Treasury)
Cc: Jackie Lynn; "^FOIA Liaison" <FOIA.Public.Liaison@ssa.gov>, <OGIS@nara.gov>
Dear Mr. Delmar,
I am attaching a couple of documents created to validate my claim that an audit/investigation/examination that involved Ms. Altemus and Mr. Guishard did, in fact exist, contrary to a claim made by Mr. Sciurba.
Within this compilation of 3 emails, you will see the request made to me by Mr. Guishard (10/16/19) for the release signed by me which enabled your office to obtain information on my account from Comerica Bank. This was characterized by Mr. Guishard as an "audit" and in Number 4 of the directions, the activity was characterized as "...in the course of investigating...
In an additional email from Ms. Altemus dated Feb 25, 2020, she stated, "...this office has a remit only to examine... so now we have three synonymous words used to describe this matter: audit, investigation, and examination.
In the email dated Tue, Mar 03, 2020, 8:01 am, Mr. Sciurba stated the above audit/investigation/examination did not exist.
On March 4, 2020, I sent Mr. Sciurba an email, copying the 10/16/19 email from Mr. Guishard to me, identifying the audit/investigation/examination referenced by Mr. Guishard.
At no time did Ms. Altemus or Mr. Guishard state that their work was part of OIG Treasury 19-041, which deflates your theory that this work was part of that report. If that were the case, this matter would have been mentioned in the preliminary edition of 19-041 on July 29, 2019.
As for the FOI submission 2020-03-070 requesting the investigation conducted by Ms. Scott, I assume Ms. Scott to be an "investigator" because she signed of as "ASAC Sonja L. Scott, US Department of Treasury, Office of Inspector General, Office of Investigations."
This validates my FOI request.
Sincerely, J.B. Simms

Thursday, March 19, 2020

Social Security had information regarding the hacker who changed my address. They were not giving men the information. The FOI that I sent to Social Security was denied.

Sunday, March 22, 2022

Conduent had contributed to the campaign of Corey Booker as well as the Democrat National Committee. We were getting nothing from Elizabeth Warren, and this was due to the fact that she was getting money from the DNC, banking money, and she was not going to rock the boat.

Thursday, March 26, 2020

Subject: Customer: J.B. Simms
From: jbsimms
Date: Thu, Mar 26, 2020, 4:55 am
To: "Teresa Brady" <teresa.brady@nara.gov>
Cc: Jackie Lynn
Dear Ms. Brady,
Thank you for your call yesterday. The initial concern involved a program of Treasury, but this has now developed into a concern of the integrity of persons at OIG Treasury who are trying to protect their reputations by concealing their work product which, by their own admission, is available via an FOI request.

This lack of transparency at Treasury (specifically Bureau of Fiscal Service) was the subject of the published GAO 17-176 report signed by Michael Clements (Jan 25, 2017). I have stumbled upon a culture of secrecy and those at Treasury are doing all they can to stop me.
I have copied your office on many exchanges with OIG Treasury.
I look forward to a reply from Ms. Murphy.
Sincerely,
Jim Simms

Ms. Brady (National Archives Record Administration) and Ms. Murphy knew I did not trust OIG Treasury.

Subject: Customer: J.B. Simms
From: Teresa Brady <teresa.brady@nara.gov>
Date: Thu, Mar 26, 2020, 5:25 am
To: jbsimms
Good morning.
Your OGIS case number is 20-1690.Teresa A. Brady, National Archives and Records Administration
The OGIS case number was 20-1690. Treasury could have been more helpful.

On Thu, Mar 26, 2020, at 7:56 AM jbsimms wrote:
Dear Ms. Brady,
Thank you for your call yesterday. The initial concern involved a program of Treasury, but this has now developed into a concern of the integrity of persons at OIG Treasury who are trying to protect their reputations by concealing their work product which, by their own admission, is available via an FOI request.
This lack of transparency at Treasury (specifically Bureau of Fiscal Service) was the subject of the published GAO 17-176 report signed by Michael Clements (Jan 25, 2017). I have stumbled upon a culture of secrecy and those at Treasury are doing all they can to stop me.
I have copied your office on many exchanges with OIG Treasury.
I look forward to a reply from Ms. Murphy. I will be working outdoors much of the morning and will not be accessible. I suggest Ms. Murphy review the email I have sent your office and send me an email to tell me her availability, maybe tomorrow.
Sincerely,
Jim Simms

Wednesday, April 1, 2020

Subject: OGIS Response - Simms
From: OGIS <OGIS@nara.gov>
Date: Wed, Apr 01, 2020, 8:11 am
To: OGIS <OGIS@nara.gov>
Cc: jbsimms
April 1, 2020—Sent via email.
Re: Case No. 20-1690
Dear J.B. Simms:
OGIS provides information to FOIA requesters and Federal agencies to increase understanding and resolve disputes.
We carefully reviewed your submission of information and we understand that you are dissatisfied with the response you received from the Department of Treasury.
It is unclear from your submission whether you appealed the Treasury's response according to the directions provided in the Treasury's response letter. If you have not done so already, we strongly encourage you to file a FOIA administrative appeal.
The appeal is an important part of the FOIA administrative process, and OGIS's assistance does not replace the appeal process. By filing an appeal, you preserve your administrative rights and give the agency a chance to look at the request anew and carefully review and reconsider every part of the initial response, from the search the agency conducted to any initial decision the agency made to withhold records in full or in part.
Sincerely,
The OGIS Staff
OFFICE OF GOVERNMENT INFORMATION SERVICES, National Archives and Records Administration

More politics. Our government has a way of keeping information away from the public. They act as though they are honest civil servants. That is not the case.

Thursday, April 2, 2020

Below is my reply to the email from OGIS received on the previous day. The battle continued.

Subject: OGIS Response - Simms
From: jbsimms
Date: Thu, Apr 02, 2020 5:07 am
To: "OGIS" <OGIS@nara.gov>
Cc: "Teresa Brady" <teresa.brady@nara.gov>, Jackie Lynn
Dear OGIS Staff,
Thank you for your reply. The wording of your email was very confusing, and it appears my narratives were not examined by your office.
You stated, "It is unclear from your submission whether you appealed the Treasury's response according to the directions provided in the Treasury's response letter." By using the word "whether" you implied there was an alternative, but you never stated the alternative.
I followed all proper procedure and protocol to challenge the refusal of OIG Treasury to lawfully adhere to my FOI requests.
Your hesitancy to act on my behalf in a direct and objective manner, while not surprising, is disconcerting. Accountability on the part of federal employees and depending upon federal employees to hold accountable the illegals acts of their peers, does not exist. The lack of integrity and by OIG Treasury noted in my appeal and my communication to your office was clear. Your office chose to send me a "brush-off" email, and the sender did not have the courage or integrity to sign their name.
I am not pursuing this matter because I am bored and in seclusion. This has been an ongoing matter for two years.
The attention given to this matter by Ms. Brady made me think that someone would attend to this, and she certainly appeared to understand the gravity of the matter. My request is that this matter be referred to a person who can understand the nuances and the facts and act appropriately.
I want a reply email to schedule a conference with the director of OGIS. I might not be able to immediately answer my telephone as I am doing major yard work for a disabled friend of 40 years.

Friday, April 3, 2020

Subject: Customer: J.B. Simms
From: Teresa Brady <teresa.brady@nara.gov>
Date: Fri, Apr 03, 2020, 4:12 am
To: jbsimms
Good morning.
I do apologize for what has happened, but I can only do what I did as an employee.
After the telephone call from you, I sent an email to my supervisor for review.
I do not have control over their (OGIS office) response, which is rooted in the policy of the Agency. Again, I am sorry, and hope that you get the assistance you need.
Thank you.
Teresa A. Brady
National Archives and Records Administration, Office of Government Information Services (OGIS)

Teresa Brady, along with Cawana Pearson, were beginning to understand what I was going through with the drama of FOI requests and the government agencies fighting to protect their information.

Thursday, April 4, 2020

Jackie was getting her congressman (Keating) involved. Michael Jackman worked for Keating.

From: Jackman, Michael [Michael.Jackman@mail.house.gov]
Sent: Thursday, April 4, 2019, 4:43 PM
To: Delmar, Richard K. (OIG Treasury)
Subject: RE: Treasury Direct Express - Inspector General action
Mr. Delmar—

It has come to my attention that Treasury's contract with Comerica for providing federal benefits to beneficiaries who are not able to receive direct deposits. Given the widespread fraud that has been reported anecdotally to this office, I wanted to ask a few follow up questions:

To your knowledge, how many federal beneficiaries receive benefits through a Direct Express card?

How many reports of fraud involving Direct Express is the Office of Inspector General aware of? How many fraud investigations involving Direct Express cards are currently underway by the OIG?

How many investigations of fraud involving the Direct Express program has the OIG completed? Of those, how many investigations found that fraud had been committed? Without identifying any individual employees, what consequences resulted from those productive investigations?

What is the current status of the Dept. of Treasury's contract with Comerica to implement the Direct Express program?

If the contract was recently renewed, was the incidence of fraud in the Direct Express program, and Comerica's ability or lack thereof to address it considered when deciding to renew this contract? Were any additional fraud safeguards written into the contract?

Thank you for your attention to this email. I look forward to your response.

Michael Jackman, District Director, Office of Congressman Keating (MA-09)

Jackie had Jackman contact Delmar. Delmar continued to delay and delay the publication of the updated OIG report detailing the investigation and audit of Comerica Bank/Conduent. The report would be delayed (on purpose) for years. No one at OIG Treasury would publish anything critical about fellow Treasury employees, especially Santaniello or Brett Smith.

Social Security inserts were not in the envelope

Subject: Looks like the SSA insert has ceased
From: jbsimms
Date: Mon, Apr 06, 2020, 6:05 pm
To: Walter Bayer (SSA OIG)
Cc: Steven Lepper (CEO-Military Banks of America), Jackie Lynn
Dear Mr. Bayer,

Information was received from Ms. Densmore (copied) that the insert in the Social Security checks touting the Direct Express program was not found to be in the latest month's check payment. I do not know if this applies to the VA disability check, but that information will be obtained by Ms. Densmore (her brother-in-law receives VA benefits as well. An endorsement of the Direct Express program was printed on the envelope, but we will accept the ceasing of the inserts as a minor victory. Hopefully SSA finally sees that the Direct Express program victimizes recipients, and the mismanagement of the program by BFS and the Fiscal Agent is a disgrace.

We are interested in knowing if you or someone else at SSA were able to get the attention of Bureau of Fiscal Service to stop this practice of having the Direct Express inserts put into the envelopes.

Thank you for your attention during this long battle. Hopefully, you and SSA OIG will be able to publish a document to reflect your findings.

Sincerely, Jim

Wednesday, April 8, 2020

Subject: Your telephone call to OGIS
From: OGIS <OGIS@nara.gov>
Date: Wed, Apr 08, 2020 12:52 pm
To: OGIS <OGIS@nara.gov>
Cc: jbsimms
April 8, 2020
Re. OGIS Case 20-1690
J.B. Simms
jbsimms

Dear Mr. Simms:

This is in response to your recent call to the Office of Government Information Services (OGIS). I understand that you are frustrated with our April 1st response to you. To address your call, I reviewed OGIS's response to the information that you provided and determined that we responded to you in a manner that is consistent with our role as the FOIA ombudsman. It may be helpful to further explain OGIS's mandate and how we process inquiries that we receive. Congress created OGIS to complement existing FOIA practice and procedure; we strive to work in conjunction with the existing request and appeal process. OGIS has no investigatory or enforcement power, nor can we compel an agency to release documents. Participation in OGIS's mediation services is voluntary and both the requester and the agency must be willing to share information and discuss the relevant issues. We hope that this information is useful in understanding OGIS's response to your request. Although this may not be the outcome you anticipated, we hope that this information is useful. Thank you for bringing this matter to OGIS. At this time, it appears that there is no further assistance OGIS can offer, and we will take no further action at this time.

Sincerely, Martha Murphy, Deputy Director, OGIS,

Another FOI roadblock by another governmental bureaucrat

Subject: Your telephone call to OGIS
From: jbsimms
Date: Wed, Apr 08, 2020, 2:59 pm
To: "OGIS" <OGIS@nara.gov>
Cc: "Teresa Brady" <teresa.brady@nara.gov>, Jackie Lynn

Dear Ms. Murphy,

I was quite clear in my appeal to the refusal of OIG Treasury to abide by my FOI requests. I was also quite clear during my telephone conversation with Teresa Brady, who appeared to understand exactly the issues involved in the appeal, and the fact that three officials at OIG Treasury gave conflicting answers in an attempt to conceal information which had previously been said to be available via an FOI request.

OGIS has been copied on emails and anyone having a modicum of intelligence can understand and see that my claim is valid. My requests have exposed the lack of integrity of the federal employees involved in my attempt to exercise my legal right. This denial can be categorized as a denial of civil rights under color of authority, and if you are familiar with civil litigation, that defines another avenue of redress.

These people (Delmar, Sciurba, Altemus) have falsified information in an attempt to avoid responsibility and culpability. Your office, by failing to even lift a finger to execute the mandate that is your purpose, has now been lumped into the same irresponsible and defiant category as is the agency which defied my legal request. You, personally, have the contact information which would enable you to contact me as did Ms. Brady. It is beneath you to contact me for any clarification which seems to be the reason you are unilaterally dismissing this appeal?

Here are your options: you can either arrange a telephone interview with me or you can pass this email up the ladder to the director of OGIS. You have failed to do your job; it is up to someone else to do your job.

Your statement at the end of your email that the matter is over was a premature statement. If you think you can summarily dismiss this matter and that I will not challenge an obvious agenda of concealment, call Richard Delmar before you call me and you will have better prepared for our conversation.

Sincerely,
J.B. Simms

Ms. Murphy was as useless as the others government employees.

Tuesday, April 14, 2020

The issues switched from Comerica Bank to Social Security, the connection was Bureau of Fiscal Service. We could not determine who was controlling the check inserts advertising the Direct Express program.

Subject: The end of the inserts?
From: jbsimms
Date: Tue, Apr 14, 2020, 5:15 am
To: Walter Bayer (SSA OIG)
Cc: Jackie Lynn, Jennifer Kreeger, Franklin Lemond
Dear Walter,

Can you brief us on the developments on the communication between SSA and BFS which led to the cessation of the inserts placed into the VA and SSA recipient envelopes?
The cessation of the inserts is something I have been promoting for months. We all know the issues with BFS giving the contract to Comerica Bank and continuing to fail to have security measures on the Direct Express debit card and I appreciate you being receptive to these facts.
Be safe.
Jim

Subject: The end of the inserts?
From: Walter Bayer (Soc Sec OIG) (Soc Sec)
Date: Tue, Apr 14, 2020 6:33 am
To: jbsimms
Jim,
I am not sure what led to the changes cited below. The Agency has its own process for making decisions about mailers (as with other parts of its operations) and the OIG would not comment on such things unless it is part of something we release to the public, such as an audit or congressional response report. That said, as I noted earlier, I always pass along concerns from the public to the appropriate parties here.
Thanks,
Walt

Subject: The end of the inserts?
From: jbsimms
Date: Tue, Apr 14, 2020, 9:08 am
To: Walter Bayer (Soc Sec OIG) (Soc Sec)
Cc: Jackie Lynn, Steven Lepper (CEO-Military Banks of America), Franklin Lemond (Plaintiff's Attorney)
Thanks for passing along the concerns of the victims of the Direct Express program. We do wish SSA, and other agencies were a bit more transparent (nothing personal). You know I have seen the worst of the worst with the BFS and Comerica Bank contract and deals.
We would like to address SSA OIG and ask direct questions of administrators outside SSA OIG, but we will have to take you being the conduit hoping they understand that SSA (as VA realized) does have a responsibility to protect recipients, even if it means SSA confront BFS.
Thanks again.
Jim

Social Security was not motivated to help. The Social Security website along with the inserts direct and even pressure SSA recipients to use the Direct Express Debit Card. They ignored the federal court filings and continued to support Comerica Bank as the Fiscal Agent.
What was the motive for supporting this corrupt program?

Thursday, April 16, 2020

We received this from Franklin this morning:

I haven't made a motion to extend discovery due to the virus just yet. We have until September to complete the initial phase of discovery. I've been meeting & conferring with opposing counsel regarding their discovery responses and pushing back against the insufficient subpoena responses as well.
If we were to ask for more time now, it would likely fall on deaf ears as the judge would likely say come talk to me closer to the deadline if you can't complete everything in the next five months.

We have to fight the government, our lawyer, and now we fight a damned virus.
Delmar was sending me to the Treasury Hotline to communicate my FOI requests. Very funny.

Monday, April 20, 2020

From: "Jackman, Michael" <Michael.Jackman@mail.house.gov>
Date: April 20, 2019, at 2:47:25 PM EDT
To: Jackie Lynn
Subject: FW: Treasury Direct Express - Inspector General action
Jackie – please see attached Treasury OIG's response to my inquiry. Please note that the final selection for the Direct Express vendor will be made by May 17, 2019.

We knew the naming of the Fiscal Agent would be soon. Santaniello refused to allow Jackie and me to approach the people at BFS who made that decision.
There would be a big surprise for everyone.

Tuesday, April 21, 2020

Social Security was hiding information about a hack into my Social Security account. If I had not gone to the Social Security office to question insurance coverage, I would have never found out I had been hacked. My information was being used by someone thirty miles from my residence in Fresno, CA.

Many emails were sent to Walter Bayer and Sara Lizama, both of SSA OIG. The FOI that I sent to Social Security was basically ignored. Someone at SSA allowed an unauthorized person to change my address. Fraud was the purpose.
SSA is refusing to tell me how this was done (phone, email, telephone).

Wednesday, April 22, 2020

Subject: Fee Notice: SSA-2020-002424
From: no-reply@foiaonline.gov
Date: Wed, Apr 29, 2020 6:34 am
To: jbsimms
Mr. Simms:
Thank you for your FOIA request, SSA-2020-002424. Attached is the fee notice applicable to your FOIA request. Please respond within 10 business days, as stated within the attached notice.
Sincerely,
The FOIA Team
Social Security Administration

SSA wanted me to pay for an FOI request.

Subject: Response I received was not applicable to my request RE 2020-001896
From: jbsimms
Date: Wed, Apr 22, 2020, 7:05 am
To: "^FOIA Public Liaison" <FOIA.Public.Liaison@ssa.gov>
Cc: Walter Bayer (SSA OIG), Sarah Lizama (Soc Sec OIG)
Dear SSA FOIA Liaison worker,
I just received an email denying my FOI request because someone decided that I needed to enlist in some type of group of persons submitting FOI requests. You people have had my FOI request for months, and this has been passed from person to person in an attempt to dissuade me from continuing to advocate my rights to this information.
This email was a "no reply" email which shows over cowardice on your part. You know you will not be able to converse with me without me exposing the lack of integrity and corruption in your agency. You know I requested this information in the proper manner, and now you want to make me think you can change the rules whenever you want.
It is unfortunate that Mr. Bayer and Ms. Lizama have to be exposed to such incredibly corrupt behavior. Both have known about my request for the information I requested, and the SSA is covering for inept employees who allowed my identity to be compromised.
I will put forth the challenge again for someone from your office to contact me via telephone. I am familiar with corruption in the public sector, and you people are a good example of corruption and cover-up. You know who allowed my address to be changed and how it was done. This same person can be part of another corrupt

criminal group which deals with identity fraud. You are so corrupt that you will cover for a criminal employee rather than protect citizens.

My request was made. Have a GS-14 or above to contact me and we will see what happens.

J.B. Simms

Subject: I received was not applicable to my request RE 2020-001896
From: ^FOIA Public Liaison <FOIA.Public.Liaison@ssa.gov>
Date: Wed, Apr 22, 2020, 12:02 pm
To: jbsimms

Mr. Simms:

Your request for a "copy of the investigation by SSA with regard to [fraud on your account] HOW the fraud was attempted, as well as the time. For example, if the contact with SSA was by email at 10:35 a.m., that would be an answer" is being processed under FOIA request SSA-2020-002424. Your first request was handled as a Privacy Act request. We now understand you are requesting a copy of an OIG report; therefore, we will handle your request under the FOIA. Thank you for your patience and understanding.

Thank you, The FOIA Team SSA

This was an exercise in futility. SSA was not going to give me any information regarding how my SSA account was hacked. I had the address used by the person. SSA was protecting themselves from me.

Thursday, April 23, 2020

Subject: Response I received was not applicable to my request RE 2020-001896
From: jbsimms
Date: Thu, Apr 23, 2020 7:16 am
To: "^FOIA Public Liaison" <FOIA.Public.Liaison@ssa.gov>
Cc: Jackie Lynn

Thank you for your reply and it appears someone is beginning to understand the nature of the inquiry. My address was changed and SSA is protecting the manner in which it was changed. I have sent police reports from two agencies to SSA and a prudent person would think that an investigation into this matter would have begun. If it happened to me, it would be happening to others, and if an SSA employee is facilitating fraud and being criminally rewarded by a third party, that should have been investigated. Remember, I conducted criminal investigations for over 25 years, and I know when I "smell a rat."

Let's see if SSA will police their own people or hide them.

J.B. Simms

Wednesday, April 29, 2020

Subject: Fee Notice: SSA-2020-002424
From: no-reply@foiaonline.gov
Date: Wed, April 29, 2020 6:34 am
To: jbsimms

Mr. Simms:

Thank you for your FOIA request, SSA-2020-002424. Attached is the fee notice applicable to your FOIA request. Please respond within 10 business days, as stated within the attached notice.

Please do not reply to this email correspondence, i.e., to this email address. If you have an account with FOIA online, you can correspond directly with us by logging into your account. If you need to correspond with us regarding your FOIA request but do not have an account with FOIA online, please send your correspondence to FOIA.Public.Liaison@ssa.gov. The FOIA Public Liaison mailbox was created to assist the public with their FOIA requests, as well as to provide assistance to individuals requesting access to their own records under the Privacy Act. When you email this mailbox, we encourage you to limit the amount of personally identifiable information you provide in your email correspondence. While SSA operates within a secure network, we have no control of the data we receive while it is in transit to or from our FOIA Public Liaison mailbox. Please include your FOIA tracking number in your email.

Sincerely,

The FOIA Team, Social Security Administration

SSA wanted me to pay for the report. I convinced Franklin Lemond to pay for a number of these SSA reports. He must have paid a few thousand dollars.

Subject: Fee Notice: SSA-2020-002424]
From: jbsimms
Date: Wed, Apr 29, 2020 6:20 pm
To: Walter Bayer (SSA OIG)
Cc: Franklin Lemond (Plaintiff's Attorney) , Jackie Lynn; "^FOIA Liaison"
<FOIA.Public.Liaison@ssa.gov>, Sarah Lizama (Soc Sec OIG)
Dear Mr. Bayer,
I am writing you and forwarding a copy of a letter I was emailed by Ms. Zimmerman of SSA.
My request was simple; I asked for the method which was illegally used to change my address on my account with the Social Security Administration. As I remember, the change was made on June 29, 2018 and I caught the fraud on July 3, 2018.
After first requesting to know the method used to illegally change my address (email, telephone, text, regular mail, etc.) Sarah Lizama directed me to another woman who refused to give me the information. During the interim, over the past 18 months, I have continued to pursue the answer which I am entitled.
I continued to ask for the information.
After submitting an FOI request to SSA, the request was denied. Again, I pursued it.
I want you to read the letter from Ms. Zimmerman and read it very carefully. Ms. Zimmerman is trying to make me believe that the "work" necessary to look at my account and derive how an address change was made took the combined efforts of people needing 29 hours of work to make a 20 second inquiry on my account.
All the reviews and consultations being made by the FOI section at SSA, comprising the 29 hours, can only be equated to an "CYA" meeting (please pardon the acronym but it was the only accurate explanation for 29 hours of consultation).
There appears to be a few things that are evident:
(1) SSA created a fraudulent invoice in the amount of $1,444.00 in order to discourage me from seeing how and/or who at SSA allowed my address to be fraudulently changed.
(2) The fee of $1,444.00 is mere retribution for my vigilance in this matter. I have been refused at least twice by SSA FOI and they, including Ms. Zimmerman, do not like citizens to make them accountable. Ms. Zimmerman is culpable in this cover-up and her attempt to illegally extort a fee from me that is not only outrageous, illegal, and without merit falls directly at her feet.
You and I have communicated for over a year with respect to other fraud matters, and you have been gained my respect for your candor and receptiveness to my advocacy for scores of persons subjected to the Direct Express program and its association with SSA. I wanted you to have firsthand knowledge of what is going on at SSA FOI, and I ask that you present this matter to SSI OIG for consideration.
It took 29 hours to do a 20 second inquiry.
It does not take a person having my professional background to see something inappropriate, but my professional background does afford me a bit more insight into suspicious behavior which those at SSA FOI have exhibited.
I will be appealing this to whomever is necessary.
Sincerely,
Jim Simms

Paying SSA $1,444.00 to tell me how my SSA account was hacked was ridiculous. SSA knew I was after them regarding the Direct Express matter.

In a later email to Ms. Zimmerman, I told her "[T]he ball is now in your court. Your motive is transparent, and your argument is without merit. Send this challenge to your fee "up the ladder" and I will be glad to make my case on a conference call with you being present for questioning."

Thursday, April 30, 2020

Subject: FOIA Appeal SSA-2020-002580 Submitted]
From: jbsimms
Date: Thu, Apr 30, 2020, 6:30 am

To: Walter Bayer (SSA OIG)
Cc: Franklin Lemond (Plaintiff's Attorney), Jackie Lynn
Dear Mr. Bayer,

I just now received the email below noting my challenge and appeal to the $1,444.00 fee for alleged 29 hours of work to expose the nature of the fraud on my account. I know you have more to do than attend to my sole dispute with SSA FOI and SSA employees, but this fraud appears to be the "smoke" from which a fire exists within SSA. The attempt by Mary Ann Zimmerman to make me believe SSA FOI spent 29 hours to do a 20 second inquiry was ludicrous.

I am not being difficult; I am a citizen who has connected dots for more years than most of these SSA workers have been alive, and God help those who do not have my experience.

Let's see what happens. Your office at SSA OIG might want to take a close look at the operation of SSA FOI and the denials of information requested. I believe you have a problem in SSA FOI.

The only reason I am getting attention is because I am not going to let them do this to me, and I will help others as I did with the fraud within the Direct Express program.

Jim

SSA wanted $1,444.00 for a report that they should give for free?

Subject: FOIA Appeal SSA-2020-002580 Submitted]
From: Walter Bayer (Soc Sec OIG) (Soc Sec)
Date: Thu, Apr 30, 2020 8:38 am
To: jbsimms

Mr. Simms,

I can certainly share your concerns about the FOIA process with the folks here (and attach it to your original issue so everyone has the full story).

I cannot remember – did SSA-OIG (other than me) ever reach out to you about the original concern or only SSA?

Thanks,
Walt

Subject: FOIA Appeal SSA-2020-002580 Submitted]
From: jbsimms
Date: Thu, Apr 30, 2020 12:56 pm
To: Walter Bayer (Soc Sec OIG) (Soc Sec)

Dear Walt,

Thank you for being receptive to this.

I visited the SSA office in Fresno CA on July 3, 2018. I was told the address on my driver license was not the same as was on my account. The clerk told me my address on my account was changed on June 29, 2018, five days before I visited the SSA office.

The clerk was kind enough to help me with information to establish an online account. When I raced back to my apartment, I went online and found the fraudulent address on my account, and I changed it.

I simply want to know HOW this change was made:

Email

Regular mail

Telephone

Visit to a different SSA office.

Or maybe a corrupt SSA employee facilitated a criminal (making the SSA employee a criminal) by changing my address, enabling the fraudster to contact Direct Express to have a new card issued and the fraudster would receive the new card before the next SS payment.

This is how some of the fraud is happening. People have had their addresses changed at SS and only SS employees can make this happen.

I had not established a My Social Security Account, so the change could not be done from that portal.

Mary Ann Zimmerman wants to charge me $1,444 for the information on MY account showing how the change was made, and it took Zimmerman's staff 29 hours to find the input information. First of all, a third grader could do this. Secondly, Zimmerman cannot use the excuse of a long-time frame when I have been asking for an investigation into this from the date it happened.

*My requests were denied more than once. FOI requests were denied. I kept on, and finally got a reply.
There is a huge problem at SSA at FOI. Zimmerman is hiding the truth. Without making accusations, my money
says SSA employee(s) are engaged with criminals and are being paid to change addresses so new debit cards
can be mailed to the new address, then the monies taken from the new card before the rightful cardholder can
try to use his card. Believe me, that story has come across my desk.
I did notice that the BFS insert was not in the latest SSA check envelope. That is a good thing, and progress.
Hopefully you or someone in your office can bring in Zimmerman and qualify the 29 hours and $1,444 fee she
wants to charge me.
Be safe. Wash your hands.
Jim*

Friday, May 1, 2020

*Subject: no inserts? good
From: jbsimms
Date: Fri, May 01, 2020 5:43 am
To: Walter Bayer (SSA OIG), Steven Lepper (CEO-Military Banks of America), Jackie Lynn; Franklin
Lemond (Plaintiff's Attorney)
Cc: Richard Delmar (OIG Treasury)
Good Morning.
I will be travelling today, en route to CA.
Jackie Densmore told me yesterday that there was no insert in the envelope of checks of VA and SSA recipients
distributed by BFS. There have been no inserts for the past 2 months. I hope this is the new normal, and that
BFS has ceased touting the Direct Express program.
I am not privy to any input of communication any of you had with BFS and Santaniello in addition to everyone
reading my disgust with the practice. Regardless, let's hope the inserts have ended and we can direct as many
people as possible from the Direct Express program to a different financial institution for deposits.
Santaniello has not contacted me to tell me that BFS ceased the insertion of the inserts, and I am not waiting for
his call.
Thank you all for supporting my efforts (and those of Jackie) to stop the inserts. The public, including our
veterans, need protection from BFS.
Jim*

If we could stop the inserts used by VA and SSA endorsing the Direct Express program, that was our goal.

Tuesday, May 5, 2020

*Subject: RE: Your telephone call to OGIS
From: jbsimms
Date: Tue, May 05, 2020, 9:25 am
To: "OGIS" <OGIS@nara.gov>
Cc: Jackie Lynn; "Teresa Brady"
<teresa.brady@nara.gov>, Richard Delmar (OIG Treasury),
Loren Sciurba (OIG Treasury), Amy Altemus (OIG Treasury)
Dear Ms. Murphy,
Below you will find copies of correspondence between us. The fact remains I have to legitimate FOI requests
having been submitted to OIG Treasury which are being blocked. The only purported justification for blocking
these requests is semantics, which is not a valid defense. Officials have chosen to equate a previously defined
exercise as an investigation and are now trying to use their version of a synonym of the word investigation
(process, inquiry, etc) to block me from two reports which were said to be available to me upon a level of
completion.
These two reports were promised to be available to me by Ms. Altemus and Ms. Scott. After submitting the FOI
requests, Mr. Sciurba and Mr. Delmar changed the narrative and now are denying access. Mr. Sciurba lied to
me and to FOI Treasury when he stated the "investigation" conducted by Ms. Altemus did not exist. He has
since recanted, stating the work performed by Ms. Altemus was not an investigation. Mr. Delmar concealed Ms.
Scott's investigation by stating that the investigation being conducted by Ms. Scott was a "process" and was to
supplement Treasury OIG 19-041 which was reported in preliminary form in July 2019.*

While my email relationship with Mr. Delmar has been contentious, candid, but quite civil, the revelation of this cover-up has resulted in a defensive posture. I find this quite disappointing.

Mr. Sciurba, on the other hand, has been found to defend and turn a blind eye to reported corruption within the Bureau of Fiscal Service, which has been interpreted as a lack of credibility. A person does not need to wear an expensive watch to know the time, and the time for honesty is now.

In early November 2019 Ms. Densmore and I were scheduled to have a conference call with Ms. Scott, and at the last moment this conference call was cancelled with no explanation after I submitted a syllabus of matters to be discussed.

This pattern of disingenuous behavior by officials at OIG Treasury is to be considered as you receive communication with regard to my FOI requests. We are not hiding from these people. They are defensive because no one has made them accountable until now.

If you call me as did Ms. Brady, you might get a better understanding of the gravity of this matter. Not only have Ms. Densmore and I been betrayed by government officials by their attempt at creative rhetoric, but they are also continuing to allow lack of accountability by employees within Treasury which can only be viewed as an incestuous relationship as they withhold the family secrets.

You can reach me at (803) 309-6850. Email me if you wish and we will schedule a conference.

Sincerely,

J.B. Simms

Updated Treasury Report 19-041 being delayed

From: jbsimms
Sent: Tuesday, May 5, 2020, 10:56 AM
To: Delmar, Richard K. (OIG Treasury)
Cc: Jackie Lynn
Subject: 19-041

Dear Mr. Delmar,

Please pardon me for what might appear to be intrusive during this time of turmoil, but can you tell us when the final version of Treasury 19-041 will be published? I looked at the index online and could see no final report. While my response to the report which was published 10 months ago was greeted with debate, the issues I raised have yet to be directly addressed.

We do hope you and your staff remain virus free so we may personally address all people involved in this investigation.

Hopefully this request will be greeted with more enthusiasm than the pending FOI requests I have submitted to your office.

Sincerely,

J.B. Simms

The missing FOI request

Subject: RE: Your telephone call to OGIS
From: jbsimms
Date: Tue, May 05, 2020, 11:29 am
To: "OGIS" <OGIS@nara.gov>
Cc: Jackie Lynn; "Teresa Brady" <teresa.brady@nara.gov>, Richard Delmar (OIG Treasury), Loren Sciurba (OIG Treasury), Amy Altemus (OIG Treasury) , Sonja Scott (OIG Treasury)

Dear Ms. Murphy,

If you question my veracity or challenge my assumptions with regard to the lack of integrity by officials at Treasury, take a look at the attached document. The attached document is a list of FOI requests for the first quarter of 2020. On Page 23 you see an entry for FOI Request 2020-03-070 by me, James Simms, requesting a copy of the investigation overseen by Ms. Sonja Scott (which Ms. Scott stated I would be entitled to at the publication of OIG Treas 19-041).

What you do not see in this attachment is the listing of FOI Request 2020-02-023 which is the investigation of dozens of fraud reports reported by victims to me during 2018. Reference to 2020-02-023 should be listed on Page 10 but is missing. The fraud incidents perpetrated upon my Direct Express account were part of this investigation, and as with Ms. Scott, Ms. Amy Altemus assured me I would be privy to the result of the investigation into my personal account. Mr. Loren Sciurba took it upon himself to deny the investigation took

place in an attempt to keep me from getting the information I was promised and am entitled. This is the type of people we are dealing with.
FOI Treasury failed to list FOI Request 2020-02-023 for a reason.
I would think that this additional revelation not only justifies my assertions but would motivate you to give me a call so we can discuss this matter.
Sincerely,
J.B. Simms

From: Richard Delmar (OIG Treasury))
Date: Tue, May 05, 2020 2:42 pm
To: jbsimms
Cc: Jackie Lynn
Mr. Simms: The final version will report Treasury OIG's findings re the financial agent's customer service and compliance with Regulation E. We expect that this report will be posted this summer.
Rich Delmar
Deputy Inspector General
Department of the Treasury

Spoiler alert: It is now April 2023 and Delmar still had not published the report. Above you see he promised the report would come out during the summer of 2020.

Word games again: investigation, audit, process

Subject: RE: 19-041
From: Richard Delmar (OIG Treasury)
Date: Tue, May 05, 2020, 5:35 pm
To: jbsimms
Cc: Jackie Lynn
As we have explained previously, sir, it is not an investigation. It's an audit. Distinct work products, conducted by distinct categories of personnel, in separate offices within the OIG.
And as I have also explained previously, Mr. Simms, please understand that Mr. Sciurba has not misled you or engaged in any improper behavior. I strongly advise you to cease your unfounded accusations against him.
Rich Delmar
Deputy Inspector General
Department of the Treasury

Date: Tue, May 05, 2020, 7:40 pm
To: Richard Delmar (OIG Treasury))
Cc: Jackie Lynn
Dear Mr. Delmar,
It has been clear from the beginning that the work product of Ms. Scott is the result of an "investigation" and I promise you I will find that definitive language in emails between Ms. Scott and me. I specifically differentiated between an investigation and an audit, and Ms. Scott's investigation was to be made available to me upon the publication of the audit. The investigation conducted by Ms. Scott was to be incorporated in the audit.
My first complaint after reading 14-031 and 17-034 was made to Paulette Battle, as you know. I believe this was February 26, 2018 (no cheating here, off the cuff, and I believe I am correct). Conversations with Ms. Battle and Ms. Scott have confirmed the fact that the "investigation" which was to have been performed and included in the aforementioned audits was insufficient. There is a difference between an audit and an investigation, and the investigation was faulty. I can only assume you agreed to some extent because OIG 19-041 was commissioned.
Ms. Altemus, along with Ms. Scott, advised me that their investigation would be available for me to read. Since Ms. Altemus' investigation involved 30 of the victims taken from the list of 105 I submitted to Ms. Scott, I would only be privy to the investigation of my particular fraud experience, as well as any part of the report which could be deemed "common to all victims" to include a preface, introduction, summation, procedure, recommendation, or any part of Ms. Altemus' report which does not reveal proprietary information of any victim information which is not mine.

As for Mr. Sciurba, the fact that he took it upon himself to defend the unethical behavior of Thomas Santaniello in the face of covert negotiations between BFS and Comerica Bank, then made what appears to be a false statement when he stated for the record that the information I requested from Ms. Altemus did not exist, leaves little to discern the intent and the agenda of Mr. Sciurba. I assume he would not treat you with condescending contempt as he has me, but he does this to me because he thinks he can and thinks that I have no recourse.

If you wish to continue to deny the differentiation between an investigation and audit, and the fact that the information from the investigation is incorporated into the audit, let me know now. I will produce "chapter and verse" from emails confirming my assertion as fact, as well as the witness who sent the emails.

At this point, I will give you my word not to copy this email to anyone except Ms. Densmore until I receive your reply. All I ask is that the investigation conducted by Ms. Scott and Ms. Altemus, as agreed, be forwarded to me upon the publication of 19-041.

I understand this matter has been put on the back burner since the viurs, and that your department is quite busy. I simply ask for a bit of honesty and sincerity from you, if from no one else.

Sincerely,

J.B. Simms

Wednesday, May 13, 2020

Delmar admits "investigating" misconduct in 2018 email

Jackie Lynn
Wed, May 13, 10:18 AM
to me
On Fri, Sep 14, 2018, at 11:11 AM Delmar, Richard K. (OIG Treasury) wrote:
Treasury OIG has been reviewing how BFS and Comerica have executed the Direct Express program for several years and has identified problems and recommended corrections in that execution.

*We continue to conduct those reviews, as well as actively investigating allegations of misconduct involving the program. To clarify, our previous Direct Express work was focused on BFS' efforts to award the FAAs and not on the details of fraud monitoring and customer service. Our new audit and investigative work focus **on issues raised by Mr. Simms and Ms. Densmore**. Mr. Simms's criticism to the contrary, our prior work, as all our work, complied with all GAO and CIGIE standards, and is objective and independent, as the Inspector General Act requires.*

Rich Delmar
Counsel to the Inspector General
Department of the Treasury

They will focus on "…[i]ssues raised by Mr. Simms and Ms. Densmore."

Subject: the kill shot
From: jbsimms
Date: Wed, May 13, 2020, 10:34 am
To: Franklin Lemond (Plaintiff's Attorney)
Cc: Jackie Lynn
Franklin,
I looked into my emails and found this one.
OIG Treas is denying the existence of investigations, referring to them as a process, inquiry, etc.
I will explain the issues tomorrow and hope you will be able to help.Jim

Sonja Scott left Treasury Investigative Division

Subject: the Investigative division
From: jbsimms
Date: Wed, May 13, 2020 1:48 pm
To: Franklin Lemond (Plaintiff's Attorney)
Cc: Jackie Lynn
Check out the menu on the left side of the home page for OIG Treasury.
There, right in front of you, is the Investigative division.

This is what Sciurba and Delmar state does not exist.
The investigations are sent to the Audit.
By the way, Jackie and I saw an email sent to victim by Sonja Scott. She is no longer working on the Hotline in the investigative division. Odd.

The "investigative division" conducts "investigations" and not audits. The audit division conducts audits.

Thursday, May 14, 2020

From: jbsimms
Sent: Thursday, May 14, 2020
To: Scott, Sonja L. <ScottS@oig.treas.gov>
Cc: Delmar, Richard K. (OIG Treasury); Loren Sciurba (OIG Treasury); Jackie Lynn; Kate Berry (American Banker); Katherine Johnson (OIG Treasury); Thomas Santaniello (Treasury Bur of Fisc Svc)
Subject: Ignoring the obvious
Dear Ms. Scott,
It was brought to my attention that you are leaving your investigative position at OIG Treasury. Hope you will remember Jackie and me in your next job.
As with the more than 100 persons who have reached out to me to interpret the crimes which are evident upon examining their statements, it is quite clear that the Fraud Department of Conduent is far from competent as they "determine" the validity of a fraud claim.
You see that Mr. Colburn's statement reflects transactions from China. During discussions with Mr. Colburn, he never indicated he has been in China or makes transactions with Chinese companies. As is the pattern with Conduent Fraud Division (Shantelle Johnson), admissions that their department examine previous transactions to invalidate the fraud claim.
It is quite clear that the investigation by your office of the Fraud Unit of Conduent will expose not only a failure by that office to perform in a logical and intelligent manner, but also expose that since Thomas Santaniello of BFS allowed Comerica Bank to be awarded the new Fiscal Agent contract, Mr. Santaniello and his "Evaluation Team" need be investigated to determine the exact parameters of the concessions made by Comerica Bank to Mr. Santaniello and his group in order for the contract to be approved.
Unless Mr. Colburn is purchasing exotic Asian aphrodisiacs from China using his Direct Express card, I see no validity in these transactions.
My best to you in your endeavors. Feel free to forward this to your successor. It has been quite an adventure engaging with you.
Sincerely,
Jim

Subject: Ignoring the obvious
From: Sonja Scott (OIG Treasury)
Date: Thu, May 14, 2020, 12:20 pm
To: jbsimms
Good afternoon. Just a clarification - I am not leaving Treasury OIG. I am just no longer responsible for complaints. Sonja
ASAC Sonja L. Scott, CFE
US Department of Treasury
Office of the Inspector General
Office of Investigations

Delmar wanted all complaints to go to the hotline. That is like the "dead letter office.

Subject: RE: Ignoring the obvious
From: Sonja Scott (OIG Treasury)
Date: Thu, May 14, 2020, 12:39 pm
To: jbsimms
Cc: Jackie Lynn
Direct Express complaints will go to the hotline like other complaints.

Tuesday, May 19, 2020

Santaniello is exposed and unethical, refusing to answer a subpoena

J B Simms
Tue, May 19, 8:15 AM
to Franklin, Jackie
Franklin,
I just texted Jackie and am sharing.
Jackie figures Santaniello is talking to Arpin, and we have to wonder "WHO" else at Comerica he is talking to.
"We need a motion to compel to make Santaniello answer the subpoena. The more pressure we put on Santaniello, the sooner that news will be trickle down to Comerica. There will be communication between Santaniello and Comerica that they will not want us to see."
I assume (hopefully) Santaniello or someone at the OIG (Delmar) should have responded by now.
Thanks
Hope the meeting goes well.
We push from other angles.

Franklin never pushed Santaniello.

A formal complaint filed against Sciurba with the Maryland Bar Association

J B Simms
May 19, 2020, 8:57 AM
to Jackie, Kate
Loren Sciurba, an atty at Office of Special Counsel at OIG Treasury lied in order to keep me from getting information as a result of an FOI request. He also defends Santaniello at BFS. A formal complaint has been filed at the Maryland Bar Grievance Committee and they should receive the physical grievance on Thursday morning. The USPS will deliver the complaint to their office, virus or no virus. Let's see what Sciurba has to say about that. He is a dirt bag (you can substitute another "d" word for dirt).
Thanks for staying in touch.
Jim

I had dealt with filing complaints against attorneys with their respective bar associations. I did not expect much, except more lies from Sciurba.

Friday, May 21, 2020

A settlement offer was made. Of course, Chally ignored this.

Chally had no intention of settling. Comerica would rather pay Chally than pay victims.

Re: Carnley, et al. v. Conduent Business Services, LLC, et al.
Case No. 5:19-cv-01075-XR (W.D. Tex.)
Dear Jon and Adam:
I am writing on behalf of Plaintiffs Joe Almon, Jon Carnley, Cynthia Clark, Jackie Densmore, Jennifer Kreegar, Harold McPhail, Kathleen Paglia, JB Simms, and Kenneth Tillman ("Plaintiffs") in connection with the aforementioned matter. This is a confidential settlement communication subject to all protections, including those set forth in Federal Rule of Evidence 408.
While Plaintiffs disagree with your suggestion that Defendants properly investigated and resolved the complaints regarding the fraudulent transactions on their accounts and strongly believe that class certification is likely in this matter, they recognize the uncertainty inherent in litigation. Therefore, I have been authorized to convey an offer of settlement on behalf of the individual Plaintiffs only. My clients are willing to dismiss their claims, with prejudice, in exchange for $1,500,000. This offer is subject to the negotiation of a settlement agreement and release acceptable to Plaintiffs.
I look forward to hearing from you.
Sincerely,
E. Adam Webb

Sunday, May 24, 2020

Jackie is involved in trying to get Bayer to do something.

Jackie Lynn
Sun, May 24, 9:40 PM
to Walter. Bayer, me
Hello Mr. Bayer,
I hope you are doing ok and staying healthy during this difficult time.
During this time, it has given me a lot of time to think and review old emails. I am following up on an email you sent me regarding the Direct Express audit. I was wondering if you had a completion date yet. I am also wondering how you are currently handling and fraud reports. Treasury has a hotline set up do you have the same or a different one or does your agency direct them to the hotline? If so, what is the number to the hotline and what company mans these calls?
JB and I have been getting an alarming number of calls lately well more than normal and I am just wondering where I can send these poor victims. I think what is going on in the world is creating a shortage of call centers reps or they are working from home and not having the calls monitored - I have been hearing horror stories. Any help would greatly be appreciated!
Jackie Densmore

Monday, May 25, 2020

Subject: Subpoenas and FOI Requests
From: jbsimms
Date: Mon, May 25, 2020 7:52 am
To: Richard Delmar (OIG Treasury),Loren Sciurba (OIG Treasury)
Cc: Jackie Lynn, Amy Altemus (OIG Treasury) , "Michael Jackman" <michael.jackman@mail.house.gov>, "Kate Berry" Kate Berry (American Banker)
Dear Mr. Delmar and Mr. Sciurba,
While we as victims of the Direct Express program and the Bureau of Fiscal Service have experienced denials of investigations by Mr. Sciurba and semantics by you to conceal developing information which was previously a acknowledged and its content be delivered to us upon request, I remind you that not only is your office ignoring FOI requests but your office as well as Thomas Santaniello of BFS are ignoring lawfully served subpoenas as well which have served upon US Treasury.
I am attaching said subpoenas for your pleasure.
The compliance by you and Mr. Santaniello will be appreciated.
Sincerely,
J.B. Simms

I attached the subpoena to the email. We had to keep pushing.

Subject: Addressing outstanding subpoena
From: jbsimms
Date: Mon, May 25, 2020, 11:24 am
To: Walter Bayer (SSA OIG)
Cc: Jackie Lynn
Dear Walt,
Independent from the failure of SSA to abide by my FOI request, attempting to charge me $1,444.00 to reveal information about the hack of my account, there appears to be another issue at hand.
A subpoena was served upon SSA probably in February 2020. It is now the end of May, 4 months later.
I see no compliance by SSA with respect to this subpoena.
Can you look into this?
Thank you.
Sincerely,
Jim Simms
 Subpoena - OIG - SSA - 2020.pdf

SSA and Bureau of Fiscal Service ignored the subpoenas. Franklin did not pursue the matter. This made Jackie and me pretty angry.

Tuesday May 26, 2020
Subject: the director of the Direct Express call center- Marquita Stevenson
From: jbsimms
Date: Tue, May 26, 2020, 8:59 am
To: Franklin Lemond (Plaintiff's Attorney)
Cc: Jackie Lynn
Dear Franklin,
Jackie found Marquita Stevenson as the director of the Direct Express call center of Conduent.
She is not qualified. Unbelievable. She never worked for a bank. She has been at Conduent 4 years and knows what is happening. She is a Bible thumper, but she should not have this job.
Subpoena her and hit her hard.

Wednesday, May 27, 2020

This was an email from 18 months ago. Sonja Scott believed she could help us with the Bureau of Fiscal Service. She could not.

Subject: DE Issues
From: Sonja Scott (OIG Treasury)
Date: Tue, November 27, 2018, 6:11 am
To: "'roussinkenneth@att.net'" <roussinkenneth@att.net>
Cc: 'Jackie Lynn' , jbsimms
We have received your complaint and have forwarded to the Bureau of Fiscal Service who oversees the DE Program. We have had very good success when working with the BFS in getting these matters resolved. Sonja
ASAC Sonja L. Scott
US Department of Treasury
Office of the Inspector General
Office of Investigations

Advising Delmar that this book would be written

Subject: Transparency and GAO 17-176
From: jbsimms
Date: Wed, May 27, 2020, 12:59 pm
To: Richard Delmar (OIG Treasury)
Cc: Loren Sciurba (OIG Treasury), Amy Altemus (OIG Treasury), Sonja Scott (OIG Treasury), Jackie Lynn, Kate Berry (American Banker), Steven Lepper (CEO-Military Banks of America), Michael Clements (US Gen Acct Office) Joe Plenzler (Wounded Warriors)
Dear Mr. Delmar,
As I begin writing the book addressing the connections between persons at BFS, Comerica Bank, and the Direct Express program (title/isbn has been registered and cover prototype has been developed) I am explaining to the readers how the three OIG Treasury reports (14-031, 17-034, and 19-041(preliminary) were pretty much ignored by the "Evaluation Team" at BFS, as was GAO Report 17-176.
I doubt I will be reaching out to a Treasury employee for quotes. There is plenty information to be gleaned from emails.
I have one question, and that relates to a quote from GAO 17-176, page 18. Mr. Clements wrote:
"Although Treasury publicly discloses the total amount of compensation paid to Fiscal Service's financial agents in its annual budget submissions, it does not provide more detailed information about these financial agents in a central location, such as on its website. For example, Treasury does not fully disclose in a central location the number of Fiscal Service's active financial agency agreements, the types of services provided to Fiscal Service under the agreements, and the amount of compensation paid to each financial agent for its services. Treasury officials told us that it is not required to and has not determined the need to publicly disclose Fiscal Service's financial agency agreements on its website. In contrast, Treasury's Office of Financial Stability has provided on its public website copies of the 27 financial agency agreements that it entered into to manage

the Troubled Asset Relief Program and the amount obligated to compensate each agent. According to Treasury officials, the Office of Financial Stability made its financial agency agreements available to the public based on a policy decision to promote the Troubled Asset Relief Program's transparency."

Since the Treasury website and/or that of Fiscal Service continues to withhold disclosure of Fiscal Service financial agency agreements on its website, can you enlighten us as to the contemplation to withhold said information and the "determination" made which prohibits Direct Express cardholder victims to enjoy full disclosure?

I am interested to know why this information is being withheld by you and was by your predecessor. The need for transparency is obvious; there should be no benefit to any person to withhold this information. With all due respect, it is a bit arrogant and condescending for any employee of Treasury to "determine the need to publicly disclose" information relative to a program which disburses funds to citizens, including disabled veterans.

Sincerely, J.B. Simms

I had to vent. If we were able to get the GAO to conduct another investigation, things would have been different. These people had no conscience.

Blocked from addressing the Evaluation Team against Comerica Bank

Subject: The FASP and BFS
From: jbsimms
Date: Wed, May 27, 2020, 4:24 pm
To: Thomas Santaniello (Bureau of Fiscal Service)
Cc: Loren Sciurba (OIG Treasury), Jackie Lynn; "Kate Berry" Kate Berry (American Banker), Michael Clements (US Gen Acct Office) Steven Lepper (CEO-Military Banks of America), Walter Bayer (SSA OIG)

Dear Mr. Santaniello,

During the process of working on the manuscript of the upcoming book, I am reviewing reports from OIG Treasury and GAO.

Below is an outtake from GAO 17-176, Page 21, by Michael Clements.

"The guidance divides the process into four phases: (1) initiation of the FASP, (2) publication of a financial agent solicitation, (3) selection of the best proposal submitted by a financial institution, and (4) designation of the financial institution as a financial agent."

During Phase 3 of the most recent section of the Fiscal Agent for the Direct Express program, Jackie Densmore and I petitioned the Bureau of Fiscal Service in an attempt to address what was said to be an "Evaluation Team" (a group of persons yet to be identified, verified, or validated). This petition, in the form of an email sent to you in the spring of 2019 during the part of the process announced by BFS which the Evaluation Team would be entertaining oral presentations from prospective bidders."

Upon submitting this petition, you took it upon yourself to shield this deliberative group from any input from any victim of Comerica Bank, Conduent, and Bureau of Fiscal Service. You denied both Ms. Densmore and myself of the opportunity to go on record with the truth about knowledge of the malfeasance of Comerica Bank and Conduent, and the culpability of BFS by failing to make corrections as pointed out to the current Director in Treasury OIG 14-031 and 17-034.

In addition, Mr. Clements further stated:

In addition, the FASP guidance highlights the need for program offices to consider as early as possible the portability of the financial agent services—that is, the ability to transfer services from one agent to another with minimum difficulty. According to the guidance, portability helps to ensure that a program can continue without interruption if services need to be transferred to another agent and promotes competitive pricing and high-quality service.

We are requesting a copy of any document, pamphlet, or any tangible evidence of policy of BFS within the Fiscal Agent Selection Process which would have prohibited Ms. Densmore and me from testifying before the Evaluation Team which you defined to me. A copy of the FASP might shed a bit of light on the subject.

We are also aware of an ally of yours within the Office of Special Counsel, Treasury OIG, who has come forth to defend your unilateral decision to block us from this deliberative group. This alliance will not stop us. We are offering you an opportunity to validate your actions with policy, not by whim, and your true motivation to allow Comerica Bank to remain the Fiscal Agent of the Direct Express program.

I am certain I am not the only person who questions this behavior.

Sincerely, J.B. Simms

Thursday, May 28, 2020

Subject: A snippet from upcoming book
From: jbsimms
Date: Thu, May 28, 2020 1:14 pm
To: Franklin Lemond (Plaintiff's Attorney) , Jackie Lynn, "Kate Berry" Kate Berry (American Banker)
Here is how Comerica Bank skirted around regulations placed upon them by Fiscal Service. Sadly, we glossed over this report, but if you concentrate on the report, lot of stuff jumps out at you.
Excuse the typos; this is rough draft.
The highlighted material came from OIG 17-176 published Jan 25, 1017, one day after the second OIG Treasury audit of Direct Express program.
What is the FASP process? The FASP (Fiscal Agent Selection Process) is a secretive process of internal documents which Mr. Clements at GAO was not able to access, but the overview of the steps is below:
The guidance divides the process into four phases: (1) initiation of the FASP, (2) publication of a financial agent solicitation, (3) selection of the best proposal submitted by a financial institution, and (4) designation of the financial institution as a financial agent.18
In addition, the FASP guidance highlights the need for program offices to consider as early as possible the portability of the financial agent services—that is, the ability to transfer services from one agent to another with minimum difficulty. According to the guidance, portability helps to ensure that a program can continue without interruption if services need to be transferred to another agent and promotes competitive pricing and high-quality service.19
The FASP guidance notes that a financial institution should describe in its proposal its ability to perform the work, which may include its
• experience in providing the same or similar services,
• ability to meet security requirements,
• personnel and infrastructure capabilities, and
• private sector and government references. 20
Private sector references are non-governmental references. You would think the deliberative group would want to hear private sector references outside the bounds of submissions from the financial institutions?
Is a financial institution mandated to reveal any litigation of which they have been named as defendant?
If Comerica Bank is to describe its ability to meet security requirements, what are those security requirements?
The Selection Phase
According to the 2015 FASP guidance, employees involved in selecting or designating the financial agent should sign a conflict-of-interest statement before evaluating proposals. 21 (page 23)
We never saw this agreement from Santaniello.
In addition, Fiscal Service has an employee conduct policy, which addresses outside activities, gifts, and other topics relevant to conflicts of interest. As discussed previously, the 2015 FASP guidance requires employees involved in selecting or designating a financial agent to complete ethics training before their involvement in a FASP and sign a conflict-of-interest statement before evaluating financial agent proposals. 22
As Mr. Clements continued, he stated that during the Selection Phase:
" [N]one of the four administrative records included acknowledgement forms signed by the financial institutions indicating that they would, if selected, accept the terms of the financial agency agreement. "23 (see page 29 of GAO 17-176)
This revelation shows that the financial institution, the prospective Fiscal Agent, if approved, would not be accountable to accept the terms of the Fiscal Agent Agreement. This was the backdoor that allowed Comerica Bank to go back to BFS and be paid for the original contract.

Friday, May 29, 2020

This book had to be delayed to see what Comerica Bank was going to do

Subject: OIG Treasury 20-028 and the anticipated audit of Comerica Bank and Conduent
From: jbsimms
Date: Fri, May 29, 2020, 1:52 pm
To: Katherine Johnson (OIG Treasury)
Cc: Jackie Lynn; "Kate Berry" Kate Berry (American Banker)
Dear Ms. Johnson,

Ms. Densmore brought to my attention today OIG Treasury Report 20-028. I was anticipating a final report of 19-041, as was promised by Mr. Delmar upon its completion in late summer. It is not clear whether that report will be named the final report of 19-041, but we anticipate its completion and publication.

I see this report, 20-028, focuses upon the Corrective Actions suggested in the previous reports, 14-031 and 17-034. It is clear BFS was not made accountable for ignoring corrective action suggestions, interpreting the word "suggestions" in a literal manner, not to be confused with The Ten Commandments being interpreted as The Ten Suggestions.

There is no accountability where there is no consequence.

As you continue to gather investigative material to complete your audit, I ask that you review GAO 17-176 which was published the day after OIG Treasury 17-034. I am reviewing this report as I add commentary and insight to be published independently. The report, submitted by Mr. Michael Clements, reveals not only the intentional lack of transparency with regard to payments made to Fiscal Agents, but the fact that the Fiscal Agent (Comerica) benefited from the covert behavior of BFS as documented on Page 30 of GAO 17-176:

"[T]he checklist omits one type of document listed in the guidance (i.e., amendments to a financial agency agreement) because such documents would not be created until after the initial FASP is completed."

This checklist refers to the checklist created by BFS to qualify Fiscal Agents. I assume you see what happened. Please review GAO 17-176 to remind yourself of the rogue activity evidenced at BFS.

We look forward to your publication.

Sincerely,

J.B. Simms

Delmar was withholding the report. As of April 2023, the report had not been published

Monday, June 1, 2020

Filed the complaint at Maryland Bar on Sciurba

Subject: gloves off
From: jbsimms
Date: Mon, Jun 01, 2020 3:34 pm
To: Jackie Lynn; "Kate Berry" Kate Berry (American Banker)
this is how I roll.
This goes to the Maryland Bar today.
The complaint has already been filed.
Looks like Sciurba and Santaniello are sharing more than pizza and pasta.

Wednesday, June 3, 2020

Subject: 2020-02-137 and 2020-03-042 and 2020-03-070
Appeal Acknowledgement Letter_FINAL.pdf
From: Cawana Pearson (FOI Treasury)
Date: Wed, Jun 03, 2020 6:41 am
To: jbsimms
Good morning,
Treasury is in receipt of your recently submitted FOIA Appeals. Thank you, Cawana
I had appealed three FOI requests:
2020-02-137
 2020-03-042
2020-03-07

Wednesday, June 10, 2020

From: jbsimms
Sent: Wednesday, June 10, 2020, 6:15 PM
To: Cawana Pearson (FOI Treasury)
Cc: Jackie Lynn; Sonja Scott (OIG Treasury) Kate Berry (American Banker)
Subject: Failure of OIG Treasury to respond to FOI Request
Dear Ms. Pearson,

I apologize for having to use you as a conduit between you and your superiors, but no one from your office has contacted me with regard to my FOI requests and the overt misrepresentation of facts purported by Mr. Loren Sciurba of Office of Special Counsel, Department of Treasury.

Below is a copy of an email sent to me from Ms. Jackie Densmore. I am copying Ms. Densmore on this email as confirmation of my permissive use of said email. Within this email, you will see the sender, Sonja Scott, stating she had received an email from Ms. Densmore. From this point forward, August 14, 2018, Ms. Scott communicated over a hundred times with me in her capacity as having been assigned to the "Office of Investigations" and not the "Office of Audit" for OIG Treasury.

I came across this email as I compose the manuscript of the upcoming book to be published on this matter. The false assertion made by Loren Sciurba to your office, that there were no "investigations" is not only false on its face but should be referred to a separate agency independent of OIG Treasury and Office of Special Counsel for an investigation of said assertion by Mr. Sciurba and the exposure of the motive for attempting to circumvent the Freedom of Information Act.

It is my wish that your superior will avail me the same courtesy as did you when you chose to call me a few months ago instead of ignoring obvious sinister behavior.

The copy of the email is below.

Sincerely,

J.B. Simms

The battle with Delmar, Sciurba, and Altemus was never-ending. The lies regarding "investigations" continued. Below is a reminder from 2018 that the Office of Investigations existed.

From: Sonja Scott (OIG Treasury)
Date: August 14, 2018 at 2:08:00 PM EDT
To: "'jackiedenzz@yahoo.com'"
Subject: Complaint re Direct Express
We have received your complaint and referring the matter to the Bureau of Fiscal Service who manages the Direct Express Program. Sonja
ASAC Sonja L. Scott
US Department of Treasury

Thursday, June 11, 2020

Subject: Failure of OIG Treasury to respond to FOI Request
From: Cawana Pearson (FOI Treasury)
Date: Thu, Jun 11, 2020, 4:35 am
To: jbsimms
Cc: , (OIG Treasury), Kate Berry (American Banker)
Good morning Ms. Simms,
I hope all is well. You may not remember Mr. Paul Levitan, the former Director of FOIA and Transparency but the two of you had a long conversation about your FOIA requests. Please rest assured that we have received your FOIA appeals, and we are in communication with the Office of Inspector General.
Thank you,
Cawana

I felt some comfort and understanding from Cawana Pearson. Our conversation was held as I sat in Hite Miller's truck got her attention.

Subject: Failure of OIG Treasury to respond to FOI Request
From: jbsimms
Date: Thu, Jun 11, 2020, 9:02 am
To: "Cawana.Pearson@treasury.gov" Cawana Pearson (FOI Treasury)
Cc: "Jacki"
Dear Ms. Pearson,

Thank you for responding. I do remember a conversation with Mr. Levitan, but I was not able to expound upon the gravity of apparent disreputable behavior of OIG Treasury as with you. I will research my emails to look for emails from him.

This refusal to abide by FOI regulations is consistent with the delinquent submission of documents requested by Jackie Densmore in October 2018. This request was conveniently "lost" for almost a year, and upon its release to Ms. Densmore, was redacted to the extent that culpability of malfeasance (or worse) by Treasury employees (or anyone) was rendered impossible.

Please forward this to Mr. Levitan and convey my request that he acknowledged receipt.

Sincerely,

Jim Simms

I was reminding Ms. Pearson that Treasury "lost" the FOI request Jackie sent them for a copy of the 2014 Fiscal Agent agreement naming Comerica Bank as the Fiscal Agent. It was almost a year before they responded, but only after mysteriously finding the request.

Wednesday, June 17, 2020

Mr. Lepper emailed me to tell me that he was planning to talk to Kate Berry. That was encouraging.

We were hoping she would write about the battle with the VA. The story (to me) is not that the VA was so smart to create the VBBP (Veterans Benefit Banking Program). The story is the "backstory" which is what the VA learned about the Direct Express program and how BFS approved Comerica and Conduent to operate the program.

The fact that I was the only person to confront the VA (confront and challenge the director of the Veterans Benefits, Paul Lawrence) was a big secret.

Sunday, June 21, 2020

The lack of integrity by Loren Sciurba, Office of Special Counsel

From: jbsimms

Date: Sun, Jun 21, 2020, 10:09 pm

To: "Cawana.Pearson@treasury.gov" Cawana Pearson (FOI Treasury)

Cc: Jackie Lynn

Dear Ms. Pearson,

During what was supposed to be "leisure time" my mind wandered to the matter of Loren Sciurba denying the existence of investigation(s) being conducted with respect to OIG Treas 19-041.

There is a document entitled the US Code Service (USCS) which is referenced as a PDF on the website of OIG Treasury. While I found the denial by Mr. Sciurba of the existence of investigations being performed by Ms. Scott and Ms. Altemus (and their assigns) to be disingenuous at the least (along with support from Director Delmar) I submit to you that investigations do take place within the Investigative Division.

Below are some outtakes from the US Code Service:

Title 5 USCS Section 2

Page 6

TITLE 5. GOVERNMENT ORGANIZATION AND EMPLOYEES

TITLE 5--APPENDIX

INSPECTOR GENERAL ACT OF

§ 2. Purpose and establishment of Offices of Inspector General; departments and agencies involved.

In order to create independent and objective units--

(1) to conduct and supervise audits and investigations relating to the programs and operations of the establishments listed in section 12(2).

"Investigations" do take place. Since Ms. Scott first contacted Ms. Densmore and me in September 2018, identifying herself as working in the Office of Investigations, we took Ms. Scott at her word that investigations were being conducted in the Office of Investigations.

2. Purpose

Purpose of Congress in enacting Inspector General Act (5 USCS Appx) was to establish independent and objective units within each department to conduct audits and investigations of its programs and operations, and to prevent and detect fraud and abuse therein. Inspector General of Department of Veterans Affairs (9/11/96) Comp. Gen. Dec. No.B-270403, 1996 US Comp Gen LEXIS 437.

We knew that OIG Treasury 19-041, published July 29, 2019, was labeled a "preliminary audit" of BFS and its relationship with Comerica Bank and Conduent. OIG Treasury published OIG Treasury 20-028 on March 2, 2020, which was labeled "Corrective Action on OIG Treasury 14-031 and 17-034" which were the reports I challenged in February 2018 to Paulette Battle. The report might be construed to be the fulfillment of OIG Treasury 19-041, but since the FOI have been made, all communication from OIG Treasury has ceased.
If OIG Treasury is going to submit a final report to OIG 19-041, the investigations will not be available until that report is published. If Sciurba and Delmar had given that answer, that would have been acceptable, but they chose a less than honest justification to deny me my request; Sciurba stated the investigations did not exist.
If this is the case, the investigation performed and submitted to the person who signed off on OIG Treasury 20-028 should be available. This published audit was not labeled "preliminary." Ms. Densmore and I are well aware that an audit "should" integrate an investigation. The reason we are all here is because I challenged that there were no investigations on 14-031 and 17-034, and my challenge was validated.

Saturday, June 27, 2020

Subject: Delmar admitting investigation
From: J B Simms
Date: Sat, Jun 27, 2020 10:53 am
To: jbsimms
From: Jackie Lynn
Date: Sat, Mar 9, 2019 at 7:23 AM
Subject: Delmar admitting investigation

On Fri, Sep 14, 2018 at 11:11 AM Delmar, Richard K. (OIG Treasury) wrote:
Treasury OIG has been reviewing how BFS and Comerica have executed the Direct Express program for several years and has identified problems and recommended corrections in that execution.
We continue to conduct those reviews, as well as actively investigating allegations of misconduct involving the program. To clarify, our previous Direct Express work was focused on BFS' efforts to award the FAAs and not on the details of fraud monitoring and customer service. Our new audit and investigative work focus on issues raised by Mr. Simms and Ms. Densmore. Mr. Simms's criticism to the contrary, our prior work, as all our work, complied with all GAO and CIGIE standards, and is objective and independent, as the Inspector General Act requires.
Rich Delmar
Counsel to the Inspector General
Department of the Treasury

I sent the above copy to Ms. Pearson, Jackie, and Mr. Lepper, proving what liars there were in OIG Treasury, claiming there were no investigations.

Dear Ms. Pearson,
Appended below please find a complete copy of an email which was sent to Ms. Densmore and me by Acting Director Delmar, OIG Treasury. While I will refrain from responding to comments made by Mr. Delmar referring to my criticism of the performance of OIG Treasury in the matter of BFS/Comerica Bank/Conduent (which in fact has been validated by the same Mr. Delmar as he commissioned an audit and investigation based solely upon fact submitted by me), I bring your attention to the admission within the text of the email within which Mr. Delmar admits the existence of "...[a]udit and investigative work focus on issues raised by Mr. Simms and Ms. Densmore."

Monday, June 29, 2020

Jackie sent this out to us.

Mon, Jun 29, 2:18 PM
to Franklin, me, Kate
Franklin, JB and Kate ,
I wanted to share the good news with you ! All of your hard work JB working with the Lepper has paid off -they are no longer endorsing the DE program they have changed the inserts as well as the envelopes. This is a huge win , JB through your dedication and Persistence Veterans have a safe way to bank and Comerica loses money !! You have saved so many from being Victimized !!!
Way to get it done 👏👏👏👏

We pushed hard and had to stop the VA from endorsing the Direct Express program by stuffing the inserts into the envelopes.

Tuesday, June 30, 2020

Subject: SSA Audit promised
From: Walter Bayer (Soc Sec OIG) (Soc Sec)
Date: Tue, Jun 30, 2020 10:31 am
To: jbsimms
Jim,
Those reports have not been issued. The audit team is currently going through their annual process to create a new audit work plan. I expect the earlier issues, as well as new issues such operations during COVID-19, will be part of the ongoing discussions. The new (FY 2021) audit work plan will be issued in late summer or early fall. At that point, you will be able to learn more about the focus of the team's audits.
Thanks,
Walt

SSA never submitted an audit or investigation of the Direct Express program. SSA was too deeply involved with BFS, almost incestuously.

Covid and more Covid and more delays.

Steven Lepper (CEO-Military Banks of America)
Tue, Jun 30, 4:24 AM (8 days ago)
to Jackie, me, Andia
Jackie,
Thanks for the very kind note and for the picture of the flyer. VBA did a lot of heavy lifting, not only to get VBBP off the ground but also to get Treasury to send out this flyer. We at AMBA are simply thankful that we've been able to help. We're now hopeful that we can get Social Security to embrace a similar approach. More later on that.
To help generate "buzz" in the veteran community, we would greatly appreciate your "tagging" VBA, Dr. Lawrence, the VBBP, and AMBA in your social media messages. Although I'm no expert on social media, I'm told that doing so will help spread the word among veterans who are plugged into Facebook, LinkedIn, and other social media channels.
All the best,
Steve

J B Simms
Tue, Jun 30, 8:31 AM (8 days ago)
to Franklin, Steven, Jackie, Andia
We, as facilitators, and veterans are pleased the VAB decided to create a program to address the problem we presented.
Hopefully, SSA will follow the lead of VA, examine the same evidence as witnessed by the VA, and come to the same conclusion.
The elimination of the BFS inserts and printed solicitation on the envelopes gives us great joy.
Sincerely,
J.B. Simms

Thursday, June 2, 2020

Subject: The real reason for exclusion from Bureau of Fiscal Services predicted centuries ago]
From: jbsimms
Date: Thu, Jul 02, 2020, 4:45 pm
To: Franklin Lemond (Plaintiff's Attorney)
Cc: "Kate Berry" Kate Berry (American Banker), Jackie Lynn
This email was sent the persons below over a year ago.
Some things never change. You might recognize the author.
Nothing could be more accurate.
Jim

Subject: The real reason for exclusion from Bureau of Fiscal Services
predicted centuries ago
From: jbsimms
Date: Tue, May 07, 2019 9:40 pm
To: Sonja Scott (OIG Treasury), Thomas Santaniello (Treasury Bur of Fisc Svc), thorsone@oig.treas.gov,
Richard Delmar (OIG Treasury)
Cc: Jackie Lynn; Kate Berry (American Banker

Below is an excerpt of a book written 500 years ago. This passage describes the Bureau of Fiscal Services. I am not advocating the remedy proposed in the last sentence of this passage, as this was written in a different era, but, the description of the appointment of corrupt persons and lack of consequence is spot on. This passage also explains why OIG Treasury has not challenged Fiscal Services for ignoring the two OIG reports as well as GAO 17-176.

Evidently human nature has not changed much. Fiscal Services has sent out Mr. Santaniello to guard against persons "expressing their views" and exposing corruption.

CHAPTER XVIII. —How a Free Government existing in a corrupt City may be preserved, or not existing may be created.

Again, as to making laws, any of the tribunes and certain others of the magistrates were entitled to submit laws to the people; but before these were passed it was open to every citizen to speak either for or against them. This was a good system so long as the citizens were good, since it is always well that every man should be able to propose what he thinks may be of use to his country, and that all should be allowed to express their views with regard to his proposal; so that the people, having heard all, may resolve on what is best. But when the people grew depraved, this became a very mischievous institution; for then it was only the powerful who proposed laws, and these not in the interest of public freedom but of their own authority; and because, through fear, none durst speak against the laws they proposed, the people were either deceived or forced into voting their own destruction.

In order, therefore, that Rome after she had become corrupted might still preserve her freedom, it was necessary that, as in the course of events she had made new laws, so likewise she should frame new institutions, since different institutions and ordinances are needed in a corrupt State from those which suit a State which is not corrupted; for where the matter is wholly dissimilar, the form cannot be similar.

But since old institutions must either be reformed all at once, as soon as they are seen to be no longer expedient, or else gradually, as the imperfection of each is recognized, I say that each of these two courses is all but impossible. For to effect a gradual reform requires a sagacious man who can discern mischief while it is still remote and in the germ. But it may well happen that no such person is found in a city; or that, if found, he is unable to persuade others of what he is himself persuaded. For men used to live in one way are loath to leave it for another, especially when they are not brought face to face with the evil against which they should guard, and only have it indicated to them by conjecture. And as for a sudden reform of institutions which are seen by all to be no longer good, I say that defects which are easily discerned are not easily corrected, because for their correction it is not enough to use ordinary means, these being in themselves insufficient; but recourse must be had to extraordinary means, such as violence and arms; and, as a preliminary, you must become prince of the city, and be able to deal with it at your pleasure.

Sunday, June 5, 2020

From: rebeccamnewton@aol.com
Sent: Tuesday, February 5, 2019 5:14 PM
To: Delmar, Richard K.
Subject: James Edward Sims Jr.
Mr. Delmar,
Per our phone conversation this afternoon attached please find the Direct Express Card statements from March 2018 through August 2018. When you look at each statement none of those charges should be there they are all fraudulent. The total amount due back to my dad is $7,043.61. I have also spoken with Susan Rutledge at Comerica, I have also spoken with Shantelle Johnson at Conduent and Alicia at Conduent. None of them are willing to help me unless I have something signed by my dad saying I'm allowed to handle this for him and in his current condition he is unable to do that. As we speak I am in an ICU room with him worthy of just taking him off all of machines and making him comfortable so that he may pass peacefully. Not only was my father victimized when his money was stolen but now he's being victimized again by Conduent and Comerica. If the direct express call center employees that my dad and I spoke to an early January add father to document the fact my father told them repeatedly that he wanted me to handle this for him I don't believe that my dad and I would be in this situation. Like I said previously my father was saving that money on his card so that when something like this did happen to him it wouldn't put me in such a financial burden. And now here I am this is still unresolved and my father is about to pass and I have absolutely no way financially to take care of him once he does pass. I am truly hoping that you can help me and at least bring some peace for me and my dad.
Also when speaking to Conduent Last Friday they put a non suspension fraud hold on my dad's Direct Express Card. So even if the money did get back to us somehow I don't even know how we would get the money. So I'm hoping you can help with that as well please.
Rebecca Newton

From: Delmar, Richard K.
Date: Tue, Feb 5, 2019 5:28 PM
To: 'rebeccamnewton@aol.com';
Cc: James Edward Sims Jr.
got it. Also get that Lutz is over 300 miles from those places in Georgia.
I will talk to the BFS Security Officer and see what can be done.
Back to you ASAP.
Rich Delmar
Counsel to the Inspector General
Department of the Treasury

Empty promises; Delmar was doing nothing.

Saturday, July 4, 2020

The following email was sent to Delmar, Santaniello, Sciurba, and Mr. Lepper.

This is the sad story of the suicide death of Nona Clarke.

On Jul 4, 2020, at 1:35 AM, jbsimms wrote:
Gentlemen,
As I review the thousands of emails beginning December 2017 which pertain to Comerica Bank, BFS, and the Direct Express program, I just want to remind you what happened at 11:37am on August 6, 2019.
Anna Martinez +52 928 117 0851 called me from a city administration office of Huatulco, Mexico. She called to say Nona Clarke had been in auto accident. My contact information was found on the body. No relatives were known.
The truth was Nona had entered a store trying to get her Direct Express card to work. Nona had first emailed me in May 2019, and we exchanged no fewer than five (5) emails and a couple telephone calls.
A few of these emails were sent to Ms. Scott, who was receptive and admittedly diligently passed the matter to a BFS Liaison. I am certain Ms. Scott and others know my response to sending a matter to the same agency which created this fiasco.

394

I received an email on August 4, 2019 from Ms. Clarke.

That was the last communication we exchanged. The story of the traffic accident was not true; Nona died from self-inflicted wounds, using a sharp object to cut her wrists. The object was found with Nona Clarke in the bathroom of the store where Nona was trying to buy provisions. After not being able to access her funds for approximately 3 months, having to barter to pay rent, live off the kindness of strangers, that walk from the counter to the restroom sent thoughts racing through her mind that you have not experienced.

For those of you whose mothers are deceased, do you remember how you learned of the passing of your mother? I was playing in a baseball game and learned of the passing when I got home. Not only do I remember that moment, but I have worked suicide cases. Nona's kids found out from the Mexican consulate.

From May 21, 2019, until August 6, 2019 a rational person would think this matter could have been solved. (I do see Ms. Clarke also contacted SSA OIG). I know you are not going to divulge the name of the person at BFS to whom Ms. Scott passed along this information to address the issue, but for those persons who think that referring an issue pertaining to Comerica Bank and Conduent to BFS will be handled in the best interest of the victim, try telling that to the daughters of Nona Clarke.

Below is the text message I received from one of Nona's daughters. I do not know what it is going to take to shake out BFS and it's supporters to expose of their motive of protecting BFS, Comerica Bank, and Conduent. We are simply looking for that one person whose conscience suddenly appears.

Sincerely,

J.B. Simms

Subject: Message from Paige Clarke
From: Steven Lepper (CEO-Military Banks of America)
Date: Sat, Jul 04, 2020, 3:56 am
To: jbsimms
Cc: Andia Dinesen <Andia.dinesen@ambahq.org>
Mr. Simms,

Thank you for sharing this tragic story. I've never questioned your passion because you've shared stories like these. Hopefully, we'll be able to connect everyone currently in the Direct Express program to financial institutions that have people who can help at the other end of their phone lines.

One update that might improve your day: On Thursday, my colleague, Andia Dinesen, and I had a call with two senior officials in VBA. The call marked the transition of VBBP from an initiative to a full, permanent VBA program. The two ladies we talked to will be VBA's full-time administrators of the program. We discussed a number of ideas we hope will target and encourage even more veterans to switch from Direct Express to direct deposit. Hopefully, we'll eliminate tragedies like this one.

Best wishes to you for a happy and safe 4th of July.

All the best, Steve

The email below was sent by Nona Clarke's daughter a month following Nona's death. I had some voice messages from Nona on my phone and sent them to Paige. This was heartbreaking.

Subject: Message from Paige Clarke
From: J B Simms
Date: Fri, August 09, 2019 11:51 am
To: jbsimms
Thank you, JB. For forwarding your communication with my mom and for your kind words.

My sister spoke with the investigator and the doctor who performed the autopsy.

I'm not sure why Anna told you it was a traffic accident; I think she felt uncomfortable telling you information without being her next of kin.

She was found in the bathroom of a grocery store with a sharp object. They were looking into foul play, but they think that it was suicide. They asked several questions about her mental health, relationships with family and if she had any sleep problems. All of that combined with stress around not being able to have access to her funds and being in physical pain could have led to her taking her own life.

I really appreciate you having supported her through this tough time, I'm sure your kindness and connection meant a lot to her.

Warmly,

Paige

Wednesday, July 8, 2020

Franklin Lemond (Plaintiff's Attorney)
Wed, Jul 8, 2020, 3:19 PM
to Jim, me
JB,
The Defendants have started asking about scheduling depositions. You will be pleased to know that they have asked to wait and take your deposition later than many of the other plaintiffs. Since I have been asking others for dates in August or September, perhaps you should let me know what your availability is in mid-to-late September or early October. Of course, we would spend plenty of time preparing for the deposition, so you know what to expect. How things progress with the pandemic will influence whether the deposition would be in person or via video conference.
We can certainly discuss this on Friday unless you have questions before then.
Franklin

Monday, June 22, 2020

Franklin talked to Steve Lepper. Depositions would begin.

Mr. Lepper told Franklin that for new applicants, more than 50% of the sign-up are going with his program and not Direct Express. He also said that in July, the inserts in the check envelopes for benefit recipients will be advertisements for the VA/AMBA program and not DE. Lepper said he knew that would be music to JB's ears.

Subject: A debt of gratitude
From: jbsimms
Date: Mon, Jun 22, 2020, 3:50 pm
To: Steven Lepper (CEO-Military Banks of America)
Cc: Jackie Lynn
Dear Mr. Lepper,
We received an abbreviated Reader's Digest/Cliff Note email debriefing from Mr. Lemond regarding your telephone communication.
I think I speak for Ms. Densmore, her brother-in-law and the veterans we have helped, when I simply say thank you for believing in what we are doing and validating what I was conveying to the VA.
Thank you again.
Sincerely,
J.B. Simms

Conduent has over 500 contracts with the US government

Subject: I told you the tail is wagging the dog
From: jbsimms
Date: Mon, Jun 22, 2020 8:42 pm
To: Franklin Lemond (Plaintiff's Attorney), Jackie Lynn
USA Spending website tells where money is spent.
Looks like Conduent has over 500 contracts with the government.
Am I wrong?
I could not find a site showing how much Comerica is getting paid for the Direct Express program. Maybe that info will be divulged from one of our subpoenas to Treasury.
Jim

Conduent was running the show. Comerica was the lapdog for Conduent.

Tuesday, June 23, 2020

Subject: Clarification of authorization of inserts into VA benefit envelopes
From: jbsimms
Date: Tue, Jun 23, 2020 11:42 am
To: Steven Lepper (CEO-Military Banks of America)
Cc: Jackie Lynn; Walter Bayer (SSA OIG)

Dear Mr. Lepper,

I am always grateful for the time you have spent addressing this issue I have created, and in no manner would want to appear intrusive.

During the debacle concerning the dreaded inserts (which I believe I raised in January 2020) my first target of inquiry was to SSA and VA, which both denied culpability with regard to having requested, placed, or endorsed the inserts. That lead me to assume that since the inserts were accompanying checks from SSA and VA, and the benefits were filtered through Bureau of Fiscal Service (BFS), that someone BFS was authorizing the inserts accompany the paper checks.

That person at BFS was never identified, nor was the department where this person is assigned.

It was learned that beginning in July 2020, the inserts in the check envelopes for benefit recipients will be advertisements for the VA/AMBA program and not Direct Express.

My questions are these:

Who at the VA authorized the new inserts accompany VA benefit checks, and why?

Who at the VA approached BFS to request BFS cease Direct Express promotional material accompany the VA checks?

Who at BFS was the liaison between the VA and BFS?

Someone at the VA realized the inserts were detrimental to veterans. Someone at the VA pulled the trigger to stop BFS from promoting the Direct Express program.

I am copying Mr. Bayer in hopes that SSA could create an insert for SSA recipients which would direct veterans to the AMBA for assistance with establishing a bank account. Many SSA check recipients are veterans. A generic insert addressing veterans to contact the AMBA might reduce the number if check recipients instead of using the passive tool of attrition at the only tool being utilized by SSA.

I will be glad to direct my inquiries to a specific person at VAB if you feel that is necessary.

Sincerely, J.B. Simms

Clarification of Freedom of Information Requests

I had to submit a dozen or more FOI requests to different agencies. No one wanted to answer questions or be accountable. The FOI requests were a big part of our success.

Subject: Clarification of outstanding FOI
From: jbsimms
Date: Tue, Jun 23, 2020, 7:36 pm
To: "Cawana.Pearson@treasury.gov" Cawana Pearson (FOI Treasury)
Cc: Jackie Lynn

Dear Ms. Pearson,

I am itemizing the FOI requests I submitted this year in an attempt to obtain copies of investigations on two matters at OIG Treasury.

Here are the requests as I see them:

2020-02-023: The initial request for copy of the investigation under the supervision of A.J. Altemus with regard to fraud claims against Comerica Bank and Conduent by thirty (30) Direct Express cardholders. This investigation commenced on or about October 2019.

This was the FOI request which kept being bantered back and forth while identity prerequisites were being fulfilled.

This request was denied by A.J. Altemus

2020-02-137: This FOI request is the appeal of the above request, 2020-02-023

2020-03-042 : This FOI request was for the report of the investigation of my personal fraud claims as a Direct Express cardholder.

This request was denied by Loren J. Sciurba, stating no investigations were performed.

2020-03-070: This FOI request was submitted to obtain the investigative report submitted by Ms. Sonja Scott to be included in OIG Treasury Audit 19-041.

It appears the FOI request outstanding are 2020-02-137, 2020-03-042, and 2020-03-070. The denials by Mr. Sciurba and Ms. Altemus are without merit, thus these three FOI requests remain outstanding.

Thank you for your indulgence and attention to this matter. There are so many files on these matters and so many emails that it becomes a blur.

Sincerely, J.B. Simms

The federal government offices never like Freedom of Information requests. I filed at least 13 requests during this case. Much of the information we developed came from FOI requests.

Wednesday, June 24, 2020

Subject: Clarification of outstanding FOI
From: Cawana Pearson (FOI Treasury)
Date: Wed, June 24, 2020 4:43 am
To: jbsimms
Good morning,
Thank you so much Mr. Simms!
Have an awesome day on purpose! Stay safe!

Subject: Clarification of outstanding FOI
From: jbsimms
Date: Wed, Jun 24, 2020 10:44 am
To: "Cawana.Pearson@treasury.gov" Cawana Pearson (FOI Treasury)
Cc: Jackie Lynn
I apologize for the confusion. The refusal of OIG Treasury to abide by the FOI requests, and the refiling of appeals, has created more drama than was necessary.
It looks like I misstated the application of case numbers and I will try to explain it now.
On Feb 24, 2020 I sent an email to Altemus requesting a copy of the investigation of fraud on my Direct Express debit card. This investigation was prompted by an email I received in October 2019 from Kevin Guishard who worked for Altemus. Upon asking for the investigative report, Altemus refused to produce the report, while directing me to submit an FOI request.
After submitting the original FOI request, and eventually satisfying prerequisites for identification, the request was accepted, acknowledged by you. I believe that was on the following day, Feb 25. That FOI submission was given the case number 2020-02-023.
I then submitted an FOI request for the investigation of the 30 victims of fraud (I was one of the thirty). That submission was given the case number 2020-02-137.
You sent me an email advising me that both requests, 02-023 and 02-137 were to be joined as 02-137.
Loren Sciurba of OIG Special Counsel denied any investigation(s) were taking place and refused to produce the requested documents. This denial was made via email, and Mr. Sciurba offered me the option to appeal. I appealed his refusal, and this appeal appears to have been given the case number 2020-03-042.
A third FOI request was submitted requesting a copy of the investigation conducted by the office of Sonja Scott, OIG Treasury, Office of Investigations. This investigation was to be included in audit Treasury OIG 19-041 published by Katherine Johnson. The preliminary 19-041 audit was published July 29, 2019. At the inception of the investigation conducted by the office of Ms. Scott, I communicated with Ms. Scott and was assured I could request a copy of said investigation.
A reply to this request was made by Richard Delmar, Acting Director of OIG Treasury. Delmar, as with Sciurba, denied an "investigation" was conducted by Ms. Scott's office. I probably have made an appeal to this particular denial but am not certain. No new case number has been assigned to an appeal to my knowledge.
As I stated previously, an investigation into the credibility and veracity of claims of the absence of an investigation being conducted by the office of Ms. Altemus is underway by a separate agency which is not connected with your office or that of the US Treasury. At this time there is no similar investigation of allegations of lack of an investigation by office of Ms. Scott having been submitted to Katherine Johnson (re: 19-041 audit) by Mr. Delmar but if this and other attempts to block my legal access to the investigations via FOI request persists, I will have no option but to proceed as was regarding Sciurba.
In summation, allow me to list the requests and the nature of the requests to you as I now see them:
2020-02-023 Request for the investigation of fraud on my personal Direct Express account by AJ Altemus
2020-02-137 Request for the investigation of the list of 30 Direct Express fraud victims
2020-03-042 Appear of denial by Loren Sciurba of FOI requests 2020-02-023 and 2020-02-137 (no know jointly as 2020-02-137)
2020-03-070 Request for the investigation conducted by Sonja Scott in reference to Treas OIG 19-041.
If you can make this more clear than I have presented, please do.
Sincerely,
J.B. Simms

The other investigation into Sciurba's claim that no investigations took place was to be conducted as a result of my filing a claim against Sciurba with the Maryland Bar Association. I knew that the Maryland Bar Association would shield Sciurba, but I had to file the grievance.

Saturday, June 27, 2020

Subject: Delmar admitting investigation: September 14, 2018
From: jbsimms
Date: Sat, Jun 27, 2020, 11:22 am
To: "Cawana.Pearson@treasury.gov" Cawana Pearson (FOI Treasury)
Cc: Jackie Lynn; Steven Lepper (CEO-Military Banks of America)
Dear Ms. Pearson,
Appended below please find a complete copy of an email which was sent to Ms. Densmore and me by Acting Director Delmar, OIG Treasury. While I will refrain from responding to comments made by Mr. Delmar referring to my criticism of the performance of OIG Treasury in the matter of BFS/Comerica Bank/Conduent (which in fact has been validated by the same Mr. Delmar as he commissioned an audit and investigation based solely upon fact submitted by me), I bring your attention to the admission within the text of the email within which Mr. Delmar admits the existence of "...[a]udit and investigative work focus on issues raised by Mr. Simms and Ms. Densmore."
The three FOI request for records pertaining to said investigation(s) do, in fact, exist, and the lack of veracity by Loren Sciurba (OIG Special Counsel) by asserting otherwise not only contradicts the admission by his superior but exposes and agenda which attempts to conceal information to which I am legally entitled.
With no disrespect to you personally or professionally, I humbly request you confer with attorneys at the US Justice Department with regard to OIG Treasury and specified persons within OIG Treasury and OIG Special Counsel to investigate and opine in this matter. I was inclined to make that contact, but you might have a more direct route.
Sincerely,
J.B. Simms

J B Simms
Sat, Jun 27, 2:28 PM (11 days ago)
to Kate, Jackie
Dear Kate,
Delmar and Sciurba are protecting Conduent. Conduent is running the day-to-day financial disbursement machine of Treasury.
Jackie was the person who got Delmar to respond. Now he and Sciurba are blocking FOI requests (redacted Jackie's until it looked like a used diaper) and denying that "investigations" exist.
Sorry to bug you on a Saturday, but I have no life until I get these emails reviewed and the text edited. Thousands of emails. Most from Jackie. No comment.

Monday, June 29, 2020

Scott meets with Comerica; Altemus cancels our meeting

Subject: make a note: 10/10/19 OIG Treasury met with Comerica
From: jbsimms
Date: Mon, Jun 29, 2020, 9:16 am
To: Franklin Lemond (Plaintiff's Attorney)
Cc: Jackie Lynn; "Kate Berry" Kate Berry (American Banker)
While reviewing emails, many forgotten things pop up.
Here is a nice nugget to ponder: Sonja Scott of OIG Treasury supposedly met with Comerica Bank on October 10, 2019.
Since that time, Jackie and I were scheduled for a conference during the first week of November. Amy Altemus, atty for OIG Special Counsel cancelled the meeting, blaming the syllabus I sent OIG Treasury as the reason. Below is confirmation of the meeting.
I want to see Sonja Scott's report of that meeting.
Jim

I knew Sonja Scott was not going to send me a report but I knew the interview would be noted in the report I was trying to get using and FOI request.

Subject: ACS as original contractor for Comerica
From: jbsimms
Date: Mon, Jun 29, 2020, 11:17 am
To: Franklin Lemond (Plaintiff's Attorney) , Jackie Lynn
Dear you two,
No, I have no life.
These two pages were taken from the proposal made by Comerica Bank to BFS in 2008.
ACS is a service agency, as is Conduent.
I want to know about the contract between Comerica and ACS, plus if Conduent got the contract away from Comerica. Jim

ACS became Conduent. ACS was a subsidiary of Xerox. This is important because the negotiations for the 2019 contract, that had not been published, will address Conduent. ACS was the original facilitator for Comerica Bank, included so Comerica Bank could get the contract.

VA inserts were changed: Jackie was happy

Jackie Lynn
Attachments
Mon, Jun 29, 2:18 PM
to Franklin, me, Kate
Franklin, JB and Kate,
I wanted to share the good news with you! All of your hard work JB working with the Lepper has paid off -they are no longer endorsing the DE program they have changed the inserts as well as the envelopes. This is a huge win, JB through your dedication and Persistence Veterans have a safe way to bank and Comerica loses money !! You have saved so many from being Victimized!!!
Way to get it done 👏👏👏👏

On Jun 29, 2020, at 5:46 PM, Jackie Lynn wrote:
Dear Mr. Lepper,
I wanted to reach out to you and personally thank you for all of your work and dedication. We received Derek's check today and to my surprise the envelope was not marked Direct Express program and the insert had been changed to your program. This truly brought tears to my eyes, to know Veterans now have a safe way is just so amazing ! You have saved some many people from being victims and I am forever thankful.
God Bless, Jackie

Tuesday, June 30, 2020

Jackie sends Lepper the new VA insert

Steven Lepper (CEO-Military Banks of America)
Tue, Jun 30, 4:24 AM
to Jackie, me, Andia
Jackie,
Thanks for the very kind note and for the picture of the flyer. VBA did a lot of heavy lifting, not only to get VBBP off the ground but also to get Treasury to send out this flyer. We at AMBA are simply thankful that we've been able to help. We're now hopeful that we can get Social Security to embrace a similar approach. More later on that.
To help generate "buzz" in the veteran community, we would greatly appreciate your "tagging" VBA, Dr. Lawrence, the VBBP, and AMBA in your social media messages. Although I'm no expert on social media, I'm told that doing so will help spread the word among veterans who are plugged into Facebook, LinkedIn, and other social media channels.
All the best,
Steve

We were getting small victories. We wanted it all.

Bayer promises SSA audit to be published

Subject: SSA Audit promised
From: Walter Bayer (Soc Sec OIG)
Date: Tue, June 30, 2020, 10:31 am
To: jbsimms
Jim,
Those reports have not been issued. The audit team is currently going through their annual process to create a new audit work plan. I expect the earlier issues, as well as new issues such operations during COVID-19, will be part of the ongoing discussions. The new (FY 2021) audit work plan will be issued in late summer or early fall. At that point, you will be able to learn more about the focus of the team's audits.
 Thanks,
 Walt

That audit team at SSA was hiding from us. They were not addressing this issue.

Subject: SSA Audit promised
From: jbsimms
Date: Tue, Jun 30, 2020 11:12 am
To: Walter Bayer (Soc Sec OIG) (Soc Sec)
Cc: Jackie Lynn
Dear Walt,
Thank you for your email.
We are excitedly anticipating the SSA OIG reports. You have been in the loop and know what we know and what we feel.
By the way, SSA has an outstanding subpoena in reference to the case against Comerica and Conduent. This subpoena was served months ago. Can you slip a note under the nose of one of the attorneys at SSA and remind them of this obligation?
Sincerely,
Jim

SSA lied to us. The investigation by SSA OIG was to take place. Nothing was published. They did nothing because the agency to blame was Bureau of Fiscal Service and Social Security would never be critical of BFS for renewing the contract with Comerica.

The inserts might not seem to be a big deal to most, but it reinforces the allegation that Social Security was endorsing a faulty program (Direct Express) and BFS was shoving it down their throat.

Tuesday, June 30, 2020

Steven Lepper (CEO-Military Banks of America)
Tue, Jun 30, 4:24 AM
to Jackie, me, Andia
Jackie,
Thanks for the very kind note and for the picture of the flyer. VBA did a lot of heavy lifting, not only to get VBBP off the ground but also to get Treasury to send out this flyer. We at AMBA are simply thankful that we've been able to help. We're now hopeful that we can get Social Security to embrace a similar approach. More later on that.
All the best,
Steve

Friday, July 3, 2020

Subject: James Edward Sims Jr.
From: jbsimms
Date: Fri, Jul 03, 2020, 9:50 am
To: Jackie Lynn; Richard Delmar (OIG Treasury)
As I review emails for the manuscript, I came across this email trail within which Rebecca Newton, whose father James Sims, had communicated with Mr. Delmar.
Mr. Sims died soon thereafter, and Ms. Newton received no further contact from BFS, Comerica, Conduent, or OIG Treasury.
Within a month after the death of Mr. Sims, the mother of Ms. Newton died.
Then Ms. Newton broke her leg in a freak accident in her front yard.
I assume the anxiety of all this must have caused her to lose her focus.
This is but one of the cases, and the reasons, we help these victims, because no one is held accountable and as in this case, nothing was done by anyone other than Ms. Densmore and me to them.
Sincerely, J.B. Simms

I was tired of the games. I was very bitter.

Below is a copy of the email noting the request by Jackie and me to address the committee that gave the renewed contract to Comerica. They did not want to hear the truth.

Subject: RE: Follow up
From: Sonja Scott (OIG Treasury)
Date: Wed, April 03, 2019 5:27 am
To: jbsimms
Thanks for speaking with us. I will send your request to our BFS liaison, but never heard of a process for the public to provide opinions re a contract bid/award.   Sonja
ASAC Sonja L. Scott
US Department of Treasury
Office of the Inspector General, Office of Investigations

No one at Treasury, either OIG or BFS, would want to see Jackie and me address them. We knew too much.

Notice that Sonja Scott worked in the Office of Investigations, where "investigations" were denied.

Tuesday, July 7, 2020

Subject: Social Security and BFS
From: jbsimms
Date: Tue, Jul 07, 2020 12:28 pm
To: Walter Bayer (SSA OIG)
Cc: Jackie Lynn; "Kate Berry" Kate Berry (American Banker)
Dear Mr. Bayer,
We noticed the SSA has ceased having promotional inserts, but a DE promo is still on the back of the SSA envelope, unlike that of the VA checks. The back of the VA check envelopes are now blank.
We are interested in knowing how SSA was able to have the DE promo inserts stopped being placed into the envelopes.
Our question(s) is this: Who at the SSA made the decision to cease the inserts, and who at BFS did an SSA official contact in order for this practice to cease?
Someone called someone, and that someone had a reason. Someone emailed someone who had to validate the request for the cessation of the inserts.
Will the SSA enact a PR program for veterans to contact the AMBA in order to obtain a bank account?
Sincerely,
Jim

Thursday, July 9, 2020

A great win at the VA, but no fanfare for Jackie and me.

Subject: Lepper and the VA, and BFS
From: jbsimms
Date: Thu, Jul 09, 2020, 9:52 am
To: "Kate Berry" Kate Berry (American Banker)
Cc: Jackie Lynn
Dear Kate,
Franklin, our esteemed attorney, had a chat with Lepper. He is revealing little.
We know the VA is making the Veterans Benefit Banking Program (VBBP) a permanent department of the VA and outwardly refuting the BFS handling of veteran benefits by directing (and sometimes unwilling enrolling) to use the Direct Express program.
We got the inserts stopped, and the fact that two lowly citizens could stop BFS from advertising the corrupt program, is a story. We can chat if you wish. There is more to the story, with OIG Treasury and Santaniello. We are indebted to you by your support.
Sincerely,
Jim

Subject; Could persons at VA contact Bayer? Could be effective
From: jbsimms
Date: Thu, Jul 09, 2020, 12:12 pm
To: "Kate Berry" Kate Berry (American Banker)
Cc: Jackie Lynn
Dear Wonderful Helpful, Magnificent, Super-Intelligent, Kate,
I found the person at the VA who would be the contact person, and that would be Joe Gurney. Gurney was on a panel in a promo video with Gen Lepper, and Gurney was the person at the VA who is said to have reached out to Lepper to help solve the problem with DE program which I so delicately presented to the VA.
Gurney can tell "how" the VBBP was created, and when. We know that nothing was done until I went after Pamela Powers and Paul Lawrence beginning around Feb 2019. They cannot deny this began because of issues being raised by Ms. Densmore and me, but they will project that they rolled over in bed one morning and thought "...BFS is profiting from the DE program and veterans are being victimized." God does not talk to these people.
Herein is the hook, Joe Gurney at the VBA. , Jim

The trail led from Pamela Powers to Paul Lawrence to Joe Gurney. Gurney was the one who ramrodded the VBBP and brought Lepper onboard. I am a bit shocked that Gurney never reached out to me.

Remember this email below naming Gurney at the VA.

Subject: Re: Could persons at VA contact Bayer? Could be effective.
From: Steven Lepper (CEO-Military Banks of America)
Date: Tue, February 18, 2020 5:08 am
To: jbsimms
Cc: Jackie Lynn
Mr. Simms,
The other gentleman who participated in the LinkedIn Live event last week was Joe Gurney, Special Assistant to the Under Secretary. He has spearheaded this entire effort to move veterans from DE and paper checks to bank accounts.
This new program is gaining momentum. We will be onboarding credit unions in the next few weeks, thereby giving veterans even more banking choices. I predict it will be only a matter of time before we extend the program to other groups — e.g., Social Security recipients.
Thanks again for all your efforts. Given everyone's desire to move veterans to mainstream banking, our focus is on educating those who still receive their benefits on prepaid cards and paper checks. We're glad you are part of that effort.
All the best, Steve

403

Subject: Issue raised outside any subpoena
From: jbsimms
Date: Thu, Jul 09, 2020 3:53 pm
To: Walter Bayer (SSA OIG)
Cc: Jackie Lynn; Steven Lepper (CEO-Military Banks of America)
Dear Walt,
We are aware of the reluctance of Mr. Lemond, in light of an outstanding subpoena duces tecum, to engage officials of Social Security in a fact-finding mission.
Our inquiries have not been, as is the context of a subpoena (What have you done?) of past events. We know the answer to the "what have you done" question (not too much). Our inquiries are directed to future events, as in "What are you going to do?" type questions.
I am reviewing thousands (literally) of emails from Dec 2017 to the present, and I do come upon you name quite often. I was reminded moments ago as I reviewed emails from early this year as Mr. Steven Lepper became involved. Mr. Lepper's involvement validated my assertions that the VA's endorsement of the Direct Express program was based upon a false premise that BFS had done their job, and that OIG Treasury had conducted adequate audits, both premises were found to be false based upon evidence presented by me.
You are well aware of the "inserts" and the promotional printing of Direct Express enticements on envelopes, both of which have ceased for VA benefit recipients. The VBBP was created, and now is a permanent and staffed program of the VA.
What is the plan for SSA to conduct a parallel program? We did notice the inserts were eliminated. I would like to discuss the cessation of that promotional program (who caused BFS to stop inserting the paraphernalia, when, and why).
One suggestion I might make, if I may, is to place an insert into SSA envelopes directing all veterans to the VBBP so they can obtain a bank account through the Association of Military Banks of America. I assume Mr. Lepper, or a person to whom he assigns this task, can, through collaboration with SSA, create an insert to alert all veterans receiving paper checks directing them to the VBBP and/or the AMBA.
I would like to know the intent of SSA with regard to future dealings with BFS and the Direct Express program, both issues certainly would be addressed in the upcoming audit, but some things can be enacted "while Rome is burning."
Sincerely,
Jim

Saturday, July 11, 2020

The person Nora Arpin dealt with at Conduent was Mitch Raymond

Subject: Communication and constructive notice
From: jbsimms
Date: Sat, Jul 11, 2020, 7:30 am
To: Franklin Lemond (Plaintiff's Attorney) , Jackie Lynn
After our chat, and the revelation of the database searches being conducted, it appears my work (with FOI requests and other inquiries) do compliment.
Remember me telling of Nora Arpin and the Conduent employee [Mitch Raymond] around April 2018 as they both looked at my LinkedIn profile? There must be emails between the two.
Jackie's revelation of the failed program which compromised Derek's money caused Arpin to make changes. That "notice" resulted in change. The "notice" I made dozens of times to Comerica, Conduent, BFS, and OIG Treasury, were ignored, evidenced by the fact that dozens of victims came forth to me (and Jackie) and continued to tell the story of the lack of investigations, immediate denial of claims, refusal to produce copies of investigations, refusal to give provisional credit (during investigation), along with other violations provisions of Reg E.
There was quite a bit of chatter between persons from Comerica and Conduent addressing the Simms character's allegations of violating federal banking regulations. The victims continued to appear even after the involvement of OIG Treasury and Sonja Scott. Comerica/Conduent had the opportunity to address and fix the problem but would not allow me the satisfaction. Now they have to deal with Franklin.

Monday, July 13, 2020

Jackie receives VBBA mailing. We won a battle.

from: Jackie Lynn
to: J B Simms
cc: Franklin Lemond (Plaintiff's Attorney) ,
Kate Berry Kate Berry (American Banker),
Steven Lepper (CEO-Military Banks of America)
date: Jul 13, 2020, 5:50 PM
subject: Very excited to see this!!!
Hi everyone!
Wanted to share what we received in the mail today about the Veterans Benefits Banking Program. This is so exciting! So glad that Veterans have a safer way to bank!!! Now we need to get social security on board to protect people from the corrupt bank - Comerica
Today is a good day!
Jackie

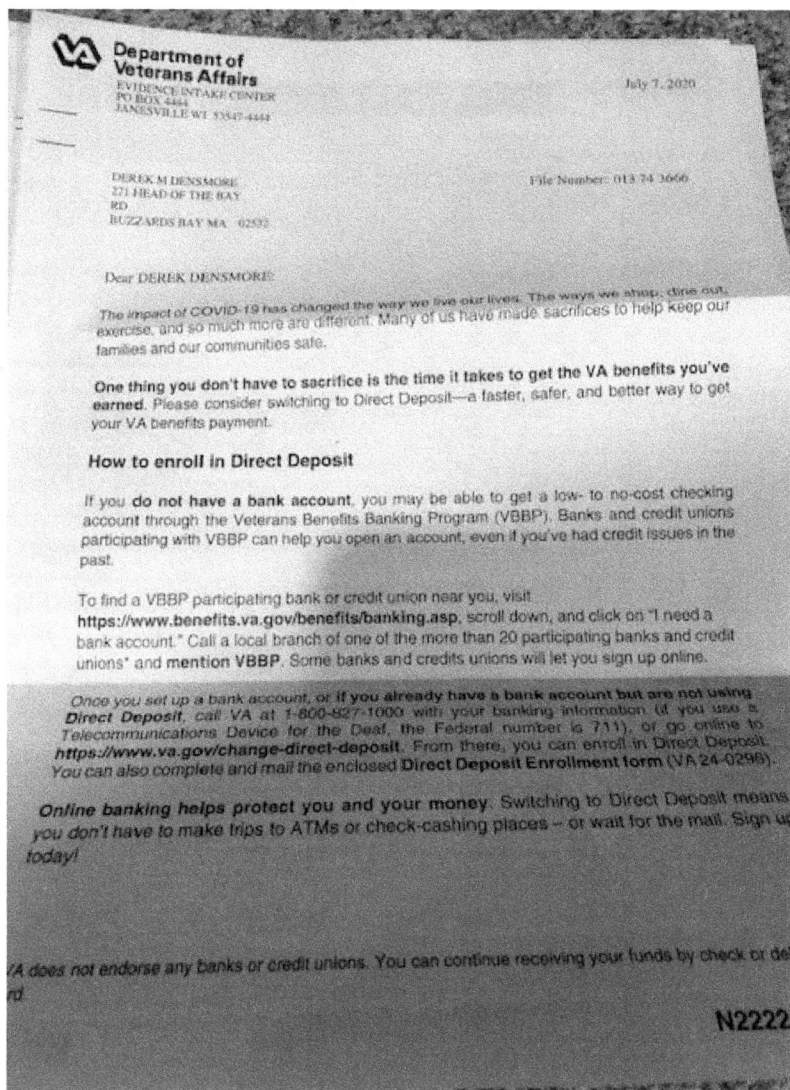

Department of Veterans Affairs
EVIDENCE INTAKE CENTER
PO BOX 4444
JANESVILLE WI 53547-4444

July 7, 2020

DEREK M DENSMORE
271 HEAD OF THE BAY
RD
BUZZARDS BAY MA 02532

File Number: 013 74 3666

Dear DEREK DENSMORE:

The impact of COVID-19 has changed the way we live our lives. The ways we shop, dine out, exercise, and so much more are different. Many of us have made sacrifices to help keep our families and our communities safe.

One thing you don't have to sacrifice is the time it takes to get the VA benefits you've earned. Please consider switching to Direct Deposit—a faster, safer, and better way to get your VA benefits payment.

How to enroll in Direct Deposit

If you do not have a bank account, you may be able to get a low- to no-cost checking account through the Veterans Benefits Banking Program (VBBP). Banks and credit unions participating with VBBP can help you open an account, even if you've had credit issues in the past.

To find a VBBP participating bank or credit union near you, visit https://www.benefits.va.gov/benefits/banking.asp, scroll down, and click on "I need a bank account." Call a local branch of one of the more than 20 participating banks and credit unions' and mention VBBP. Some banks and credits unions will let you sign up online.

Once you set up a bank account, or if you already have a bank account but are not using Direct Deposit, call VA at 1-800-827-1000 with your banking information (if you use a Telecommunications Device for the Deaf, the Federal number is 711), or go online to https://www.va.gov/change-direct-deposit. From there, you can enroll in Direct Deposit. You can also complete and mail the enclosed Direct Deposit Enrollment form (VA 24-0296).

Online banking helps protect you and your money. Switching to Direct Deposit means you don't have to make trips to ATMs or check-cashing places – or wait for the mail. Sign up today!

VA does not endorse any banks or credit unions. You can continue receiving your funds by check or debit card

N2222

J B Simms

Jul 13, 2020, 9:59 PM
Conduent was running the show. Comerica was the lapdog for Conduent.
Thank goodness the work I began on behalf of veterans, which began in March 2019, bore fruit before my involvement became a "vanishing role."
Mr. Delmar, this program mostly benefits enlisted personnel who are in lower socioeconomic lifestyle than that of commissioned officers. I do hope you have some reverence for the enlisted veterans who will be aided by this program.
I believe Pamela Powers related to me that the VA met with your office, so I assume you know my involvement. If you have any questions about my involvement, contact General Lepper.
Let's hope everyone is up to speed on this matter.J.B. Simms

Joe Plenzler (Wounded Warriors)
Jul 14, 2020, 8:18 AM
to me
Congrats, JB. This wouldn't have happened w/o your advocacy!
JOE PLENZLER, APR, communications director, Wounded Warrior Project

This was great to receive from Joe Plenzler.

Franklin Lemond (Plaintiff's Attorney)
Tue, Jul 14, 2020, 9:07 AM
to Jackie, Kate, Steven, me
Very cool!

Tuesday, July 21, 2020

We got an email from the AMBA and Lepper. Here is the new insert. We beat BFS.

Jackie got an email from Treasury regarding her FOI filed to get the contract Comerica got from BFS. Treasury wanted $57,000 in fees to get her the information. Treasury did not want us to see the information.

Chapter Nine
Inserts, FOI Requests, and Flipping the VA

Monday, August 3, 2020

from: J B Simms
to: Walter Bayer (SSA OIG), Richard Delmar (OIG Treasury),
Thomas Santaniello (Treasury BFS), Loren Sciurba (OIG Treasury)
cc: Jackie Lynn
Kate Berry (American Banker)
Steven Lepper (Military Banks of America)
Sonja Scott (OIG Treasury)
date: Aug 3, 2020, 9:53 PM
Gentlemen,
This parlor game between SSA and BFS is not amusing to victims of the Direct Express debit card program.
The VA came to the correct conclusion after continual bombardment with facts; BFS should cease inserting and printing endorsements of the Direct Express program. After learning moments ago from Ms. Densmore that her brother-in-law's Social Security check, it became necessary to determine who would take responsibility for marketing this snake oil elixir, which cures nothing and is toxic.
I was told by Mr. Steven Lepper, upon learning of inserts placed in the VA benefit envelopes of veterans, that the VA did not place the inserts nor did the VA print any marketing messages on the envelopes. (A copy of this email is being sent to Mr. Lepper if I am to be challenged.) If the SSA denies any knowledge of this marketing printing on the envelopes, culpability falls into the lap of BFS, Thomas Santaniello, and whomever else was/were "influenced" by persons from Comerica Bank or Conduent to provide Comerica Bank and Conduent with this free advertisement. I seriously doubt Comerica Bank technically "reimbursed" BFS for this printing in a manner that would not pass "the smell test."
Please advise me of your understanding of the reversal of BFS to print this promotional material on the envelopes and avoid an FOI request dance.
Sincerely,
J.B. Simms

August 2020 insert

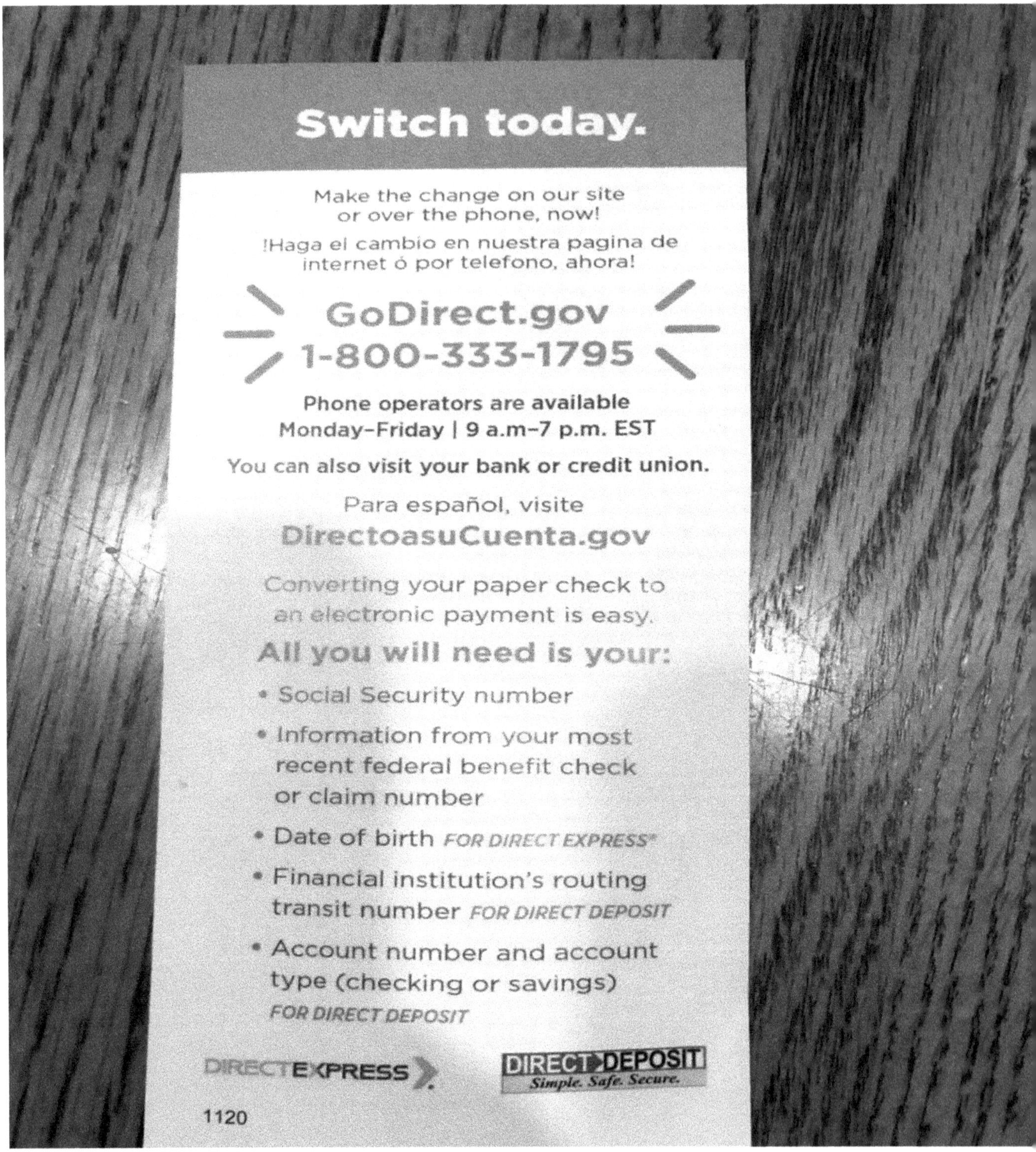

Switch today.

Make the change on our site
or over the phone, now!

!Haga el cambio en nuestra pagina de
internet ó por telefono, ahora!

GoDirect.gov

1-800-333-1795

Phone operators are available
Monday–Friday | 9 a.m–7 p.m. EST

You can **also visit your bank or credit union.**

Para español, visite
DirectoasuCuenta.gov

Converting your paper check to
an electronic payment is easy.

All you will need is your:

- Social Security number
- Information from your most recent federal benefit check or claim number
- Date of birth *FOR DIRECT EXPRESS®*
- Financial institution's routing transit number *FOR DIRECT DEPOSIT*
- Account number and account type (checking or savings) *FOR DIRECT DEPOSIT*

DIRECT EXPRESS

DIRECT DEPOSIT
Simple. Safe. Secure.

1120

Tuesday, August 11, 2020

I did not trust Treasury, BFS, or Social Security to give up any information, which is why I wanted subpoenas sent to them. Franklin asked me to send him the list of documents the subpoena would include.

Franklin Lemond
Tue, Aug 11, 2020, 12:50 PM
to me, Jackie
I've left additional messages with the US Attorney's Office requesting a discussion regarding the subpoenas but have yet to receive a response.
I'm going to send something in writing to their office by tomorrow afternoon, and if I do not receive a timely response to that, the time for a motion may be getting near.
Franklin

Everyone needed to be reminded of this statement from Nora Arpin:
August 31, 2018
To better support individuals who lose their card, yet need immediate access to their funds, the program added the Cardless Benefit Access feature in 2017. Under the Cardless Benefit Access program, many who lose their cards are given the option to access their funds through MoneyGram. When learning that fraudsters were using the feature to improperly access cardholders' funds, Comerica Bank temporarily shut down the feature and is working with the Fiscal Service and law enforcement to address the fraud and consumer complaints, and review ways to enhance fraud protection.

Jackie gets credit for the dismantling of the Cardless Benefit Program.

I sent an email to Franklin asking these questions:
Any information on subpoenas?
Is it time to file motions to compel on all of them?
When would that be an option?

Friday, August 21, 2020

Subject: Honor and Integrity
From: jbsimms
Date: Fri, Aug 21, 2020, 10:30 am
To: Richard Delmar (OIG Treasury), Michael Jackman (Aide to Rep. Keating)
Cc: Jackie Lynn, Steven Lepper (Military Banks of America), Walter Bayer (SSA OIG), Kate Berry (American Banker)
Dear Mr. Delmar and Mr. Jackman,
As I review the thousands of email records exchanged during this two-and-a-half-year (and counting) mission to expose the Direct Express program, and those federal employees culpable of "covering" for their fellow Treasury employees' malfeasance, I came across this exchange between you.
It was only after my "shot across the bow" moment with OIG Treasury Paulette Battle on February 26, 2018, that anyone recognized that the two OIG Treasury reports which were supposed to have "investigated and audited" the Direct Express program were amateurish at best.
It was Kate Berry who exposed that OIG Treasury received confirmation from Mr. Delmar that four (4) months after my talk with Ms. Battle that OIG Treasury did implement another investigation/audit of the program, BFS, Comerica Bank, and Conduent. While the preliminary report (OIG Treasury 19-041) was published a year ago and has had many false assertions in that report countered by me, the final report (audit), including the investigation complementing said report/audit is anxiously anticipated.
The promise made by Mr. Delmar to Mr. Jackman, saying, " I'll keep you advised of developments," seems to have fallen flat.
Mr. Jackman, let me, if I may tell you of the developments:
Over one hundred victims personally contacted me after having experience fraud and fraud claim denials. I was able to direct these victims, and at times intercede, and over 70 percent of the victims were reimbursed after having first been denied by Conduent and Comerica Bank.

One victim communicated with me from Mexico, where she moved from Atlanta and communicated with me. Comerica Bank and Conduent ignored her. I received a call from a local town official that the victim had killed herself in a grocery bathroom, having slit her wrists.

Another victim, bedridden and disabled, was a victim of over $7,000 in fraud as he lay dying. Comerica Bank and Conduent ignored the evidence of fraud, and the victim died. The daughter of the victim had to use a municipal gesture to bury her father. This victim's last words were "I am sorry" as he apologized for being a victim of this program.

A third, a retired E-8 Army veteran, a black female from Mississippi, called me while she was en route to a hospital for her cancer treatment. She had accumulated all evidence of fraud, was ignored by Comerica Bank and Conduent, and her claim was denied. I brought this matter to the attention of OIG Treasury. Two days later I received a text message from her husband that this retired Senior NCO died the day after we talked. I was later told the fraud claim had been paid. This lady died knowing that the fraud claim, which was money used to care for her disabled wheelchair-bound son, had not been paid.

Lastly, Ms. Densmore and I communicated with another former enlisted person, experiencing PTS, who verbally and textually expressed his desire to commit suicide. Ms. Densmore sent money to the victim to save his life.

This, Mr. Jackman, is your update. I have seen no retired military officers being victims, but having seen retired military officers ignore former enlisted personnel does give me pause.

What you will not hear is that after a yearlong battle with the VA, I received notification from Gen. Steven Lepper (USAF Ret) in December 2019 notified me that the VA was in the process of ceasing the endorsement of the failed program. This gesture protects former enlisted personnel, unlike the Department of Treasury (to include BFS and OIG Treasury).

We have yet to learn if SSA will, as did the VA, cease all endorsement of the Direct Express program.

This, Mr. Jackman, is the "update" that you were promised. Below is the promise given to you by Mr. Delmar.

Sincerely,
J.B. Simms

Monday, August 31, 2020

Big day today. Jackie sent me an email showing that Derek's insert in his VA check was endorsing the Association of Military Banks of America (AMBA) and relegating the Direct Express program as a third option. Progress was being made.

The insert touted the VBBA and AMBA, but the envelope still had a Direct Express logo on it. We had to get that printing off the envelope.

From: Jackie Lynn
Date: August 31, 2020, at 2:44:02 PM PDT
To: Franklin Lemond (Plaintiff's Attorney)
Cc: Jbsimms, Kate Berry (American Banker)
Subject: So nice to see this in Derek's monthly check - grateful they broke from DE now we just need them to get new envelopes
Jbsimms
Aug 31, 2020, 5:27 PM
to Steven, Pamela, Jackie, Kate
Dear Mr. Lepper
I just got this from Jackie Densmore.
Do you think Dr. Lawrence or Mr. Gurney could make a call to Santaniello at BFS and stop them from printing this endorsement of the corrupt Direct Express program?
We thank you for supporting our effort to save veterans from being victimized. We would like to see a more proactive effort on the part of the VA rather than Ms. Densmore and I having to point out obvious self-serving behavior by BFS. We have subjected ourselves to the ire of the VA as we point out that BFS does not have the interest in mind by continuing to endorse the Direct Express program. We do apologize that you are our only conduit for our concerns and corrective measures, but no one at the VA has the motivation necessary to engage us.
Thank you again.
Sincerely,
JB Simms

Tuesday, September 1, 2020

Steven Lepper remained loyal and helpful

Steven Lepper (Military Banks of America)
Tue, Sep 1, 2020, 5:04 AM
to Jackie, Kate, Pamela, me
Mr. Simms,
Thanks for the note; I understand your frustration. However, there are three silver linings to this mailing:
1. It did contain an advertisement for the Veterans Benefits Banking Program promoting direct deposit.
2. It includes a statement, printed on the back of the envelope, indicating the recipient is "required to replace [his] paper check with direct deposit. This leads me to ask: Why is Derek still receiving paper checks?
3. If you go to www.GoDirect.gov, you'll see that Treasury has now included a new link on that page. It takes veterans to the VA's VBBP page.
I will certainly pass your note to VBA; however, I think our energy would be better spent focusing on the message this envelope was intended to convey — the "important notice" Treasury wants to communicate here: "You are required to replace your paper check with direct deposit." That requirement is a huge step in the right direction. It's part of VA's proactive effort to get all the veterans it supports "banked."
Thanks,
Steve

Switch to Direct Deposit

- **Protect** your benefits
- **Get** your money faster
- **Bank** securely

• • •

How to Enroll

If you **do not have** a bank account

- Visit benefits.va.gov/banking
- Call one of the participating banks and mention Veterans Benefits Banking Program

If you **have** a bank account but are not using Direct Deposit

- Visit va.gov/change-direct-deposit
- Call 1-800-827-1000 (711 for TDD)

VA | U.S. Department of Veterans Affairs

VA0920 VA does not endorse any banks or credit unions. You can continue receiving benefits by check or

412

Important Notice

You are required to replace your paper check with direct deposit.

GO DIRECT

www.GoDirect.gov
(800) 333-1795

DIRECT EXPRESS

Contact Us

J B Simms
Tue, Sep 1, 2020, 6:38 AM
to Richard, Jennifer, Steven, Jackie, Kate, Pamela
Dear Mr. Lepper,
Thank you for your reply.
I will go to the link and see that Go Direct leads veterans to the VBBP.
It appears that the fact that Treasury (BFS) has included a new link directing veterans to the VBBP has validated the supposition made by Ms. Densmore and me that the Direct Express program, as operated by Comerica Bank and Conduent, is not a viable manner from which veterans to receive veteran benefits. Veterans who are employed at Treasury should feel a sense of duty to other veterans, but it has taken our non-apologetic effort to make anything happen at Treasury, VA, and Social Security.
I do hesitate to speak for Derek's decision to continue to receive checks. My understanding is his debilitation has resulted in trust only in checks. We are aware of other veterans receiving checks. The number of these recipients will diminish through transition and attrition.
In a broader view, maybe Derek's decision gives us a direct and immediate view of change, or lack thereof, by VA, BFS, Social Security, and inertia being overcome at OIG Treasury.
Derek is the monitor of these agencies.
I knew there must have been a reason I awakened at 4 am, and I found your email. The universe is working. Thank you for being a voice for disabled enlisted veterans.
Sincerely,Jim

J B Simms
Sep 1, 2020, 6:49 AM
to Franklin
Franklin,
Jackie and I got things done. Look at the changes made. These bastards did not change because they liked us. I feel you can use the changes we made happen to validate our case. Changes are being made dynamically. We constantly make things happen.Jim

Friday, September 4, 2020

Jbsimms
Fri, Sep 4, 2020, 12:13 PM
to Walter, Jackie, Steven
Dear Walter,
Below is the insert found accompanying the Social Security check for MS. Densmore's brother-in-law. While we profess this insert is an attempt to validate a corrupt and unsafe financial program created by BFS (a practice ceased by the VA), we want to know who directed this insert be placed in the envelope.
We have no other option than to reach out to social media to determine the answers to our questions. Hopefully someone of good conscience will respond, as was the case with the VA.
We only ask for transparency and accountability.
Sincerely,Jim

We did not know who was directing the inserts to be put in the SSA checks trying to get SSA recipients to enroll in the Direct Express program. The SSA was ignoring the VA's decision to separate from the BFS program (Direct Express). Walter Bayer made us think he supported us, but he ultimately would betray us.

Tuesday, September 8, 2020

Bayer, Walter Office of the Inspector General <Walter Bayer (SSA OIG)>
Tue, Sep 8, 2020, 1:00 PM
to me
Hi Jim,
This is a question you will need to direct to the Agency given that these mailings are part of its operations.
I may have already provided you with some public affairs contact information, but just in case I am providing it again.
Thanks,Walt

Thursday, September 10. 2020

The depositions of the plaintiffs began. John Carney was deposed by Comerica's lawyers.

It was evident that Carnley's lack of education and sophistication was used against him by the defense attorneys. It was like cattle led to the slaughter. The attorneys for Comerica could see that Carnley was not intellectually ready for a deposition, but this did not dismiss the fact that he had been victimized.
Most of the victims using the Direct Express card were of a lower socioeconomic group, and less educated.

Thursday, October 1, 2020

from: J B Simms
to: Steven Lepper (Military Banks of America)
cc: Jennifer Kreegar,
Jackie Lynn
Walter Bayer (SSA OIG)
date: Oct 1, 2020, 10:58 AM
subject: VA disability check inserts
Dear Mr. Lepper,
It is that time of the month when we anticipate the inserts.
This came from Ms. Kreegar, who just now sent me this copy of the insert accompanying her disability check. There is no mention of Direct Express.
Please pass along to persons at the VA the glee of Ms. Densmore and me.
We are hoping the understanding we imparted to the you and the VA will be absorbed be the Social Security Administration, and the SSA will cease endorsement of the BFS program (Direct Express) as administered by Comerica Bank and Conduent. Many veterans receive SSA payments and should be protected along with other citizens.
Again, thank you for believing and having the integrity to validate and endorse our position to the VA of the dangers of the Direct Express program.
Sincerely,
Jim Simms

Social Security check insert

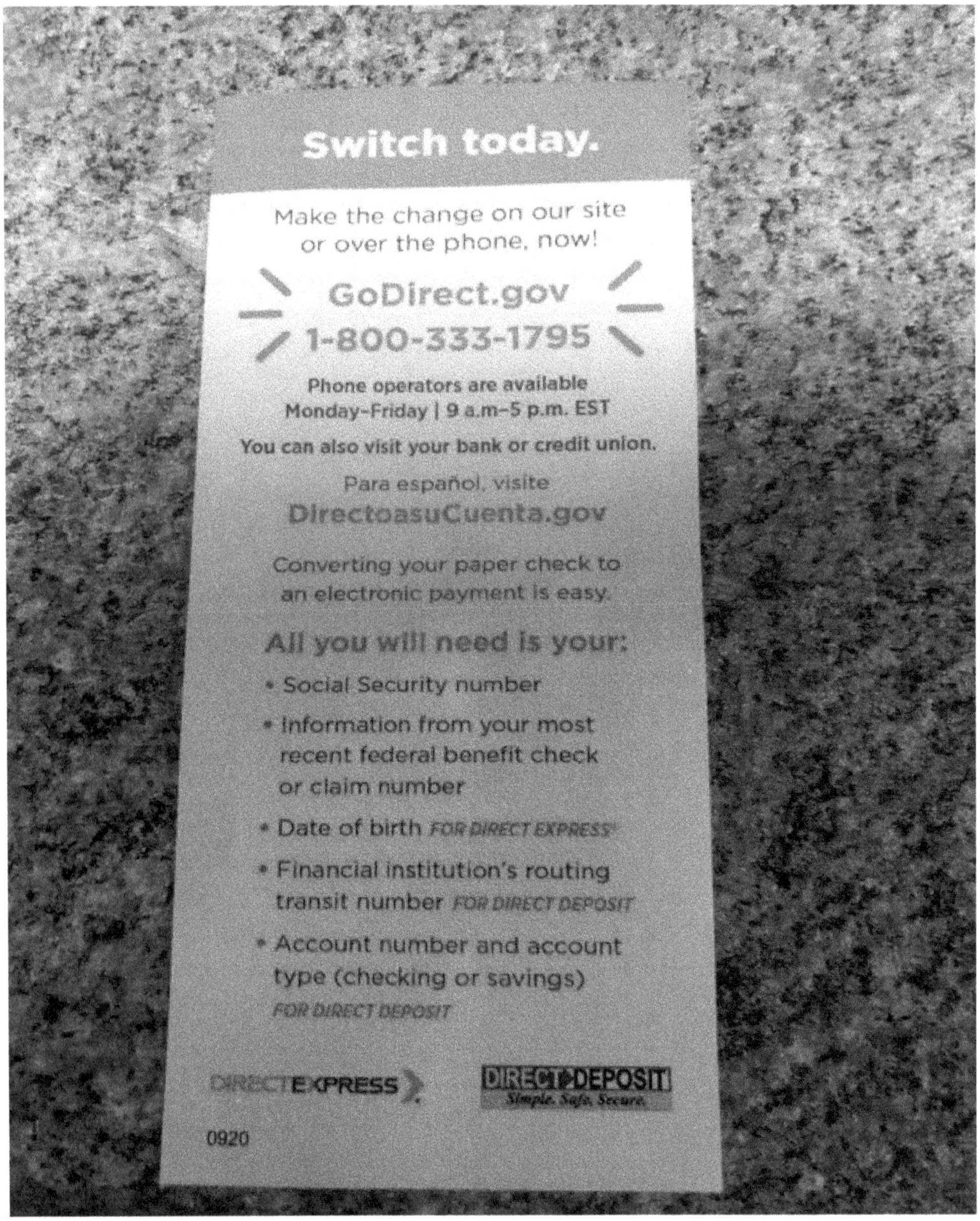

Switch to Direct Deposit

☆ **Protect** your benefits
☆ **Get** your money faster
☆ **Bank** securely

• • •

How to Enroll

If you **do not** have an account

🖵 Visit benefits.va.gov/banking

📞 Call one of the participating banks/ credit unions and **mention Veterans Benefits Banking Program**

If you **have** an account but are not using direct deposit

🖵 Visit va.gov/change-direct-deposit

📞 Call 1-800-827-1000 (711 for TDD)

VA | U.S. Department of Veterans Affairs

VA does not endorse any banks or credit unions. You can continue receiving benefits by check or card.

VA0721

Friday, October 2, 2020

from: *Jbsimms*
to: *Steven Lepper (Military Banks of America)*
cc: *Jackie Lynn*
date: *Oct 2, 2020, 1:02 PM*
subject: Look at this crap-threatening inserts.
Mr. Lepper,
Thank you for being receptive.
I am glad the VA changed their inserts. Now if we can just get the VA to create a policy wherein all persons applying for VA benefits will be directed to your organization via the VBBP, and the words "Direct Express" will be eliminated from all documents at the VA for persons getting benefits.
Attrition, transition, and application are the keywords. This is not just about sticking a finger into the eye of Comerica and Conduent; this is about protecting veterans from financial abuse and anxiety.
It appears Mr. Bayer is a bit reluctant to discuss the matter of the inserts in contrast with his many cordial communications. That is no deterrent for us. Social Security has the same obligation to veterans as does the VA to protect veteran recipients of either VA benefits or any Social Security benefits. If you can convey our concerns to Mr. Gurney or others at the VA, maybe they will contact Social Security and convince them to act as did the VA and stop endorsing and promoting the Direct Express program.
Thank you for your well wishes, and I wish you the same. My weekend will be spent preparing for my upcoming deposition with Comerica/Conduent attorneys, which hopefully will be in person.
Sincerely,
Jim

Cardholder Guide to Direct Express Fraud Procedures

Comments on Laws Protecting Debit Cardholders

Regulation E- Electronic Fund Transfers
Title 12 Code of Federal Regulations, Section 205
Overview of Paragraphs 205.6 and 205.11
The duties of the financial institution (Direct Express/Comerica Bank): (A) Must acknowledge the first call to the call center giving notice of the fraud. (B) Can decide to conduct no investigation; noticing fraud immediately and reimbursing the cardholder (C) Must begin the investigation immediately upon receiving verbal notice. (D) Cannot wait for written reports from the cardholder to begin the investigation. (E) Must give full provisional credit within 10 days of reporting fraud if the investigation will take up to 45 days. (F) Cannot hold cardholder liable for knowing about fraudulent activity if circumstances such as hospitalization or travel are a factor. (G) Must give a record of the complete investigation if requested. (H) Cannot hold cardholder liable for any negligence or trusting behavior, i.e., give access information to a family member, or caregiver, to access funds on behalf of the cardholder.

Jackie had gotten Michael Jackman, the aide to Representative Keating, to talk to Delmar and others in 2018 on her behalf (as a constituent of Keating). Delmar continues to make excuses and was never accountable.

From: Richard Delmar (OIG Treasury)
Sent: Monday, September 24, 2018, 10:51 AM
To: Michael Jackman (Aide to Rep. Keating)
Subject: Treasury Direct Express - Inspector General action
Mr. Jackman – following up on our previous communications about Treasury OIG's oversight of the Direct Express program.
In addition to our current audit work, our Office of Investigations is meeting with responsible officials at BFS and Comerica to discuss the Direct Express program and the fraudulent activities affecting it.
We will evaluate the steps already taken by Comerica and their sub-contractor to make the system and its processes more robust and resistant to identity theft and other frauds.
In addition, we will review what they are doing to analyze frauds and their own possible vulnerabilities, as well as how they report problems.
With our financial crime and forensic expertise, we will add value by identifying security gaps and proactive steps they can take, including the provision of more real-time information to us.

Thank you for your interest. I'll keep you advised of developments.
Rich Delmar
Counsel to the Inspector General
Department of the Treasury

From: Michael.Jackman@mail.house.gov
Sent: Monday, September 24, 2018, 1:14 PM
To: Richard Delmar (OIG Treasury)
Subject: RE: Treasury Direct Express - Inspector General action
Thank you, Rich. I appreciate your response and would ask that, as best you can, please keep me abreast of any developments from these meetings.
Michael Jackman, District Director
Office of Congressman Keating (MA-09)

Saturday, October 3, 2020

from: *Jackie Lynn*
to: *Franklin Lemond ((Plaintiff's Attorney)*
cc: *Jbsimms*
date: *Oct 3, 2020, 3:56 PM*
Reading over Martisha's deposition something really stood out that she said - she said the call center rep told her that even with a new card fraudster could still access the acct because they knew the acct number. Which means that we all have assigned acct numbers that when our accts were hacked Comerica still left our accts vulnerable and that is why I believe ppl got hit twice.
Is there any way to find out for the plaintiffs if any of the account numbers were changed after the fraud happened?
Just a thought I need to get with you and go over dates at some point.
Thanks Jim
J
How would persons at the call center know the fraudsters had Mr. McPhail's account number?

Thursday, August 15, 2020

Jackie sees the result of us defeating the VA

from: *Jackie Lynn*
to: *Jbsimms*
Franklin Lemond ((Plaintiff's Attorney), Walter Bayer (SSA OIG), Steven Lepper (Military Banks of America), Cate Mahan <casework@warren.senate.gov>, Kate Berry (American Banker)
date: *Oct 15, 2020, 6:55 PM*
subject: So grateful for this program!!

Department of Veterans Affairs

EVIDENCE INTAKE CENTER
PO BOX 4444
JANESVILLE WI 53547-4444

October 5, 2020

File Number: 013 74 3666

DEREK M DENSMORE
271 HEAD OF THE BAY
RD
BUZZARDS BAY MA 02532

Dear DEREK DENSMORE:

You can't stop storms from blowing in, but you can help protect your VA benefits. **Direct Deposit** allows you to manage your benefits from the comfort of your home.

You currently get your VA benefits by prepaid card or check. Please consider switching to **Direct Deposit**—a faster, safer, and better way to get your VA benefit payments.

How to enroll in Direct Deposit

If you **do not have a bank account**, you may be able to get a low- to no-cost checking account through the Veterans Benefits Banking Program (VBBP). Banks and credit unions participating with VBBP can help you open an account, even if you've had credit issues in the past.

To find a VBBP participating bank or credit union near you, visit **https://www.benefits.va.gov/benefits/banking.asp**, scroll down, and click on "Find a bank." Call a local branch of one of the more than 30 participating banks and credit unions* and **mention VBBP**. Some banks and credits unions will let you sign up online.

Once you set up a bank account, or **if you already have a bank account but are not using Direct Deposit**, call VA at 1-800-827-1000 with your banking information (if you use a Telecommunications Device for the Deaf, the Federal number is 711), or go online to **https://www.va.gov/change-direct-deposit**. From there, you can enroll in Direct Deposit.

Online banking helps protect you and your money. Switching to Direct Deposit means neither bad weather nor mail delays will keep you from getting your benefit payments on time. Sign up today!

The VBBP is mentioned in the letter above. Pamela Powers was instrumental in starting the process, Joe Gurney did the work for the VA, and Steven Lepper validate my message to the VA.

The email below identifies an Assistant U.S. Attorney (AUSA) who would be handling the subpoenas we had served on federal employees and agencies.

From: Treadwell, Trish (USAGAN)
Date: Wed, Oct 16, 2019, at 2:45 PM
Subject: Almon v. Conduent and Comerica Bank -- FS/Treasury Subpoena
To: Franklin Lemond
Franklin:
I am hoping to set up a call this week or early next week regarding the Subpoenas that Plaintiffs served on the Bureau of Fiscal Services in this matter. I am the N.D. Ga. AUSA who will be handling any filed responses or litigation, although I am hopeful that we can discuss a solution that allows for the production of some subset of documents that will obviate the need for any motion to quash or to compel.
Please let me know if there is a time tomorrow or next week that you all are available to discuss. (I will be in meetings out of the office all day on Friday.)
Trish Treadwell
Trishanda L. Treadwell | Assistant United States Attorney | Civil Division
United States Attorney's Office | Northern District of Georgia

Franklin was trying to push the federal agencies to respond to subpoenas. Santaniello was refusing to abide by his subpoenas. He never did.

Sunday November 1, 2020

JD sent me an insert for SSA, promoting DE.
Thelma Leatherbarrow has been contacting Schmitt. Thelma got provisional credit from both Conduent and the merchant.

Tuesday, November 3, 2020

Freedom of Information requests continue to be filed

Below is an email from the Freedom of Information section of the Social Security Administration acknowledging the Freedom of Information request I submitted. See the "Description" section of the request to the documents I was requesting.

from: admin@foiaonline.gov
to: jb.simms10@gmail.com
date: Nov 3, 2020, 11:59 AM
subject: FOIA Request SSA-2021-001175 Submitted
mailed-by: foiaonline.gov
This message is to confirm your request submission to the FOIA online application: View Request. Request information is as follows:
Tracking Number: SSA-2021-001175
Requester Name: James B Simms
Date Submitted: 11/03/2020
Request Status: Submitted
Description: 1. The identity of the federal agency, department, office, and person(s) charged with creating, editing, developing, or having any creative input with regard to the printed paper inserts (endorsing and promoting the Direct Express program) which accompany checks being mailed to Social Security recipients from January 2020 the present.
2. The identity of the federal agency, department, office, and person(s) which/who directed the paper inserts be inserted into the envelopes to accompany Social Security checks.
3. The name of the person at Bureau of Fiscal Service or the Social Security Administration who directed the inserts be placed in the envelopes to accompany Social Security checks.

4. Copies of any emails, transcripts of telephone conversations, notes of any meetings, witness statements or any tangible evidence of communication between the Bureau of Fiscal Service, Comerica Bank, Conduent, SSA OIG, OIG Treasury and the Social Security Administration with regard to the paper inserts endorsing the Direct Express program and the insertion into the check envelopes.

5. Copies of emails, transcripts of telephone conversations, notes from meetings, witness statements or any tangible evidence of any or all illegal payments being made to federal employees at Bureau of Fiscal Service, OIG Treasury, Social Security OIG, Bureau of Fiscal Service Office of Legislative Affairs, by Comerica Bank or Conduent to promote the Direct Express program or to protect against inquiries.

Thursday, November 10, 2020

The FOI section of US Treasury denied my request for a waiver to make payment for documents generated from an FOI request.

The public has "the right to know" information withheld by our government

from: *Jbsimms*
to: *"Cynthia A. Sydnor" <Cynthia.Sydnor@fiscal.treasury.gov>*
date: *Nov 5, 2020, 11:30 AM*
subject: Re: FOIA # 2020-10-016 (Simms)
Dear Ms. Syndor-Jones,
Quoting from your email of earlier this morning, allow me to post the following sentence from your email:
You must demonstrate that disclosure of the information is in the public interest and is likely to contribute significantly to the public's understanding of the operations or activities of the government.
The "[u]nderstanding of the operations or activities..." to which you refer is the matter at hand.
The public has a right to know the information I requested. I know more than the general public does about the operations of Bureau of Fiscal Service and the secretive manner in which processes are conducted. My telephone number was flagged by your agency (an employee of your agency identified me by name upon answering a call without the call having been forwarded; this employee has been identified with date and time of the conversation noted) and promised return calls never materialized.
You stated the waiver was denied, but you did not identify the person making the denial nor the legal justification for said denial. This leads a citizen to believe the denial is standard operating procedure by BFS in their attempt to avoid and evade exposure and accountability.
I request you bring this matter to the attention of Commissioner Gribben. His appointment, upon the retirement of Commissioner McCoy, comes on the heels of investigations and audits commissioned with regard to revelations by me. I assure you Commissioner Gribben is unaware of all he inherited. I will welcome an appointment to discuss this matter with Commissioner Gribben.
Sincerely,
J.B. Simms

Thursday, November 5, 2020

Santaniello was exposed again for "what" he was

from: *Jbsimms*
to: *Kate Berry (American Banker)*
Jackie Lynn
date: *Nov 5, 2020, 10:30 AM*
subject: one last epiphany
Office of Legislative and Public Affairs
Bureau of the Fiscal Service
U.S. Department of the Treasury
Guess who works in the same office? You got it; Santaniello.
They want me to pay $473, which they know I will not pay.
Jackie submitted a challenge to the redacted contracts between Comerica and BFS.
No word on their reply.
Jim

Subject: Re: Today's agenda
From: Franklin Lemond ((Plaintiff's Attorney)
Date: Thu, November 05, 2020 4:18 pm
To: Jim Simms jbsimms
Cc: Jackie Lynn
JB,
Regarding the subpoenas, I have been working with the US Attorney's office regarding the requested information. I am finalizing a letter to them that will go out tomorrow and am optimistic that I will have documents this month. Fingers crossed.
I have received two productions from Defendants in the past two weeks and have about 35,000 new pages of documents to review. An additional (smaller) production is coming soon and then I will be able to see where we are with respect to what they have produced versus what is outstanding that I have requested.
As far as plaintiff depositions, you two and Ms. Paglia are all that is left for defendants to depose. They would like to get them all done this month, which I think is possible. Before we schedule your depositions I want to make sure that we have produced all documents you have, so we will need to work on that soon.
As for deposing the Defendants, in addition to deposing their designated corproate representative, I envision deposing Nora Arpin, Shantelle Johnson, Marquite Stevenson, and at least a couple of the following execs Joe Froderman, Mitch Raymond, Sam Marzano, Rachelle Denman, Deborah Srour, and Ellen McMahon. Which of those I depose will depend on what the document review flushes out. I'd like to start taking some of these in December and then finish up in January if necessary.
Franklin

Monday, November 9, 2020

The focus will change from the inserts (which we believed had been changed because Jackie and I raised a little hell about this).

FOI revelation: the conspiracy to retain Comerica Bank as Fiscal Agent

Three emails came from Richard Ha.
Mr. Ha was in the FOI office of the Veterans Administration.
These emails exposed "The White Paper"

Ha, Richard <Richard.Ha1@va.gov>
jbsimms
|Email 1 of 3 due to size limitations|
November 9, 2020
In Reply Refer To: 001B
FOIA Request: 20-09821-F
Dear Mr. Simms:
This is the Initial Agency Decision (IAD) to your Freedom of Information Act (FOIA) request to the Office of the Secretary, U.S. Dept. of Veterans Affairs (OSVA), dated September 3, 2020, received September 25, 2020, and assigned FOIA tracking number 20-09821-F. You requested:
"Copies of all communication between the following persons employed at the VA and Bureau of Fiscal Service (to include Mr. Santaniello and Mr. Gribben) beginning February 1, 2019 to the present: Pamela Powers, Paul Lawrence, Joe Gurney.
These communications will include documented records of telephone calls, emails, faxes, notes from meeting between the VA employees and Bureau of Fiscal Service, directives, or any tangible publication regarding the Direct Express program.
Copies of all communication between the VA employees and representatives of the Association of Military Banks of America, to include communication between VA and Major General Steven J. Lepper (USAF Retired), CEO of Association of Military Banks of America.
Copies of all inter-department email, texts, letters, faxes, communication logs, notes from meetings, briefings, or any tangible record of any communication between and not limited to Pamela Powers, Paul Lawrence, Joe Gurney, and Secretary Wilkie from February 1, 2019 to the present with regard to the Direct Express debit card program and the administration of said program by the Bureau of Fiscal Service, Department of Treasury."

As a reminder, the VHA FOIA office is processing your FOIA request 20-09883-F for any responsive emails to or from VBA employees Paul Lawrence and Joe Gurney. OSVA is processing only the responsive emails to or from Secretary Wilkie or Acting Deputy Secretary Pam Powers.

IAD & Reasonable Searches Dated 9/29/20, 10/6/20, & 10/9/20

On September 29, 2020, an OSVA FOIA Officer requested that the OIT office provided all responsive emails within its possession. On October 6, 2020, the OIT office provided such, with an OSVA FOIA Officer to conduct secondary searches.

On October 9, 2020, an OSVA FOIA Officer conducted the four (4) below key term searches within the email boxes of Robert Wilkie with the date timeframe of February 1, 2019, to October 9, 2020, our search cut-off date.

Search 1

From: Powers or Wilkie or RLW To: Santaniello or Gribben or Lepper

Date: 2/1/19 to 9/29/20

Search 2

To: Powers or Wilkie or RLW From: Santaniello or Gribben or Lepper

Date: 2/1/19 to 9/29/20

Search 3

To: Powers or Wilkie or RLW Date: 2/1/19 to 9/29/20

Key term: "Direct Express"

Search 4

From: Powers or Wilkie or RLW Date: 2/1/19 to 9/29/20

Key term: "Direct Express"

The four (4) aforementioned emails searches yielded one hundred thirty-six (136) responsive pages.

From: jbsimms

Date: Mon, November 09, 2020 1:45 pm

To: "Ha, Richard" <Richard.Ha1@va.gov>

Cc: Jackie Lynn

Dear Mr. Ha,

Thank you very much for your expeditious reply and the document attached. There are many moving parts (Ms. Powers, Dr. Lawrence, Treasury operatives and employees from Comerica Bank and Conduent).

While I am pleased that the VA responded to my involvement after Sec Wilkie responded to Sen Warren. My assertion that the Direct Express program, as administered by Bureau of Fiscal Service, victimized veterans and other citizens while subjecting victims cardholders to unnecessary psychological/mental stress which endangers the lives of veterans.

I have glanced at the first document, and look forward to reading the second document. The communication from Ms. Powers was refreshingly candid. Communication from me is sprinkled within the document, which again validates my assertions.

Give my regards to Ms. Powers for her cooperation in this matter. There might be a few challenges to identify some persons, but I feel I know this matter very well and can connect some dots.

Sincerely,

J.B. Simms

Tuesday, November 10, 2020

An FOI request was sent to the Social Security Administration

Below is the response from Social Security, Freedom of Information office, for information noted as "Request Description" within the text of the email.

Notice the reason for requesting the request be expedited. I knew they were going to turn down my request, but I had to try.

I was sending FOI requests to different agencies and asking for much of the same information. It was an effective plan.

from: admin@foiaonline.gov
to: jb.simms10@gmail.com
date: Nov 10, 2020, 3:17 PM
subject: FOIA Expedited Processing Disposition Reached for SSA-2021-001175
mailed-by: foiaonline.gov.
Your request for Expedited Processing for the FOIA request SSA-2021-001175 has been denied. Additional details for this request are as follows:
Request Created on: 11/03/2020.
Request Description:
1. The identity of the federal agency, department, office, and person(s) charged with creating, editing, developing, or having any creative input with regard to the printed paper inserts (endorsing and promoting the Direct Express program) which accompany checks being mailed to Social Security recipients from January 2020 the present.
2. The identity of the federal agency, department, office, and person(s) which/who directed the paper inserts be inserted into the envelopes to accompany Social Security checks.
3. The name of the person at Bureau of Fiscal Service or the Social Security Administration who directed the inserts be placed in the envelopes to accompany Social Security checks.
4. Copies of any emails, transcripts of telephone conversations, notes of any meetings, witness statements or any tangible evidence of communication between the Bureau of Fiscal Service, Comerica Bank, Conduent, SSA OIG, OIG Treasury and the Social Security Administration with regard to the paper inserts endorsing the Direct Express program and the insertion into the check envelopes.
5. Copies of emails, transcripts of telephone conversations, notes from meetings, witness statements or any tangible evidence of any or all illegal payments being made to federal employees at Bureau of Fiscal Service, OIG Treasury, Social Security OIG, Bureau of Fiscal Service Office of Legislative Affairs, by Comerica Bank or Conduent to promote the Direct Express program or to protect against inquiries.

Reason submitted for Expedited Processing

Expedited Processing Original Justification*: The continued endorsement of the Direct Express program endangers the financial, mental, and emotional conditions of veterans and other persons receiving this material. The persons involved in the perpetuation of this promotion need to be exposed.*
Expedited Processing Disposition Reason: This request is being closed as a duplicate of SSA-2021-000274. Your expedited processing decision will come attached to that case number.

Thursday, November 12, 2020

The FOI document from the VA opened the door to expose the conspiracy to retain Comerica Bank including the White Paper on Page 20

From: jbsimms
Date: Thu, November 12, 2020, 2:27 pm
To: "Richard.ha1@va.gov" <Richard.ha1@va.gov>
Dear Mr. Ha,
Thank you for forwarding the three (3) attachments with regard to my FOI request.
I do not know if you are privy to the nature of this issue to which the FOI requests was made so I will refrain from commenting at length on the matter. As can see no one from the VA chose to contact me after my communication with Ms. Powers began in March 2019. This reluctance and refusal allowed the VA to buy into the false narrative presented by Comerica Bank and Bureau of Fiscal Service that the nature of the issue was a "data breach" or "security breach."
Since I could not interact with the VA, only communicating "to" Pamela Powers, I was trying to enlighten the VA to the fact that the issue was (and is) a violation of Regulation E (15USC1693) and associated federal regulations by Comerica Bank and the subcontractor Conduent. The attempt to downplay the significance of this malfeasance by the perpetrators (persons and entities) was not lost on me. This matter could have been cleared up quickly if only Ms. Powers or Mr. Lawrence chose to communicate.
I am pleased the VBBP was created as a result of my communication with Ms. Powers.
The matter being addressed today is missing data from the FOI request, specifically the "White Paper" report to Ms. Powers. For some reason, the "Recommendations" referenced at the top of the page 20 was redacted. I

respectfully fail to see your motive to validate the redaction of this section since recommendations by the person writing this White Paper is relevant to my request.

The second matter with information reference in the White Paper is in the second paragraph of the same White Paper, noting that the VHA and VBA met with a Comerica employee noted as the Director of Government Electronic Solutions. The minutes/notes/transcription of this meeting falls under my FOI request, and I am requesting this document, to include the identity of all persons in attendance and all statements made by persons at the meeting.

Again, it is assumed that the "recommendations" would append to the record of the meeting (which I assume was forwarded to Ms. Powers since the synopsis was sent to her) and those recommendations are being requested.

Thank you again for supplying me the limited documents as a result of my request, and I look forward to receiving the balance of the requested documents.

Sincerely,
J.B. Simms

Friday, November 13, 2020

From: jbsimms
Sent: Friday, November 13, 2020 11:04 AM
To: VACO FOIA Service Inbox <vacofoiase@va.gov>
Subject: FOI 20-09821-F and attachments
Dear MS. Holley,
You misunderstood my reply to my response to the FOI information I received. I believe a different person sent the information to me. I am not in disagreement with the submission; I stated the submission was incomplete and I specifically noted that information from a specific meeting was absent from the documents I received. Your suggestion of a referral of my revelation of a failure to comply by VA OIG is insulting and dismissive. I suggest you either forward this email to your supervisor, to the person originally responding, or to Pamela Powers.
Sincerely,
J.B. Simms

After sending this letter to appeal and get more info about the White Paper, I submitted another FOI request.

Sunday, November 15, 2020

from: Franklin Lemond ((Plaintiff's Attorney)
to: Jackie Lynn
cc: Jbsimms
date: Nov 15, 2020, 11:33 AM
subject: Re: Ugh
Franklin Lemond ((Plaintiff's Attorney)
Nov 15, 2020, 11:33 AM
to Jackie, me
As I explained to JB when we spoke on November 5, I expect to get meaningful responses to the subpoenas from the agencies by the end of this month. As I told JB during that same conversation, if I do not get them by then, then I will move to compel. I am supposed to speak with the US Attorney's office further regarding the subpoena production on Monday and will update you later in the week.
Franklin

Santaniello and Delmar blocked us.

from: Jbsimms
to: Jackie Lynn
date: Nov 15, 2020, 8:57 PM
I saw this. BFS did not comply with the recommendations of OIG Treasury and suffered no consequences. (This was regarding the Treasury OIG 20-028 audit)

December 2020 Social Security insert (front and back)

427

Get your payments directly.

Convert your paper checks to electronic payments with direct deposit or a Direct Express® card.

Tuesday, November 24, 2020

from: *Franklin Lemond ((Plaintiff's Attorney)*
to: *Jackie Lynn*
cc: *Jbsimms*
date: *Nov 15, 2020, 11:33 AM*
subject: Re: Ugh

As I explained to JB when we spoke on November 5, I expect to get meaningful responses to the subpoenas from the agencies by the end of this month. As I told JB during that same conversation, if I do not get them by then, then I will move to compel. I am supposed to speak with the US Attorney's office further regarding the subpoena production on Monday and will update you later in the week.
Franklin

The focus was now on the "White Paper."

From: jbsimms
Sent: Tuesday, November 24, 2020, 12:24 PM
To: OGC FOIA Appeals <ogcfoiaappeals@va.gov>
Cc: VACO FOIA Service Inbox <vacofoiase@va.gov>; Jackie Lynn; Jennifer Kreegar
Subject: FOI 20-09821-F and attachments
Attn: VA FOI Appeals Office
Below is a copy of the correspondence between Ms. Holley and myself with regard to my FOI Request 20-09821. I am grateful for the expeditious manner in which my request was addressed. As for the limited information forwarded to me as a result of my FOI request, you see below I have requested more definitive information concerning a few issues referenced in the documents provided by the VA FOI office.
One issue is, as stated below, is reference made on Page 20 of the attached document, the first of three documents submitted to me by the VA FOI office. Documentation on this page references a "White Paper" with regard to a meeting on March 19, 2019, between VBA, VHA, and Comerica Bank officials. The synopsis offered to me was not a copy of the White Paper but was an overview of the meeting, lacking documentation of interaction between participants or referencing to documents presented by persons present at the meeting.
I feel it is within the scope of my FOI request that the entirety of the White Paper submitted to Ms. Pamela Powers be forwarded to me in its entirety.
I am copying a caregiver of a veteran and a veteran who both receive VA benefits. Both persons have suffered as a result of the association of the VA with Comerica Bank, and we are pleased that the relationship has ended.
Sincerely,
J.B. Simms

The secrets of the White Paper

The White Paper made reference to a request for scheduled meetings with employees of the VA (notably the Veterans Benefit Association), Social Security, Bureau of Fiscal Service, and OIG Treasury.
No employee of these agencies had told anyone outside their circle about the meetings that occurred in the spring of 2019. This was the time (May 2019) that the Bureau of Fiscal Service was to award the fiscal agent contract for the Direct Express program. This announcement was delayed for six months, until January 2020.
It will be shown that there was a problem that I exposed, Pamela Powers mandated the meetings and BFS had to delay awarding the renewed fiscal agent contract to Comerica Bank.

The "White Paper" was huge. It showed the VA (Pamela Powers) mandated meetings, which began March 16, 2021. These meetings were attended by people from OIG Treasury, SSA, VA, and Comerica.
I needed to find the original White Paper revelation.

Depositions are beginning. Jackie will be deposed before me.
UDOC <udoc@dcodc.org>
jbsimms erikpublishing.com
Good afternoon,
This email contains a letter from Office of Disciplinary Counsel. Please see attached.

Ashley White
Administrative Assistant
Office of Disciplinary Counsel
515 5th Street, NW, Superior Court Building A, Room 117, Washington, DC 20001

This was for the complaint filed against Delmar with the Washington DC Bar Association. The Bar Association did not solicit a reply from Delmar. They denied my claim outright. Delmar made no statement. This was a big political move on the part of Delmar to avoid me.

Another FOI request to the VA- the unredacted White Paper

Knight, Tracy (OGC) tracy.knight@va.gov
To: jbsimms
Attached.
From: OGC FOIA Appeals
Sent: Tuesday, November 24, 2020 2:03 PM
To: jbsimms
Subject: FOI 20-09821-F and attachments
 Hello,
Your FOIA Appeal has been received. Attached is our acknowledgment letter for your appeal.
Thank you,
OGCFOIAAppeals@va.gov
Office of General Counsel (024)
Information & Administrative Law Group
Department of Veteran Affairs

I filed an appeal in order to get an unredacted copy of the White Paper.

Below is an FOI request sent to the Social Security Administration. I knew SSA persons attended meetings with the VA and Treasury.

admin@foiaonline.gov
Nov 29, 2020, 1:40 PM
to me
This message is to confirm your request submission to the FOIA online application: View Request. Request information is as follows:
Tracking Number: SSA-2021-002188
Requester Name: James B Simms
Date Submitted: 11/29/2020
Request Status: Submitted

My Reply:
Description: Citing the Freedom of Information Act, and in reference to the attached document, I am requesting the following records, which should be readily available with no expectation of a fee being levied because the documents being requested are in the public interest.
The attached document is a redacted brief of a meeting that was attended (as noted in the document) by representatives of the VBA, VHA, DT (Department of Treasury), and a representative of Comerica Bank. As you read, the meeting was conducted to address issues with regard to Comerica Bank as the Fiscal Agent of the Direct Express Program.
I bring your attention to the last paragraph, where is it noted, "[O]utcome: Due to the increase in account takeover and benefit payment fraud, Comerica agreed to a monthly group with VA, USDT, and SSA to track and find better ways to serve our customers."
With regard to the above outtake of the noted brief, I respectfully submit this FOI request to be furnished the following documents:
(1) Notes, minutes, summaries, email interaction, and documents produced from the "monthly working group" from the date of the agreement by Comerica Bank, being March 12, 2019, to the present.

(2) The identity of any and all representatives of persons identified as employees of "USDT" (US Department of Treasury) to include employees of OIG Treasury and Bureau of Fiscal Service, SSA (Social Security Administration), and VA (Veterans Administration) who were present at any and all of the meetings. Thank you for your attention, and for your expected compliance.
Sincerely,
J.B. Simms

Friday, November 27, 2020

FOI requests had been sent to the VA and we were receiving information. The VA revelations changed our case.
November 27, 2020
12:22pm
Jones, Quanisha <noreply@ains.com>
jbsimms
Dear Mr. Simms,
Please find attached our interim response to your recent FOIA request assigned case number 20-09883-F. We estimate our next response being provided to you by December 11, 2020, if not sooner.
Feel free to contact our office if you have any questions at FOIA.vbaco@va.gov.
VBA FOIA/PA Office

I had to submit another FOI request to the VA.
The first one that Ha responded to was 20-09821F. The first FOI request revealed communication regarding the White Paper. The copy supplied to me was redacted.
The subsequent one was 20-09883F.

Monday, November 30, 2020

Jackie got notice that her deposition was to be on December 8, 2020.
Here is the Notice of Deposition for Jackie.
NOTICE OF VIDEOTAPED DEPOSITION
PLEASE TAKE NOTICE that, pursuant to Rule 30 of the Federal Rules of Civil Procedure, the undersigned attorneys will take the videotaped deposition of Jackie Densmore at 10:00 a.m. ET on Tuesday, December 8, 2020 via remote video Zoom application (or similar remote video application), hosted by Veritext Reporting, upon oral examination pursuant to the Federal Rules of Civil Procedure. The access link to this remote video deposition will be sent electronically by Veritext Reporting to the following email addresses for participation in this deposition:
Deponent: Jackie Densmore (c/o Plaintiffs' Counsel listed below)
Plaintiffs' Counsel: E. Adam Webb, adam@webbllc.com
Plaintiffs' Counsel: G. Franklin Lemond, Jr, franklin@webbllc.com
Defendants' Counsel: Jonathan R. Chally, jchally@kslaw.com
Defendants' Counsel: Adam Reinke, areinke@kslaw.com
The deposition will be taken, remotely, before a notary public or an officer authorized to administer oaths, and will be recorded by video and stenographic means. The oral examination will continue from day to day until completed.
Dated: November 30, 2020

Tuesday, December 8, 2020

Below is the confirmation of an FOI request sent to the Bureau of Fiscal Service on November 30, 2020. The "monthly working group" that was created by Pamela Powers was the subject I was pursuing.
I submitted this FOI request to BFS at the same time I submitted an FOI request to the VA (requesting some of the same information and an unredacted copy of the White Paper.
DEPARTMENT OF THE TREASURY
BUREAU OF THE FISCAL SERVICE
WASHINGTON, DC 20227
December 8, 2020
James Simms

Re: FOIA # 2020-11-035

Dear Mr. Simms:

This is in response to your Freedom of Information Act (FOIA) request that was received by the Department of the Treasury's (Treasury) Bureau of the Fiscal Service (Fiscal Service) on November 30, 2020. In reference to the document provided with your FOIA request, you requested the following:

1. Notes, minutes, summaries, email interaction, and documents produced from the "monthly working group" from the date of the agreement by Comerica Bank, being March 12, 2019 to the present; and

2. The identity of all representatives of persons identified as employees of Treasury to include employees of OIG Treasury, the Fiscal Service, Social Security Administration, and Veterans Administration who were present at any of the meetings.

Your FOIA request has been assigned the number listed above.

Your request for a fee waiver has been denied. You must demonstrate that disclosure of the information is in the public interest and is likely to contribute significantly to the public's understanding of the operations or activities of the government. Your fee waiver justification did not explain in detail how disclosure of the requested records would satisfy the requirements for a fee waiver. In considering a request for a fee waiver, Fiscal Service follows the longstanding Department of Justice guidelines on this subject, found in FOIA Update Vol. VIII, No. 1, dated January 1, 1987, which is available on DOJ's Office of Information Policy website.

Page 2 – FOIA # 2020-11-035

The Fiscal Service estimates that the fees for processing your FOIA request amount to approximately $534.74. The breakdown is:

Search and Review $534.74, Duplication $ 0.00, Total Costs $534.74

Upon receipt of your payment, the requested records will be processed and sent to you.

You may make your FOIA payment online using Pay.gov. Paying online with Pay.gov is safe, secure, and the preferred method to make a payment. Please go to the following link to pay online: https://pay.gov/public/form/start/72294391. Using Pay.gov, you may make a payment using one of the following methods: Bank account (ACH), PayPal account, Amazon Pay, debit or credit card.

As an alternative to making an online payment, you may submit a check or money order for $534.74 made payable to the Department of the Treasury. Direct your payment to the Department of the Treasury, Bureau of the Fiscal Service, Attn: FOIA Disclosure Office/Room 508B, 3201 Pennsy Drive, Building E, Landover, MD 20785. Please include your FOIA identification number on all related correspondence.

If you have any questions pertaining to this request, you may contact the FOIA Disclosure Office at FOIA@fiscal.treasury.gov or 202-874-5602.

If I do not hear from you within 15 business days from the date of this letter, your FOIA request will be closed.

Sincerely,

Cynthia A. Sydnor-Jones

BFS was charging me over $500.00 for work they are paid to do. SSA also denied FOI fee waivers.
Franklin paid probably $5,000 in FOI fees to SSA and BFS.
FOI requests had been sent to the VA and I was receiving information. The VA revelations changed our case. The VA did not charge me any fee for the FOI request.

Thursday, December 10, 2020

from: Jbsimms
to: ^FOIA Public Liaison <FOIA.Public.Liaison@ssa.gov>
date: Dec 16, 2020, 1:08 AM
subject: Status of FOI Request 2021 001175

I submitted an FOI request, having been given the number 2021-000274 on October 12, 2020. Having not had a reply in the appropriate time from SSA, I submitted the same request on November 3, 2020, and was given the FOI number 2021-001175.

A request was made to expedite 2021-001175 because the first request was ignored or lost. That request was denied.

I am requesting a status briefing of FOI request 2021-001175. As you are aware, it is not necessary to postpone the delivery of the entire request when the request can be satisfied in segments. I believe the request included four (4) separate sections. After the completion of each section requested the information can be delivered separately.
Your reply giving the status of said request is highly appreciated. If there is a fee, please state such.
Sincerely,
J.B. Simms

Jbsimms
Dec 10, 2020, 8:56 AM
 FOIA # 2020-11-035 [Bureau of Fiscal Service]
Dear Ms. Jones,
Thank you for your email.
I see that your office is trying to make me pay not only for work the GS persons are paid to do but to place a hardship upon citizens wishing for transparency. I will be calling the telephone number you gave me later today or tomorrow to speak with your supervisor.
Sincerely,
J.B. Simms

Friday, December 11, 2020

from: Jbsimms
to: Franklin Lemond ((Plaintiff's Attorney),
Jackie Lynn
date: Dec 11, 2020, 1:37 PM
from: Cynthia A. Sydnor <Cynthia.Sydnor@fiscal.treasury.gov>
to: jb.simms
cc: "Cynthia A. Sydnor" <Cynthia.Sydnor@fiscal.treasury.gov>
date: Dec 16, 2020, 7:41 AM
subject: FOIA # 2020-11-035 (Simms)
mailed-by: fiscal.treasury.gov
Attached is a copy of the FOIA Receipt of Payment Letter.

Franklin paid $535.74 in FOI fees to the Bureau of Fiscal Service.

Wednesday, December 16, 2020

Franklin Lemond paid over $3,000 to SSA for FOI information.

from: J B Simms
to: ^FOIA Public Liaison <FOIA.Public.Liaison@ssa.gov>
date: Dec 16, 2020, 1:08 AM
subject: Status of FOI Request 2021 001175
I submitted an FOI request, having been given the number 2021-000274 on October 12, 2020. Having not had a reply in the appropriate time from SSA, I submitted the same request on November 3, 2020, and was given the FOI number 2021-001175.
A request was made to expedite 2021-001175 because the first request was ignored or lost. That request was denied.
I am requesting a status briefing of FOI request 2021-001175. As you are aware, it is not necessary to postpone the delivery of the entire request when the request can be satisfied in segments. I believe the request included four (4) separate sections. After the completion of each section requested the information can be delivered separately.
Your reply giving the status of said request is highly appreciated. If there is a fee, please state such.
Sincerely,
J.B. Simms

Thursday, December 17, 2020

from: Jbsimms
to: Jackie Lynn
date: Dec 17, 2020, 10:32 PM
subject: Re: First set of questions for Rich Delmar.docx
Jbsimms
Thu, Dec 17, 2020, 10:32 PM
to Jackie
just plain nasty. He hated you then, and he hates you now.
I am not trying to disrespect Franklin by using the FOI tactic, but evidently, he and his partners read what i was asking for and thought it was valid.
You and I have been going after these people (not real people) and have been in the trenches against them. My God, they hate us.

First set of questions for Rich Delmar, Chief Counsel for Fiscal Services

The following was emailed to Richard Delmar from Jackie:

After either of the two OIG reports were issued ((14-031 ands 17-034), and the Commissioner of Fiscal Services (David A Lebryk and Sherly R. Morrow, respectively) submitted their letter of acknowledgement (included in the OIG report), where is evidence of Fiscal Services having addressed or corrected any issue presented by OIG within their report?

Who were the persons within Fiscal Services making contact with Comerica officers (including Ralph Babb, and Nora Arpin) subsequent to Comerica being awarded the first bid, who accepted the changes to the original FAA, allowing Comerica to be paid in conflict with the original FAA?

Who are the persons within Fiscal Services to whom the OIG report is referring who had undocumented discussions and negotiations (referred to as documentation that was "lacking") with Comerica regarding changing the original FAA? See below a paragraph from Page 11 of OIG report 14-031:

OIG Comment
We acknowledge the importance of Direct Express to achieve the goal of DCIA and Treasury's "all electronic mandate." However, as discussed in our report, we are concerned with Fiscal Service's administration of the Direct Express program, its enforcement of the terms of the FAA, and its overreliance on the financial agent for decision-making information. Also, we found that Fiscal Service's documentation supporting key decisions and the ongoing monitoring of a program involving tens of millions of taxpayer dollars and the delivery of payments to millions of Federal beneficiaries was often lacking.

Where is evidence of specific communication between Comerica and Direct Express employees with OIG auditors?

Who are the compliance officers employed by Comerica and Direct Express, and where is evidence of communication and reports to Fiscal Services from these persons?
Who are the top four (4) persons in charge of the Fraud Unit of Direct Express, and what is their professional qualifications?

What evidence is there of communication between Nora Arpin, Susan Schmidt, or any Comerica officer with the Direct Express Fraud Unit during either of the audits?

Where is the evidence of casework and reports of fraud completed by the Direct Express Fraud Unit?

J.B. Simms submitted two complaints to the Consumer Financial Protection Bureau (to be referred to as CFPB) with respect to the absence of performance by the Direct Express Fraud Unit and violation of Regulation E, Section 226.12(b)(2)(iii)(3) upon his Direct Express account in December 2017. The CFPB complaint numbers are 171229-2740881 and 180127-2811418. Mr. Simms' claim that the Fraud Unit of Direct Express failed to abide by Regulation E and immediately credit his account was confirmed and validated within the response of Susan Schmidt, SVP of Comerica Bank to the CFPB. Ms. Schmidt acknowledged that Mr. Simms was forced to make contact with merchants from whom the fraudsters made purchases, and the merchants refunded the purchase amount to Mr. Simms' Direct Express Account. Mr. Simms then conducted an interview with Tasha, a telephone attendant at the CFPB, on Thursday February 22, 2018. Tasha told Mr. Simms there were 414 complaints against Direct Express/Comerica comprising 17 pages on her screen. Since Mr. Simms' complaint to CFPB landed on the desk of Susan Schmidt, it is safe to assume that other complaints of victimization and violation of regulations against Comerica/Direct Express resulted to being forwarded to the same destination for "attention." Where are the records of all reports from the CFPB to Susan Schmidt or any officer of Comerica?

Who is the liaison between the Social Security Administration and Fiscal Services? What evidence is there of any security measures being communicated between Treasury Fiscal Services and the Social Security Administration directed to Direct Express Fraud Unit or the call centers, which are operated by Conduent?

Where is there any evidence of an investigation of Direct Express or Fiserv employee who was fired as a result of compromising the identity of Paul J. Katynski on or about January 16, 2018? Where are the reports to law enforcement concerning the firing of this individual? Where is the log of telephone calls and emails made by this individual during the time of this fraud? Where is the arrest report of this individual? Why was Mr. Katynski not given the opportunity to press charges against this individual?

In the matter of my brother in-law, Derek Densmore, a disabled Veteran, where is the evidence that Direct Express/Comerica made any contact with the security personnel at the Walmart store located in Hollywood, FL to determine the identity of the person who victimized Derek and impersonated me, Jackie Densmore? Where is the evidence that the call center employee of Conduent (dba Direct Express) who received the call from the female fraudster, identifying herself as me, made any attempt to validate the identity of the caller? I received no alert, no telephone call, or email to advise me that the funds which were intended for the use of Derek had been redeemed at a Walmart store located approximately 2,000 miles from my home? I spent my time (and the time of J.B. Simms) to track down the fraudster and obtain visual proof of the crime. I did the job of the Fraud Unit, and I question if it even exists.

Why would Comerica/Direct Express victimize a recipient named Nancy Hernandez of Los Angeles, whose account was victimized by a fraudster in Nigeria, by withholding her funds for 45+days to "investigate" the matter? Over $1,400 was withheld from this mother of two dependent disabled children, and it was not until Ms. Hernandez contacted Mr. Simms that she received the credit she legally deserved. The fraudster was in Nigeria. Nancy Hernandez lives in Los Angeles. This is pure cruelty on the part of Comerica/Direct Express. Kenneth Tillman was victimized recently by Comerica/Direct Express until he contacted Mr. Simms. Mr. Tillman's fraudster was in San Francisco, not in Aurora, Colorado where Mr. Tillman lives. Mr. Tillman suffered physical pains which caused him to need immediate medical attention. Comerica/Direct Express ignored him until he reached out for help. Comerica/ Direct Express and their mysterious fraud unit did nothing to report this federal crime to law enforcement, as is their mandate in the Fiscal Services Agreement. Comerica/Direct Express violated Regulation E. Mr. Tillman is entitled to damages from Comerica/Direct Express, and Fiscal Services is accountable. The CEO of Comerica, Ralph Babb, called Mr. Tillman to apologize. What a comfort that was. Where is the police report generated by the Direct Express Fraud Unit? Where is any documentation that the Fraud Unit did any work on this matter? Where is the documentation of accountability by Susan Schmidt of Comerica Bank?
Mr. Simms and Mr. Katynski also were proactive in determining the identity of the persons who victimized them, before they were subsequently victimized again by Comerica/Direct Express.
Mr. Simms has assisted other victims to rightfully receive monies from Comerica/Direct Express which had been illegally withheld in violation of Regulation E. Nora Arpin (Comerica) and Mitch Raymond (Conduent) conducted due diligence on Mr. Simms, learning that Mr. Simms conducted financial crime investigations as the owner of an investigative agency, and a bank employee.

This list of questions and issues to be answered and addressed is the first of a continuum of communication between you and me. You are in receipt of an email from Mr. Simms to which you stated to me you would reply, but you seem not to want to engage Mr. Simms. So, I guess since you agreed to communicate with me, you are

435

stuck with me, and be assured that I will be channeling many others as we communicate. I will give you, personally, and Fiscal Services, an opportunity to account for your behavior, be accountable to the victims of Comerica/Direct Express and be accountable to the taxpayers of my country who pay your salary.

Friday, December 18, 2020

from: Jbsimms
to: ^FOIA Public Liaison <FOIA.Public.Liaison@ssa.gov>
date: Dec 18, 2020, 10:21 AM
subject: RE: FOI request 2021-002188
Thank you for your email requesting clarification. Below are the issues you presented:
the names or positions of the employee(s) whose emails you would like us to search;
search terms applicable to your request for emailed correspondence; and
the timeframe applicable to your search for the requested emailed correspondence.
Here are my responses as best as I can offer:
1. Walter Bayer (SSA), Sara Lizama (SSA), Richard Delmar (Treasury), Thomas Santaniello (BFS, Treasury), Nora Arpin (Comerica Bank), and any person from Comerica Bank, Bureau of Fiscal Service, the Veterans Administration, and OIG Treasury. Also all persons attending the monthly meetings, and the duration of said meeting (as if the meetings are ongoing or have been suspended).
2. Emails copied to any and all persons noted as joint participants in the monthly meetings.
3. The monthly meetings were mandated to have begun in March 2019. I do not know if these meetings are ongoing. Information requested will be confined to only the monthly meetings until there was an agreement between the VA, BFS, OIG Treasury, Comerica Bank (and maybe Conduent), as well as SSA. We do not know if the meetings are still taking place.
Thank you again for reaching out to me. This gesture of transparency is recognized.
Sincerely,
J.B. Simms

Wednesday, December 23, 2020

from: Jbsimms
to: Cawana.Pearson@treasury.gov
cc: Jackie Lynn
date: Dec 23, 2020, 10:41 AM
subject: Outstanding FOI requests
Dear Ms. Pearson,
While you are aware of the outstanding FOI requests having been submitted to OIG Treasury, I have received no communication from OIG Treasury or from your office with respect to progress in this matter or acknowledgment of false statements made by officials at OIG Treasury in their attempt to deny access to the requested material.
If I am correct, it was March 2020 when talked to you on the telephone about this matter. I was sitting in the vehicle of my disabled friend as he sat spellbound hearing me explain the corruption and malfeasance experienced from OIG Treasury subsequent to my audacity to request documents that precipitated their behavior. A dozen or more documents have been submitted to your office validating my position that documents pertaining to procedures identified as "investigations" were performed and documented.
Please address this matter at your earliest possible convenience, then enjoy your holiday.
Sincerely,
J.B. Simms

Thursday, December 24, 2020

from: FOIA <FOIA@fiscal.treasury.gov>
to: "jb.simms10@gmail.com" <jb.simms10@gmail.com>
cc: "Cynthia A. Sydnor" <Cynthia.Sydnor@fiscal.treasury.gov>
date: Dec 24, 2020, 6:52 AM
subject: FOIA # 2020-12-037 (Simms)
mailed-by: fiscal.treasury.gov
signed-by: fiscal.treasury.gov

Attached is a copy of the FOIA Receipt of the Payment Letter.

Franklin paid for the FOI info from Treasury.

Thursday, December 31, 2020

No inserts in the Social Security check envelope

Jackie sent the following email to Mr. Lepper:

Dear Mr. Lepper,

To my surprise the Social Security check my disabled brother in law got today had no insert promoting the Direct Express program. Nothing was in the envelope except for the check.

Both VA and SSA initially denied any knowledge of the inserts or how they were placed into the envelopes. Both blamed BFS, which was a poor excuse.

Since the VA stopped promoting Direct Express with the inserts, and the VA does not respond to Jim or me, we thanked you for being the advocate for the vets and our mouthpiece.

Somehow SSA might have gotten the message, but they do not respond to Jim or me like the VA.

We thank you for all you have done to protect veterans from the Direct Express program from the VA and now SSA. They hear us but act like they don't. Your work behind the scenes has done more than you can imagine for many people.

Sincerely,

Jackie

The year ended and we were continuing to battle the inserts, FOI requests, and now the White Paper. The White Paper presented to Pamela Powers (Chief of Staff at the VA) mentioned meeting, and I was sending FOI requests to all agencies hoping I would find a leak.

Switch today.

Make the change on our site
or over the phone, now!

!Haga el cambio en nuestra pagina de
internet ó por telefono, ahora!

GoDirect.gov
1-800-333-1795

Phone operators are available
Monday–Friday | 9 a.m–7 p.m. EST

You can also **visit your bank or credit union.**

Para español, visite
DirectoasuCuenta.gov

Converting your paper check to
an electronic payment is easy.

All you will need is your:

- Social Security number

- Information from your most
  recent federal benefit check
  or claim number

- Date of birth *FOR DIRECT EXPRESS*

- Financial institution's routing
  transit number *FOR DIRECT DEPOSIT*

- Account number and account
  type (checking or savings)
  FOR DIRECT DEPOSIT

DIRECTEXPRESS

DIRECT DEPOSIT
Simple. Safe. Secure.

1120

438

Chapter Ten
The farce of the deposition of J.B. Simms

Depositions were taking place in our federal civil suit. In December (2020) I was deposed, and it was scheduled to last 6 hours. Jon Chally, the attorney for Comerica Bank, made a statement regarding the credit give me on my bank account after the fraud was exposed. Chally stated that Conduent (partner with Comerica) reversed the fraudulent transaction, but that was false. The merchant reversed the transaction because I proved the fraudulent transaction. I told Chally that his client was a liar.

We went on a break during the deposition after this revelation. My deposition was terminated. Chally did not want to hear any more from me. I had stacks of documents lined up on the desk in front of me. I was ready to attack.

After the deposition ended, I drafted a treatise based upon information I had planned to enter into the record. After Chally ended the deposition and I was not given the opportunity to speak further (it is not clear of Franklin Lemond could have interjected), I drafted the document below, sent it to Franklin Lemond, and asked that this document be filed with the case. Franklin would not file the document.

The document is attached below.

The Treatise submitted after the suspension of the deposition of J.B. Simms

Declaration of J.B. Simms

At the moment of the abrupt termination of my deposition (Joe Almon, et al. vs Conduent Business Services, LLC and Comerica Bank, US District Court, Western District of Texas, San Antonio Division, Case No. 5:19-cv-01075-XR) on December 10, 2020 conducted by Jonathan R. Chally, (attorney for the defense) it became evident that many of the documents which were presented to me by the defense prior to the deposition, to be validated or to illicit response, were not addressed. Having been fully prepared to defend the assertions made in support of the Complaint and Amended Complaint of this matter, the termination of the deposition was a deliberate act by opposing counsel to skew and limit the perception of facts which were originally meant to be revealed and attempt to validate false assertions made by the Defendants in this matter.

The deposition ended after a break requested by defense counsel approximately three and a half hours into the deposition, which was scheduled for seven-plus hours. Immediately prior to the break, defense counsel was asserting that a credit to my Direct Express debit card balance was a "credit generated by Conduent" (subcontractor for federal contractor/Fiscal Agent Comerica Bank) and not the merchant credit. It was pointed out to defense counsel the obvious contradictions regarding my contact with the merchant (Zulily) versus the assertion made by Conduent that the dollar amount of the fraud transaction (there were two made involving merchant Zulily) was credited to my account in accordance with adherence to Regulation E by Conduent. The fact is Conduent never contacted the merchant and presented no evidence of having conducted an investigation to validate making the credit, in addition to the fact that one of the two fraudulent transaction was obviously credited by the merchant. Thus, Conduent was in violation of Regulation E and encouraged defense counsel to become a party to this false allegation.

I will now list some of the documents the defense counsel failed to present and comment within this declaration.

Email/letter was received on January 18, 2018 from Susan Schmidt (Comerica Bank Corporate Quality Process Department)

"On December 26, 2017, a dispute was opened for an unauthorized mail order/telephone order transaction in the amount of $165.07 that was processed to your Direct Express card account on December 22, 2017. In addition, your dispute paperwork was also received on December 26, 2017. Further, a representative from the Cardholder Advocacy Group contacted you and explained the time frames for your claim.
On December 29, 2017, your claim was closed as the merchant issued a credit. The merchant "Zulily" issued a credit to your card account in the amount of $165.07. On January 2, 2018, a letter (copy attached) was mailed advising you of the credit issued by the merchant."

Part of the information presented by Ms. Schmidt was false. The fraud on my Direct Express account was reported to Conduent when noticed on December 10, 2018. A Conduent call center employee acknowledged the $165.07 fraudulent transaction was "pending" and I told them this was fraud. This is confirmed by my bank statement. I was told I could not contest the charge until the merchant debits the account. I contacted the merchant, and the credit was issued by the merchant (as is stated by Schmidt in this letter). Ms. Schmidt wrote that the fraud dispute was opened on December 26, 2017 when in fact the dispute was opened 16 or so days prior. Conduent/Comerica ignored the notice given

on December 10, 2017. Said notice was effective as defined in Regulation E and this assertion by Susan Schmidt confirms a violation of Regulation E.

Attorney Chally stated during the deposition that the defendant Conduent credited the fraud amount. That claim by Mr. Chally on behalf of his clients is false, and is contradicted by one of his client's employees, Susan Schmidt.

It was also learned that Conduent can manipulate data entries to make merchant credit appear to be a credit generated by Conduent. This practice was validated in a letter from the Texas Banking Association, noting that Comerica Bank has no direct knowledge of the validity of data entries made by Conduent. The cessation of the deposition prohibited me from revealing this information.

Subsequent to an exchange between opposing counsel, and me exposing Conduent as having made a false data entry on my account, the deposition ended.

I was confidently awaiting the continuation of the deposition in order to comment on said documents. The suspension of my deposition prohibited me from completing my planned testimony.

Pending Transactions: Withholding funds from cardholder
Mr. Chally argued the point that a fraudulent purchase dated December 9, 2017 was reimbursed sometime after December 22, 2017 and struggled to understand why this was upsetting to me. I was trying to explain that Conduent froze my account because of the "pending transaction" (which was fraudulent) even after I reported the fraud on December 10, 2017. I had no access to my money, and Conduent violated Regulation E by ignoring notice of the fraud (as evidenced by the email from Susan Schmidt) and conducted no investigation. The fraud was obvious, this being the second fraudulent transaction involving this merchant, and as per Regulation E, Conduent had the authority to acknowledge the fraud and immediately make my funds available to me without escalating the matter to necessitate an investigation. This exclusion of my funds during a holiday season was traumatic.

Pissed Consumer
Postings relating to violations of Regulation E by the defendants and other victims were made on the Pissed Consumer website. Mr. Chally presented my counsel with copies of postings. Victims of the Direct Express debit card program began contacting me for assistance in February 2018. Within a year or so, over 100 persons had contacted me.

Mr. Chally questioned the veracity of those who contacted me. I found no alleged victim to have falsified any representation to me.I was unable to comment further on the victims.

Facebook
Mr. Chally did not challenge postings or membership of Facebook page, Direct Express Cardholder Victims, which had 1,168 members on the document which I was given. (As of this writing, the membership of this page exceeds 1,500 persons). I was fully prepared to address these postings and systemic violations of Regulation E by Conduent/Comerica Bank.

Federal Corruption blog
Mr. Chally did not challenge postings on a Federal Corruption blog site of which I am the owner.

Email on behalf of defendant Jennifer Kreegar, January 2, 2019
A copy of an email sent to people at OIG Treasury, Comerica Bank, journalist, attorneys, General Accounting Office, and Conduent was submitted for discussion. The blatant violations of Regulation E by Conduent and Comerica Bank experienced by Plaintiff Ms. Kreegar, were exposed. Mr. Chally did not challenge this email I wrote on behalf of Ms. Kreegar, nor was I

able to comment further on this violation of Regulation E suffered by Ms. Kreegar. It was later learned that Nora Arpin, a bank official employed by Comerica Bank who was copied on this email.

Email sent to the staff of Senator Elizabeth Warren and others (dated January 11, 2019)

Defendant Jackie Densmore, and journalist Kate Berry were copied in this email, and was not challenged by Mr. Chally. This email addressed the fact that the Bank of Montreal debit card had security parameters which were never offered by Comerica Bank. This further proved Comerica Bank not only did not have the infrastructure in place to offer customers protection from fraud, but the lack of infrastructure was also evident when the subcontractor Conduent repeatedly violated Regulation E when dealing with fraud victims. Conduent was not a bank, and their employees had no knowledge of Regulation E. (I have evidence of two Conduent Fraud Department employees denying knowledge).

Telephone call to the Fraud Department of Conduent. (My verbatim notes are below)

Thursday October 25, 2018
1104am T (888) 545-5577 DE Fraud
Tt
Emanuel
He dnk
Reg E
Asked for all my identifying info before would talk. My number is on the screen, but need verify. My account has been referred to Soc Sec, consent based process. This is call center, he admit works for Conduent.
Cannot fax or email to the Fraud Unit.
This is legitimate department of Direct Express. They handle disputes but work for Conduent.
Asked: does debit card fall under Regulation E ?
"cannot disclose.
Ask: who pays you ? "cannot give you my personal information. That is absurd."
Admit his Conduent employee number is 8382002
Call was referred to supervisor: Gustav
Immediately asked "are you a private investigator?"
Got employee number of 8382002
"There is an alert on your account; need to go to Soc Sec office"
Is my debit card covered under Regulation E?
"I suppose so. Cannot discuss company policy, must go to website.:
20 min conversation

Neither attendant knew anything about Regulation E or federal banking law.

Email to Maj Gen Steven Lepper (Ret, USAF) January 17, 2020

Subject: RE: Warren press release, and failure to produce responses to letters
Date: Fri, January 17, 2020 :55am
To: "Steven Lepper" <Steven.Lepper@ambahq.org>
Cc: "Jackie Lynn" Dear Mr. Lepper,
Thank you from our hearts.
Jackie and I had a conversation yesterday concerning the inserts which were included with paper checks. The inserts from last month noted the Direct Express program, and we questioned that.

Was that subject brought up, the endorsing of the Direct Express program on the inserts? Jackie was thinking these were printed some time ago and simply added to the checks with no mention of AMBA. As you see there is great controversy with respect to the awarding of this contract by BFS to Comerica Bank. BFS is refusing to reveal the contents of the agreement which would be compared to the old agreement.

Security features such as immediate transaction notification and the ability to immediately challenge obvious fraudulent transactions are two features which Comerica Bank does no offer. The transaction notification can alert the cardholder of fraud within moments of the transaction, allowing the victim to contact the bank and stop subsequent transactions. These subsequent fraudulent transactions caused much distress to cardholders. This happened to me also.

Thank you again. If you can drop us a note concerning the marketing plan of the VA and the inserts (which seems to be a small issue, but very obvious), we would be grateful.

Sincerely, Jim

Subject: Re: Warren press release, and failure to produce responses to letters
From: Steven Lepper <Steven.Lepper@ambahq.org>
Date: Fri, January 17, 2020 5:24 am
To: jbsimms Cc: Walter Bayer <Walter.Bayer@ssa.gov>, Jackie Lynn
Mr. Simms,
Thanks for the note. I just finished a week in DC, during which I met a couple of times with VBA. Our Veterans Benefits Banking Program is getting up to speed and VBA is fully behind it. In the coming weeks, they will be engaging in more outreach with veterans who still use Direct Express and paper checks to encourage them to migrate to more reliable, less expensive bank accounts. Our VBBP banks are simply some of the choices they can make among banks that understand the financial needs and challenges of veterans.
All the
best,
Steve

The Veterans Administration broke from BFS because of violations of Regulation E and evidence of lack of infrastructure in the call center (again, falsification of application for the contract by DefendantComerica Bank). In July 2020 the VA created their own inserts, not using the propaganda printed by BFS on behalf of Comerica Bank.

Mr. Chally failed to ask any questions about the Veterans Administration, or any veterans being victimized as a result of Reg E violations relating to my involvement with Mr. Lepper.

Rebecca Newton email February 1, 2019

Conduent failed to give provisional credit to James Sims whose account was hacked for over $7,000.00. The thieves bought pizza while Mr. Sims was in a hospital room in Georgia. Then Conduent refused to talk to Rebecca, his daughter, when the telephone was handed to Rebecca. Mr. Sims died soon thereafter. Conduent also failed to conduct an investigation into the fraud, which was obvious.

Email from Sonja Scott March 28, 2019

From: "Scott, Sonja L." <ScottS@oig.treas.gov>
Date: Thu, March 28, 2019 8:30 am
To: "'jbsimms
Mr. Simms – You mentioned yesterday that you have list now of 90 victims. Can you forward me the new list? Thanks. Sonja
ASAC Sonja L. Scott

Nona Clarke suicide in Mexico, a result of stress caused by Conduent

From:<jbsimms>
Date: Fri, Aug 9, 2019 at 8:46 AM
Subject: the narrative of your mom's issue with Direct Express

To: Paige Clarke

Dear Paige,

I was very happy to be able to talk with you.

Attached is the narrative which your mom sent to me, as well as the office at OIG Treasury. I will go back and find emails she sent me and forward to you.

Hopefully you can talk to Anna Martinez, the lady who called me from Mexico. Hopefully she can get info to you about the accident, or maybe some of her friends.

The narrative makes reference to others and friends who were in the area of your mom. She did tell me she did not hang out much with the America ex-pats in the area. She had planned to come back to the US but I am not certain if she was going back to Atlanta or not.

This matter with Direct Express program (operated by Comerica Bank and Conduent) caused her much stress. I am not sure if she received or got access to all her money.

Hopefully you can make contact with the Soc Sec Admin to determine your next step.

Jim

The lack of infrastructure, and the falsification of the application submitted by Comerica, caused Nona Clarke to be deprived of her funds, and her ultimate suicide. Conduent, Comerica Bank, and BFS have blood on their hands.

Attorney Chally declined to discuss this incident which stifled my exposure of the truth regarding malfeasance on the part of the Defendants.

Email from JB Simms to Cynthia Clark, November 21, 2018

Cynthia Clark was a victim of fraud, is a Plaintiff in this matter, and reached out to me when the fraud occurred. The monies lost by Ms. Clark was for the disabled child of Ms. Clark, not personally for Ms. Clark. Ms. Clark was a resident of Conyers, GA when the fraud was discovered having been committed in Minnesota. Conduent ignored her notice of fraud. The fraud was blatant and obvious as to shock the conscience. My email to Ms. Clark included the law, Regulation E, which she used to confront Conduent and Comerica Bank to have her monies reimbursed. My email and support were necessary to make the defendants in this matter abide by the law.

Ms. Clark was told by the merchant that law enforcement would be contacted on behalf of Ms. Clark. Comerica Bank and Conduent did ignore the Plaintiff, in violation of Regulation E, having never contacted the merchant or law enforcement.

Attorney Chally declined to discuss the fact that Ms. Clark has to reach out to me when she was ignored by the Defendants, and that Ms. Clark ultimately had to contact OIG Treasury for relief.

These are but a few of the dozens exhibits presented to our attorney by defense counsel in preparation for my deposition. I was well prepared to address each document to validate our claim of violations of Regulation E by the defendants as well as the falsification of the applications submitted by Comerica Bank to the Bureau of Fiscal Services in order to become the Fiscal Agent for the Direct Express program.

This document is hereby being submitted to be made part of the record of this case, Case No. 5:19-cv-01075-XR.

Franklin Lemond did not file this declaration by me into the record. Franklin claimed it would be unusual for a plaintiff to submit such a document regarding a deposition. I told Franklin that I was not an ordinary plaintiff.

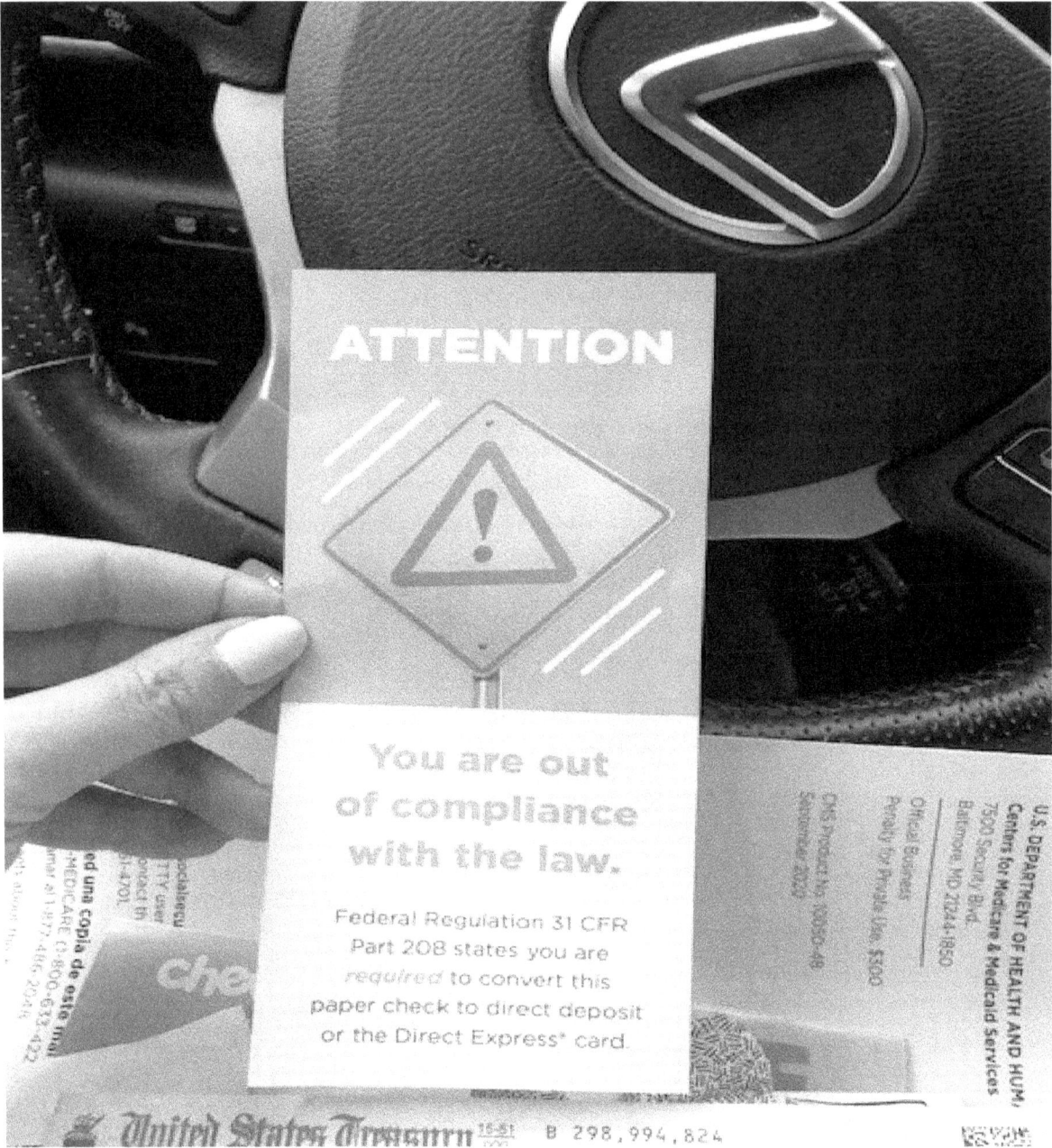

ATTENTION

You are out of compliance with the law.

Federal Regulation 31 CFR Part 208 states you are *required* to convert this paper check to direct deposit or the Direct Express® card.

United States Treasury   B 298,994,824

U.S. DEPARTMENT OF HEALTH AND HUM.
Centers for Medicare & Medicaid Services
7500 Security Blvd.
Baltimore, MD 21244-1850

Official Business
Penalty for Private Use, $300

CMS Product No. 10050-48
September 2022

Chapter Eleven
Secret Meetings, the "Deal" and Inserts

Insert from SSA Jan 2021

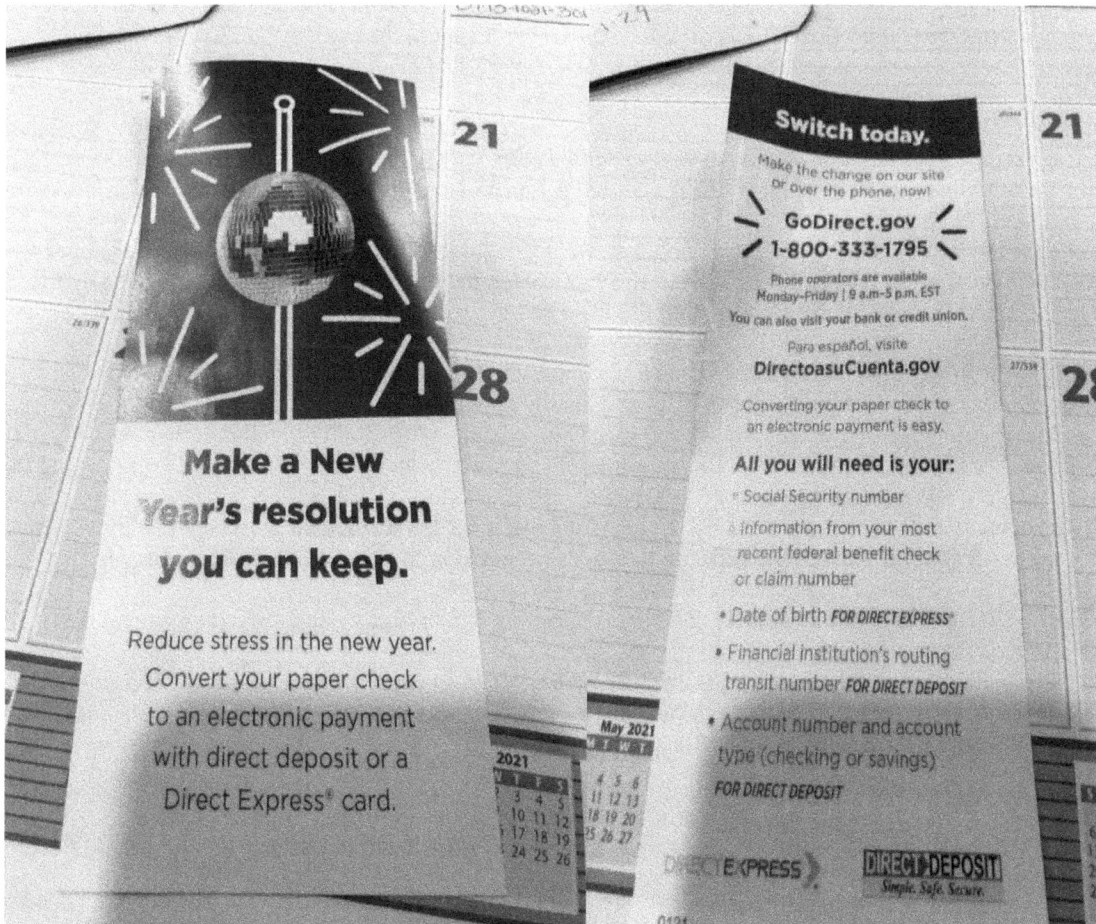

Monday, January 4, 2021

jbsimms
to: Cawana.Pearson@treasury.gov
Jackie Lynn
Dear Ms. Pearson,
I would like to discuss the FOI requests submitted to your office well over a year ago. We had a conversation in March 2020, I submitted proof of the lies and attempted deception by the attorneys at OIG Treasury, and still nothing has happened. You have been gracious in your responses, but it appears your office is not an independent arbitrator of the truth, thus it appears your "hands are tied."
I look forward to speaking with you again.
Sincerely,
J.B. Simms

Tuesday, January 5, 2021

jbsimms
to: Franklin Lemond, Jackie Lynn
Jackie called me, said you have meeting with Conduent attys. I hope they know I was waiting to resume the deposition when they unexpectedly ended it.'
Ask them if their clients are ready to come to the table.
Jackie and I did discuss confirming her phone call on Aug 3, 2018. That was notice. That information will deflate another argument, just like Conduent intentionally entering a merchant refund as a bank credit. This is consistent with the letter to the Texas Banking Assoc; Comerica is kept in the dark as Conduent cooks the books. Jackie can request the records from her carrier first, before subpoena.
We need to get the motion to compel done.
I am after 4 FOI reports, three of which your firm paid the fee. There is one more coming.
I am sure the attys, Comerica, and Conduent have seen LinkedIn and the Facebook page. The SSA FOI material that cost $3000 was for info and the link of BFS, Comerica, and SSA on the inserts. This is big.

Jon Chally, the attorney for Comerica Bank/Conduent, went to a "break" during the deposition in December 2020 immediately after I exposed Comerica Bank lied while claiming the money I lost was reimbursed by the bank. The merchant reimbursed my money, whom I had to contact, rather than the Fraud Department of Conduent.

Two violations of Regulation E were committed on the fraud I experienced in December 2017: (1) No provisional credit was extended to me (Comerica immediately giving me credit until an investigation took place), and (2) the reimbursement could have been given immediately with no investigation if there was obvious fraud. People from India were sending perfume and a brown leather jacket to India and I was paying for it.

Chally was stating that Conduent refunded my money. That was a lie. I contacted the merchant (Zulily), spoke to the customer service reps, communicated with the attorneys working for Zulily, and Zulily acknowledged the fraud. Zulily contacted Conduent and the reimbursement was conducted.

I told Chally, "Your client is a liar." Chally ended the deposition 3 hours early. He must have known I had much information that would hurt his client.

Comerica denied that Jackie called them on August 3, 2018, after learning of the fraud on her brother-in-law's debit card account. Operators at the Conduent call center were purposely not answering the calls. A source told me repeat calls from cardholders was ignored.

Wednesday, January 6, 2021

Looking for information about the "monthly meetings"

Within the White Paper, it was observed that Pamela Powers was requesting monthly meetings with all agencies that had a hand in creating or administering the Direct Express debit card program. I had her attention. It appeared I would have to submit a separate FOI request to get information about the monthly meetings. No information was ever given without having to file an FOI request.

jbsimms
Date: January 6, 2021
To: Quanisha Jones (FOI VA)
Jackie Lynn
Dear Ms. Jones,
It appears the last email to you concerning the above FOI request was sent to you on December 11, 2020. The date of my submission was November 27, 2020.
This request was given the above FOI number subsequent to the original request VAFOI 20-09821, submitted to me by Mr. Ha.
I believe my request was for documents pertaining to the monthly meetings which were referenced in the White Paper document submitted to me by Mr. Ha. If my memory serves me, that White Paper and the reference to the monthly meeting was found on Page 20 of what Mr. Ha sent me.
Please determine the status of this FOI request and let me know when I can expect to receive the minutes of the referenced meetings.
Sincerely, , Jim Simms

This was correct. The revelation of the monthly meetings requested by Ms. Powers came through the FOI documentation sent to me by Mr. Ha. Now that I had information that the meetings were planned, I needed to know information about the meeting, the participants, and the agenda.

The monthly meetings will expose Comerica Bank and BFS corruption.

jbsimms
to: Quanisha Jones (VA FOI), Jackie Lynn
Dear Ms. Jones,
Thank you very much for your reply.
The FOI requests seem to run together and it is challenging to keep them straight.
After the revelation of the FOI response from Mr. Ha, I submitted a request for redactions to be removed (I believe that was immediate of the response) as well as one other important matter; records of the meetings noted in the White Paper which was noted on Page 20 of the FOI document sent to me.
The communication between officials (Gribben, Santaniello, Powers, Lawrence, Gurney, Lepper) are quite important. There were a few emails from Ms. Powers to Mr. Gurney in reference to the White Paper as well as one in November 2019 from Ms. Powers asking a VA official to update me on the progress of the VA addressing the matter which I presented to them.
If you are able to find the records of the minutes or debriefing documents pertaining to the monthly meetings held involving SSA, VA, Treasury, BFS, Comerica (and probably Conduent) that would be very helpful. If these documents can be submitted as incremental submission to me, I will be glad to wait for other revelations.
Thank you again.
Sincerely,
J.B. Simms

I did not want Ms. Jones to take forever to accumulate documents. I wanted her to send me what she found and go find more.

From: Quanisha Jones (VA FOI)
Date: Mon, January 11, 2021 7:59 am
To: jbsimms
You're correct the last email you sent me regarding FOIA Request 20-09883-F was December 11, 2020. I am unaware of request VAFOI 20-09821. If Mr. Ha has been assigned to process the request then it is assigned to the Office of the Secretary (OSVA) which is outside of my purview. I am still processing your request seeking: Copies of all communication between the following persons employed at the VA and Bureau of Fiscal Service (to include Mr. Santaniello and Mr. Gribben) beginning February 1, 2019 to the present: Paul Lawrence and Joe Gurney.
Copies of all inter-department email, texts, letters, faxes, communication logs, notes from meetings, briefings, or any tangible record of any communication between and not limited to Paul Lawrence and Joe Gurney from February 1, 2019, to the present with regard to the Direct Express debit card program and the administration of said program by the Bureau of Fiscal Service, Department of Treasury.
The records search returned a voluminous number of documents and I am still reviewing them to see which documents are responsive to the information you have requested from the Veterans Benefits Administration.
I thank you for your patience as I continue my review.
Please feel free to contact me with any more questions or concerns.
Respectfully,
Quanisha Jones
FOIA/Privacy Program Specialist
Department of Veterans Affairs

The FOI response that Jackie sent to Treasury regarding the initial Fiscal Agent Agreement that Comerica Bank bid on in 2008 was so heavily redacted that I had to fire off a letter to Cynthia Syndor of Treasury on January 11, 2021.

Below is Jackie's response to the report she received:
> from: Jackie Lynn
> to: Jbsimms
> subject: Re: 2020-12-037 FOIA Response
> The shit heads blacked it all out what a joke

Below is my response in support of Jackie's FOI request
jbsimms
to: Cynthia Syndor (BFS Treasury), Jackie Lynn
Dear Ms. Syndor,
Attached please find a letter/email sent to your office with regard to the above referenced FOI request submitted by Ms. Densmore, of which a copy of this was sent to me.
The document emailed to your office detailed redactions which appeared to be gratuitous, shielding federal workers from accountability and exposure of questionable ethical behavior.
Please allow me to recap the experience Ms. Densmore has suffered as a result of submitting this FOI request to BFS/Treasury: The original FOI request was "lost" by BFS/Treasury, having been submitted in September/October 2018 only to be found 10 months later. Ms. Densmore's original request was given a subsequent tracking number as BFS ignored their culpability by ignoring the original submission. Ms. Densmore submitted a request to challenge the redactions on October 9, 2020 (via mail) and this submission was also ignored by BFS/Treasury FOI. The contract between Comerica Bank and BFS created approximately 2008 is 12 years old, and the massive redactions cannot be validated.
While I do appreciate your responses and attention to FOI requests I have submitted, I would hope your office would afford Ms. Densmore the courtesy of addressing her submissions in a timely manner. If there is a person other than yourself who has been tasked to receive and acknowledge FOI Request referenced above, please forward this email to their attention and copy Ms. Densmore in the communication. Ms. Densmore deserves to know who is addressing this matter and the reasons for the delays.
Sincerely,
J.B. Simms

Friday, January 8, 2021

After reviewing the redacted documents sent to Jackie (the original application filed by Comerica Bank to bid on the DirectExpresss contract) I drafted this appeal for Jackie to send to OIG Treasury.
US Department of the Treasury
Bureau of Fiscal Service (Fiscal Service)
Attn: FOI Disclosure Office
CC: Ms. Martha Murphy, Office of Government Information Services, National Archives and Records
Email transmission: ogis@nara.gov
Re: FOI Request 2019-08-012
Document Number One: Application to Serve as Financial Agent and to Provide Debit Card Services
The U.S. Department of the Treasury, Financial Management Service, October 2, 2007
Dear Ms. Syndor and Ms. Murphy,
Attached to this letter is a copy of my appeal and request to eliminate redactions from documents I received from your office.
This request was sent over three (3) months ago and no response has been received.
Please address this matter.
Sincerely,
Jacqueline Densmore

The Bureau of Fiscal Service knew I was looking for information that would be detrimental to BFS and Comerica Bank. This is one page of redactions which we were challenging:
> *Document Redaction Challenges*
> *Document Number One Application to Serve as Financial Agent and to Provide Debit Card Services*
> *The U.S. Department of the Treasury, Financial Management Service October 2, 2007*
> *Page 19 Section (1) Qualifications Comerica's Subcontractor Contacts Key Personnel-all entries*
> *Page 20 Section (1) Qualifications Key Personnel (continued from previous page)- all entries*
> *Page 27 Section (7) Debit Card Features Regulation E-Entire paragraph*

Page 33 Section (10) Settlement Processing/Reconciliation Entire section/paragraphs Section (13) Cardholder Customer Services Entire paragraph
Page 34 Section (13) Cardholder Customer Services (Continued from previous page)- Entire paragraph
Page 35 Section (13) Cardholder Customer Services Complaint Resolution-Entire paragraph
Page 36 Section (13) Cardholder Customer Services Complaint Resolution (Continued from previous page)- Entire paragraph Error Resolution- entire paragraph Training Customer Service Personnel- entire paragraph
Page 37 Section (13) Cardholder Customer Services Training Customer Service Personnel (Continued from previous page) – entire paragraphs
Page 38 Section (14) Fraud Monitoring and Investigation Entire section
Page 39 Section (14) Fraud Monitoring and Investigation (Continued from previous page)- Entire section

Friday, January 15, 2021

As seen in the first paragraph, the original FOI regarding the origin of the inserts was sent on October 13, 2020. The initial response was November 5, 2020. The request was denied by citing "personal and medical files..." and circumvention of the law. BFS did not want me to know who was creating the inserts (because it was them doing it).

DEPARTMENT OF THE TREASURY
BUREAU OF THE FISCAL SERVICE
WASHINGTON, DC 20227
January 15, 2021
Mr. James Simms
Re: FOIA # 2020-12-037
Dear Mr. Simms:
This is in response to your Freedom of Information Act (FOIA) request that was originally received by the Department of the Treasury's Bureau of the Fiscal Service (Fiscal Service) on October 13, 2020. As stated in our initial response dated November 5, 2020, we are responding to your request for the following:
1. Copies of any emails, transcripts of telephone conversations, notes of any meetings, witness statements, or any tangible evidence of communication between the Fiscal Service, Comerica Bank, Conduent, SSA OIG, OIG Treasury, and the Social Security Administration with regard to the paper inserts endorsing the Direct Express program and the insertion into the check envelopes.
The Fiscal Service conducted a search of its records and has enclosed a copy of the responsive records that were located. We have withheld portions of the responsive records pursuant to exemptions (b)(6) and (b)(7)(E) of the FOIA, 5 U.S.C. §552. Exemption (b)(6) protects from disclosure "personnel and medical files and similar files the disclosure of which would constitute a clearly unwarranted invasion of personal privacy." Exemption (b)(7)(E) exempts from disclosure certain records or information, "if such disclosure could reasonably be expected to risk circumvention of the law." We have also withheld portions of the records because they are non-responsive to your FOIA request.
This is a partial denial of your request. You may administratively appeal this partial denial within 90 calendar days from the date of this letter.
Sincerely,
Cynthia A. Sydnor-Jones
Co-Disclosure Officer

Notice the standard disclaimer underlined above. Federal agencies will withhold documents and make their rules to justify their actions. They make the rules. There is no accountability among federal employees. We just had to be persistent and creative.
One way to find out more about what the agencies were withholding was to send FOI requests to multiple agencies requesting the same information. This plan worked. The VA was more cooperative than the Bureau of Fiscal Service, Treasury, or Social Security. The only way I found out about the monthly meetings was from the VA. An FOI request was submitted to the VA regarding the inserts, and I found out about the "White Paper." I then had to submit another FOI request regarding the White Paper and the meetings.

Another email was received from the Bureau of Fiscal Service on the same day. This request concerned the "monthly meetings" that began on March 12, 2019. These were the meetings that Pamela Powers of the VA requested be conducted. You can also see they withheld documents citing:

> *"Exemption (b)(5) protects from release "inter-agency or intra-agency memorandums or letters which would not be available by law to a party other than an agency in litigation with the agency."*

This denial meant they were not going to give me information "unless" I were suing the agency in court (thus the use of the word "litigation").

January 15, 2021
Mr. James Simms
Re: FOIA # 2020-11-035
Dear Mr. Simms:
This is in response to your Freedom of Information Act (FOIA) request for information regarding the last paragraph of a Direct Express® White Paper, which read, "[O]utcome: Due to the increase in account takeover and benefit payment fraud, Comerica agreed to a monthly group with VA, USDT, and SSA to track and find better ways to serve our customers." You specifically requested:
1. Notes, minutes, summaries, email interaction, and documents produced from the "monthly working group" from the date of the agreement by Comerica Bank, being March 12, 2019, to the present; and
2. The identity of any and all representatives of persons identified as employees of "USDT" (U.S. Department of the Treasury) to include employees of OIG Treasury and Bureau of the Fiscal Service, SSA (Social Security Administration), and VA (Veterans Administration) who were present at any and all of the meetings.
The Fiscal Service conducted a search of its records and has enclosed a copy of the responsive records that were located. We have withheld portions of the responsive records pursuant to exemptions (b)(6) and (b)(7)(E) of the FOIA, 5 U.S.C. §552. We have also withheld 7 pages in their entirety pursuant to exemption (b)(5) of the FOIA, 5 U.S.C. §552. Exemption (b)(5) <u>*protects from release "inter-agency or intra-agency memorandums or letters which would not be available by law to a party other than an agency in litigation with the agency."*</u>
This is a partial denial of your request. You may administratively appeal this partial denial within 90 calendar days from the date of this letter.
Sincerely,
Cynthia A. Sydnor-Jones
Co-Disclosure Officer

I removed some of the 'fluff' from the above two emails. At the end of the emails, I was told I could appeal the FOI ruling within 90 days. Treasury FOI was sending me what they wanted to send, not what they were supposed to send.

Saturday, January 16, 2021

Below is my response to the denial of my FOI request regarding the origin of the inserts:

U.S. Department of the Treasury, Bureau of the Fiscal Service
Attn: FOIA Disclosure Office/Room
Submitted by email: Cynthia Syndor (BFS Treasury)
Office of Government Information Services National Archives and
RE: FOI 2020-11-035 and 2020-12-037
Dear Ms. Syndor Jones and OGIS,
At first glance, and having read the documents, two things immediately came to mind:
1. The documents regarding monthly meetings (2020-11-035) were woefully incomplete. These meetings were to begin in April 2019. There is no definitive list of meetings, and minutes were redacted.
2. The names of persons at BFS, Comerica, VA, and SSA were redacted. One of the purposes of the FOI requests was to identify persons responsible for both the inserts (2020-12-037) and those in attendance at the meetings (2020-11-035).
These redactions should never have happened. The person/persons at BFS who was/were tasked to abide by the Freedom of Information Act and redact the requested documents became complicit in a cover-up of malfeasance and improper conduct by BFS officials.
I will review each document and submit a synopsis of each of the 19 documents I received. It shocks the conscience to think BFS charged $534.74 and $473.65 only to have suspicions of lack of accountability and a

criminal mindset validated. Laws and regulations mean nothing to persons at BFS who are involved (past and present) with Comerica Bank and subcontractor Conduent, and the awarding of the Fiscal Agent contract.
This letter is a notice of appeal of FOI submissions 2020-12-037 and 2020-11-035.
Sincerely,
J.B. Simms

Treasury was covering for Comerica's violations and continued to give Comerica the contract.
We were experiencing all sorts of redactions of FOI requests.

Saturday, January 16, 2021

from: *Jbsimms*
to: *Cynthia Syndor (BFS Treasury), OGIS <ogis@nara.gov>*
cc: *Jackie Lynn*
date: *Jan 16, 2021, 7:19 PM*
subject: Appeal FOI documents 2020-12-037 and 2020-11-035
Dear Ms. Syndor-Jones and OGIS officials,
Attached please find my appeal of the above two FOI requests. While there is no way to validate the cost of said documents, your submission to me was a gesture of arrogance and lack of impunity.
In a few days, I will be calling both of your offices to put this matter into context. Hopefully, people at either of your offices will understand the magnitude of the charade presented to me by BFS.
Sincerely,
J.B. Simms.

Monday, January 18, 2021

The "Meetings" and the Coverup

Jbsimms
Attachments
Mon, Jan 18, 2021, 11:00 AM
to Jackie, Franklin
I reviewed the FOI documents.
Although they are incomplete, it is interesting that the VA told BFS that the VA was going to create its own inserts in July 2020. Kudos to the VA.
This revelation of the break with BFS on the inserts, and the establishment of the VBBP at the VA validates all Jackie and I have been doing.
Let me point out a big issue:
Comerica/Conduent has a mantra that the meetings and the subject are all about fraud prevention; this is the red herring put out in a PR move to avoid the real issue. The real issue is the violation of Reg E. Although Comerica Bank could have instituted the same security parameters for DE cardholders as for their proprietary customers, which would have protected cardholders a bit more, the issue of Conduent violating Regulation E was the genesis of this suit as well as the basis from which my argument defending VA beneficiaries was based. Thankfully Mr. Lepper validated the assertions made by Jackie and me, and we will forever be in his debt since no one at the VA was allowed to communicate directly with me.
We await further documents from the VA which might reveal more.
This limited information can be used during depositions of Comerica (Arpin, Schmidt) and Conduent (Mitch Raymond, Shantelle Johnson, Marquita Stevenson, and more) to further define the "working group" and documents pertaining to the group.

Tuesday, January 19, 2021

January 19, 2021
jbsimms
Franklin Lemond (Plaintiff's Attorney), Jackie Lynn
Franklin,
I want you to look at the caption of our case.
You see Conduent listed, as dba Direct Express?

Comerica has the contract with BFS, not Conduent.
I will look at the Sec of State in Texas to see if Conduent IS dba Direct Express.
Conduent is not a bank.
Conduent employees are not trained to abide by Reg E.
What provision allowed Conduent to attain the dba?
This DBA matter requires a bit of research.
I told you a long time ago that the tail was wagging the dog. Conduent runs the show, but is not a bank. Some Conduent employees have said to victims "we are not a bank."

Friday, January 22, 2021

Reply from: Jbsimms
to: FOI SSA <FOIA.Public.Liaison@ssa.gov>
cc: Jackie Lynn
date: Jan 22, 2021, 11:36 AM
subject: Fwd: Payment for 2021-000274 $3,085.50
Dear Ms. Zimmerman,
Please update me on the progress of the submission of documents pertaining to FOI request 2021-001175. SSA has received the fee of $3,085.50 almost a month ago and I have seen no evidence of any compliance with SSA by submitting the documents.
Sincerely,
J.B. Simms

From: jbsimms
Sent: Friday, January 22, 2021, 12:53 PM
To: Quanisha Jones (VA FOI)
Cc: Jackie Lynn
Subject: FOI request 20-09883F
Dear Ms. Jones,
While reviewing emails, I see an email dated January 11, 2021, from you stating the information I am requesting appears to be quite voluminous and you are reviewing said documents.
Within the list of documents submitted as the "1st Interim Response" page 20 refers to meetings that were said to have been set up with representatives from VA, SSA, BFS, and Treasury to address issues concerning the BFS debit card program, administered by Comerica Bank and Conduent, known as Direct Express. I believe I submitted a request for information concerning each meeting subsequent to this "White Paper" reference on Page 20, along with the attendees and notes from each meeting which were probably sent to Ms. Pamela Powers.
Please update me on the approximate date of submission of the document search which you are conducting and if the information concerning the meetings will be included in your submission.
Thank you for your assistance in this matter.
Sincerely,
J.B. Simms

Thursday, January 28, 2021

SSA sent an email Re: 2021-002188 regarding a fee for FOI request documents. Franklin agreed to pay. The fee notice came from Mary Zimmerman.

Friday, January 29, 2021

Quanisha Jones (VA FOI)
To: jbsimms
Mr. Simms,
Thank you for your patience while I continue my review of the record. Though I cannot provide an approximate date when I will be releasing the next interim response I can assure you that I will be in contact with you by February 12, 2021, with any update.

I'm unaware of your request for information concerning each meeting subsequent to this "White Paper" reference on Page 20, along with the attendees and notes from each meeting which were probably sent to Ms. Pamela Powers.

I am still working on the request 20-09883F seeking:

1. Copies of all communication between the following persons employed at the VA and Bureau of Fiscal Service (to include Mr. Santaniello and Mr. Gribben) beginning February 1, 2019 to the present: Pamela Powers, Paul Lawrence, and Joe Gurney.

2. These communications will include documented records of telephone calls, emails, faxes, notes from a meeting between the VA employees and the Bureau of Fiscal Service, directives, or any tangible publication regarding the Direct Express program.

3. Copies of all communication between the VA employees and representatives of the Association of Military Banks of America, including communication between VA and Major General Steven J. Lepper (USAF Retired), CEO of the Association of Military Banks of America.

4. Copies of all inter-department emails, texts, letters, faxes, communication logs, notes from meetings, briefings, or any tangible record of any communication between and not limited to Pamela Powers, Paul Lawrence, Joe Gurney, and Secretary Wilkie from February 1, 2019, to the present with regard to the Direct Express debit card program and the administration of said program by the Bureau of Fiscal Service, Department of Treasury.

Anything outside of the information requested in FOIA request 20-09883F will need to be submitted in the form of a new FOIA request. Have you submitted a new request for the "White Paper" information? If so has it been assigned a FOIA request number? If it has you should follow up with the point of contact on the acknowledgment letter to inquire about that request.

I thank you again for your patience.

Please feel free to contact me with any other questions or concerns regarding FOIA request 20-09883F.

Respectfully,

Quanisha Jones, FOIA/Privacy Program Specialist, Department of Veterans Affairs

Quanisha Jones was great to work with and she understood the issues.

Sunday, February 7, 2021

Franklin was going to pay for an SSA FOI report. That was good of Franklin.

Franklin Lemond (Plaintiff's Attorney)

To: Jbsimms

See email below and attached payment form, which I sent to the FOIA department on Jan. 28.

Franklin

Wednesday, February 10, 2021

I had three (3) FOI submissions to Treasury. The email below addresses the emails.

Wednesday, February 10, 2021

FOIA@treasury.gov

jbsimms

Mr. Simms,

Wrapping up our telephone call I wanted to provide you with a status update on your FOIA requests and subsequent appeals. At this time our office has three FOIA appeals on file related to your requests which have been assigned case numbers 2021-APP-00010/2020-03-070, 2021-APP-00009/2020-03-042, and 2021-APP-00008/2020-02-137. Each of these appeals has been directed to Treasury's appellate authority, the Deputy Assistant Secretary for Privacy, Transparency, and Records, for a review of the processing of your initial requests and the additional documentation that you provided challenging the adequacy of the search conducted by the Office of the Inspector General. You will be notified of your appeal decision through a response letter.

As a FOIA requestor, you have the ability to contact the Office of Government Information Services (OGIS) to discuss your request. OGIS also mediates disputes between FOIA requesters and federal agencies as a non-exclusive alternative to litigation.

Sincerely,

Mark BittnerDirector, FOIA & Transparency, Office of Privacy, Transparency, and Records

U.S. Department of the Treasury

Appeal, appeal, appeal. These people protect themselves from the citizens who pay them.

Wednesday, February 17, 2021

Treasury and Soc Sec dodged and redacted our FOI requests. The VA was more open with information than Soc or Treasury. But, we did get information regarding the meetings coordinated by Pamela Powers (supposedly attended by Joe Gurney for the VA).

Thursday, February 25, 2021

From: jbsimms
Sent: Thursday, February 25, 2021, 1:07 PM
To: Quanisha Jones (VA FOI)
Cc: Jackie Lynn
Subject: 20-098837
Thank you for taking the time to discuss this FOI request. I know it appears broad, but the focus is the communication to Ms. Powers from Lawrence and Gurney which resulted in the creation of the Veterans Benefit Banking Program. Lawrence and Gurney, or other designated VA persons, had to be present at the meetings subsequent to the March 2019 meeting referenced in the "White Paper."
Interestingly enough, the renewal of the Fiscal Agent contract with Comerica Bank by BFS was ongoing at the same time these meetings were taking place.
You have been very helpful. I will gladly receive installments of FOI material, especially noting Mr. Powers, Nora Arpin (Comerica Bank), and Thomas Santaniello (BFS).
Sincerely,
J.B. Simms

I was willing to take whatever I could get by offering to receive any information in increments rather than waiting for a huge report. We knew Santaniello was keeping Jackie and me from testifying before the committee that gave the fiscal agent contract to Comerica Bank. BFS did not want to give us a forum from which to expose malfeasance.

Friday, February 26, 2021

FOIA.Public.Liaison@ssa.gov
Fri, Feb 26, 2021, 2:25 PM
to FOIA, OGIS, me, Jackie
Good Afternoon, Mr. Simms:
Thank you for your email and for providing the clarification we requested. We will provide the applicable components with the updated information so that we can issue you a new fee estimate. Please know that the amount of $3,085.50 was the estimated fee based on estimated search and review time. It is our policy not to charge until the FOIA request is closed; therefore, the agency did not charge you $3,085.50 for your request. With our letter emailed to you from FOIA online this morning, we returned your credit card payment of $3,085.50. Once we have the necessary information from the applicable components, we will issue you a revised fee notice.
Thank you,
The FOIA Team. SSA

The email below is a response from Treasury OIG regarding my request for information about the monthly meetings. Representatives Treasury were supposed to be at the meetings. I deleted the disclaimer. Franklin Lemond paid for the SSA information.

DEPARTMENT OF THE TREASURY, BUREAU OF THE FISCAL SERVICE, WASHINGTON, DC 20227
Mr. James Simms
Sent via electronic mail to:
Re: FOIA # 2020-11-035
Dear Mr. Simms:
This is in response to your Freedom of Information Act (FOIA) request for information regarding the last paragraph of a Direct Express® White Paper, which read, "[O]utcome: Due to the increase in account

takeover and benefit payment fraud, Comerica agreed to a monthly group with VA, USDT, and SSA to track and find better ways to serve our customers." You specifically requested:

1. Notes, minutes, summaries, email interaction, and documents produced from the "monthly working group" from the date of the agreement by Comerica Bank, being March 12, 2019, to the present; and

2. The identity of any and all representatives of persons identified as employees of "USDT" (U.S. Department of the Treasury) to include employees of OIG Treasury and Bureau of the Fiscal Service, SSA (Social Security Administration), and VA (Veterans Administration) who were present at any and all of the meetings.

The Fiscal Service conducted a search of its records and has enclosed a copy of the responsive records that were located. We have withheld portions of the responsive records pursuant to exemptions (b)(6) and (b)(7)(E) of the FOIA, 5 U.S.C. §552.

This is a partial denial of your request. You may administratively appeal this partial denial within 90 calendar days from the date of this letter.

There was more. These meetings were requested by Pamela Powers of the VA. We found out about the meetings via an FOI request to the VA. We learned what info Treasury has about these meetings.

Monday, March 1, 2021

I had to send an email to Cawana Pearson to clear up the matter of all the FOI requests.

From: jbsimms
Sent: Monday, March 1, 2021 10:42 PM
To: Pearson, Cawana <Cawana.Pearson@treasury.gov>
Subject:] Clarification of FOI requests (2020-02-023 and 2020-02-137)
Dear Ms. Pearson,
A list of the FOI request is being compiled with regard to the matters involving federal agencies and their relationship with the Treasury and the Direct Express debit card program.
There are more than a dozen outstanding FOI requests outstanding with Treasury, BFS, VA, and SSA. The FOI requests I made with Treasury beginning February 20 and 21, 2020 were the first of four (4) requests with Treasury. With respect to the above-referenced attachment, this is a letter from you stating the convergence of FOI 2020-02-137 with an unnamed and unnumbered FOI request. I am assuming the request being joined with 2020-02-137 would be 2020-02-023. I am at a disadvantage by not having copies of the original FOI requests. The other two FOI requests were as follows:

> *2020-03-042*
> *Request for records of the investigation by OIG Treasury of 30 fraud victims by Comerica/Conduent.*
> *2020-03-070*
> *Request for the investigation conducted and submitted to inform Katherine Johnson as she published OIG Treasury audit 19-041.*

Would you be able to clarify the matter of FOI requests 2020-02-023 and 2020-02-137? I assume 2020-02-023 was created then joined with the latter, and no longer exists.I appreciate you clarifying this issue and confirming that only 3 FOI requests exist.
Sincerely, , J.B. Simms

Monday, March 2. 2021

March 2, 2021
Cawana.Pearson@treasury.gov
jbsimms
Good morning Mr. Simms,
I hope this email finds you well.
The FOIA request you referenced, 2020-02-023 is associated with another FOIA requester. Below are the FOIA requests you submitted to Department of the Treasury. All cases are closed.

> *2020-03-070 – Under the name of James Simms*
> *2020-02-146 – Under J.B. Simms*
> *2019-08-184 – J.B. Simms/Erik Publishing Co.*
> *2020-03-042 – J.B. Simms/ Erik Publishing Co.*
> *2020-02-137 – J.B. Simms / Erick Publishing Co.*

Thank you, Cawana

The biggest find: the unredacted White Paper

An email from the VA regarding an FOI request is below;

Barnes, Deborah (OGC) <debi.barnes@va.gov>
Mr. Simms,
Good morning. Please see attached OGC's Decision for J.B. Simms, FOIA Tracking #20-09821-F, OGC Case #152331.
Deborah C. Barnes
Legal Assistant
Office of General Counsel (024), Room 1157A
Information and Administrative Law Group

The attachment sent by Debi Barnes was a letter and the WHITE PAPER (UNREDACTED)

The unredacted White Paper sent to Pamela Powers, VA COS

Direct Express White Paper

BLUF: Recommend that VA take no action to distance the agency from the U.S. Department of Treasury or its contractor Comerica, Inc. VA's authority and influence on benefits delivery ends at the successful transmission of benefits to Treasury.

Background: Direct Express is a pre-paid debit card program administered by the U.S. Department of Treasury (USDT) through contracted services provided by Comerica Bank. The program was initiated to give US citizens, to include veterans, that cannot get bank accounts
(due to homelessness, credit issues, skepticism, etc.) a way to electronically receive federal benefits payments. As customers of USDT, neither VHA nor VBA have a direct business relationship with Comerica Inc., nor have influence on the contract administered by USDT. The alternative decision for VA to execute its contract for a separate pre-paid debit card would subject VA to incur startup and implementation costs as well as imposing a higher level of payment risk on the veteran. The Direct Express contract is funded by USDT and operates with a fraud rate of approximately .01 %, whereas the industry standard is between .03%-.05%.

VHA and VBA representatives met with USDT and Nora Arpin, Comerica Senior Vice President and Director of the Government Electronic Solutions Team on March 12, 2019, to discuss the referenced instances of fraud, potential data breaches, and the impact the situation has had on veterans. Nora reiterated that there has been no data breach at Comerica and the three veterans referenced were victims of an account takeover and payment redirect scam, where criminals steal identities and then use the personal information to compromise accounts and steal money. Account takeover and payment redirect fraud schemes are on the rise in both the public and private sectors. Even with the rise in electronic benefits theft, it is still easier to steal paper checks out of someone's mailbox, than it is to illegally obtain an individual's identity from the dark web and use that to identify and compromise each of the online benefits accounts.

VA has approximately 131,711 veterans who use the Treasury Direct Prepaid Debit Card program as their banking solution for VHA and VBA benefits payments. Comerica had 480 out of 4.5M (.13%) Direct Express accounts that were compromised; 30 of those were veterans who had federal benefits stolen. Comerica reaffirmed that all veterans that were deemed victims of account takeover and payment redirect fraud have been repaid. The veterans involved in the class action lawsuit chose litigation to solve their disagreements with Comerica and therefore are reliant on the U.S. court system for final resolution.

Outcome: Due to the increase in account takeover and benefit payment fraud, Comerica agreed to a monthly working group with VA, USDT, and SSA to track and find better ways to serve our customers.

This was the document that changed everything. The information about the meetings was hidden from us. No one told us why there was a six-month delay in announcing that Comerica Bank was to remain the Fiscal Agent. The reason was Comerica Bank brought in i2c to take over new Conduent debit card accounts. The only reason Comerica Bank kept the contract was to get rid of Conduent, and that is because we (Jackie and I) exposed them. There was too much heat on Comerica Bank to keep Conduent.

Monday, March 15, 2021

Jbsimms
Mon, Mar 15, 2021, 11:37 AM
to Jackie, Franklin
I will not stop.
They keep pushing back on the FOI requests. I have submitted a dozen requests and information from yours and mine has helped our case.
You and I are so weary of this and hopefully, the subpoenas will be pursued to gain more info to be used in the depositions.
A big issue we forgot to ask Mitchell about is the meetings orchestrated by the VA in March-June 2019. We will not forget this when Nora Arpin is deposed.
Jim

March 18, 2021

Jackie found this on the internet at the Comerica website.

> *Partners*
> *Home/Partners*
> *The Direct Express® program is run on behalf of the U.S. Treasury's Fiscal Service by Comerica Bank, which serves as Treasury's Financial Agent. The Direct Express® Debit Mastercard® card is issued by Comerica Bank, pursuant to a license by Mastercard International Incorporated. Comerica Bank operates the Direct Express® program with support from its contractors, i2c, Inc., and Conduent Corporation.*
>
> **<u>Conduent Corporation</u>**
> *Conduent Incorporated (Nasdaq: CNDT), a global technology-led business process solutions company, delivers mission-critical services and solutions on behalf of businesses and governments – creating exceptional outcomes for its clients and the millions of people who count on them. Through its dedicated people, processes, and technologies, Conduent solutions and services enhance customer experience, increase efficiencies, reduce costs, and improve performance for most Fortune 100 companies and more than 500 government entities.*
> *Learn more at www.conduent.com.*
>
> **<u>i2c, Inc</u>**
> *i2c, Inc. drives innovation to the global digital payments and open banking industry with a multi-function platform built for endless possibilities. Advanced "building block" processing technology at its core provides a vast suite of credit, debit and prepaid solutions—all from a single global SaaS platform. This enables clients to dynamically configure payment solutions with unparalleled flexibility, agility and performance while maintaining highly secure and reliable payments. Founded in 2001, and headquartered in Silicon Valley, i2c's next-generation technology helps organizations drive revenue growth, scale and adapt to change while supporting millions of users in more than 200 countries and territories and all time zones.*
> *Learn more at www.i2cinc.com and follow i2c on Twitter at @i2cinc.*

Comerica Bank saved itself by having to bring in i2c. We had discredited Conduent, but the rumor was no other bank bid on the contract so BFS had to give the contract to Comerica.

Thursday, March 18, 2021

Franklin Lemond (Plaintiff's Attorney)
jbsimms
Jackie Lynn
Sorry for the delayed email on this.
I deposed Al Taylor[Comerica Bank] last week, who is the "new Nora" although he said Conduent was responsible for everything.
A few interesting notes that he did reveal - to say Nora retired is not exactly accurate. Her position was eliminated in part due to issue with compliance (obviously including Regulation E).

Also, as part of the renewed contract from Fiscal Services, Comerica was required to bring on a second card servicer, which is i2c. i2c gets all new cards that are issued and Conduent continues to administer the legacy accounts they have had but is not allowed to get any new accounts. Mr. Taylor admitted this was a performance issue, but tried to say it was a server stability issue, not a Reg E performance issue.
Reminder - Shantelle's second deposition is on March 26.
Nora's may be April 9, but that isn't confirmed.
Franklin

The company named i2c came up again. We did our job.

Nora Arpin's departure was shrouded in secrecy. Nora was the link between Comerica Bank and BFS. She was the contact for Santaniello, Brett Smith, and the director of BFS (a position that changed 3 times during her tenure being associated with Comerica Bank.)

We made Comerica blink.

Saturday, March 20, 2021

Occasionally, I would send a victim to Delmar just to keep him aware of the problems he caused by publishing inadequate OIG Treasury reports regarding Comerica Bank and the Direct Express debit card system.
Just Mike <pitcher8inmi@yahoo.com>
Richard Delmar (OIG Treasury)
jbsimms
Mr. Richard Delmar
Acting Inspector General
Dept of the Treasury
I wanted to thank you for taking the time on your Saturday and help me get this situation resolved. I didn't expect to hear back from you until Monday per your email. Like so many people, we assume that financial institutions are there for us, until a situation of fraud. I became Leary to trust anyone, but not for the help of Mr. Jim Simms and taking the time to read the information on consumer rights. Mr. Simms could see that the bank was negligent, and asked me to get ahold of you. Again thank you so much for everything you've done.
Mike Smolka

Sunday, April 4, 2021

Better Business Bureau ceases reporting on the Direct Express program

Sun, Apr 4, 2021, 10:18 AM
to Tiffany,
Good morning on this Easter morning.
Jackie Densmore just sent me this email and I wanted to share it with you. If your news contacts see this, as well as the follow-up email from Richard Delmar (I will send in the next email), they should want to run with the story.
The reason the BBB is not taking complaints against the Direct Express program is that it is a government program, operated by the Bureau of Fiscal Service, Comerica Bank, and Conduent.
Have your news sources make contact with me and I will give them the story.
Jim

Jbsimms
Sun, Apr 4, 2021, 11:50 AM
to Kate
Ya think BFS is blocking complaints?

Bureau of Fiscal Service must have gotten to the BBB. Comerica Bank was not going to receiving complaints about the corrupt Direct Express program.

458

Jackie Lynn
Sun, Apr 4, 2021, 12:26 AM
to Franklin, me
According to the BBB people are no longer allowed to make complaints on Direct Express , this was recently changed and I want to know by whom and why ?!?!
This is huge as we all know it had an F rating with multiple complaints warning cardholders.
Now the complaints are being blocked from getting reported I want to know how many complaints have called that phone number listed from when this was put into place and to today's date.
Why and who had the authority to change this and what is this phone number all about, who takes these calls, Conduent?
We need to investigate this ASAP!
Jbsimms

Tuesday, April 6, 2021

Another victim of Comerica Bank and Conduent

From: Cricket Keene
Sent: Tuesday, April 6, 2021, 6:40 PM
To: Richard Delmar (OIG Treasury)
Cc: Jim Simms jbsimms
Subject: Direct express freeze of account since fraudulent activity.
 Dear Mr. Delmar,
 On the eve of receiving a stimulus check, I find myself in a ghastly position.
Starting on November 14 after a robbery, I have had several bad workings with direct express.
I have had my account frozen and then literally opened by people who have milked the account. While traveling at that. I spent 127 hours of which no one but Susan Schmidt of Comerica was able to help.
Once resuming the account and credit given to me for only particle amounts of the fraud I thought the nightmare was over.
In January just after the second stimulus check the account was locked up again. This time for really no reason explained to me.
I have received my benefits to that account for 3 months now and also a stimulus check is said to be going there.
I changed my account benefits to go to various bank as of last month but still direct express won't release my money to me.
Know tomarrow a stimulus check also
That is roughly 4000.00
I live on my benefits.
I have been in a shelter with now income and destitute.
Direct express has said that I have to get a special memorandum of understating from social security.
Social security doesn't understand the issues.
I have talked myself blue.
I have a case manager names Cassandra that has been helping me from the path navigation center where I live.
She can be reached at +1 213-590-0994 to verify the length of which this has caused a problem.
Jim Simms has tried to help me along the way and i am seriously near taking my life.
Honestly I have no more excuses for the bad service and impossible directions for direct express holding this money from me.
I need attention to the account. The fact that my stimulus money is going there also after I have in fact a different account for which my benefits are sent is beyond reproach.
Please tell me that you are able to see my balance be obtained by the treasury and recent to the proper account for which I currently have access.
For anything about the account through direct express in have been talking with donna Williams of whom has been very difficult to deal with. Offering no help. Meanwhile I have been penniless.
Immediate action is called for.
 In all sincerity,
Cricket Keene

I was surprised to see that Richard Delmar responded, but not surprised to see that the response was almost "clinical." Delmar referred the victim to a government website that we knew was a waste of time.

From: Richard Delmar (OIG Treasury)
Date: Wed, April 07, 2021, 12:32 pm
To: Cricket Keene
Cc: Jim Simms
I recommend that you contact both Treasury's Bureau of the Fiscal Service, and the Consumer Finance Protection Bureau, which take and resolve these issues. Here are their email addresses:
direct.express@fiscal.treasury.gov
https://www.consumerfinance.gov/complaint/
Rich Delmar
Acting Inspector General
Department of the Treasury

From: jbsimms
Date: Wed, April 07, 2021, 12:59 pm
To: Richard Delmar (OIG Treasury), Cricket Keene, Cc: Jackie Lynn
Dear Mr. Delmar,
Thank you for responding directly to victim Cricket Keene..
While we are aware that the CFPB is a repository for consumer complaints against Comerica Bank and Conduent with regard to violations of Regulation E (15USC1693) as well as regulations 12CFR205 (6 and 11) and FDIC Regulation Title 6500 Sections 1005.6 and 1005.11, I have established and confirmed that although the mandate of the CFPB does authorize enforcement of law and regulation violations, the CFPB has refused to enforce any violations against a Fiscal Agent having been awarded a contract by Treasury. The CFPB has decided not to engage a fellow federal agency as a respondent or make any fellow federal employee accountable or liable.
Considering the conditions in which Ms. Keen-Dickinson is currently living, and considering the fact she has asked for my assistance, I respectfully request you submit to Ms. Keen-Dickinson a specific person at the Bureau of Fiscal Service and the Consumer Financial Protection Bureau to whom she can directly make contact. Judging by the evidence presented in the last three (3) OIG Treasury audits, and the failure of BFS to adhere or comply to any corrective measures presented in said audits, the anticipated response from BFS will be flaccid at best and will continue to confirm that BFS cannot and will not mandate compliance of the FAA upon Comerica Bank.
Again, thank you for your direct response and please direct Ms. Keen-Dickinson to specific persons (name and telephone number) to whom she can request relief.
Sincerely,
J.B. Simms

Delmar's interaction with Keene shows he knew of the neglect of the cardholder.
Now the connection between Comerica Bank and BBB will be exposed. The BBB will no longer rate Comerica and the Direct Express debit card program.

Wednesday, April 7, 2021

The BBB changes policy and stops reporting Direct Express complaints

Wednesday, April 7, 2021
1032am
Tiffany Novak- BBB
(210) 212-1117
Ms. Novak acknowledged BBB was no longer processing Direct Express complaints.
A recent memo was received making the Direct Express program outside their purview. Management made notations. She could not share the documents or who provided the information which led to this decision, or exactly when the decision was made.
The BBB regulations do not allow complaints to be made against government program. I advised my complaint to Ms. Ann Atkinson was made December 13, 2017 and it took them over 3 years of reports and communication

with Susan Schmidt of Comerica Bank to determine Comerica Bank was a Fiscal Agent of BFS. Comerica Bank and Conduent are contractors, not part of the government.)

There are notes from supervisors at BBB who are more aware of the issue.

Julie Barlow-BBB

The telephone call was transferred to Ms. Barlow.

Once it "was determined" that the Direct Express program is a "government program" the BBB...?. This determination came during reviews of complaints against the Direct Express program.

There was no call from any person at Comerica Bank or Conduent. This revelation came about as complaints about the Direct Express program were being reviewed. We do not know who at BBB called which source that made that revelation (maybe a person at BFS).

This apparent conflict was presented to the International Association from the BBB office which covers many counties of Texas. The "memo" evidently was generated and distributed by the BBB International Association. There are two different BBB entities in Texas: one for the "Heart of Texas (Ft. Worth-San Antonio-Houston) and another for the Dallas area.

The office of Ms. Barlow in Dallas which communicated with the BBB International Association. Ms. Barlow was not part of the discussions.

She referred me to her VP, Chelsea Ellis, VP of Operations for the BBB of the Heart of Texas, and a message was being left for Ms. Ellis to contact me.

Monday, April 12, 2021

On Mon, Apr 12, 2021, at 11:39 AM jbsimms wrote:

To: Franklin, Jackie Lynn

Good morning ya'll..

Here is what I gathered from our chat:

Nora Arpin will be served with deposition subpoena

Offer will then be made to defense for settlement

In the meantime, contact will be made with Richard Delmar (OIG Treasury) to intercede (I am handing off the ball) as my attorney of record to get Treasury to give up the "investigations" associated with the following FOI requests:

> *2020-02-137 Investigation of JBS DE fraud Jan 2017 and Dec 2017*
> *2020-03-042 Investigation of 30 specific fraud victims (findings, synopsis, etc)*
> *2020-03-070 Investigation associated with OIG Report 19-041.*

There is a definitive difference between an audit and an investigation. All reports submitted by the Office of Investigations to Katherine Johnson (Chief Auditor for this audit), submitted primarily from Sonja Scott, were promised to be released. OIG recanted and refused.

In all three FOI requests, the response has been that no investigations were conducted. Loren Sciurba made that statement to the Maryland Bar in defense of my complaint against him. The Washington DC Bar (where Delmar's license is registered) refused to even elicit a response from Delmar. Both complaints were accompanied by at least 13 pieces of evidence where both Sciurba and Delmar used the word "investigation(s)" in correspondence to me.

The information in these investigations will expose more malfeasance and the coverup and help our case as has the other FOI requests I and Jackie have sent.

Also. OIG Treasury 19-041 was listed as an "interim" audit report. It was published on or about July 29, 2019. I questioned Delmar about the "interim" and he emailed me stating he would send the final report to me when it is completed. That never happened. The audit was sent to Commissioner Gribben of BFS, and six months later Comerica got a renewed contract (Jan 2, 2020), and as we know, Conduent was out of the picture.

I was told my only recourse was to file suit in federal court against Delmar and Sciurba. I am not advocating that, but I have the evidence and they know it.

I am ready to be proactive.

Jim

The Holy Grail of Exposure: The i2c connection with Comerica Bank

I researched i2c. A telephone number was found, and messages left, but no answer was received. I decided on another approach. I would email the president of i2c.

From: jbsimms
Date: Mon, April 12, 2021 9:46 am
To: "jmccarthy@i2c.com" <jmccarthy@i2c.com>
Cc: Jackie Lynn
Dear Mr. McCarthy,
I and Ms. Densmore (being copied) are familiar with debit cards and the servicing of said cards. Our experience has produced evidence that cardholders had no security parameters (no proactive fraud deterrent) nor adherence to Regulation E (15USC1693).
While we are familiar with the fact that banks which issue debit cards are ultimately liable for the training and supervision of administrators of said debit cards pertaining to Reg E, fraud resolutions are normally not obtained by a cardholder reporting the fraud to a call center manned by personnel not literate in the law and regulations pertaining to the resolution of errors (as stated by the Federal Reserve and FDIC regulations).
At your convenience, would you be willing to discuss these issues in generic terms without encroaching upon any current contracts you have?
I can make myself available to you at any time. I am in California as it appears you are. Your reply is gratefully anticipated.
Sincerely,
J.B. Simms

McCarthy never replied to the email. I guessed he found out I was the one who called him.

Thursday, April 15, 2021

The exposure of i2c and failure of Conduent

On Apr 15, 2021, at 5:59 PM, I sent an email to Jackie Lynn and Franklin Lemond regarding the call I received from Jim McCarthy, president of i2c
1130am I received a call from Jim McCarthy- I2c (415) 734-8120
Below are notes from the call.

> *President, i2c.*
> *Conduent had "issues" and I2C bid with Comerica to get new contract.*
> *McCarthy had been with Visa for 18 years.*
> *I2c is a card processor.*
> *2 different apps for DE- Conduent and I2c depending when account was opened.*
> *He has a call with BFS waiting while we are talking.*
> *Has a fraud unit within I2c- does interact with merchants and cops*
> *Have new app that allows text message every time card is used.*
> *Built into system.*
> *I2c is more advanced platform than Conduent.*
> *I mentioned the security notices were never integrated by Comerica and Conduent.*
> *BFS made decision for Comerica to use i2c*
> *"We bid with Comerica to get the contract."*
> *Comerica had to bring in i2c to keep contract.*
> *I2c got a third, Conduent got 2/3.*
>
> *McCarthy was not here when contract was made.*

This was huge. Conduent is being pushed out. Treasury is hiding this.
BBB people have not replied.

Friday, April 16, 2021

Franklin Lemond (Plaintiff's Attorney)
To: jbsimms; Jackie Lynn
Nora isn't happy that she has been served with the subpoena....
See Below
Franklin

> *From: Cowboy Couriers <cowboycouriers@yahoo.com>*
> *Date: April 16, 2021, at 12:35:15 PM EDT*
> *To: Franklin Lemond (Plaintiff's Attorney)*
> *Subject: Re: Service of Subpoena*
> *Hi there, all set I just served her. She said she does not work for Comerica anymore. And that she shouldn't be subpoenaed. I told her to call you if she has the paperwork. I will send an invoice and the proof later today. Thank you so much!*

So Nora got served.

Sun, Apr 18, 2021, 11:02 PM
to Franklin, Jackie
We need to see the new FAA
Also, see the part about hiring experienced and trained call center personnel.
Part of the terms of the old Fiscal Agency Agreement had the following provisions:
Extension-6 months
 Services-B use qualified individuals- Conduent employees must have financial experience
Compensation and performance-payment to Comerica Bank and performance criteria
 Reduction in Compensation- if Comerica did not perform, money would be withheld.
(Had to hire a new contractor, i2c, and did not publicize this)
 Financial Agent's Fiduciary Duty (A) A Fiduciary Duty ...impede from complying with legal obligations comply with lawful instructions
Key Personnel: Albert Taylor-SVP- National Card Services, Nora Arpin- SVP- Government Electronic Solutions, Shelly Denman- VP
Government Electronic Solutions
7. Debit card Features:c. Must meet or exceed Reg E protection
8. Enrollment: b. FA has no liability for Fraudulent Enrollment except FA failed to utilize reasonable commercially available tools to validate caller's identity.
9. Card Distribution/Management: f. The FA will staff its call center with experienced customer service representatives and will provide the staff with the training necessary to operate the call center which meets the requirements of the FA.
(Marquita Stevenson had zero experience. Fraud unit employees did not know Reg E).
15. Cardholder Customer Services
e. The Financial Institution shall provide cardholders with the option of receiving a "Proactive Deposit Notification." "Low Balance Alert Services" and OTHER notices via email, telephone, or text message on a mobile phone or account management service via mobile application.
h. Walmart and cardless benefit
(ended in August 2018 when Jackie Densmore confronted Nora Arpin regarding fraud.)
16. Fraud Monitoring and Investigation
The determination that fraud or misuse has occurred shall be based on and consistent with the FA's usual and customary criteria.
Service level requirements: 14- 20 Customer service reps
Call response time: 37.
Customer satisfaction survey
(Comerica did the customer satisfaction survey "in-house" and did not hire an outside company.)

Monday, April 19, 2021

Better Business Bureau creates an excuse not to report on Comerica Bank

Woods, Richard <rwoods@iabbb.org>
jbsimms
Jackie Lynn
Dear J.B. Simms,
I am happy to discuss BBB policy regarding the types of complaints that we can accept and attempt to resolve. Should we arrange a call?
Thank you.
Richard P. Woods
Vice President and General Counsel, International Association of Better Business Bureaus, Inc.
FOIA Public Liaison <FOIA.Public.Liaison@ssa.gov>

Mon, Apr 19, 2021, 8:13 AM
to me, Jackie
Good morning:
Thank you for your email. Is it your intention to appeal the decision? Please let us know so that if you do wish to appeal, we can begin the appeal process.
Thank you,
The FOIA Team, SSA/OPD

Jbsimms
Mon, Apr 19, 2021, 10:07 AM
to ^FOIA, Jackie
Dear FOI Team,
Yes, I will appeal this particular decision of SSA FOI team to block this and any "decision" to lawful requests for information to which I am entitled.
I would like immediate confirmation of this appeal from your office and direct contact information with the person in charge, as well as the expected timeline of the procedure.
Sincerely,
J.B. Simms

Thursday, April 22, 2021

Jbsimms
Thu, Apr 22, 2021, 9:05 AM
to Franklin, Jackie
Jackie and I thought about Nora trying to delay or postpone. We would not agree with that.
Delmar (FOI requests) and McClary (i2c) should be interviewed.
Let us know your intentions about calling Delmar and McCarthy.
Delmar knew Conduent was dumped, and he might think the preliminary audit 19-041 is now complete. Not so.
Jim

Friday, April 23, 2021

Jbsimms
Fri, Apr 23, 2021, 8:48 AM
to Jackie, Franklin
I adjust.
Santaniello, Delmar, and McCarthy are quite silent on the deal with i2c.
Courtney Maebus can get no reply.
"Shantelle, do you feel personally responsible for Conduent losing the Fiscal Service contract with Comerica Bank and Bureau of Fiscal Service."
"If not, who would you say is responsible?"
The contract was lost because of Reg E violations.
Boom

BFS was covering up information about the April meeting. Here is a copy of a request I sent to challenge FOI submissions to me.

There is no evidence of law enforcement interaction (Carnley) or proactive fraud measures (all Plaintiffs, specifically Densmore, Kreegar, Tillman).

Manual date May 2019: This is when Comerica joined with i2c and presented FAA application.

Regarding Jennifer Kreager: Nothing proactive ever. Fraud 12/6, Post card mailed weeks later,

Postcard received 12/27

The email above referred to plaintiff Jennifer Kreeegar's claim against Comerica. Conduent sent a postcard to Jennifer that arrived 3 weeks later.

April 23 email from Jackie:

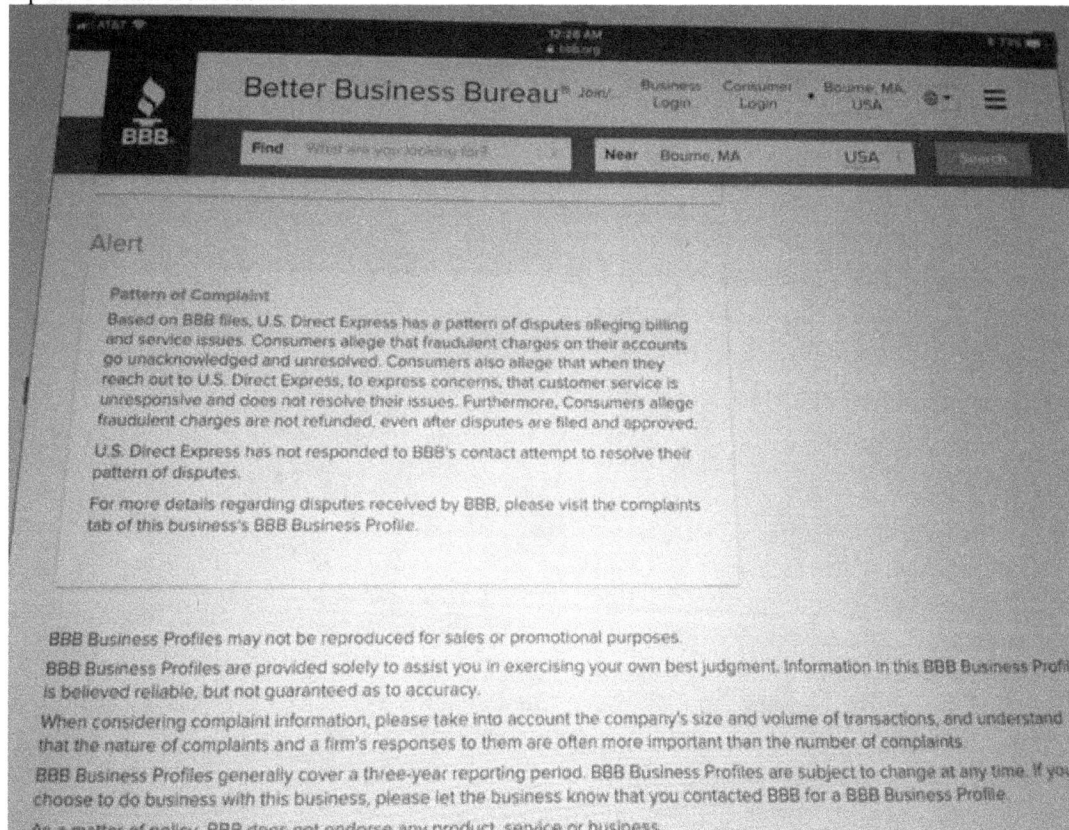

Get Accredited   For Business   Join/Apply

📍 My BBB

BBB.

≡

🔍

ℹ️ **Looking for more information? Access the headquarters listing for U.S. Direct Express** here   ✖

⚠️ **CURRENT ALERTS FOR THIS BUSINESS**

Alert:
"Better Business Bureau (BBB) cannot process complaints against Direct Express as it is a government program of the U.S. Treasury - Bureau of Fiscal Service. BBB encourages consumers with payment issues to contact the U.S. Treasury Electronic Payment Solution Center by email at DirectExpress@fiscal.treasury.gov. For all other matters, BBB encourages consumers to use the Direct Express Complaint Line at 313-222-3435. BBB will maintain copies of existing complaints on file for internal recordkeeping purposes only.
Read Less

Contact Information

⌐

Tuesday, February 16, 2021

Jbsimms
Tue, Feb 16, 2021, 5:50 PM
to Jackie, Franklin
I spent 30 min on the phone with the head of the FOI office of Treasury last week. I am appealing the refusal of Treas to give up "investigations" which were conducted (and submitted as basis for published audits). There is no accountability and I have gone after Treasury as a whole and personally after Delmar and Sciurba.

Sunday, March 7, 2021

Steven Lepper (Military Banks of America)
Mar 7, 2021, 6:20 AM
to me, Jackie
Mr. Simms,
Thanks for the note and the photo. While I understand your concern that veterans who are encouraged to GoDirect.org may sign up for the Direct Express card rather than Direct Deposit, our current situation makes me far less concerned. The current situation I'm talking about is the media blitz VA has deployed to encourage veterans to get bank accounts
Here's a press release the VA issued last week announcing that it had just hit a major milestone for the VBBP: 50,000 veterans opening bank accounts:
In short, VA is doing all it can to promote Direct Deposit and the VBBP, including advertising these programs on the GoDirect.org website. If you go to that website, see the yellow icon under "Are you a veteran?" That icon takes you to the VA's VBBP website.
Hope you're having a good weekend.
Steve

Jbsimms
Mar 7, 2020, 7:08 AM
to Franklin
Franklin,
I will continue to push, and let OIG Treasury continue to fight my FOI request.
Sciurba contradicts his subordinates.
This exposes the Comerica/BFS allies at OIG Treasury.
We can discuss other options.Jim

Jbsimms
Mar 7, 2021, 11:01 AM
to Steven, Jackie
Dear Mr. Lepper,
Thank you for taking the time to reply on a Sunday morning and sending us these informative links.
We are very happy the inserts were discontinued, but the language on the face of the check appears to be an "end run" to avoid our scrutiny. We are interested in the genesis of the decision to print the notation on the check
If you could, during any conversation with Mr. Gurney, pass along our concerns, we would be grateful.
Enjoy the balance of your weekend.
Jim

Tuesday, March 9, 2021

Franklin was going to depose Mitch Raymond of Conduent. Raymond was the supervisor of the Conduent Fraud department, including Shantelle Johnson. Below is an email making suggestions regarding questions to ask Raymond.
Jbsimms
Tue, Mar 9, 2021, 11:40 AM
to Franklin
RE: Questioning Mitch Raymond at Conduent
His interaction with Nora Arpin from March 22 2018 onward
His interaction with Shantelle Johnson and Alisha re fraud narratives.
Denying the acceptance of fraud narratives by the terms of agreement (created by Comerica) is in violation of Reg E. This means Raymond has to get permission from a Comerica person for Alisha and Shantelle to change their email and stop taking fraud narratives, again, in violation of Reg E.
Shantelle Johnson blocked the email account to stop persons from sending fraud complaints.
This was quite dirty.
I have to get the date she stopped this.
Jbsimms

Mitch Raymond got his marching orders from Nora Arpin (first) and others at Comerica Bank. The fact Conduent was automatically dismissing fraud claims was covered up by Conduent and Comerica Bank.

Tue, Mar 9, 2021, 1:57 PM
to Franklin, Jackie
Thank you Franklin.
You were able to connect some dots and point the finger of accountability. The excuse of stopping the emails to Shantelle (not able to track and give proper service) was sent in an appropriate manner and was lame.
You were looking at your papers when you mentioned the plaintiff J.B. Simms. You should have seen atty Chally open and roll his eyes[at the mention of J.B.Simms]
Interesting that all the emails I copied Nora were sent to Raymond, plus there have been emails between the two.
Raymond claimed I gave erroneous info on the internet. What else was he going to say?
The chart you presented that showed 24.9% of claims got provisional credit (I saw no date parameters) was shocking.
The ultimate compliance with Reg E was in the 99-100 percent range which we all know is not true.
BTW, I had done no videos or interviews prior to the LinkedIn viewing on March 22, 2018. So, he lied again with respect to why he viewed the profile. I do not think I knew of Arpin at that time; only Schmidt and OIG Treasury.
The fraud experienced by our plaintiffs was so obvious that no investigation would be necessary and immediate provisional credit should have been given. It appears they have no one who can discern obvious fraud; all claims go to investigations, all claims have to receive "their fraud packet (illegal), and only 24.9% receive provisional credit. I'm glad my microphone was muted.
Jim

Fraud victims were given direct access to the Conduent Fraud unit after I published the email address and telephone number leading directly to the Conduent Fraud unit. Shantell Johnson got so overwhelmed with victims, she shut down the email, at the direction of Mitch Raymond.
Jbsimms
Attachments
Thu, Apr 1, 2021, 8:56 AM
to FOI, Walter, Jackie, Kate
Dear Ms. Zimmerman,
I am in receipt of your email today which I attached.
The creative and faulty attempt to justify avoidance with my FOI request is insulting, an attempt at condescension, arrogant, and illegal.
I asked for the names of the persons employed by SSA who attended the specified meetings and reports/summations generated from these meetings. FOI documents supplied by the Veterans Administration contain the email address of SSA employees (specifically SSA OIG). I have these addresses and documents. The next person I contact if this matter is not settled today.will be Mr. Saul, and more. You caused the escalation of this.
Sincerely,
J.B. Simms

Sunday, April 4, 2021

Jbsimms
Sun, Apr 4, 2021, 10:34 AM
to Jackie, Franklin
Jackie,
Bless you for finding this and sending this.
Franklin, you stated you would be willing to step into the fray of the FOI debacle. Here is your chance. There are two issues here (1) Delmar denied 3 of my FOI requests when I asked for "investigation" reports for OIG 19-041 (which is referenced as the audit and investigation based upon info from Jackie and me), the investigation of the 30 victims audited in October 2019, and my 2 personal fraud experiences with the Direct Express program.

Delmar does not communicate with me since I reported him to the Bar of Washington DC attaching 13 pieces of evidence branding him as a liar.
Delmar is covering for BFS.
Since BFS and Treasury are ignoring your subpoenas, I am authorizing you to address the FOI requests which Delmar denied.
Happy Easter.Jim

Jackie Lynn
Sun, Apr 4, 2021, 12:26 AM
to Franklin, me
According to the BBB people are no longer allowed to make complaints on Direct Express , this was recently changed and I want to know by whom and why ?!?!
This is huge as we all know it had an F rating with multiple complaints warning cardholders.
Now the complaints are being blocked from getting reported I want to know how many complaints have called that phone number listed from when this was put into place and to today's date.
Who had the authority to change this and what is this phone number all about , who takes these calls, Conduent?
We need to investigate this ASAP!
Someone got to the BBB and made them change their policies., Jbsimms

Friday, April 23, 2021

Jbsimms
Apr 23, 2021, 8:48 AM
to Jackie, Franklin
I adjust.
Santaniello, Delmar, and McCarthy are quite silent on the deal with i2c.
Courtney Maebus can get no reply.
"Shantelle, do you feel personally responsible for Conduent losing the Fiscal Service contract with Comerica Bank and Bureau of Fiscal Service."
"If not, who would you say is responsible?"
The contract was lost because of a Reg E violation.
Boom
I was emailing Franklin when he was deposing Shantelle Johnson on April 23
Jbsimms

Fri, Apr 23, 2021, 10:24 AM
to Franklin
Manual date May 2019.
This is when Comerica joined with i2c and presented FAA application.. Jbsimms

Thursday, April 29, 2021

I received some OIG documents from SSA relating to the meetings requested by Pamela Powers of the VA. In these documents, the following is the first evidence that i2c was involved in the meetings. Comerica, and most notably Nora Arpin, brought in i2c to replace Conduent. I wonder how Conduent felt, having been thrown under the bus, and Comerica ignoring their guilt.

> *From: @ssa.gov>*
> *Sent: Thursday, April 18, 2019 10:25 AM*
> *To:(redacted)*
> *Cc:; @ssa.gov*
> *Subject: RE: [EXTERNAL] Direct Express - Agency Outreach - Fraud Mitigation*
> *Hi*
> *Sorry for the disconnect on today's i2c call. The SSA attendees will be,*
> *and (possibly).May 14*
> *9am-12pm*
> *Fiscal Service HQ (401 14th St SW Washington DC)*

The company i2c was calling into the meeting of April 18, 2019. This company replaced Conduent as the administrator of the Direct Express debit card program. This information was hidden from the public and Direct Express customers.

See the date of the meeting, April 18, 2019. Within a month the determination of the fiscal agent of the Direct Express program would be announced. The announcement did not happen. The VA was having secret meetings at this time to revamp the Veterans Benefits Association to create the Veterans Benefit Banking Program.

from: *Jbsimms*
to: *FOIA.Public.Liaison@ssa.gov, cc: Jackie Lynn, Franklin Lemond (Plaintiff's Attorney)*
date: *Apr 29, 2021, 11:29 AM*
Thank you for your email.
This matter could be clarified and the unwarranted delay of receipt of requested documents could have been avoided if your office, Ms. Zimmerman, or anyone from this office contacted me by telephone.
While I have not researched my original submission of SSA-2021-000274 or appeal SSA-2021-007229, it appears at first glance appeals and FOI request submissions are designated different notations. I draw your attention to the numerical sequence of 000274 versus 007229. If "appeal 007229" is a reference to an FOI request having the same digits, then I suggest you find the original submission of 000274 and 007229.
While your office purposely delays, avoids and refuses to abide by the Freedom of Information Act, any "confusion" on the part of the employees in the SSA Public Liaison Office could have been eliminated by simply adhering to the request for information duly noted in your email to me.
If it is necessary for me to submit evidence of the meetings to which I refer, I will do so.
There appear to be two issues:
(1) a request for documentation concerning monthly inserts into the check envelopes for SSA recipients
(2) documentation relating to the meetings beginning March 2019 and continued for at least the next four (4) months regarding the Direct Express debit card program.
I draw your attention to the attached inserts. You will see emails dated April 18 and 22 from and copied to SSA employees. These employees attended and/or were privy to these meetings. SSA OIG evidently had representatives at these meetings, most notably Walter Bayer, with whom I have been in contact for well over a year.
If someone in your office would be receptive to an oral explanation rather than this English printed version, my telephone number is (803) 309-6850. I respectfully request you contact me via email to arrange a definitive date and time for the call. While I have accepted that I might never learn the actual agenda and motivation for SSA to delay adherence to my requests, it is clear to me there is no accountability where there is no consequence, and that appears to be the escape route used to justify a lack of integrity.
Just use the search terms related in the email I received, and forward the entitled information to me as requested.
Sincerely,
J.B. Simms

On Apr 29, 2021, at 4:36 PM,
FOIA.Public.Liaison@ssa.gov
Mr. Simms:
My apologies. 11am EST on Monday, May 3rd, works for me, as well. If anything changes, I will let you know. I have blocked off a half hour on my calendar. I will call you at 11am EST.
Thank you,
Sarah Reagan
FOIA Division Director (Detail)
Office of Privacy and Disclosure
Social Security Administration

Friday, April 30, 2021

From: Richard Delmar (OIG Treasury)
Sent: Friday, April 30, 2021 3:27 PM
To: Jackman, Michael <Michael.Jackman@mail.house.gov>
Subject: RE: Sept 20, 2018 -response to Mr. Jackman's questions rewarding the direct express program

We have four completed reports, posted at Reports | Office of Inspector General (treasury.gov), and attached here.
We have a fifth report underway, which we expect to be issued in Fall 2021.
Rich Delmar
Acting Inspector General
Department of the Treasury

Monday, May 3, 2021

Jbsimms
Mon, May 3, 2021, 11:19 AM
to Jackie, FOIA SSA
Dear Ms. Reagan,
Thank you for your call and allowing me to explain a bit of the history regarding the two FOI requests. I find it amazing that SSA, after being privy to and attending the 2019 meetings, never challenged BFS or the fiscal agent Comerica Bank regarding the fiduciary responsibility of protecting SSA recipients and continued endorsing the inept program by blindly being the advertising arm of BFS by allowing inserts be placed into recipient envelopes and printing on the envelopes.
I can furnish you copies of the inserts and envelopes.
I can also furnish you copies of emails created among the attendees of the 2019 monthly meetings which specifically note SSA employees being present at these meetings.
Thank you again., J.B. Simms

It seemed futile to find any federal employee who would have the integrity to stand up against BFS, SSA, or OIG Treasury.
I sent an email to Jackie and Franklin regarding the following OIG Treasury reports: 14-031, 17-034, 19-041, 20-028

Jbsimms
Fri, Apr 30, 2021, 5:44 PM
to Franklin, Jackie
The first two were the ones I challenged in Feb 2018.
The third, 19-041, is the product of my challenge of the first two audits (14-031 and 17-034), commissioned in June 2018 and published July 2019 (right after BFS decided to renew the contract with Comerica, but that was not made public until Jan 2020).
The fourth is a follow-up to 19-041. One of my FOI requests was for the investigative report submitted by the office of Sonja Scott of the Investigative Division of OIG Treasury. Delmar lied to the FOI office stating there was no investigation performed. I have challenged this to the point of being told to file a federal lawsuit for my grievance. Franklin stated to me he would now intercede, contact Delmar, and talk lawyer to lawyer. Franklin has failed to contact Delmar. The investigation is crucial to our case and will prove continued violations of Reg E, a pattern of violations, and a pattern of deceit on the part of BFS and OIG Treasury. This fight is not for the faint of heart or a passive attitude.
You will see from the last two published audits that Comerica Bank (under the charge of BFS) has failed to make corrective measures. No one at Comerica or Conduent was contacted during the first two audits, and I forcefully challenged their "investigative and audit" protocol, and I prevailed.
I will critique this final audit again (I am certain I have referenced this and will look through my database), forward it to Jackie, and she can use it as a template to respond to Jackman.
The fact that BFS "had concerns" with Conduent, and made the association of i2c with Comerica a prerequisite of retaining the contract, is "fresh meat" for our case. That is why I asked Franklin to interview the president of i2c, Jim McCarthy, and forwarded email and telephone contact information. As of yet, I have seen no evidence this contact has been done, and we are days away from deposing Nora Arpin, who would be the person who would have made the deal for Comerica and i2c to "jointly" bid for the contract. By jointly, I mean McCarthy said they submitted the bid together. I cannot paint the picture any more clear than this.
I would like to see a more proactive than passive approach to this matter. No one is going to bring us anything; we have to go get it, and Jackie and I have been doing just that, for almost 3 years, with no prompting from anyone other than ourselves.
Jim

Tuesday, May 4, 2021

FOI SSA denied the existence of documents regarding the meeting in the spring of 2019. SSA employees were at the meeting. The Direct Express debit card program was being used exclusively by SSA to send benefits to recipients. The denials were exhausting.

Jbsimms
Attachments
May 4, 2021, 10:22 AM
to FOI SSA, Jackie
Dear Ms. Reagan,
Pursuant to our conversation, and the assertions made that SSA employees were aware of meetings on March 16, April 22, and May of 2019 (and most probably June and July 2019) regarding the Direct Express debit card program, I am attaching documents obtained via an FOI request to Treasury. You will see redactions, but you see the suffix of the email addresses being "ssa.gov" indicating that the aforementioned meetings which SSA has denied any knowledge did in fact occur and SSA employees were in fact in attendance.
The denials by SSA employees to your office appear to be disingenuous at best.
Hopefully, this evidence will empower your office to extricate the truth from those previously in denial.
Sincerely, , J.B. Simms

Franklin was to call Delmar. Delmar referred Franklin to Amy Altemus. Below is his reply to us regarding the call.

May 14, 2021
Franklin Lemond (Plaintiff's Attorney)
Jbsimms. Jackie Lynn
Altemus is a piece of work. She's still trying to play hardball and is basically daring you to file a lawsuit against them challenging their FOIA responses.
I am going to be in the office on Sunday prepping for Nora and finishing up my taxes (ugh!). Do you guys have time for a call on Sunday to catch up?
Franklin

This was the only account of Franklin's chat with Altemus that Franklin gave me.

Below are emails recovered from the FOI request. These emails were exchanged between attendees of the "meetings "requested by Pamela Powers, Chief of Staff, Veterans Affairs:

> *From: @fiscal.treasury.gov>*
> *Sent: Tuesday, May 21, 2019 9:13 AM*
> *To:[Social Security, VA, BFS, Comerica]*
> *Subject: Re: SSA/VA/Treasury Fraud Mitigation*
> *Below are the attendees that I am aware will be attending in person (without strikethroughs).*
> *Sorry for the delay. If anyone sees errors, please respond to this email*
> *chain.*
> *Thanks,*
> *-------*
>
> *Subject: SSA/VA/Treasury Fraud Mitigation*
> *When: Wednesday, May 22, 2019 11:00 AM-1:15 PM (UTC-05:00) Eastern Time (US & Canada).*
> *Where: SSA - 6401 Security BLVD Baltimore*
> *Importance: High*
> *Do we need to put these folks into safe and send a note up the line? Also, do we have a*
> *conference room reserved?*
> *Thanks-*
> *-----Original Appointment-----*
> *From: @fiscal.treasury.gov>*
> *Sent: Thursday, May 16, 2019 4:36 PM*
> *To:@va.gov*
> *Subject:] SSA/VA/Treasury Fraud Mitigation*
> *When: Wednesday, May 22, 2019 11:00 AM-1:15*

472

Above you see that BFS, Comerica, Soc Sec, and the VA had representatives at the meetings. The revelation from these meetings was that Nora Arpin conducted one meeting and revealed that I2c would be the new administrator of the Direct Express program.

Jbsimms
May 4, 2021, 10:32 AM
to FOI, Jackie
Dear Ms. Reagan,
Attached please find further evidence of the involvement in the monthly meetings by SSA employees. This document was submitted to Pamela Powers, then COS of the VA, referencing the meeting on March 16, 2019. Thank you for your attention to this matter, and being receptive to facts that contradict the replies you received from fellow SSA employees.
J.B. Simms

Jbsimms
May 4, 2021, 10:50 AM
to FOI, Jackie
Dear Ms. Reagan,
Attached please find reference to the collaboration between BFS and SSA regarding inserts to be placed into the envelopes of disadvantaged persons being coerced into subscribing to the Direct Express program.
The fact that the VA divorced itself from the Direct Express program while SSA continues to embrace this less-than-efficient program makes a person ponder the motivation of the SSA employees who continue to endorse or fail to question the motives of certain employees of BFS.
Sincerely,
J.B. Simms

Wednesday, May 5, 2021

Jbsimms
Wed, May 5, 2021, 1:27 PM
to Franklin, Jackie
Our job is to hit her with questions of which she has not prepared or been briefed.
I smelled the "prep" postponement. Now we need the date for Marquita Stevenson, and motions to compel subpoena responses from Feds.
An interview with McCarthy of i2c will be helpful. I got my foot into the door and got valuable info (end of Conduent, phone call to April 22 meeting from i2c, and joint submission of contract renewal application). Delmar needs to be interviewed re FOI submissions for investigative reporting used in OIG Treasury 19-041 audit report.
All before Nora is deposed.
I had called McCarthy. He told me that "we" (Comerica and I2C) submitted the application for renewal of the DE contract. I2C was at the meeting. They knew Conduent was done.
I got an email from the VBBP on May 6, 2021. The program worked. It was created to get veterans away from the Direct Express program. The following is data from the email:

> VeteransBenefitsBanking.org Website Analytics Overview - MARCH
> In March the website averaged about 350 visitors each day, totaling over 10,800 for the month.
> 1- 31 March 2021-10,821 visitors, who viewed an average of 2.17 pages
> Most referrals came from benefits.va.gov
> Top page views included: Homepage (54%), Banks/Credit Unions (37%), Resources (3%)
> 4,667 visitors clicked on individual bank or credit union URLs.
> In April the website averaged about 266 visitors each day, totaling over 8,000 for the month.

Thursday, May 6, 2021

Below is the acknowledgment of an FOI that I submitted investigative material used in OIG Report 20-028. A subsequent report was to be filed.
I wanted them to answer to blocking Jackie and me from reporting to the committee that awarded the contract to Comerica Bank along with all investigative documents submitted by persons in OIG Treasury and BFS.

Cawana.Pearson@treasury.gov
Thu, May 6, 2021, 7:21 AM
to me
RE: Your FOIA Request to Treasury, Case Number 2021-FOIA-00566
Dear Mr. Simms:
This email acknowledges the receipt of your FOIA request dated 05/03/2021 seeking copies of the following records:
Citing the Freedom of Information Act, I am requesting the following documents: (1) A copy of all documents submitted to the Auditing Department of OIG Treasury from the Office of Investigations regarding the investigation and audit, Treasury OIG 20-028, which was published on or about March 2, 2020. (2) A copy of all documents submitted to the Auditing Department of OIG Treasury from the office of Richard Delmar (OIG Treasury) regarding the investigation and audit, Treasury OIG 20-028, which was published on or about March 2, 2020. (3) A copy of all documents submitted to the Auditing Department of OIG Treasury from the office of Loren Sciurba (OIG Treasury) regarding the investigation and audit, Treasury OIG 20-028, which was published on or about March 2, 2020. (4) A copy of all documents submitted to the Auditing Department of OIG Treasury from the office of Sonja Scott (Office of Investigations, OIG Treasury) regarding the investigation and audit, Treasury OIG 20-028, which was published on or about March 2, 2020. (5) A copy of all documents submitted to the Auditing Department of OIG Treasury from the office of Thomas Santaniello (Bureau of Fiscal Service) regarding the investigation and audit, Treasury OIG 20-028, which was published on or about March 2, 2020, to include prohibiting citizens J.B. Simms and Jackie Densmore to address a deliberative group charged with awarding/renewing the fiscal agent contract for the Direct Express program during the dates between January 2019 and June 2019. (6) A copy of all communication (email, fax, text, etc.) between any employee of OIG Treasury and Bureau of Fiscal Service regarding in inclusion of company i2c as a subcontractor/administrator for fiscal agent Comerica Bank (regarding the Direct Express program), and the exclusion of company Conduent as the subcontractor/administrator for Comerica Bank for accounts created subsequent to January 2020. (7) A copy of all communication between OIG Treasury auditor Katherine Johnson and any employee of Conduent between November 2018 to the present.
This request has been issued with tracking number 2021-FOIA-00566. Please reference this number in all future correspondence with this office when communicating regarding this request. Please see the attached letter for more information.
Sincerely,
Cawana Pearson
Case Manager, FOIA and Transparency
Office of Privacy, Transparency, and Records

Jbsimms
Fri, May 7, 2021, 12:50 PM
to Franklin, Jackie
Giving notice for deposition of Marquita Stevenson
Question Delmar on FOI requests regarding denial of "investigations
[I want you to] Interview with McCarthy (i2c) regarding new contract, adherence to Reg E (which caused Conduent to lose the contract), and i2c relationship with Nora. (McCarthy might have come onboard after contract).
Motions to compel for subpoenaed documents.

I wanted McCarthy interviewed. He would shed light on why and when Comerica contacted them. They knew we would challenge the new contract.
Jbsimms
Thu, May 6, 2021, 9:18 AM
to FOIA, FOI
The following text of the email seen below was delivered via the Treasury portal using my account. Please address this matter at your earliest convenience.
Thursday May 6, 202, 7:15 am PDT
I recently submitted two FOI requests:
May 2, 2021 Confirmation number 214586 directed to BFS for documents in reference to the fiscal agent evaluation team and a company named "i2c."

No response or FOI file number has been received.

May 3, 2021 Confirmation number 214636 directed to OIG Treasury. This submission was acknowledged and an FOI file number 2021-00566 was assigned and confirmed via email.

Please address the submission having Confirmation Number 214586

Sincerely,, J.B. Simms

Wednesday, May 12, 2021

Jackie had Jackman making inquiries on our behalf.

From: Jackie Lynn
Date: May 12, 2021, at 8:42:20 AM EDT
To: Michael Jackman <michael.jackman@mail.house.gov>
Subject: when this will be completed
Mr. Jackman,
I thank you for your inquiry into treasury's oig report related to the direct express fraud, as you can imagine I, as well as hundreds of other victims, are disappointed the report has not been completed but do thank you for your continued help in this matter
I remember that you had put me in contact with Walter Bayer head of OIG SSA around January of last year, upon reviewing my emails I found this one below
In this email, he tells me that a report was going to be published but as Delmar has done he too has refused to respond to my emails asking for information concerning the direct express fraud.
I am asking your office since you were able to originally put me in contact with his office and reach out to him asking for information on their reports. He stated that audits were also going on concerning the direct express program so I would like to know when they would be available to the public
I'm not sure why SSA still has not broken away from Condunet or Comerica considering the VA did.
I find that making that change saved thousands of people from becoming victims of direct express fraud and I applaud them for protecting our service men and women!
I have been in contact with Sen Warren's office and they are quite alarmed that SSA still chooses to do business with such a corrupt bank.
Any help on this matter would be most appreciated!, Thank you, Jackie Densmore

Jackie's emails, many I wrote, were more of an annoyance to the recipients than effective. This was the same for my emails. She was all after Jackman, who worked for Rep Keating. Elizabeth Warren was useless and took money from banks. Jackie kept after Warren to do something.

Now for some back and forth with Ms. Reagan regarding FOI requests and the redaction of records.

FOIA Public Liaison <FOIA.Public.Liaison@ssa.gov>
May 12, 2021, 10:30 AM
to me
Mr. Simms:
Thank you for the conversation on Monday, May 3rd. Last week, I met with a representative from OIG regarding your requests. OIG will provide me with a status this week. In the interim, please confirm my understanding of your request and appeal. For SSA-2021-000274, the request is for information on SSA's involvement/participation/decision to use the inserts. Someone at SSA made the decision to allow use of the inserts; therefore, the request is for notes/memos about SSA's use of the inserts.
Appeal SSA-2021-007279, request is as follows:
OIG notes from meetings attended by SSA OIG and the Veterans Administration that took place in March, April, May, and June of 2019, as well as the emails of Walter Bayer and Sara Lizama concerning these meetings. Requested search terms are Direct Express, Comerica Bank, Conduent, Monthly Inserts, Nora Arpin, Pamela Powers (COS Veterans Administration), Dr. Paul Lawrence (Veterans Benefits Association), Joe Gurney (Veterans Administration), Thomas Santaniello (Bureau of Fiscal Service), and Richard Delmar (Commissioner of OIG Treasury). The applicable timeframe is January 2019 through August 2019.
I appreciate confirmation and continued patience.
Thank you,
Sarah Reagan, , FOIA Division Director (Detail), Office of Privacy and Disclosure, Social Security Administration

Jbsimms
May 12, 2021, 11:20 AM
to ^FOIA, Jackie, Franklin
Dear Ms. Reagan,
Thank you for your email.
This response is confirmation of my request and the appeal.
Documents were submitted to you via email validating my assertion that SSA employees were present at meetings held March, April, May, and June 2019. These meetings were originally commissioned by Pamela Powers, former COS of VA.
SSA employees were not only present, one or more meetings were held at a site hosted by SSA.
Walter Bayer of SSA OIG has been intimately aware this matter of malfeasance on the part of the Fiscal Agent (Comerica) the subcontractor/administrator (Conduent) and failure of BFS to make Comerica Bank abide by the Fiscal Agent Agreement, to include adherence to Regulation E. This victimization of veterans and disadvantaged persons was ignored by BFS, and since the VA became aware of the aforementioned indiscretions, and divorced itself from the Direct Express program, it shocks the conscience that SSA continues to endorse the program by continuing using inserts and encouraging persons to use the program.
SSA saw the same evidence as did VA.
I bet I know why.
Sincerely
Jim Simms
Sent from my iPhone

I responded on my phone many times. I could not wait to get back to my computer. Reagan was hiding stuff just as she was told to do.

Thursday, May 13, 2021

Jbsimms
Thu, May 13, 2021, 1:59 PM
to FOI, FOIA
Thursday May 13, 2021
Ryan Law
FOI Public Liaison- BFS Treasury
Email Transmission: FOIA@treasury.gov
RE: FOI submission to BFS on May 2, 2021, Confirmation number 214586
Dear Mr. Law,
Pursuant to voice messages left with the FOIA voicemail portals of your department (none of which have been answered) and your voicemail, I am emailing and faxing you regarding the FOI request submitted May 2, 2021. The text of the acknowledgment of the receipt is attached at the end of this transmission/letter.
As you see, the submission was made Sunday May 2, 2021. As a side note, a subsequent FOI request transmission was made on the following day to US Treasury. Communication from FOI Treasury has been received, an FOI case number has been assigned, while your office has failed to do so since the submission was made to your office eleven (11) days ago.
The fact the telephone numbers referenced for citizens to access live persons within FOI Treasury are not functional is a disservice to citizens who submitted FOI requests and perpetuates frustration and distrust with your office. Having had experience with FOI Treasury and the cavalier attitude/performance of FOI employees regarding the collection of requested documents disclosing malfeasance within your brother agency, it is easy to understand how citizens simply give up, which seems to be the agenda of your office.
I would like an immediate response.
Sincerely,
J.B. Simms
jb.simms10@gmail.com

Jbsimms
Thu, May 13, 2021, 5:33 PM
to Franklin, Jackie
1) findings on the 30 victims
2) finding on my personal fraud
3) investigation on OIG Treasury 19-041
4) filed May 3- investigation of OIG Treasury 20-028
Altemus also canceled the meeting Jackie and I had with Sonja Scott in November 2018.
If they deny the last FOI, stating no "investigation" took place, Delmar will hate me more. I will be after his law license again.
Wannna bet?
I should be present for Altemus. She lied about the first two FOI requests. I have the names of her minions who contacted me.
I then talked to her personally and was assured I would get a copy of the investigation.
The investigation of the 30 victims has a conclusion without giving out personal information.
Sonja Scott's office conducted the investigations.
I would have Altemus so twisted she would scream for her mother before I let up on her.
She, Delmar, and Sciurba are all in this to protect OIG Treasury. I exposed their incompetence and their agenda.
Scooby Doo could see this.
The email to Jackie and Franklin was a reminder that Amy Altemus at OIG Treasury stopped us from being interviewed in November 2019. This is the kind of thing, and people we had to battle.

> *From: OIG Counsel <OIGCounsel@oig.treas.gov>*
> *Date: November 5, 2019 at 4:56:33 PM EST*
> *To: "'jbsims@erikpublishing.com'", "'jackiedenzz@yahoo.com'"*
> *Subject: Cancellation*
> *Dear Mr. Sims, Ms. Densmore:*
> *I'm writing to cancel the meeting I understand had previously been scheduled for tomorrow. Upon review, it appears the agenda you have submitted is beyond the scope of our work and our jurisdiction. However, if you feel you have additional material for our review that documents specific problems and deficiencies in how BFS and its current financial agent are operating the Direct Express program, we would appreciate your providing that information in writing or electronically. All such submissions will be reviewed, applied as appropriate to our investigative and audit work, and made part of our records. You may submit such information to the Office of Counsel at OIGCounsel@oig.treas.gov, or to the Office of Inspector General at the address below. While we surely appreciate your investment in this matter, our mandate is to provide impartial and dispassionate review of the programs and whatever issues it faces, and ensuring that the process is seen as such, including the avoidance of any potential appearance of impropriety or partiality in our work and ensuring that the work is completed timely and with all necessary attention and expertise on the issues and findings.*
> *My apologies for the late notice, and thank you for your understanding and assistance-*
> *Sincerely,*
> *Amy*
> *A. J. Altemus*
> *Attorney-Advisor*
> *Office of the Inspector General*
> *U.S. Department of the Treasury*

Jbsimms
May 13, 2021, 6:59 PM
to Franklin
These are dirty people.

Friday, May 14, 2021

Jbsimms
Attachments
Fri, May 14, 2021, 9:31 AM
to Franklin, Jackie
After emailing and faxing BFS yesterday with a nice nastygram, BFS finally acknowledged receipt of the FOI submission of Sunday May 2.
Franklin is to talk to Altemus today.
The lawyers at OIG Treasury refused to talk to me, or Jackie.
Nice club, but all cowards hiding their failures.
I have no patience with people not doing their jobs or being dishonest.
Franklin did talk to Altemus. She ran all over him. He got nothing from her and refused to give Jackie and me a report of exactly what Altemus said to Franklin. I wanted a report of the conversation.

Jbsimms
Fri, May 14, 2021, 5:25 PM
to Franklin, Jackie
Franklin,
I want a written synopsis of the interview with Amy Altemus. Having to take notes of your monologue of the event will not be sufficient.
Also, it was agreed at the time subpoenas were issued to federal agencies that information derived would be viable and assist in our case. Your reasoning that the subpoenaed information would not assist in a class action matter has no bearing on Jackie, me, or other original plaintiffs. What you do for future plaintiffs is of no concern to me, and this posture of complacency in enforcement of subpoenas jeopardizes our case. Information from these subpoenas affected Arpin's deposition. The defense is in bed with the Feds and is fighting for their clients. We simply ask the same., Jim

Monday, May 17, 2021

Jbsimms
Mon, May 17, 2021, 10:03 AM
to Cawana Pearson, Jackie
Dear Ms. Pearson,
After OIG Treasury refused to produce documents pertaining to three FOI requests a year ago, and after acknowledging receipt of the current FOI request 2021-0566 a few weeks ago, it has come to my attention that an attorney operating within OIG Treasury is planning to continue this illegal behavior and deny my most recent submission.
With all due respect and based upon my limited understanding of the "procedure," I am requesting the identity and contact information of the person to whom you forward the request and determining the person at FOI to whom my request would ultimately be directed to accumulate the requested documents.
Correct me if I am wrong, but my understanding is a person within an FOI office determines the most applicable source at OIG Treasury to whom the request is to be directed. In the matter of the previous three requests, and now the current request, this person could be you. My requests seem to have been directed to OIG Treasury attorneys instead of the Office of Investigations where the records of the requested "investigations" reside.
Hopefully, this will not be replicated regarding this most recent submission. Attorneys at OIG Treasury "ran interference" to avoid complicity regarding the previous requests.
The only response/remedy offered by OIG attorneys is "sue us." This response was received Friday, May 14, 2021, by an attorney designated to speak on behalf of OIG Treasury. This person knows your office has no oversight or enforcement authority and has exhibited the utmost disrespect for your office and the law.
I would like to have direct communication with not only counsel within your office and liaison personnel at the office of Secretary Yellen. If you can forward this to me, I would be grateful.
You have seen the evidence I submitted to you which validated my assertions within my previous submissions.
I anticipate a replication of the same behavior from OIG Treasury regarding my most recent submission. Thank you for your time and indulgence.
Sincerely, , JB Simms

FOI request reveal Reg E violations

Jbsimms
Mon, May 17, 2021, 10:22 AM
to Franklin, Jackie
There is information within these four FOI requests which will show that Reg E had been violated.
Another FOI has been sent to BFS regarding the 2019 meetings. The FOI requests, while seemingly a waste of time, have generated more evidence than the subpoenas. Hopefully, the enforcement of the subpoenas will reverse the script.
As soon as you can compose a narrative of your chat with Ms. Altemus, please forward this to Jackie and me. I continue to send a list of issues regarding Arpin's deposition to Jackie. The big issues are the 2109 contract, the 2019 meetings, the April 22, 2019 "call-in" by an unidentified i2c employee at the meeting, and the admission by McCarthy that Comerica and i2c jointly submitted the bid for the new contract.
Jim

Cawana Pearson was always polite, and I saw her hands were tied. She listened to me when I was in the truck with Hite Miller. She knew the OIG Treasury was not being honest.

Jbsimms
Mon, May 17, 2021, 10:03 AM
to Cawana Pearson, Jackie
Dear Ms. Pearson,
After OIG Treasury refused to produce documents pertaining to three FOI requests a year ago, and after acknowledging receipt of the current FOI request 2021-0566 a few weeks ago, it has come to my attention that an attorney operating within OIG Treasury is planning to continue this illegal behavior and deny my most recent submission.
With all due respect and based upon my limited understanding of the "procedure," I am requesting the identity and contact information of the person to whom you forward the request and determines the person at FOI to whom my request would ultimately be directed to accumulate the requested documents.
Correct me if I am wrong, but my understanding is a person within an FOI office determines the most applicable source at OIG Treasury to whom the request is to be directed. In the matter of the previous three requests, and now the current request, this person could be you. My requests seem to have been directed to OIG Treasury attorneys instead of the Office of Investigations where the records of the requested "investigations" reside.
Hopefully this will not be replicated regarding this most recent submission. Attorneys at OIG Treasury "ran interference" to avoid complicity regarding the previous requests.
The only response/remedy offered by OIG attorneys is "sue us." This response was received Friday, May 14, 2021 by an attorney designated to speak on behalf of OIG Treasury. This person knows your office has no oversight or enforcement authority and has exhibited the utmost disrespect for your office and the law.
I would like to have direct communication with not only counsel within your office and liaison personnel at the office of Secretary Yellen. If you can forward this to me, I would be grateful.
You have seen the evidence I submitted to you which validated my assertions within my previous submissions. I anticipate a replication of the same behavior from OIG Treasury regarding my most recent submission. Thank you for your time and indulgence.
Sincerely,
JB Simms

We were dealing with media writers who would be interested, then we heard nothing. All delays and excuses. All scared.
The meetings were to be held March 12 and April 22, 2019 and May 19, 2021.
Here is what Jackie was getting from Mastercard. They denied any liability.

Direct express / MasterCard

Seth Eisen   10:52 PM   **SE**
To: Jackie Lynn   Details

Ms. Densmore:

Apologies for the delay. I have shared your messages with our internal teams and will be following up with them on Wednesday. Once I have an opportunity to speak with them, we will follow up with you.

Seth

Seth Eisen
Senior Vice President
Communications

Mastercard
2000 Purchase Street | Purchase, NY 10577-2509
tel 914-249-3153 | mobile 914-325-5932

mastercard

⚐   🗂   🗑   ↩   ✎

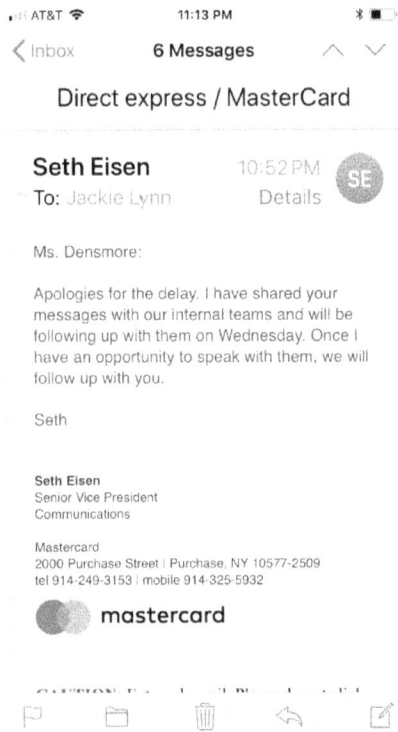

Wednesday, May 19, 2021

I got a copy of the 2019 Fiscal Agent Agreement submitted by Comerica Bank to the Bureau of Fiscal Service regarding the notes I made after reading the contract below. These notes were emailed to Jackie, Franklin, and Kate Berry:

> Page 25, Section 6, Paragraph 3, in which Comerica is complaining of challenges with social media: Social media has made the task of managing media, congressional and reputational risk more challenging.
> What would have been deemed a minor incident in the past (e.g., normal fraud impacting a small number of cardholders), can escalate into a very challenging media and congressional relations situation because of cardholder activists and their use of social media.

Well, they never addressed the violations of Reg E which necessitated the social media posts.

> Page 15: Brett Smith of BFS was said to have knowledge of recent performance (positive) of Comerica.

This report was dated March 8, 2019. I have a record of me leaving messages for Brett Smith on the following dates:

> Wed April 10, 2019, 7:02 am
> Thursday April 11, 2019, 10:50 am
> Friday, April 12, 2019, 9:54 am

Friday, April 12, 2021

10:14 am Tammy Breeden of BFS observed Brett Smith on a phone call. She left him a message via Skype.

> Thursday, April 18, 2019, 805am and 828am, which were dates just after the March 12 meeting.
> April 18, 2019 - Meeting when i2c called into meeting
> May 22, 2019- Meeting when Nora Arpin did presentation

Nora never addressed violations of Reg E and dismissed complaints via social media as insignificant.

The Federal Election Commission website was inspected. The following contributions were found:

> Conduent 2017-2018 $5000 to DNC
> Cory Booker- $10,000

Conduent was in the bag with Democrats.

Tuesday, May 25, 2021

On Tue, May 25, 2021, at 10:29 PM jbsimms wrote:
Jackie called and we talked.
There were hundreds of issues to be addressed, and I am adding more.
1) Jackie mentioned there is no mention of the break of the VA from the DE program.
2) There is no mention of the monthly meetings (March, April, May, and maybe June) that Nora and other Comerica officers attended which were initiated by the VA.
3) There is no mention of any emails between Nora and Brett Smith before or after the submission of the FA renewal presentation. You know there was chat before and after.
4) We see no mention of losing the VA accounts in ANY emails between Nora, Comerica employees, Conduent, or i2c.
5) We see no email communication or reports between Nora/Comerica and i2c.
Documents regarding the above issues that should have been included in the FOI documents were "suspiciously absent."
One caveat is the subpoena to Comerica/Nora predated the information obtained by me via the FOI requests. The monthly meetings were not revealed until late 2020. There was no way anyone knew of the meetings or to ask about them. We now know i2c called into the meeting on April 18, 2019.
Below again is the list of the meetings:

> March 12, 2019- white paper is the exhibit; Need email notes from Treas and VA
> April 18, 2019- i2c called in. Might have been Scott Galit- CEO (646) 465-9558
> May 22, 2019- Baltimore-SSA headquarters

Jackie was able to sit through the deposition of Nora Arpin. Below is the email Jackie sent after watching Nora Arpin's deposition.

Wednesday, May 26, 2021

Jackie Lynn
Wed, May 26, 2021, 6:56 PM
to Franklin, me
Franklin,
Looking forward to seeing what Nora has to say.
I also wanted to make sure we have direct communication with each other during the deposition as well as the breaks what is the best way to get in touch with you during the deposition?
I would like the opportunity to reach out to you during the deposition.
Please let me know before the deposition starts about these questions I have in the email
Thanks
Jackie

From: Jackie Lynn
Date: May 27, 2021 at 9:05:51 PM EDT
To: Franklin Lemond (Plaintiff's Attorney)
Subject: Today
Good job today it was painful for all the listen and watch her lie through her teeth, I thank you for being available during and before the deposition and preparing us with all the documentation.
Would love to set up a call to review, I'm curious why al Taylor would lie about her position being removed vs her being retired. think it's time we find that employee that was fired and interview her.
At the beginning of the deposition, Nora recommended this employee be referred to another part of the agency, however, Conduent made the final decision on firing her why would Nora want an employee to be in another part of the agency if she didn't follow the protocol and handled the call correctly in the first place?
I would also like to know if this other employee had any other violations on her record or had an impeccable record and was fired so quickly.
The employee will definitely know inside information and won't be as well coached however in my opinion she looked like a complete ass by saying she can't talk about the investigation or for that matter give me a copy of the investigation but she can certainly disclose exact and rehearsed information five minutes before the deposition is to end.
I'm also curious and still a little confused with her comments regarding Mastercard.

481

She stated when it came to the email to Mitch Raymond about Jennifer Kreegar that Jb's email did not have any effect on Jennifer getting her money back but rather documents that she reviewed prior to that the decision making of her being refunded her money she also said that she has a team that she reaches out to you to find these documents.

Who was she talking to at 9 p.m. from her team to verify the information if it wasn't JBs email? Which is lie

The fact that she ran the prepaid debit card program but didn't know that the Veterans Affairs administration opened up another program for them is just ridiculous especially if she was monitoring the Facebook page which she admitted was doing per Bretts' recommendation

She stated she has an agreement with consumer affairs however stated she has no idea about the Better Business Bureau both consumer affairs and Better Business Bureau complaints were listed on Elizabeth Warren's letter as reference

Lots to talk about , what day / time works for you

Jackie

Friday, May 28, 2021

Fri, May 28, 2021, 1:19 AM

to Jackie

Arpin was an apologist (excuse maker) for Comerica, but she ran out of problems (ignoring Reg E violations by Conduent) to explain away. She had outlived her usefulness. She must have signed a non-disclosure agreement, and the personal lawyer she named should be contacted to confirm this. Arpin is a selfish narcissist and she gained her position through manipulation and extortion. She is the kind of person to "have stuff on people" which keeps them quiet, while she uses a false squeaky demeanor to make you look like a bully when she is made accountable.

Finding issues that she lied about in the deposition might be time-consuming but I will know the particulars about the Arpin v Arpin found in the index.

Chally had to know Nora was the loaded gun and could compromise the case if some of her personal emails or conversations were exposed.

Time expired before the March 2019 meetings could be addressed.

Chally said he was privy to the Facebook page. Chally is not a member of that page unless he is a member of the SSI Direct Express Facebook page, of which I am not the administrator. I became the administrator after being asked to administer the site in late 2018 by Rob Ferry.

Filing the motion to compel on the heels of this deposition would be tactically effective, letting Nora and Chally know answers from these subpoenas would impeach Nora's testimony.

Nora would not fare well in front of a jury.

Let me dive into the civil case of "Nora L. Arpin" and Mark Arpin. If this proves to be helpful, how would you present this to Chally?

Also, you seem to be conversant with Chally, so why can't you ask him how he was able to view the Facebook page? I see how gathering the comments using fake identities were done (we have 1400 persons) and I would have done the same thing if I were them.

Jim

Tuesday, June 1, 2021

On Jun 1, 2021, at 13:59, jbsimms:

Mr. Lepper,

After extensive interviews with the reporter (including both Jennifer Kreegar and Jackie Densmore), I was told today that the article regarding the DE program, the VA, and veterans will be published Thursday.

Hopefully, the VA will be able to use the article to validate the VBBP and continue the transition of DE cardholders to bank accounts, and for your involvement I am grateful.

The VA, Comerica, i2c, and Conduent refused to comment. Hopefully, the readers will infer the real reason the change was made at the VA (without naming Jackie and me of course).

One question: is there any published document that will give us an up-to-date total of the transitioned cardholders from the DE program through the VBBP or AMBA?

Sincerely,

Jim

Wednesday, June 2, 2021

Our efforts were paying off- 70,000 conversions were made

June 2, 2021
Steven Lepper (Military Banks of America)
jbsimms
Jackie Lynn; Jennifer Kreegar
Mr. Simms,
Thanks for the note and the news. To answer your question, we were told today that over 70,000 veterans have opened bank accounts or otherwise started direct deposit of their VA benefits since we began the VBBP. I don't have a document describing that fact; we heard it today from a VA official. VA is solidly behind this program.
Best,
Steve

Franklin had info through discovery of the person who got Marteshia's dad's money.
I ran a database and found the guy living near Marteshia. Never saw a connection to the McPhail family.
Conduent still owed them $30,000 and implied the McPhail family took the money. Comerica Bank accused the McPhail family of fraud by allowing the teenage son of Mr. McPhail to use the card.
The person who stole the money has worked at a Walmart and lived fewer than 20 miles from Marteshia. The fraudster took the $30,000 and deposited the money into a Green Dot debit card account.
The Green Dot people refused to give info on the card.

Wednesday, July 14, 2021

Jackie had to create a declaration to be submitted to the Court.
Here is the text.

DECLARATION OF JACKIE DENSMORE

I, Jackie Densmore, do hereby declare:

1.   I am an adult resident of the State of Massachusetts over the age of 18 and testify to the facts set forth in this Declaration based on my own personal knowledge.

2.   I am one of the named Plaintiffs in this lawsuit.

3.   I am the caregiver for my brother-in-law, Derek Densmore, a disabled Marine, who receives federal benefits which were provided to him through his Direct Express Debit MasterCard Card.

4.   At the time fraudulent charges were made on my brother-in-law's Direct Express card, Conduent and Comerica offered what was known as the "Cardless Benefit Access Service," which would allow cardholders to access the money on their card in certain instances where they did not have their card in their possession.

5.   Even though neither Derek nor I had ever used the "Cardless Benefit Access Service," in August 2018, an unknown individual or individuals were able to utilize this service to withdraw $814 from Derek's Direct Express account via a MoneyGram at a Walmart Superstore in Hollywood, Florida.

6.   This transaction was approved by Conduent even though Derek and I reside in Massachusetts.

7.   On August 3, 2018, I called the number on the back of the Direct Express card to see if Derek's monthly benefits had been deposited into his account.

8.   I received a recorded statement informing me that a new Direct Express card had been mailed out to Derek: neither I nor Derek had requested a new Direct Express debit card and the recording did not allow me to make contact with any employee of Conduent to give constructive notice of the issue, nor did the recorded statement give me any indication of any unusual activity on Derek's account.

9.   After a couple days, having not received the debit card which the recording of August 3, 2018, revealed, I tried to contact Direct Express (Conduent) about the new card and to determine the reason for the new card being issued.

10.   After trying unsuccessfully for several days to get someone on the phone who could assist me, I was able to reach a live person (who identified themselves as a supervisor) employed by Conduent on August 10, 2018, seven (7) days after my original call to Conduent to question the delay in funds being paid to Derek.

11.   The supervisor informed me someone had called Direct Express on August 2, 2018, claiming to be me – even providing my name, address, and social security number – and stated that "they" had damaged the card and wanted Direct Express to send a MoneyGram so they could access the funds.

12.   I advised the supervisor that neither she nor her disabled brother-in-law had made such a request and no attempt was made by any Conduent employee to confirm the fraudulent allegation of the claim.

13.   The supervisor stated that a fraud claim was being opened and that I needed to fill out paperwork and return it back to Direct Express so that the fraud department could investigate.

14.   After Direct Express failed to send me the paperwork as promised by the supervisor, I put together a hand-written narrative outlining the fraudulent transaction that my brother-in-law's account had experienced and submitted it to Direct Express via facsimile. I also filed a police report with the City of Hollywood, Florida, where the Wal-Mart where Derek's money was transferred to was located.

15.   After submitting the paperwork to support the fraud claim, I continued to contact Direct Express/Conduent on numerous occasions about the fraudulent withdrawal from Derek's account, but Direct Express/Conduent refused to provide a provisional credit, make an immediate reimbursement to Derek's account, or submit a copy of any investigation despite the obvious fraudulent nature of the charges, all in violation of Regulation E.

16.   Therefore, I escalated the situation by contacting my Senator, Elizabeth Warren, my Congressman, William Keating, and Kate Berry, a reporter with the American Banker.

17.   As a result of these escalations, several things happened. First, Direct Express shut down the "Cardless Benefit Access Service" to ensure that other cardholders were not victimized in the same fashion. Second, Senator Warren submitted a Letter of Inquiry to Comerica Bank regarding their handling of the Direct Express program. Third, the American Banker ran a story about the fraud that occurred on Derek's account.

18.   Additionally, as a result of my efforts, Direct Express eventually refunded the money that was stolen from Derek's account.

19.   However, despite my explicit request that they do so, Direct Express failed to provide me with the results of their investigation into the fraud on my brother-in-law's account.

20.   The fact that my brother-in-law's account was compromised put Derek under an increased level of stress. As a result, I had to take Derek to additional doctor's appointments.

21.   I understand that I am one of the proposed class representatives in this lawsuit. As a class representative, I understand I would be representing a class of other persons whose fraud claims were handled improperly by Conduent and Comerica.

21.   Given the media attention that Derek's fraud case attracted, numerous other Direct Express cardholders, including many of the other named plaintiffs, contacted me regarding their issues with Direct Express. As such, I have been intimately involved in this case from the outset, spending many hundreds of hours assisting fellow victims.

22.   I have communicated with my attorneys during this case on a regular basis. I often speak with to my counsel about suggestions or thoughts I have about the case as well as a potential litigation strategy. I also attended the deposition of a defense witness.

23.   In connection with my discovery obligations, I provided my counsel with documents prior to joining this case and assisted my attorneys in preparing responses to interrogatories and requests for the production of documents. I have communicated with my attorneys during the case. I was also deposed for several hours on December 8, 2020. Before and after my deposition I conferred with counsel.

24.   I, along with fellow plaintiff J.B. Simms, put pressure on the Treasury Department to investigate how the Direct Express program was being run by Comerica and Conduent. We also changed how veterans received their benefits going forward so other Cardholders do not have to go through the same things Derek and I did, resulting in the Veterans Administration to create the Veterans Benefit Banking Program and withdrawing any endorsement of the Direct Express program, Comerica Bank, and Conduent.

25.   I have also been contacted by several attorneys also wanting to assist in their individual cases against Direct Express.

26.   I do not mind spending time and effort on the litigation. I am dedicated to this case and feel that my efforts serve an important purpose.

27.   I understand that, from time to time throughout the rest of the case, I need to confer with my attorneys and perform tasks upon their request. I also understand that I may be called as a witness to testify at trial. I am willing and able to fulfill all of my duties as a class representative.

28.   If this case were not certified as a class action, I could not afford to pay an attorney to bring an individual lawsuit on my behalf.

_____
Jackie Densmore

484

Monday, July 19, 2021

I submitted my declaration to the Court.
UNITED STATES DISTRICT COURT
WESTERN DISTRICT OF TEXAS
SAN ANTONIO DIVISION

JOE ALMON, JON CARNLEY, CYNTHIA CLARK, JACKIE DENSMORE, JENNIFER KREEGAR, HAROLD MCPHAIL, KATHLEEN PAGLIA, JB SIMMS, and KENNETH TILLMAN on behalf of themselves and all others similarly situated, Plaintiffs, v. § Case No. 5:19-cv-01075-XR CONDUENT BUSINESS SERVICES, LLC d/b/a DIRECT EXPRESS, COMERICA, INC., and COMERICA BANK, Defendants.

DECLARATION OF J.B. SIMMS
I, J.B. Simms, do hereby declare:
1. I am an adult resident of the State of California over the age of 18 and testify to the facts set forth in this Declaration based on my own personal knowledge.
2. I am one of the named Plaintiffs in this lawsuit.
3. I formerly received federal Social Security benefits through my Direct Express Debit MasterCard Card, a program administered by the Defendants.
4. In January 2017, I discovered fraudulent transactions on my account, namely, the purchase of Caribbean vacation packages and gaming programs.
5. I disputed these transactions with Direct Express and was informed that I would be sent a "fraud packet" so that I could formally dispute these charges.
6. Because Direct Express did not deliver the Questionnaire of Fraud to me, I mailed a written narrative outlining the fraudulent transactions to Direct Express.
7. The Defendants denied my fraud claim.
8. Despite my request, Defendants failed to provide me with a copy of the documents upon which they relied in making their determination that the transactions were not fraudulent.
9. I validated my fraud claim directly with the merchants, and the merchants reimbursed the fraud loss to my Direct Express debit card.
10. The Defendants conducted no investigation regarding the fraud on my Direct Express account and did not furnish me a copy of the investigation, both being violations of Regulation E.
11. I was victimized by fraudulent transactions a second time in December 2017.
12. On this occasion, I discovered an unauthorized pending charge on my account and immediately reported the fraud to Direct Express via facsimile.
13. Unauthorized fraudulent charges for perfume, a leather jacket (both being mailed to India), online dating services, and Google services were discovered.
14. The charge for the leather jacket was discovered as a pending charge and the Defendant refused to acknowledge the fraudulent charge nor the reporting of the charge.
15. Defendants denied my fraud claim a second time and failed to provide me with a copy of the documents upon which they relied in making their determination to once again deny my claim in violation of Regulation E.
16. Further, despite the fact that I promptly contacted Direct Express regarding the fraudulent transactions, Defendants refused to provide me with a provisional credit and failed to timely provide me with the results of their purported investigation in violation of Regulation E.
17. Defendants also failed to validate the obvious fraud claim with no need of investigation, and make immediate reimbursement, as provided in Regulation E.
18. It was only after I escalated the situation by contacting the merchants involved in these disputed transactions did I eventually receive a refund, receiving approximately 80 percent refund directly from the merchants, and token service charges reimbursed by the Defendant.
19. It was only after the merchants made refunds that the Defendant made what they considered a conciliatory gesture and reimbursing a token amount of the fraud loss.

485

20. After my less than satisfactory experience with the Defendant(s), I decided to assist other cardholders who experienced fraud, by demanding the Defendants abide by Regulation E (15USC1693), having their denied claim status of their disputes reversed and obtaining reimbursement of funds.

21. I was contacted by and directly assisted 103 victims between February 2018 and March 2019, advocating for victims by legally contacting the Defendants on behalf of fraud victims after being victimized by the Defendants, recovering full reimbursement for approximately 70 percent of said victims totaling over $400,000 in reimbursements.

22. The Office of Investigations within the Office of Inspector General of the US Treasury requested a copy of the narratives of the original 103 victims which detailed personal contact information, fraud experience, violations of Regulation E by both Defendants and the outcome of my involvement.

23. From May 2018 until April 2019, I was spending no fewer than 8-10 hours daily receiving telephone calls and writing emails on behalf of victims.

24. In the fall of 2018, I was asked to become an administrator of a Facebook page where people who experienced fraud on their Direct Express account could go and get information on Regulation E, FDIC, and Federal Reserve regulations, how to file or challenge their fraud claims and how to confront Comerica Bank and Conduent employees into abiding by Regulation E by refunding money to cardholders whose claims were originally denied.

25. I also posted my contact information on various websites like PissedConsumer.com.

26. By making myself available to Direct Express cardholders in these fashions, I personally helped well over the original 103 cardholders receive fraud reimbursement, when the Conduent employees initially denied fraud claims by default.

27. I worked with my fellow plaintiff Jackie Densmore to pressure officials at the Department of Treasury, Social Security, Bureau of Fiscal Service, and the Veterans Administration to investigate how Comerica Bank and Conduent, which administers the Direct Express program, handles fraud claims and violates Regulation E as an established behavior.

28. I also pressured officials at the Veterans' Administration to create an alternative program that Veterans could use to receive their benefits, so they did not have to use the Direct Express program.

29. On February 26, 2018, I challenged the integrity of two investigative audits published by the Office of Inspector General of US Treasury, which lead to the commissioning of two further audits. This was performed before counsel was secured for the Plaintiffs.

30. Evidence of my activity independent of my counsel is the twelve or more FOI requests submitted to agencies to include the VA, Social Security Administration, Bureau of Fiscal Service, and Office of Inspector General of US Treasury.

31. My involvement also included Wounded Warriors and a number of media outlets.

32. Steven Lepper (Maj Gen USAF Ret.), CEO of the Association of Military Banks of America (AMBA) became my liaison with the Veterans Administration, communicating to me in December 2019 regarding the pending press release announcing the Veterans Benefit Banking Program which never would have occurred except for my endless daily communication with the Chief of Staff of the VA, all conducted with no involvement of my attorney.

33. The Veteran Administration has since ceased endorsing the Direct Express program (to include the Bureau of Fiscal Service) by changing the inserts being placed into the envelope of check recipients directing recipients to the VA and the Veterans Benefit Banking Program, which was the result of the pressure exerted by Jackie Densmore and myself, all conducted without the involvement of our attorney.

34. As such, I have been intimately involved in this case from the outset, exposing corruption from the outset of the Direct Express program.

35. I am more knowledgeable of the manner in which the Defendants obtained the Direct Express contract, and the fact that the Defendants ignored violations of Regulation E than anyone involved in this litigation.

36. I understand that I am one of the proposed class representatives in this lawsuit. As a class representative, I understand I would be representing a class of other persons whose fraud claims were handled improperly by Conduent and Comerica Bank.

37. I have communicated with my attorneys during this case on a regular basis. I often speak with my counsel about suggestions or thoughts I have about the case as well as potential litigation strategy. I also attended the deposition of several defense witnesses.

38. In connection with my discovery obligations, I provided my counsel with documents prior to joining this case and assisted my attorneys in preparing responses to interrogatories and requests for the production of

documents. I have communicated with my attorneys during the case. I was also deposed for several hours on December 10, 2020. Before and after my deposition I conferred with counsel.

39. I am dedicated to this case and have invested well over a thousand hours on behalf and as an advocate for persons victimized by the Defendants after being victimized by fraud.

40. I understand that, from time to time throughout the rest of the case, I needed to confer with my attorneys and perform tasks upon their request. I also understand that I may be called as a witness to testify at trial. I am willing and able to fulfill all of my duties as a class representative and lead Plaintiff in this matter.

41. If this case were not certified as a class action, I could not afford to pay an attorney to bring an individual lawsuit on my behalf.

J.B. Simms

The VA changed their inserts. The insert above was for the disability check Derek received for his July 2021 VA check.

We were happy about that.

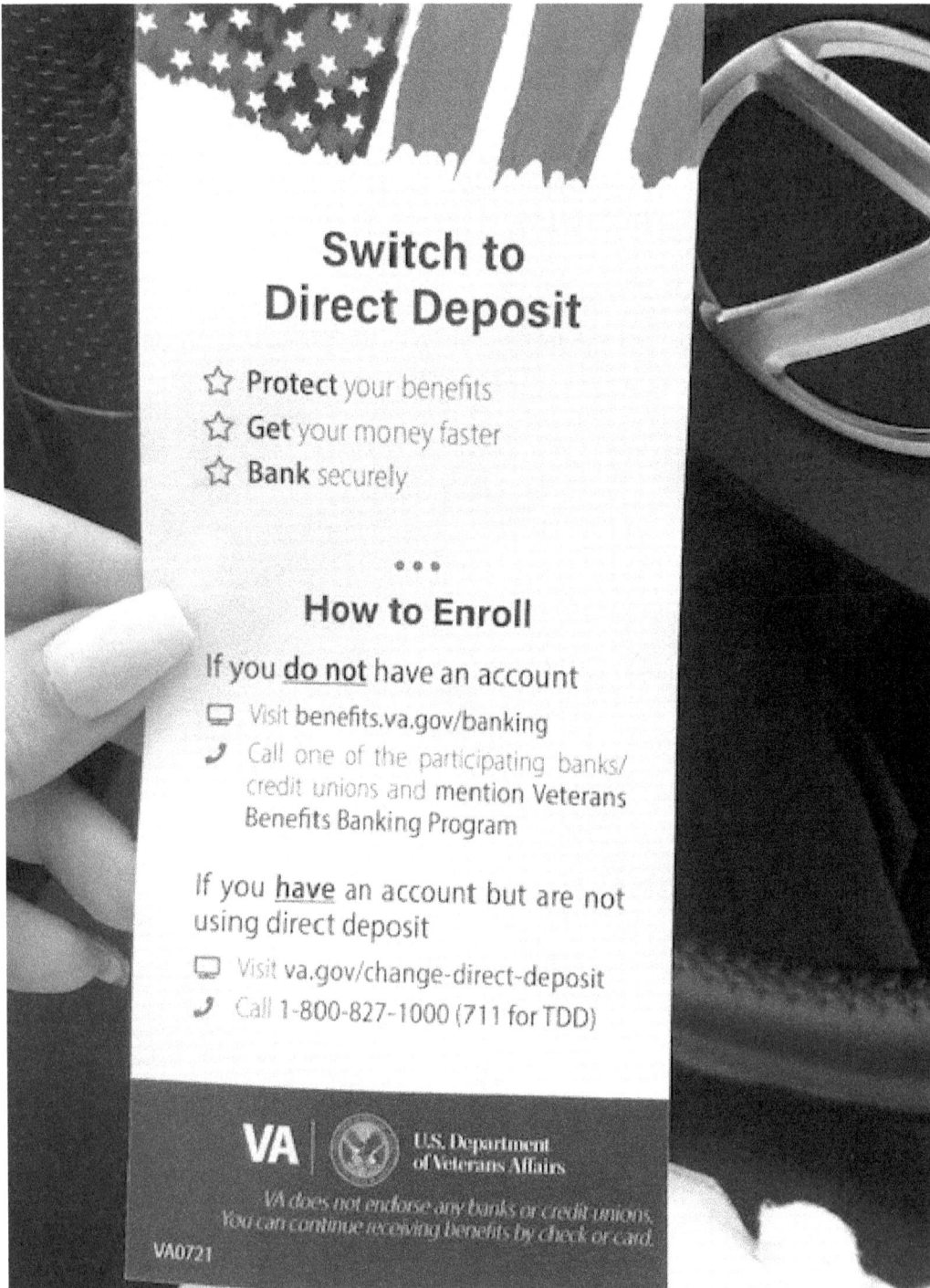

Wednesday, August 11, 2021

I wanted to know why documents and filings on the federal case website were sealed. Franklin responded below.

From: Franklin Lemond (Plaintiff's Attorney)
Date: August 11, 2021 at 10:42:59 AM EDT
To: jbsimms
Cc: Jackie Lynn
Subject: Re: status
Jim,

The motion and exhibits were filed under seal because they quote, refer to, and attach documents that were marked "confidential" and/or "attorneys' eyes only" and pursuant to the confidentiality order, such items must be filed under seal until opposing counsel has a chance to review the items and designate what redactions are necessary before the document can be filed publicly. I would expect that process to take another few weeks. Comerica and Conduent do have an opportunity to contest the motion and their deadline is September 3, 2021. We get to file a reply to their opposition by September 27.
Franklin

Franklin filed the motion for class action certification.
All we could do was wait.

Monday, September 6, 2021

Jbsimms
Mon, Sep 6, 2021, 9:09 AM
to Franklin, Jackie
What is the status of Discovery after class certification?
Treasury still ignores the subpoenas you sent and I see no proactive gestures on behalf of the plaintiffs.
If I file an FOI to Treasury regarding the subpoenas, I bet I will get more response than the US Attorney is giving you.
Jim Simms

The VA gets on board with a new division to serve veterans.

Steven Lepper (Military Banks of America)
jbsimms
Jackie Lynn
Mr. Simms,

We just got the green light from VA to proceed on version 2.0 of the VBBP — a new website that will include financial and credit counseling as well as enhanced financial education. I'll let you know when we flip the switch. We're also testing a new alternative for the Direct Express debit card. It's a new financial product that can be used around the world and avoids all the problems that have given veterans such fits. Look for that soon, too.
I'll keep you posted on our progress.
All the best,
Steve

Wednesday, September 22, 2021

Franklin Lemond (Plaintiff's Attorney)
jbsimms
Jackie Lynn
Jim,
The defendants did file their opposition brief last Friday as scheduled.
Franklin

Litigation is killing us. Long drawn-out process. The lawyers for the defendant, Comerica Bank, filed an opposition to everything that was filed. That is their job, to oppose. This aggravates us with more delay, but there was no avoiding it.

Thursday, September 30, 2021

I continued to press Social Security about the inserts. The inserts were one of the issues we had that we had to fight. Social Security was promoting the Direct Express debit cards while Comerica Bank was allowing Conduent to violate banking laws.

Refer to: S9H: SSA-2021-000274

September 30, 2021

Mr. James Simms

Dear Mr. Simms:

This letter is in response to your October 11, 2020 Freedom of Information Act (FOIA) request for the following:

1. The identity of the federal agency, department, office, and person(s) charged with creating, editing, developing, or having any creative input with regard to the printed paper inserts (endorsing and promoting the Direct Express program) which accompany checks being mailed to Social Security recipients from January 2020 the present;

2. The identity of the federal agency, department, office, and person(s) which/who directed the paper inserts be inserted into the envelopes to accompany Social Security checks;

3. The name of the person at Bureau of Fiscal Service and/or the Social Security Administration (SSA) who directed the inserts be placed in the envelopes to accompany Social Security checks;

4. Copies of any emails, transcripts of telephone conversations, notes of any meetings, witness statements, or any tangible evidence of communication between the Bureau of Fiscal Service, Comerica Bank, Conduent, SSA Office of the Inspector General (OIG), OIG Treasury, and SSA with regard to the paper inserts endorsing the Direct Express program and the insertion into the check envelopes; and

5. Copies of emails, transcripts of telephone conversations, notes from meetings, witness statements, or any tangible evidence of any or all illegal payments being made to federal employees at Bureau of Fiscal Service, OIG Treasury, Social Security OIG, Bureau of Fiscal Service Office of Legislative Affairs, by Comerica Bank or Conduent to promote the Direct Express program or to protect against inquiries.

Per your telephone meeting on May 3, 2021 with the Acting Division Director for the FOIA and Transparency Division – and confirmed via email on May 12, 2021 – you revised your request as follows:

Page 2 – Mr. Simms

"any notes/memos regarding SSA's use of the printed-paper inserts (endorsing and promoting the Direct Express program) which accompany checks being mailed to Social Security recipients from January 2020 to the present."

We located five emails and seven attachments responsive to your request; however, we are withholding three "draft" attachments pursuant to the FOIA Exemption 5 (deliberate process). FOIA Exemption 5 (5 U.S.C. § 552(b)(5)) protects from disclosure privileged information, specifically inter- or intra-agency memorandums or letters which would not be available by law to a party other than an agency in litigation with the agency. We have determined that the release of the information withheld under the FOIA Exemption 5 (deliberate process) would cause foreseeable harm to agency interests protected by this exemption.

The breakdown of the enclosed documents are as follows:

1. Email Doc 1- draft attachment withheld (FOIA exemption 5);

2. Email Doc 2- draft attachment withheld (FOIA exemption 5);

3. Email Doc 3- 2 attachments;

4. Email Doc 4- draft attachment withheld (FOIA exemption 5); and

5. Email Doc 5- no attachments.

The origin of the inserts sent out by the SSA was the nature of the FOI request.

I looked through the emails. Some of the response was helpful. Some were redacted. SSA was useless in responding to FOI requests. I was able to glean information from the VA FOI requests.

We had caught them in a lie anyway. We knew that Comerica had to bring in i2c to keep the contract.

Thursday, October 14, 2021

On Oct 14, 2021, at 5:53 PM, Franklin Lemond (Plaintiff's Attorney) wrote:
I'll gladly share a draft of the response, but the deadline is 10/25 rather than 10/18.
Jackie Lynn

Jbsimms
Oct 15, 2021, 6:33 PM
to Jr., Jackie
What is the issue with the outstanding OIG Treasury report?
We know Delmar is in the bag for Chally and not to produce the audit before class action certification.
Will the audit be admissible after the certification? You never went after treasury for ignoring the subpoenas.
You want to call Delmar and ask him about the OIG audit or do you think you will get blasted again by his
underling, Ms Altemus? You never sent us the narrative of that conversation from a year ago. You never gave us
the plan for future discovery. I feel like we are talking to Chally. Jim Simms

Friday, October 22, 2021

Fri, Oct 22, 2021, 1:32 PM
to me, Franklin
Sent from my iPhone
Begin forwarded message:
From: "Jackman, Michael" <Michael.Jackman@mail.house.gov>
Date: October 22, 2021, at 1:19:38 PM EDT
To: Jackie Lynn
Subject: FW: Request for OIG report
FYI, Mr. Bayer's email came back as undeliverable, he may have retired. I am trying to track down a good
email for the SSA OIG.
Also, Mr. Delmar informs me that the final Treasury report is due in February 2022.
--Mike Jackman

From: Jackman, Michael
Sent: Friday, October 22, 2021, 12:56 PM
To: walter.bayer@ssa.gov
Subject: Request for OIG report
Good afternoon Mr. Bayer:
On behalf of our constituent Jackie Densmore, I am requesting any information from the OIG's FY 2021 and/or
FY2022 Audit Work Plans pertaining to audits/investigations of the Direct Express Program.
Also, if any reports have been issued regarding audits or investigations of the Direct Express Program, please
provide those as well.
Michael Jackman, District Director
Office of Congressman Keating (MA-09)
It looked like Bayer had retired and was no longer with SSA. We could not get a reply from Bayer.
Franklin filed his Opposition to the Motion filed by Chally in federal court. This back-and-forth continued.

Sunday, November 7, 2021

Here is an example of the games played by SSA. They closed an FOI request before sending documents. They
took Franklin's money and did nothing until I exposed them.
FOIA Public Liaison <FOIA.Public.Liaison@ssa.gov
RE: SSA-2021-000274
Inbox
Jbsimms
Nov 7, 2021, 1:19 AM
to FOI
It looks like you people got paid $1,600.00
I do not think I received my documents. J.B. Simms

Monday, November 8, 2021

FOIA Public Liaison <FOIA.Public.Liaison@ssa.gov
Nov 8, 2021, 6:01 AM
to me
Good morning:
Thank you for your email. We closed your request, SSA-2021-000274, on September 30, and transmitted the responsive records as well as a response letter, to this email address. Please check your spam or junk folders for an email with the subject line, "SSA-2021-000274 -Final Response Letter- 9-30-21," which was sent through FOIAonline.
If you did not receive this email, please let us know and we will transmit the response and documents to you again.
Thank you,
The FOIA Team
SSA

Jbsimms
Nov 8, 2021, 10:15 AM
to Franklin, Jackie, ^FOIA
Please bring to the attention of Ms. Zimmerman that your office redeemed a payment from attorney Franklin Lemond and the FOI material should and will be delivered as requested.
If Ms. Zimmerman has any questions, I can be reached at (803) 309-6850.
Sincerely,
JB Simms

Wednesday, November 10, 2021

Below is more drama from Social Security FOI office. Treasury and Social Security were the worst regarding compliance with FOI inquiries.
Nov 10, 2021, 7:53 AM
To: FOIA, Franklin, Jackie
Dear Ms. Zimmerman,
There has been no response to the email I sent on November 10 regarding the dismissal of my FOI request and the debiting of the bank account from the account of Mr. Lemond regarding the same request.
While I am familiar with unilateral decisions made regarding citizens having been denied lawfully entitled information from your office, the withdrawal of funds from the account of Mr. Lemond must have been credited to an unknown fund within your agency because someone refused to acknowledge the request.
Please address this matter at your earliest convenience.
J.B. Simms

FOIA Public Liaison <FOIA.Public.Liaison@ssa.gov>
Nov 10, 2021, 10:31 AM
to me
Good morning:
As previously indicated, your requested records were emailed to you via our FOIA processing system, FOIA online, on September 30, 2021. The credit card provided was charged the cost of searching for and reviewing the requested records, per the SSA-714 you submitted on June 10, 2021.
Enclosed in this email are the documents that were transmitted to you.
Please let us know if you have further questions.

Jbsimms
Nov 10, 2021, 10:44 AM
to Franklin, Jackie, FOIA
The email stated the matter was closed.
Are you trying to say the requested documents were submitted and subsequently the matter was closed?
If I missed seeing the requested documents which were paid by debiting the credit card of attorney Mr. Lemond, that would be my error, and I am requesting the same FOI documents be re-submitted. J.B. Simms

FOIA.Public.Liaison@ssa.gov
Nov 10, 2021, 11:20 AM
to me
Good afternoon:
Thank you for your reply. The requested documents were emailed to you again, attached to our 10:31 email today (we previously sent them with our September 30 email as well).
We did not reopen your request; we transmitted the documents to you at the time the request was closed, and transmitted them again today.
Please let us know if you have any issues accessing the PDFs we have emailed you.

From: Jbsimms
Sent: Wednesday, November 10, 2021 11:45 AM
To: FOIA.Public.Liaison@ssa.gov
Cc: Franklin Lemond (Plaintiff's Attorney); Jackie Lynn
Subject: SSA-2021-000274
The email stated the matter was closed.

FOIA.Public.Liaison@ssa.gov
Nov 10, 2021, 12:51 PM
to Franklin, Jackie, me, ^FOIA
Good Afternoon, Mr. Simms:
Please know that we closed SSA-2021-000274 and sent final correspondence from FOIAonline on September 30, 2021. We did not receive notification that the email and its attachments were not received; however, we apologize if you did not receive them. Please know that we are reopening the request so we can send you a courtesy copy of the response letter and attachments again. After we do so, we will close the request. Please expect to receive the email from FOIAonline this afternoon.
Thank you,
The FOIA Team
SSA/OPD

Jbsimms
Nov 10, 2021, 12:57 PM
to ^FOIA, Franklin, Jackie
Thank you for your kind gesture of reopening the request.
I am certain attorney Franklin Lemond will be pleased to know how his money was used.
J.B. Simms

Monday, December 6, 2021

Chally files a Reply to Motion for Summary Judgement.
More legal delays.

Wednesday, December 8, 2021

Jbsimms
Wed, Dec 8, 2021, 7:34 PM
to Jackie
Read them all. All about SSA. The last email was a link to the first article.
The second article shows how 32 of 36 people had their info hacked and Comerica pointed its finger at "hackers."
Conduent was never named.

Switch today.

Make the change on our site
or over the phone, now!

!Haga el cambio en nuestra pagina de
internet ó por telefono, ahora!

GoDirect.gov
1-800-333-1795

Phone operators are available
Monday–Friday | 9 a.m–7 p.m. EST

You can also visit your bank or credit union.

Para español, visite
DirectoasuCuenta.gov

Converting your paper check to
an electronic payment is easy.

All you will need is your:

- Social Security number

- Information from your most
  recent federal benefit check
  or claim number

- Date of birth FOR DIRECT EXPRESS*

- Financial institution's routing
  transit number FOR DIRECT DEPOSIT

- Account number and account
  type (checking or savings)
  FOR DIRECT DEPOSIT

DIRECTEXPRESS ❯

DIRECT DEPOSIT
Simple. Safe. Secure.

1120

494

Chapter Twelve
The Win

Tuesday, February 8, 2022

8:01 am
jbsimms erikpublishing.com
To: Richard Delmar (OIG Treasury)
Jackie Lynn, Michael Jackman (Rep Keating aide) Franklin Lemond (Plaintiff's Attorney)
Dear Mr. Delmar,
While it appears consequential that the failure of publication of the highly anticipated and questionable postponement of the latest OIG report (appearing to be 20-028) detailing the investigation of Comerica Bank, BFS, and Conduent, has benefited the defendants in the federal lawsuit by OIG Treasury refusing to publish said report, it also appears your office has not been relating accurate or believable information to Mr. Jackman regarding these postponements.
Isn't it odd that the preliminary report by Katherine Johnson was published well over a year and the final report has been secreted during the litigation of the federal lawsuit? Other OIG reports do not take this long to finish.
Sincerely,
J.B. Simms

Monday, March 28, 2022

Mon, Mar 28, 2022, 9:43 PM
to me, Jackie
JB & Jackie,
See attached order from the court issued earlier today. Some good, some bad. The fact that he asks us to re-file for class certification with amended class definitions is certainly a good thing.
It is a lot to digest, but we can discuss after you've had a chance to review.
Franklin
The judge was telling Franklin to restate his argument. This was a bit scary, but Franklin did refile.

Thursday, March 31, 2022

Thu, Mar 31, 2022, 6:05 AM
to Franklin, Jackie
The fact that investigations did not commence immediately is apparent.
The fact that Jackie and I got our money as quickly as we did was because we did the work Conduent was supposed to have done, as well as Cynthia Clark.
I went after the merchants, as did Jackie and Cynthia. I was on the phone with Cynthia on a Saturday morning identifying the fraud, the stores, and going after the store security people. I did this for many victims. (No, I am not Batman, but very close.)
The issue of dismissing us from the case involving reimbursement is in error, as cited above.

Thu, Mar 31, 2022, 5:05 AM
to Franklin, Jackie
I have read the Order.
Some things should be addressed. Some things are encouraging.
The finding of lack of specificity regarding the commonality of all class action plaintiffs can be remedied by noting by zeroing in on the Reg E stipulations of the following (I have a document regarding these stipulations and the cites):
1) Constructive notice is effective when contact is made by mail, email, fax, or telephone to the financial institution. (The shutting down of the email to the Fraud Unit was done with malice. Noted also was that the Terms of Use did not include contact information for the Fraud Unit.)
2) The investigation of the reporting of fraud must begin immediately.
3) Provisional credit must be given within 10 days.
4) A copy of the investigation must be made available.

There is also a cite that states if the fraud is obvious (as is the case with Clark, Densmore, and Kreeger) "no investigation is necessary."

There is also the issue of the Kreegar postcard being sent a week after the fraudster made the changes of address. Seems the change was made on Dec 6, the notice postcard mailed a week later, and Kreegar did not get notice until late December. I followed the law by giving notice of the Kreegar fraud myself via lovely email. Arpin had a fit and told Conduent to repay Kreegar immediately.

Sunday, April 3, 2022

J B Simms
Sun, Apr 3, 2022, 7:58 AM
to Franklin, Jackie

If Plaintiffs were not proactive (Kreegar, Simms, Densmore, Clark) beyond simply giving notice, the Defendants would have, based upon patterns of behavior, violated Reg E and 12CFR with more regularity.

Plaintiffs are subjected to double jeopardy; actual losses of money, and lack of redress for civil damages as a result of being proactive.

This case exposed the Defendants as having no regard for the consumer (failure to give contact information regarding the fraud department) and no regard for regulations.

The defendants falsely stated in their application submitted to BFS that they would abide by Reg E and other regs.

They did not.

The five tenants of the Reg E violations experienced by all defendants were sent to you both.

Wednesday, April 13, 2022

Jackie Lynn
Wed, Apr 13, 2022, 7:48 AM
to me, Franklin

I also see no mention of the cardless benefit program being shut down

I would also like to point out that the phone number the only phone number given to customers is restricted once the fraudsters get a hold of it making it impossible for cardholders to reach level 2

There is also no mention of a third OIG report being issued that was prompted by us

J B Simms
Wed, Apr 13, 2022, 8:54 AM
to Jackie, Franklin

That is a great point.

More mention of 1)the careless benefit program being shut down and the 2) creation of the VBBP at the VA. Both events were prompted by us and both were validated by Nora and the VA.

Monday, July 18, 2022

Davis, Angela C., VBAVACO <Angela.Davis14@va.gov>
Good afternoon Mr. Simms:

On or about September 20, 2020, you submitted a FOIA request to the VBACO FOIA Office. The previous FOIA Officer is no longer with this office and your request has been re-assigned.

Please see the attached correspondence and let me know if you are still interested in this request no later than August 17, 2022.

Angela C. Davis

Saturday, July 23, 2022

The Social Security Administration was never going to cooperate with FOI requests. They charged exorbitant amounts to get information or simply delayed responses.

SSA FOI office was a joke, married to Comerica and BFS. Bayer had betrayed us by making us think he was taking the Direct Express issue to SSA OIG. He never did.

Wednesday, July 27, 2022

I was getting tired of Delmar's delays and misleading statements. Delmar denied my FOI requests by claiming there was no "investigation" when we knew Sonja Scott, a Treasury Agent, worked in the Office of Investigations. We knew the corruption ran deep at OIG Treasury.

J B Simms
Wed, Jul 27, 2022, 7:27 PM
to Richard, Michael, Jackie, Kate
Dear Mr. Delmar,
Is there any truth that Comerica Bank and Conduent have been dictating to OIG Treasury officials to delay the release of the OIG report for the past 18-24 months or more to benefit Comerica Bank?
This last OIG report was to be published well over 18 months ago. We gave you all the incriminating evidence and amazingly the evidence has been ignored.
Sincerely,
JB Simms

Thursday, September 8, 2022

Jackie and I helped Ron Wilcox in his case. We got statements from him and his client.
Wilcox got a win for his client against Comerica; $125,000 for his client.

J B Simms
Thu, Sep 8, 2022, 1:38 PM
to Franklin, Jackie
Hi,
We won the appeal. The Court then entered Judgment against Comerica for $1.2 million+.
It refused to pay. We then had court order it to appear and tell us where its assets were.
Before the hearing, Comerica paid, with interest.
Good luck,
Ron

Wednesday, September 28, 2022

The Ruling for Class Action Certification: We win 3 of 4 violations

We got class action certification. Franklin sent us an email with the Order attached.

Franklin Lemond (Plaintiff's Attorney)
Attachments
Wed, Sep 28, 2022, 11:37 AM
to Jackie, me
Guys,
See the attached order hot off the presses. The Judge split the baby somewhat, certifying the 3 proposed EFTA classes, but not certifying the breach of contract class. Obviously, I would have loved for him to certify all of the classes, but getting certification in three classes is a big win. There is a lot to digest here and I need some time to think about our next steps, so let's plan to chat tomorrow or Friday.
Franklin

We (Franklin and the plaintiffs) asked for a class action claim in four areas; provisional credit, investigations to be conducted, copies of investigations to be furnished, and breach of contract regarding the Terms of Agreement we were given. The Terms of Agreement is the sheet of paper sent to cardholders that supposedly explain the conditions of use and liability of cardholders. We asserted Comerica Bank and Conduent violated Regulation E in a number of places, but the judge did not agree. He gave us three of the four, which was not bad. We won.
We have to tell Kate.

JB Simms
Wed, Sep 28, 2022, 12:24 PM
to Kate, Jackie
Dear Kate,
4 years. 4 long years.
If you read the ruling, we got class action cert on failure to provide provisional credit, failure to provide timely investigation report, and failure to provide an investigative report when requested.
Breach of contract was denied.
So, here is your story.
Franklin will chat with us on Friday, but if you read the end of the ruling I sent you, you will see the cert that I mentioned above.
Now let's get paid.
Jim

Chapter Thirteen
Validation From American Banker

From August 2018, Kate Berry of American Banker had been an faithful ally and supporter of the fight Jackie and I waged on behalf of the victims of the Direct Express program. The fight exposed Comerica Bank, Conduent, U.S. Treasury OIG, and the Bureau of Fiscal Service as the cabal of abuse of veterans and other users of the Direct Express debit card.

The Veterans Administration officially stopped endorsing the Direct Express program in December, 2019 but not without my fight against Paul Lawrence of the Veterans Benefit Association who ignored my attempts engage him. VA Chief of Staff Pamela Powers was instrumental in exposing the complicity in all agencies. She is to be applauded and we owe her a debt of gratitude for exposing the wrongdoing in her own agency.

Jackie and I had been trying to get Kate Berry to write another article. Kate had been telling us for months that she had been receiving information from sources that would be shocking, confirming the suspicions of Jackie and me.

Below is the article from American Banker Magazine, written by Kate Berry, and published on May 29, 2023.

Internal communications obtained by American Banker indicate that bank officials were concerned about the legality of the bank's third-party vendor relationships retained as part of its contract with the Treasury Department to operate Direct Express, a public benefits payment system. Bloomberg News

By Kate Berry

May 29, 2023, 9:00 p.m. EDT

Comerica Bank officials privately acknowledged significant compliance failures in their operation of a Treasury Department program that provides federal benefits on prepaid cards to millions of unbanked Americans, according to internal documents obtained by American Banker.

A Comerica executive said the Dallas bank faced a "serious contract violation" for allowing fraud disputes and data on Direct Express cardholders to be handled out of a vendor's office in Lahore, Pakistan, the documents show.

Personally identifiable information on veterans, Social Security and disability recipients were routinely shared and handled by i2c Inc., a vendor based in Redwood City, Calif., with an office in Lahore, Pakistan — in violation of the government contract, the Comerica executive said. The Treasury's agreement with the bank states that all services
provided "shall be performed in the United States or its territories."

Paul Lawrence, who served as under secretary for benefits in the Department of Veterans Affairs from 2018 to 2021, said he was in "complete shock and disgust" after being told of
the information contained in the internal Comerica documents.

"All of these government contracts basically say you have to be in the U.S. and the program has to be run by U.S. citizens," Lawrence, a longtime government consultant, said in an interview. "This has all the makings for a really, really bad situation."

The internal documents, in addition to court documents filed in a class action last year, paint a broader picture of the $91.2 billion-asset Comerica's strategy and third-party oversight of Treasury's Direct Express program, which serves 4.5 million Americans.

Comerica has been mired in litigation and yearslong disputes over Direct Express, which it has operated under a contract with the Treasury since 2008. Direct Express deposits roughly $3 billion a month electronically on prepaid cards to millions of federal government beneficiaries who do not have a bank account. The program is part of a government effort to reduce potential fraud and costs by weaning people off paper checks.

Comerica has contracted out the day-to-day operations of Direct Express to two vendors: i2c and Conduent Inc., a publicly-traded conglomerate based in Florham Park, N.J.

The internal documents include a 2020 email from a Comerica executive, who described sweeping violations of Regulation E, which governs how a financial institution addresses errors reported by consumers including for theft or fraud. Nora Arpin, Comerica's then-senior vice president and director of government electronic solutions, said the bank was in breach of its Treasury contract but that it was unable to get its third-party vendor to make changes.

"Management for Reg E dispute processing is in Lahore which means that cardholder information is being shared with/sent to Lahore, which is a serious contract violation," Arpin wrote.

Arpin no longer works at Comerica. Arpin and an attorney who had represented her in the past did not respond to requests for comment.

David P. Weber, a clinical assistant professor of accounting at Salisbury University and a former supervisory counsel and enforcement chief at the Federal Deposit Insurance Corp., said the bank would need to inform its regulator about the activities of third-party service providers.

"It was a clear violation of the contract Comerica held with the Department of the Treasury to locate the vendor in a foreign country when part of the consideration for them being awarded this federal contract was to use American employees and vendors," said Weber, who served as special counsel for enforcement for more than 10 years at the Office of the Comptroller of the Currency.

"Separate and aside from contract fraud, it is inappropriate for a federally-insured depository institution to locate third-party service provider activities in a foreign nation without informing their regulator, and locating the operations in a country in which there are questions about rule of law, which would make supervisory and exam activities as well as protections of American consumers questionable."

The bank previously had been criticized by the Federal Reserve Bank of Dallas in a "matters requiring attention" order a year earlier, which described "weaknesses" in Comerica's risk monitoring of Direct Express, according to court documents. Examiners said Conduent, the bank's primary vendor, did not provide cardholders reporting fraud on their cards with information on how to receive a provisional credit, documents show.

Comerica was paid $151 million in 2020 to operate Direct Express, and received roughly $770 million in total gross revenue over a six-year period, from 2015 to 2020, to run the program, Albert Taylor, a Comerica senior vice president and director of National Bankcard Services, said in court documents.

In response to questions from American Banker, a Comerica spokeswoman said the bank is "proud to have served as financial agent for the Treasury Department's Direct Express Program since its inception in 2008."

"Should an issue arise with a third-party vendor involving compliance with the Financial Agency Agreement, Comerica works closely with the vendor to address the situation, in accordance with Comerica's obligation under the FAA to ensure its vendors' compliance with the FAA," the Comerica spokeswoman said in an email. "Additionally, Comerica promptly notifies [Treasury's Bureau of] Fiscal Service of issues impacting the program and keeps Fiscal Service apprised until they are fully resolved."

Conduent declined to comment. Executives at i2c declined an interview but instead provided a written statement disputing allegations it had violated its contract.

"As a global provider of banking and payment services, we naturally employ a global workforce. One that spans more than six countries — a fact that we are proud of and that our partners are actively made aware of and accept," i2c said.

"Let it also be known that i2c's compliance regarding the access, use, storage, and transmission of cardholder information is independently certified by third parties including, but not limited to an annual [Payment Card Industry Data Security Standard] certification, which requires the encryption or masking of personal identifiable information regardless of geographic location," reads the statement.

The Treasury's Bureau of Fiscal Service did not return calls seeking comment. The Treasury's Office of Inspector General said it had no comment.

Inadequate fraud reporting

In a key internal 2020 email, Arpin, the former Comerica executive, listed 13 bullet points describing the practices of i2c. Among the bank's "serious concerns," she wrote:

- "We are having significant difficulty getting adequate fraud reporting."
- "We can't get the Call Center statistics we need."
- "Reg E adjudication is an issue"
- "Fraud prevention is a serious issue."
- "Reporting in general is an issue — we aren't getting the reporting that the [Treasury's Bureau of] Fiscal Services requires."

Arpin also wrote in the internal email that i2c's CEO Amir Wain "doesn't have plans to fix those issues."

Cardholders have complained for years about fraud, poor customer service and high fees in the Direct Express program.

Last year, a federal judge certified a class action against Comerica and Conduent brought by Direct Express cardholders who claimed their accounts were drained of thousands of dollars from 2015 to 2022 due to fraud. The class action, filed in the U.S. District Court for the Western District of Texas, alleges that Comerica and Conduent denied refunds to cardholders who alleged fraud on their accounts.

The court documents, combined with internal documents that were received anonymously in the mail, provide a better understanding of Comerica's private and public responses to various inquiries. Comerica executives were repeatedly warned about vendor oversight, potential breaches of the Treasury contract and deficiencies in the bank's compliance management system, said sources familiar with the matter who asked that they remain anonymous out of fear of retaliation. In-house lawyers escalated their concerns to the bank's senior leadership, including Susan Joseph, Comerica's head of compliance; Jay Oberg, senior executive vice president and chief risk officer; and Peter L. Sefzik, senior executive vice president and chief banking officer.

The Treasury's Office of Inspector General issued reports in 2014, 2017 and 2020 that were critical of compliance, chargeback and dispute processing at Direct Express, which Comerica manages, in addition to the bidding process for the government contract. The OIG investigates waste, fraud and abuse in the agency and programs it oversees.

In August 2018, Sen. Elizabeth Warren, D-Mass., launched an investigation into Direct Express after cardholders complained about not being reimbursed for fraud. In a letter to the Veterans Administration, Warren said fraudsters had used "stolen data to impersonate benefit recipients, made fraudulent purchases, and drained the prepaid cards of the federal benefits."

Comerica's Executive Chairman Ralph W. Babb responded to Warren by stating that Comerica has taken appropriate steps to root out fraud.

Comerica "follows all laws and regulations including the [Federal Financial Institutions Examination Council] guidelines for supplier oversight," Babb said in a 21-page response in October 2018.
'

Reg E Lite'

Yet, within a month of Sen. Warren's inquiry, a Comerica lawyer tried to convince a Texas bank examiner that Regulation E does not apply to the bank or to federal government beneficiaries, the internal documents show.

The Comerica lawyer was responding to a query from the Texas Department of Banking by claiming that the bank was not fully required to abide by the Electronic Fund Transfer Act, which is implemented by Regulation E. The regulation sets strict timelines for banks to resolve errors including investigating fraud and reimbursing harmed consumers with provisional credit when money is stolen.

"Program customers only get 'Regulation E Lite,' benefits," a Comerica executive in the bank's legal department wrote in 2018. That lawyer described "why [the] program's customers are not entitled to all of the provisions and benefits of Regulation E."

In the email, the Comerica lawyer wrote that "...neither the Federal Electronic Funds Transfer nor its Regulation E applies to the Comerica Bank under the Program as a 'financial institution."

Comerica argued that the Treasury, not the bank, was considered to be the financial institution for Direct Express, "which is why we generally state that Program customers are only entitled to 'Regulation E lite' benefits."

By August 2019, Joseph, the chief risk officer, had forwarded the email about 'Reg E Lite," to another Comerica lawyer.

Comerica submitted a glossy, 67-page application to the Treasury in early 2019 in which it described the vendor, i2c, "as a leader in transaction processing, security, fraud prevention and innovation."

In 2020, Treasury **renewed Comerica's contract** after i2c was hired to handle new cardholders. The agreement with the Treasury was signed by Babb, who retired in 2019. Babb was succeeded by Curt C. Farmer, Comerica's chairman and CEO.

Experts say banks have a general obligation to act in good faith when dealing with customers.

Weber, the accounting professor and former regulator, said the bank's legal and compliance obligations far exceed Regulation E. He also called into question Comerica's third-party risk management and operational risk standards.

"The unbanked people already are more vulnerable than ordinary bank customers because they don't have the skill set or financial acumen to know what their rights are, and it's compounded when they are victims of fraud," Weber said. "At the end of the day, federally insured depository institutions are required to have appropriate third-party risk management processes in place, and it isn't new to prepaid cards or benefits."
Weber noted that Bank of America was hit with a $225 million **consent order** last year for failing to investigate fraud claims in unemployment benefits.

"The idea in a perfect world is that somehow the third-party vendor can do it faster and cheaper than the bank because they think they're not obligated to follow the same rules," said Weber, who analyzes counterproductive work behavior. "It's an operational risk issue if the third-party doesn't have the policies, procedures and controls to identify systemic issues."

VA finds a way out

The myriad problems in the Direct Express program, which Comerica managed, forced the Veterans Administration to devote resources to helping
veterans find an alternative. By 2019, the VA helped create the Veterans Benefit Banking Program, a consortium of banks and credit unions that offer free checking accounts so veterans can receive their monthly payments via direct deposit.

"We made a super-conscientious effort to get veterans off Direct Express because the bad experiences were just gut-wrenching," said Lawrence, the VA's under secretary for benefits.

Steve Lepper, a retired U.S. Air Force Major General who is president and CEO of the Association of Military Banks of America, a trade group, worked with the VA to create the program.

"The complaints the VA was getting finally pushed them to the point where we needed to create an alternative to the Direct Express program," Lepper said. "Veterans were apoplectic about all of the problems that they were experiencing with the Direct Express program and, of course, Comerica was responsible for all of the management of the program —including the fraud investigation and resolution processes."

Roughly 240,000 veterans have migrated away from Direct Express and now have bank accounts with direct deposit, Lepper said. About 80,000 unbanked or underbanked veterans still receive their benefits on Direct Express prepaid cards or paper checks.

Lepper credited J.B. Simms, an author and private investigator in Brighton, Tenn., who recently published a book titled, "Comerica, Conduent and the U.S. Treasury Betrayed Veterans and Other Victims." Simms says he first discovered fraudulent charges on his Direct Express account in January 2017 and a second time later that year. He then sought to help other veterans recover money that was stolen due to fraud, including those in which veterans' claims were denied.

Alleged violations

Simms and others say Comerica's failure to address problems with Direct Express should get a public airing.
"The Direct Express cardholders are the most vulnerable population of all Social Security recipients, and most do not have bank accounts and lack the sophistication to challenge any authority," said Simms. He is one of just eight named plaintiffs in the case.

Another plaintiff, Harold McPhail, a Vietnam veteran, reported that $30,000 was stolen from his Direct Express account in 2018. But he died before getting a resolution, said his daughter Martisha McPhail, who said Conduent initially denied her father's fraud claim.

Some Social Security recipients who reported fraud have lost hope that they will ever be reimbursed for thousands of dollars they say was stolen off their prepaid cards. Some said they have not been notified of the class action or any efforts by the bank to reimburse them.

Mike Colburn, a retired Las Vegas businessman, alleged that $5,500 was stolen from his Direct Express account in 2018. Colburn said he was unable to make his mortgage payment and had to borrow money from relatives to avoid defaulting. He ultimately was reimbursed $500 by Conduent but was never able to get all of his money back.

"I gave up on talking to that bank," Coburn said. "They don't return phone calls, they don't return emails and Conduent accused me of stealing the money from myself."

After money was allegedly stolen from his Direct Express account, Colburn called the Social Security Administration to sign up for paper checks. Now his monthly Social Security check comes with an insert stating that he is breaking the law for not using Direct Express, he said.

Cardholders allege in the class action that they were not given provisional credit when errors were reported and were not sent the results of investigations in a timely manner. Regulation E requires that a financial institution investigate fraud within 10 days of being notified by a cardholder, but the *bank can* take up to 45 days to investigate if they provide provisional credit in the amount of the alleged error.

"Nobody could get through to the call center and most of the time people never filed a claim because they got locked out of their accounts," said Jackie Densmore, a plaintiff in the class action, who is a caregiver for her brother-in-law, Derek Densmore, a disabled Marine. She alleged $800 was stolen from his Direct Express card in 2018 and described hours spent trying to get through to   Conduent on the phone and being told to submit a claim in writing.

"There are all these people out there who were never able to complete a fraud packet and actually file a claim," Densmore said.

The vendor had run into problems before with government oversight. Conduent was fined by the Consumer Financial Protection Bureau in 2019 for unfair student
loan practices, and in 2017 for sending incorrect information to credit reporting agencies. In 2019, Conduent, which at the time was owned by Xerox Corp., agreed to a $235 million settlement with the Texas attorney general
for Medicaid-related claims.

Densmore also switched to paper checks for her brother-in-law, who has post- traumatic stress disorder. Symptoms resurface every month, she said, when he sees the insert from Social Security that states: "Notice of noncompliance. You are required by law to convert your paper check to direct deposit or the Direct Express card."

"Every month we relive the nightmare from five years ago," she said. "Since   Derek has a medical condition, I have to explain to him every month about the situation that we have gone through with Direct Express and that he is allowed to get a paper check."

What's next for Comerica customers?

Court documents show that in May 2019 alone, Comerica received 15,712 fraud disputes, according to Taylor, Comerica's director of National Bankcard Services. Taylor said in court documents that Comerica did not have any data to identify cardholders that reported fraud, and the bank didn't keep track of money refunded or denied for fraud.

The supervisory letter from the Federal Reserve Bank of Dallas in early 2019 identified potential consumer harm, program deficiencies and customer service issues in Comerica's handling of Direct Express. Specifically, examiners at the Dallas Fed said that Conduent's call centers were not trained in Regulation E and did not tell cardholders who reported fraud that they could receive provisional credit as part of the process of filing a dispute.

"Only those callers who specifically asked for instructions or inquired about the provisional credit process received any guidance," the Dallas Fed stated in
the supervisory letter sent to Joseph, Comerica's head of corporate compliance.
In addition, Conduent required that cardholders provide documents and a written statement but did not state that cardholders had 10 days to do so or they may not receive provisional credit.

"While [an] explanation of provisional credit is not a regulatory requirement, the recurring consumer complaints regarding provisional credit indicate consumers are adversely affected," the Dallas Fed stated.

It also noted more systemic problems in the collection of data.

"There is no root cause analysis of complaints to identify systemic issues and trends that warrant immediate correction," according to the supervisory letter "Comerica must establish a method of identifying root causes of complaints originating at Conduent and track complaints with serious allegations or high compliance risk, such as [unfair, deceptive acts and practices.]"

A problem of incentives

In its bid for the Treasury contract, Comerica said it is "committed to delivering a low-cost solution, while providing ready access to funds and protecting both the Direct Express cardholder and the overall program."

Comerica receives fees, interchange revenue and annual payments from the Treasury that rose to $151 million in 2020, the most recent data available, according to court documents. Of that total, Conduent received $105 million in 2020 from Comerica, Mitch Raymond, a senior director in account management at Conduent, said in court documents.

Comerica also benefits from an estimated $3 billion a month in low-cost, non- interest-bearing deposits from the Direct Express program, sources familiar with the program said. The deposits boost the bank's liquidity at little cost and can be leveraged, allowing the bank to lend to more customers, sources said.

Last year, Comerica disclosed that the Consumer Financial Protection Bureau is investigating some of its business practices. The Texas bank stated in a regulatory filing in February 2022: "Remedies in these proceedings or settlements may include fines, penalties, restitution or alterations in the corporation's business practices and may result in increased operating expenses or decreased revenues."

Weber, the former FDIC enforcement chief, said that regulators typically take into account whether information exists to indicate that a bank "is willfully in noncompliance with the law." To deter misconduct, regulators may factor into a civil money penalty whether a bank's executives and board directors believed a potential fine would be lower than the cost of compliance.

"It's a mixture of misplaced financial incentives combined with failing to have appropriate board and management oversight over different operational areas of the bank," said Weber, who also served as a former assistant inspector general for investigations at the Securities and Exchange Commission. "When evidence indicates that individual officers or directors have made decisions to allow misconduct and violations of the law to occur, it is well past time to not only hold the bank accountable but to hold the individual officers and directors and the entire board personally accountable."

Simms, one of the plaintiffs in the class action, lays the blame for the problems on shoddy third-party oversight by the Treasury.

"The Bureau of Fiscal Service, as a part of the U.S. Treasury, allowed Comerica Bank to continue violating federal banking laws and endorsed the contract with Comerica knowing inaccurate information was submitted by Comerica to obtain the contract," Simms said, citing the OIG reports.

Lepper, who helped create the alternative option for veterans; said he didn't understand why the most vulnerable citizens were not getting the attention of
Comerica top executives.

"Why didn't they make the obvious improvements to their program to avoid all of this?" Lepper said.

There were some interesting points made by Kate Berry in her article.

In May, 2019, there were 15,712 fraud disputes. The class action suit against Comerica Bank involved the call center, Conduent. If you multiply the number of disputes for that one-month times 12 (months in a year) and then times 3 (for the three years of disputes between 2017 through 2019) the total fraud disputes would be 565,632. The class action suit was based upon three different premises: not paying provisional credit upon reporting fraud, not beginning investigations, and not giving copies of investigations.

When a bank needs money for liquidity, or to make loans, they have to borrow from the Federal Reserve. An interest rate is established, and banks pay interest on borrowed money. Ms. Berry's statement that Comerica Bank was using Social Security deposits as an interest-free loan is shocking. Comerica Bank was receiving three billion dollars at the beginning of each month as Direct Express money from Social Security.

The issue with the veterans was big. Paul Lawrence refused to speak to me, and it was Pamela Powers, along with Steven Lepper, who made the changes. Paul Lawrence had ignored the problem.

Jackie Densmore was on target regarding victims who never reached the call center by phone.

There was no mention of the shelving of the OIG report (19-041) by Richard Delmar in order to protect Comerica Bank. An inside source confirmed my suspicion, revealing to my source that Delmar never had any intention of publishing the new report. If this is true, Delmar lied to a congressional aide and to others regarding the date OIG 19-041 would be published.

We know that Nora Arpin was the moderator of the third secret meeting held in 2019. Nora Arpin presented the case for Comerica to keep the contract but she knew that i2c was not compliant. Does that mean

I was very happy Kate Berry wrote this article. I would say she wrote it "for Jackie and me" but she had a story that we gave her and she explored many avenues that led her to information we did not have.

Please Select the Starting Number of Your Card

Log in to check your balance, view account activity, transfer funds, and use a variety of additional services.

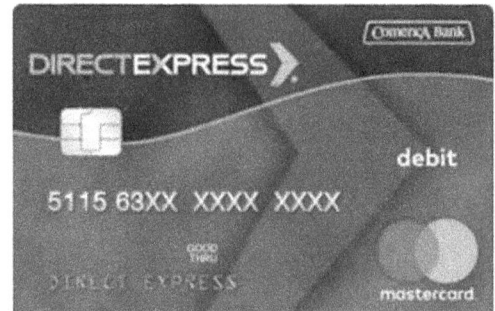

○ 5332 48

○ 5115 63

Terms of Use

Terms of Use

PROCEED TO LOGIN →

Notice the card on the left has a different six digit preface number than the one on the right. This is because one of the cards is for Direct Express cardholders managed by Conduent, and the other is the card used by cardholders whose account is managed by i2c.

Direct Express White Paper

BLUF: Recommend that VA take no action to distance the agency from the U.S. Department of Treasury or its contractor Comerica, Inc. VA's authority and influence on benefits delivery ends at the successful transmission of benefits to Treasury.

Background: Direct Express is a pre-paid debit card program administered by the U.S. Department of Treasury (USDT) through contracted services provided by Comerica Bank. The program was initiated to give US citizens, to include veterans, that cannot get bank accounts (due to homelessness, credit issues, skepticism, etc.) a way to electronically receive federal benefits payments. As customers of USDT, neither VHA nor VBA have a direct business relationship with Comerica Inc., nor have influence on the contract administered by USDT. The alternative decision for VA to execute its own contract for a separate pre-paid debit card would subject VA to incur startup and implementation costs as well as imposing a higher level of payment risk on the veteran. The Direct Express contract is funded by USDT and operates with a fraud rate of approximately .01%, whereas the industry standard is between .03%-.05%.

VHA and VBA representatives met with USDT and Nora Arpin, Comerica Senior Vice President and Director of the Government Electronic Solutions Team on March 12, 2019, to discuss the referenced instances of fraud, potential data breaches, and the impact the situation has had on veterans. Nora reiterated that there has been no data breach at Comerica and the three veterans referenced were victims of an account takeover and payment redirect scam, where criminals steal identities and then use the personal information to compromise accounts and steal money. Account takeover and payment redirect fraud schemes are on the rise in both the public and private sector. Even with the rise in electronic benefits theft, it is still easier to steal paper checks out of someone's mailbox, than it is to illegally obtain an individual's identity from the dark web and use that to identify and compromise each of the online benefits accounts.

VA has approximately 131 , 71 1 veterans who use the Treasury Direct Prepaid Debit Card program as their banking solution for VHA and VBA benefits payments. Comerica had 480 out of 4.5M (. 13%) Direct Express accounts that were compromised; 30 of those were veterans who had federal benefits stolen. Comerica reaffirmed that all veterans that were deemed victims of account takeover and payment redirect fraud have been repaid. The veterans involved in the class action lawsuit chose litigation to solve their disagreements with Comerica and therefore are reliant on the U.S. court system for final resolution.

Outcome: Due to the increase in account takeover and benefit payment fraud, Comerica agreed to a monthly working group with VA, USDT, and SSA to track and find better ways to serve our customers.

Epilogue

I was tired. Jackie was tired. We saw the corruption within Bureau of Fiscal Service, OIG Treasury, Comerica Bank, Conduent, and the Social Security Administration. We saw audits that were crafted to protect the malfeasance of fellow Treasury employees. We were lied to and saw audits postponed protecting a corrupt contractor. We were excluded from the contractor (fiscal agent) selection process. Employees from all agencies listed above lied and were involved in the coverup, to include lawyers.

The only agency that reluctantly cooperated (in a limited fashion) was the Veterans Administration through the Veterans Benefit Association. Paul Lawrence was aware of my work, ignored me, was exposed, and left the Veterans Benefit Association.

There was to be a long road ahead to address settlement issues. The legal wrangling of the class action settlement was a hard battle for Jackie and me.

We fought everyone, including Comerica Bank, Conduent, government employees, and our lawyers. No one understood what we did to make this case work; no one.

Our best allies were Kate Berry (American Banker) and Steven Lepper (Association of Military Banks of America). Kate helped expose the Direct Express issue, and Steven Lepper was instrumental in the Veterans Administration. We owed them both a debt of gratitude.

Our fellow plaintiffs were great, helpful, and insightful. One plaintiff was a pain in the ass, calling for updates, and when Jackie and I would tell that plaintiff what was going on, the plaintiff would call Franklin and bother him.

This was a difficult matter to explain to friends and family. It took almost 5 years to get our win in federal court, and I am sure no one understood how hard it was to keep going.

I appreciated the support I received from my son, Joe. He knew his father very well and knew the battles I had fought.

Jackie will always be in my heart. We spent thousands of hours talking and making this victory possible. We cursed at each other and everyone, and we got it done. We knew all our family issues and how this affected our families.

This victory will help hundreds if not thousands of people, and hopefully, save them heartache.
The government works. Federal agencies work. Regulations and laws are there for a reason, and if they are enforced, "people" become accountable.

The "human element" destroyed the federal programs. It was the humans employed by the US Treasury, Social Security, Veterans Administration, Comerica Bank, and Conduent who caused the Direct Express program to become a nightmare to US citizens who had no accountability. These were corrupt people.

The problem was unelected bureaucrats, agency officials, and other government employees who ignored laws and created programs to benefit themselves.
We exposed some of them, but we are not done.

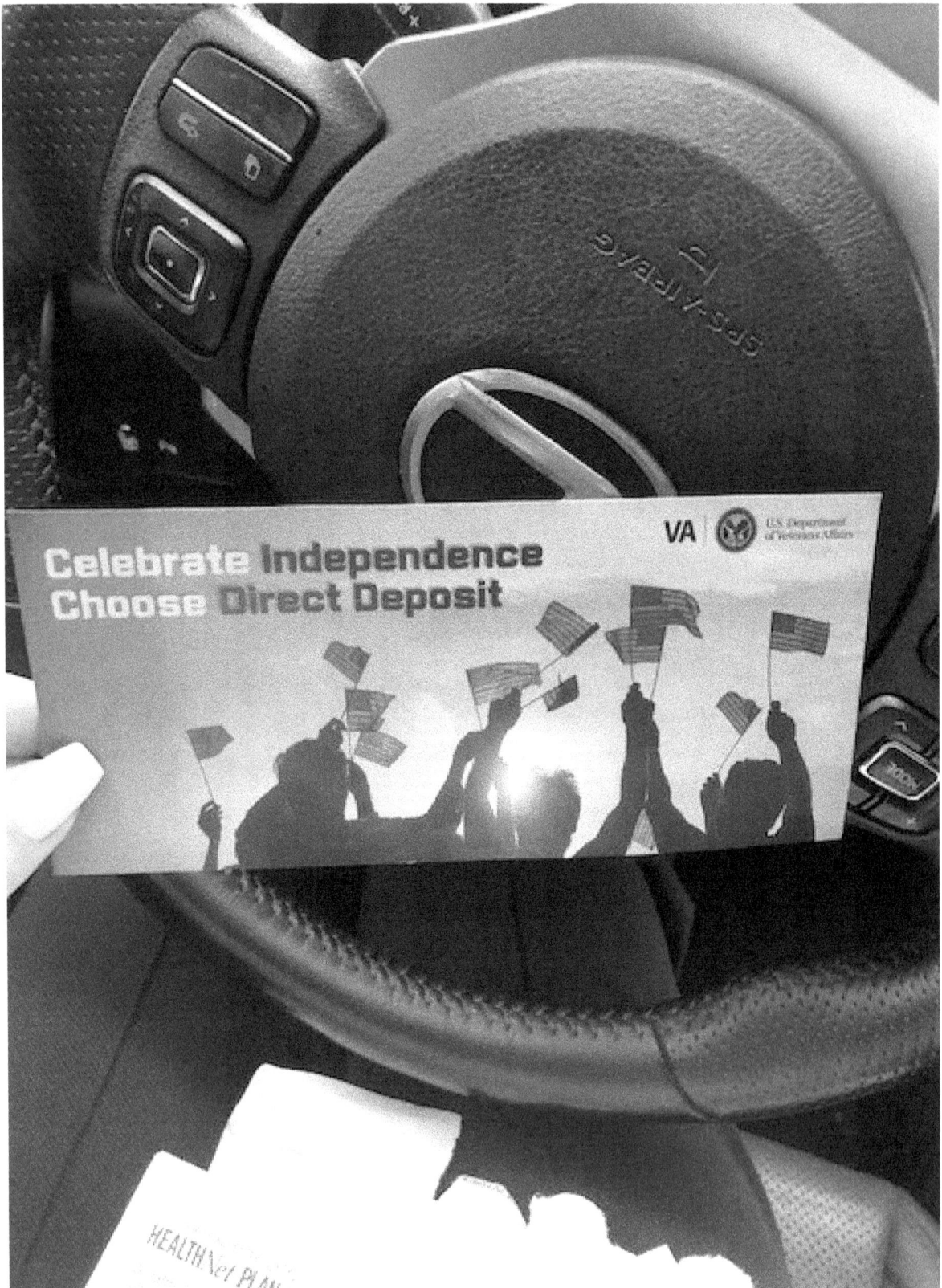

Endnotes

Introduction:

Page 1
(1) OIG 14-031
(2) OIG 14-031

Chapter 1

Page 1
(3) OIG 14-031
(4) OIG 14-031
(5) OIG 14-031
(6) OIG 14-031
Page 2
(7) OIG 14-031
(8) OIG 17-034
(9) OIG 17-034
(10) OIG 17-034
(11) OIG 17-034
Page 3
(12) OIG 17-034
(13) OIG 17-034
Page 4
(14) OIG 17-034
Page 5
(15) OIG 17-034

Chapter 2

Page 10
(16) OIG 14-031
(17) OIG 14-031
(18) OIG 14-031
(19) OIG 14-031
(20) OIG 14-031
Page 11
(21) OIG 14-031
(22) OIG 14-031
(23) OIG 14-031
Page 12
(24) OIG 14-031
(25) OIG 14-031
(26) OIG 14-031
(27) OIG 17-034
Page 13
(28) OIG 17-034
(29) OIG 17-034
(30) OIG 17-034
Page 14
(31) OIG 17-034
(32) OIG 17-034
(33) OIG 17-034
(34) OIG 17-034
(35) OIG 17-034
Page 15
(36) OIG 17-034
(37) OIG 17-034

(38) OIG 17-034
Chapter 3
Page 4
(39) American Banker webpage www.american.banker.com/author/nora.arpin accessed June 10, 2020
Page 15
(40) Kate Berry article August 26, 2018 American Banker
Chapter 5
Page 15
(41) FDIC 6500
Page 35
(42) Shaw v United States (SCOTUS)

Notes

Notes